Dietrich/Pilniok

European Security Union

European Security Union

Law and Policies

edited by

Jan-Hendrik Dietrich

Arne Pilniok

2024

BECK • HART • NOMOS

Published by
Verlag C.H.Beck oHG, Wilhelmstraße 9, 80801 München, Germany,
email: bestellung@beck.de

Co-published by
Hart Publishing, Kemp House, Chawley Park, Cumnor Hill, Oxford, OX2 9PH, United Kingdom,
online at: www.hartpub.co.uk

and

Nomos Verlagsgesellschaft mbH & Co. KG, Waldseestraße 3–5, 76530 Baden-Baden, Germany,
email: nomos@nomos.de

Published in North America by Hart Publishing
An Imprint of Bloomsbury Publishing 1385 Broadway, New York, NY 10018, USA

beck.de

ISBN 978 3 406 81045 9 (C.H.BECK)
ISBN 978 1 5099 6543 4 (HART)
ISBN 978 3 7560 1930 4 (NOMOS)

Printed in Germany by
Beltz Grafische Betriebe GmbH
Am Fliegerhorst 8, 99947 Bad Langensalza

Typeset by
Reemers Publishing Services GmbH, Krefeld
Cover: Druckerei C.H.Beck Nördlingen

myclimate
shape our future

chbeck.de/nachhaltig

Preface

The Member States of the European Union are moving closer together in ensuring internal and external security. To achieve this goal, the EU Security Union Strategy (COM(2020) 605 final) outlines a comprehensive framework and mission statement. However, a closer examination reveals several areas that require further clarification, particularly regarding the scope and significance of Member State sovereignty. The reservation stated in the third sentence of Art. 4(2) TEU is significantly ambiguous in terms of legal interpretation. Following the recent judgments of the European Court of Justice on data retention, it remains unclear, how far the 'sole responsibility of the Member States' for their 'national security' extends and which contradictions between Member States and the European Union could arise.

Against this backdrop, an international symposium, sponsored by the European Parliament and funded by the German Federal Ministry of the Interior and Community, was held in Brussels in June 2022. The symposium provided valuable insight into the potential and limitations of European security cooperation, leading to a more substantial discussion and a clearer understanding of the constraints placed on action by both the European Union and its Member States.

The contributions in this book are based on the outcomes of the symposium. We are grateful that we were able to attract so many renowned experts from politics, academia, administrative practice and civil society as authors. The contributions first address political approaches, structures and principles of governance in the European Security Union (Parts 1 and 2). This is contrasted in the following contributions with the role of 'national security' as an expression of the sovereignty of the Member States (Part 3). Part 4 is dedicated to the modes and conditions of European security cooperation, whereas Part 5 emphasizes key domains for implementing the European Security Union. Part 6 explores perspectives for developing the European Security Union. In all chapters, political, social, and historical analyses are contextualized with legal discourse. The book is thus aimed at researchers of various disciplines and a broad specialist audience in the fields of national and European administration and justice.

The publication is the work of many helping hands. We would like to thank all the authors for their contribution to this project and their wonderful, patient collaboration. We are also particularly grateful to *Jutta Keller-Herder* and *Dietmar Marscholleck* from the Federal Ministry of the Interior and Community. They played a key role in making both the above-mentioned symposium and this handbook possible. Without their support, neither would have been realised. Further thanks are due to *Thomas Klich* and *Jonathon Watson* of C.H.Beck Publishers for their careful guidance and advice on this project. Finally, we would like to thank *Ute Reusch* for language editing and translations as well as our research assistants *Steffen Zanger* and *Jannik Luhm* for their organizational support of the book.

Berlin and Bielefeld
April 2024

Jan-Hendrik Dietrich
Arne Pilniok

Table of contents

PART VI
PERSPECTIVES

Abbreviations

AFIS	Automated Fingerprint Identification System
AFSJ	Area of Freedom Security and Justice
AI	Artificial Intelligence
AJCL	American Journal of Comparative Law
AöR	Archiv des öffentlichen Rechts
API	Advanced Passenger Information
APuZ	Aus Politik und Zeitgeschichte
BBC	British Broadcasting Corporation
BMS	Biometric Matching Service
BND	Bundesnachrichtendienst (German Foreign Intelligence Service)
BVerfG	Bundesverfassungsgericht (Federal Constitutional Court of the Republic of Germany)
BYU L. Rev	Brigham Young University Law Review
BayVBl.	Bayerische Verwaltungsblätter
CBRN	Chemical, Biological, Radiological and Nuclear
CEPS	Centre for European Policy Studies
Cf.	compare
CFR	Charter of Fundamental Rights of the European Union
CFSP	Common Foreign and Security Policy
CIR	Common Identity Repository
CISE	Common Information Sharing Environment
CJEU	Court of Justice of the European Union
CLSR	Computer Law & Security Review
CMS	Comparative Migration Studies
Coreper	Committee of Permanent Representatives
CSDP	Common Security and Defence Policy
CTG	Counter Terrorism Group
CyCLONe	European Cyber Crises Liaison Network
DÖV	Die öffentliche Verwaltung
DPA	Data Protection Authorities
DuD	Datenschutz und Datensicherheit
DV	Die Verwaltung
ed.(s)	editor(s)
e.g.	for example
EAS	Europol Analysis System
EASO	European Asylum Support Office
EAW	European Arrest Warrant
ECCC	European Cybersecurity Competence Centre and Network
ECGFF	European Coast Guard Functions Forum
ECHR	European Convention on Human Rights
ECJ	European Court of Justice
ECLR	European Constitutional Law Review
ECRIS-TCN	European Criminal Records Information System for TCNs and stateless persons
ECtHR	European Court of Human Rights
EDA	European Defence Agency
edn	edition
EDPB	European Data Protection Board
EDPL	European Data Protection Law Review
EDPS	European Data Protection Supervisor
EEAS	European External Action Service
EES	Entry Exit System

EFAR	European Foreign Affairs Review
EIS	Europol Information System
EJRR	European Journal of Risk Regulation
ELJ	European Law Journal
EMPACT	European Multidisciplinary Platform Against Criminal Threats
EMSA	European Maritime Safety Agency
ENISA	European Network and Information Security Agency
EP-JMN	European Papers Jean Monnet Network
EPL	European Public Law
EPPO	European Public Prosecutor's Office
EPRS	European Parliament Research Service
ERA Forum	Europäische Rechtsakademie Forum
ERGA	European Regulators' Group for Audiovisual Media Services
ESP	European Search Portal
et seq(q).	and the following
ETIAS	European Travel Information and Authorization System
EU FIU	European Union Financial Intelligence Unit
EUAA	European Union Asylum Agency
EUDPR	European Union Data Processing Regulation
EuGRZ	Europäische Grundrechte-Zeitschrift
eu-LISA	European Union Agency for the Operational Management of Large-Scale IT Systems in the AFSJ
EUMC	European Union Military Committee
EuR	Europarecht
Eur. J. Crim. Policy Res	European Journal on Criminal Policy and Research
Eur. J. Int. Relat	European Journal of International Relations
Eur. J. Secur. Res	European Journal for Security Research
EURODAC	European Asylum Dactyloscopy Database
EUROSUR	European Border Surveillance System
EuZW	Europäische Zeitschrift für Wirtschaftsrecht
FAZ	Frankfurter Allgemeine Zeitung
FDI	Foreign Direct Investment
FIMI	Foreign Information Manipulation and Interference
FRA	Fundamental Rights Agency
Frontex	European Border and Coast Guard Agency
GDPR	General Data Protection Regulation and the
GG	Grundgesetz (Basic Law of the Federal Republic of Germany)
HRLR	Human Rights Law Review
IBM	Integrated Border Management
ICT	Information and Communication Technology
IDEA	International Institute for Democracy and Electoral Assistance
i.e.	that is
IJICI	International Journal of Intelligence and CounterIntelligence
IJMBS	International Journal of Medical and Biomedical Studies
Int. J. Law Inf. Technol	International Journal of Law and Information Technology
IntCen	European Union Intelligence and Situation Centre
IntDir	European Union Military Staff Intelligence Directorate
InTeR	Zeitschrift zum Innovations- und Technikrecht
Interpol	The International Criminal Police Organization
ISF	Internal Security Fund
J	Multidisciplinary Scientific Journal
J. Intellect. Prop. Inf. Technol. E-Commer. Law	Journal of Intellectual Property, Information Technology and Electronic Commerce Law
JCER	Journal of Contemporary European Research
JCMS	Journal of Common Market Studies
JEPP	Journal of European Public Policy
JHAAN	The Justice and Home Affairs agencies' network
JIPITEC	Journal of Intellectual Property, Information Technology and Electronic Commerce Law

JIT	Joint Investigation Team
JöR	Jahrbuch des öffentlichen Rechts
JZ	JuristenZeitung
KritV	Kritische Vierteljahresschrift für Gesetzgebung und Rechtswissenschaft
LED	Law Enforcement Directive
MID	Multiple Identity Detector
MJIL	Michigan Journal of International Law
mn.	margin number
N.Y.U. L. Rev	New York University Law Review
NALL	Netherlands Administrative Law Library
NCC	National Coordination Centre
NJW	Neue Juristische Wochenschrift
NVwZ	Neue Zeitschrift für Verwaltungsrecht
NZI	Neue Zeitschrift für Insolvenz- und Sanierungsrecht
p.	page
PFI	EUAA Push Factor Index
PNR	Passenger Name Records
RAS	Rapid Alert System
sent.	sentence
SIAC	Single Intelligence Analysis Capacity
SIS	Schengen Information System
SLTD	Interpol Stolen and Lost Travel Document database
SSRN	Social Science Research Network
StratCom	Strategic Communication Division
StV	Strafverteidiger
SWIFT	Society for Worldwide Interbank Financial Telecommunication
TCN	Third Country National
TDAWN	Interpol Travel Documents Associated with Notices database
TEC	Treaty Establishing the European Community
TEU	Treaty on European Union
TFEU	Treaty on the Functioning of the European Union
UNEP	United Nations Environment Programme
Va. L. Rev	Virginia Law Review
VVDStRL	Veröffentlichungen der Vereinigung der Deutschen Staatsrechtslehrer
WHI-Paper	Walter Hallstein Institut Paper
ZaöRV	Zeitschrift für ausländisches öffentliches Recht und Völkerrecht
ZAR	Zeitschrift für Ausländerrecht und Ausländerpolitik
ZEuS	Zeitschrift für europarechtliche Studien
ZPol	Zeitschrift für Politikwissenschaft
ZRP	Zeitschrift für Rechtspolitik

Contributors

Katarina Barley is Vice-President of the European Parliament and a member of the Committee on Civil Liberties, Justice and Home Affairs. Previously, she has served as Germany's Federal Minister of Justice and for Consumer Protection as well as a Member of the German Parliament.

Raphael Bossong works at the German Institute for International and Security Affairs.

Johannes Buchheim is Professor of Public Law and the Law of Digitalization at the University of Marburg.

Iain Cameron is Professor of Public International Law at Uppsala University.

Gerhard Conrad is a lecturer at King's College London, the Federal University of Applied Administrative Sciences in Berlin and Sciences Po Paris. From 2016 until retirement in 2019 he was Director EU INTCEN. As retired director at the German Foreign Intelligence Service (BND) he currently is Intelligence Advisor to the Munich Security Conference (MSC).

Jan-Hendrik Dietrich is Professor of Public Law and Security Law at the Federal University of Administrative Sciences, Berlin.

Päivi Leino-Sandberg is Professor of Transnational European Law at the University of Helsinki.

Carolyn Moser is the Research Group Leader of ENSURE (European Security Revisited) at the Max Planck Institute for Comparative Public Law and International Law (Heidelberg) and holds the Alfred-Grosser Chair at Sciences Po (Paris).

Olivier Onidi is Deputy Director-General for Migration and Home Affairs at the European Commission.

Arne Pilniok is Professor of German and European Public Law and Administrative Sciences at the University of Bielefeld.

Teresa Quintel is Administrator for the European Parliament Committee on Civil Liberties, Justice and Home Affairs.

Oliver Rüß is Head of Division at the federal administration.

Bettina Schöndorf-Haubold is Professor of German, European and International Administrative Law, Administrative Science and Comparative Law at the Justus-Liebig University Giessen.

Rita Schwarzelühr-Sutter is Parliamentary State Secretary at the German Federal Ministry of the Interior and Community.

Markus Sehl is a Lawyer and the deputy editor-in-chief for Legal Tribune Online. Regularly he works as journalist for the German weekly newspaper Die Zeit.

Satish Sule is legal officer in the Directorate General of Human Resources and Security of the European Commission.

Jörg Philipp Terhechte is Professor of Public Law, European and International Law as well as Antitrust and Regulatory Law at the Leuphana University Lüneburg.

Teija Tiilikainen is Director of The European Centre of Excellence for Countering Hybrid Threats (located in Helsinki, Finland).

Bertrand Warusfel is Professor at the University Paris 8 (Vincennes-Saint-Denis) and an Attorney at Law. He is also Vice-Chairman of the French Association for Security and Defence Law.

Thomas Wischmeyer is Professor of Public Law and Information Law at the University of Bielefeld.

Steffen Zanger is a Governmental Advisor in NATO Mission Iraq's Political Advisory Group in Baghdad.

PART I
POLITICAL APPROACHES

§ 1
The European Security Union between Member State interests and necessities of European integration*

Rita Schwarzelühr-Sutter

The central bodies of the European Union, i.e. the European Parliament, the European Commission and the governments of the Member States, cooperate when it comes to security in Europe. When they, with their different perspectives, enter into a dialogue, discuss their various interests and integrate them, it is in general to the benefit of Europe and the citizens of the EU. Europe means: listening to each other, seeking a balance, working to accommodate diverging interests.

I am grateful to Professor Pilniok and Professor Dietrich, the editors of this publication, for putting the spotlight on these issues with the support of the Federal Ministry of the Interior and Community was able to provide support, as I am happy to mention.

Of course, the illegitimate war of aggression against Ukraine is very much on all our minds. It is an attack on our peacetime order; it is an attack on Europe as a whole. This is why the Member States can and must respond to it together.

It proves how crucial the security dimension of the process of European integration is. Security, by its very nature, requires an integrated approach, not a blinkered mindset that separates domestic from foreign aspects. This is why you can find topics such as cyber security and hybrid threats in this book. The focus of this symposium is neither the Common Foreign and Security Policy nor the Common Security and Defence Policy, but the European Security Union.

What is this Security Union? Building on the European Agenda on Security, in 2016 the Commission presented the first Security Union concept. It proposed a new approach for internal security based on shared responsibility between the European Union and its Member States.

Part of the strategy is to establish the necessary tools, infrastructure and framework conditions at European level to enable national authorities to cooperate efficiently and to respond to common threats. Frans Timmermans, Executive Vice-President of the European Commission, was right when he said: 'Terrorism knows no borders.'

I agree with Frans Timmermans that national authorities are responsible for internal security, but they need to be able to cooperate seamlessly to prevent terrorism and track down the perpetrators. The EU must provide the right framework and tools for this, but what will make the difference is how the Member States use them. Law enforcement authorities in all our Member States should both 'think European' and 'act European', as internal security is a shared responsibility, which requires joint action.

---

* This contribution is based on a keynote speech delivered at the international symposium on European Security in Brussels on 16 June 2022.

The current EU Security Union Strategy covers the period from 2020 to 2025. It focuses on helping Member States to foster security. The Commission regularly informs about progress made.

The EU strategy pursues four objectives:

1. ensuring that EU security policy reflects the changing threats landscape
2. building long-term, sustainable resilience
3. engaging the EU institutions and agencies, governments, the private sector and individuals in a whole-of-society approach
4. bringing together the many policy areas with a direct impact on security.

The European Security Union also focuses on four strategic priorities. They emphasize, among other things, protecting people against terrorism and organized crime and building a stronger security ecosystem.

This approach adopted by the Commission is useful and necessary. It is obvious that greater integration is needed to achieve a genuine European Security Union.

Member States cannot guarantee the protection of their citizens on their own because threats are of an increasingly cross-border nature. This is true not only of more 'traditional' forms of crime like terrorism and organized crime, but also of cybercrime in particular where even the means used to commit the crime are borderless.

At the same time, we are aware that we are talking within and about a common area of freedom, security and justice. The rule of law itself is based on a normative foundation. Power is contained within a clear structure of competences. The legitimacy of our common project, the Security Union, rests on a foundation of treaties. This foundation is stable so that the Commission and the Member States can work together to ensure our common security.

The division of competences codified in the EU's primary law forms the legal framework for the democratically legitimized exercise of competences by the EU. Art. 4(2) sent. 3 TEU explicitly states: 'In particular, national security remains the sole responsibility of each Member State.'

I am aware that this sentence creates a conflict with the aim of the Security Union. It is exactly this conflict that this volume is aiming to shed light on. It makes sense to intertwine competences, not to hamper integration, but to create added value.

It would, however, not be good for the Union and its Member States to exacerbate this conflict. Especially when I look at the recent decisions by the European Court of Justice and the Member States' reactions to them it becomes clear why this debate is so necessary.

This book is to my mind particularly suited to address the most urgent questions in a transparent and objective way. We want to highlight the great benefits of the Security Union, but also the limits of these competences that always go hand in hand with any legitimate exercise of power.

I can think of the following questions:

- What is 'national security" in the sense of Art. 4(2) sent. 3 TEU? Could we try and define this term from a functional perspective that focusses on the purpose of taking action? Does the term have an institutional component implying a specific organizational structure for authorities to perform certain state functions? These are open questions.

  We have not yet finished discussing the question as to whether a Union competence is needed to regulate access of intelligence agencies to information. Another example is the E-Privacy Directive where we still have to find effective solutions while keeping in mind fundamental rights.

- What is after all the significance of Art. 4(2) sent. 3 TEU? The competences conferred to the Union by the treaties do not establish any EU competence in this field. Why then explicitly rule out responsibility for national security?
- Currently there is much debate over the Commission's proposal for an EU Regulation on Artificial Intelligence. The discussion is still in full swing. The aim of Germany's Federal Government is to make sure that it remains possible for security agencies and migration authorities to use AI in a practicable way. We therefore consider it necessary for this to be regulated in a separate legal instrument or a separate final chapter.
- This shows that there are many diverse open and urgent questions, also of course regarding the substance of conferred competences and how they are limited by the principles of proportionality and subsidiarity. This is why this academic debate is important: among other things, when we clarify our understanding of this system of competences we reduce frictions and thus strengthen our security.
- A question that I would like to address regards the Court of Justice of the European Union. A fundamental tenet is the autonomy of Union law and the CJEU's competence, conferred to it by the treaties, to give rulings and interpret the law. How does this relate to Art. 4(2) sent. 3 TEU? Doesn't it rule out any possibility for EU competence once and for all? On the other hand, it is also clear to me that 'national security' cannot serve as a pretext for Member States to single-handedly decide that they are not bound by Union law. Above all, it cannot serve to justify abandoning those values on which the Union is based: respect for human dignity, freedom, democracy, equality, the rule of law and human rights. This raises fundamental questions regarding the institutional balance of this values-based integration project. I expect that we will inevitably have to deal with this topic in all its complexity.

These are only some of the questions that spring to mind in this area which is highly interesting in legal and political terms. But this also illustrates that we are dealing with a very complex issue for which there are not really any simple answers.

Despite all these questions, I am firmly convinced: the Security Union is a success story – in many areas and for all citizens. The aim is to push ahead with this successful project.

In particular in the areas covered by the Security Union, there is further potential for more freedom and security, which for me are two sides of the same coin. To tap this potential, we in the Union must reach a common understanding of who is responsible for what.

Under the rule of law, competences are not a matter for formalists, but are just as binding as any other form of legitimization of state power. Upholding this lies at the heart of the rule of law. And this is what this book is all about: the successful project, its prospects and also its framework.

It is necessary to look at the overall picture to create a solid foundation for continuing the successful integration in an ever-closer European Union, for a united Europe. We can only achieve this together – academia, civil society and government, the European Parliament, the Commission and the Member States.

§ 2
Crime doesn't stop at the border post – European security in a multi-level system

Katarina Barley

A. Challenges

European unification has allowed people and economies in Europe to grow ever closer together. At the same time, others who we would rather not see doing so are also joining forces in Europe. It is not only employees and businesspeople who use open borders to their advantage: crime no longer stops at the border post either.

The European Union (EU) and its Member States grant unprecedented freedom to individuals. With that great freedom comes a great challenge, as that kind of freedom can be abused. The EU and its Member States therefore need to think about ensuring security within the Union and beyond.

It is not only the task of reconciling freedom and security that keeps bringing up new challenges. In a multi-level system like the EU, it is also a matter of determining which level can best deal with a security threat. Here the Treaty on European Union (TEU) provides for an apparently far-reaching limitation of the Union's exercise of competence in the area of national security. Under Art. 4(2) sent. 3 TEU, 'national security remains the sole responsibility of each Member State.' At the same time, in order to ensure effective pan-European security the Union is and must be active in regulating many areas that are relevant to security.

B. An ongoing project: environmental crime

In this intertwined situation, the contours of the European Security Union need constant reassessing. One area that can illustrate the need for a multi-level approach is the protection of the environment under criminal law.[1]

The EU and its Member States face a common challenge as regards the protection of the environment. Protecting the environment by means of incentives – such as a CO_2 emissions trading system – is crucial. However, there also need to be criminal sanctions. Environmental crime is increasingly a problem for Member States. Very different areas such as the illegal trade in timber, illegal ship recycling, the extraction of groundwater or the discharge of pollutants are showing a growing momentum. The European

[1] The EU's competency derives from Art. 83(2) TFEU, according to which the EU may establish minimum rules with regard to the definition of criminal offences and sanctions in an area which has been subject to harmonization measures if the approximation of criminal laws and regulations of the Member States proves essential to ensure the effective implementation of a Union policy.

Commission estimates that criminal activities related to the environment are increasing by between five and seven per cent annually.[2]

Environmental crime is often cross-border or has cross-border effects. Therefore, EU-wide coordination can have a variety of advantages, especially in relation to the Member States' aim of ensuring security. The harmonization of criminal offences under the Environmental Crime Directive[3] provides all the EU Member States with the certainty that the other members of the common market are also taking action against environmental crime. The Union thus helps to protect the exercise of freedom against abuse, thereby creating a level playing field for the benefit of all and preventing safe havens for criminals.

However, particularly in the area of environmental crime the best laws may be of little use if they are not strictly enforced. The Commission's proposal for a revision of the Environmental Crime Directive attempts to counterbalance the fact that enforcement is a national competence that possibly creates loopholes and grey areas in which crime can thrive.[4] To that end, the Commission proposes that Member States must ensure effective enforcement of the provisions of criminal law. They must ensure that their enforcement authorities cooperate with each other and are equipped with the necessary resources.[5] From the national perspective, it may appear as if the Commission is displaying a degree of distrust towards the Member States. However, this reading is misguided. Such requirements are a necessary tool in the face of Member States that try to undermine common rules by not enforcing them.

At the same time, the Commission's proposal – like the first Directive of 2008 – seeks to preserve national legal traditions. For example, it stipulates that Member States need not introduce criminal sanctions against legal persons.[6]

In addition to the hard law requirements, the EU also takes on a softer, coordinating role. In 2018, the Commission set up a high-level group of experts – the Environmental Compliance and Governance Forum – to facilitate exchange with Member States and with European networks of environmental inspectors, police officers, prosecutors, judges, and environmental agencies.[7] Such networks help Member States to share knowledge, experience and insights. The EU itself provides funding to support the work of the Forum. Finally, the EU sees the need to fight environmental crime beyond its borders and to cooperate internationally in this regard.

C. European contributions to the Security Union

In other areas, too, the European Union is taking on a more active role as part of the ever-evolving European Security Union. This is a direct response to changing threat

[2] UNEP-INTERPOL, 'Rapid Response Assessment: The Rise of Environmental Crime – A Growing Threat to Natural Resources Peace, Development and Security' (2016).

[3] Directive 2008/99/EC on the protection of the environment through criminal law (Environmental Crime Directive) and the Commission's proposal for a new Directive replacing the old Directive of 1999; European Commission, Proposal for a Directive of the European Parliament and of the Council on the protection of the environment through criminal law and replacing Directive 2008/99/EC, 15.12.2021, COM(2021) 851 final. See Köllner/Otto, 'Strafrechtliche Durchsetzung des "Green deal"', NZI 2022, 602.

[4] European Commission, 'Commission Staff Working Document, Evaluation of the Directive 2008/99/EC of the European Parliament and of the Council of 19 November 2008 on the protection of the environment through criminal law (Environmental Crime Directive), Part 1 of 2', 28.10.2020, SWD(2020) 259 final, 33.

[5] Art. 16 et seqq. COM(2021) 851 final.

[6] Art. 7(2)(a) COM(2021) 851 final.

[7] European Commission, 'Commission Decision of 18 January 2018 setting up a group of experts on environmental compliance and governance', 2018/C 19/03.

situations in many areas. Not so long ago, some might have seen these areas as a domain of the Member States, at least in part. There are many recent examples.

First, the EU is becoming a more active player in the area of criminal justice and law enforcement itself. It is responding to cross-border policing challenges, for example, by steadily developing Europol's mandate.[8] In addition, in connection with Russian war crimes in Ukraine, the EU is providing Eurojust and Joint Investigation Teams (JITs) with the means and procedures to coordinate investigative work.[9] Furthermore, the Union continues to expand those areas in which it can set minimum criminal sanctions. It will, for instance, add sanctions violations[10] to the list of EU crimes under Art. 83 TFEU. Similar plans exist as regards hate crime and hate speech.[11] For more than a year now, the EU has also been taking law enforcement into its own hands in areas that are particularly sensitive. By establishing the European Public Prosecutor's Office (EPPO), the EU has created a law enforcement agency that can look back on a very successful first year.[12]

Second, the EU is engaging in broader areas of security that have EU-wide significance. The Commission's proposal for the NIS 2 Directive[13] and work done by the European Agency for Cybersecurity (ENISA) aim at creating a secure digital infrastructure. The EU seeks to protect citizens and Member States' democratic systems from abuses of power by national security agencies – as can be seen in the Pegasus scandal in the aftermath of which the European Parliament is investigating Member States' practices in relation to violations of EU law. In addition, the EU is engaged in the prevention of terrorism and right-wing extremism. It is stepping in with a range of tools, from the Regulation on Addressing the Dissemination of Terrorist Content Online to information sharing and stricter anti-money laundering rules.[14]

Finally, the EU is playing a growing role in ensuring national security more broadly. It works to counter external threats, such as foreign interference in democratic processes. In addition, it is helping Member States to counter military threats. The EU is creating a more integrated defence and foreign policy, as well as a more integrated and competitive European defence market.

---

[8] Regulation (EU) 2022/991 amending Regulation (EU) 2016/794, as regards Europol's cooperation with private parties, the processing of personal data by Europol in support of criminal investigations, and Europol's role in research and innovation and Regulation (EU) 2022/1190 amending Regulation (EU) 2018/1862 as regards the entry of information alerts into the Schengen Information System (SIS) on third-country nationals in the interest of the Union.

[9] Eurojust, 'Press Release: Estonia, Latvia and Slovakia become members of joint investigation team on alleged core international crimes in Ukraine', 31.5.2022 <https://www.eurojust.europa.eu/news/estonia-latvia-and-slovakia-become-members-joint-investigation-team-alleged-core-international> (last accessed: 21.9.2023).

[10] European Commission, 'Commission Proposal for a Council Decision on adding the violation of Union restrictive measures to the areas of crime laid down in Article 83(1) of the Treaty on the Functioning of the European Union', 25.5.2022, COM(2022) 247 final.

[11] European Commission, 'Annex to the Communication from the Commission to the European Parliament and the Council, A more inclusive and protective Europe: extending the list of EU crimes to hate speech and hate crime', 9.12.2021, COM(2021) 777 final.

[12] European Public Prosecutor's Office, '1 year of EPPO operations: larger and faster EU fraud investigations, 1 June 2022', <https://www.eppo.europa.eu/en/news/1-year-eppo-operations-larger-and-faster-eu-fraud-investigations> (last accessed: 21.9.2023).

[13] European Commission, 'Proposal for a Directive of the European Parliament and of the Council on measures for a high common level of cybersecurity across the Union, repealing Directive (EU) 2016/1148', 16.12.2020, COM/2020/823 final.

[14] See European Commission, 'Anti-money laundering and countering the financing of terrorism legislative package', 20.7.2021, <https://finance.ec.europa.eu/publications/anti-money-laundering-and-countering-financing-terrorism-legislative-package_en> (last accessed: 21.9.2023).

D. Outlook

All these examples make one thing clear: The threats to national security are changing and becoming more European. The area of environmental crime exemplifies the EU's central and, at the same time, case-specific role in the European Security Union. Environmental criminal law makes clear what the potential of such an integrated approach is. Transnational challenges arise from both European integration and from the nature of the threats themselves. They call on Member States and the Union alike to jointly seek the best possible ways to integrate the EU and national level while striking a balance between security and freedom.

§ 3
Building a strong and effective Security Union

Olivier Onidi

A. Introduction

Globalization, free movement and the digital transformation have brought and continue to bring prosperity to the EU, but alongside these benefits come inherent risks and costs. They can be manipulated by terrorism, organized crime, drugs trade and human trafficking. Security threats are also becoming more complex as the boundaries between the physical and digital world are increasingly blurred and the actor behind the threat often hides in vulnerable groups. Citizens cannot be protected only through Member States acting on their own. While primary responsibility for security remains solely with Member States, recent years have brought an increasing understanding that the security of one Member State is the security of all. Indeed, the Commission's role in ensuring the safety of all EU citizens at the EU level has evolved from a rather modest beginning under the so-called third-pillar to a quite central role under the current Treaties. Nevertheless, this does not mean that the Commission will become a law enforcement authority with operational responsibilities on the ground. Instead, the Commission's institutional role in this area clearly developed into one of key policy maker as well as concrete facilitator and supporter of Member States' operational needs. The Security Union Strategy framework highlights the priority areas where the EU can bring added value to support Member States in fostering security for all those living in Europe. The strategy lays out the tools and measures that have been and will be developed for 2021–2025.

B. Law enforcement cooperation

The European Union supports the Member States and their law enforcement authorities in combating cross-border crime and terrorism. For that, the Commission provides instruments and tools for national authorities to coordinate their actions across Member States, to share information across borders and to engage together in operational police cooperation. For instance, in December 2021, the Commission adopted three legislative proposals to improve police cooperation inside the EU: the so-called police cooperation package. The first proposal is for a Council Recommendation on operational police cooperation.[1] This proposal will make it easier for police officers to work with other EU countries and intervene in other Member States if need be. It will create common standards for better cooperation between police officers acting in the territory of another Member State with clearer rules for working across borders, effective access to information during cross-border operations and promoting a com-

[1] European Commission, 'Proposal for a Council Recommendation on operational police cooperation', 8.12.2021, COM(2021) 780 final.

mon EU culture of policing. Second is the proposal for a Regulation revising the rules on automated exchange of certain categories of data (the so-called Prüm II) that will help establish links between crimes across the EU much more effectively.[2] Prüm II will help close information gaps, boost the prevention, detection and investigation of criminal offences in the EU and foster security for everyone in Europe. Lastly, the Police cooperation package includes a proposal for a Directive on information exchange between police authorities.[3] The proposed Directive provides new rules on information exchange between law enforcement authorities of Member States. Police officers in one Member State should have equivalent access to the information available to their colleagues in another Member State, under the same conditions. However, for EU police cooperation to work, law enforcement officers from different Member States need to work together in a trusted and efficient way. At EU-level, CEPOL (European Union Agency for Law Enforcement Training) is the main tool to nurture this common EU law enforcement culture through training. Together with the Executive Director at CEPOL and with the CEPOL Management Board, the Commission has started a reflection on how best to equip the Agency for its important tasks.

I. Europol

Europol is the cornerstone of the EU's security architecture as the information hub on criminal activities and centre for law enforcement expertise. As the EU is facing more and more cross border offline and online crimes, under Europol's recently revised mandate, Europol will be able to cooperate effectively with private entities. It will have the right tools and safeguards to support police forces in analysing big data to investigate crime and in developing pioneering methods to tackle cybercrime. These changes come with a reinforced data protection framework and stronger parliamentary oversight and accountability. Furthermore, the implications of the war in Ukraine have only underlined the benefit of Europol. For instance, regarding the risk to the security of the EU posed by suspicious individuals entering the EU at its external borders, Europol is now present in all Member States neighbouring Ukraine and in Moldova with guest officers to support secondary security checks and information gathering, and with deployed Europol staff to support information sharing and analysis. On sanctions and economic crime, Europol has launched Operation Oscar to support financial investigations by Member States targeting criminal assets owned by individuals and legal entities EU-sanctioned.

II. EMPACT

Additionally, one of the key Europol and Commission supported instruments to fight organized and serious international crime that should be highlighted is EMPACT, the European Multidisciplinary Platform Against Criminal Threats. EMPACT develops partnerships between law enforcement authorities and helps build a framework for a more integrated EU security architecture. Through a four-year cycle, EMPACT delivers

[2] European Commission, 'Proposal for a Regulation of the European Parliament and of the Council on automated data exchange for police cooperation ("Prüm II"), amending Council Decisions 2008/615/JHA and 2008/616/JHA and Regulations (EU) 2018/1726, 2019/817 and 2019/818 of the European Parliament and of the Council', 8.12.2021, COM(2021) 784 final.

[3] European Commission, 'Proposal for a Directive of the European Parliament and of the Council on information exchange between law enforcement authorities of Member States, repealing Council Framework Decision 2006/960/JHA', 8.12.2021, COM(2021) 782 final.

operational results and training, capacity building, prevention, cooperation with non-EU partners and joint investigations against high-value targets. It regularly strikes some heavy blows on organized crime across Europe, including during 'Joint Action Days supported' by EU Agencies such as Europol and Frontex. For instance, in February 2022, a coordinated strike took place in EMPACT, involving the German Police Inspectorate Emsland/Bentheim, the German Dortmund Police, the Austrian Criminal Police Office and the Bosnian Ministry of Interior Affairs Canton Sarajevo, with the support of Europol. The strike led to the dismantlement of a gang of car thieves operating across Germany. This criminal network comprised Bosnian nationals who were residing illegally in Germany and committing crimes in the federal states of Lower Saxony, North-Rhine Westphalia and Hesse. They are suspected of breaking into residential buildings at night to steal the keys of expensive vehicles before driving off with them. The total value of the stolen vehicles exceeds EUR 1.5 million.

III. Drugs trafficking

Another area with a clear EU-added value is drugs policy. No Member State can intervene alone to address trafficking of drugs or drug demand. This can only be done efficiently at EU level, where national initiatives are supported and coordinated. In this context, for example, the European Monitoring Centre for Drugs and Drug Addictions (EMCDDA) provides the EU and its Member States with factual, objective, reliable and comparable information at European level on drugs, drug addiction and their consequences. It provides evidence to inform policymaking and guide initiatives to tackle drugs by monitoring the drugs problem in Europe (including emerging trends), solutions applied to drug-related problems, providing information on best practice in EU countries and encouraging them to share it, assessing the risks of new psychoactive substances and running an early warning system on new psychoactive substances, etc. In January 2022, the Commission proposed a targeted revision of the mandate of the current European Monitoring Centre for Drugs and Drug Addiction, transforming it into the European Union Drugs Agency.[4] It is the Commission's intention to update the mandate of the Agency for it to be appropriately equipped to deal with the current and future challenges posed by drugs in the EU and to continue to be the centre of excellence it is today.

IV. Counter-terrorism and violent extremism

Lastly, while Member States retain the primary responsibility in the fight against terrorism and radicalization, the undeniable cross-border dimension of the threat has called at several times for further steps in EU cooperation and coordination. This was the case with the Madrid and London bomb attacks in 2004 and 2005, after which important initiatives such as the current Critical Infrastructure Directive[5] were pushed forward. However, also after the more recent attacks, notably in France (Charlie Hebdo, Bataclan, Nice) important steps were taken to reinforce Europol (European Counter-Terrorism Centre), strengthen the EU criminal law framework with the Directive on combating terrorism and to take more vigorous action to protect public spaces and

---

[4] European Commission, 'Proposal for a Regulation of the European Parliament and the Council on the European Union Drugs Agency', 12.1.2022, COM(2022) 18 final.

[5] Directive 2008/114/EC on the identification and designation of European critical infrastructures and the assessment of the need to improve their protection.

places of worship.[6] All this evolution over the last 15–20 years is also well reflected in the EU strategy adopted at the end of 2020: the Counter-Terrorism Agenda for the EU.[7] The Counter-Terrorism Agenda has four key pillars: anticipate, prevent, protect and respond. These work strands reflect the different dimensions in which the EU Counter-Terrorism work has developed to offer solutions to an ever-evolving threat situation, reinforced now by new technologies.

[6] Directive (EU) 2017/541 on combating terrorism and replacing Council Framework Decision 2002/475/JHA and amending Council Decision 2005/671/JHA.

[7] European Commission, 'A Counter-Terrorism Agenda for the EU: Anticipate, Prevent, Protect, Respond', 9.12.2020, COM(2020) 795 final.

PART II
STRUCTURE AND PRINCIPLES

§ 4
Governance of the European Security Union*

Arne Pilniok

Bibliography: Aden, 'Der Zufall und andere "Themenmacher" – Problemdefinition und Agendagestaltung in der Kriminalpolitik', Monatsschrift für Kriminologie und Strafrechtsreform 2003 (86), 105; Aden, Police cooperation in the European Union under the Treaty of Lisbon, Baden-Baden 2015; Aden, 'Europäische Rechtsgrundlagen und Institutionen des Polizeihandelns' in Lisken/Denninger (eds), Handbuch des Polizeirechts, 7th edn, Munich 2021, p. 1809; Aden, 'Wie beeinflusst der Gerichtshof der EU die Politik öffentlicher Sicherheit?' in Rehder/Schneider (eds), Gerichtsverbünde, Grundrechte und Politiken in Europa, Baden-Baden 2016, p. 233; Aden, 'Europäisierung der Polizeiarbeit – ein Sonderfall im europäischen Verwaltungsraum?' in Kopke/Kühnel (eds), Demokratie, Freiheit und Sicherheit: Festschrift zum 65. Geburtstag von Hans-Gerd Jaschke, Baden-Baden 2017; Aden, 'Die Europäische Union als "Sicherheitsunion"? Die gemeinsame Innen- und Justizpolitik' in Müller-Graff (ed.), Kernelemente der europäischen Integration, Baden-Baden 2020, p. 457; Aden, 'Interoperability Between EU Policing and Migration Databases: Risks for Privacy', EPL 2020 (26), 93; Albi, 'The European Arrest Warrant, constitutional rights and the changing legal thinking' in Fletcher/Herlin-Karnell/Matera (eds), The European Union as an Area of Freedom, Security and Justice, London 2017, p. 137; Arzt, 'Das neue Gesetz zur Flugdatenspeicherung', DÖV 2017, 1023; Augsberg, 'Agencification der Kommissionsverwaltung' in Terhechte (ed.), Internationale Dimensionen des europäischen Verwaltungsrechts, Europarecht Beiheft 1/2016, 119; Baele/Jalea, 'Twenty-five Years of Securitization Theory: A Corpus-based Review', Political Studies Review 2023 (21:2), 376; Baldus, 'Staatliche Gewaltmonopole' in Mehde/Ramsauer/Seckelmann (eds), Festschrift für Hans Peter Bull zum 75. Geburtstag, Berlin 2011, p. 3; Baldus, 'Entgrenzungen des Sicherheitsrechts – Neue Polizeirechtdogmatik?', DV 2014, 1; Baldus/Heger, 'Recht auf Freiheit und Sicherheit' in Heselhaus/Nowak (eds), Handbuch der EU-Grundrechte, 2nd edn, Munich 2020, § 18; Barczak, 'Die Staatsanwaltschaft als „Justizbehörde"', JZ 2020, 1125; Bendiek, Europa verteidigen: Die Gemeinsame Außen- und Sicherheitspolitik der Europäischen Union, Stuttgart 2019; Blanke/Mangiameli (eds), Treaty on the Functioning of the European Union – A Commentary, Vol. 1, Berlin 2021; Böttner, 'The size and the structure of the European Commission – legal issues surrounding project teams and a (future) reduced college', European Constitutional Law Review 2018 (14), 37; Bossong, The Evolution of EU Counter Terrorism, London 2012; Bossong, 'Peer reviews in the fight of terrorism: A hidden dimension of European security governance', Cooperation and Conflict 2012 (47), 519; Bossong, 'Public Good Theory and the 'Added Value' of the EU's Counterterrorism Policy' in Brzoska (ed.), European peace and security policy, Baden-Baden 2014, p. 67; Bossong, 'Informelle Governance zur Inneren Sicherheit in Europa' in Frevel/Wendekamm (eds), Sicherheit zwischen Staat, Markt und Zivilgesellschaft, Wiesbaden 2017, p. 97; Bossong, 'Intelligente Grenzen und interoperable Datenbanken für die innere Sicherheit der EU', SWP-Studie 2018 (4); Bossong/Rhinard, 'Terrorism and transnational crime in Europe' in Economides/Sperling, EU Security Strategies, London 2018, p. 181; Brummund, Kohärenter Grundrechtsschutz im Raum der Freiheit, der Sicherheit und des Rechts, Baden-Baden 2011; Buckler, 'Auf dem Weg zu einer digitalen europäischen Grenzkontrollarchitektur?', BayVBl. 2018, 73; Buckler, 'Schengen-Grenzmanagement 2022', DÖV 2020, 749; Bull, Die Staatsaufgaben nach dem Grundgesetz, 2nd edn, Kronberg 1977; Buraczyński, Die Herstellung von Sicherheit an der EU-Außengrenze, Wiesbaden 2015; Bures, 'EU Counter-Terrorism' in Ripoll Servent/Trauner (eds), The Routledge Handbook of Justice and

* This is a revised and updated version of a contribution that was originally published in German in Dietrich/Fahrner/Gazeas/v. Heintschel-Heinegg (eds), Handbuch Sicherheits- und Staatsschutzrecht, Munich 2022.

Home Affairs, London 2018, p. 157; Buzan/Wæver/de Wilde, Security: A New Framework for Analysis, Boulder (CO) 1998; Calliess, 'Europäisierung der Staatsaufgabe Sicherheit' in Müller/Schneider (eds), Die Europäische Union im Kampf gegen den Terrorismus, Baden-Baden 2006, p. 83; Calliess, Öffentliche Güter im Recht der Europäischen Union, Gütersloh 2021; Calliess/Ruffert (eds), EUV/AEUV: Das Verfassungsrecht der Europäischen Union mit Europäischer Grundrechtecharta, 5th edn, Munich 2016; Calliess/Ruffert (eds), EUV/AEUV: Das Verfassungsrecht der Europäischen Union mit Europäischer Grundrechtecharta, 6th edn, Munich 2022; Cameron, 'European Union Law Restraints on Intelligence Activities', IJICI 2020 (33), 452; Carraçico/Farrand, 'Cyber Crime as a Fragmented Policy Field in the Context of the Area of Freedom, Security and Justice' in Ripoll Servent/Trauner (eds), The Routledge Handbook of Justice and Home Affairs, London 2018, p. 146; Carrapiço/Farrand, 'The European Union's fight against cybercrime' in Fletcher/Herlin-Karnell/Matera (eds), The European Union as an Area of Freedom, Security and Justice, London 2017, p. 459; Ceccorulli/Lucarelli, 'Securing borders, savings migrants: The EU's security dilemma in the twenty-first century' in Economides/Sperling (eds), EU Security Strategies: Extending the EU system of security governance, London 2018, p. 162; Coman-Kund, European Union Agencies as Global Actors, London 2018; Conrad, 'Europäische Nachrichtendienstkooperation – Entwicklungen, Erwartungen und Perspektiven' in Dietrich/Gärditz/Graulich/Gusy/Warg (eds), Reform der Nachrichtendienste zwischen Vergesetzlichung und Internationalisierung, Tübingen 2019, p. 161; Cross, 'The European space and intelligence networks', Journal of Transatlantic Studies 2020 (18), 209; Curtin, 'Overseeing Secrets in the EU: A Democratic Perspective', JCMS 2014 (52), 684; Curtin, 'Second order secrecy and Europe's legality mosaics', West European Politics 2018 (41), 846; Curtin/Bastos, 'Interoperable Information Sharing and the Five Novel Frontiers of EU Governance', EPL 2020 (26), 59; Czaika/Trauner, 'EU Visa Policy' in Ripoll Servent/Trauner (eds), The Routledge Handbook of Justice and Home Affairs, London 2018, p. 110; Dalby, 'Sicherheitsgesetzgebung unter dem Eindruck von Terror' in Gusy/Kugelmann/Würtenberger (eds), Rechtshandbuch Zivile Sicherheit, Wiesbaden 2017, p. 87; Dann, 'Programm- und Prozesssteuerung im europäischen Entwicklungsverwaltungsrecht' in Bartelt/Dann (eds), Entwicklungszusammenarbeit im Recht der Europäischen Union, Europarecht Beiheft 2/2008, Baden-Baden 2008, p. 107; Dann, Entwicklungsverwaltungsrecht: Theorie und Dogmatik des Rechts der Entwicklungszusammenarbeit, untersucht am Beispiel der Weltbank, der EU und der Bundesrepublik Deutschland, Tübingen 2012; Dankowski, Expertengruppen in der europäischen Rechtsetzung: Sachverständige Beratung der Europäischen Kommission im Spannungsfeld von Funktionalität und Gemeinwohlorientierung, Berlin 2019; De Capitani, 'Progress and Failure in the Area of Freedom, Security, and Justice' in Bignami (ed.), EU Law in Populist Times, Cambridge 2020, p. 375; De Hert/Papakonstantinou, 'Data Protection Policies in EU Justice and Home Affairs' in Ripoll Servent/Trauner, The Routledge Handbook of Justice and Home Affairs, London 2018, p. 169; de Waele, 'Priority 7: Justice, Fundamental Rights and the Juncker Commission: Qui trop embrasse, mal étreint?' in Stüwe/Panayotopoulos (eds), The Juncker Commission, Baden-Baden 2020, p. 157; Deubner, Security and Defence Cooperation in the EU, Baden-Baden 2018; Dörig/Langenfeld, 'Vollharmonisierung des Flüchtlingsrechts in Europa: Massenzustrom erfordert EU-Zuständigkeit für Asylverfahren', NJW 2016, 1; Eckes, 'External Relations Law: How the Outside Shapes the Inside' in Arcarazo/Murohy (eds) EU Security and Justice Law, Oxford 2014, p. 186; Esser, 'Eurojust vor neuen Aufgaben?', StV 2020, 636; Egeberg/Gornitzka/Trondal, 'Organization theory' in Ansell/Torfing (eds), Theories of governance, 2nd edn, Cheltenham 2022, p. 29; Egeberg/Trondal, An Organizational Approach to Public Governance: Understanding and Design, Oxford 2018; Fastenrath/Skerka, 'Sicherheit im Schengen-Raum nach dem Wegfall der Grenzkontrollen – Mechanismen und rechtliche Probleme grenzüberschreitender polizeilicher und justizieller Zusammenarbeit', ZeuS 2009, 219; Fichera, 'Sketches of a theory of Europe as an Area of Freedom, Security and Justice' in Fletcher/Herlin-Karnell/Matera (eds), The European Union as an Area of Freedom, Security and Justice, London 2017, p. 34; Fink, Frontex and Human Rights: Responsibility in 'Multi-Actor Situations' under the ECHR and EU Public Liability Law, Oxford 2018; Finke, 'Notwendigkeit und Grundlagen eines transnationalen und globalen Katastrophenschutzrechts' in Pünder/Klafki (eds), Risiko und Katastrophe als Herausforderung für die Verwaltung, Baden-Baden 2016, p. 211; Fisch, 'Verwaltungskulturen – Geronnene Geschichte?', DV 2000 (33), 303; Franzius, 'Recht und Politik in der transnationalen Konstellation', AöR 2014 (136:2), 205; Fritz, Die Bindung an die Europäische Grundrechtecharta bei operativen Einsätzen im Rahmen der gemeinsamen Außen- und Sicherheitspolitik und der Grenzschutzagentur Frontex: zugleich eine vergleichende Betrachtung des unionskoordinierten operativen Handelns, Berlin 2020; Funke, 'Primärrechtliche Grundlagen, Raum der Freiheit, der Sicherheit und des Rechts' in Ferdinand Wollenschläger (ed.), Europäischer Freizügigkeitsraum – Unionsbürgerschaft und Migrationsrecht, Baden-Baden 2021, § 16; Gärditz,

'Europäisches Regulierungsverwaltungsrecht auf Abwegen', AöR 2010 (135), 251; Gatti, 'The Role of the European External Action Service in the External Dimension of the Area of Freedom Security and Justice' in Flaesch-Mougin/Rossi (eds), La dimension extérieure de l'Espace de liberté, sécurité et de justice, Brussels 2013, p. 171; Gatti, European External Action Service: Promoting Coherence through Autonomy and Coordination, Leiden 2016; Gerbig, Grundrecht auf staatlichen Schutz: Ein Vergleich von Grundgesetz für die Bundesrepublik Deutschland und Verfassung der Vereinigten Staaten von Amerika, Berlin 2014; Giegerich, 'Die Unabhängigkeit der Gerichte als Strukturvorgabe der Unionsverfassung und ihr effektiver Schutz vor autoritären Versuchungen in den Mitgliedstaaten', ZEuS 2019, 61; Görisch, Demokratische Verwaltung durch Unionsagenturen, Tübingen 2009; Grabitz/Hilf/Nettesheim (eds), Das Recht der Europäischen Union: EUV/AEUV, 80th edn, Munich 2023; Grauvogel/Diez, 'Framing und Versicherheitlichung: Die diskursive Konstruktion des Klimawandels', Zeitschrift für Friedens- und Konfliktforschung 2014 (3), 203; Groß, 'Defizite des Grundrechtsschutzes bei FRONTEX-Einsätzen', ZAR 2020 (2), 51; Grimheden/Kjaerum/Toggenburg '"Administering Human Rights": The Experience of the EU's Fundamental Rights Agency' in Harlow/Leino/della Cananea (eds), Research Handbook on EU Administrative Law, Cheltenham 2017, p. 113; Gundel, 'Vorratsdatenspeicherung und Binnenmarktkompetenz: Die ungebrochene Anziehungskraft des Art. 95 EGV', EuR 2009, 536; Gusy, 'Sicherheitsrecht als Rechtsgebiet? – Ein Streit um Worte oder um die Sache und wenn ja, um welche Sache?' in Dietrich/Gärditz (eds), Sicherheitsverfassung – Sicherheitsrecht, Festgabe für Kurt Graulich zum 70. Geburtstag, Tübingen 2019, p. 9; Gusy/Ebeling, 'Die grundrechtliche Basis öffentlicher Sicherheit in Europa' in Kugelmann/Rackow (eds), Prävention und Repression im Raum der Freiheit, der Sicherheit und des Rechts, Baden-Baden 2014, p. 25; Härtel, 'Die Europäische Grundrechteagentur: unnötige Bürokratie oder gesteigerter Grundrechtsschutz?', EuR 2008, 489; Haltern, Europarecht: Dogmatik im Kontext, Bd. I: Entwicklung, Institutionen, Prozesse, 3rd edn, Tübingen 2017; Hecker, 'Die Europäisierung der inneren Sicherheit', DÖV 2006, 273; Hegemann, International counterterrorism bureaucracies in the United Nations and the European Union, Baden-Baden 2014; Heger, 'Einführung der Europäischen Staatsanwaltschaft in das deutsche Recht', ZRP 2020, 115; Herlin-Karnell, 'Constitutional Principles in the Area of Freedom, Security and Justice' in Arcarazo/Murohy (eds), EU Security and Justice Law, London 2014, p. 38; Herlin-Karnell, 'The EU as a Promoter of Preventive Criminal Justice and the Internal Security Context' in Léonard/Kaunert (eds), Searching for a Strategy for the European Union's Area of Freedom, Justice and Security, London 2017, p. 73; Herlin-Karnell, 'The European Court of Justice as a Game Changer: Fiduciary obligations in the area of freedom, security and justice' in Servent/Trauner, The Routledge Handbook of Justice and Home Affairs Research, London 2018, p. 396; Herlin-Karnell, The Constitutional Structure of Europe's Area of 'Freedom, Security and Justice' and the Right to Justification, Oxford 2019; Herrnfeld/Brodowski/Burchard, European Public Prosecutor's Office, Munich 2021; Hill, 'Innovation Labs: Neue Wege zu Innovation im öffentlichen Sektor', DÖV 2016, 493; Hofmann, 'Das Gewicht der Sicherheit als Herausforderung des liberalen Verfassungsstaates', GSZ 2020, 233; Huisjes/Tosza, 'Eurojust: mechanisms controlling the agency for coordination and cooperation in criminal matters' in Scholten/Brenninkmeijer (eds), Controlling EU Agencies, Cheltenham 2020, p. 234; Isensee, Das Grundrecht auf Sicherheit, Berlin 1983; Jann, 'Verwaltungskulturen im internationalen Vergleich. Ein Überblick über den Stand der Forschung', DV 2000 (33:3), 325; Jansen/Schöndorf-Haubold, The European Composite Administration, Antwerp 2011; Jong, 'EU agency tort law and its limited role in controlling agencies' in Scholten/Brenninkmeijer (eds), Controlling EU agencies, Cheltenham 2020, p. 117; Karamanidou, 'The Securitisation of European Migration Policies' in Lazaridis/Wadia (eds), The Securitisation of Migration in the EU, Basingstoke 2015, p. 37; Karpenstein/Sangi, 'Nationale Sicherheit im Unionsrecht', GSZ 2020, 162; Kastler, Föderaler Rechtsschutz: Personenbezogene Daten in einem Raum der Freiheit, der Sicherheit und des Rechts, Wiesbaden 2017; Kaufhold, 'Gegenseitiges Vertrauen: Wirksamkeitsbedingung und Rechtsprinzip im Raum der Freiheit, der Sicherheit und des Rechts', EuR 2008, 408; Kaufmann, Sicherheit als soziologisches und sozialpolitisches Problem, 2nd edn, Stuttgart 1973; Kaunert, 'The Area of Freedom, Security and Justice: Commission policy entrepreneurship?', Journal of European Security 2010 (19), 169; Kellerbauer/Klamert/Tomkin (eds), Commentary on the EU Treaties and the Charter of Fundamental Rights, Oxford 2019; Kirst, 'Firearms Regulation in the European Union: Striking a Delicate Balance Between Single Market and Security', Fordham Journal of International Law 2020 (439), 855, Klement, Verantwortung, Tübingen 2006; Kloepfer, Handbuch des Katastrophenrechtsschutzrecht, Baden-Baden 2015; Knelangen, Das Politikfeld innere Sicherheit im Integrationsprozess: Die Entstehung einer europäischen Politik der inneren Sicherheit, Wiesbaden 2001; Knodt/Große Hüttmann/Kobusch, 'Die EU in der Polykrise: Folgen für das Mehrebenen-Regieren' in Grimmel (ed.), Die neue Europäische Union, Wiesbaden 2020, 119; Konstdinides/

O'Meara, 'Fundamental Rights and Judicial Protection' in Arcarazo/Murohy (eds) EU Security and Justice Law, Oxford 2014, p. 77; Krüper, 'Legitimation durch Evaluation' in Gusy (ed.), Evaluation von Sicherheitsgesetzen, Wiesbaden 2015, p. 171; Kotzur, 'Grundfragen einer europäischen Sicherheitspolitik' in Hatje/Nettesheim (eds), Sicherheit in der Europäischen Union, EuR-Beiheft 3/2009, Baden-Baden 2009, p. 7; Kruse, Der Europäische Auswärtige Dienst zwischen intergouvernementaler Koordination und supranationaler Repräsentation, Berlin 2014; Kuskonmaz, 'The Grand Gala of PNR Litigations', European Constitutional Law Review 2023 (19), 294; Ladenburger, 'Das Verhältnis von Verwaltungsrechtswissenschaft und Verwaltungsrechtspraxis' in Kahl/Mager (eds), Verwaltungsrechtswissenschaft und Verwaltungsrechtspraxis, Baden-Baden 2019, p. 69; Ladenburger, 'The Principle of Mutual Trust between Member States in the Area of Freedom, Security and Justice', ZeuS 2020, 373; Lahl/Varwick, Sicherheitspolitik verstehen: Handlungsfelder, Kontroversen und Lösungsansätze, 2nd edn, Frankfurt 2021; Lauer, Informationshilfe im Rahmen der polizeilichen und justiziellen Zusammenarbeit in Strafsachen, Baden-Baden 2018; Lehner, 'Rechtliche Möglichkeiten zur Schaffung einer EU-Asylbehörde', in Lehner/Wapler (eds), Die herausgeforderte Rechtsordnung: Aktuelle Probleme der Flüchtlingspolitik, Berlin 2018, p. 183; Lehnert, Frontex und operative Maßnahmen an den europäischen Außengrenzen, Baden-Baden 2014; Lenaerts, 'The Contribution of the European Court of Justice to the Area of Freedom, Security and Justice', The International and Comparative Law Quarterly 2010 (59), 255; Léonard/Kaunert, Refugees, Security and the European Union, London 2019; Léonard/Kaunert, 'The development of Europol's external relations', Maastricht Journal of European and Comparative Law 2021 (28:2), 229; Leuschner, 'EuGH und Vorratsdatenspeicherung', EuR 2016, 431; Leuschner, 'Sicherheit als chartarechtliches Gewährleistungsziel in der EU' in Gusy/Kugelmann/Würtenberger (eds), Rechtshandbuch Zivile Sicherheit, Wiesbaden 2017, p. 173; Leuschner, Sicherheit als Grundsatz, Tübingen 2018; Lohse, Rechtsangleichungsprozesse in der Europäischen Union, Tübingen 2017; MacKenzie/Kaunert/Léonard, 'Counter-terrorism' in Trauner/Ripoll Servent (eds), Policy Change in the Area of Freedom, Security and Justice, London 2015, p. 93; Matera, 'An external dimension of the AFSJ?' in Fletcher/Herlin-Karnell/Matera (eds), The European Union as an Area of Freedom, Security and Justice, London 2017, p. 359; Matera/Gatti, 'Facultative Mixity in the Area of Freedom, Security and Justice' in Chamon/Govaere (eds), EU External Relations Post-Lisbon, Leiden 2020, p. 187; Menz, 'EU Labor Immigration Policy' in Ripoll Servent/Trauner (eds), The Routledge Handbook of Justice and Home Affairs, London 2018, p. 124; Mitsilegas, 'EU Criminal Competence after Lisbon' in Arcarazo/Murohy (eds), EU Security and Justice Law, Oxford 2014, p. 110; Mitsilegas, 'The Preventive Turn in European Security Policy' in Bignami (ed.), EU Law in Populist Times: Crises and Prospects, Cambridge 2020, p. 301; Mitsilegas/Guild/Kuskonmaz/Vavoula, 'Data retention and the future of large-scale surveillance: The evolution and contestation of judicial benchmarks', ELJ 2022, 1; Mitsilegas/Vavoula, 'Criminal law' in Trauner/Ripoll Servent (eds), Policy Change in the Area of Freedom, Security and Justice, London 2015, p. 133; Monar, The External Dimension of the EU's Area of Freedom, Security and Justice, Stockholm 2012; Möstl, Die staatliche Garantie für die öffentliche Sicherheit und Ordnung: Sicherheitsgewährleistung im Verfassungsstaat, im Bundesstaat und in der Europäischen Union, Tübingen 2002; Mrozek, Grenzschutz als supranationale Aufgabe, Baden-Baden 2013; Müller-Graff, 'Europäische Zusammenarbeit in den Bereichen Justiz und Inneres: Funktion, Ausgestaltung und Entwicklungsoptionen des dritten Pfeilers der Europäischen Union' in Müller-Graff (ed.), Europäische Zusammenarbeit in den Bereichen Justiz und Inneres, Baden-Baden 1996, p. 11; Müller-Graff, 'Der Raum der Freiheit, der Sicherheit und des Rechts in der Lissabonner Reform' in Schwarze/Hatje (eds), Der Reformvertrag von Lissabon, Europarecht Beiheft 1/2009, Baden-Baden 2009, p. 105; Müller-Graff, 'Der Raum der Freiheit, der Sicherheit und des Rechts: Integrationswert für Bürger und Gesellschaft, Mitgliedstaaten und Union', Integration 2012, 100; Nettesheim, 'Grundrechtskonzeptionen des EuGH im Raum der Freiheit, der Sicherheit und des Rechts', EuR 2009, 24; O'Neill, 'The development of the external dimension of the AFSJ – new challenges for the EU legal and policy framework' in Léonard/Kaunert (eds), Searching for a Strategy for the European Union's Area of Freedom, Justice and Security, London 2017, p. 24; Orator, Möglichkeiten und Grenzen der Einrichtung von Unionsagenturen, Tübingen 2017; Pache, 'Die Union als Raum der Freiheit, der Sicherheit und des Rechts' in Niedobitek (ed.), Europarecht: Grundlagen und Politiken der Union, 2nd edn, Berlin 2020, § 21; Palacios, 'On the Road to a European Intelligence Agency?', IJICI 2020 (33), 483; Pechstein/Nowak/Häde (eds), Frankfurter Kommentar zu EUV/GRC/AEUV, Tübingen 2017; Peers, 'Justice and Home Affairs Law since the Treaty of Lisbon' in Arcarazo/Murohy (eds) EU Security and Justice Law, London 2014, p. 17; Peers, 'The rise and fall of EU justice and home affairs law' in Fletcher/Herlin-Karnell/Matera (eds), The European Union as an Area of Freedom, Security and Justice, London 2016, p. 11; Peers/Hervey/Kenner/Ward (eds), The Charter of

Fundamental Rights, Munich/Oxford/Baden-Baden 2014; Pernice, 'Europäisches und nationales Verfassungsrecht', VVDStRL 2000, 148; Pernice, 'Der Europäische Verfassungsverbund auf dem Weg der Konsolidierung', JöR 2000, 205; Pernice, Der Europäische Verfassungsverbund, Baden-Baden 2020; Peuker, 'Datenschutz als Annexkompetenz', ZfDR 2023, 384; Peuker, 'Unionsrechtliche Regelungskompetenzen im Bereich der nationalen Sicherheit. Zur Auslegung von Art. 4 Abs. 2 S. 3 EUV unter kritischer Würdigung der EuGH-Rechtsprechung', EuR 2023, 535; Pilniok, Governance im europäischen Forschungsförderverbund: Eine rechtswissenschaftliche Analyse der Forschungspolitik und Forschungsförderung im Mehrebenensystem, Tübingen 2011; Pilniok, 'Zwischen Wissenschaft, Politik und Verwaltung: Die Gemeinsame Forschungsstelle der Europäischen Kommission als Element der europäischen Wissensinfrastruktur', DÖV 2012, 662; Pilniok, 'Struktur, Funktionen und Probleme der Expertengruppen der Europäischen Kommission: legitime Expertise oder unzulässige Einflussnahme?', EuR 2014, 62; Pilniok, 'Europäisches Wissenschaftsverwaltungsrecht' in Terhechte (ed.), Europäisches Verwaltungsrecht, 2nd edn, Baden-Baden 2021, § 38; Pilniok, Parlamentarisches Regieren: Theorie, Dogmatik und Praxis der Organisationsverfassung demokratischer Herrschaft unter dem Grundgesetz (forthcoming); Poli, 'The EU anti-terrorism policy in the external AFSJ dimension' in Ripoll Servent/Trauner (eds), The Routledge Handbook of Justice and Home Affairs, London 2018, p. 389; Rademacher, Rechtsschutz gegen Realakte im Rechtsschutzsystem der EU, Tübingen 2014; Rasmussen, 'Plädoyer für ein Ende des judikativen Schweigens' in Haltern/Bergmann (eds), Der EuGH in der Kritik, Tübingen 2012, p. 113; Reimer, Verwaltungsdatenschutzrecht: Das neue Recht für die behördliche Praxis, Baden-Baden 2019; Revelas, 'Permanent Structured Cooperation: not a panacea, but an important step for consolidating EU security and defence cooperation' in Waechter/Vérez (eds), Europe, Baden-Baden 2020, p. 53; Rieckhoff, Der Vorbehalt des Gesetzes im Europarecht, Tübingen 2007; Rijpma, 'Brave New Borders' in Cremona (ed.), New Technologies and EU Law, Oxford 2017, p. 197; Rijpma, 'Institutions and Agencies: Government and Governance after Lisbon' in Arcarazo/Murphy (eds), EU Security and Justice Law, Oxford 2014, p. 54; Ripoll Servent, 'The European Parliament in Justice and Home Affairs' in Ripoll Servent/Trauner (eds), The Routledge Handbook of Justice and Home Affairs, London 2018, p. 385; Robbers, Sicherheit als Menschenrecht: Aspekte der Geschichte, Begründung und Wirkung einer Grundrechtsfunktion, Baden-Baden 1987; Röhl, 'Die Beteiligung der Bundesrepublik Deutschland an der Rechtsetzung im Ministerrat der Europäischen Union', EuR 1994, 409; Roos, 'The Council and European Council in EU Justice and Home Affairs Politics' in Ripoll Servent/Trauner (eds), The Routledge Handbook of Justice and Home Affairs, London 2018, p. 421; Rüß, 'Internationale nachrichtendienstliche Zusammenarbeit' in Dietrich/Eiffler (eds), Handbuch des Rechts der Nachrichtendienste, Stuttgart 2017, § 4; Sauer, '"Solange" geht in Altersteilzeit – Der unbedingte Vorrang der Menschenwürde vor dem Unionsrecht', NJW 2016, 1134; Saurer, 'Die Errichtung von Europäischen Agenturen auf der Grundlage der Binnenmarktharmonisierungskompetenz des Art. 114 AEUV', DÖV 2014, 549; Scheffel, 'Auf dem Weg zu einer europäischen Verteidigungsunion', NVwZ 2018, 1347; Schmidt, The European Court of Justice and the Policy Process: The Shadow of the Case Law, Oxford 2018; Schmidt-Aßmann, 'Der Europäische Verwaltungsverbund und die Rolle des Europäischen Verwaltungsrechts' in Schmidt-Aßmann/Schöndorf-Haubold (eds), Der europäische Verwaltungsverbund, Tübingen 2005, p. 1; Schmidt-Aßmann/Schöndorf-Haubold, Der europäische Verwaltungsverbund, Tübingen 2005; Schneider, 'Informationssysteme als Bausteine des Europäischen Verwaltungsverbundes', NVwZ 2012, 65; Schnettger, Verbundidentität: Schutzgehalt, Funktionen und gerichtliche Durchsetzung des Art. 4 Abs. 2 S. 1 Var. 2 EUV, Tübingen 2021; Schöndorf-Haubold, Europäisches Sicherheitsverwaltungsrecht, Baden-Baden 2010; Schöndorf-Haubold, 'Das Recht der Zivilen Sicherheit an der Schnittstelle von nationaler, europäischer und internationaler Zuständigkeit' in Gusy/Kugelmann/Würtenberger (eds), Rechtshandbuch Zivile Sicherheit, Wiesbaden 2017, p. 691; Schöndorf-Haubold, 'Europäisches Polizei- und Sicherheitsrecht' in Terhechte (ed.), Verwaltungsrecht der Europäischen Union, 2nd edn, Baden-Baden 2022, § 35; Schoppa, Europol im Verbund der europäischen Sicherheitsagenturen, Berlin 2013; Schwarze/Becker/Hatje/Schoo (eds), EU-Kommentar, 4th edn, Baden-Baden 2019; Schwartz, Das Katastrophenschutzrecht der Europäischen Union, Baden-Baden 2012; Stoll, Sicherheit als Aufgabe von Staat und Gesellschaft, Tübingen 2003; Schuppan, 'Shared Service Center' in Veit/Reichard/Wewer (eds), Handbuch zur Verwaltungsreform, 5th edn, Wiesbaden 2019, p. 297; Sule, Spionage: Völkerrechtliche, nationalrechtliche und europarechtliche Bewertung staatlicher Spionagehandlungen und besonderer Berücksichtigung der Wirtschaftsspionage, Baden-Baden 2006; Sule, 'National Security and EU law restraints on Intelligence Activities' in Dietrich/Sule (eds), Intelligence Law and Policies in Europe, Munich/Oxford/Baden-Baden 2019, p. 335; Tabbara/v. Achenbach, 'Der gemeinsame parlamentarische Kontrollausschuss für Europol: Innovative Verwaltungskontrolle in der EU', DV 2021, 73; Thörner,

Der Nexus von innerer und äußerer Sicherheit, Tübingen 2022; Trute, 'Katastrophenschutzrecht – Besichtigung eines verdrängten Rechtsgebiets', KritV 2005 (88:4), 342; Trute, 'Demokratische Legitimation der Verwaltung' in Voßkuhle/Eifert/Möllers (eds), Grundlagen des Verwaltungsrechts, 3rd edn, Munich 2022, § 9; van Middelaar, Das europäische Pandämonium, Berlin 2021; Vara, 'The EU's Agencies' in Ripoll Servent/Trauner (eds), The Routledge Handbook of Justice and Home Affairs, London 2018, p. 445; Vavoula, 'Databases for Non-EU Nationals and the Right to Private Life: Towards a System of Generalised Surveillance of Movement?' in Bignami (ed.), EU Law in Populist Times, Cambridge 2020, p. 227; Vavoula, Immigration and Privacy in the Law of the European Union, Leiden 2022; v. Achenbach, Demokratische Gesetzgebung in der Europäischen Union, Wiesbaden 2014; v. Achenbach, 'Verfassungswandel durch Selbstorganisation: Triloge im europäischen Gesetzgebungsverfahren', Der Staat 2016 (55), 1; v. Bogdandy, 'Grundrechtsschutz durch die Europäische Grundrechteagentur' in Merten/Papier (eds), Handbuch der Grundrechte in Deutschland und Europa VI/1, Munich 2010, p. 1249; v. Bogdandy/Hering, 'Die Informationsbeziehungen im europäischen Verwaltungsverbund' in Voßkuhle/Eifert/Möllers (eds), Grundlagen des Verwaltungsrechts, 3rd edn, Munich 2022, § 25; v. Bogdandy/Schill, 'Die Achtung der nationalen Identität unter dem reformierten Unionsvertrag', ZaöRV 2010 (70), 701; von der Groeben/Schwarze/Hatje (eds), Europäisches Unionsrecht, 7th edn, Baden-Baden 2015; Vorrath/Zoppei, 'Africa-EU Relations on Organized Crime' in Ripoll Servent/Trauner (eds), The Routledge Handbook of Justice and Home Affairs, London 2018, p. 323; Wæver, 'Securitization and Desecuritization' in Lipschutz (ed.), On Security, New York 1995, p. 46; Walus, 'Europäischer Katastrophenschutz', EuR 2010, 564; Weiembergh/Brière, 'EU Criminal Law' in Ripoll Servent/Trauner (eds), The Routledge Handbook of Justice and Home Affairs, London 2018, p. 192; Weinzierl, 'Die EU-Task-Force für Griechenland: Internationale Beratung am Beispiel der griechischen Steuerverwaltung' in Klemm/Schultheiß, Die Krise in Griechenland, Frankfurt am Main 2015, 448; Weiß, Der Europäische Verwaltungsverbund: Grundfragen, Kennzeichen, Herausforderungen, Berlin 2010; Wieczorek, 'Understanding JHA Agencies in context: Where does Eurojust lie in the constitutional architecture of the Area of Freedom, Security and Justice' in Fletcher/Herlin-Karnell/Matera (eds), The European Union as an Area of Freedom, Security and Justice, London 2017, p. 441; Wischmeyer, Informationssicherheit, Tübingen 2023; Wischmeyer, 'Regierungs- und Verwaltungshandeln durch KI' in Ebers/Heinze/Krügel/Steinrötter (eds), Künstliche Intelligenz und Robotik, Munich 2020, § 20; Wolff, 'Der EU-Richtlinienentwurf zum Datenschutz in Polizei und Justiz' in Kugelmann/Rackow (eds), Prävention und Repression im Raum der Freiheit, der Sicherheit und des Rechts, Baden-Baden 2014, p. 61; Wolff, 'Terrorismus als Katalysator der Rechtsentwicklung' in Kugelmann (ed.), Polizei und Menschenrechte, Bonn 2019, p. 417; Wood, 'Mapping EU Agencies as Political Entrepreneurs', European Journal of Political Research 2018 (57), 404; Zalnieriute, 'A Struggle for Competence: National Security, Surveillance and the Scope of EU Law at the Court of Justice of the European Union', Modern Law Review 2021 (85:1), 198; Zaun, 'The European Commission in Justice and Home Affairs' in Ripoll Servent/Trauner (eds), The Routledge Handbook of Justice and Home Affairs, London 2018, p. 409.

A. Guaranteeing security: a joint undertaking

1 The task of guaranteeing security, traditionally the responsibility of the nation-state,[1] has been comprehensively Europeanised.[2] This development is a fairly novel aspect of European integration whose importance can hardly be overestimated[3] and for which there is no blueprint in the history of modern statehood. It is given concrete expression in a variety of

[1] Bull, p. 347 et seqq.; Knelangen, p. 34 et seqq.; Hecker DÖV 2006, 273 et seqq.; Funke in Wollenschläger, Europäischer Freizügigkeitsraum – Unionsbürgerschaft und Migrationsrecht, § 16 mn. 7.

[2] Calliess in Müller/Schneider, Die Europäische Union im Kampf gegen den Terrorismus, p. 83 et seqq.; Calliess, p. 20. See also European Council, 'European Council meeting (20 June 2019) – Conclusions', 20.6.2019, EUCO 9/19, 6, which in particular emphasises the need for cooperation in the security policy dimensions.

[3] On historical developments in that regard, see, e.g. Peers in Fletcher et al., The European Union as an Area of Freedom, Security and Justice, p. 11 et seqq.

facets: The state's monopoly on power[4] is developing into a duopoly including EU officials also empowered (though so far only in certain instances) to exert sovereign powers. The responsibility of the nation-states for internal and external security[5] is eclipsed by the EU Member States' responsibility for guaranteeing security within the territory of the Union as established under EU constitutional law. The existence of a borderless internal market renders this just as necessary as do various transnational phenomena that can be described as the 'drivers of insecurity', such as cross-border terrorism, migration flows, climate change, pandemics, biosecurity and cybersecurity.[6] The guarantee of security is therefore a public good,[7] the provision of which has become a joint undertaking of the Union and the Member States within an integrated European constitutional order.[8] The focus is thereby placed on the creation of an Area of Freedom, Security and Justice, one of the Union's explicit objectives under EU constitutional law. Yet even beyond that, diverse Union competences touch on security issues, from legal harmonization in the internal market to civil protection and the Common Foreign and Security Policy (CFSP). Nevertheless, there is one feature that sets apart the division of competences between the Union and the Member States, as laid down in primary EU law from other EU policies, which is its impact on governance structures. Despite all the Europeanization and interconnectedness, there is an integration-proof core. Art. 4(2) sent. 3 TEU states 'national security remains the sole responsibility of each Member State.' In view of the momentum behind EU law – in particular when it comes to regulating digital systems and markets – this issue is central to the constitution of the European Security Union (→ § 8).

The evolving guarantee of security in the EU's multi-level system has also led to governance structures becoming comprehensively Europeanized. The institutionalization of EU agencies is an essential element when it comes to realizing the Security Union. The EU agencies have only limited operational competences and personnel to deploy, though. That is why the Member States' resource-intensive administrative infrastructures still form the core when it comes to guaranteeing security in Europe. Nevertheless, the Member States' security authorities are to a large extent integrated into the EU's administrative order. They are substantially shaped and determined by EU legislation, EU funding programmes, and specific coordination and cooperation mechanisms that involve the EU's security authorities. An extensive 'composite administration' has emerged within the security administration, as it has in all other policy fields.[9] Taking this perspective indicates that – due to the distribution of competences – the integrated administration cannot be built on the Union's hierarchical control of the security administration but on horizontally and vertically agreed collaboration within 2

[4] See Baldus Mehde/Ramsauer/Seckelmann, Festschrift für Hans Peter Bull zum 75. Geburtstag, p. 3 et seqq.

[5] The German Federal Constitutional Court ruled on this decades ago: 'The security of the state as a constitutional power of peace and order and the security of its population to be guaranteed by it are constitutional values which […] are indispensable because the institution of the state derives its actual and ultimate justification from them.' (BVerfG 1.8.1978 – 2 BvR 1013/77, NJW 1978, 2235 (2237), [own translation]; reference is also made to this ruling in Leuschner, p. 173 (174), fn. 6.

[6] For the citation and more details relating to the development of these phenomena, see Lahl/Varwick, p. 75 et seqq. See also European Council, 'European Council meeting (20 June 2019) – Conclusions', 20.6.2019, EUCO 9/19.

[7] Calliess, p. 20 et seqq.

[8] More generally on the term 'constitutional union' (*Verfassungsverbund*), see Pernice, VVDStRL 2000, 148 (163 et seqq.); Pernice, JöR 2000, 205 et seqq.; Pernice, p. 1 et seqq.

[9] See, more generally, on this, Jansen/Schöndorf-Haubold; see Aden in Kopke/Kühnel, Demokratie, Freiheit und Sicherheit: Festschrift zum 65. Geburtstag von Hans-Gerd Jaschke, p. 239 et seqq.; on the 'composite administration'in general, see Schmidt-Aßmann/Schöndorf-Haubold, p. 1 et seqq. and Weiß, p. 1 et seqq.; on the 'composite security administration' (Verbund der Sicherheitsverwaltung), see Schöndorf-Haubold, p. 1 et seqq.

different networks of authorities. Since the Union's actions either supplement, supersede or superimpose the Member States' sector-specific activities, a new distribution of tasks is emerging that is shaped by ever more detailed EU secondary law.

3 As a result, complex cooperative governance structures in relation to the guarantee of security have evolved in the European setting. They are characterized by various institutional factors: First, the EU bodies' organizational structures need to be aligned to the task of guaranteeing security. Second, the institutionalization of new players with responsibility for these issues represents a key mode of governance in the Union. Once a new body or a new authority has been established, that body not only has a lasting impact in terms of the performance of its tasks, but also in terms of shaping the discourse and perceiving problems.[10] Besides establishing authorities at the EU level, setting up several informal and formal cooperation platforms is a key aspect of integration for the Member States' administrations. Close cooperation leads to the creation of epistemic communities of officials that are an important factor when it comes to integration within the Security Union.[11] Besides the harmonization of legislation, which has a direct or indirect impact on the guarantee of security, the incentives created by allocating funding to certain EU measures are another key mode of governance that has grown significantly in dimension in the field of internal security – though thus far largely unnoticed by the general public. These instruments all become politically and legally more plausible if they are geared to an overarching goal. Being guided by a common idea is thus a key instrument of European governance, that is an idea that is initially legally non-binding but has an indirect impact on account of secondary lawmaking being aligned to it. In the field of security, this strategy – which is well-known in other policy areas – is intended to bring together different aspects and legal bases in one highly recognisable term – the European Security Union.[12]

B. The European Security Union: a legal and political objective

4 The term 'security' is ambiguous and can be assigned various meanings. The first step must therefore be to analyse how the term is concretized in the EU context.[13] The guarantee of security is one of the Union's key objectives in primary EU law. As set out programmatically in Art. 3(2) TEU, the EU offers its citizens an Area of Freedom, Security and Justice without internal borders. This wording fits seamlessly into the diverse area-specific approaches to integration that have been adopted in other policy areas, such as the European Higher Education Area or the European Research Area,[14] and contains 'territorial claim and a symbolic claim'.[15] Art. 3(2) TEU expresses the functional link between security and integration that is based on a logic of compensation.[16] Because the EU constitutes an area without internal borders, compensatory measures need to be put in place. Taking a historical perspective on the integration process, the creation of the

[10] See Egeberg/Gornitzka/Trondal in Ansell/Torfing, Theories of governance, p. 29 et seq.

[11] See, with reference to the EU's internal security, Cross, Journal of Transatlantic Studies 2020, 209 et seq.

[12] See European Council, 'European Council meeting (20 June 2019) – Conclusions', 20.6.2019, EUCO 9/19, 6.

[13] See also Kotzur in Hatje/Nettesheim, Sicherheit in der Europäischen Union, p. 7 et seqq.

[14] See Müller-Graff in Schwarze/Hatje, Der Reformvertrag von Lissabon, p. 107; on the European Research Area, see Pilniok (2011), p. 63 et seqq.; for a critical analysis, see Funke in Wollenschläger, Europäischer Freizügigkeitsraum – Unionsbürgerschaft und Migrationsrecht, § 16 mn. 7, see also Thörner, p. 60 et seqq.

[15] Fichera in Fletcher/Herlin-Karnell/Matera, The European Union as an Area of Freedom, Security and Justice, p. 40.

[16] On this term and line of argument, see Thörner, p. 59 et seq.

internal market and the associated free movement of people within the Schengen Area were therefore central to deepening cooperation on internal security and subsequently to developing the idea of a European Security Union.[17] Listing the Area of Freedom, Security and Justice as the first of the Union's four main objectives serves to attach particular importance to the dimension of integration going forward.[18] It is thus clear that, under primary EU law, security is a key factor for integration.[19] Since the Treaty of Lisbon, at the latest, it has no longer been focused on market integration[20] and now even ranks the guarantee of security above the common market.[21] The Union is therefore designed to be a comprehensive political community. This evolution of the objectives and the related competence structure has a lasting impact on the Union's definition of 'security' on which the EU bodies base their actions.

Consequently, the Council and especially the European Commission developed this abstract objective as set out in EU constitutional law programmatically into the Internal Security Strategy for the European Union.[22] Since 2016 the goals and measures set out in that Strategy have been summarized under the pithy concept of a 'European Security Union'.[23] Semantically, it expresses the EU's comprehensive aspiration in relation to the guarantee of security that, naturally, has to be measured against the division of competences between the Union and the Member States. At the same time, the definition of 'security' is broad – although there are differences in the details between how the (European) Council and the Commission apply the term. According to the European Council's Internal Security Strategy, '[t]he concept of internal security must be understood as a wide and comprehensive concept which straddles multiple sectors in order to address these major threats and others which have a direct impact on the lives, safety and well-being of citizens, including natural and man-made disasters such as forest fires, earthquakes, floods and storms.'[24] Major threats, as the European Council understands them, are terrorism, serious and organized crime, illicit drug trafficking, computer crime, trafficking in human beings, sexual exploitation of children and child pornography, white-collar crime and corruption, illicit arms trafficking and cross-border crime.[25] Similarly, the Commission also has a broad understanding of the 5

[17] Knelangen, p. 101: 'Catalyst for cooperation in the policy field of internal security'; in a similar vein, Calliess, p. 21.

[18] Terhechte in Grabitz/Hilf/Nettesheim, EUV Art. 3 mn. 33: 'the operational part of Union law [will] take a central position in the further course of integration in the years to come.'

[19] See also Müller-Graff, integration 2012, 100 et seqq.

[20] Müller-Graff in Schwarze/Hatje, Der Reformvertrag von Lissabon, p. 111, which uses the term 'transnational community'; likewise Terhechte in Grabitz/Hilf/Nettesheim, EUV Art. 3 mn. 33.

[21] On the central objective of guaranteeing safety, see European Council, 'European Council meeting (20 June 2019) – Conclusions', 20.6.2019, EUCO 9/19, 6.

[22] See European Council, 'Internal security strategy for the European Union, March 2010; Council of the European Union, Draft Council Conclusions on the Renewed European Union Internal Security Strategy 2015–2020', 10.6.2015, Doc. 9798/15; most recently, Council of the European Union, 'Council Conclusions on Internal Security and European Police Partnership', 24.11.2020, Doc. 13083/1/20.

[23] See European Commission, 'Delivering on the European Agenda on Security to fight against terrorism and pave the way towards an effective and genuine Security Union', 20.4.2016, COM(2016) 230 final; European Commission, 'EU Security Union Strategy', 24.6.2020, COM(2020) 605 final and, most recently, on the current state of play European Commission, 'Sixth Progress Report on the implementation of the EU Security Union Strategy', 18.10.2023, COM(2023) 665 final.

[24] European Council, 'Internal security strategy for the European Union', March 2010, 7120/10; the strategy was prepared by Justice and Home Affairs Council and subsequently adopted by the European Council according to Art. 68 TFEU.

[25] The areas mentioned in the Council's strategy largely correspond to the areas of crime referred to in Art. 83(1) TFEU.

Security Union's areas of activity without offering a similarly concise definition.[26] The EU's approach is thus strongly characterized by its abstract orientation towards prevention. Under the Union's concept, no clear distinction is drawn between protection against threats and law enforcement.[27] Its point of reference was initially to protect each individual from interference, by other private actors or states, with their legally protected rights – in particular life, liberty, physical integrity and property – but it goes significantly beyond that. The Union's definition of 'security' covers more than the management of risks posed by people, things and nature,[28] and is increasingly focusing on safeguarding the proper functioning of society, for instance by means of the supply of essential public goods.[29]

6 The above definition and other documents make it clear that various other EU policy areas that go beyond the traditional field of 'internal security' as the term is understood by the Member States need to be incorporated into the guarantee of security.[30] Seen in that way, security policy is thus an overarching cross-sectional task.[31] This conceptual approach illustrates the multi-layered contexts in which the term 'security' is used. This is based on the approaches developed in the political sciences, which regard 'security' from a constructivist perspective (though with differences when it comes to the details). The notion of 'securitization' draws attention to the fact that virtually every political issue can be described as a security issue, that is insofar as society accepts that fact.[32] Such 'framing'[33] of certain issues leads to a shift in competences, media attention and political feasibility. One such example is the attitude that is prevalent in the EU that migration is a security issue.[34] A structurally similar debate is gaining in importance, which is whether climate change and its consequences should now be defined as a security issue.[35] The Commission, Council and Parliament, the EU's security agencies and the various actors in the Member States continuously work towards finding a shared discursive understanding of what problems need to be addressed within security policy. A tendency towards delimitation is thus intrinsic to the broad term 'security'.[36] This also has repercussions for governance structures within the European Security Union: Every policy area may potentially be relevant to security, meaning that wide-ranging competences are available to Union lawmaking. Also, diverse authorities can be empowered to contribute to the European Security Union.

---

[26] COM(2020) 605 final.

[27] Mitsilegas in Bignami, EU Law in Populist Times: Crises and Prospects, p. 308 et seqq.

[28] See Stoll, p. 13 et seqq., for whom, in addition to internal security, occupational health and safety as well as the security of facilities, technologies and products form part of the guarantee of security.

[29] Lahl/Varwick, p. 19; for a detailed description, see Buraczyński, p. 27 et seqq.

[30] Fichera in Fletcher/Herlin-Karnell/Matera, The European Union as an Area of Freedom, Security and Justice, p. 38.

[31] See conceptually Kaufmann, p. 1 et seqq.

[32] For a fundamental analysis, see Wæver in Lipschutz, p. 46 et seqq.; Buzan/Wæver/de Wilde, p. 1 et seqq.; for a comprehensive review of the literature, see Baele/Jalea, Political Studies Review 2023, 376 et seqq.; for a legal perspective, Kotzur in Hatje/Nettesheim, Sicherheit in der Europäischen Union, p. 11 et seqq.

[33] On this approach, Grauvogel/Diez, Zeitschrift für Friedens- und Konfliktforschung 2014, 203 et seqq.

[34] Buraczyński, p. 55 et seqq.; Karamanidou in Lazaridis/Wadia, p. 37 et seqq.; Ceccorulli/Lucarelli in Economides/Sperling, EU Security Strategies, p. 162 et seqq.; Léonard/Kaunert, p. 1 et seqq; for a more cautious approach, see European Council, 'European Council meeting (20 June 2019) – Conclusions', 20.6.2019, EUCO 9/19, 7.

[35] Grauvogel/Diez, Zeitschrift für Friedens- und Konfliktforschung 2014, 203 et seqq.

[36] See Baldus DV 2014, 1 et seqq.; on the difficulties of defining the concept of security from a jurisprudential perspective; Gusy in Dietrich/Gärditz, Sicherheitsverfassung – Sicherheitsrecht, Festgabe für Kurt Graulich zum 70. Geburtstag, p. 9 et seqq.

At the same time, the EU's security-policy objectives are also always shaped by actual developments.[37] Isolated, random events that attract wide social and media attention – such as terrorist attacks,[38] longer crises like the COVID-19 pandemic and the large numbers of refugees seeking entry at the EU's external borders – are usually dealt with at short notice in the Commission's strategy papers and legislative proposals.[39] The 9/11 attacks in the United States, for instance, and the various terrorist attacks perpetrated in the EU Member States since 2004 have acted as a catalyst for the EU's security policy.[40] This periodically creates new options in terms of political action. Previously debated proposals thus become capable of gaining a majority when the factual premises change.[41] As a consequence, European security policy and how its legal bases are interpreted are constantly evolving. Whilst a dynamic response to previously unknown phenomena does appear desirable, it also runs the risk of calling forth kneejerk legislative reactions (including in the Member States) that are not based on a thorough assessment of and reflection on the existing legal framework.[42] 7

The fact that changing *leitmotifs* have a lasting impact on the political debate is closely linked to this development. Whilst at the start of the integration process in the 1990s security policy focused on cross-border crime[43] – in response to the internal market and the Schengen regime – the safeguarding of the Union's external borders, terrorism and cybersecurity (→ § 16) have now become the dominant issues and narratives in the political discourse.[44] These phenomena, which are cross-border in nature, legitimize the EU's actions by promising to give them added value.[45] That also gives expression to the fact that, despite general objectives such as the establishment of the Security Union and not least on account of the division of competences within its multi-level system, the Union must focus on certain security-related issues and phenomena.[46] Put another way, the Union has competences and modes of action in various policy areas that give it more opportunities to act than it has in those areas that were traditionally linked to internal security, given that they are largely shaped by the Member States' personnel, financial and legal resources.[47] 8

Furthermore, Art. 3(5) sent. 1 and Art. 21 TEU also expressly define the goal of protecting the Union's citizens in the context of its external actions. This objective thus takes up the traditional distinction drawn between 'internal' and 'external' security, which empowers different authorities to act depending on the source of the threat.[48] 9

---

[37] See, more generally, also Dalby in Gusy/Kugelmann/Würtenberger, Rechtshandbuch Zivile Sicherheit, p. 87 et seqq.; Wolff in Kugelmann, Polizei und Menschenrechte, p. 417 et seqq.

[38] For a general take, see Aden, Monatsschrift für Kriminologie und Strafrechtsreform 2003, 105 et seqq.

[39] On the transformative effects for the Union as a whole, see van Middelaar, p. 1 et seqq.

[40] Bossong, p. 38 et seqq., 73 et seqq., 92 et seqq.; Aden in Rehder/Schneider, Gerichtsverbünde, Grundrechte und Politiken in Europa, p. 233.

[41] See on 'windows of opportunity' MacKenzie/Kaunert/Leonard in Trauner/Servent, Policy Change in the Area of Freedom, Security and Justice, p. 93 et seqq.; Aden in Rehder/Schneider, Gerichtsverbünde, Grundrechte und Politiken in Europa, p. 235, referring to the garbage can theory applied in administrative research.

[42] See Krüper in Gusy, Evaluation von Sicherheitsgesetzen, p. 171 et seqq.

[43] On this development, see Knelangen, p. 101 et seqq.

[44] European Council, 'European Council meeting (20 June 2019) – Conclusions', 20.6.2019, EUCO 9/19.

[45] Bossong uses the example of counter-terrorism: Bossong in Brzoska, European peace and security policy, p. 67 et seqq.

[46] Pache is critical of the concept of a Security Union on account of its competence structure: Pache in Niedobitek, Europarecht: Grundlagen und Politiken der Union, § 21 mn. 41.

[47] See also Schöndorf-Haubold in Gusy/Kugelmann/Würtenberger, Rechtshandbuch Zivile Sicherheit, p. 691 (696).

[48] Lahl/Varwick, p. 61.

However, this outdated dichotomy has undeniably become extremely questionable from both a theoretical, factual and legal perspective.[49] Both Member States' national and the EU's security guarantees focus on phenomena that are not limited to a specific territory and thus create interdependencies between internal and external security.[50] Instead, the 'security nexus' that encompasses both dimensions is stressed in the political and legal discourse.[51] That creates a new need to coordinate activities to achieve a coherent policy and institutional cooperation. Despite the existence of various legal regimes, the boundaries between internal and external security are thus fluid – a characteristic feature of security policy in the EU.[52] Various points of intersection have emerged. This is, for example, evident in the fact that EU missions under the Common Security and Defence Policy (CSDP) also serve to guarantee security at the EU's external borders (→ mn. 24). Internal and external security also overlap in the area of cybersecurity (→ § 16) and when it comes to the protection of critical infrastructure. The term 'hybrid threats'[53] (→ § 17) describes a phenomenon where third states use covert military and civilian means to destabilize the EU Member States' social order and, thus indirectly, the Union itself as well, for instance by means of targeted disinformation campaigns or cyber attacks on public infrastructure.[54] In terms of 'internal' security, that means that EU law must also be ready to address external threats, although limited by the Union's competences.

C. The EU constitutional law framework for the EU's guarantee of security

I. EU competences for guaranteeing security

1. Competences for realizing the Area of Freedom, Security and Justice

10 One of the focuses of the Union's competences in relation to guaranteeing security is set out in Title V of the Treaty on the Functioning of the European Union (TFEU), which further constitutionalizes the Area of Freedom, Security and Justice. This overarching objective, as expressed in Art. 3(2) TEU, is substantiated in the subgoals that precede the chapter 'Area of Freedom, Security and Justice' (Art. 67(1) to (3) TFEU), although they still need to be rendered more precisely. Pursuant to Art. 4(2)(j) TFEU, it is one of the areas of shared competence between the Union and the Member States. As laid down in Art. 2(2) TFEU, the Member States exercise their competence 'to the extent that the Union has not (yet) exercised its competence.' The Union's actions are therefore only substantively limited by the principles of proportionality

[49] ibid., p. 62 et seq.; Calliess, p. 21; Fichera in Fletcher/Herlin-Karnell/Matera, The European Union as an Area of Freedom, Security and Justice, p. 43.

[50] See Monar, p. 13 et seqq.

[51] Thörner, esp. p. 18 et seqq.; see also Deubner, p. 173 et seq.

[52] Mitsilegas in Bignami, EU Law in Populist Times: Crises and Prospects, p. 308 et seqq.

[53] See European Commission and High Representative, 'Joint Framework on countering hybrid threats', 6.4.2016, JOIN(2016) 18 final; the emergence of this rarely used category for joint communications of the High Representative for the Common Foreign and Security Policy and the European Commission expresses the intersection of the categories institutionally; see also COM(2020) 605 final, 18 et seqq.

[54] COM(2023) 665 final, 7 et seqq. For more on hybrid threats, see Bendiek, p. 119 et seqq.

and subsidiarity.[55] However, the Member States' special sensitivity in relation to lawmaking in the Area of Freedom, Security and Justice is manifested in several limitations that have been imposed. The role of the Member States' national parliaments when it comes to oversight of the principle of subsidiarity, for instance, is explicitly laid down in primary EU law (Art. 69 TFEU), in contrast to other policy areas. Nevertheless, the mechanisms of the subsidiarity protocol can have only a limited structural impact on account of the functional logic of the parliamentary systems of government that exist in most Member States.[56] In addition, pursuant to Art. 67(1) TFEU, the Union is to respect the Member States' different legal systems and traditions when exercising its competences. Furthermore, Art. 72 TFEU emphasizes the fact that the Member States' responsibilities as laid down in Art. 67 et seqq. TFEU may not affect the exercise of the responsibilities incumbent upon them with regard to the maintenance of law and order and the safeguarding of internal security. That provides the basis for Art. 276 TFEU ruling out jurisdiction on the part of the Court of Justice of the European Union (CJEU).[57] It limits the competence of the Court in relation to judicial cooperation in criminal matters and police cooperation within the Area of Freedom, Security and Justice in two ways. First, reviewing the applicability or proportionality of police measures or measures by other law enforcement authorities is excluded from the Court's control function, which only covers individual actions, but not legislative acts.[58] Second, the Court's control of Member States' activities to maintain public order or to protect internal security is also limited. The Court can only conduct a review of whether it is competent,[59] which it always is where implementation of Union law is concerned (on the role of the CJEU → mn. 47).

Title V of the TFEU (Area of Freedom, Security and Justice) sets out key competences in relation to European security law, but also goes beyond that. First, they encompass those competences that relate to 'policies on access'[60] to the territory of the EU, that is border controls, asylum and migration. Here, EU policy can, to varying degrees, regulate issues related to the guarantee of security, i.e. governance of its borders (→ § 19 and → mn. 63). The territory of the EU is to be protected at its external borders against unauthorized access by people and things that do not per se, but may pose a security risk. However, under EU law, controlling access to the territory of the EU is essentially seen from the perspective of security. For instance, large quantities of resulting data collected during border checks and entries into the EU are stored and analysed on the basis of EU law (→ mn. 91). Nevertheless, one should also not ignore the fact that EU legislation on migration is also determined by other factors, such as implementation of human rights safeguards and opening up the 11

[55] See extensively Herlin-Karnell in Arcarazo/Murohy, EU Security and Justice Law, p. 38 (45 et seqq.); see also Müller-Graff in Schwarze/Hatje, Der Reformvertrag von Lissabon, Europarecht Beiheft 1/2009, p. 105 (111); Aden in Lisken/Denninger, Handbuch des Polizeirechts, mn. 3.

[56] For a closer look at the German example, see Pilniok (forthcoming), § 9.

[57] Kotzur in Geiger/Khan/Kotzur, AEUV Art. 276 mn. 2; Dörr in Grabitz/Hilf/Nettesheim, AEUV Art. 276 mn. 2: 'has an internal connection with Art. 72 TFEU in this respect'; Pechstein in Pechstein/Nowak/Häde, AEUV Art. 276 mn. 6: 'procedural safeguarding' of Art. 72 TFEU; Schima in Kellerbauer/Klamert/Tomkin, TFEU Art. 276 mn. 4 et seqq.

[58] Kotzur in Geiger/Khan/Kotzur, AEUV Art. 276 mn. 3 et seq.; Dörr in Grabitz/Hilf/Nettesheim, AEUV Art. 276 mn. 13.

[59] Kotzur in Geiger/Khan/Kotzur, AEUV Art: 276 mn. 3 et seq.; Pechstein in Pechstein/Nowak/Häde, AEUV Art. 276 mn. 8.

[60] The term '*Zugangspolitiken*' was coined by Müller-Graff, Müller-Graff in Schwarze/Hatje, Der Reformvertrag von Lissabon, p. 114.

internal market to third-country skilled workers.[61] Second, rules on judicial cooperation in civil matters are enabled that concern the 'Area of Justice' and not the guarantee of security per se.[62] Third, various bases are laid for assigning competence for judicial cooperation in criminal matters, including the establishment of a European Public Prosecutor's Office, and thus a core institution of security governance. Amongst other things, these enable limited harmonization of criminal procedure legislation according to Art. 82 TFEU and substantive criminal law according to Art. 83 TFEU (→ mn. 84)[63]. Because of the Member States' sensitivity when it comes to EU lawmaking on criminal law,[64] various restrictions have been imposed. For example, harmonization is only possible in relation to certain serious cross-border crimes. Moreover, to compensate for the required majority decision in the ordinary legislative procedure, procedural rules apply so as to limit the expansion of Union access. The German parliament can, for example, use an 'emergency brake mechanism' to veto legislation adopted on the basis of Art. 82 and 83 TFEU. It permits a Member State to refer a matter to the European Council if it feels that its system of criminal law is threatened by a legislative proposal; the European Council can, however, also decide to continue with the procedure. Fourth, Title V of the TFEU lays the legal foundations so that police cooperation in the EU can be concretized in secondary EU law. This provides the primary law basis for institutionalizing cooperation, above all information cooperation (→ mn. 88).[65] The following applies to all four areas: Either explicit or implicit competence bases have been created for institutionalizing the European security administration, which has gained significant importance in terms of the Union's contribution to providing security (→ mn. 49).

12 Besides those competences that are shared between the Union and the Member States, Title V of the TFEU also sets out the Union's competences when it comes to coordinating and supporting the Member States (Art. 6 TFEU).[66] They include, on the one hand, the Council's competence to regulate administrative cooperation within the Area of Freedom, Security and Justice, which can be used to set the conditions for an integrated administration of comprising the Member States' security authorities (Art. 74 TFEU). This horizontal and vertical cooperation is of very great practical relevance (→ mn. 67). In addition, the Union can support the Member States in the field of crime prevention (Art. 84 TFEU). Considering the diverse causes of criminality, this gives the Union a wide field of action. Since this competence relates to coordination measures – ruling out the harmonization of legislation – that action is of course limited to making recommendations, institutionalizing cooperation and exchange forums, and financing projects.

---

[61] For the state of play on this issue see Czaika/Trauner, EU in Ripoll Servent/Trauner, The Routledge Handbook of Justice and Home Affairs, p. 110 et seqq.; Menz in Ripoll Servent/Trauner, The Routledge Handbook of Justice and Home Affairs, p. 124 et seqq.

[62] They will, therefore, not be dealt with in the following.

[63] For a detailed analysis see Mitsilegas in Arcarazo/Murohy, EU Security and Justice Law, p. 110 et seqq.

[64] See BVerfG 30.6.2009 – 2 BvE 2/08, NJW 2009, 2267 (2274): 'Particularly sensitive for the ability of a constitutional state to democratically shape itself are decisions on substantive and formal criminal law, on the disposition of the monopoly on the use of force by the police within the state and by the military towards the exterior.'

[65] Information cooperation is also a focus of the European Council, 'European Council, European Council meeting (20 June 2019) – Conclusions', 20.6.2019, EUCO 9/19, 6.

[66] Pache in Niedobitek, Europarecht: Grundlagen und Politiken der Union, § 21 mn. 50 et seq.

2. Specific security-related competences

Furthermore, there are various individual provisions of primary law that can be regarded as covering those competences that relate to the guarantee of security. One little noted area is the provision of security by the customs authorities, which are, amongst other things, responsible for protecting the Union against illegal or dangerous goods and certain financial crimes. Following implementation of the internal market and the full communitization of customs legislation,[67] an intensive level of cooperation between Member States' customs authorities was the next logical step,[68] for which Art. 33 TFEU lays the foundation. According to that provision, the Union may structure horizontal and vertical cooperation between the customs authorities as *lex specialis* in relation to Art. 197 TFEU[69] and Art. 87 TFEU in the ordinary legislative procedure. Art. 33 TFEU thereby provides one of the primary EU law bases for the composite administration in general and the 'composite security administration' in particular.[70] It is thus supplementary, at the procedural level, to those competences on harmonization in the field of criminal law, which concern those crimes that the customs authorities focus on – such as money laundering – amongst others.[71] 13

Additionally, several competences are able to contribute to guaranteeing security in a crisis.[72] Art. 196 TFEU, for example, makes provision for the Union to support, supplement and promote the Member States' national civil protection activities.[73] Both extreme events caused by natural disasters and human-induced events that cause widespread damage are categorized as 'disasters'.[74] European civil protection legislation can contribute to mitigating the consequences of security risks as well as to protecting against such events becoming a security risk,[75] for example on account of looting. As the climate crisis is leading, inter alia, to more extreme weather events which have possible consequences for the internal security of the EU, this power will continue to gain significantly in importance going forward. Furthermore, Art. 222 TFEU is another provision that is closely related to Art. 196 TFEU. It establishes a duty, on the part of the Union and the Member States, to act in a spirit of solidarity, especially when it comes to terrorist attacks. Despite this EU-internal character of this norm, it has been erroneously contextualized in the TFEU together with the Union's competences for 14

---

67 Art. 3(1)(a) TFEU.

68 Kotzur in Geiger/Khan/Kotzur, AEUV Art. 33 mn. 1: 'Such provisions on cooperation were, however, necessary even before Art. 33 TFEU had been introduced'. See also Kerikmäe/Särav/Hamul'a' in Blanke/Mangiameli, TFEU Art. 33 mn. 4 et seq.

69 Terhechte in Schwarze et al., AEUV Art. 33 mn. 2; Haltern/Janson in Pechstein/Nowak/Häde, AEUV Art. 33 mn. 3.

70 Kotzur in Geiger/Khan/Kotzur, AEUV Art. 33 mn. 1; Haltern/Janson in Pechstein/Nowak/Häde, AEUV Art. 33 mn. 6; Kerikmäe/Särav/Hamul'a' in Blanke/Mangiameli, TFEU Art. 33 mn. 5 et seqq.

71 Waldhoff in Calliess/Ruffert, AEUV Art. 33 mn. 8.

72 The 'New strategic agenda 2019–2024' also focuses on civil protection law, which will continue to gain in importance, especially in view of ongoing global warming; European Council, 'European Council meeting (20 June 2019) – Conclusions', 20.6.2019, EUCO 9/19, 6.

73 For more details on civil protection law, see Trute, KritV 2005, 342 et seqq.; Schwartz, p. 1 et seqq.; Kloepfer, § 5; Walus, EuR 2010, 564 et seqq.; Finke in Pünder/Klafki, Risiko und Katastrophe als Herausforderung für die Verwaltung, 211 et seqq.

74 On the use of the term 'disaster' in Union law, see Kotzur in Geiger/Khan/Kotzur, AEUV Art. 196 mn. 2.

75 On how this is put in more concrete terms in secondary EU legislation, see European Parliament and the Council of the European Union, 'Decision No 1313/2013/EU on a Union Civil Protection Mechanism', 17.12.2013, amended by European Parliament and Council, 'Decision (EU) 2019/420 amending Decision No 1313/2013/EU on a Union Civil Protection Mechanism', 13.3.2019, and Regulation (EU) 2021/836 amending Decision No 1313/2013/EU on a Union Civil Protection Mechanism.

foreign affairs.[76] The obligation applies in the case of attacks by non-state actors and is thus complementary to the obligation to provide aid and assistance in the face of armed aggression by third parties laid down in Art. 42(7) TEU.[77] In view of the concomitant wide-ranging measures, such as the deployment of other Member States' armed forces, it presupposes that the government concerned has submitted a corresponding request.[78] On account of the Union's coordinating role, the provision also does not permit direct access, by the Union, to Member States' security authorities.[79] The general clause was put in concrete terms in a legislative act so that actors are ready to apply the solidarity clause in the event of an emergency.[80] However, to what extent such preventive legislation will actually be of any use in relation to the Union's actions in situations of crisis has yet to be proven in an actual emergency.

15 The extent to which this competence allows the Union to take preventive action well ahead of any potential terrorist attacks is a controversial matter. In contrast to police cooperation, the Union has not yet been assigned any explicit competences in relation to cooperation between the Member States' intelligence services (→ § 18) or the establishment of an EU intelligence agency.[81] That is why there is an ongoing debate as to whether the wording used in Art. 222 TFEU – 'the Union shall mobilize all the instruments at its disposal, including the military resources made available by the Member States, to prevent the terrorist threat in the territory of the Member States [and to] protect democratic institutions and the civilian population from any terrorist attack' – encompasses the power to establish an EU intelligence service.[82] However, this goal can only be pursued on the basis of legislative and administrative competences that must be worded differently.[83] The establishment of an EU intelligence service with its own operational powers thus requires an amendment of the EU treaties.[84] The same is likely to be the case when it comes to the creation of an agency to coordinate the work of the Member States' services that does not itself engage in any operational activities or gather intelligence.[85] From the perspective of EU primary law, the EU Intelligence Analysis Centre (EU INTCEN) thus operates in a grey area. Although it is for now reliant on intelligence supplied by the Member States on a voluntary basis, the fact that it only forms part of the European External Action Service (EEAS) and does not have a legal basis of its own is questionable from the point of view of the rule of law.[86] That applies all the more since the current legal structure does not institutionalize parliamentary oversight by the European Parliament. However, whether the Member States would be willing to give the EU a stronger legislative and practical role when it comes to intelligence-gathering is an extremely debatable issue. Since, according to the majority

---

[76] Geiger in Geiger/Khan/Kotzur, AEUV Art. 222 mn. 3.

[77] ibid. mn. 2; Thym in Grabitz/Hilf/Nettesheim, AEUV Art. 222 mn. 11.

[78] Point (a) indent 3 of Art. 222(1) TFEU.

[79] Geiger in Geiger/Khan/Kotzur, AEUV Art. 222 mn. 6; Thym in Grabitz/Hilf/Nettesheim, AEUV Art. 222 mn. 23.

[80] Council Decision 2014/415/EU on the arrangements for the implementation by the Union of the solidarity clause.

[81] Aden in Müller-Graff, Kernelemente der europäischen Integration, p. 460.

[82] See in detail Sule in Dietrich/Sule, Intelligence Law and Policies in Europe, p. 335 et seqq.; Palacios, IJICI 2020, 483 et seqq.

[83] Frenz in Pechstein/Nowak/Häde, AEUV Art. 222 mn. 23 expressly states that there is no competence to implement an EU secret service.

[84] On such calls, see Rüß in Dietrich/Eiffler, Handbuch des Rechts der Nachrichtendienste, § 4 mn. 15 et seqq.; Palacios IJICI 2020, 483 et seqq.

[85] Sule, p. 404; however, referring to the identical wording used in the failed Constitutional Treaty, Sule sees a basis for cooperation amongst the EU intelligence services.

[86] The Council Decision establishing the EEAS does not even mention this part of the organization.

of interpretations, Art. 4(2) sent. 3 TEU at any rate protects the military and the intelligence services against access under EU law (as they are national institutions), the Member States could at any rate not be placed under any obligation in that regard. Both institutional developments would, therefore, require amendments to EU constitutional law. At this time, it appears extremely doubtful whether the majority of the Member States would be in favour of that.

3. Security-related cross-cutting competences

Besides more specific competences laid down in the TFEU, the Union has various reasons for making frequent use of its competence for the internal market as laid down in Art. 114(1) TFEU as the basis for its competence for providing security.[87] Although the Union cannot harmonize the Member States' legislation on internal security, it can, on the basis of its key internal market competence, regulate important conditions and contexts for this policy area as well as set an EU framework for the Member States' security authorities. This is facilitated by the fact that the general criteria for relying on that competence base are difficult to determine given the vague wording used in the Treaty. The European Court of Justice has developed hardly any concrete standards in that regard.[88] That is why it tends to be generous when it comes to accepting Art. 114(1) TFEU as a legal basis. It has, for instance, confirmed that the Data Retention Directive could be based on this provision even though it was motivated by security policy issues.[89] The European Court of Justice considers it decisive that a Member State's legislation at any rate also creates unequal rules for the affected businesses and thus leads to distortions of competition in the internal market.[90] Using the Union's competence for the internal market can thus above all be considered where security-related obligations are to be introduced for private parties (esp. businesses).[91] Since access to data has become a key tool for guaranteeing security and businesses have to collect large amounts of relevant data, the Union is given large scope for legislation in this respect.[92] **16**

Product safety legislation, for example, the aim of which is to avoid distortions of competition, is one point of reference for Union lawmaking. It is not limited to product-related security in the narrow sense, as the ECJ made clear in its ruling on weapons law. It was specifically in response to several terrorist attacks that were perpetrated in the EU **17**

---

[87] Gundel uses a vivid term: Gundel, EuR 2009, 536: 'unbroken attraction' of the Regulation.

[88] The ECJ requires that it must be objectively and actually apparent from the legislative act that its purpose is to improve the conditions for the functioning of the internal market. In doing so, the ECJ grants the EU legislature a wide margin of discretion 'depending on the general context and the specific circumstances of the matter to be harmonised' (ECJ 6.12.2005 – case C-66/04, ECLI:EU:C:2005:743 para. 45 – *United Kingdom v European Parliament and Council*).

[89] ECJ 10.2.2010 – case C-301/06, ECLI:EU:C:2009:68 para. 80 – *Ireland v European Parliament and Council of the European Union*, which makes reference to the fact that what is being regulated are the obligations incumbent on enterprises and not access by the security authorities. However, in a later decision, the ECJ found the Directive to be incompatible with EU fundamental rights; see ECJ 8.4.2014 – case C-293/12, ECLI:EU:C:2014:238 – *Digital Rights Ireland and Seitlinger and Others*.

[90] ECJ 10.2.2010 – case C-301/06, ECLI:EU:C:2009:68 para. 62 et seqq. – *Ireland v European Parliament and Council of the European Union*.

[91] Where reference is made in Art. 114(3) TFEU to 'safety', it does not relate to 'public safety', but to 'product safety'; see Khan/Eisenhut in Geiger/Khan/Kotzur, AEUV Art. 114 mn. 21.

[92] Moreover, Art. 114 TFEU is not only used as a competence base for the approximation of legislation, but also for institutionalization processes – which are particularly important within the security architecture; see ECJ 2.5.2006 – case C-217/04, ECLI:EU:C:2006:279 – *United Kingdom v Parliament and Council as regards the European Union* Agency for Cybersecurity (ENISA); see also→ mn. 66; see critically Gärditz, AöR 2010 (135), 251 (272 et seqq.), which includes reference to the wording 'approximation of such laws, regulations or administrative provisions'. On Art. 114 TFEU as the basis for EU agencies, see also Saurer, DÖV 2014, 549 et seqq.; Orator, p. 214.

that the (at that time) relevant Directive on control of the acquisition and possession of weapons, which was based on Art. 114(1) TFEU,[93] was tightened and provision was made for broader bans and duties of registration to be imposed on gun owners. Despite the Directive's purposes being the prevention of violence, in the Court's view it could still be based on the Union's competence for the internal market.[94] The Court rightly pointed out that dynamic adaptations in previously harmonized areas must be possible when the circumstances change, without the basis for that competence being called into question as a result. According to the ECJ's broad interpretation, Art. 114(1) TFEU not only contributes to harmonization but also to the standardization of legislation by means of bans.[95] Both aspects give the Union quite considerable leeway when it comes to regulating matters that are relevant to security law.

18 Several examples illustrate a clear indication of just how relevant Art. 114(1) TFEU is for the Security Union in relation to the evolving regulation of the digital sphere by the EU, which mainly has its basis in Art. 114(1) TFEU. Given digital societies' vulnerabilities, it has become imperative for the Union and the Member States to impose corresponding requirements on private parties, since, even when private infrastructures fail, there is a risk of considerable public security problems arising. Thereby, cybersecurity has become an indispensable part of security law, and its key legislative acts were likewise enacted on the basis of Art. 114(1) TFEU.[96] This example shows that the internal market clause (the wording of which has not changed for a considerable period of time) also has an important function when it comes to responding to new challenges in the Security Union. The internal market clause is thus an important part of the regulatory structures in this area.[97]

19 More recently, the AI Act has given rise to considerable controversy between the Union and the Member States (on the use of AI in the Member States → § 9). Among other things, it raises the question of the scope of the reservation under Art. 4(2) sent. 3 TEU. This piece of legislation, which is based on the EU's competence for the internal market and is modelled on product safety law, prohibits certain uses of AI systems and imposes a detailed list of obligations on the authorities using them.[98] The Union's desire to comprehensively regulate this area is at odds with the Member States' considerable interest in security authorities being able to use AI systems, for example in biometric facial recognition or advanced lie detectors.[99] The fact that Member States' national public administrations, including their security authorities, will be subject to direct obligations is one of the differences between the AI Act and other internal market legislation, where Union law aims to regulate the rights and

---

[93] Directive (EU) 2017/853 amending Council Directive 91/477/EEC on control of the acquisition and possession of weapons, which has since been replaced by Directive (EU) 2021/555 on control of the acquisition and possession of weapons.

[94] ECJ 3.12.2019 – case C-482/17, ECLI:EU:C:2019:1035 – *Czech Republic v Parliament and Council.*

[95] Khan/Eisenhut in Geiger/Khan/Kotzur (eds) AEUV Art. 114 mn. 18. It is argued that banning products does not promote the internal market and that these are therefore inadmissible; see, on the current state of the debate, Classen in von der Groeben/Schwarze/Hatje (eds) AEUV Art. 114 mn. 146 et seq.; Kellerbauer in Kellerbauer/Klamert/Tomkin (eds) TFEU Art. 114 mn. 6.

[96] Directive (EU) 2022/2555 on measures for a high common level of cybersecurity across the Union, amending Regulation (EU) No 910/2014 and Directive (EU) 2018/1972 and repealing Directive (EU) 2016/1148 (NIS 2 Directive).

[97] In more detail, Wischmeyer, p. 1 et seqq.

[98] European Commission, 'Proposal for a Regulation of the European Parliament and the Council laying down harmonised rules on artificial intelligence (Artificial Intelligence Act) and amending certain Union legislative acts', 21.4.2021, COM(2021) 206 final; see the positions adopted by the Council and the Parliament.

[99] In more detail, Wischmeyer in Ebers et al., Künstliche Intelligenz und Robotik, § 20 mn. 15 et seqq.

obligations of private parties and not to limit the activities of security authorities. This conflict is also exacerbated by the fact that the EU's own security administration is, at least for a few years, exempted from these rules, resulting in asymmetrical regulation. However, the Member States insisted on an explicit exemption in the AI Act for those authorities that fall under the category of 'national security' according to Art. 4(2) TEU. In any case, the implementation of the AI Act is likely to become a test case for the balance between the Union's wish to regulate this matter and the Member States' desire for autonomy.

4. The external dimension of competences for internal security

In view of the challenges and global interconnections that phenomena such as **20** terrorism or securing the external borders of the EU pose, providing security within the Union is hardly likely to succeed without cooperation with third countries.[100] That is why a stronger integration in the field of internal security was from the outset linked to the Council's demand that 'all competences and instruments at the disposal of the Union, and in particular, in external relations must be used in an integrated and consistent way to build the area of freedom, security and justice.'[101] The different competence bases and modes of governance come into play in this context.[102] Their use has developed gradually in the last decade.[103]

Concluding international treaties is a traditional mode of EU cooperation with **21** third countries. Art. 216(1) TFEU bestows upon the Union the competence to conclude such agreements if they are necessary to achieve the Union's goals or provided for in secondary EU law. Regarding the competencies established within the Area of Freedom, Security and Justice, only Art. 79(3) TFEU is relevant, which creates an explicit basis for the external dimension of migration policy, while the significant amount of discretion produced by the implied powers is especially significant in this context. The objectives to be pursued are not so much to be derived from the very general wording of Art. 3 TEU, but rather from the competences relating to individual policies in order to still be able to do justice to the principle of limited individual powers.[104] In addition, when it comes to the second alternative of Art. 216(1) TFEU, the element of necessity is sometimes interpreted narrowly in the ECJ's case-law.[105] Thus, the most important alternative in Art. 216(1)

---

[100] See, for a general account, European Commission, 'A strategy on the external dimension of the Area of freedom, security and justice', 12.10.2005, COM(2005) 491 final; more recently and programmatically, European Commission, 'Fifth Progress Report on the implementation of the EU Security Union Strategy', 13.12.2022, COM(2022) 745 final, 18 et seqq.; Monar, p. 13 et seqq.; Eckes in Arcarazo/Murohy. EU Security and Justice Law, p. 186 et seqq.; Matera in Fletcher/Herlin-Karnell/Matera, The European Union as an Area of Freedom, Security and Justice, p. 359 (363).

[101] European Council, 'Conclusions of the Tampere European Council', 15/16.10.1999, para. 59.

[102] See the list of potential instruments in European Commission, 'A strategy on the external dimension of the Area of freedom, security and justice', 12.10.2005, COM(2005) 491 final; see also Matera in Fletcher/Herlin-Karnell/Matera, The European Union as an Area of Freedom, Security and Justice, p. 359.

[103] See e. g. O'Neill in Léonard/Kaunert, Searching for a Strategy for the European Union's Area of Freedom, Justice and Security, p. 24 et seqq.; Poli in Ripoll Servent/Trauner, The Routledge Handbook of Justice and Home Affairs, p. 389 et seqq.

[104] Geiger in Geiger/Khan/Kotzur, AEUV Art. 216 mn. 5 et seqq.; Vöneky/Beylage-Haarmann in Grabitz/Hilf/Nettesheim, AEUV Art. 216 mn. 10; on the restrictive interpretation of this version of Art. 216(1) TFEU, see also Giegerich in Pechstein/Nowak/Häde, AEUV Art. 216 mn. 95 et seqq.; Erlbacher in Kellerbauer/Klamert/Tomkin, TFEU Art. 216 mn. 4 seqq.

[105] Vöneky/Beylage-Haarmann in Grabitz/Hilf/Nettesheim, AEUV Art. 216 mn. 11; Giegerich in Pechstein/Nowak/Häde, AEUV Art. 216 mn. 101.

TFEU are references in secondary EU law, in particular legal acts based on the competences in Art. 67 et seqq. TFEU. They can to a very large extent be realized by means of international agreements as a result: The internal and external dimensions of these competences run in parallel, at any rate when it comes to security law, without being identical. As the competences regarding the Area of Freedom, Security and Justices are shared competences, mixed agreements of both the EU and the Member States are a legal option and often concluded in practice.[106] The procedure for adopting such agreements is governed in detail in Art. 218 TFEU, which is complex and therefore often also time-consuming in practice. At EU level, foreign policy is a matter of executive action; in accordance with this provision, the Commission and the Council are the key actors (on the role of the EEAS → mn. 47).[107] Besides rights to information, the European Parliament above all retains rights of oversight on account of its right to reserve consent under Art. 218(6) TFEU. The Union has made comprehensive use of these competences in relation to external affairs, for instance securing its external borders[108] and including third countries in the European security architecture.[109] Agencies such as Frontex and Europol in particular are also active at the global level.[110] The Frontex Regulation, for instance, makes provision for the conclusion of cooperation agreements with third countries based on a standardized model.[111]

22 Besides concluding international treaties, other security-related cooperation measures can also be founded on other general competence bases relating to the Union's external activities. Art. 8 TEU requires the Union to engage in a neighbourhood policy that regulates its cooperation with its closest neighbours. Amongst other provisions, Art. 212 TFEU enables cooperation with third countries by means of providing financial support, inter alia. Moreover, pursuant to Art. 209(1) TFEU, the Union may also adopt 'measures' for the implementation of its development cooperation policy. This is generally done by initiating and funding projects that are incorporated into complex programmes. Secondary EU legislation specifies 'security' as a thematic funding priority, for example in relation to the fight against terrorism and organised crime, because of the need to establish state structures capable of effective action (on funding as one of the Security Union's modes of action → mn. 92). Finally, Art. 220 TFEU empowers the Union to cooperate with international organizations. That also gives rise to security-related aspects, such as when it comes to the United Nations' and other actors' counter-terrorism activities.[112]

---

[106] See Matera/Gatti in Chamon/Govaere, EU External Relations Post-Lisbon, p. 187 et seqq.

[107] In this context, see Gatti in Flaesch-Mougin/Rossi, La dimension extérieure de l'Espace de liberté, sécurité et de justice, p. 171 et seqq.

[108] For a detailed account, see Matera in Fletcher/Herlin-Karnell/Matera, The European Union as an Area of Freedom, Security and Justice, p. 359 et seqq.

[109] See, e.g., Council Decision (EU) 2018/1549 on the signing, on behalf of the Union, of the Arrangement between the European Union, of the one part, and the Kingdom of Norway, the Republic of Iceland, the Swiss Confederation and the Principality of Liechtenstein, of the other part, on the participation by those States in the European Agency for the operational management of large-scale IT systems in the area of freedom, security and justice; see as an example further Vorrath/Zoppei in Ripoll Servent/Trauner, The Routledge Handbook of Justice and Home Affairs, p. 323 et seqq.

[110] On Frontex, see European Commission, 'establishing the multiannual strategic policy for European integrated border management', 14.3.2023, COM(2023) 146 final, 6; Coman-Kund, p. 1 et seqq.

[111] Art. 73 et seqq. of the Regulation (EU) 2019/1896.

[112] COM(2020) 605 final, 22.

5. Competences for external security

In view of the internal and external security nexus, competences in relation to external security can also gain relevance for the European Security Union. A 'Defence Union' as a goal of integration to stand alongside the Security Union[113] has gained in momentum in the current geopolitical context. Despite the semantic parallels, the legal differences are striking. The traditional distinction between 'internal' and 'external' security is reflected in the Treaties' governance regimes.[114] It is no coincidence that the CFSP was regulated together with the CSDP in the TEU and not in connection with the chapter on internal security (Art. 67 et seqq. TFEU). The legal bases, modes of action and the Member States' degree of obligation vary all too considerably.[115] Art. 40 TEU expressly delimits the two areas. **23**

First, the competences relating to external security facilitate institutionalization in this especially sensitive area of integration. Besides the possibility of establishing a European Defence Agency that is set out in Art. 45 TEU (for more details on this → mn. 72), this in particular refers to the creation of an EU legal framework for deeper integration in relation to defence policy by means of permanent structured cooperation pursuant to Art. 46 TEU, which was first made use of in 2018.[116] Even more than in other policy areas, the CFSP and, in particular, the CSDP are built on the idea of differentiated integration, as Art. 46 TEU explicitly shows. Second, the Union's competence as set out in Art. 43 and 44 TEU to carry out civilian and military missions in third countries is highly relevant for the European Security Union because of the interdependencies between internal and external security. The possibility of reducing security risks in this way is important in various areas of security policy, such as border security and counter-terrorism.[117] Such overlaps between communitized internal security policy and intergovernmental external security policy conflict with Art. 40(1) TEU, which aims to establish clear-cut competences. Given the different decision-making procedures and access to justice, this has wide-ranging consequences. In other cases, the ECJ has ruled that measures can only be based on CFSP competences, even if they pursue both internal and external objectives, thus forcing the European Parliament to play a more limited role as prescribed in Art. 36 TEU.[118] **24**

---

[113] In more detail, Scheffel, NVwZ 2018, 1347 et seqq.

[114] This distinction between the legal regimes of internal and external security also corresponds to that of the German Basic Law (*Grundgesetz*). Several other Member States, including France and Italy, do not have such a hard border, which is given institutional expression by the fact that they have a 'gendarmerie' that is incorporated into the military.

[115] In detail, Thörner, p. 57 et seqq.

[116] The English acronym 'PESCO' is generally used, not least in secondary EU law: Council Decision (CFSP) 2017/2315 establishing permanent structured cooperation (PESCO) and determining the list of participating Member States; Council Decision (CFSP) 2018/909 establishing a common set of governance rules for PESCO projects; Council Decision (CFSP) 2020/1639 establishing the general conditions under which third States could exceptionally be invited to participate in individual PESCO projects. See, for more details, Scheffel, NVwZ 2018, 1347 et seqq.; Revelas in Waechter/Vérez, Europe, p. 53 et seqq.

[117] However, the principle of unanimity in the Council laid down in Art. 31(1) TEU in relation to such operational decision-making gives all the Member States a right of veto.

[118] For a critical perspective, De Capitani in Bignami, EU Law in Populist Times, p. 375 et seqq., with reference to ECJ 24.6.2014 – case C-658/11, ECLI:EU:C:2014:2025 – *Parliament v Council* and ECJ 14.6.2016 – case C-263/14, ECLI:EU:C:2016:435 – *Parliament v Council.*

II. Regulation of the exercise of competences in EU constitutional law

25 The competences of the Union and the Member States to guarantee security as outlined above are constrained in several dimensions by EU law. Limits are imposed on the Union's actions by means of the specific limit on the exercise of powers that is 'national security' as well as by fundamental EU rights. In the light of its duty to protect, the latter naturally also constitute one of the grounds for the EU's actions.

1. 'National security' as a limit to the exercise of the Union's powers

26 The topos of 'national security' first of all serves to delimit the Union's and the Member States' competences. Art. 4(2) sent. 2 TEU reflects a traditional perspective on the functions of the nation-state. Accordingly, the Union 'respects' essential state functions, including ensuring territorial integrity of the state, maintaining law and order, and safeguarding national security. Sentence 3 goes beyond 'respect' in stating that national security remains the 'sole responsibility' of each Member State. This sentence was lifted from the practically identically worded unsuccessful Treaty establishing a Constitution for Europe and included in the Lisbon Treaty. The aim was to grant the Member States' request for clarification in response to the Union stepping up its counter-terrorism activities.[119] That, in turn, took up discussions in the Constitutional Convention, which, in view of greater integration, sought to constitutionalize a negative list of competences – a not unproblematic issue for a constitution.[120] 'National security' was the only item on the list to subsequently be included in the Treaty text.

27 Interpreting the general concept of 'national security' is, of course, not without its difficulties and it is only on account of the ECJ's most recent case-law that it has attracted more attention in the legal discourse (→ § 8).[121] Despite the extensive literature on the plurality of constitutional identities in the common European legal area as outlined in Art. 4(2) TEU,[122] the legal scholarship up to now largely ignores the specific relevance of sentence 3 and its implications for EU law. Although much has been written from the perspective of constitutional theory about the plurality of constitutional identities in the common European legal area as set out in Art. 4(2) TEU, the specific relevance of sentence 3 and its impact on EU law is generally ignored in the legal literature. There is as of yet insufficient clarity, in terms of the theory of legal norms, as to what the function of Art. 4(2) sent. 3 TEU is. On the one hand, it can be regarded as a justification clause that allows the Member States not to apply EU law in specific sectors. If the provision is understood in that sense, it supplements the more specific clauses in Art. 346 TFEU that have formed part of EU law for a considerable amount of time.[123] Accordingly, a Member State may refuse to supply information to EU institutions, to the general public or to individuals on the basis of EU law if that is contrary to the essential interests of its security.[124] Further, the provision allows Member States to derogate from internal market

[119] Callies in Calliess/Ruffert, EUV Art. 4 mn. 45; Obwexer in von der Groeben/Schwarze/Hatje, EUV Art. 4 mn. 46.

[120] Karpenstein/Sangi, GSZ 2020, 162 (165).

[121] See, for the current state of the literature, ibid. 162 et seq. Peuner, ZfDR 2023, 384 et seqq; Peuner, EuR 2023, 535 et seq.

[122] See, e.g., De Witte, EPL 2021, 559 et seqq.

[123] Karpenstein/Sangi, GSZ 2020, 162 (167).

[124] Khan/Eisenhut in Geiger/Khan/Kotzur, AEUV Art. 346 mn. 4.

regulations when it comes to the production of or trade in military goods. The intention, from a regulatory perspective, is thus to create tightly delimited exemptions to primary and secondary EU law. The EU's exercise of the competences enshrined in the TFEU is thus not restricted. In the Privacy International case (on this ruling → § 10), the ECJ thus examined Art. 4(2) sent. 3 TEU in this way, without explicitly revealing or reflecting on any specific interpretation of its wording.[125] However, interpreting the clause without elaborating on its content is problematical because it creates legal uncertainty for future lawmaking as well as for Member States' actions. As soon as a Member State erroneously – in the Union's opinion – invokes the provision, the Commission is required to initiate time-consuming and resource-intensive procedures, such as infringement proceedings, to reinstate the primacy of EU law.

On the other hand, Art. 4(2) sent. 3 TEU can also be interpreted as a competence 28
provision, an interpretation which is much more convincing from a systemic point of view.[126] This understanding can, first, be based on the wording itself, because 'responsibility' implies the assignment of competence.[127] It is also systematically correct that the binding nature of the Member States' responsibility is kept separate from the Union's respect for the Member States' national identities (to which reference is made in sentence 2). Account can be taken of the origin of this provision – a negative list of Union competences – when choosing this definition.[128] While the Union is limited to acting within the framework of conferral of powers and cannot assign competences to Member States, the latter can nonetheless include both substantiating and limiting competences in the Treaties. As a meta-provision on competences, Art. 4(2), sent. 3 TEU plays a key role in imposing limits on the Union's competence. This applies less to those competences that are specifically set out in, for instance, Art. 67 et seqq. TFEU, but primarily to the cross-cutting competences in competition and internal market law[129] – in particular Art. 114 TFEU. Further, the reservation in Art. 4(2) sent. 3 TEU is interpreted to mean that it is not possible to fall back on flexible, open Union competences such as Art. 352 TFEU when security-related matters are legislated.[130] The limitation of the Union's competences must therefore be taken into account when determining the areas of application and exceptions in secondary EU law because it must also be possible to concretise the precise meaning of this reservation in different areas. Art. 4 (2) sent. 3 TEU is regarded primarily as a task and obligation for the design of secondary EU law to determine the scope of application. However, even if there are provisions introduced by secondary EU law, these norms may increase legal uncertainty by creating a need for further interpretation. This is particularly the case when secondary legislation simply introduces an exception for matters of 'national security', such as the AI Act.

Notwithstanding its diverse usages in various contexts, no definition of 'national 29
security' is in sight.[131] Given that it is a term that is applied in EU law, how it is put in concrete terms cannot be left to the Member States' understanding of themselves, since

[125] ECJ 6.10.2020 – case C-623/17, ECLI:EU:C:2020:790 mn. 44 – *Privacy International*; for more details, see also Zalnieriute, Modern Law Review 2021, 205.

[126] For a detailed interpretation of Art. 4(2) sent. 1 TEU as a competence principle, see Schnettger, p. 216 et seqq.

[127] Karpenstein/Sangi, GSZ 2020, 162 (163 et seq.), with further references.

[128] v. Bogdandy/Schill, ZaöRV 2010, 701 et seqq.; Karpenstein/Sangi, GSZ 2020, 162 (165), with further examples besides national security, the standardization of which was discussed at the Constitutional Convention.

[129] Karpenstein/Sangi, GSZ 2020, 162 (164).

[130] Puttler in Calliess/Ruffert, EUV Art. 4 mn. 21.

[131] Sule in Dietrich/Sule, Intelligence Law and Policies in Europe, mn. 23.

that would lead to the primacy of EU law being undermined.[132] What is thus needed is a separate understanding of the provision as used in EU law compared to other similar legal terms. 'National security' must be delimited from 'public security' as used, for example, in Art. 36 TFEU.[133] What the two terms have in common is that they cover both internal and external security. The wording of the draft Treaty of a Constitution for Europe was specifically expanded to include both dimensions of this outdated distinction.[134] That is what distinguishes Art. 4(2) sent. 3 TEU from Art. 72 TFEU, which, in light of its regulatory context, only refers to 'internal security'.[135] Even if a distinction is then also drawn in secondary legislation between 'public security', 'public order', 'national defence' and 'national security',[136] military defence always forms part of 'national security'. Beyond that, 'national security' is also generally defined more narrowly than 'public security'.[137] Various phrases are used to describe the fact that only a core area of state sovereignty is to be protected. What we are dealing with here is the 'security of the state'[138] per se, its 'essential security interests',[139] or rather the 'fundamental vested interests of the Member State in question'.[140] Based on a historical and comparative analysis, Sule proposes that 'national security' should encompass four aspects, namely securing a state's territorial integrity, its constitutional order, a fully-functional state and business sector, and public services.[141] This definition applies in particular to the intelligence services of the Member States. Even when the term is substantiated in that way, concrete rules still need to be established and interpreted for specific scenarios, as the ECJ's most recent case-law shows.[142] Delimiting competences in individual cases will thus require further clarification by judicial decisions and legal scholarship.

2. Fundamental rights guarantees

30 The grounds for and limits to EU action in the area of security law derive from EU fundamental rights.[143] Art. 6 of the Charter of Fundamental Rights (CFR) lays down an explicit right to 'security of person'. This is a fundamental right against state interference that seeks to protect individuals, in the tradition of habeas corpus rights, against illegal detention by state agencies.[144] It is thereby the right to legal security against state arbitrariness.[145] That is also the core of the right to security under Art. 5 of the European Convention on Human Rights (ECHR), which is practically identical in terms

[132] ibid., mn. 28.

[133] ibid., mn. 71.

[134] Karpenstein/Sangi GSZ 2020, 162 (166), including reference to an initiative by the United Kingdom.

[135] ibid.

[136] See recital 67 of Directive (EU) 2016/680 on the protection of natural persons with regard to the processing of personal data by competent authorities for the purposes of the prevention, investigation, detection or prosecution of criminal offences or the execution of criminal penalties, and on the free movement of such data, and repealing Council Framework Decision 2008/977/JHA.

[137] Karpenstein/Sangi GSZ 2020, 162 (166); Schnettger, p. 164.

[138] Karpenstein/Sangi GSZ 2020, 162 (166).

[139] ibid.

[140] ibid., 167.

[141] Sule in Dietrich/Sule, Intelligence Law and Policies in Europe, mn. 72.

[142] ECJ 6.10.2020 – case C-623/17, ECLI:EU:C:2020:790 – *Privacy International*.

[143] For an overview of older jurisprudence, see Nettesheim, EuR 2009, 24; see also Brummund, p. 1 et seqq.; Gusy/Ebeling in Kugelmann/Rackow, Prävention und Repression im Raum der Freiheit, der Sicherheit und des Rechts, p. 25 et seqq.; Konstdinides/O'Meara in Arcarazo/Murohy, EU Security and Justice Law, p. 77 et seqq.

[144] Wilsher in Peers et al., CFR Art. 6 mn. 22; Baldus/Heger in Heselhaus/Nowak, Handbuch der EU-Grundrechte, § 18 mn. 7; Lock in Kellerbauer/Klamert/Tomkin, CFR Art. 6 mn. 1 et seqq.

[145] The phrase is taken from Schöndorf-Haubold, mn. 4.

of its wording;[146] via Art. 6(3) TEU it also gains relevance for EU law. Since, pursuant to Art. 51 CFR, the CFR is only applicable to the actions of the EU institutions and the Member States when it comes to implementing EU law, but operative action is primarily the task of the Member States' authorities based on their national legislation, its scope has so far been narrow. With the expansion of the Security Union and, in particular, with the independent exercise of operative powers by EU officials in Frontex, this guarantee will, however, gain in importance (→ mn. 56).

The public guarantee of the physical security and freedom of individuals is incomplete without state obligations to protect against interference by private third parties, which are derived from fundamental rights. The justification and scope of such a duty to protect are the subject of controversial debate in the legal systems of the Member States.[147] There are differing opnions on whether the Union's obligation to act in this regard can be deduced from Art. 6 CFR.[148] Considering the legislative institutions' prerogatives, restraint is in order here (at any rate as regards the derivation of general duties to take action), as is generally the case in relation to duties to protect. However, the ECJ generally succinctly derives a corresponding duty to protect from Art. 6 CFR:[149] **31**

> It is apparent from the case-law of the Court that the fight against international terrorism in order to maintain international peace and security constitutes an objective of general interest […]. The same is true of the fight against serious crime in order to ensure public security […]. Furthermore, it should be noted, in this respect, that Art. 6 of the Charter lays down the right of any person not only to liberty, but also to security.

Here, the Court deviated from its otherwise reticent case-law on duties relating to fundamental rights protection.[150] However, that duty to protect – where it can actually be made out in previous case-law – serves more as a topos in the reviews of proportionality the Court conducts than to derive concrete legislative duties on the part of EU institutions. It can, however, also gain relevance when it comes to the legal and political legitimation of legislative proposals. **32**

Moreover, European fundamental rights set a limit to the exercise of public authority. As clarified by the ECJ, this applies not only to the Union but also to the security legislation of the Member States.[151] The Court made this clear in case-law that relied on EU fundamental rights when it declared that various Member States' rules **33**

---

[146] Wilsher in Peers et al., CFR Art. 6 mn. 8.

[147] Baldus/Heger in Heselhaus/Nowak, Handbuch der EU-Grundrechte, § 18 mn. 12, who, though, point out the need for comparative law research; on the German discussion, see Isensee, p. 1 et seqq.; see also Robbers, p. 1 et seqq.; see also Möstl, p. 1 et seqq; Gerbig, p. 33 et seqq.; Hofmann, GSZ 2020, 233 et seqq.

[148] With reference to the replication of the corresponding standardization in the ECHR against the assumption that there is a duty to protect, Augsberg in von der Groeben/Schwarze/Hatje, GrCh Art. 6 mn. 6; for a comprehensive take as regards the duty to protect, including further evidence, see Leuschner, p. 1 et seqq.; Leuschner in Gusy/Kugelmann/Würtenberger, Rechtshandbuch Zivile Sicherheit, p. 173 et seqq. Germany's Federal Administrative Court assumes that the Member States have a duty to act that derives from Art. 6 of the CFR, see a preliminary ruling by the Federal Administrative Court of 25 September 2019, BVerwG 25.9.2019 – NVwZ 2020, 1108, mn. 31 et seqq.; see also Lock in Kellerbauer/Klamert/Tomkin, CFR Art. 6 mn. 3.

[149] ECJ 8.4.2014 – case C-293/12, ECLI:EU:C:2014:238 mn. 42 – *Digital Rights Ireland and Seitlinger and Others.*

[150] Leuschner in Gusy/Kugelmann/Würtenberger, Rechtshandbuch Zivile Sicherheit, p. 175, which includes the plausible assumption that this is because there was little reason for it when the traditional division of labour between the Union and the Member States applied.

[151] ECJ 6.10.2020 – case C-623/17, ECLI:EU:C:2020:790 – *Privacy International.*

on data retention were contrary to EU law.[152] In view of the fact that, in a digital society, Member States' national and the EU's security administrations are highly dependent on collecting, storing and analysing data (on security databases → mn. 89), the emphasis here is on Art. 7 CFR (Respect for private and family life) and on Art. 8 CFR (Protection of personal data).[153] Thus, the focus of legal issues shifts to the question of proportionality of legislation in the light of these provisions.[154] Further, the ECJ uses the argument of the indirect impact of security law on other fundamental rights, for example the deterrent effect when it comes to the exercise of the freedom of opinion and information under Art. 11 CFR.[155] Unlike Art. 8(2) ECHR – and despite its wording being largely similar to Art. 7 CFR – the CFR contains no explicit reservations in relation to national or public security. Justification for any interference with fundamental rights for the benefit of public security can, therefore, only be derived from general regulations. Art. 51(1) sent. 2 and (2) CFR in particular should be called to mind here, since a link is created between fundamental rights and the Union's constitutional organizational rights. The provision determines that the CFR may not be used to expand the Union's competences.[156] In the case of security law, account must thus in particular be taken of the Member States' general responsibility for national security as laid down in Art. 4(2) sent. 3 TEU, although consideration must also be given to the aforementioned narrow interpretation of 'national security' (→ § 8).

III. Rule-of-law requirements under primary EU legislation in relation to Member States' security authorities

34 The rule-of-law requirements under EU constitutional law (Art. 2 TEU) not only apply to the actions of the Union itself, for example its agencies, but also to the Member States. They impose limits on the activities of the Member States' security authorities within the European composite administration (→ § 6). For example, the actions of the national security authorities in the prevention and prosecution of criminal offences are a particularly sensitive issue from a fundamental rights point of view restrained by the rule-of-law requirements. Although they must be translated into specific legislative provisions,[157] they have thus a significant role to play in determining security within the multi-level EU system.[158] That should be reason enough in a Union of shared values to pay close attention to how the principle of the rule of law is realized. However, these primary-law requirements for the Member States are especially important within the system of composite administration. As in other areas, cooperation can only work smoothly if decisions can be, as a matter of principle, mutually recognized, as is required under Art. 82(1) TFEU. This, in turn, presupposes that the Member States

[152] Leuschner, EuR 2016, 431 et seqq.; ECJ 6.10.2020 – case C-623/17, ECLI:EU:C:2020:790 – *Privacy International.*

[153] ECJ 8.4.2014 – case C-293/12, ECLI:EU:C:2014:238 mn. 42 – *Digital Rights Ireland and Seitlinger and Others*; ECJ 6.10.2020 – case C-623/17, ECLI:EU:C:2020:790 – *Privacy International.*

[154] In more detail, Herlin-Karnell, p. 73 et seqq.

[155] ECJ 6.10.2020 – case C-623/17, ECLI:EU:C:2020:790 – *Privacy International.*

[156] Lock in Kellerbauer/Klamert/Tomkin, CFR Art. 51 mn. 1; Ward in Peers et al., CFR Art. 51 mn. 97.

[157] On the individual elements, see European Commission, 'A new Framework to strengthen the Rule of Law', 11.3.2014, COM(2014) 158 final.

[158] European Council, 'European Council meeting (20 June 2019) – Conclusions', 20.6.2019, EUCO 9/19, 6.

have sufficient mutual trust that rule-of-law standards will be upheld.[159] It is only then that loyal cooperation within the Union will be possible and that the bases of each individual decision do not have to be called into question.

Nevertheless, the Commission's often limited knowledge of the concrete situation in each Member State is likely to be a problem, as generally the case in infringement procedures. The Commission's mechanisms for monitoring the Member States are one response to this, which addresses the problems associated with the rule of law arising in and through the security authorities. The Commission's annual Rule of Law Report is prominent amongst them. It includes both country reports and an aggregated assessment by the Commission.[160] Consequences can then be drawn from these reports, that is whether to institute infringement proceedings or proceedings under Art. 7 TEU. However, the fact that the rule of law has therefore become a criterion of national and EU jurisprudence is equally relevant. These general requirements are made concrete in the EU's practice as regards the European arrest warrant.[161] This instrument of EU law, whose purpose is to enable and facilitate cross-border criminal prosecution, is used as a measure of the relevant criteria both at the national and EU level. The consistent past decisions of the German Federal Constitutional Court on the European arrest warrant have served to sound out the limits of EU law in relation to domestic law.[162] And, vice versa, the European arrest warrant has given the ECJ considerable influence, meaning that it can rule on those of the Member States' structures that relate to the guarantee of security.[163] For example, the (lack of) independence of the Member States' law enforcement authorities, amongst other things, has been regarded as being determined by EU law.[164] **35**

D. The EU's security architecture

The core of the EU's security architecture is formed of the Member States' security authorities. They have both powers to take action and personnel and material resources, whilst the EU's security administration can only draw on operative capacities to a limited degree (→ mn. 2). However, comprehensively incorporating the Member States' national security authorities into the EU's governance structures in relation to the guarantee of security presupposes that they are prepared to cooperate within the Security Union on a permanent basis by adapting to the EU's internal organizational structures. The relevant organizational changes have thus been made both within ministries and in the operational authorities, for example by establishing separate divisions and departments responsible for EU and international **36**

---

[159] For a fundamental approach to trust in the Area of Freedom, Security and Justice, see Kaufhold, EuR 2008, 408 et seqq.; Herlin-Karnell in Arcarazo/Murohy, EU Security and Justice Law, p. 38 (41 et seqq.); Ladenburger, ZeuS 2020, 373 et seqq.; see also Franzius, AöR 2014, 205 (295 et seqq.).

[160] Most recently, European Commission, '2023 Rule of Law Report', 5.7.2023, COM(2023) 800 final, with the corresponding country reports.

[161] See only Albi in Fletcher/Herlin-Karnell/Matera, The European Union as an Area of Freedom, Security and Justice, p. 137 et seqq.; Herlin-Karnell in Servent/Trauner, The Routledge Handbook of Justice and Home Affairs Research, p. 400 et seqq.; Pache in Niedobitek, Europarecht: Grundlagen und Politiken der Union, § 21 mn. 25 et seqq.

[162] See, e.g., Sauer, NJW 2016, 1134 et seqq.

[163] Aden in Rehder/Schneider, Gerichtsverbünde, Grundrechte und Politiken in Europa, p. 233 et seqq.

[164] For a detailed analysis, see Barczak, JZ 2020, 1125 et seqq.; see also Giegerich, ZEuS 2019, 61 (97 et seqq.).

cooperation.[165] This Europeanized security architecture in the Member States contrasts with an increasingly highly differentiated complex of actors at the EU level. Besides the EU institutions, which will be analyzed in more detail in the following, and their specific tasks within the complex configuration of the Security Union, there are, above all, EU agencies that have been established under secondary EU legislation and form the core of the EU's security administration. There are diverse cooperation structures involving the various actors at Union and Member State level that contribute significantly to the complexity of its governance structures (→ mn. 49).

I. EU institutions

1. European Council and Council of the European Union

37 The basic tension between intergovernmentalism and supranationalism within the EU is especially apparent in the Security Union's institutional structure. The emphasis on the role of the Member States within the constitutional division of competences is due to the fact that the European Council and the Council of the European Union are assigned prominent security policy tasks, in comparison to other policy areas.[166] Pursuant to Art. 68 TFEU, the European Council – which consists of the heads of state or government of the EU Member States – is tasked with defining 'the strategic guidelines for legislative and operational planning' within the Area of Freedom, Security and Justice. That goes beyond its function in relation to defining 'general political directions' within the meaning of Art. 15(1) TEU.[167] Primary EU law thus spells out the Member States' entitlement to shape security policy at the conceptual level, in particular in relation to the otherwise dominant Commission.[168] The legal, institutional and actual bases of this key area, namely EU security law, are to be developed not only incrementally but also systematically. Yet this aspiration can be upheld in constitutional practice only to a limited degree. This is due to the dynamic nature of security-related events, the European Council's need to take decisions based on consensus against the backdrop of extremely heterogeneous Member State objectives[169] and the Commission's typically incrementalist style of doing politics.[170] The multiannual planning guidelines published in 2014 and 2019 set out rather succinct general goals,[171] whilst previous programmes appeared more detailed and thereby more ambitious.[172] It was in connection with those guidelines that the

[165] Thus, a separate department dealing with 'International Matters' has been set up at Federal Police Headquarters that oversees EU cooperations, see the organization chart dated 29.6.2020 <https://www.bundespolizei.de/Web/DE/05Die-Bundespolizei/03Organisation/01Praesidium/Praesidium_node.html> (last accessed: 17.8.2023).

[166] See also Roos in Ripoll Servent/Trauner, The Routledge Handbook of Justice and Home Affairs, p. 421 et seqq.

[167] Kotzur in Geiger/Khan/Kotzur, AEUV Art. 68 mn. 3; Chevallier-Govers in Blanke/Mangiameli, TFEU Art. 68 mn. 5 et seqq.

[168] Matera in Fletcher/Herlin-Karnell/Matera, The European Union as an Area of Freedom, Security and Justice, p. 361.

[169] De Capitani in Bignami, EU Law in Populist Times, p. 402.

[170] Bossong/Rhinard in Economides/Sperling, EU Security Strategies, p. 96.

[171] See the Operational and Legislative Planning Guidelines for 2015–2020, European Council, 'European Council 26/27 June 2014 Conclusions', 27.6.2014, EUCO 79/14, 1 to 6 and European Council, 'European Council 20 June 2019 Conclusions, A New Strategic Agenda 2019–2024', 20.6.2019, EUCO 9/19.

[172] See European Council, 'The Stockholm Programme – An open and secure Europe serving and protecting citizens', 4.5.2010, which is almost 40 pages long.

Commission stepped up its Communications on security policy both in terms of frequency and scope (for examples → mn. 42). As a result, the more progress is made on institutionalization, the more the Commission is taking the political initiative – as is the norm in other communitized policy areas. In addition, the guidelines adopted by the European Council are only politically but not legally binding. Consequently, the Commission is not obliged to implement its right of initiative on the basis of the goals set out in the guidelines.[173] However, in derogation from the Commission's general monopoly on the right of initiative[174] and in view of judicial cooperation in criminal matters and police cooperation, legislative acts may also be adopted based on the initiative of a quarter of the Member States (Art. 76(b) TFEU). The Member States thus also have opportunities under primary EU law to implement the strategic guidelines adopted by the European Council. However, in view of the specific challenges that legislative proposals at the European level have to meet, there are likely to be significant barriers to exercising this right in EU practice.

Because the Member States have primary responsibility for guaranteeing security, **38** their representatives in the Council of the European Union play a special role. It is mainly the Justice and Home Affairs (JHA) Council that is responsible for lawmaking in this policy field. However, a distinction is made at the institutional level between 'justice affairs' on the one hand and 'home affairs' on the other – reflecting the fact that these areas are usually also kept distinct in the Member States. In line with these ministerial structures in the Member States, the rules provide that the justice and interior ministers meet as separate configurations for Council meetings. Where other competence bases are drawn on, such as Art. 114(1) TFEU (→ mn. 16), other configurations, for instance the Competitiveness Council, may be competent as well. The different responsibilities have an impact on the legislative work because each group of actors has different agendas and worldviews. Internal market regulators, which for example, discussed the AI Act, do not attach priority to security concerns. That applies all the more to the preparatory bodies than to the Council members themselves. Given the complexity of EU legislative acts and the complex and time-consuming trilogue negotiations, which include the Commission and the European Parliament[175] (on the consequences of this for the European Parliament → mn. 45), the legislative procedures are highly dependent on the Permanent Representatives Committee (COREPER) and on the relevant supporting bodies. These are made up of seconded national officials in line with the national ministerial structures, who thus often also adopt the priorities and perspectives of their countries of origin.[176] In addition to lawmaking, the function of the Council is to develop soft law, in which common standards and agreements on cooperation can be manifested (→ mn. 87).

Alongside its concrete involvement in legislative procedures, one of the Council's **39** ongoing tasks is to draw up general opinions as part of the Council Conclusions as well as thematic strategies. These strategies serve two purposes: firstly, to assist Member States in reaching agreement on politically implementable solutions, and secondly, to foster dialogue with EU institutions. The Council has, for instance, put forward a general strategy on the Commission's concepts relating to the Security Union that sets

[173] Kotzur in Geiger/Khan/Kotzur, AEUV Art. 68 mn. 3; Chevallier-Govers in Blanke/Mangiameli, TFEU Art. 68 mn. 13 et seq.

[174] See Haltern, mn. 503, 1081 et seqq.

[175] On EU practice, see v. Achenbach, p. 1 et seqq.; v. Achenbach, Der Staat 2016, 1 et seqq.

[176] See Röhl, EuR 1994, 409 (418 et seqq.).

out milestones for a five-year period.[177] The Council also adopts thematic, security-related EU strategies, for instance the Cybersecurity Strategy.[178] Finally, the Council is the institutional point of reference for a multitude of networks connecting security administrations within the EU (→ mn. 88).

40 Besides that, the Council has institutionalized a specific role within the framework of its right to organize its own affairs by creating the post of EU Counter-Terrorism Coordinator.[179] Despite the job title including the terms 'EU' and 'Coordinator', the incumbent is part of the General-Secretariat of the Council and subordinate to its Secretary General.[180] According to the decision on which the creation of the post was based, the Coordinator's task is to coordinate the Council's counter-terrorism activities.[181] Close institutional cooperation within the EU's political system is of course necessary to achieve this goal. According to the Coordinator's job description,[182] one key function is a communicative and performative one, namely constantly drawing attention both to the issue of counter-terrorism and its diverse aspects in the Council, Parliament and general public, for instance by making proposals, conducting analyses, organizing events and undertaking studies.[183]

2. European Commission

a) College and Directorates-General

41 The European Commission is active on various levels in relation to the EU's guarantee of security and plays a role as 'motor of integration'.[184] The Commission is composed of the College of Commissioners and has one Member – the Commissioner for Home Affairs – who is responsible for overseeing security policy and who acts as the contact person for the Member States' interior ministers. Giving the Commissioner responsibility for only a single issue focuses the incumbent's perspective on internal security. Nevertheless, that competence has been qualified since the introduction, in 2014, of the Commission's multi-layered organizational structure. A Vice-President is responsible for several Commissioners' portfolios, including home affairs, and is tasked with coordinating and networking them.[185] Given the available administrative resources, the Directorates-General of the European Commission play a central role

[177] <https://data.consilium.europa.eu/doc/document/ST-13083-2020-REV-1/en/pdf.> (last accessed: 17.8.2023).

[178] <https://data.consilium.europa.eu/doc/document/ST-8665-2021-INIT/en/pdf> (last accessed: 17.8.2023); see also the EU Drugs Strategy <https://www.consilium.europa.eu/en/press/press-releases/2020/12/18/council-approves-the-eu-drugs-strategy-for-2021-2025/> (last accessed: 17.8.2023).

[179] See European Council, 'Statement by the members of the European Council on the fight against terrorism', 25.3.2004, Doc. 7906/04, 14; for more detail on its position, see Rüß in Dietrich/Eiffler, Handbuch des Rechts der Nachrichtendienste, § 4 mn. 31 et seqq.; on the context of the EU policies in this realm see Bures in Ripoll Servent/Trauner, The Routledge Handbook of Justice and Home Affairs, p. 157 et seqq.

[180] See the organization chart of the Council General Secretariat <https://www.consilium.europa.eu/media/35512/gsc-organisation-chart-en.pdf> (last accessed: 17.8.2023).

[181] For a more detailed analysis of activity profile, see Hegemann, p. 242 et seqq.

[182] <https://www.consilium.europa.eu/de/policies/fight-against-terrorism/counter-terrorism-coordinator/> (last accessed: 17.8.2023).

[183] See, as an example, EU Counter-Terrorism Coordinator, 'Terrorism in Times of Corona', 14.5.2020, Doc. 7838/1/20; for an analytical approach, see Hegemann, p. 251 et seqq.: Coordinator as 'Entrepreneur', 'Manager' and 'Think-Tank'.

[184] See also Zaun in Ripoll Servent/Trauner, The Routledge Handbook of Justice and Home Affairs, p. 409 et seqq.

[185] On the related legal issues, see Böttner, European Constitutional Law Review 2018, 37 et seqq.

within the EU security architecture (→ § 13).[186] At the institutional level, the importance of security policy within the diversity of European policy areas was expressed in the establishment of a Directorate-General (DG) for Migration and Home Affairs. Its acronym – HOME – is reminiscent of the traditional designations given to interior ministries in the Member States. A comparison of the Directorates-General shows that the DG HOME is one of the smaller units within the Commission in terms of staffing.[187] However, the financial resources available to this policy field in general have been rising steadily and significantly for some time now. This above all benefits staff recruitment in the operational agencies (→ mn. 56), whilst the Commission is responsible for quasi-ministerial policy development, which is less resource-intensive. On account of the broad definition of 'security' as well as the interdependencies between the various policy fields, there are numerous other Directorates-General that deal with security issues, for instance the DG Justice and Consumers, the DG Taxation and Customs Union, the DG for European Civil Protection and Humanitarian Aid Operations and the DG Communication Networks, Content and Technology.

Given the highly differentiated system of agencies and the Commission's functions as **42** set out under primary EU law, the Commission's tasks above all focus on policymaking. To achieve this, it provides regular evaluations of legislation on non-legislative measures related to the internal security policy field.[188] Moreover, new initiatives and goals, in the form of Commission Communications, build upon the political impetus generated by the Council and the European Council as well as by the EU agencies and current events.[189] These communications always also reflect the priority areas of EU action. The Commission has, for instance, recently published Communications containing conceptual ideas on counter-terrorism in the EU,[190] on the EU Strategy to Tackle Organised Crime[191] and on the EU Strategy on Combatting Trafficking in Human Beings[192].

The Commission thus contributes substantially to the evolution of the secondary- **43** legislative framework by exercising its monopoly of initiative.[193] Even though the Member States may, by way of exception, exercise a right of initiative in the Area of Freedom, Security and Justice to a limited degree (→ mn. 37), in the EU's constitutional practice it is also virtually always the Commission that avails itself of this option. Further, pursuant to Art. 290 TFEU, the Commission may be empowered in the legislative acts relating to security and within the bounds of the legal reservation[194] to adopt delegated legislative acts and thus to engage in lawmaking (for an example of legislation on funding the guarantee of security → mn. 93). In addition, the Commission has established expert groups to engage in discussions on the current political para-

---

[186] What is not addressed here is the fact that the Commission, like all the other EU institutions, needs to protect itself in order to ensure its offices remain fully functional in the face of external attacks. This in particular applies to cybersecurity, for which the Directorate-General for Human Resources and Security is responsible.

[187] See European Commission, 'Human Resources Key Figures Staff Members 2023' <https://commission.europa.eu/system/files/2023-04/HR-Key-Figures-2023-fr_en.pdf> (last accessed: 17.8.2023).

[188] Most recently, e.g., COM(2023) 665 final.

[189] For a theoretical perspective of policymaking in that regard, see Kaunert, Journal of European Security 2010, 169 et seqq.

[190] See, e.g., European Commission, 'A Counter-Terrorism Agenda for the EU: Anticipate, Prevent, Protect, Respond', 9.12.2020, COM(2020) 795 final.

[191] European Commission, 'on the EU Strategy to tackle Organised Crime 2021–2025', 14.4.2021, COM (2021) 170 final.

[192] European Commission, 'on the EU Strategy on Combatting Trafficking in Human Beings 2021–2025', 14.4.2021, COM(2021) 171 final.

[193] On the monopoly on the right of initiative in general, see Haltern, mn. 490 et seqq.

[194] In more detail, Rieckhoff, p. 1 et seqq.

digms, to advise the Commission on developing legislative acts and to create networks of EU and Member State actors within the security authorities.[195] The Commission can use these expert groups as it sees fit in accordance with the requirements set out in a general framework.[196] Further, the Commission (and its subordinate executive agencies) also has a major influence on shaping the use of funding instruments to guarantee security, because the relevant programmes often create leeway as regards implementation (→ mn. 92).[197]

b) High Representative and European External Action Service

44 The external security dimension is also institutionally linked to the Commission. The High Representative of the Union for Foreign Affairs and Security Policy's portfolio is largely shaped by issues relating to the provision of security; the High Representative is also Vice-President of the Commission. The High Representative is responsible for the European External Action Service (EEAS),[198] which has a hybrid organizational structure somewhere between the Commission and the Council.[199] Various units within the EEAS are involved in guaranteeing security. EU INTCEN is part of the EEAS and is tasked with compiling information and analyses forwarded by the Member States' civilian and military intelligence services. These are secondary analyses that serve the generation of situation assessments, reports, etc. that are relevant to EU policies, primarily its external action.[200] However, the EEAS has no EU legal basis beyond the general decision relating to its establishment. Accordingly, there are also no specific forms of parliamentary oversight (→ § 14) over EU INTCEN, which would have to balance control with the authorities' need for confidentiality. That lack of oversight may, at most, be acceptable where only secondary analyses of the Member States' information are concerned, but not if EU INTCEN were to gather information independently. Moreover, the EU Military Staff is also assigned to the EEAS;[201] a Military Planning and Conduct Capability was established within the EU Military Staff[202] to support military missions, although it does not itself engage in combat missions. The EU Military Staff is also engaged in intelligence activities, amongst other things.[203] These raise legal concerns relating to the link between internal and external

[195] On the functions of these expert groups, see Pilniok, EuR 2014, 62 (72 et seqq.); Dankowski, p. 200 et seqq.

[196] Commission Decision establishing horizontal rules on the creation and operation of Commission expert groups, 30.5.2016, C(2016) 3301 final.

[197] On the executive agencies in general, see Pilniok in Terhechte, Europäisches Verwaltungsrecht, § 38 mn. 15.

[198] Council Decision 2010/427/EU establishing the organisation and functioning of the European External Action Service.

[199] In more detail, Kruse, p. 228 et seqq.; on the EEAS's legal status and scope of its autonomy, see Gatti, p. 103 et seqq.

[200] On these tasks, see Rüß in Dietrich/Eiffler, Handbuch des Rechts der Nachrichtendienste, § 4 mn. 20 et seqq.; in more detail from a stakeholder perspective, Conrad in Dietrich et al., Reform der Nachrichtendienste zwischen Vergesetzlichung und Internationalisierung, p. 161 et seqq.

[201] Council Decision (CFSP) 2005/395/amending Decision 2001/80/CFSP on the establishment of the Military Staff of the European Union.

[202] Council Decision (EU) 2017/971 determining the planning and conduct arrangements for EU non-executive military CSDP missions and amending Decisions 2010/96/CFSP on a European Union military mission to contribute to the training of Somali security forces, 2013/34/CFSP on a European Union military mission to contribute to the training of the Malian armed forces (EUTM Mali) and (CFSP) 2016/610 on a European Union CSDP military training mission in the Central African Republic (EUTM RCA).

[203] Rüß in Dietrich/Eiffler, Handbuch des Rechts der Nachrichtendienste, § 4 mn. 26 et seqq., which also refers to the EU Satellite Centre.

security, for instance regarding information obtained during the EU's civilian and military missions in the context of the CSDP and situation reports drawn up by the Union's security authorities, which the Member States are also allowed to use.

3. European Parliament

For a long time, the role of the European Parliament was characterized by the fact that it struggled to exert an equal level of influence on EU security law. The institutionalization of the Area of Freedom, Security and Justice as part of the 'third pillar' under the Maastricht Treaty assigned virtually all decision-making competences to the Council.[204] This fundamentally changed following the dissolution of the previous architecture of the EU's primary law. Even though more special legislative procedures and reserve approvals by the Member States' parliaments can be found in this policy area than in other policies, the European Parliament often acts as co-legislator in the ordinary legislative procedure, especially where security-related legislation is based on competence bases that are set out elsewhere than in Title V of the TFEU (Art. 67 et seqq.). The regulatory structures of the ordinary legislative procedure have created informal negotiation structures within the trilogues, within which the European Parliament's rapporteurs have substantial negotiating power.[205] **45**

On the one hand, the majority of the European Parliament backs an integration-friendly approach, including deepening the European Security Union.[206] On the other hand, though, the Parliament emphasizes the tension between liberty and security more than the Council and the Commission do. That is symbolically expressed in the name given to the relevant committee, the Committee on Civil Liberties, Justice and Home Affairs (LIBE). The functions of the Parliament and of its Committees go well beyond their involvement in lawmaking. Specifically, the highly differentiated agency structure requires ever more intensive parliamentary oversight, not least on account of the associated level of civil liberties and the personnel and financial resources granted to them. The rapid differentiation among specialization of the EU's agencies in this policy field poses a particular challenge for the Parliament's modus operandi regarding time and attention for oversight and scrutiny. The LIBE committee, for example, created 'scrutiny working groups' for Frontex's activities. Parliamentary oversight is also conducted within the joint institutional setting of the European Parliament and Member States' national parliaments, thus transferring the hybrid nature of an EU security agency, whose function is to support the Member States' authorities, to the Parliament (→ § 14). So far, Europol has remained the only example that has such a structure,[207] though other agencies such as Frontex and the European Union Asylum Agency are potential candidates. **46**

4. Court of Justice of the European Union

Finally, the CJEU has also become an important actor when it comes to the EU's guaranteeing of security, at any rate since its competences were expanded under the **47**

[204] On the legal situation at that time, see, e.g., Müller-Graff in Müller-Graff, Europäische Zusammenarbeit in den Bereichen Justiz und Inneres, p. 11 et seqq.; Ripoll Servent in Ripoll Servent/Trauner, The Routledge Handbook of Justice and Home Affairs, p. 385 et seqq.

[205] v. Achenbach, p. 1 et seqq.; v. Achenbach, Der Staat 2016, 1 et seqq.

[206] Ripoll Servent in Ripoll Servent/Trauner, The Routledge Handbook of Justice and Home Affairs, p. 390 et seqq. is deriving explanations from different integration theories for these developments.

[207] Tabbara/v. Achenbach, DV 2021, 73.

Lisbon Treaty.[208] The Court's case-law not only adjudicates individual cases, it also shapes strategic options for the legislative institutions' future activities;[209] it can be a 'game-changer'.[210] It influences various aspects of the guarantee of security: First, the CJEU delimits the Member States' security legislation by interpreting secondary legislation. Its rulings on data retention are an important example of this.[211] These rulings have led to Art. 4(2) sent. 3 TEU gaining considerable relevance from the Member States' perspective. Further, numerous EU legislative acts that are not directly based on security-related competences can influence the conditions under which the security authorities can function. The Court's interpretation of those acts regularly contributes to that legal framework. Examples include the EU's anti-discrimination law[212] or its labour and working time legislation, as the Court's ruling on the applicability of the Working Time Directive to armed forces recently showed[213]. Second, the Court conducts reviews of the Union's competences. Its case-law on this is quite generous, as it is in other policy areas, too. Third, EU acts are always measured against EU fundamental rights, which have as yet only been defined in outline. Given that the focus of EU law is on establishing and shaping EU-wide information networks in relation to security law, Art. 7 and 8 CFR are of key importance here.[214] The Court is thus increasingly taking on the role of 'watchdog' vis-à-vis steadily expanding security law.

48 The Court's importance when it comes to shaping security law in the European setting has without a doubt grown considerably.[215] This development increases the potential for conflict between the Member States' institutional interests in the autonomy of security-related decision-making on the one hand and the Court's interests in the wide-ranging application of EU law and thus its oversight competences on the other. Nevertheless, the Court's succinct style of decision-making, which largely avoids including detailed derivations and grounds,[216] does not contribute to lawmaking such that policymakers can generalize it and take it as a point of reference going forward. That is why the Court has so far only resolved some of the conflicts over competences within the multi-level system. The lack of dissenting opinions in the Court's rulings also limits the wealth of arguments applied to the cases. Eventually, the Advocates-General's opinions in some cases indicate that there may be other ways of interpreting the law. However, the different possible interpretations of the EU's constitutional law, which is written in rather vague language, cannot be sufficiently acknowledged in the legal discourse. That makes it more difficult for the Court's rulings to gain acceptance, which must above all be based on its authority.

---

[208] On previous case-law, see Lenaerts, The International and Comparative Law Quarterly 2010, 255 et seqq.; see also Peers in Arcarazo/Murohy, EU Security and Justice Law, p. 25 et seqq.

[209] Schmidt, p. 10 et seq.

[210] Herlin-Karnell in Ripoll Servent/Trauner, The Routledge Handbook of Justice and Home Affairs, p. 396 et seqq.

[211] See recently ECJ 20.9.2022 – case C-793/19, ECLI:EU:C:2022:702 – *SpaceNet*; for a summarising analysis, Mitsilegas et al., ELJ 2022, 1 et seqq.

[212] See ECJ 11.1.2000 – case C-285/98, ECLI:EU:C:2000:2 – *Kreil*, on opening up service in the Bundeswehr to women.

[213] ECJ 15.7.2021 – case C-742/19, ECLI:EU:C:2021:597 – *Ministrstvo za obrambo*.

[214] See, e.g., Reference for a preliminary ruling from Amtsgericht Köln made on 16 March 2020 regarding Directive (EU) 2016/681 (PNR Directive).

[215] See also the diagnosis reached in Cameron, IJICI 2020, 452 (460): 'For security and intelligence agencies the CJEU is a new, and presumably unwelcome, actor that has appeared on the scene.'

[216] This criticism of the ECJ is old, but still applies; see Rasmussen in Haltern/Bergmann, Der EuGH in der Kritik, p. 148.

II. EU agencies in the Area of Freedom, Security and Justice

The decentralised EU agencies[217] have taken on an extremely important role as independent administrative bodies in relation to guaranteeing security (→ § 13).[218] Institutionalizing specialized actors is one of the key modes of EU action. This is not only, but especially, the case in regard to those policy areas in which lawmaking competences are structurally limited. The EU agencies are not subordinate to the Commission, but they are independent administrative bodies that are subject to different requirements in terms of democratic legitimization and constitutional accountability.[219] About 35 agencies have been established in very different policy areas in recent decades.[220] Whilst they were initially primarily geared to supporting the Commission in knowledge-intensive areas, such as the administration in the environmental or medicines sector, their remit has rapidly and significantly expanded to ensure the Commission is not overburdened with administrative functions. The following are agencies in the Area of Freedom, Security and Justice:[221] 49

- Europol, which is responsible for police cooperation;
- Eurojust, which is responsible for criminal justice cooperation;
- Frontex, the Border and Coast Guard Agency;
- the European Union Agency for Asylum;
- CEPOL, which is responsible for developing, implementing and coordinating training for law enforcement officials;
- the European Monitoring Centre for Drugs and Drug Addiction;
- eu-LISA, which is responsible for operating the security-related IT infrastructure;
- and the European Union Agency for Fundamental Rights.

As they are decentralized institutions, the aforementioned agencies are based in different EU Member States and thus also geographically at a distance from the Commission.[222] They are rightly regarded as the 'cornerstones' of the EU's security policy[223] and will thus be analyzed in more detail in the following. 50

During the first phase of their establishment, which was based on the principles of intergovernmental cooperation, independent security authorities such as Europol were, at any rate partly, set up outside the EU legal framework. After the Lisbon Treaty created comprehensive primary legal bases subject to the Community/Union method, the decisions to establish the agencies were successively revised. They thus also became subject to the general framework the legislative bodies agreed on to coherently shape the 51

---

[217] For general information on the EU agencies, see Görisch, p. 185 et seqq.; Orator, p. 33 et seqq. and passim; Augsberg in Terhechte, Internationale Dimensionen des europäischen Verwaltungsrechts, Europarecht Beiheft 1/2016, p. 119 et seqq.

[218] See also Vara in Ripoll Servent/Trauner, The Routledge Handbook of Justice and Home Affairs, p. 445 et seqq.

[219] See Trute in Voßkuhle/Eifert/Möllers, Grundlagen des Verwaltungsrechts, § 9 mn. 107 et seqq.

[220] See <https://european-union.europa.eu/institutions-law-budget/institutions-and-bodies/search-all-eu-institutions-and-bodies_en> (last accessed: 17.8.2023).

[221] Based on how the agencies see themselves, those agencies relevant to the Area of Freedom, Security and Justice include, in addition to the bodies already mentioned, the European Institute for Gender Equality, see JHAAN, 'Final report on the JHA agencies network activities 2022', February 2022 <https://www.cepol.europa.eu/api/assets/media/downloads/2023/jhaan-final-report-2022.pdf> (last accessed: 17.8.2023).

[222] On these effects, see Egeberg/Trondal, p. 101 et seqq.

[223] Council of the European Union, Council Conclusions on Internal Security and European Police Partnership, 24.11.2020, Doc. 13083/1/20.

EU agencies at the institutional level.[224] It is thus possible to describe general aspects of the agencies' structure, although the security agencies in particular sometimes deviate from these for functional reasons. Based on the interinstitutional blueprint, the agencies' decision-making structures comprise a management board, which usually includes representatives of the Commission and of all the Member States, and an executive director, who is appointed by the management board and is responsible for the agency's ongoing administrative business. The management board's steering instruments include the budget and, above all, multi-year strategies and annual work programmes. Besides the typically detailed descriptions of tasks and powers that are included in their constituting acts as well as the modes of cooperation they engage in with the Member States' authorities, provision is also made for diverse oversight structures. The European Parliament and its Committees, the European Court of Auditors, the European Ombudsman, the European Data Protection Officer and others are involved in that oversight with their respective institutional perspective. The agencies, like the EU institutions, are themselves subject to EU regulation on access to official documents,[225] although protection of confidentiality plays a more important role here, even though it has so far been little defined.[226] In principle, according to sentence 2 of Art. 263(1) TFEU, the CJEU shall provide legal protection against decisions by the EU agencies. More specifically, however, various problems arise around legal protection, for example legal protection against real acts or against the actions of EU agencies and national authorities in the European setting.[227]

1. Europol

52 Europol was the first of the institutions within the differentiated EU security architecture to be established in the context of integration.[228] Although Europol was first established as an international organization on an international law basis,[229] Art. 88 TFEU now makes provision for the establishment of Europol as a European Police Office. The article defines the agency's task as providing support to and strengthening action by the Member States' police authorities when it comes to combating certain serious cross-border crimes. In line with the general reservations laid down in primary legislation that benefit the Member States, Art. 88(3) TFEU emphasizes the limited operational competences of the EU agencies. Europol may only take operational action together with the Member States' authorities, not on its own. Developing the authority into a 'European FBI', which is being debated in the political realm and in public, will thus require amendments to primary EU legislation, that is if the move is in fact deemed sensible.[230] The recently adopted reform of the Europol Regulation provides for Europol

[224] See the Joint Statement of the European Parliament, the Council of the European Union and the European Commission, 'on decentralised agencies', 19.7.2012.

[225] Regulation (EC) No 1049/2001 regarding public access to European Parliament, Council and Commission documents.

[226] See Curtin, JCMS 2014, 684 et seqq.; Curtin, West European Politics 2018, 846 et seqq., including reference, inter alia, to the interoperable security databases (in more detail → mn. 88).

[227] Rademacher, p. 1 et seqq.

[228] On how the debate has evolved since the 1970s, see Knelangen, p. 189 et seqq.; see in general, though in detail outdated, Schoppa, p. 1 et seqq.

[229] In more detail, Schöndorf-Haubold in Terhechte, Verwaltungsrecht der Europäischen Union, § 35 mn. 34 et seq.

[230] Lingenfelter/Miettinen, Maastricht Journal of European and Comparative Law 2021, 182 et seqq.; Léonard/Kaunert, Maastricht Journal of European and Comparative Law 2021, 229 et seqq. For the German perspective on integration, especially under Chancellor Helmut Kohl, see König/Trauner, Journal of European Integration 2021, 175 et seqq.; more recently, see the motion tabled by the FDP parliamentary group in the Bundestag, BT-Drs. 19/10164.

to access private parties for information-gathering purposes. By strengthening the operational mandate, it is getting close to reaching the limits of the competences laid down in primary law.

Further, primary EU law (i.e. Art. 88(2) TFEU) includes a legislative mandate to shape Europol's organizational structure in more detail in the ordinary legislative procedure. The Europol Regulation[231] takes essential aspects of the decentralized agencies as its point of departure, although it also has various special features. It includes the regulation of organizational structures, of procedure and of operational law and constitutes a monitoring regime for Europol's activities. Like the other agencies, Europol has a management board and an executive director, though the distribution of competences within it is somewhat different. Europol's management board – which, as in the other agencies, comprises one representative of each of the Member States and a representative of the Commission[232] – has numerous responsibilities to fulfil that gives the management board a higher-profile role than the management boards in the other agencies. Amongst other tasks, it adopts the Europol budget and work programme and exercises its powers according to the EU's Staff Regulations of Officials.[233] The management board also has the right to propose candidates for election as executive director and his deputy and it monitors the executive director in the exercise of his or her duties.[234] Oversight over Europol deviates from the standard model of parliamentary oversight as well: The European Parliament and the national parliaments are jointly responsible for this task, emphasizing the role of the Member States in this regard as well (→ mn. 46).[235] Characteristic of Europol's organizational structure are its various 'centres', though their legal status remains unclear. Such centres have, for instance, been established to deal with cybercrime[236], smuggling and trafficking of human beings, terrorism and cross-border economic crime. Amongst other things, these centres differ from a department in an authority on account of the so-called 'programme boards' that have also been set up. The Commission, Council and other affected EU institutions are represented on these programme boards, which are, amongst other things, responsible for setting priorities in relation to task fulfilment. 53

Europol is constantly evolving. The focus of that process is only ever on expanding its possible legal and factual actions, some of which are based more on a specific situation, i.e. security incidents. Recently, the Union strengthened various aspects of Europol's role within the EU security architecture.[237] The focus here was above all on incorporating Europol into an information network that encompasses all the EU security authorities and on expanding Europol's possible independent actions in its relationship with the Member States' authorities. This successive expansion of EU powers under- 54

---

231 Regulation (EU) 2016/794 on the European Union Agency for Law Enforcement Cooperation (Europol).

232 Art. 10(1) Regulation (EU) 2016/794.

233 Art. 11(1)(a), (b) and (g) Regulation (EU) 2016/794; on the functioning of the Management Board, see the Rules of Procedure of the Management Board of Europol <https://www.europol.europa.eu/sites/default/files/documents/management_board_of_europol_rules_of_procedure_.pdf> (last accessed: 17.8.2023).

234 Art. 11(1)(j) and (k) Regulation (EU) 2016/794. In contrast to other agencies, the Executive Director is elected by the Council, a special feature that expresses the national prerogatives in this policy field.

235 Tabbara/v. Achenbach, DV 2021, 73.

236 See on the larger context of Europol's role Carrapiço/Farrand in Fletcher/Herlin-Karnell/Matera, The European Union as an Area of Freedom, Security and Justice, p. 459 et seqq.; see also Carrapico/Farrand in Ripoll Servent/Trauner, The Routledge Handbook of Justice and Home Affairs, p. 146 et seqq.

237 Regulation (EU) 2022/991 amending Regulation (EU) 2016/794, as regards Europol's cooperation with private parties, the processing of personal data by Europol in support of criminal investigations, and Europol's role in research and innovation.

mines the intended limitation under Art. 4(2) TEU.[238] However, in the ordinary legislative procedure, the national governments – as well as, via participatory mechanisms, the parliaments[239] – regularly agree to the proposed reforms or at any rate raise no objections.

2. Eurojust

55 The second agency in the Area of Freedom, Security and Justice whose legal bases are established directly in primary EU law is Eurojust, the European Union Agency for Criminal Justice Cooperation.[240] Under Art. 85(1) TFEU, it is the agency's task 'to support and strengthen coordination and cooperation between national investigating and prosecuting authorities in relation to serious crime affecting two or more Member States or requiring a prosecution on common bases'. It thus complements the work of Europol when it comes to repressive law enforcement.[241] To that end, where certain crimes have been committed[242] the agency is responsible for facilitating mutual information sharing between the law enforcement authorities, coordinating their work and organizing Joint Investigation Teams. Eurojust's organizational structure also differs significantly from the model applied to the other agencies (→ mn. 51). Its key decision-making body is its College,[243] which is made up of national members of law enforcement agencies.[244] The Eurojust Presidency is elected from amongst the national members; the monocratic leadership (i.e. only one director) that is customary in other agencies is thus significantly reduced because the agency's administrative director is dependent on the College. The collegiate structure reflects the Member States' particular sensitivity and responsibility when it comes to law enforcement. For the same reasons, the guiding principle of self-administration is also applied in the area of law enforcement to the organizational structure of the European Public Prosecutor's Office (EPPO) (→ mn. 70). Specific features can also be made out when it comes to oversight structures:[245] A complex oversight regime has been put in place in regard to data protection that links the European Data Protection Officer with the national data protection authorities.[246] The establishment of the EPPO raises the question of its relationship to Eurojust. Under Art. 86(1) TFEU, the EPPO may be established 'from Eurojust', thus giving expression to an institutional evolution. Notwithstanding that, the tasks of these two agencies as laid down in primary EU law already differ significantly:[247] Whilst Eurojust supports the national law enforcement authorities' investigations into diverse crimes, the EPPO itself conducts investigations, though these

---

[238] See Schöndorf-Haubold in Terhechte, Verwaltungsrecht der Europäischen Union, § 35.

[239] For more details, see Pilniok (forthcoming), § 9.

[240] Regulation (EU) 2018/1727 on the European Union Agency for Criminal Justice Cooperation (Eurojust).

[241] Aden, mn. 154 et seqq.

[242] Annex 1 to Regulation (EU) 2018/1727.

[243] In contrast to other agencies, Eurojust thus has its own rules of procedure <https://www.eurojust.europa.eu/document/eurojust-rules-procedure> (last accessed: 17.8.2023).

[244] Art. 7(1) and 10 Regulation (EU) 2018/1727; as regards Germany, see. § 2 Eurojust Act (Eurojust-Gesetz): The Federal Ministry of Justice, in consultation with the German Länder departments of justice, appoints a national member who must be a federal civil servant qualified to hold judicial office and is bound by the Ministry's instructions.

[245] See for an overview Wieczorek in Fletcher/Herlin-Karnell/Matera, The European Union as an Area of Freedom, Security and Justice, p. 441 et seqq.; Huisjes/Tosza in Scholten/Brenninkmeijer, Controlling EU Agencies, p. 234 et seqq.

[246] Art. 40 et seqq. Regulation (EU) 2018/1727.

[247] See also Aden, mn. 154 et seqq., 163 et seqq.; on the relationship between Eurojust and the EPPO, see Vogel/Eisele in Grabitz/Hilf/Nettesheim, AEUV Art. 85 mn. 39.

are still limited to offences against the interests of the EU. Consequently, there is a justification for two separate agencies. However, since there may be overlaps and opportunities to develop the agencies' cooperation further, secondary EU legislation logically sets out their duties of cooperation in detail.[248]

3. Frontex

Frontex, the European Border and Coast Guard Agency, has gained considerable **56**
attention on account of its joint responsibility with the Member States for implementing operational measures at the EU's external borders. Its establishment was based on the competence to introduce an 'Integrated Border Management' system (→ § 19) at the external borders pursuant to Art. 77(2)(b) and (d), and Art. 79(2)(c) TFEU.[249] Frontex's organizational structure and oversight mechanisms are very much in line with the general blueprint that is also applied to the other EU agencies (→ mn. 51). It was established in 2004, is based in Warsaw and was originally only intended to support the Member States.[250] In the meantime it has gained significantly in importance, primarily on account of experience gained during the 2015/16 'migration crisis'.[251] Its restructuring more clearly indicates that securing the EU's external borders is a common task of the EU that must be based on the principle of solidarity, even though, as laid down in EU law, the Member States bear primary responsibility for this task. There are various aspects to Frontex's new role: Its tasks were expanded by means of a rapid succession of amendments to its constituting act. The funding allocated to the agency's budget has been significantly increased and is used, amongst other things, to purchase large amounts of technical equipment. Finally, the establishment of an independent standing corps of 10,000 uniformed and armed EU officers is especially significant from the structural perspective, since it means that for the first time it will not only be staff seconded from the Member States that will be deployed at the EU's external borders to guarantee security.[252] As a result and based on previous budget planning, Frontex is to become the largest of all the EU agencies and the second-largest EU institution in terms of personnel (only the Commission is larger).[253] This has numerous consequences for the EU's staffing structure and raises follow-up questions, for instance as regards the legal standards, access to justice and democratic accountability.[254]

Frontex's diverse tasks sit at the 'politically disputed interface between migration **57**
policy, border protection and security'.[255] The Frontex Regulation emphasizes the European Border and Coast Guard's contribution to ensuring a high level of internal

---

[248] See Art. 50 Regulation (EU) 2018/1727, amongst other things, provision is made for information about and participation in College meetings. For more details on the relationship between the institutions, see Esser, StV 2020, 636 et seqq.

[249] Regulation (EU) 2019/1896 on the European Border and Coast Guard. Although its official name is 'European Border and Coast Guard Agency', it continues to be referred to as 'Frontex', its previous name. (see recital 3 of Regulation (EU) 2019/1896 and the Agency's website <https://frontex.europa.eu/> (last accessed: 17.8.2023).

[250] See its initial name 'European Agency for the Management of Operational Cooperation at the External Borders of the Member States of the European Union', Regulation (EC) No 2007/2004.

[251] The term 'polycrisis' was coined by then Commission President Jean-Claude Juncker; see, more generally, on the consequences for the EU, Knodt et al. in Grimmel, Die neue Europäische Union, p. 119 et seqq. On account of the momentum of EU lawmaking, previous studies are now only partially relevant; for older literature, see Lehnert, p. 1 et seqq.; Mrozek, p. 1 et seqq.

[252] See also Ladenburger in Kahl/Mager, Verwaltungsrechtswissenschaft und Verwaltungsrechtspraxis, p. 78.

[253] ibid., p. 80.

[254] ibid., p. 78.

[255] Aden in Lisken/Denninger, Handbuch des Polizeirechts, mn. 180 [own translation].

security within the Union. Its mandate includes contributing to the detection, prevention and combating of serious cross-border crime at the external borders.[256] To that end, the agency has become the key player within the system of Integrated Border Management.[257] Together with the Member States' border authorities, Frontex is responsible for coordination, information and monitoring tasks, as well as for organizing and cooperating in operational missions.[258] However, the European Court of Auditors recently gave a very critical assessment of Frontex, both in terms of the level of implementation of its mandate and of its share in providing security in the EU, and urged it to improve both its organizational structure and its cooperation with the Member States in order to better realize its diverse responsibilities.[259]

58 Both in terms of the objectives set out in secondary EU law and institutional practice, migration is above all regarded as a security problem in EU law.[260] That creates tension with fundamental rights and international law requirements for the protection of refugees.[261] Since it has been involved in operational missions to a previously unknown degree, and increasingly more so in cases with a high degree of relevance for fundamental rights, whether the agencies' standard oversight arrangement is therefore also appropriate to Frontex thus appears to be a question that is rightly discussed critically[262] and has not yet been fully answered. Nevertheless, the commitment made in the Frontex Regulation to protect fundamental rights has been implemented within Frontex by adopting various measures in relation to the agency's organizational structure, which otherwise follows the standardized model (→ mn. 51).[263] Provision was made for the appointment of a fundamental rights officer, for example;[264] Frontex officials are deployed on the ground as fundamental rights monitors;[265] and a consultative forum has been established to advise on fundamental rights issues[266]. In addition, the European Parliament's parliamentary oversight vis-à-vis Frontex has in particular been stepped up as part of constitutional practice. However, unlike in the case of Europol (→ mn. 53) and despite the intensive level of cooperation between Frontex and the Member States' border authorities, there is no institutionalized form of joint parliamentary oversight involving the European Parliament and the Member States' national parliaments. Future reforms should take this institutional setup, as well as the powers of oversight actually assigned, into close consideration.[267] Finally, accountability can in principle be established on the basis of court rulings. However, the General Court decided that Frontex in joint operations with Member States cannot be held accountable in terms of non-contrac-

---

[256] Art. 1 Regulation (EU) 2019/1896.

[257] See European Commission, 'establishing the multiannual strategic policy for European integrated border management', 14.3.2023, COM(2023) 146 final.

[258] See the list of tasks in Art. 8 Regulation (EU) 2019/1896.

[259] European Court of Auditors, Frontex's support to external border management: not sufficiently effective to date, Special Report, August 2021.

[260] Léonard/Kaunert, p. 1 et seqq.; Buraczyński, p. 55 et seqq.; Ceccorulli/Lucarelli in Economides/Sperling, EU Security Strategies, p. 162 et seqq.

[261] On the complex fundamental rights standards, see Fink, p. 1 et seqq.; Fritz, p. 197 et seqq.

[262] For more details, see Groß, ZAR 2020, 51 et seqq.

[263] See Art. 99 et seq. Regulation (EU) 2019/1896.

[264] Art. 109 Regulation (EU) 2019/1896.

[265] Art. 110 Regulation (EU) 2019/1896.

[266] Art. 108 Regulation (EU) 2019/1896.

[267] See Aden in Lisken/Denninger, Handbuch des Polizeirechts, mn. 189: 'Regulations [are] thus deficient'.

tual liability.[268] Not only in this case,[269] the CJEU will in the future have to decide to what extent Frontex's contributions within the framework of cooperation based on the division of labour with the Member States' agencies are to be attributed to the agency itself and what requirements result from Frontex's involvement.

Given that Frontex developed rapidly from being a unit that was responsible for providing support to Member States into the EU's largest agency with its own operative staff, the question arises of whether, going forward, its officials could take the place of the national border guards in those Member States that have an external border. The Frontex Regulation, which references the gradual European Integrated Border Management at the external borders, can be interpreted in that way. However, the origin of the term 'Integrated Border Management' speaks against this, since the underlying objective was to establish a cooperative support facility not to supranationalize executive powers.[270] Account would also have to be taken of Art. 4(2) sent. 3 TEU (→ mn. 26). Switching from the indirect provision of support by an EU agency to direct provision by the EU would therefore require a Treaty amendment.[271] Of course, that would lead to increased demands to legally secure individual access to justice and democratic accountability. 59

Border management is also an important example of the fact that the boundaries between internal and external security are becoming blurred in EU practice. Frontex has diverse ongoing cooperation projects with third parties that are based on mandates in secondary EU legislation (→ mn. 21 on competences).[272] A web of agreements with neighbouring third countries, known as 'status agreements', have also been concluded on that basis.[273] They make provision for the establishment of 'antenna offices' in third countries, for the deployment of coordinating officers and sharing of information, but they also permit operational cooperation. The third countries' willingness to cooperate is also promoted by means of funding measures in the third countries. Further, it is not only Frontex that is responsible for the management of borders and migration, as missions are also conducted within the framework of the CSDP (→ mn. 23). One example was a military operation conducted in the Southern Central Mediterranean whose express aim was to combat crime, specifically human smuggling and trafficking.[274] The ECJ has in principle permitted legislative acts with links to internal and external affairs to be based exclusively on the competences set out in the CSDP, even though that largely rules out the involvement of the European Parliament.[275] 60

---

[268] GC 6.9.2023 – case T-600/21, ECLI:EU:T:2023:492 – *WS v European Border and Coast Guard Agency*; see also de Jong in Scholten/Brenninkmeijer, Controlling EU agencies, p. 117 et seqq.

[269] An appeal is pending against the decision of the General court in the case *Kocner v Europol* (ECLI: EU:T:2021:631), ECLI:EU:C:2023:481; also the case *Hamoudi v European Border and Coast Guard Agency* is before the General court (T-136/22).

[270] Kotzur in Geiger/Khan/Kotzur, AEUV Art. 77 mn. 8; Thym in Grabitz/Hilf/Nettesheim, AEUV Art. 77 mn. 37.

[271] Thym in Grabitz/Hilf/Nettesheim, AEUV Art. 77 mn. 37.

[272] Art. 71 et seqq. Regulation (EU) 2019/1896.

[273] European Commission, 'Model status agreement as referred to in Regulation (EU) 2019/1896 of the European Parliament and the Council of 13 November 2019 on the European Border and Coast Guard and repealing Regulations (EU) No 1052/2013 and (EU) 2016/1624', 21.12.2021, COM(2021) 829 final.

[274] See the recitals in Council Decision (CFSP) 2015/778 on a European Union military operation in the Southern Central Mediterranean (EUNAVFOR MED), which is no longer in force.

[275] For a critical perspective, see De Capitani in Bignami, EU Law in Populist Times, p. 375 (404 et seq.).

4. CEPOL

61 The European Union Agency for Law Enforcement Training, or CEPOL,[276] which is based in Budapest, was established on the basis of Art. 87(2)(c) TFEU.[277] It was originally set up under the 'third pillar', which disappeared with the signing of the Treaty of Lisbon.[278] Like other agencies, though, it now has its basis in a regulation adopted in accordance with the ordinary legislative procedure, thus giving the European Parliament substantial influence on the institutional design. Its purpose is to support the Member States' authorities through training on the EU framework of security law and its institutions, to facilitate cross-border cooperation and the use of information systems, and to share know-how on particularly relevant topics such as terrorism.[279] The aim is to create a shared knowledge base within the Union, to contribute to knowledge-sharing between the various agencies and authorities, and to promote the creation of a sector-specific administrative culture.[280] In view of this narrow mandate and its limited staff resources,[281] the question of the need for such a separate agency naturally arises. However, a proposal put forward by the Commission to integrate CEPOL into Europol, which appeared very appropriate, was unable to gain political acceptance.[282]

5. European Union Drugs Agency

62 The oldest of the independent administrative units relevant to the security realm in the EU, the European Monitoring Centre for Drugs and Drug Addiction (EMCCDA),[283] was established in 1993; it now operates under the name of 'European Union Drugs Agency' (EUDA) and its mandate has been expanded.[284] The agency's tasks include generating the necessary knowledge bases for the relevant agencies in the Union and the Member States, but not operational activities.[285] The tasks in the relevant regulation include collecting, analysing and distributing information about drugs, coordinating with the Member States' authorities and operating an EU information network.[286] Best practices are to be shared, for instance, and an early warning system for new psychoactive substances is to be set up and their risks assessed.[287] It is based on those risk assessments that the security agencies can then develop their strategies and

---

[276] This acronym for the agency's original French designation – Collège Européen de Police – is also used on its website, whilst Regulation (EU) 2015/2219 on the European Union Agency for Law Enforcement Training (CEPOL) and replacing and repealing Council Decision 2005/681/JHA establishes 'CEPOL' as the shorthand.

[277] Regulation (EU) 2015/2219.

[278] Schöndorf-Haubold in Terhechte, Verwaltungsrecht der Europäischen Union, § 35.

[279] See the description of objectives in Art. 3(1) and (2) Regulation (EU) 2015/2219.

[280] For a general take on administrative culture, see Jann, DV 2000 (33:3), 325 et seqq.; Fisch, DV 2000 (33), 303 et seqq.

[281] According to its Annual Budget 2020, the agency had financial resources of just under 10m euros and around 30 permanent posts, see CEPOL, 'Statement of revenue and expenditure of the European Union Agency for Law Enforcement Training (CEPOL) for the financial year 2020', 31.5.2022, 2022/C 216/01.

[282] See European Commission, 'Proposal for a Regulation of the European Parliament and the Council on the European Union Agency for Law Enforcement Cooperation and Training (Europol) and repealing Decisions 2009/371/JHA and 2005/681/JHA', 27.3.2013, COM(2013) 173 final.

[283] Regulation (EC) No 1920/2006 on the European Monitoring Centre for Drugs and Drug Addiction.

[284] Regulation (EU) 2023/1322 on the European Union Drugs Agency (EUDA).

[285] During the 'first wave' in which agencies were established it was mainly knowledge-generating institutions that were set up; for details, see Orator, p. 67 et seq., with further references.

[286] Art. 4 and 5 Regulation (EU) 2023/1322 and, on the Reitox network, Art. 32 et seq.

[287] Art. 7 and 8 Regulation (EU) 2023/1322.

activities, for example to combat the risks posed by new drugs. The agency sits at the interface between health policy and security policy. This is evident from the fact that it is, on the one hand, based on the EU's competence for supporting the Member States' health policies as set out in Art. 168(5) TFEU[288] whilst, on the other hand, forming part of the group of security-related agencies (on the 'JHA agencies' → mn. 49). The institution's primarily knowledge-generating function has been given concrete expression in the establishment of a scientific committee,[289] something which quite rare amongst the agencies within the Area of Freedom, Security and Justice.

6. European Union Agency for Asylum

Given the relevance of migration to security,[290] the European Union Agency for Asylum (EUAA)[291] is included in the group of agencies in the Area of Freedom, Security and Justice. Following a wide-ranging reform of the regulatory structures of migration law, the EUAA is to contribute to overcoming the EU's structural problems in this policy area. One of its core competences is EU-wide knowledge-generation about the situation in asylum seekers' countries of origin regarding persecution.[292] Since administrative and judicial asylum procedures are a knowledge issue,[293] the provision of relevant information takes the burden off national actors and at the same time leads to greater homogenization in decision-making practice. Hence, the concept of 'safe countries of origin' plays a key role in EU law (and is also to be further strengthened). That even applies although secondary EU law ultimately does not impose an obligation to follow these country assessments. The agency's second important task is to monitor the Member States' migration administrations. During the 2015/16 'migration crisis', the fact that the burden was unilaterally placed on some Member States meant that their migration administrations became overstretched. The EUAA is thus to ensure, on an ongoing basis, the proper functioning of the Common European Asylum System (CEAS) by means of wide-ranging monitoring obligations.[294] Supporting the Member States' authorities through asylum support teams comprising staff from the agency and other Member States is a central mechanism. This codifying of previous administrative practice means that asylum procedures are fully executed in the individual Member States by the supports teams, excluding the final decision made by the competent Member State authority, so as to relieve the burden on them.[295] Despite this leading to growing interconnections between the Union's and Member States' migration management, the Member States still have primary responsibility for enforcing EU migration law. Moreover, there have been repeated calls both in the political[296] and academic realm[297] to transition to direct implementation of asylum law by the EU administration at the external borders. This demand is particularly relevant if, as part of the reform of the CEAS, the implementation 63

---

288 Kotzur in Geiger/Khan/Kotzur, AEUV Art. 168 mn. 13; Schmidt am Busch in Grabitz/Hilf/Nettesheim, AEUV Art. 168 mn. 70.

289 Art. 31 Regulation (EU) 2023/1322.

290 See, for a fundamental approach, Wæver in Lipschutz, On Security, p. 46 et seqq.; Buzan/Wæver/de Wilde, p. 1 et seqq.; for a comprehensive review of the literature, see Baele/Jalea, Political Studies Review 2023, 376 et seqq.; Léonard/Kaunert, p. 55 et seqq.; Ceccorulli/Lucarelli in Economides/Sperling, EU Security Strategies, p. 162 et seqq.

291 Regulation (EU) 2021/2303 on the European Union Agency for Asylum.

292 Art. 10 to 12 Regulation (EU) 2021/2303.

293 See e.g. Mitsch, p. 1 et seqq.

294 Art. 14 and 15 Regulation (EU) 2021/2303.

295 Ladenburger in Kahl/Mager, Verwaltungsrechtswissenschaft und Verwaltungsrechtspraxis, p. 78.

296 See the Franco-German Meseberg Declaration of 19.6.2018, available in German <https://www.bundesregierung.de/breg-de/service/archiv/erklaerung-von-meseberg-1140536> (last accessed: 17.8.2023).

297 Dörig/Langenfeld, NJW 2016, 1 (3 et seq.).

of asylum procedures directly at the EU's external borders is considered.[298] First, it is not clear whether Art. 78 TFEU creates a sufficient legal basis for this.[299] Second, and much more importantly, having to deal with several tens of thousands of administrative proceedings each year, including legal redress, would represent a paradigm shift within the EU administration. Whether that would be a sensible distribution of tasks between the Union and the Member States is a question that would need to be answered on the basis of detailed public administration studies.[300]

7. eu-LISA

64 The Security Union is primarily intended to be an information network comprising the diverse actors in the Member States and at the EU level (→ mn. 88). That has become manifest in the creation of databases whose effectiveness is to be increased by making them largely interoperable (→ mn. 89).[301] The individual agencies, in cooperation with the Member States' national authorities, are responsible for maintaining the content of these databases. However, operating them whilst cooperating with the Member States' authorities also poses a considerable technical challenge. The European Union Agency for the Operational Management of Large-Scale IT Systems (eu-LISA), was set up so that sufficient expertise would be available to fulfil these tasks.[302] The fact that it has overarching responsibility for the EU's IT systems emphasizes the legislative goal of security policy of ensuring that various information systems are linked up and of giving the security authorities extensive access to all the available databases (→ § 20). The task of eu-LISA can thus be described as that of a 'shared service' facility that renders services to other agencies.[303] That, too, naturally goes hand in hand with its potential to independently shape those services. Realizing access to the relevant applications shapes their usability. By incorporating AI systems into its operations, the databases also potentially gain a new dimension that goes beyond merely providing a service to other agencies and determines what technical options are actually available.[304]

8. European Union Agency for Fundamental Rights

65 According to their self-definition, the group of nine agencies in the Area of Freedom, Security and Justice[305] includes the European Union Agency for Fundamental Rights (FRA).[306] Given the great relevance of the security agencies' powers to act according to EU fundamental rights, it is obvious that that should be one of the FRA's work

[298] See e.g. Dörig/Langenfeld, NJW 2016, 1 (3).

[299] For more on the legal requirements, see Lehner in Lehner/Wapler, Die herausgeforderte Rechtsordnung: Aktuelle Probleme der Flüchtlingspolitik, p. 183 et seqq.

[300] Ladenburger in Kahl/Mager, Verwaltungsrechtswissenschaft und Verwaltungsrechtspraxis, p. 77.

[301] Regulation (EU) 2019/817 on establishing a framework for interoperability between EU information systems in the field of borders and visa.

[302] Regulation (EU) 2018/1726 on the European Union Agency for the Operational Management of Large-Scale IT Systems in the Area of Freedom, Security and Justice (eu-LISA).

[303] For more details on shared services in the public sector, see Schuppan in Veit/Reichard/Wewer, Handbuch zur Verwaltungsreform, p. 297 et seqq.

[304] See eu-LISA, 'Artificial Intelligence in the Operational Management of Large-Scale IT-Systems', July 2020, <https://www.eulisa.europa.eu/Publications/Reports/AI in the OM of Large-scale IT Systems.pdf> (last accessed: 17.8.2023).

[305] For more on how the JHAAN sees itself and on its activities, see 'Final report on the JHA agencies network activities 2020', February 2021 <https://fra.europa.eu/sites/default/files/2021-03/2021_02_15_final_report_jhaan_2020.pdf> (last accessed: 17.8.2023).

[306] Council Regulation (EC) No 168/2007 establishing a European Union Agency for Fundamental Rights; Council Regulation (EU) 2022/555 amending Regulation (EC) No 168/2007 establishing a European Union Agency for Fundamental Rights.

priorities.[307] The tasks of the agency, which was established in 2007, include generating knowledge about fundamental rights and observing legal practice in the Union and the Member States.[308] This is reflected in its organizational structure on account of the establishment of a number of scientific committees of legal experts. The agency thus aims to continuously address fundamental rights issues, for instance by putting out opinions and publications, by organizing events and above all by addressing other actors' actions. As a result, like the European Data Protection Officer, it can be regarded as a discursive supervisory entity on account of its interaction with the EU's security-related agencies.

9. Other agencies

There are other security-related agencies beyond the group of agencies within the Area of Freedom, Security and Justice. Given the importance that cybersecurity plays in the EU's security strategy (→ § 16),[309] the focus of attention has now turned to the European Union Agency for Cybersecurity (ENISA).[310] ENISA is tasked with working towards a 'high common level of cybersecurity across the Union'. The more this issue has gained in importance, the more ENISA's tasks and responsibilities have diversified. Also, a legislative procedure is ongoing to create an agency that will be tasked with combating money laundering.[311] It is then, at the latest, though, that the question would arise as to how far the process of differentiation amongst the agencies can go before it reaches its functional limits. A considerable need for coordination has already arisen on account of these numerous agencies, which could prove an obstacle to effective task fulfilment. 66

10. Horizontal networks within the EU security architecture

This process of differentiation within the EU authorities to establish various agencies creates the need for coordination and cooperation, since their mandates often overlap. That is why provision has been made in secondary EU law for the agencies to cooperate with the institutions, facilities and other bodies that have become institutionalized in the 67

---

[307] See, e.g., European Union Agency for Fundamental Rights, 'Programming Document 2020–2022' <https://fra.europa.eu/sites/default/files/fra_uploads/fra-2020-programming-document-2020-2022_en.pdf> (last accessed: 13.8.2023), which, e.g., refers to issues such as the examination of criminal justice systems, fundamental rights issues in relation to migration and AI regulation. Recital 3 of Council Regulation (EU) 2022/555 amending Regulation (EC) No 168/2007 establishing a European Union Agency for Fundamental Rights clarifies that its range of tasks also includes judicial cooperation in criminal cases.

[308] More generally on the work of the agency, see Härtel, EuR 2008, 489 et seqq.; v. Bogdandy in Merten/Papier, Handbuch der Grundrechte in Deutschland und Europa VI/1, p. 1249 et seqq.; Grimheden/Kjaerum/Toggenburg in Harlow/Leino/della Cananea, Research Handbook on EU Administrative Law, p. 113 et seqq.

[309] See COM(2020) 605 final, 9, which designates cybersecurity as one of the strategic priorities of the Security Union; on the major initiatives of the Commission see COM(2023) 665 final, 2 et seqq.

[310] Regulation (EU) 2019/881 on ENISA (the European Union Agency for Cybersecurity) and on information and communications technology cybersecurity certification (Cybersecurity Act); the agency was originally established by Regulation (EC) No 460/2004 establishing the European Network and Information Security Agency; on compatibility with primary EU law, see ECJ 2.5.2006, case C-217/04, ECLI:EU:C:2006:279 – *United Kingdom v Parliament and Council.* Several subsequent legislative acts extended the Agency's originally temporary mandate and broadened its range of competences, before Regulation (EU) 2019/881 was then adopted.

[311] European Commission, 'Proposal for a Regulation of the European Parliament and the Council establishing the Authority for Anti-Money Laundering and Countering the Financing of Terrorism and amending Regulations (EU) No 1093/2010, (EU) 1094/2010, (EU) 1095/2010', 20.7.2021, COM(2021) 421 final.

Area of Freedom, Security and Justice.[312] And it is also why the agencies set up the JHA Agencies Network (JHAAN) (comprising the agencies referred to in → mn. 49), which is oriented to the public as well and whose presidency rotates annually amongst the member agencies.[313] The JHAAN focuses on political and strategic action. It publishes joint papers and press releases, for instance, and aims to present a uniform front vis-à-vis the Standing Committee on Internal Security of the Council (for more on COSI → mn. 77). Further, EU law provides for practice-based forms of bilateral cooperation as part of the agencies' operative activities. These are dependent on the nature and level of intensity of the necessary cooperation. For example, it has become EU practice for the agencies to conclude bilateral cooperation agreements amongst themselves. Depending on the relevant tasks, competences and thematic overlaps, these agreements contain rules on cooperation mechanisms, for instance joint activities or information-sharing working groups. Naturally, the limits imposed under data protection legislation as regards passing information on to other agencies must be observed.

68 Moreover, the institutionalization of this cooperation by means of projects can also be observed. The EU Innovation Hub for Internal Security is an insightful example. The project group is organized by Europol and comprises representatives of nine EU agencies in the field of security, of the Commission, of the Council and of the EU Counter-Terrorism Coordinator.[314] Its aim is to create a network of agencies that are engaged, to varying degrees, in operational activities and that conduct practical research and innovation within their area of responsibility. The focus is on the use of new technologies to guarantee security at the EU level. In line with the European Commission's general political targets,[315] the use of AI systems plays a key role (→ § 9).[316] The ongoing creation of extensive, interlinked databases under EU law (→ § 20 and → mn. 89) creates a need for automated technical analyses. So that Europol can actually make use of its new powers,[317] not only legal but also technical conditions have to be met, and that is to be done via this collaborative network. The term 'Innovation Hub' references the active role the EU administration has in the creation of such options as well as the concomitant requirements to be made of the involved administrative structures.

III. Other EU bodies involved in guaranteeing security

69 Other EU bodies have also been established on different EU legal bases, but cannot be classified as EU agencies due to specific aspects of their organisational structure. This includes entities established within the confines of the CSDP, in addition to the EPPO.

---

[312] For an example, see Art. 4(1)(b) Regulation (EU) 2018/1727.

[313] See on the institutional development Rijpma in Arcarazo/Murohy, EU Security and Justice Law, p. 73 et seqq.

[314] Europol, 'EU Innovation Hub for Internal Security – state of play', 17.2.2021, Doc. 5905/21, 2; EU Inoovation Hub for Internal Security – Annual Report 2022 <https://www.europol.europa.eu/cms/sites/default/files/documents/Eu%20Innovation%20Hub%20Annual%20event%20report%202023.pdf> (last accessed: 21.11.2023); see generally on such organisational arrangements Hill DÖV 2016 (12), 493 et seqq.

[315] COM(2020) 605 final, 15, 31.

[316] Europol, 'EU Innovation Hub for Internal Security – state of play', 17.2.2021, Doc. 5905/21, 4 cites this as one of the panel's priorities, along with encryption techniques.

[317] Regulation (EU) 2022/991 amending Regulation (EU) 2016/794, as regards Europol's cooperation with private parties, the processing of personal data by Europol in support of criminal investigations, and Europol's role in research and innovation.

1. European Public Prosecutor's Office

The most recent iteration of the ongoing supranationalization of the guarantee of security was the establishment of the European Public Prosecutor's Office (EPPO), which is evidence of the asynchronicities in the field of police and judicial cooperation.[318] Judicial cooperation in criminal matters, for instance, was institutionalized later than administrative cooperation between the police authorities was, although the two are functionally very closely linked. Eurojust (→ mn. 55) was set up long after Europol. Following lengthy and intense political discussions,[319] the EPPO was established on the basis of Art. 86 TFEU.[320] It was founded in the framework of closer cooperation, which additionally slowed down the necessary procedures on account of the requisite interstate decision-making processes.[321] A total of 22 of the 27 EU Member States are currently involved in the EPPO.[322] The level of regulation of the body's internal collegiate structure, its tasks and powers are quite complex.[323] 70

The innovative step that was taken when the EPPO was set up represents a new mode of Europeanization: The European Public Prosecutors, who are appointed by the Council, conduct independent investigations and act as counsel for the prosecution before the Member States' courts. That is the difference between the work of the European Public Prosecutors and that of Eurojust, because formal acts of judicial procedure are the reserve of the Member States' law enforcement authorities (Art. 85 (2) TFEU). Originally, this paradigm shift was justified on the basis of the idea that an EU authority could serve to overcome deficits in criminal prosecution by the national authorities in relation to offences against the financial interests of the Union. Given the multitude and diversity of investigations to be conducted, the EU was of the opinion that resources were not always being deployed as desired and required.[324] EPPO's competences are also likely to be expanded, depending on the positive assessment the EPPO gives of its work so far. Even before the EPPO took up its work, the Commission had already come out in favour of extending its competences to include cross-border terrorism offences.[325] As in the case of other agencies such as Europol, the EPPO will likely have set in motion institutionalization processes that will gradually lead to it being 71

[318] See Aden in Müller-Graff, Kernelemente der europäischen Integration, p. 460.

[319] See, for an early text, Fastenrath/Skerka, ZeuS 2009, 219 (260); de Waele in Stüwe/Panayotopoulos, The Juncker Commission, p. 157 et seqq.

[320] Council Regulation (EU) 2017/1939 implementing enhanced cooperation on the establishment of the European Public Prosecutor's Office ('the EPPO'). On the resulting need for amendments to German legislation, see Heger, ZRP 2020, 115 et seqq.

[321] Although the legislative act was adopted back in 2017, the EPPO was not established until 2021.

[322] Recital 8 of Regulation (EU) 2017/1939 lists 20 Member States; after the Regulation was promulgated, the Netherlands (Commission Decision of 1 August 2018 confirming the participation of the Netherlands in the enhanced cooperation on the establishment of the European Public Prosecutor's Office) and Malta (Commission Decision of 7 August 2018 confirming the participation of Malta in the enhanced cooperation on the establishment of the European Public Prosecutor's Office) also joined. Hungary, Poland and Sweden have explicitly not joined the EPPO, and Denmark and Ireland are not part of the Area of Freedom, Security and Justice.

[323] See the extensive commentary on the regulation in Herrnfeld/Brodowski/Burchard, p. 1 et seqq.

[324] See European Public Prosecutor's Office, 'Annual Report 2022' <https://www.eppo.europa.eu/sites/default/files/2023-02/EPPO_2022_Annual_Report_EN_WEB.pdf> (last accessed: 17.8.2023).

[325] European Commission, 'A Europe that protects: an initiative to extend the competences of the European Public Prosecutor's Office to cross-border terrorist crimes. A contribution from the European Commission to the Leader's meeting in Salzburg on 19–20 September 2018', 21.9.2018, COM(2018) 641 final, including a draft decision by the European Council; see also COM(2020) 605 final, 16: 'It remains an objective to extend the mandate of the European Public Prosecutor's Office to cross-border terrorist crimes.'

given a bigger role on cross-border crimes.[326] However, especially against the backdrop of the EPPO's independence under EU law,[327] attention would have to be paid to questions of democratic legitimacy and accountability. Owing to increased cooperation, the European Parliament is only involved in approving regulations to a very limited extent, whilst the Council has decision-making competence. That raises the question of whether the EPPO has a suitable oversight regime.

2. European Defence Agency

72 The European Defence Agency (EDA) also has a special status compared to the other EU agencies in the field of security. The EDA is closely linked to the High Representative for Foreign Affairs and Security Policy (→ mn. 44);[328] its basis in primary EU law can be found in Art. 42 and 45 TEU. It differs considerably from the other EU security agencies since it is part of the CSDP.[329] The EDA is headed by the High Representative instead of an Executive Director.[330] That is why, unlike the other agencies, it is not a decentralized agency that is based in one of the Member States but has its seat in Brussels as the Commission and the Council.[331] The EDA acts under the Council's authority and reports directly to it.[332] It is thus not subject to parliamentary oversight by the European Parliament. At the same time, the EDA represents a mode of enhanced cooperation, since the Member States' commitment to the agency is voluntary. All the Member States make use of this possibility, including, since 1 July 2022, Denmark. The participating Member States are represented on the EDA's Steering Board, which means they are involved in managing the agency.[333] Its tasks are to promote cooperation in the area of defence, with a focus on military equipment, in particular by means of creating common standards on procurement, cooperative tenders, and initiating research and development projects.

3. European Union Institute for Security Studies

73 Finally, the European Union Institute for Security Studies (EUISS) is another body that was established in the framework of the CFSP.[334] It is one of the Union's knowledge-generating institutions and serves to compile studies and analyses for the EU's external action. It is thus a type of EU-level 'departmental research institute'. With only 24 members of staff, it is one of the Union's smallest independent administrative units. That raises the question of whether it makes sense to have such an independent agency or whether it would not be more appropriate to incorporate the Institute into another facility, for example the EEAS or the Joint Research Centre.[335]

---

[326] See also Aden in Müller-Graff, Kernelemente der europäischen Integration, p. 460.

[327] See Art. 6 Regulation (EU) 2017/1939.

[328] Council Decision (CFSP) 2015/1835 defining the statute, seat and operational rules of the European Defence Agency.

[329] This agency's specific status is also reflected in the fact that it has its own organizational framework: Council Decision (EU) 2016/1351 concerning the Staff Regulations of the European Defence Agency, and repealing Decision 2004/676/EC; Council Decision (EU) 2016/1352 concerning the rules applicable to national experts seconded to the European Defence Agency, and repealing Decision 2004/677/EC; Council Decision (EU) 2016/1353 concerning the financial rules of the European Defence Agency and repealing Decision 2007/643/CFSP.

[330] Art. 7(1) Council Decision (CFSP) 2015/1835.

[331] Art. 1(5) Council Decision (CFSP) 2015/1835.

[332] Art. 1(2) Council Decision (CFSP) 2015/1835.

[333] Art. 8 and 9 Council Decision (CFSP) 2015/183.

[334] Council Decision (CFSP) 2014/75 on the European Union Institute for Security Studies.

[335] See on the JRC Pilniok, DÖV 2012, 662 et seqq.

E. Modes of governance in the Security Union

The above stock-taking and analysis of the competence structures and institutional architecture in relation to the EU's guarantee of security have undeniably indicated the complexity and diversity of the Security Union. The same goes for its modes of governance, which derive from the modes of action that are provided for under constitutional EU law (Art. 288 TFEU) and the possibilities for which provision is made in the respective policy areas. These modes of action will be summarized in the following in order to be able to describe key features of the modes of governance, though these should not to be regarded as exhaustive. Integration for the purpose of providing security occurs by means of institutionalization, networks and mutual observation (I.), by means of harmonizing legislation (II.), by means of operating databases and other knowledge infrastructures (III.) and by means of funding (IV.). 74

I. Integration by means of institutionalization, cooperation and mutual learning

1. Institutionalization of EU security agencies

Any analysis of the EU security architecture reveals the European Security Union's key mode of action: the institutionalization of security-related actors at the EU level.[336] The creation of administrative capacities can, first of all, be observed from a functionalist perspective, in that they are to serve certain purposes and tasks, for instance improving border security or police cooperation. It is only autonomous administrative capacities that enable the Union to pursue its agenda on integration by collecting information, making proposals and implementing decisions.[337] This is accompanied by dynamic vertical specialization in the European multi-level setting.[338] In addition, some of the Member States' national officials are seconded to all the EU's institutions and administrative bodies, the Commission as well as the agencies for a limited time. This established approach has a substantial socialization effect that is beneficial when it comes to generating a genuine European perspective. Nevertheless, these aspects only cover some of the relevant effects of developments at the institutional level. To varying degrees, the EU's institutions have great symbolic value. They make integration visible and function as something onto which both the proponents and opponents of integration can project their ideas. Being authorities, the administrative bodies are required to constantly justify their raison d'être, not only in the course of fulfilling their tasks but also through their external communication. As a result, the EU dimension of the guarantee of security becomes continuously visible. Furthermore, as soon as the agencies are established they begin undertaking efforts to expand, something which is even underlined on account of the agencies' autonomy from the Commission. This not only applies to their personnel and financial resources, but also to their powers. The agencies are aptly referred to generally as 'political entrepreneurs'[339] that develop their own agenda and attempt to 75

336 On institutionalization as a mode of guaranteeing security in the EU, see also Schöndorf-Haubold in Gusy/Kugelmann/Würtenberger, Rechtshandbuch Zivile Sicherheit, p. 704 et seqq.

337 For a general approach, see Pilniok (2011), p. 90.

338 Egeberg/Trondal, p. 87.

339 Wood, European Journal of Political Research 2018 (57), 404 et seqq.

enforce it vis-à-vis EU institutions, the Member States and their authorities. That, too, is the likely explanation for the great dynamic when it comes to expanding the agencies' legal bases in secondary EU law. The legislative acts by which the agencies were established and where central aspects of the respective policy field, such as border control in the case of Frontex, are regulated are one cornerstone of the secondary legislation that constitutes the European Security Union. However much the administrative resources are expanded at the EU level, they remain finite. The Security Union's governance structures will remain asymmetrical in terms of form, support and coordination on the one hand and operational action by the Member States' authorities on the other.

76 The institutionalization of the security actors' networks is promoted in various ways by the Commission in particular. Characteristic for the European Security Union is the creation of extensive networks and cooperation at different levels and in different contexts.[340] These networks are both formal and informal in nature, and their remits can thus vary greatly. EU-level actors are regularly part of these networks, as they simultaneously act as these networks' organizational and institutional hub. By facilitating cooperation and coordination, the networks also fulfil other functions in addition to the tasks that are officially assigned to them. In particular, they give rise to far-reaching socialization effects: The Member States' officials come into contact with the other national authorities' and EU institutions' ways of seeing things, which in turn influences their own view of those problems that need to be tackled jointly.[341]

2. Cooperation between the security authorities

77 The list of formal cooperation bodies includes the Standing Committee on Operational Cooperation on Internal Security (COSI). It was established within the Council on the basis of Art. 71 TFEU.[342] The existence of such a norm in constitutional EU law is a symbol, at the institutional level, of the Member States' particular sensitivity regarding security policy. COSI is not involved in the Council's legislative activities, but is to promote operational cooperation between the Member States on internal security.[343] That in particular encompasses collaboration between the police, customs and judicial authorities as well as shared responsibility for protecting the EU's external borders. COSI comprises officials from the Member States' national ministries. The Commission, the EEAS and the EU security agencies are also represented in COSI. One of COSI's functional problems is that its meetings are regularly attended by almost 100 people and it is thus not suited to operational coordination purposes. Another criticism that has been raised is that COSI members are not always present more than temporarily.[344] Nevertheless, the Standing Committee contributes to the adoption of a common view of the problems that exist in the Union. The same goes for other Council committees, which were set up without any explicit primary or secondary EU law basis but on the basis of the Council's right to conduct its own affairs. Thus, there is inter alia a Coordinating Committee in the area of police and judicial cooperation in criminal matters as well as working parties (or Council preparatory bodies) that deal, for example, with information exchange and data protection, civil protection, criminal law, law enforcement, terrorism, customs coop-

[340] See also the contributions in Aden, Police cooperation in the European Union under the Treaty of Lisbon.

[341] On this function of the Council committees, see Pilniok (2011), p. 171 et seqq.

[342] Council Decision 2010/131 on setting up the Standing Committee on operational cooperation on internal security.

[343] See on COSI also Rijpma in Arcarazo/Murohy, EU Security and Justice Law, p. 69 et seqq.

[344] Bossong/Rhinard in Economides/Sperling, EU Security Strategies, p. 190.

eration and cooperation in criminal matters.[345] These structures, which are difficult to analyse from an outside perspective, can raise questions of accountability, even though the committees have no formal decision-making powers. Whether regularly submitting a report to the European Parliament is enough – albeit at very large intervals – is something that has been criticized.[346]

The Commission, too, with its comitology committees and expert groups, represents **78** a hub of formal and, more often, informal networks in the area of security policy.[347] Some European networks that have been set up by liaison officers on the basis of secondary EU law seek to facilitate subject-specific cooperation with the Member States.[348] Aside from this, agencies are above all reliant on establishing the relevant cooperation structures with the Member States' authorities. In some cases, provision has been made for this under secondary EU law, for example in the case of the European Border Surveillance System (EUROSUR), within whose communications network Frontex shares situation reports and intelligence with the Member States.[349] Alternatively, they can be based on the authorities' right to organize their own affairs and the cooperation tasks assigned to them under primary EU legislation; the Frontex Risk Analysis Network is one such example. Its purpose is to conduct risk assessments based on the different bodies of knowledge that Frontex and national experts have.[350] This example already gives an indication of the different functions that such informal cooperation structures are assigned. They mainly serve information-sharing purposes, though some also take on executive tasks such as conducting risk assessments as well as regulative functions such as reaching agreement on common technical standards.[351] Unlike in other areas, the networks that have been set up in the Security Union almost always comprise representatives of the Member States' national authorities and of the EU authorities, whilst enterprises and other private actors are only involved in certain individual cases.[352] Transparency and accountability are not always adequate in the case of those networks that were initiated by the Commission and the agencies.[353]

Moreover, cooperation frameworks are also promoted by means of the establishment **79** of institutional formats for joint training or mutual exchange as part of military training. These have been institutionalized in very diverse forms for the police (by CEPOL → mn. 61) and the military[354] and as EU-funded projects (on funding → mn. 96). Training is also provided to the judiciary.[355] As is the case with other policy areas, the Union thus hardly noticeably contributes to the integration process by developing joint perspectives and experiences, thereby addressing the epistemic dimension of integration that is vital to the Security Union.

Administrative assistance and operative cooperation, which is structured on the basis **80** of secondary EU law, are geared more directly to the security authorities' actions.

---

[345] See the list of Council preparatory bodies <https://www.consilium.europa.eu/de/council-eu/preparatory-bodies/> (last accessed: 17.08.2023).

[346] For a critical take, see De Capitani in Bignami, EU Law in Populist Times, p. 401 et seq.

[347] See <https://home-affiars.ec.europa.eu/networks_en> (last accessed: 17.08.2023).

[348] See, e.g., Regulation (EU) 2019/1240 on the creation of a European network of immigration liaison officers.

[349] Art. 18 et seq. Regulation (EU) 2019/1896.

[350] Bossong in Bernhard/Wendekamm, Sicherheit zwischen Staat, Markt und Zivilgesellschaft, p. 107.

[351] ibid. 108 et seq.

[352] ibid., 110 et seq.

[353] ibid., 113.

[354] Council Decision (CFSP) 2020/1515 establishing a European Security and Defence College, and repealing Decision (CFSP) 2016/2382.

[355] For more details, see Pache in Niedobitek, Europarecht: Grundlagen und Politiken der Union, § 21 mn. 214 et seq., 248.

Administrative assistance often relates to a specific individual case and is already an obligation given the duty of loyal cooperation according to Art. 4(3) TEU within the European integrated administration. In order nevertheless to be able to create reliable conditions that take account of sector-specific particularities, administrative assistance has also been elaborated in secondary EU law, mainly and specifically as regards information exchange in law enforcement,[356] although it goes well beyond that, too.[357] Operative cooperation goes yet further. EU law not only regulates cooperation in specific crisis situations and prepares the ground for such cooperation through exchange and joint exercises,[358] it above all also creates the conditions for permanent structural cooperation within joint teams. In varying levels of detail, secondary EU law already, for example, makes provision for Europol's Joint Investigation Teams[359] as well as Frontex's and the European Union Asylum Agency's Joint Support Teams[360]. Besides changing the temporal dimension of cooperation, this in particular leads to Member States contributing to such teams and to security-related tasks thus being jointly performed, in the spirit of solidarity, in another Member State.

3. Mutual observation and learning

81 The above-mentioned cooperation structures are supplemented by various mutual observation and evaluation mechanisms that are detailed in the Member States' national security policies. Here, too, legally established and more informal modes of cooperation can be made out. In addition, a distinction can be drawn between whether evaluations are done at the supranational level by the Commission, an agency or else by the other Member States. Supranational evaluations based on secondary EU legislation can, for example, be found in the EU framework on border management. According to the relevant Regulation,[361] the Commission and Frontex evaluate the performance of the Member States' border authorities. Those evaluations are, in turn, used to draw up the Union's funding programmes, which amongst other things are to enable the Member States to eliminate any deficiencies (→ mn. 93). The European Semester applies a similar mechanism, insofar as there are any links to security issues. The Commission's country reports, for instance, assess the level of

[356] Art. 39 et seqq. of the Convention implementing the Schengen Agreement; Directive (EU) 2023/977 on the exchange of information between the law enforcement authorities of Member States; European Commission, 'Proposal for a Regulation on automated data exchange for police cooperation ("Prüm II")', 8.12.2021, COM(2021) 784 final.

[357] For an example with reference to the fight against fraud in the internal market, see Council Regulation (EC) No 515/97 on mutual assistance between the administrative authorities of the Member States and cooperation between the latter and the Commission to ensure the correct application of the law on customs and agricultural matters in the version of Regulation (EU) 2015/1525 of the European Parliament and of the Council of 9 September 2015 amending Council Regulation (EC) No 515/97 on mutual assistance between the administrative authorities of the Member States and cooperation between the latter and the Commission to ensure the correct application of the law on customs and agricultural matters.

[358] Council Decision 2008/617/JHA on the improvement of cooperation between the special intervention units of the Member States of the European Union in the crisis situations.

[359] Council Framework Decision 2002/465/JHA on joint investigation teams; see also Regulation (EU) 2023/969 establishing a collaboration platform to support the functioning of joint investigation teams and amending Regulation 2018/1726.

[360] Art. 40 et seqq. Regulation (EU) 2019/1896; for more details, see Schöndorf-Haubold in Gusy/Kugelmann/Würtenberger, Rechtshandbuch Zivile Sicherheit, p. 708 et seq.; Art. 19 et seqq. Regulation (EU) 2021/2303.

[361] Council Regulation (EU) 2022/922 on the establishment and operation of an evaluation and monitoring mechanism to verify the application of the Schengen acquis.

corruption;[362] countermeasures are eligible for EU funding if they make explicit reference to those findings.

Moreover, the EU uses yardstick competitions and mutual observation mechanisms in almost all policy areas – in various forms and under different names – to promote its integration goals.[363] The aim of the reciprocal peer reviews that Member States conduct in certain subareas of security policy make a contribution to finding best-practice solutions (although the question of what criteria are applied always arises here) and to enable Member States to learn from each other. These processes are typically initiated and moderated by the Commission. A peer review was conducted in the field of counter-terrorism, for instance.[364] In addition, following around ten years of practical implementation, the Council has long since established, as a permanent instrument, a comprehensive coordination and cooperation procedure in relation to combating crime, namely the European Multidisciplinary Platform Against Criminal Threats (EMPACT). The basic idea is that goals and priorities are jointly agreed for several years (called 'cycles') following in-depth preparation by the Council. The areas most recently adopted by the Council include, for example, environmental crime, weapons and drugs smuggling, and cyber attacks.[365] Following adoption, the Commission, the agencies and the Member States draw up multi-year strategy plans to substantiate the subgoals and measures. **82**

II. Integration by means of harmonizing security law

The term 'security law' covers a wide range of different subject matters, namely criminal and regulatory offences law, police law, military and civil defence law, intelligence services law and civil protection law. As analyzed above (→ mn. 10 et seqq.), the EU has competences to harmonize legal matters in only some of these areas. It is on that basis that a portfolio of EU security law has selectively evolved that needs to be incorporated into each Member State's regulatory structures.[366] The following areas in particular can be made out by way of example: **83**

1. Harmonization of criminal law

Fostered by the new competences in the Area of Freedom, Security and Justice in the Treaty of Lisbon, a separate (sub)legal area has emerged in the last two decades: EU criminal law.[367] The Union applies its traditional range of instruments in various subareas, for example the harmonization of the Member States' laws, by setting minimum requirements in the relevant directives and the corresponding consequences under EU law.[368] The range of harmonized subject matters is now very broad. The first of these is **84**

---

362 On this criterion in general, European Commission, 'Assessment of progress on structural reforms, prevention and correction of macroeconomic imbalances, and results of in-depth reviews under Regulation (EU) No 1176(2011)', 16.2.2020, COM(2020) 150 final, 4.

363 More generally on such mechanisms, Pilniok (2011), p. 200 et seqq.

364 For an instructive analysis, see Bossong, Cooperation and Conflict 2012, 519 et seqq.

365 Council of the European Union, 'Council conclusions setting the EU's priorities for the fight against serious and organised crime for EMPACT 2022–2025', 12.5.2021, Doc. 8665/21.

366 See the overview in Pache in Niedobitek, Europarecht: Grundlagen und Politiken der Union, § 21 mn. 262 et seqq.; for a general take on the causes of harmonization processes Lohse, p. 1 et seqq.

367 For an overview, see Mitsilegas/Vavoula in Trauner/Ripoll Servent, Policy Change in the Area of Freedom, Security and Justice, p. 133 et seqq.; Weiembergh/Brière in Ripoll Servent/Trauner, The Routledge Handbook of Justice and Home Affairs, p. 192 et seqq.

368 De Capitani in Bignami, EU Law in Populist Times, p. 394 et seqq.

criminal procedure law, where specific EU instruments are created,[369] the principle of mutual recognition is defined more precisely,[370] a response is provided to cases with a cross-border reference[371] and key building blocks of rule-of-law proceedings, the right to instruction and information[372] and access to legal counsel are harmonized[373] to ensure that minimum standards apply under EU law[374]. Second, EU law makes requirements regarding the law of sanctions[375] and certain crimes as defined in substantive criminal law.[376] Harmonization in criminal law is dynamic and being continued by the Commission.[377] Moreover, the definition of 'criminal law' applied in EU law is broad and also covers legal provisions that are preventive in nature.[378] Thus, for instance, the Directive on airline passenger data retention was based on the EU's competences in relation to criminal law.[379]

2. Harmonization of threat prevention and regulatory law

85 Some of the EU legislative acts that are closely linked to the harmonization of criminal law are geared to protection against threats, for instance those relating to the fight against money laundering and the financing of terrorism. Here, preventive measures are also taken to preclude the relevant offences, for example by setting up monitoring systems.[380] Further, regulatory provisions can also be classed as being preventative in nature and as serving threat prevention purposes. Based on Art. 114 TFEU (→ mn. 16), provisions relating to security-related products in the internal market have been harmonized, for instance in relation to the purchase and possession of weapons,[381] to pyrotechnical products[382] as well as to the sale of explosives precursors in the internal market.[383] The Regulation on addressing the dissemination of terrorist content online is a far-reaching example.[384]

---

[369] Directive 2011/99/EU on the European protection order; Directive 2014/41/EU regarding the European Investigation Order in criminal matters.

[370] Regulation (EU) 2018/1805 on the mutual recognition of freezing orders and confiscation orders.

[371] Directive 2010/64/EU on the right to interpretation and translation in criminal proceedings.

[372] Directive 2012/13/EU on the right to information in criminal proceedings.

[373] Directive 2013/48/EU on the right of access to a lawyer in criminal proceedings and in European arrest warrant proceedings, and on the right to have a third party informed upon deprivation of liberty and to communicate with third persons and with consular authorities while deprived of liberty.

[374] See, in addition to the aforementioned legislative acts, Directive (EU) 2016/343 on the strengthening of certain aspects of the presumption of innocence and of the right to be present at the trial in criminal proceedings; Directive (EU) 2016/800 on procedural safeguards for children who are suspects or accused persons in criminal proceedings; Directive (EU) 2016/1919 on legal aid for suspects and accused persons in criminal proceedings and for requested persons in European arrest warrant proceedings.

[375] Directive 2014/42/EU on the freezing and confiscation of instrumentalities and proceeds of crime in the European Union.

[376] Directive 2011/36/EU on preventing and combating trafficking in human beings and protecting its victims; Directive 2011/93/EU on combating the sexual abuse and sexual exploitation of children and child pornography; Directive (EU) 2017/1371 on the fight against fraud to the Union's financial interests by means of criminal law; Directive (EU) 2018/1673 on combating money laundering by criminal law.

[377] See e. g. European Commission, 'Proposal for a Regulation of the European Parliament and the Council on the transfer of proceedings in criminal matters', 5.4.2023, COM(2023) 185 final.

[378] See Herlin-Karnell in Léonard/Kaunert, Searching for a Strategy for the European Union's Area of Freedom, Justice and Security, p. 73 et seqq.

[379] Directive (EU) 2016/681 on the use of passenger name record (PNR) data for the prevention, detection, investigation and prosecution of terrorist offences and serious crime.

[380] Regulation (EU) 2018/1672 on controls on cash entering or leaving the Union.

[381] Directive (EU) 2021/555 on control of the acquisition and possession of weapons; for how the legal situation has evolved, see Kirst, Fordham Journal of International Law 2020, 855 et seqq.

[382] Directive 2013/29/EU on the harmonisation of the laws of the Member States relating to the making available on the market of pyrotechnic articles.

[383] Regulation (EU) 2019/1148 on the marketing and use of explosives precursors.

[384] Regulation (EU) 2021/784 on addressing the dissemination of terrorist content online.

Amongst other things, it allows the Member States' authorities to adopt transnational administrative acts to oblige hosting providers in other Member States to delete terrorist content from their platforms. From the Member States' perspective, the Regulation can thus be regarded as serving to protect against threats; from the EU's perspective, it represents an obstacle in the common digital internal market. The provisions that serve to protect critical infrastructure are likewise based on Art. 114 TFEU and are also of considerable relevance to public security[385] (→ § 16).

3. Harmonization of security-related data protection law

The work of the security authorities is very essentially based on what they know about dangerous individuals, situations and places. The more paradigmatic a new definition of 'security' is (which already seeks to comprehensively prevent threats arising), the more the collection and processing of data comes to the fore. That also raises wide-ranging legal questions regarding data protection.[386] Whilst the General Data Protection Regulation (GDPR) created a comprehensive legal data protection framework that applies directly in the Member States (including the public administration on account of the aforementioned competences), the Union was forced to exercise legislative restraint when regulating data protection in relation to the Member States' national security authorities.[387] This is manifested in both the mode of legislation and the content of the Data Protection Law Enforcement Directive.[388] It is the practical consequence of Declaration No. 20 on Art. 16 TFEU, namely that due account needs to be taken of national security whenever rules on the protection of data are to be adopted.[389] This declaration can also be regarded as echoing Art. 4(2) sent. 3 TEU, even though it sets a framework and there can, therefore, be no question of sole responsibility. On the one hand, the declaration grants the Member States additional leeway. On the other hand, data protection monitoring is also strengthened by taking recourse to the independent national data protection structures that were created on the basis of the GDPR. Contrary to EU law, the Directive 2016/680 on data protection in the JHA realm had (at the time of writing) not yet been implemented in all member states.[390] This in particular prevents the data protection authorities from effectively protecting fundamental rights under administrative law vis-à-vis the security authorities. **86**

4. Soft law

Finally, integration through legislative harmonization not only occurs by introducing binding modes of action in accordance with Art. 288 TFEU, but also by means of soft **87**

---

[385] Directive (EU) 2022/2555 on measures for a high common level of cybersecurity across the Union (NIS 2 Directive); see on the state of play and planned reforms COM(2023) 665 final, 2 et seqq.

[386] See Kastler, p. 1 et seqq.; De Hert/Papakonstantinou in Ripoll Servent/Trauner, The Routledge Handbook of Justice and Home Affairs, p. 169 et seqq.

[387] For more details as regards this distinction, see Reimer, mn. 29 et seqq.

[388] Directive (EU) 2016/680 on the protection of natural persons with regard to the processing of personal data by competent authorities for the purposes of the prevention, investigation, detection or prosecution of criminal offences or the execution of criminal penalties, and on the free movement of such data; on the draft, see Wolff in Kugelmann/Rackow, Prävention und Repression im Raum der Freiheit, der Sicherheit und des Rechts, p. 61 et seqq. On the implemenation see European Commission, 'First report on application and functioning of the Data Protection Law Enforcement Directive (EU) 2016/680', 25.7.2022, COM(2022) 364 final.

[389] OJ 2008 C 115, 345.

[390] The Commission therefore sent Germany a reasoned opinion in May 2020, which was followed by infringement proceedings under Art. 258 TFEU. See European Commission, 'May infringements package: key decisions', 14.5.2020.

law.[391] From the Commission's perspective, this has advantages in terms of cutting the length of procedures and increasing flexibility when amendments are made. Provisions can therefore be found in various policy areas that are non-binding but claim to be normative in nature, for example on account of being published in the Official Journal of the European Union. These rules – which are often developed with the intensive cooperation of expert groups – have a symbolic function, but often also act as a precursor drafting legislation. The Code of Conduct on countering illegal hate speech online[392] is one such example in the area of security law. It is based on the Code of Conduct, for which the European Commission was responsible, that various corporations that operate online communications platforms have undertaken to implement certain measures to combat hate crimes. By publishing regular reports on the level of implementation of the Code of Conduct, the Commission is to put sufficient pressure on these corporations to act accordingly, despite them not being legally obliged to do so.[393] However, because soft law was unable to achieve the desired effects, provision has now been made under EU law for the introduction, in the Digital Services Act,[394] of more extensive rules on that basis.

III. Integration by means of information systems

1. Interoperable personal data files in the composite security administration

88 As has been highlighted for some time now,[395] the European composite administration largely constitutes an information network. The sharing of information and shared, cross-border and inter-institutional access to information are two key cooperation mechanisms.[396] They are also, and especially, applied in the Security Union (→ § 20). That is why their core elements include establishing and operating extensive security-related information systems, in particular to secure the EU's external borders and guarantee freedom of movement within the territory of the EU.[397] Whilst the EU sets the legal framework and safeguards operations, the Member States' security authorities are largely responsible for the entries made in the relevant databases and their use to guarantee security. Like other aspects of the Security Union, there is great momentum in terms of lawmaking and administrative practice on this form of integration. The relevant legal bases are constantly being expanded and the issue of making better use of the available data is addressed – for instance through the use of AI (→ § 9). The following information systems have been established to date:[398]

---

[391] More generally on this, Pilniok (2011), p. 234 et seqq., with further references.

[392] European Commission, 'The Code of conduct on countering illegal hate speech online', 22.6.2020.

[393] See, most recently, European Commission, '7th monitoring round of the Code of Conduct', November 2022.

[394] Regulation (EU) 2022/2065 on a Single Market For Digital Services (Digital Services Act).

[395] See Schmidt-Aßmann in Schmidt-Aßmann/Schöndorf-Haubold, Der europäische Verwaltungsverbund, p. 15: 'All administration of the common European space is first and foremost information administration.'[own translation]; Schneider, NVwZ 2012, 65 et seqq.; see, in detail, v. Bogdandy/Hering in Voßkuhle/Eifert/Möllers, Grundlagen des Verwaltungsrechts, § 25, especially mn. 78 et seqq.

[396] See, e.g., Lauer, p. 1 et seqq.

[397] This is, e.g., expressed in Regulation (EU) 2017/458 amending Regulation (EU) 2016/399 as regards the reinforcement of checks against relevant databases at external borders.

[398] It is on the basis of Council Regulation (EC) No 515/97 on mutual assistance between the administrative authorities of the Member States and cooperation between the latter and the Commission to ensure the correct application of the law on customs and agricultural matters that an Anti-Fraud Information System is also operated, which is primarily directed at the customs authorities; it is not described in more detail in the following. The focus continues to be on further developments as regards

- The first to be established was the Schengen Information System (SIS)[399] (→ § 19). The system was originally established in 1995 on the basis of the Schengen Convention to compensate for the discontinuation of checks at the EU's internal borders.[400] The SIS serves the tracing of people and things (e.g. vehicles) in the territory of the EU, mainly for repressive purposes. Diverse data, including photographs and fingerprints, may be stored when alerts are issued.[401] Not only the Member States' security authorities have access to the SIS, but, in certain circumstances, Europol, Eurojust and Frontex as well.[402] The SIS's central unit is operated by eu-LISA (→ mn. 64); the Member States are required to set up national systems. However, the SIS is not a centralized database, but a netlike structure within which the Member States' systems are constantly synchronized via the central unit, thus facilitating shared access.[403]
- The Europol Information System (EIS) is long-established but differs conceptually from the SIS. It is a centralized database that is operated by Europol into which a multitude of security-related personal data can be entered;[404] it also encompasses working files set up for only a limited period.[405] However, unlike other EU legislative acts, instead of taking the technical infrastructure as its point of reference, the applicable rules take the EU institutions as their starting point. The Europol Regulation makes comprehensive provision as regards its powers to act (incl. on data collection and processing) and as regards the related internal competences and safeguards. The aim is to ensure that solutions are technically neutral[406] and that the specific technical details are left to Europol, thus providing greater flexibility. The national units to be established by the Member States are under the obligation to transmit the information that Europol needs to fulfil its tasks. Following the most recent reform of its powers, Europol is now also permitted to collect more data itself, including from private parties.[407] This is a further step towards giving the agency an independent role that goes well beyond coordinating the Member States' authorities. The Member States' security authorities can search the SIS, but are reliant on their national units' mediating role when it comes to transmitting more extensive information. Europol makes available a specific communication system that facilitates cooperation between the Member States' authorities.
- Then there is the European Criminal Records Information System (ECRIS),[408] which is supplemented by a database that keeps a record of convictions of third-country nationals and stateless persons (ECRIS-TCN).[409] This system is based on

---

the Schengen Area, European Council, 'European Council meeting (20 June 2019) – Conclusions', 20.6.2019, EUCO 9/19, 6.

[399] Regulation (EU) 2018/1861 on the establishment, operation and use of the Schengen Information System (SIS) in the field of border checks.

[400] Schöndorf-Haubold in Terhechte, Verwaltungsrecht der Europäischen Union, § 35 mn. 73.

[401] Art. 20 and 32 et seq. Regulation (EU) 2018/1861.

[402] Art. 35 et seq. Regulation (EU) 2018/1861.

[403] Schöndorf-Haubold in Terhechte, Verwaltungsrecht der Europäischen Union, § 35 mn. 73.

[404] See the list in Annex II to Regulation (EU) 2016/794.

[405] For more details, see Schöndorf Schöndorf-Haubold in Terhechte (ed), Verwaltungsrecht der Europäischen Union, § 35 mn. 81.

[406] On the background to this, ibid., § 35 mn. 80.

[407] Art. 26a Europol Regulation.

[408] Directive (EU) 2019/884 amending Council Framework Decision 2009/315/JHA, as regards the exchange of information on third-country nationals and as regards the European Criminal Records Information System (ECRIS), and replacing Council Decision 2009/316/JHA.

[409] Regulation (EU) 2019/816 establishing a centralised system for the identification of Member States holding conviction information on third-country nationals and stateless persons (ECRIS-TCN) to supplement the European Criminal Records Information System and amending Regulation (EU) 2018/

a complex and detailed architecture whose centralized system is also operated by eu-LISA.[410] In addition to data identifying an individual, fingerprints, facial images and information about whether a criminal registry entry has been made are also stored in the system. Member States' security authorities then have to request information about concrete individuals from the Member State in which those data are stored.

- Eurodac's database stores data (incl. biometric data) on asylum seekers and third-country nationals.[411] The database is operated by eu-LISA and the Commission. The Member States' authorities as well as Frontex and Europol can use it. As is apparent from the extremely lengthy title given to the Regulation establishing Eurodac,[412] the database has a twofold function. First, it is to improve the EU's extensively reshaped migration management by identifying double entries, for instance; second, it is to serve the protection against threats and criminal prosecution by the relevant security authorities. In the context of a wide-ranging amendment to EU migration legislation, the Commission initiated a proposal that aims to expand the data that may be stored and extend retention periods to be able to better fulfil both functions.[413]
- The purpose of the Visa Information System (VIS)[414] is to create an information network that encompasses the embassies and consulates of those of the Member States' agencies that issue visas, as well as their asylum and border authorities. A large amount of data on those third-country nationals who need a visa to enter a Member State on account of the length of their stay or their country of origin are collected for identification purposes, including photographs and fingerprints, as well as visa-related information. The VIS is also operated by eu-LISA. The purpose of the most recent reform of its legal basis was to expand the kinds of data that may be stored, above all, though, to create the conditions for comprehensive interoperability so that the VIS can be linked up to the other information systems.

1726; last amended by Regulation (EU) 2019/818 on establishing a framework for interoperability between EU information systems in the field of police and judicial cooperation, asylum and migration and amending Regulations (EU) 2018/1726, (EU) 2018/1862 and (EU) 2019/816.

[410] For more details, see Schöndorf-Haubold in Terhechte, Verwaltungsrecht der Europäischen Union, § 35 mn. 88.

[411] See also ibid., § 35 mn. 85.

[412] Regulation (EU) No 603/2013 on the establishment of 'Eurodac' for the comparison of fingerprints for the effective application of Regulation (EU) No 604/2013 establishing the criteria and mechanisms for determining the Member State responsible for examining an application for international protection lodged in one of the Member States by a third-country national or a stateless person and on requests for the comparison with Eurodac data by Member States' law enforcement authorities and Europol for law enforcement purposes, and amending Regulation (EU) No 1077/2011 establishing a European Agency for the operational management of large-scale IT systems in the area of freedom, security and justice.

[413] See Regulation (EU) 2024/1350 of the European Parliament and of the Council on the establishment of 'Eurodac' for the comparison of biometric in order to effectively apply Regulations (EU) 2024/1351 and (EU) 2024/1350 of the European Parliament and of the Council and Council Directive 2001/55/EC and to identify illegally staying third-country national or stateless person and on requests for the comparison with Eurodac data by Member States' law enforcement authorities and Europol for law enforcement purposes, amending Regulations (EU) 2018/1240 and (EU) 2019/818 of the European Parliament and of the Council and repealing Regulation (EU) No 603/2013 of the European Parliament and of the Council.

[414] Regulation (EC) No 767/2008 concerning the Visa Information System (VIS) and the exchange of data between Member States on short-stay visas (VIS Regulation).

- The Entry/Exit System (EES)[415] serves the realization of a smart borders concept[416] and is an important building block in securing the EU's borders.[417] The EES is used to record all entries and exits of third-country nationals, regardless of whether they require a visa to stay or not.[418] Accordingly, the system's architecture needs to be rather complex so that all the involved actors can be incorporated into it.[419] Personal data, including fingerprints and photographs, are stored in the EES.[420] Data matching with the VIS is to be possible, as is the automated monitoring of dates on which the third-country nationals are required to leave.[421] Provision has expressly been made for the Member States' national security authorities and Europol to access the EES.[422]
- In terms of its objectives, the EES is closely linked to the European Travel Information and Authorisation System (ETIAS),[423] which (at the time of writing) was soon to take up operations.[424] Following the example set by the United States, the ETIAS subjects all those who are permitted visa-free entry to a – generally automated – authorization process prior to entry. That generates large amounts of data about all those entering the territory of the EU. One objective is to protect against threats, in that it is to be possible to refuse entry to those individuals who might pose a security risk. Another is that the security authorities are to be given extensive access to the data in the ETIAS system. Reviewing entry authorization already suggests that the data are matched with those in other EU databases.[425] However, over and above that the ETIAS database is also to be incorporated into the extensive network of EU databases.[426]

In recent years the legal requirement of interoperability between the various EU **89**
security databases has gained particular relevance and has been extensively legislated (on interoperability → § 20). This development began with the Commission's finding that the databases were too strongly fragmented and that, as a result, they were not fully functional. Different types of information on specific individuals are not available

---

[415] Regulation (EU) 2017/2226 establishing an Entry/Exit System (EES) to register entry and exit data and refusal of entry data of third-country nationals crossing the external borders of the Member States and determining the conditions for access to the EES for law enforcement purposes.

[416] On this, see Rijpma in Cremona, New Technologies and EU Law, p. 197 et seqq.; Bossong, SWP-Studie 2018 (4); see also Schöndorf-Haubold in Terhechte, Verwaltungsrecht der Europäischen Union, § 35 mn. 87.

[417] See the related amendments made to the Schengen Borders Code on the basis of Regulation (EU) 2017/2226 establishing an Entry/Exit System (EES) to register entry and exit data and refusal of entry data of third-country nationals crossing the external borders of the Member States and determining the conditions for access to the EES for law enforcement purposes.

[418] Regulation (EU) 2018/1806 listing the third countries whose nationals must be in possession of visas when crossing the external borders and those whose nationals are exempt from that requirement.

[419] See Art. 7 Regulation (EU) 2017/2226: 'the system shall be composed of a Central System operated by eu-LISA (EES Central System), a National Uniform Interface (NUI) in each Member State based on common technical specifications and identical for all Member States, enabling the connection of the EES Central System to the national border infrastructures in Member States in a secure manner and a web interface for private individuals.'

[420] Art. 14 et seqq. Regulation (EU) 2017/2226.

[421] Art. 8 and 11 Regulation (EU) 2017/2226.

[422] Art. 1(2) and 29 et seqq. Regulation 2017/2226.

[423] Regulation (EU) 2018/1240 establishing a European Travel Information and Authorisation System (ETIAS).

[424] See, for an extensive account, Vavoula, p. 467 et seqq.; for more details, see Buckler, BayVBl 2018, 73 et seqq.; Buckler, DÖV 2020, 749 et seqq.

[425] Regulation (EU) 2021/1151 amending Regulations (EU) 2019/816 and (EU) 2019/818 as regards the establishment of the conditions for accessing other EU information systems for the purposes of the European Travel Information and Authorisation System.

[426] See also Schöndorf-Haubold in Terhechte, Verwaltungsrecht der Europäischen Union, § 35 mn. 91 et seqq.

in the same way to the relevant authorities.[427] 'Interoperability' is generally understood to be the creation of shared networks and data matching between otherwise separate databases. Put in more simple terms, the data sets on individual people or things are to be drawn together so as to be able to thoroughly identify potential risks. To that end, two regulations (known as the Interoperability Regulations) were adopted to create the extensive legal bases for the interoperability of almost all the aforementioned databases.[428] Interoperability not only needs a legal framework, but a considerable number of technical conditions relating to the required interfaces also need to be put in place. Given the number of involved authorities, which are in turn integrated into different national infrastructures, that is a complex challenge. One of the key outcomes is to be a European Search Portal, which is to give the security authorities simultaneous access to various databases via a single user interface.[429] To that end, identity data and biometric data are to be stored together.[430] The main aim of pooling data in this way is to be able to automatically identify people who are using multiple identities.[431]

90 The comprehensive interoperability of EU databases creates a number of problems. First, the already highly complex legal bases underlying the individual information systems have become significantly more multi-layered on account of the Interoperability Regulations and the concomitant changes, making them very intransparent.[432] That constitutes a rule-of-law problem, in particular for the authorities applying the law as well as in terms of those (potentially) affected being able to understand how the law is applied. Whether the precautions put in place to safeguard fundamental rights as well as data protection monitoring are sufficient at the institutional level is at the very least questionable.[433] In particular, the fact that the data concerned relate to third-country nationals causes problems.[434] Accordingly, the rise of databases also leads to more intensive cooperation with third countries and their security authorities, which may cause a shift in the Union's relevance compared to the Member States.[435] Moreover, these networks exacerbate a problem that the databases already have when they operate independently. Decentralized information-gathering by the Member States' authorities carries the risk of generating poor-quality data. False or imprecise entries may be used in other Member States as the decision-making basis for administrative action has extremely significant repercussions for fundamental rights. This is thus a very specific example of a general problem of mutual trust within the European composite administration.[436] Issues around legal protection against the act of data entry and storage have only been insufficiently addressed.[437] In view of the large amounts of data stored in the information systems and their interconnectedness, the guarantee of security will also become an important area as regards the extent to which using protective measures will in future be analysed by technological means, especially AI systems (which is already

[427] European Commission, 'Stronger and Smarter Information Systems for Borders and Security', 6.4.2016, COM(2016) 205 final.

[428] Regulation (EU) 2019/817 on establishing a framework for interoperability between EU information systems in the field of borders and visa.

[429] Art. 6 et seqq. Regulation (EU) 2019/818.

[430] Art. 12 et seqq. and 17 et seqq. Regulation (EU) 2019/818.

[431] Art. 25 et seqq. of Regulation (EU) 2019/818.

[432] For a critical take, see also Schöndorf-Haubold in Terhechte, Verwaltungsrecht der Europäischen Union, § 35 mn. 92.

[433] ibid., § 35 mn. 91; Aden EPL 2020, 93 et seqq.

[434] For more details, see Vavoula in Bignami, EU Law in Populist Times, p. 227 et seqq.

[435] Curtin/Bastos, EPL 2020, 59 (68).

[436] ibid. 66 et seq.

[437] On this more generally, see Rademacher, p. 76 et seqq., 220 et seqq.

being planned), and then used as the basis for the actions on the part of the Member States' security authorities.[438]

2. Institutionalization of other information systems

Other building blocks of EU security law include the storage of data on airline passengers, at least on flights to and from third countries, which is to serve the prevention and combating of terrorist and other serious criminal offences. However, in structural terms this is regulated differently than the other databases, because the focus here is not on transnational data sharing. The PNR Directive[439] obliges the Member States[440] to involve the airlines by putting in place national data transmission legislation and to establish a central data storage unit. The data transmitted by the airlines are matched with a variety of databases and then other measures are taken on that basis. Airline passenger data storage is highly controversial, both politically and legally, in particular on account of the long data retention period of five years. In a ruling that interpreted the Directive restrictively,[441] the ECJ positioned itself on this matter as befits its role of watchdog over all fundamental rights (→ mn. 47), in particular Art. 7 and 8 CFR. What is striking is the length of that judgment, which is unusually long for the ECJ. As in its previous decisions on data retention, the Court is against the groundless storage of airline passenger data. It is to be limited to those connections for which there are at any rate indications of an actual or foreseeable terrorist threat. It is not permissible to use such data to improve border checks, for example, or to combat illegal migration. The Court's case-law has implications beyond the concrete matter in hand and also impacts on automated decision-making, which both the Member States and the Union are moving forward with, including in relation to the use of AI systems in the security sector. The relevant passages of the PNR Directive are often interpreted to mean that only semi-automated decision-making involving humans is permissible.[442] **91**

IV. Integration by means of financing the guarantee of security

The EU also uses its 'financial reins' to allocate funding on various levels to achieve **92** its integration goals within the Security Union. The Union has various programmes through which it allocates financial resources and sets uniform standards for the allocation of these resources. The Member States' authorities and other actors have to apply for this funding by submitting programmes and concepts; in some cases, cross-border cooperation is a prerequisite. At any rate, to be eligible to receive funding, a Member State's national policies must be aligned with the standards and criteria laid down in EU law. Even though these are adopted as part of the legislative procedure

[438] Curtin/Bastos, EPL 2020, 59 (69).

[439] Directive (EU) 2016/681 on the use of passenger name record (PNR) data for the prevention, detection, investigation and prosecution of terrorist offences and serious crime; The Commission's proposal goes even further, European Commission, 'Proposal for a Regulation on the collection and transfer of advance passenger information for the prevention, detection, investigation and prosecution of terrorist offences and serious crime, and amending Regulation (EU) 2019/818', 13.12.2022, COM(2022) 731.

[440] Implemented in Germany by means of the Act Implementing Directive (EU) 2016/681 (Gesetz zur Umsetzung der Richtlinie (EU) 2016/681), BGBl. I 2017, p. 1484. According to § 1 of that Act, the Federal Criminal Police Office is the central office, whilst data processing is carried out by the Federal Office of Administration. See, for more details, Arzt, DÖV 2017, 1023 et seqq.

[441] ECJ 21.6.2022 – case C-817/19, ECLI:EU:C:2022:491 – *Ligue des droits humains.*

[442] See e.g. Kuskonmaz, European Constitutional Law Review 2023, 294 et seqq.

and a subsequent specification phase, for example in expert groups and comitology committees and with the Member States' involvement, the result is a significant degree of harmonization. Accepting EU funding thus comes at a price: If a national authority accepts EU funding, it becomes accountable to the Commission under complex budgetary regulations. While the EU has long used the 'power of the purse' for example to fund research and development aid, it is still remarkable to what extent various security-related areas are funded for the administrative structures of the member states.

1. Funding Member States' security resources

93 The EU has various programmes that are aimed at the Member States' security authorities, and it puts a considerable amount of effort into funding the guarantee of security through these programmes. This funding is, of course, bound by medium-term budgetary planning,[443] and the programmes were all updated in 2021, in some cases with a considerable increase in the funding and the setting of new priorities. The aim in creating incentives through the use of EU funding is to be able to strictly set the course, for example as regards cooperation between police authorities. Another key concern of the programmes is to set the administrative framework so that the authorities are able to do their share of the tasks within the Security Union, on the basis of the division of labor.[444] Drawing up national programmes in close cooperation with the Commission – the precondition for receiving EU funding – leads to a critical stock-taking of the Member States and ensures that the Commission has a considerable influence on the way in which personnel and financial resources are used in the area of internal security, especially in those Member States in which the funding of public security is a precarious matter. This does to some extent stand in contradiction to the Member States' emphasis on their autonomy, for which they invoke Art. 4(2) sent. 3 TEU. At least three relevant funding programmes were created under the multiannual financial framework 2021–2027 that are linked to the guarantee of security and are all defined by over-arching rules on funding allocation[445] and therefore share structural features. In principle, drawing EU funding always requires national co-financing.

94 The focus of this multiannual financial framework is on setting up an Internal Security Fund,[446] which is to contribute to ensuring a high level of security by providing the Member States with funding within the framework of the EU's competences. A total of almost two billion euros is to be allocated in that way.[447] The Member States are required to draw up programmes detailing how the funding is to be used, and these have to be coordinated with the security agencies and then evaluated and approved by the Commission.[448] EU funding is available to a very broad spectrum of measures and items, ranging from local crime prevention strategies to equipment for the security

---

[443] Council Regulation (EU, Euratom) 2020/2093 laying down the multiannual financial framework for the years 2021 to 2027.

[444] See Ladenburger in Kahl/Mager, Verwaltungsrechtswissenschaft und Verwaltungsrechtspraxis, p. 79; For a similar example of support for national administrative reforms, see Weinzierl in Klemm/Schultheiß, Die Krise in Griechenland, p. 448 et seqq.

[445] Regulation (EU) 2021/1060 laying down common provisions on the European Regional Development Fund, the European Social Fund Plus, the Cohesion Fund, the Just Transition Fund and the European Maritime, Fisheries and Aquaculture Fund and financial rules for those and for the Asylum, Migration and Integration Fund, the Internal Security Fund and the Instrument for Financial Support for Border Management and Visa Policy.

[446] Regulation (EU) 2021/1149 establishing the Internal Security Fund.

[447] Art. 7(1) Regulation (EU) 2021/1149.

[448] Art. 13 Regulation (EU) 2021/1149 in conjunction with Art. 23 Regulation (EU) 2021/1060.

authorities and training measures. Particular emphasis is placed on remedying deficits that have been identified as part of various mutual monitoring and oversight mechanisms. Funding is above all also made available to put in place the infrastructural conditions for, and to use, EU security databases (→ mn. 88). Various coordination and cooperation projects are also eligible for funding. The Member States are required to compile annual performance reports, for which various performance indicators (e.g. the quantity of drugs confiscated) are defined.[449] Part of the Fund is administered under the shared management of the EU budget, where a national agency is responsible for funding allocation within a Member State.

A Fund for Integrated Border Management has been established, too. This Fund **95**
encompasses two instruments that have different legal bases. The first is a financial assistance instrument in relation to border management and visa policy, which was established on the basis of Art. 77(2) and Art. 79(2)(d) TFEU.[450] The instrument is very similar to the Internal Security Fund in terms of its basic content and procedure. Funding is also available for diverse measures (e.g. to prevent and detect crime at the external borders), although the focus is on large-scale IT systems and the relevant local infrastructure. Given the various competence bases, the EU also adopted a complementary instrument to fund equipment needed for customs control purposes based on Art. 33, 114 and 207 TFEU.[451] In view of the importance of customs authorities in the management of external borders, EU funding shall contribute to the availability of a common level of equipment and thus to rebalance the different burdens on member states. However, emphasis is placed on the relevance of the customs authorities when it comes to fighting crime on the one hand and the importance of the multifunctionality of the equipment to be purchased (e.g. body scanners) for border checks on the other.[452] Finally, the customs programme for cooperation in regard to customs checks was established by Regulation (EU) 2021/444.[453] It is to be used to promote both structured cooperation between the Member States' customs authorities and the establishment and operation of EU-wide IT customs systems, for instance for risk management purposes.[454] The Justice Programme is directed at public prosecution offices and criminal courts, amongst others, but has less available funding than other programmes.[455] Among other things, the EU finances measures for mutual learning and the sharing of best practices, as well as measures to enhance knowledge of the applicable EU legislation, to establish EU-wide networks, to digitize the judiciary and facilitate interoperable cross-border systems.[456]

---

449 Art. 30 and Annex V Regulation (EU) 2021/1149.

450 Regulation (EU) 2021/1148 establishing, as part of the Integrated Border Management Fund, the Instrument for Financial Support for Border Management and Visa Policy.

451 Regulation (EU) 2021/1077 establishing, as part of the Integrated Border Management Fund, the instrument for financial support for customs control equipment.

452 Recitals 11 and 18 Regulation (EU) 2021/1077.

453 Regulation (EU) 2021/444 establishing the Customs programme for cooperation in the field of customs and repealing Regulation (EU) No 1294/2013.

454 European Commission, 'on the EU Strategy and Action Plan for customs risk management: Tackling risks, strengthening supply chain security and facilitating trade', 21.8.2014, COM(2014) 527 final; European Commission, 'Report from the Commission to the Council and the European Parliament. Progress Report on the implementation of the EU Strategy and Action Plan for customs risk management', 19.7.2016, COM(2016) 476 final; European Commission, 'Report from the Commission to the Council and the European Parliament. Second Progress Report on the implementation of the EU Strategy and Action Plan for customs risk management', 20.7.2018, COM(2018) 549 final; European Commission, 'Report from the Commission to the Council and the European Parliament. Third Progress Report on the implementation of the EU Strategy and Action Plan for customs risk management', 18.1.2021, COM (2021) 9 final.

455 Regulation (EU) 2021/693 establishing the Justice Programme.

456 Art. 8 of Regulation (EU) 2021/693.

2. Funding security research

96 Security is also fostered by funding security research through research framework programmes. Under the current Horizon Europe programme, which supports predefined topics, 'civil security' is regarded as one of the EU's global challenges[457] and funding is allocated to research projects in that field. The designation of the relevant funding line in the research framework already emphasizes the social relevance of security research. Research is to be conducted into responses to ongoing security threats, including cybercrime, as well as to both natural and man-made disasters.[458] The funding available under this programme is allocated to cooperative research projects conducted by both universities and non-university research institutes in conjunction with small and medium-sized enterprises and industry. Approximately 1.3 billion euro has been allocated for the current funding period (2021–2027).[459] The Member States' authorities are also given the right of access to the research findings.[460] Other funding lines also make reference to security research; cybersecurity, for example, is a funding priority in those funding lines that are geared to the digital transformation.

97 One example of EU research funding that has garnered a great deal of attention are those projects that come under the heading 'smart borders'.[461] The Commission has supported various projects in which research facilities cooperated with security authorities and aimed to develop and test, in practice, technical means for improving border checks. They are linked to the setting up of extensive interoperable databases in the EU (→ mn. 88). The focus is on AI technologies (→ § 9). It is hoped that, along with facilitating analyses of the extensive databases, these will lead to the introduction of facial recognition systems so as to be able to identify those people who pose a potential threat to the security of the EU and, simultaneously, to swifter checks. Allocating funding and development by means of projects financed by the EU creates downstream pressure to act – at any rate if the systems prove their worth and are fit for purpose – because their potential to actually or allegedly increase security creates the need to justify why some do not make use of EU funding. It is clear that a number of legal questions have so far not been sufficiently discussed, in particular as regards the subsequent use of algorithms.

3. Funding security-related projects in third countries

98 Since security in the EU is dependent on various conditions being met in third countries, security is also guaranteed by funding measures in those third countries. The funding available under the EU's Neighbourhood Policy and as part of its development aid has now been conflated under one programme[462] that has various security-related

---

[457] Research projects in the field of military security are entrusted to an independent research funding programme due to the special nature of the European Defence Fund; see recital 54 of Regulation (EU) 2021/695 establishing Horizon Europe – the Framework Programme for Research and Innovation, laying down its rules for participation and dissemination. The European Defence Fund will allocate 8bn euro to such research in the period 2021 to 2027, see, for more details, Regulation (EU) 2021/697 establishing the European Defence Fund.

[458] Annex I to and second paragraph, point (c) of Regulation (EU) 2021/695.

[459] Art. 12(2) Regulation (EU) 2021/695.

[460] Art. 41(9) Regulation (EU) 2021/695.

[461] See Wischmeyer in Ebers et al., Künstliche Intelligenz und Robotik, § 20 mn. 18; see for the failed attempt to get access to the documents related to this project the judgment of the Court of 7 September 2023, ECJ 7.9.2023 – case C-135/22 P, ECLI:EU:C:2023:640 – *Patrick Breyer v European Research Executive Agency.*

[462] Regulation (EU) 2021/947 establishing the Neighbourhood, Development and International Co-operation Instrument – Global Europe.

objectives, including in relation to combating terrorism, organized crime and cybersecurity.[463] To that end, various measures are funded both in the EU's neighbouring states and as part of development cooperation. Amongst other things, the aim is to provide support in overcoming global and transregional threats as well as to contribute to creating fully functional security authorities based on the rule of law.[464] The assumption is that stabilizing the relevant third countries will at the same time have positive effects as regards the guarantee of security in the EU. The programmes are fleshed out and promoted within complex governance structures.[465]

F. Outlook: trends in the Security Union

Taking stock of the current state of play as regards the European Security Union, **99**
what is particularly striking is the considerable momentum and high degree of differentiation in this area (for an outlook and on that momentum → § 21). Since the turn of the century, and then accelerated by the new competence bases laid down in the Lisbon Treaty, as well as on account of actual threat scenarios, integration within the Security Union has evolved into one of the EU's most important policy areas. That almost inevitably goes along with a considerable level of complexity, which means that some parts of European security law have already become fairly intransparent. One reason for this is the general trend in EU law towards comprehensive and – on account of the need to reach compromises between the Member States and the EU institutions – extremely detailed EU legislative acts. This is evident, for instance, in the emergence of EU criminal law, which within the space of a few years has become a separate subarea of criminal law and requires bulky reference material to be properly understood. The *acquis communautaire* of EU security law draws together the heterogeneous subject matters of criminal and regulatory offences law, police and regulatory law, intelligence services law, military and civil defence law, and civil protection law. These individual subareas differ considerably as regards their depth of regulation and the available instruments. This is on account of the differences between the competences available to the EU in relation to legislative acts and the available modes of action, as well as the Member States' different ambitions as regards integration. Finally, the momentum of integration has, not least, increased because of the EU's changed geopolitical situation.

Overall, besides partial harmonization and the considerable increase in the amount of **100**
allocated funding, it is above all the institutionalization of the EU security agencies that has contributed to the emergence of a European Security Union. In recent years, the different agencies have been the subject of a significant expansion of powers, competences and resources. Within the multi-level system that is the EU security architecture, they are embedded in complex coordination and cooperation relationships with the Member States' security authorities, although there are considerable differences between them. The resulting follow-up problems as regards accountability and oversight within the composite security administration have only been touched upon and by no means finally resolved. In particular, these problems arise when it comes to cooperative

[463] Recital 53 Regulation (EU) 2021/947.

[464] See, e.g., the areas of intervention set out in Annex III Regulation (EU) 2021/947.

[465] For more details on the regulatory structures, see Dann in Bartelt/Dann, Entwicklungszusammenarbeit im Recht der Europäischen Union, p. 107 et seqq.; Dann, p. 147 et seqq.

activities involving the Union's and the Member States' authorities, to which they make different contributions, in particular within joint teams. Given the large number of cases involving significant interference with fundamental rights, the problems are especially acute in relation to Frontex.

101 Particular attention also deserves to be paid to the Security Union on account of the close cooperation between the national and EU authorities in relation to the digital transformation. The EU has created various extensive databases that are to be fed and used by the Member States' authorities. That presupposes a considerable level of trust that all the authorized authorities will make correct, legal entries, and it raises questions around legal protections in the context of cooperation based on the division of labour. Two aspects will in future considerably exacerbate this basic problem. First, the legislative acts have for some time now been shaped by the principle of interoperability. That creates extensive links between the different databases. Incorrect or even deliberately inaccurate entries can, thus, have considerable EU-wide consequences. Second, the Commission and the agencies are very much interested in improving the analysis of these extensive databases using new digital technologies or at any rate digital technologies, such as AI, that have made big development strides. Such a development would significantly expand the importance of informational security governance within the Union and thus create new challenges as regards democratic legitimacy and rule-of-law accountability. That raises the question of whether the use of digital innovations by private parties creates new security risks that the Security Union will need to address. Diverse phenomena are imaginable that can as yet only be made out in outline. When one considers the possibilities that AI systems create in terms of generating artificial images and voices, or 3D printers, which can also print weapons, then all new technologies intrinsically come with security risks that need to be countered both legally and in practice. To that extent the EU's policies on promoting innovation and research also potentially have a downside, and these consequences need to be monitored in the European setting.

102 The challenges the EU's security architecture will face on account of the climate crisis is another matter only the contours of which can currently be made out. For example, civil protection law and solidarity mechanisms will gain in importance in relations between Member States because extreme weather events, for instance, are on the increase and Member States will not always be able to handle them on their own. Both EU law and EU institutions are expected to continue to evolve as a result. The scarcity of resources (e.g. drinking water) that is already being felt will also give rise to new socio-political conflicts that will likewise raise security-related questions. Finally, the previously discussed global consequences of climate change will have repercussions for the Security Union, too. The climate crisis will, in all probability, increase migratory pressure on the EU, either directly on account of its leading to the loss of livelihoods or indirectly owing to it triggering violent geopolitical conflicts. Taking that perspective, the efforts the EU is undertaking in regard to climate legislation (i.e. the EU Green Deal) also represent an important preventative security policy measure. Nonetheless, the European Security Union will need to adapt to these and other as yet unforeseeable challenges.

PART III
NATIONAL SECURITY AND SOVEREIGNTY OF MEMBER STATES

§ 5
National security and sovereignty of Member States – an introduction*

Satish Sule

Bibliography: Bodin, Les six livres de la Republiques (1583), German translation: Über den Staat, Stuttgart 2011; Calliess, 'Konfrontation statt Kooperation zwischen BVerfG und EuGH?', NVwZ 2020, 897–904; Craig/de Búrca, EU law, 7th edn, Oxford 2020); Dearlove, 'National Security and Public Anxiety' in Johnson (ed.), The Oxford Handbook of National Security Intelligence, Oxford 2010, p. 33–40; Goodman/Ischebeck-Baum, 'Intelligence in Modern European History', in Dietrich/ Sule (eds), EU Intelligence Policies and Law, Munich/Oxford/Baden-Baden 2019, p. 1–37; Hobbes, Leviathan (1651), edited by Richard Tuck, Cambridge 1996; Isensee, Grundrecht auf Sicherheit, Munich 1983; Omand, Securing the State, London 2010; Röhner, 'Sicherheit als rechtswissenschaftliche Praxis', KritV 2015, 153–169; Ruffert/Walter, Institutionalisiertes Völkerrecht, 2nd edn, Munich 2015; Schmitt, Politische Theologie, 7th edn, Berlin 1996 (1922); Sule, 'National Security and EU Law Restraints on Intelligence Activities' in Dietrich/Sule (eds), EU Intelligence Policies and Law, Munich/Oxford/Baden-Baden 2019; Sule, Spionage, Baden-Baden 2006; Vedder/Heintschel von Heinegg (eds), Europäisches Unionsrecht, 2nd edn, Baden-Baden 2018; von der Groeben/Schwarze/ Hatje (eds), Europäisches Unionsrecht, 7th edn, Baden-Baden 2017.

A. Overview

There is still a strong need to further develop the European Union's common security policy to counter threats that affect all the Member States. The need to further develop this common security policy has been established in recent decades, and previous chapters illustrate this amply. Any further development in this sensitive area can only be based on voluntary cooperation among the Member States. Such cooperation requires common ground, i.e. a political and legal framework. The latter, however, is only defined by the depth of such a common security policy. This depth, then, will yield the common minimum of political goals and legal requirements for cooperation. By placing it in the second and third pillar within the system of the Maastricht Treaty, such cooperation was clearly given an intergovernmental character.[1] Parts of criminal law enforcement and police cooperation, however, have since been institutionalized within supranational EU law.[2] 1

Thus, any further integration of security cooperation will depend on how much Member States are willing to submit it to the European integration process. While some Member States will prefer intergovernmental cooperation between their authorities, 2

* This chapter expresses only the personal opinion of the author and does not bind in any way the European Commission.

[1] See, e.g., the description provided by Craig/de Búrca, p. 10–13.

[2] See ibid., p. 21 and → § 4 mn. 83 et seq.

others may be prepared to go further and harmonize certain rules or even institutionalize at least parts of such a policy.

3 The depth and longevity of efficient security cooperation between the Member States will, ultimately, depend on their common values and political goals.[3] Short-term security cooperation may always be possible in any international context, as long as the cooperating states have parallel interests. Any long-term cooperation, though, must be founded on the common ground of those societies that such a security cooperation is meant to protect. Such values would include similar state political structures and beliefs in a society, for example the principles of democracy, the rule of law, the separation of powers and fundamental rights (→ § 7 mn. 6 et seq.). The more these principles converge, the easier it should be to develop cooperation mechanisms.

4 That being said, all Member States will insist on being the sole party in control of national security. This control will also include the definition of the concept of 'national security'. Even though all the Member States may claim to respect the same fundamental values of democracy, the rule of law and fundamental rights, each of them may have different approaches to balancing them with national security interests. Furthermore, national security can be viewed as the core reason for the nation-state itself. Thus, sharing information about it or even institutionalising tasks that impact it would mean transferring essential powers to the EU in this context. While such a transfer of powers has happened in other areas in recent decades, in the area of security it would have a fundamental impact on the nation-state. It is small wonder that the Member States insisted on including a provision in the Treaty on European Union (TEU) on carving out any (legislative) powers concerning national security from EU law. Accordingly, Art. 4(2) sent. 3 TEU reads: 'In particular, national security remains the sole responsibility of each Member State' (→ § 8).

5 At the same time, if Member States use the provision to impede implementation of EU law, they may risk disintegration of the latter and of the European Union itself.

6 In the light of the above, it is imperative to map out where cooperation between the Member States and possibly EU institutions can be broadened and deepened and what red lines need to be observed by EU institutions as well as the Member States. This chapter gives an overview of the relevant questions raised in this context. Subsequent chapters of this part of the book will then look at these questions from different angles and in more detail.

B. Common legal approach to deepening EU Security cooperation

I. Central common values as a precondition

7 Security cooperation may be feasible between states that do not share the same basic state principles and values. However, such cooperation will most probably not go beyond protecting current common interests of an ad-hoc character. Often, they will focus on a concrete threat, for example to territorial integrity (an aggressor state as in the case of the Ukraine war) or to the lives of a state's population in the case of a terrorist attack. In both cases, security measures may target a common enemy. However, the common interest in providing protection will constitute what has already been

[3] The long-term intelligence cooperation between the US and the UK, both democratic systems built on the rule of law, may serve as an example of this. See, e.g., Goodman/Ischebeck-Baum in Dietrich/Sule, EU Intelligence Policies and Law, mn. 48.

referred to as 'parallel interests', meaning that they might run parallel for a while but may diverge at any moment. This makes it difficult to develop any deep and long-term security cooperation, because a minimum of trust is necessary and this is often based on shared core state principles and values in a society.

Therefore, any phrasing of legal provisions aimed at deepening long-term security **8** cooperation at EU level will depend not only on common identified security needs but will also be dictated by those common assets and interests that are deemed worthy of protection. These will include the lives of the population in a Member State, the integrity of its territory, its political system, all the institutions and procedures needed to keep it and its society running, and its critical infrastructure. At an underlying level, however, assets requiring specific protection include a Member State's core state principles and values. These constitute the very essence the Member States are based on, particularly democracy, the rule of law and fundamental rights to protect individuals within society, namely the right to human dignity.[4] They also provide the basis for a genuine minimum level of trust between the Member States that have joined the EU, thereby transferring some of their powers to this international organization and rendering it supranational in its areas of competence.

II. National and EU legal provisions on security

The aforementioned Member States' common core values and state principles thus **9** constitute the common base for any legal provisions empowering state or even EU actors to take security decisions. They are relevant for security law both at national and at EU level.

1. National law

At national level, legal provisions outlining the state's tasks and powers in relation to **10** providing security to its society and individuals are of key importance. With the advent of modern States in the 16th and 17th century, modern philosophers underlined the state's main purpose of providing their citizens with security. *Bodin*, back in 1583, named the protection and defence of its subjects as one of the State's existential matters.[5] *Hobbes* – who is regularly referred to in security debates[6] – went further by proclaiming that not only one but the State's (or 'commonwealth's') final cause was to ensure preservation of its citizens.[7] This, would in particular, allow them to be defended both from foreign invasion as well as injury caused by internal conflicts, that is by other citizens.[8] The State's main purpose was, thus, to guarantee peace and defence,[9] i.e. protection from both external threats and internal turmoil. It is to this essential core function of the state that Member States come back when they insist on their sole competence for national security, as referred on in Art. 4(2) sent. 3 TEU.

This is reflected in the Member States' numerous laws that form the legal bases for **11** establishing security, intelligence and law enforcement authorities, as well as the different powers they are allowed to exercise. All Member States need to put this on a strong legal

---

[4] As referred to in Art. 2 and 6 TEU and in Art. 1 of the Charter of Fundamental Rights of the European Union (CFR).

[5] Bodin, p. 9, 101 (original page numbering).

[6] Röhner, KritV 2015, 153 (157).

[7] Hobbes, chapter 17, mn. 117.

[8] ibid., mn. 120.

[9] ibid., chapter 18, mn. 6 and 10, 124, 126.

foundation, since they have committed to adhere to the principles of the rule of law and fundamental rights of individuals. This is further reflected by the fact that all the Member States are parties to the European Convention on Human Rights (ECHR). Therefore, any public measures taken to ensure security must be foreseeable and proportionate to their aim, specifically since the measures may often restrict individual fundamental rights.[10] As regards such national legal frameworks, it is interesting to note that most Member States have extended them to include the intelligence services.[11] Traditionally, the intelligence services have led a secretive existence, often regulated by internal administrative guidelines rather than publicly promulgated (parliamentary) legislation. Following the end of the Cold War, in the 1990s some of the Member States started putting their intelligence services on a more solid legislative basis.[12]

2. EU law

12 Within EU law there are evidently few legal provisions that deal with security issues. This stems from the Member States' original focus solely on economic market integration and their subsequent reluctance to allow any supranational intrusion into the area of security.

13 However, political integration increased with the adoption of the Single European Act of 1986 and the three-pillar structure of the Maastricht Treaty, which for the first time saw European intergovernmental cooperation in the areas of Common Foreign and Security Policy ('second pillar') and Justice and Home Affairs ('third pillar').[13] The second and third pillar mechanisms required unanimity among all the Member States in all their decision-making. This reflected the clear will of the Member States to remain solely responsible for the areas of security, foreign and home affairs, i.e. opposing any supranational EU rules in this area. As European integration continued, several provisions concerning security cooperation entered into the framework of primary EU law, namely provisions on judicial cooperation in criminal matters and police cooperation.[14]

14 That being said, the legal framework for Europol serves as an example of growing integration and the move from an intergovernmental to a supranational approach in some areas of security law: Whereas Europol was originally established by an international convention that was unanimously adopted by all Member States under the third pillar of the Maastricht construct,[15] the latest update of its legal framework (the Europol Regulation[16]) is based on Art. 88 TFEU, which provides for an ordinary legislative procedure and thus only a qualified majority of votes in the Council (→ § 4 mn. 52 and → § 7 mn. 9).

15 At a more general level, the TEU refers to *national* security: Art. 4(2) sent. 2 TEU states that the Union will respect the essential State functions of its Member States, including ensuring the territorial integrity of the State, maintaining law and order, and safeguarding national security (for an extensive treatment of Art. 4(2) TEU → § 8). The provision thus establishes a clear obligation on the part of the EU vis-à-vis its Member States, namely the

---

[10] As, e.g., reflected in Art. 8(2) ECHR.

[11] See the overview by FRA, 'Report – Surveillance by intelligence services: fundamental rights safeguards and remedies in the EU – Mapping Member States' legal frameworks', 18.11.2015, 20 et seqq.

[12] See Sule, p. 111–239 regarding Germany, France and the UK (that was a Member State at the time).

[13] See the description by Craig/de Búrca, p. 10–13.

[14] Title 5, Area of Freedom, Security and Justice, Chapters 4 and 5 TFEU.

[15] Council of the European Union, 'Council Act of 26 July 1995 drawing up the Convention based on Article K.3 of the Treaty on European Union, on the establishment of a European Police Office (Europol Convention)'.

[16] Regulation (EU) 2022/991 amending Regulation (EU) 2016/794, as regards Europol's cooperation with private parties, the processing of personal data by Europol in support of criminal investigations, and Europol's role in research and innovation.

obligation not to interfere in the areas mentioned. Art. 4(2) sent. 3 TEU then explicitly recalls that national security remains the sole responsibility of the Member States. This particular emphasis was inserted into the Lisbon Treaty at the 2007 conference. It was due to the Member States' concern that increasing cooperation in terms of counterterrorism action at EU level might impinge on their competence to maintain internal security at national level.[17] This limitation of EU competences is, furthermore, actionable before the Court of Justice of the European Union (CJEU), representing progress from the former three-pillar structure, which had denied the CJEU any jurisdiction in the areas of Common Security and Defence policy under the old Art. 46 TEU.[18]

C. Member States' 'red lines': competence issues arising from the term 'national security'

Nevertheless, any security measures taken at national level may have an impact on areas that fall under EU law. This is due to the ongoing integration of EU law and policies in the decades since the foundation of the European Communities. The origins of EU law, that is the 1951 European Coal and Steel Community (ECSC) Treaty and the European Economic Community (EEC) and the Euratom Treaties, revolved around closer cooperation between and the integration of (certain) economic activities of the Member States. Their framework was, thus, designed to only cover specific areas of Member States' policies. Consequently, at that time any potential overlaps with security issues were less obvious. **16**

I. Practical issues flowing from a conflict around competence

Yet, ongoing development in terms of the further integration of EU policies has parallels with the increase in potential overlaps between EU law and Member States' security activities. Hence, specific national security measures have had an impact on internal market freedoms, that is where they were invoked for reasons of 'public security' as a ground for an exemption. The exemption clauses included in the Treaty permitted Member States to diverge from internal market regulation on the ground of public interest, including public security (for a further discussion → § 8 mn. 2 et seq., 30).[19] Such measures had a direct impact on market freedoms and allowed the *CJEU* to scrutinize them under EU law,[20] including measures taken under the more restrictive concept of national security, as more recent case law shows.[21] **17**

---

[17] See Obwexer in von der Groeben/Schwarze/Hatje, EUV, Art. 4 mn. 46.

[18] See also Vedder in Vedder/Heintschel von Heinegg, EUV, Art. 4 mn. 16.

[19] See, e.g., Art. 36, 45(3), 52, 65, 202 TFEU.

[20] See the established case law of the ECJ on restrictions of the freedoms under the TFEU, e.g. cases ECJ 4.12.1974 – case C-41/74, ECLI:EU:C:1974:13 – *Van Duyn v Home Office*; ECJ 27.10.1977 – case C-30/77, ECLI:EU:C:1977:172 – *Regina v Bouchereau*; ECJ 22.5.1980 – case C-131/79, ECLI:EU:C:1980:131 – *Regina v Secretary of State for Home Affairs, ex parte Santillo*; ECJ 10.2.2000 – case C-340/97, ECLI:EU:C:2000:77 – *Nazli and Others*; more recently: ECJ 23.11.2010 – case C-145/09, ECLI:EU:C:2010:708 – *Land Baden-Württemberg v Panagiotis Tsakouridis*.

[21] ECJ 4.6.2013– case C-300/11, ECLI:EU:C:2013:363 – *ZZ v Secretary of State for the Home Department*; ECJ 6.10.2020 – case C-623/17, ECLI:EU:C:2020:790 – *Privacy International v Secretary of State for Foreign and Commonwealth Affairs and Others*.

18 This case law shows where the overlaps between EU and national law and policies lead to a conflict that could be viewed as existential for both legal systems. This is because it concerns questions of the supremacy of law and state sovereignty within the core competence of the Member States.

II. Need to outline the scope of Art. 4(2) sent. 3 TEU

1. Definition of 'national security'[22]

19 Any starting point for resolving the above-mentioned conflict first requires a definition of the term 'national security'. Two different approaches to such a definition are conceivable: formal and substantive.

a) Formal definition of 'national security'

20 Whereas a substantive definition might list or abstractly describe elements that are essential to national security, a formal one focusses on the procedure and the role of the actor claiming the case of national security. For instance, the fact that Art. 4(2) sent. 3 TEU refers to the Member States' sole responsibility for national security, without describing the term further, may suggest that it is left to the Member States to define it. In that case, the definition of 'national security' is purely a formal one. It only comprises one procedural element: It requires that the actor wishing to use the term 'national security' simply decide himself or herself to which areas it applies and to which it does not. He or she only needs to *formally* take this decision. This 'decisionist' approach echoes the political legal thinking of the German constitutional lawyer *Carl Schmitt* of the 1920s and 1930s, who famously stated: 'Sovereign is he who decides on the state of exception.'[23]

21 Applying this approach to Art. 4(2) TEU clearly (re)asserts the sovereign character of the Member States. However, it at the same time flatly contradicts the concept of EU law as a supranational legal order in which Member States have actually limited their sovereignty in specific areas. Hence, this approach does not address the matter of overlapping competences, i.e. where a Member State claims to be acting in the interest of national security, thereby preventing the implementation of EU law. Also, it ignores the CJEU's monopoly to rule on questions of interpretation of Member States' obligations under EU law as manifested in Art. 267 TFEU.

22 How international law treats a similar phenomenon appears to underline this interpretation. Art. 2(7) of the UN Charter forbids 'the United Nations to intervene in matters which are essentially within the domestic jurisdiction of any State'. However, it is not for the state to decide what falls within such a domestic jurisdiction. Rather, that has to be defined by international law. Otherwise, each state could unilaterally define the scope of competence of the UN.[24]

b) Substantive definition of 'national security'

23 On the other hand, though, any attempt to define national security on the basis of substantive elements would have to refer back to the main purpose of the state, as is, for instance, extrapolated by political philosophers and theorists. Building on these main

---

[22] On national security in the context of EU law, see Sule in Dietrich/Sule, EU Intelligence Policies and Law, p. 335–387 and → § 7 and § 8.

[23] Schmitt, p. 1.

[24] Ruffert/Walter, mn. 199; see also Permanent Court of International Justice 7.2.1923 – Advisory Opinion No. 4, 4, 24 – *Nationality Decrees Issued in Tunis and Morocco.*

elements, some academics and intelligence practitioners either refer to abstract elements and/or list a number of concrete institutions and legally protected rights and principles that seem to recur. They could be seen as the common core of what constitutes national security.

Taking such a substantive approach, a distinction needs to be drawn between subjective and objective concepts of security. One school of thought seems to equate citizens' subjective perception of safety in their everyday life with national security. Another school tends to refer to objective criteria that indicate a threat to safety in order to claim applicability of national security.[25] Thus, Sir *David Oman*, former UK Intelligence and Security Coordinator in the Cabinet Office, sees a shift in national security interests from the traditional aim of ensuring territorial integrity during the Cold War[26] to a more general aim of establishing a high level of trust of the public so that risks and hazards to everyday life – such as terrorist attacks or pandemics – are adequately managed, thereby allowing society to continue functioning properly.[27] This suggests using citizens' subjective perception of security as an indicator for the case of national security. *Sir Richard Dearlove*, former Chief of the UK Security and Intelligence Service, also refers to citizens' general fear of a threat to their own safety regardless of its source. At the same time, though, he highlights the lack of precision if this fear were the only defining element of national security.[28] In fact, even if subjective fear and objective threats overlap,[29] they will never be identical, and the former bear the risk of being manipulated politically.[30] Subjective fears may be created and heightened with a few or even without any concrete objective grounds. The increase in false and fake news underlines this.[31] 24

It is not surprising that most substantive definitions rely on objective elements. Thus, there are examples of national law that refer to certain elements that form part of national security.[32] The European Court of Human Rights (ECtHR) similarly listed a number of elements of national security that, in its view, allowed some of the rights enshrined in the ECHR to be restricted, such as the protection of state security and constitutional democracy from the threats of espionage, terrorism,[33] threats to territorial integrity (separatism)[34] and threats to the operational effectiveness of the army.[35,36] 25

---

[25] See the overview by Röhner, KritV 2015, 155 et seqq.

[26] Omand, p. 10.

[27] ibid., p. 9.

[28] Dearlove in Johnson, The Oxford Handbook of National Security Intelligence, p. 39.

[29] ibid., p. 37.

[30] ibid., Isensee, p. 26; Röhner, KritV 2015, 155 et seqq.

[31] See, e.g., BBC Trending, 'The rise and rise of fake news' (BBC, 6.11.2016); Georgetown SCS, 'When Everything Is "Fit to Print": The Rise of Fake News' (Georgetown SCS, 25.1.2017) <https://scs.georgetown.edu/news-and-events/article/5933/when-everything-fit-print-rise-fake-news> (last accessed: 25.9.2023); Hofseth, 'Fake news propaganda and influence operations' (Reuters institute, 14.3.2017) <http://reutersinstitute.politics.ox.ac.uk/risj-review/fake-news-propaganda-and-influence-operations-guide-journalism-new-and-more-chaotic> (last accessed: 25.9.2023); Bender/Lohse, 'Das Netz ist ein Einkaufsparadies für Hetzer' (FAZ, 13.6.2017) <https://www.faz.net/aktuell/politik/inland/fake-news-hetzer-im-internet-fuer-wenig-geld-kaufbar-15059708.html> (last accessed: 25.9.2023).

[32] See Sule in Dietrich/Sule, EU Intelligence Policies and Law, mn. 62–68.

[33] ECtHR 6.9.1978 – Series A App. No. 28, paras. 45–48 – *Klass and Others v. Germany*; EctHR 29.6.2006 – App. No. 54934/00, para. 104 – *Weber and Savaria v. Germany.*

[34] ECtHR 30.1.1998 – App. No. 133/1996/752/95, paras. 40–41 – *Case of United Communist Party of Turkey and others v. Turkey.*

[35] ECtHR 27.9.1999 – App. Nos. 31417/96 and 32377/96, paras. 67, 82 – *Lustig Prean and Beckert v. United Kingdom*; ECtHR 27.9.1999 – App. Nos. 33985/96 and 33986/96, paras. 74, 87 – *Smith and Grady v. United Kingdom*; ECtHR 22.3.2012 – App. No. 30078/06, paras. 134 et seqq. – *Konstantin Markin v. Russia.*

[36] See also Research Division ECtHR, 'National security and European case-law' (2013) <https://rm.coe.int/168067d214> (last accessed: 25.9.2023), para. 5 and ECtHR 18.5.2010 – App. No. 26839/05, para. 159

26 Finally, the ECJ, after sidestepping the issue in several decisions,[37] finally offered its own definition in the la *Quadrature du Net* case:

> Article 4(2) TEU provides that national security remains the sole responsibility of each Member State. That responsibility corresponds to the primary interest in protecting the essential functions of the State and the fundamental interests of society and encompasses the prevention and punishment of activities capable of seriously destabilising the fundamental constitutional, political, economic or social structures of a country and, in particular, of directly threatening society, the population or the State itself, such as terrorist activities.[38]

27 This definition lists a number of explicit elements that reflect essential components that guarantee the 'functioning of a state' and 'fundamental interests of society'. The definition may not be far off from what Member States might declare to be 'national security elements'. Yet, the fact that the ECJ has claimed the monopoly on the definition. More importantly, the competence to judge whether a Member State is justified in applying the national security clause to derogate from applicable EU law sets the scene for substantial conflicts.

2. Consequences of the definition: Member States' courts' responses

28 Two decisions by national courts followed the *Quadrature du Net* case: one by the *French Conseil d'État* and one by the *Belgian Constitutional Court*. They showed different responses to the *ECJ's* approach.

29 First, the Belgian Constitutional Court was required to rule on the validity of certain provisions of a national Belgian law on the general and indiscriminate retention of personal data, that is traffic and location data for law enforcement and national security purposes. It followed the ECJ's approach in the *Quadrature du Net* case and annulled the provisions in question. It concluded that the provisions were not covered by the exceptions to a ban on retention that the ECJ had developed in its case law.[39] Furthermore, it ordered the Belgian legislature to redraft the provisions on personal data retention taking into account the guidelines established by the ECJ in the *Quadrature du Net* case. Thus, the Belgian court unreservedly followed the ECJ line of argument.

30 Second, the French *Conseil d'État* was also asked to rule on the validity of French legal provisions on the retention of personal data in the context of national security following the ECJ's decision.[40] In this case, the French government, following its line of argument before the ECJ, argued that the *Conseil d'État* should find the ECJ to have exceeded its prerogatives when deciding that European Union law prevailed over national law in the area of national security (for an extensive analysis of the decision given by the *Conseil d'État* → § 10 mn. 19 et seq.). The *Conseil d'État*, however, refused to do so.[41] Given that the ECJ left it up to the Member States to use national security reasons to justify derogating from concrete EU legal provisions, it seems that the *Conseil d'État* was unable to find an ultra vires act by the ECJ. It therefore accepted the competence of the ECJ when it came to defining the concept of 'national security' as mentioned in Art. 4(2) TEU. Seemingly, it also confirmed the primacy of EU law.

– *Kennedy v. United Kingdom*; ECtHR 13.9.2018 – App. No. 58170/13, 62322/14 and 24960/15, paras. 333, 335 – *Big Brother Watch and others v. United Kingdom*.

[37] For an overview, see Sule in Dietrich/Sule, EU Intelligence Policies and Law, mn. 46–55.

[38] ECJ 6.10.2020 – joined cases C-511/18, C-512/18 and C-520/18, ECLI:EU:C:2020:791 paras. 134–135 – *La Quadrature du Net and others v. Premier ministre and others*.

[39] Cour Constitutionnelle 22.4.2021, arrêt no. 57/2021.

[40] Conseil d'État – Assemblée 21.4.2021, no. 393099.

[41] ibid., para. 8.

However, the *Conseil d'État* at the same time upheld the importance of French constitutional requirements when it comes to safeguarding fundamental interests, such as the prevention of breaches of public order and the prosecution of the perpetrators of criminal offences. It held that if the application of EU law, as interpreted by CJEU case law, were to adversely affect guarantees relating to one of these constitutional requirements, then the judge in a *French administrative court* would have to disregard EU law.[42] This in particular applied where such constitutional requirements did not benefit from equivalent protection under EU law.[43] Thus, the *Conseil d'État,* while not finding an ultra-vires act by the CJEU, at the same time established a constitutional reserve, recalling the *Solange* judgments handed down by the German Federal Constitutional Court.[44] Hence, it seems that, in substance, the *Conseil d'État* retained the possibility of derogating from EU law for national security reasons, even where the CJEU interprets such a derogation as breaching EU law in a concrete case. 31

Clearly, the latter decision already highlights the potential for future conflict between the CJEU and the national courts when it comes to the interpretation and application of EU law. This, in turn, could lead to the national courts in the Member States applying EU law differently, thereby putting in jeopardy both the CJEU's monopoly and its role as designated in the Treaties. The result could be the steady disintegration of the internal market and the EU. These dangers have already been reflected in previous decisions by national constitutional courts, such as the German Federal Constitutional Court in the *PSPP* case[45] and, even more bluntly, by the Polish Constitutional Court,[46] which denied EU law supremacy at the general level. 32

D. Conclusion

National security remains the sole responsibility of each Member State, as is clearly stated in Art. 4(2) sent. 3 TEU. However, the CJEU will continue to rule on the definition of national security and on whether a Member State was justified in applying it to derogate from EU law. This has already led to inconsistencies among the Member States, particularly on account of the fact that in the case of one Member State's supreme court (the Polish Constitutional Court) who has only accepted the CJEU's ruling in a very limited way. More generally, the number of Member States' supreme courts that disagree with the CJEU's approach to the supremacy of EU law has increased. This may, in the future, endanger EU coherence and adherence to its laws. Consequently, there is a strong need for ongoing dialogue between the CJEU and the Member States' supreme courts,[47] as well as between Member States and EU institutions in general – not only in the area of (national) security. Such an ongoing dialogue between EU actors is arguably also one of its strongest assets when it comes to finding workable compromises. And such compromises will have to be found if an efficient and effective common security policy is to continue growing in the EU. 33

---

[42] ibid., para. 5.

[43] ibid., para. 8.

[44] BVerfG 29.5.1974 – 2 BvL 52/71, NJW 1974, 1697 and BVerfG 22. 10.1986 – 2 BvR 197/83, NJW 1987, 577.

[45] BVerfG 5.5.2020 – 2 BvR 859/15, NJW 2020, 164, mn. 1–237.

[46] Polish Constitutional Tribunal 7.10.2021, K 3/21.

[47] As, for example, suggested by Calliess, NVwZ 2020, 897–904.

§ 6
Rule-of-law provisions in primary law and Member States' security agencies

Jörg Philipp Terhechte

Bibliography: Allan, The Sovereignty of Law: Freedom, Constitution and Common Law, Oxford 2013; Bendiek, 'European Cyber Security Policy', SWP Research Paper 13/2012, 1; von Bogdandy, 'Ways to Frame the European Rule of Law: *Rechtsgemeinschaft*, Trust, Revolution, and Kantian Peace', ECLR 2018 (14:4), 675; Blanke/Mangiameli (eds), The Treaty on European Union (TEU), Berlin/Heidelberg 2013; Bossong/Rhinard, 'The internal and external security nexus in Europe. Exploring and problematising its emergence' in Haar/Christiansen/Lang/Vanhoonacker (eds), The Making of European Security Policy, Oxford/New York 2021, p. 104; Calliess/Ruffert (eds), EUV/AEUV, 6th edn, Munich 2022; De Capitani, 'The Democratic Accountability of The EU's Area of Freedom, Security and Justice Ten Years On' in Guild/Carrera/Eggenschwiler (eds), The Area of Freedom, Security and Justice Ten Years On, Brussels 2010, p. 23; Dobbs, 'Sovereignty, Article 4(2) TEU and the Respect of National Identities: Swinging the Balance of Power in Favour of the Member States?', Yearbook of European Law 2014 (33:1), 298; Douglas-Scott, 'The European Union and Human Rights after the Treaty of Lisbon', HRLR 2011 (11), 645; Eckes, 'The CFSP and Other EU Policies: A Difference in Nature?', EFAR 2015 (20:4), 545; Fahey, 'The EU's Cybercrime and Cyber-Security Rulemaking: Mapping the Internal and External Dimensions of EU security', EJRR 2014 (4), 46; Fernández-Rojo, EU Migration Agencies, The Operation and Cooperation of Frontex, EASO and EUROPOL, Cheltenham 2021; Grabbe, 'Six lessons of enlargement ten years on: the EU's transformative power in retrospect and prospect', JCMS 2014 (52), 40; Fink-Hooijer, 'The common foreign and security policy of the European Union', European Journal of International Law 1994 (5), 173; Giegerich, 'The Rule of Law in the European Union: Countering Recent Challenges to Self-Evident Truths Politically, Judicially and Financially', Saar Expert Papers 12/21, 1; Groussot/Pech/Petursson, 'The Scope of Application of Fundamental Rights on Member States' Action: In Search of Certainty in EU Adjudication', Eric Stein Working Paper 2001 (1), 1; Hatje/Schwarze, 'Der Zusammenhalt der Europäischen Union', EuR 2019, 153; Hobbes, Leviathan, London 1651; Hollis, 'The necessity of protection: Transgovernmental networks and EU security governance', Cooperation and Conflict 2010 (45:3), 312; Ioannides, 'Rule of Law in European External Action: Guiding Principles, Practices and Lessons Learned', IDEA 2014, 1; Kellerbauer/Klamert/Tomkin (eds), The EU Treaties and the Charter of Fundamental Rights: A Commentary, Oxford/New York 2019; Ketvel, 'The jurisdiction of the European Court of Justice in respect of the Common Foreign and Security Policy', International & Comparative Law Quarterly 2006 (55:1), 77; Krajewski/Weber, 'Binnenorganisation der EU-Außenpolitik' in von Arnauld/Bungenberg (eds), Europäische Außenbeziehungen, 2nd edn, Baden-Baden 2022, § 4; König, Der Äquivalenz- und Effektivitätsgrundsatz in der Rechtsprechung des Europäischen Gerichtshofs, Baden-Baden 2011; Lang, 'The Rule of Law, the Force of Law and the Power of Money in the EU', Croatian Yearbook of European Law 2019 (15), 26; Lautenbach, The Concept of the Rule of Law and the European Court of Human Rights, Oxford 2013; Lenaerts, 'National Remedies for Private Parties in the Light of the EU Law Principles of Equivalence and Effectiveness', Irish Jurist 2011 (46), 13; Lenaerts, 'New Horizons for the Rule of Law Within the EU', German Law Journal 2020 (21), 29; Lonardo, 'Common Foreign and Security Policy and the EU's external action objectives: an analysis of Article 21 of the Treaty on the European Union', ECLR 2018 (14:3), 584; Marin, 'Policing the EU's External Borders: A Challenge for the Rule of Law and Fundamental Rights in the Area of Freedom, Security and Justice? An Analysis of Frontex Joint Operations at the Southern Maritime Border', JCER 2011 (7:4), 468; Mendez-Pinedo, 'The principle of effectiveness of EU law: a difficult concept in legal scholarship', Juridicial Tribune (Tribuna Juridica) 2021 (11:1), 5; Mickonytė, 'Effects of the Rule-of-Law Crisis in the EU: Towards Centralization of the EU System of Judicial Protection', ZaöRV 2019, 815; De Moor, Europol, Quo Vadis? Critical Analysis and Evaluation of the Development of the European Police Office, Antwerp/Apeldoorn/

Portland 2012; Müller/Schwabenbauer, 'Unionsgrundrechte und Datenverarbeitung durch nationale Sicherheitsbehörden', NJW 2021, 2079; Nunzi, 'Cybercrime – A new challenge for the European Union', Revue Inernationale de Droit Pénal 2012 (83), 289; Orlovska/Stepanova, 'Cross-Border Crimes: Problems of Definition and Features (Ukrainian Criminal Law experience)', Krakowskie Studia Małopolskie 2021 (30:2), 100; Pech, 'The Rule of Law as a Well-Established and Well-Defined Principle of EU Law', Hague Journal on the Rule of Law 2022 (14), 107; Pech, 'A Union Founded on the Rule of Law: Meaning and Reality of the Rule of Law as a Constitutional Principle of EU Law', ECLR 2010 (6), 359; Runcheva/Stepanoska/Ognjanoska, 'Union based on the rule of law: the Court of Justice of the European Union and the (future of) European integration', Eastern Journal of European Studies 2020 (11:2), 396; Salomon/Rijpma, 'A Europe Without Internal Frontiers: Challenging the Reintroduction of Border Controls in the Schengen Area in the Light of Union Citizenship', German Law Journal 2023 (24), 281; Scheppele/Kochenov/Grabowska-Moroz, 'EU Values Are Law, after All: Enforcing EU Values through Systemic Infringement Actions by the European Commission and the Member States of the European Union', Yearbook of European Law 2020 (39:1), 3; Sielmann, Governing Difference: Internal and External Differentiation in European Union Law, Baden-Baden 2020; Spieker, 'Breathing life into the Union's common values: on the judicial application of Article 2 TEU in the EU value crisis', German Law Journal 2019 (20:8), 1182; Szwart, 'The pillars of the European Union still exist?', ECLR 2015 (11), 357; Theobald (ed.), Von der Europäischen Union zur "Europäischen Sicherheitsunion"?: Die gemeinsamen Politiken der inneren Sicherheit in der EU, Berlin 1997; Terhechte, Europäische Verfassungsstudien, Baden-Baden 2020; Terhechte (ed.), Verwaltungsrecht der Europäischen Union, 2nd edn, Baden-Baden 2022; van Elsuwege, 'Judicial review and the common foreign and security policy: Limits to the gap-filling role of the Court of Justice', Common Market Law Review 2021 (58:6), 1731; Wagner, 'The European Union's model of Integrated Border Management: preventing transnational threats, cross-border crime and irregular migration in the context of the EU's security policies and strategies', Commonwealth & Comparative Politics 2021 (59:4), 424; Zalnieriute, 'A Struggle for Competence: National Security, Surveillance and the Scope of EU Law at the Court of Justice of European Union', The Modern Law Review 2022 (85:1), 198; Zelyova, 'Restrictive measures – sanctions compliance, implementation and judicial review challenges in the common foreign and security policy of the European Union', ERA Forum 2021, 159; Ziller, 'L'État de droit, une perspective de droit comparé', EPRS 2023, 1.

A. Introduction

1 The rule of law as a 'value' of the European Union (EU) (Art. 2 TEU) has gained increasing importance in recent years.[1] Not only does it ensure that EU action is in line with the rule of law (i.e. the actions of the EU institutions),[2] it also specifies those requirements of the EU rule-of-law guarantees that apply in relation to the actions of the Member States' authorities[3] and courts.[4] Of course, national security authorities such as the police, customs authorities and intelligence services are bound to some

[1] See, e.g., Terhechte, p. 69 et seqq. and 217 et seqq.; Mickonytė, ZaöRV 2019, 815 et seqq.; Lenaerts, German Law Journal 2020, 29 et seqq.; Giegerich, Saar Expert Papers 12/21, 1 et seqq; Pech, Hague Journal on the Rule of Law 2022 (14), 107 et seqq. and Ziller, EPRS 2023, 1 et seqq.

[2] Gatta, 'Between Rule of Law and Reputation: Frontex's withdrawal from Hungary' (Verfassungsblog, 8.2.2021) <https://verfassungsblog.de/between-rule-of-law-and-reputation/> (last accessed: 25.9.2023) and Ioannides IDEA 2014, 1 et seqq.

[3] For a comprehensive treatment of this, see Terhechte; Verfassungsstudien, p. 34 et seqq. Pech, Hague Journal on the Rule of Law 2022, 107 (122 et seqq.).

[4] See, e.g., ECJ 11.7.2019 – case C-619/18, ECLI:EU:C:2019:615 – *Commission v Poland*; ECJ 5.11.2019 – case C-192/18, ECLI:EU:C:2019:924 – *Commission v Poland*; ECJ 19.11.2019 – joined cases C-585/18, case C-624/18 and case C-625/18, ECLI:EU:C:2019:982 – *A. K. v Krajowa Rada Sądownictwa* and *CP/DO v Sąd Najwyższy*; ECJ 2.3.2021 – case C-824/18, ECLI:EU:C:2021:153 – *A.B. and Others v Krajowa Rada Sądownictwa*; ECJ15.7.2021 – case C-791/19, ECLI:EU:C:2021:596 – *Commission v Poland*.

extent by these EU rule-of-law guarantees when acting within the scope of EU law. However, it is unclear what role is attributed to the various exceptions to EU law in favour of 'national security' (Art. 4(2) sent. 2 and 3 TEU) or 'public security' (e.g. Art. 36 TFEU) in this context and, specifically, how they are to be treated by the Member States' authorities in the light of the EU rule-of-law guarantees. Do these exceptions challenge the binding nature of the EU rule-of-law guarantees in relation to national security authorities? Moreover, what is the consequence of Art. 2 TEU interacting with the EU rule-of-law guarantees and its integration into the field of security (law), where a sharp distinction must be drawn between the *guarantee of external security* (Common Foreign and Security Policy (CFSP), Art. 21 et seqq. TEU) and the *guarantee of internal security* (Area of Freedom, Security and Justice (AFSJ), Art. 67 et seqq. TFEU)? Is the area of EU security policy particularly sensitive or integration-averse from the perspective of EU law? Is it even possible to speak of the reduced binding nature of EU rule-of-law guarantees in the area of the EU's CFSP?

These questions will be explored in the following. To this end, the importance of the **2** EU's rule-of law-guarantees will first be discussed and the very concept of the Union's 'rule of law' elaborated. The next step will be an analysis of the significance of these guarantees in the context of the so-called Security Union. It is noteworthy that in some areas of the EU's security policy, national security authorities are explicitly bound by EU law, for instance the fundamental rights of the Union (Art. 67(1) in conjunction with Art. 87 TFEU). But the EU rule-of-law guarantees still apply, even in those areas of security policy that are not subject to such clear obligations, unless Union law provides for explicit exceptions. And even within the framework of these exceptions, the 'value' of the rule of law in the light of the wording of Art. 2 of the TEU cannot be completely ignored. Starting from this position, the characterization of the EU as a 'Union […] founded […] on the rule of law' has a certain persuasive power, even if there is a need for action in some areas of security policy from the perspective of the rule of law.

B. The increasing importance of EU rule-of-law guarantees

I. A Union based on the rule of law

The great importance that the EU rule-of-law guarantees play today is not least due to **3** the role that law in general plays for European integration. Early on, the European Community was referred to as a '*Community based on the rule of law*', (in German *Rechtsgemeinschaft*) by the first President of the European Commission, *Walter Hallstein*. After the entry into force of the Lisbon Treaty, the term was adapted by the Court of Justice of the European Union (CJEU) to the new conceptual situation. Thus, it is referred to as a 'union based on the rule of law'.[5] In its jurisprudence, the CJEU assumes that 'the European Union is a union based on the rule of law in which all acts of its institutions are subject to review of their compatibility with, in particular, the Treaties, general principles of law and fundamental rights'.[6]

---

[5] On this, see von Bogdandy, ECLR 2018, 675 et seqq.; Terhechte, p. 534 et seqq.; Runcheva/Stepanoska/Ognjanoska, Eastern Journal of European Studies 2020, 396 et seqq.

[6] ECJ 6.10.2015 – case C-362/14, ECLI:EU:C:2015:650, para. 60 – *Schrems v Data Protection Commissioner* and ECJ 18.7.2013 – joined cases C-584/10 P, C-593/10 P and C-595/10 P, ECLI:EU:C:2013:518, para 66 – *Commissions and Others v Kadi*; ECJ 3.10.2013 – case C-583/11 P, ECLI:EU:C:2013:625,

4 This description shows that the (different) concepts seem to be vague. In fact, such a characterization of the 'union based on the rule of law' has many elements that are assigned to the rule of law principle at the level of the Member States. What, then, is the relationship between the EU's 'rule of law' and the rule of law guaranteed at Member State level?

5 The EU Treaties always focus on the level of the EU as well as that of the Member States: According to the first sentence of Art. 2 TEU, the EU is founded, among other things, on the 'value' of the rule of law. While the 'union based on the rule of law' serves as a self-descriptive formula for the EU, the value of the 'rule of law' is also aimed at the Member States. The second sentence of Art. 2 TEU underlines the fact that the values mentioned in the first sentence of Art. 2 TEU are common to all Member States. Thus, when we speak about the EU as being founded on the value of the rule of law, the reference is to its own rule of law and that of its Member States.

6 The EU rule-of-law guarantees not only play a significant role in the accession process (of Member States) to the EU pursuant to Art. 49 TEU, in the context of which Art. 2 TEU is particularly relevant, but also for the EU's neighbourhood policy and enlargement negotiations, as well as in connection with the sanction mechanism of Art. 7 TEU.[7] Moreover, with this so-called rule of law mechanism, the EU has created a new instrument that is likely to be of considerable significance for the effective enforcement of EU rule-of-law guarantees.[8] In this respect, it is important to note that the EU is not only concerned with its own 'rule of law', but also with protecting the rule of law in the Member States. The dispute between Poland and the EU, for example, shows how vigorously the EU safeguards its values in 'rule of law conflicts'.

II. Formal und substantive EU rule-of-law guarantees

7 What can be inferred from the value of the 'rule of law' at the EU level? What are the concrete guarantees hidden behind this 'magic term'? In this context, it might be useful to distinguish between formal and substantive guarantees. Accordingly, the *formal rule of law* is guaranteed by the (constitutional) principles of the separation of powers, the reservation of the law and the requirement of regulated procedures (due process); the *substantive rule of law* is guaranteed by the protection of fundamental rights and the principle of proportionality.[9] These guarantees are, however, interpreted quite differently and autonomously in Union law. Their role can differ from the role they play in the legal systems of the Member States (e.g. the German term '*Rechtsstaat*' describes something different than the English term 'rule of law'). However, this does not change the fact that these guarantees have gained considerably more attention in recent years than during other phases of European integration. The synopsis of the guarantees thus also shows that further integration at the EU level is almost inseparably linked to the expansion and further development of its own concept of the 'rule of law'.

---

para 91 – *Inuit Tapiriit Kanatami and Others v Parliament and Council*; ECJ 19.12.2013 – case C-274/12 P, ECLI:EU:C:2013:852, para 56 – *Telefónica v Commission*; see also Pech, ECLR 2010, 359 (361 et seqq.).

[7] Mickonytė, ZaöRV 2019, 815 (816); see also Scheppele/Kochenov/Grabowska-Moroz, Yearbook of European Law 2020, 3 et seqq.

[8] ECJ 16.2.2022 – case C-156/21, ECLI:EU:C:2022:97 – *Hungary v Parliament and Council* and ECJ 16.2.2022 – case C-157/21, ECLI:EU:C:2022:98 – *Poland v Parliament and Council*; Regulation (EU, Euratom) No. 2020/2092 on a general regime of conditionality for the protection of the Union budget; Hatje/Schwarze EuR 2019, 153 (180); cf. Runcheva/Stepanoska/Ognjanoska, Eastern Journal of European Studies 2020, 396: 'Purely political mechanisms to safeguard the Rule of Law, such as those in Art. 7 Treaty of European Union (TEU), do not work.'

[9] Lautenbach, p. 18 et seqq.

Another example: The traditional, state-focused principle of the separation of powers 8
cannot simply be transferred to the supranational level of the EU, and never has been. Rather, what is at stake here is the principle of *institutional balance*. Yet, whether institutional balance serves to secure the 'rule of law' in the EU remains an open question. Today, any interpretation that places it in the context of European democracy is more convincing.

Other rule-of-law guarantees play a very important role in the EU context, especially 9
with regard to the EU Security Union (Strategy). For example, *fundamental rights* (see Art. 67(1) TFEU; keywords: data processing by security authorities,[10] removal orders according to the new regulation to combat the dissemination of terrorist online content[11]) as well as *effective judicial protection* (Art. 67(4) TFEU) are central for the rule of law in the EU. In addition, the value and importance of the *principle of proportionality* can hardly be ignored in current debates in relation to further developing the EU Security Union (Strategy).

Finally, it is quite obvious that questions of competence will (again) come up in the 10
context of the Security Union in the coming years. In particular, since some legal acts are not based on any of the relevant competence provisions of Title V TFEU, but on Art. 114 TFEU (examples: the adopted AI Regulation;[12] the Regulation on preventing the dissemination of terrorist content online[13]). It is thus foreseeable that, if not a matter of time, before the CJEU will have to shed light on the tension between security policy and the internal market (keyword: data retention).

C. Rule-of-law guarantees and the Security Union

I. Foundations of the security union in primary EU law

The guarantee of internal and external security has always been a central – perhaps 12
the central – function of a Member State.[14] Ongoing EU integration in the field of security, however, constitutes a remarkable transformation that is creating a situation in which not only Member States are but also the supranational EU is now supposed to guarantee security – internally and externally.[15] This transformation towards a European Security Union is laid down in the EU Treaties and, programmatically, is concretized in legal acts and various communications from European institutions.[16] However, its focus has changed considerably since Russia's war of aggression against

---

[10] ECJ 6.10.2020 – case C-511/18, ECLI:EU:C:2020:791 – *La Quadarture du Net and Others v Premier ministre and Others*; ECJ 6.10.2020 – case C-623/17, ECLI:EU:C:2020:790 – *Privacy International v Secretary of State for Foreign and Commonwealth Affairs and Others*; ECJ 1.3.2021 – case C-746/18, ECLI: EU:C:2021:152 – *H.K. v Prokuratuur*.

[11] Müller/Schwabenbauer, NJW 2021, 2079.

[12] Not yet published. See European Commission, 'Proposal for a Regulation of the European Parliament and of the Council laying down Harmonised Rules On Artificial Intelligence (Artificial Intelligence Act) and Amending Certain Union Legislative Acts', 7.4.2021, COM(2021) 206 final.

[13] Regulation (EU) 2021/784 on addressing the dissemination of terrorist content online, OJ L 172, 79.

[14] On this, see Hobbes, Leviathan, Chapter 17, p. 85 et seqq.

[15] See, in more detail, Bossong/Rhinard in Haar et al., The Making of European Security Policy, p. 104 et seqq.; Sielmann, p. 222 et seqq.; Theobald.

[16] European Commission, 'Communication [...] on the EU Security Union Strategy', 24.7.2020, COM (2020) 605 final.

Ukraine. Recently, EU security policy centred around fighting cross-border crime[17] and cyber security[18] and thus more on guaranteeing internal security. Its current focus seems to be more on guaranteeing external security. This also has consequences from a legal perspective and as regards the question of to what extent national security agencies are bound by Art. 2 TEU, since the CFSP is committed to a completely different 'governance model' (avoiding the term 'intergovernmental') than the AFSJ.

13 First, the foundations of the Security Union (internal focus) in primary law must be considered. Today in particular, the objective of guaranteeing internal security is reflected in the AFSJ (Art. 67 et seqq. TFEU); in addition, the EU Charter of Fundamental Rights (CFR), for example, guarantees everyone the right to freedom and security (Art. 6 CFR).[19] Furthermore, Art. 3(2) TEU already states that the EU is to 'offer its citizens an Area of Freedom, Security and Justice without internal frontiers, in which the free movement of persons is ensured in conjunction with appropriate measures with respect to external border controls, asylum, immigration and the prevention and combating of crime'.[20]

14 In contrast, it is the task of the CFSP (Art. 21 et seqq. TEU) to guarantee external security, a task – as already mentioned – that has become considerably more important in recent months (see also Art. 42 TEU). In this area, however, the EU's rule-of-law guarantees may play a different role than they do within the framework of the AFSJ, even though, pursuant to Art. 21(1) TEU, the EU is to be guided by the principle of the rule of law within the framework of the CFSP.[21] Despite that, the limited role that is reserved to the CJEU (Art. 24(1) sent. 6 TEU) within the CFSP already demonstrates that time moves at a different pace in this area than, for example, in the AFSJ. Moreover, the CFSP does not require any commitment that is comparable to the role of fundamental rights as in Art. 67 (1) TFEU, more specifically there is no provision in the CFSP that explicitly refers to the binding nature of the relevant provisions on Member States' authorities.

II. The context of freedom and security

15 Guaranteeing security always means jeopardising freedom; the two are, ultimately, closely linked. Without security, freedom becomes useless; without freedom, security degenerates, becomes unrelated and arbitrary. In this context, rule-of-law guarantees have the important task of balancing security and freedom.[22] This approach is directly reflected in primary EU law. The commitment to the guarantees of the rule of law is of particular importance within the framework of the AFSJ. For example, Art. 67(1) TFEU emphasizes that the EU constitutes an area of freedom, security and justice in which fundamental rights and the various legal systems and traditions of the Member States are respected.[23] This article has an impact on all of the provisions of Title V of the TFEU, in particular in relation to police cooperation pursuant to Art. 87 et seqq. TFEU,

---

[17] Wagner, Commonwealth & Comparative Politics 2021, 424 et seqq.; Orlovska/Stepanova, Krakowskie Studia Małopolskie 2021, 100 et seqq.; European Commission, 'First Progress Report on the EU Security Union Strategy', 9.12.2020, COM(2020) 797 final.

[18] Fahey, EJRR 2014, 46 (49 et seqq.); Bendiek, SWP 2012, 1 et seqq.; Nunzi, Revue Inernationale de Droit Pénal 2012, 289 et seqq.; COM(2020) 797 final.

[19] Douglas-Scott, HRLR 2011, 645 (656).

[20] On this, see Salomon/Rijpma, German Law Journal 2023, 281 (300).

[21] In this regard, see Lonardo, ECLR 2018, 584 et seqq.

[22] Allan, p. 88 et seqq.; Marin, JCER 2011, 468 (479 et seqq.).

[23] ECJ 12.1.2023 – case C-583/22 PPU, ECLI:EU:C:2023:5, para 65 – *MV Confusion des peines*; ECJ 7.6.2012 – case C-27/11, ECLI:EU:C:2012:326, para 36 – *Vinko*; De Capitani in Guild/Carrera/Eggenschwiler (eds), The Area of Freedom, Security and Justice Ten Years On, p. 23 (23 et seq.).

which is expressly based on cooperation between Member States' authorities (→ mn. 15). A synopsis of Art. 87(1) and Art. 67(1) TFEU demonstrates that the binding nature of some rule-of-law guarantees addresses both the EU and its Member States and is laid down in primary EU law, which gives it special significance.

III. Member States' security authorities within the system of the AFSJ

The fact that Member States' authorities play an important role, especially in the AFSJ, is no coincidence but ultimately a clear consequence of the design or the structure of the Union's security policy. *Thomas Hobbes* already knew it back in 1651: 'And Covenants, without the Sword, are but Words, and of no strength to secure a man at all.'[24] And here lies one of the central problems of the EU: With a few exceptions (Europol,[25] Frontex[26]), the EU is dependent on the Member States and their authorities when it comes to implementing its security policy and enforcing the relevant provisions. In other words, for the most part, the *EU lacks the sword for the important task of guaranteeing security*. And that is why it is crucial – as it is in other areas of EU administrative law – to oblige Member States' authorities to comply with the EU's guarantees of the rule of law when enforcing EU law. 16

IV. Police cooperation as an example

The fact that the Security Union, as a concept, is based to a decisive degree on the willingness of the Member States' authorities to enforce and implement it is underlined by Art. 87(1) TFEU, according to which the EU is to establish police cooperation between all competent authorities of the Member States, including the police, customs and other law enforcement authorities specialized in the prevention or detection of criminal offences and related investigations.[27] The 'administrative network of national and supranational security authorities' is already enshrined in primary Union law and thus explicitly includes the Member States' authorities.[28] This inevitably raises the question of whether and to what extent these authorities are bound by Union law and, if that is the case, by the EU's rule-of-law guarantees. 17

D. Member States' security authorities and EU rule-of-law guarantees

The fact that the Member States' security authorities are bound by EU rule-of-law guarantees presupposes that they act within the scope of the Treaties (i.e. that they 'implement' EU law). To the extent that this is the case, however, they are bound by the 18

[24] Hobbes, Leviathan, Chapter 17, p. 85.
[25] On this, see De Moor, p. 1 et seqq. and Fernández-Rojo, p. 1 et seqq.
[26] Marin, JCER 2011, 468; Fernández-Rojo, p. 1 et seqq.
[27] On this, see Szwart, ECLR 2015, 357 (359 et seqq.).
[28] Hollis, Cooperation and Conflict 2010, 312 et seqq.

general enforcement principles of EU administrative law, which in the first instance implies full commitment to EU rule-of-law guarantees.

I. Acting within the scope of the Treaties

19 Hardly any question has preoccupied European legal scholarship in recent years as much as the question of the conditions under which EU law is to be applied. In the EU Treaties themselves no provision is made for dealing with the application of EU law. By contrast, Art. 51(1) CFR contains an important reference. Accordingly, the Charter applies to the Member States (and to its security authorities) 'only when they are implementing Union law'.[29]

20 It is not surprising that the somewhat ambiguous concept of 'implementation' has led to controversies that have gradually been resolved by the CJEU.[30] However, this aspect will not to be pursued further here. Rather, it is sufficient to assume, for the time being, that national security authorities are initially also bound by the EU guarantees of the rule of law insofar as they 'implement' EU law. Yet, it is obvious that difficult questions of demarcation can arise here and will require more detailed discussion.

II. General enforcement principles of EU law

21 Insofar as national security authorities 'implement' EU law in the situations referred to in Art. 51(1) CFR, they are not only bound by EU fundamental rights but also by a number of principles of enforcement that the CJEU has gradually developed in its case law (principle of effectiveness,[31] principle of equivalence[32]). Member States' security authorities not only have to apply EU law – if necessary in full compliance with the EU guarantees of the rule of law – they also have to enforce it just as effectively and with the same scope as national (security) law.[33]

III. EU rule-of-law guarantees between full commitment and relaxation

22 Against this backdrop, national security authorities are obliged to apply EU rules effectively and uniformly in the AFSJ, insofar as no exceptions are available (as regards the exceptions, → mn. 22 et seqq.). However, the different governance models of the two pillars of EU security policy take effect here: While full commitment to Art. 2 TEU and thus to the rule of law, fundamental rights and the principle of proportionality seems self-evident in the AFSJ, this cannot automatically apply to the CFSR owing to explicit exceptions in EU law as well as in the light of its special design and structure

---

[29] On this, see Groussot/Pech/Petursson, Eric Stein Working Paper 2011, 1 (2).

[30] ECJ 7.5.2013 – case C-617/10, ECLI:EU:C:2013:280, para. 19 – *Åklagaren v Hans Åkerberg Fransson*; ECJ 10.7.2014 – case C-198/13, ECLI:EU:C:2014:2055 para. 37 et seqq. – *Julian Hernández and Others v Reino de España and Others*.

[31] ECJ 16.5.2002 – case C-63/00, ECLI:EU:C:2002:296, para. 24 – *Schilling and Nehring*; König, p. 105 et seqq.; Mendez-Pinedo, Juridicial Tribune (Tribuna Juridica) 2021, 5 (11 et seqq.).

[32] Lenaerts, Irish Jurist 2011, 13 et seqq.

[33] Zalnieriute, Modern Law Review 2022, 198 (207 et seqq.).

(→ mn. 28 et seqq.). In this respect, there are definitely relaxations or relativizations in the area of the CFSP that lead to some (rule-of-law) contradictions.

E. Exceptions

The above raises the question of which exceptions EU law recognizes in the area of security policy. A distinction must be drawn between exceptions in the entire area of 'national security' (Art. 4(2) sent. 3 TEU), exceptions in the AFSJ (Art. 72 TFEU) and exceptions related to the internal market (e.g. within the framework of the fundamental freedoms or based on Art. 347 TFEU). **23**

It should be noted that whether Member States can be bound by the EU rule-of-law guarantees on the basis of Art. 2 TEU even in constellations that are not related to the implementation of EU law (i.e. outside the scope of application of EU law) or when acting on the basis of an exception is an entirely different matter. It is likely that this question will become more important in the coming years and that it ultimately relates to the 'transformative power' of the Union's values. Unfortunately, the issue cannot be further explored here.[34] Still, it should be highlighted that the wording of Art. 2 TEU does not give Member States' authorities *carte blanche* in the exercise of powers – regardless of whether these powers are granted by EU or national law.[35] **24**

I. Art. 4(2) sent. 3 TEU as a general exception in relation to security policy

Pursuant to Art. 4(2) sent. 3 TEU, 'national security' in particular remains the sole responsibility of the individual Member States. This provision is to be seen in the context of Art. 4(2) sent. 2 TEU, which contains the requirement that the Union respect 'essential State functions', including the protection of national security. Art. 4(2) sent. 3 TEU has so far led a shadowy existence. This could change very quickly, especially since it not only applies to the AFSJ but possibly also to the CFSP. In terms of its content, Art. 4(2) sent. 3 TEU is sometimes understood as a 'competence brake' on the EU or, more generally, as a comprehensive reservation of competence in favour of the Member States.[36] It also seems obvious that a narrow interpretation of the concept of national security is to be preferred here, that is one that focuses on the 'existential interest of the state'.[37] **25**

However, the provision cannot be used to ensure that national security authorities disregard the EU rule-of-law guarantees when enforcing existing law. As a 'competence brake', the provision does not deal with the details of existing law but with the creation of (new) law. This is, of course, debatable (on the function and scope of Art. 4(2) sent. 3 TEU → § 8). **26**

---

[34] See Lang, Croatian Yearbook of European Law 2019, 26 (29 et seqq.); Grabbe, JCMS 2014, 40 (42 et seqq.); Börzel/Risse, KFG Working Paper Series 2009, 28.

[35] Spieker, German Law Journal 2019, 1182 (1199 et seqq.).

[36] Dobbs, Yearbook of European Law 2014, 298 (301 et seqq.).

[37] BVerfG 30.6.2009 – 2 BvE 2/08, NJW 2009, 2267 (2280); Klamert in Kellerbauer/Klamert/Tomkin, TEU Art. 4 mn. 35 et seqq.

II. Art. 72 TFEU in relation to the AFSJ

27 In relation to the AFSJ, Art. 72 TFEU clearly establishes that the relevant provisions of the Title 'shall not affect the exercise of the responsibilities incumbent upon Member States with regard to the maintenance of law and order and the safeguarding of internal security.' This provision is generally understood as a public policy reservation that, under certain circumstances, allows Member States to adopt their own measures in derogation from measures under Title V TFEU (e.g. identity checks).[38] When implementing these measures, national security authorities clearly act within the scope of EU law. Hence, they cannot ignore their commitment to the values of the EU and thus remain bound by the EU rule-of-law guarantees. In this respect, corresponding measures must be proportionate and respect the EU standards of human rights, etc.[39]

III. Exemptions to the Single Market Programme

28 It can only be pointed out briefly here that there are also exceptions to the Single Market Programme, such as to the fundamental freedoms in favour of public security in the Member States (Art. 36, 45(3), 52, 62 TFEU (fundamental freedoms) or Art. 347 TFEU as a general exception). However, the EU rule-of-law guarantees are also binding in these cases. This is likely to be even more far-reaching in relation to the fundamental freedoms than in relation to Art. 72 TFEU, which is related to the strong competences of the EU in the area of the internal market.

IV. Special structure of the Common Foreign and Security Policy/ Common Security and Defence Policy

29 Finally, reference should be made to the special structure of the Common Foreign and Security Policy/Common Security and Defence Policy, which differs fundamentally from the AFSJ not only conceptually but also with regard to the mode of application and the applicable procedures.[40] Art. 40 TEU clarifies that implementation of the CFSP must be without prejudice to the other areas of Union law. It is to be separated from the other areas of Union law by a 'partition wall' (*Scheidewand*),[41] which also puts the question of being bound by the EU's guarantees of the rule of law in a different light.[42] At the very least, the competence of the CJEU is limited within the framework of the CFSP,[43] just as the role of other EU rule-of-law guarantees needs to be assessed differently here.

30 What does this mean for the enforcement of the CFSP by Member States' authorities? At least in sub-areas that rely on Member State enforcement (e.g. economic sanctions),

---

[38] Blanke in Blanke/Mangiamelids, TEU Art. 4 mn. 230–231; ECJ 21.6.2017 – case C-9/16, ECLI:EU:C:2017:483, para. 30 et seq. – *A.*

[39] ECJ 15.5.1986 – case C-224/84, ECLI:EU:C:1986:206, para. 18 et seqq. – *Marguerite Johnston v Chief Constable of the Royal Ulster Constabulary.*

[40] Fink-Hooijer, European Journal of International Law 194, 173 (174 et seqq.).

[41] Cremer in Calliess/Ruffert, EUV Art. 40 mn. 8.

[42] Eckes, EFAR 2015, 537 et seqq. (545).

[43] Van Elsuwege, Common Market Law Review 2021, 1731 (1733 et seqq.); Ketvel, International & Comparative Law Quarterly 2006, 77 (83 et seqq.).

the CJEU has consistently held that the role of fundamental rights (see Art. 24(2) sent. 6, with reference to Art. 40 TEU and Art. 275(2) TFEU) are potentially relevant for national security authorities.[44] However, the comprehensive protection of fundamental rights or judicial review remain a desideratum when it comes to the CFSP.[45]

F. Conclusions

31 It should come as little surprise that national security authorities are bound by EU rule-of-law guarantees when implementing or enforcing EU law. Nevertheless, on closer inspection, this is not self-evident, because there are different facets to the EU's security policy that are based on different pillars. In this respect, a distinction especially needs to be drawn between whether the EU wants to guarantee security externally or internally. While the inward-looking area of the AFSJ (Art. 67 et seqq. TFEU) in particular is extensively bound to the EU rule-of-law guarantees (including national security authorities), the outward-looking CFSP (Art. 21 et seqq. TEU), despite its clear commitment to the rule of law (Art. 21 TEU), is built on a governance model that is characterized by a certain amount of distance from rule-of-law guarantees. This distance cannot be overcome by the CJEU alone, but may require an amendment to primary law when it comes to important questions of the separation of powers (keyword: the role of the European Parliament and the CJEU) or the binding nature of fundamental rights. This 'split system' may be considered unavoidable in view of the policy areas covered in each case, but it is certainly at odds with the clear commitments in the Treaties in this respect and can lead to confusion (including for national security authorities).

[44] ECJ 14.1.1997 – case C-124/95, ECLI:EU:C:1997:8, para. 25 – *The Queen, ex parte Centro-Com v HM Treasury and Bank of England.*

[45] Krajewski/Weber in von Arnauld/Bungenberg, Europäische Außenbeziehungen, § 4, mn. 172; Zelyova, ERA Forum 2021, 159 (173 et seqq.).

§ 7
The national security assumption under Art. 4 TEU and its interdependence with secondary legislation requirements and limits for the Member States' intelligence agencies*

Oliver Rüß

Bibliography: Bergmann, 'INTCEN (EU-Intelligence [Analysis] Centre)' in Bergmann (ed.), Handlexikon der Europäischen Union, 5th edn, Baden-Baden 2015, p. 597; Cameron, 'European Union Law Restraints on Intelligence Activities', IJIC 2020 (33:3), 452; Cameron, 'Metadata retention and national security: Privacy International and La Quadrature du Net', Common Market Law Review 2021 (58:5), 1433; Calliess/Ruffert (eds), EUV/AEUV, 6th edn, Munich 2022; Cross, 'A European Transgovernmental Intelligence Network and the Role of IntCen', Perspectives on European Politics and Society 2013 (14:3), 388; Dürig/Herzog/Scholz (eds), Grundgesetz Kommentar, 99. Suppl., Munich 2022; Friess, 'Der Anwendungsvorrang des Unionsrechts und nationale Souveränität – Anmerkung zur Entscheidung des französischen Conseil d'État v. 21.4.2021, N°393099', EuR 2022, 504; Gärditz, 'Sicherheitsverfassungsrecht und technische Aufklärung durch Nachrichtendienste', EuGRZ 2018, 6; Geiger, 'Rechtliche Grenzen der Europäisierung nachrichtendienstlicher Aufgaben' in Jäger/Daun (eds), Geheimdienste in Europa, Wiesbaden 2009, p. 240; Grabitz/Hilf/Martin Nettesheim (eds), Das Recht der Europäischen Union: EUV/AEUV, 78. Suppl., Munich 2023; Hillgruber, 'Vom souveränen Nationalstaat zur souveränen Europäischen Union? – Souveränitätsverlagerung durch supranationale Rechtsprechung', JZ 2022, 584; Jäger/Daun, 'Intelligence in der EU' in Jäger/Daun (eds), Geheimdienste in Europa, Wiesbaden 2009, p. 213; Kirchhof, 'Die Rechtsarchitektur der Europäischen Union', NJW 2020, 2057; Karpenstein/Sangi, 'Nationale Sicherheit im Unionsrecht: Zur Bedeutung von Art. 4 II 3 EUV', GSZ 2020, 162; Lledo-Ferrer/Dietrich, 'Building a European Intelligence Community', IJIC 2020 (33:3), 440; Nomikos, 'A European Union Intelligence Service for Confronting Terrorism', IJIC 2007 (18:2), 191; Palacios, 'On the road to a European Intelligence Agency?', IJIC 2020 (33:3), 483; Polzin, 'Pandora or Montesquieu? Die Ultra-vires-Kontrolle von Völker- und Unionsrecht durch nationale Verfassungsgerichte', AöR 2021 (146), 1; Rüß, 'Internationale nachrichtendienstliche Zusammenarbeit' in Dietrich/Eiffler (eds), Handbuch des Rechts der Nachrichtendienste, Munich 2017, p. 453 et seqq; Sandhu, 'Datenschutzrecht: Anlassbezogene Vorratsdatenspeicherung nur bei erheblicher Gefahrenlage', EuZW 2012, 209; Scheren, 'Vernetzte Sicherheit – Zusammenarbeit der Inlandsnachrichten- und Sicherheitsdienste in Europa' in Jäger/Daun (eds), Geheimdienste in Europa, Wiesbaden 2009, p. 168; Skouris, 'Der Vorrang des Europäischen Unionsrechts vor dem nationalen Recht. Unionsrecht bricht nationales Recht', EuR 2021, 3; Stepanek, 'Diplomatie à la française?', EuZW 2021, 701; Storbeck, 'Ansätze und Entwicklungsmöglichkeiten europäischer Intelligencestrukturen' in Jäger/Daun (eds), Geheimdienste in Europa, Wiesbaden 2009, p. 155; Sule, 'National Security and EU law restraints on Intelligence Activities' in Dietrich/Sule (eds), Intelligence Law and Policies in Europe, Munich/Oxford/Baden-Baden 2019, p. 335; Wollenschläger/Krönke, 'Telekommunikationsüberwachung und Verkehrsdatenspeicherung – eine Frage des EU-Grundrechtsschutzes?', NJW 2016, 906.

A. Introduction

With continuing European integration, the law of the European Union has become 1
highly determinative of everyday life in the community. Notwithstanding the principle

* The following is intended as a contribution to the academic debate and only represents the views of the author. The chapter is based on a presentation given at the 'European Security Responsibility of Member States in the European Security Union' Symposium held in Brussels in June 2022.

of conferred powers, EU law quite comprehensively regulates the business sector, the life of its citizens and, not least, the actions of the Member States, including their lawmaking. In the areas under Union competence, secondary legislation requirements and limits are to be unproblematically and uncontroversially determined. Union law enjoys primacy of application.

2 This chapter deals with the special status of the intelligence agencies and the special rule set out in Art. 4(2) sent. 3 TEU, which excludes national security from the scope of EU law. The consequences of this competence reservation for secondary legislation requirements and limits for the intelligence agencies will be discussed in the following on the basis of this provision as introduced by the drafters of the TEU. The special provision set out in Art. 4(2) sent. 3 TEU rules out any direct regulation under secondary legislation of the functioning, organization or work of the intelligence agencies. Furthermore, its approach is functional: The fact that the intelligence agencies are not to be bound in any way whatsoever in anything they do to the requirements or limitations of secondary law does not, however, correspond to the intentions of the Treaty makers, nor would it be justified. Rather, the objective is to ensure that the intelligence agencies perform their tasks to protect national security. In line with its own Treaty limitations, the EU cannot enact any secondary-legislation requirements or limitations in that regard. What legislative requirements and limits under EU law exist in relation to the work and working methods of the intelligence agencies, what impact secondary legislation regulations, terminology and lawmaking have and how the interpretation and evolution of Union law impacts the non-Europeanized area of the intelligence services are controversial matters, and they also have an impact on issues relating to jurisdiction.

3 As will be illustrated in the following, the intelligence agencies at any rate perform their tasks within neither a legal nor a value vacuum, since they are subject to their respective Member State's legislation, nor are they exempt from EU requirements in the performance of their tasks or measures beyond the actual performance of tasks related to achieving the legitimate goals of national security. Besides, the intelligence agencies' remit in relation to guaranteeing national security is limited in the integration process. The sector-specific exemption from the EU Treaties can, for instance from a functional point of view, not encompass the performance of any tasks that uses the competence reservation as an excuse to infringe any of the Union's overarching goals or to intentionally circumvent regulations in areas that have been communitized.

4 Providing a legal definition and judicial control pose a challenge given the various specified competences that stand alongside each other in the Treaties. Democratic scrutiny and oversight of the intelligence services is of existential importance in our democratic legal order. The work of the intelligence services can seriously interfere with individual fundamental rights. That is why a legal framework, legitimacy and oversight structures are of elementary importance in this area. And that calls for a solution which the national and EU level must work together closely on and – not least – judicial control.

B. Secondary legislation requirements and limits for intelligence agencies – primary law aspects

I. Preliminary remarks

5 Although the subject under investigation in this chapter are the secondary-legislation requirements and limits for Member States' intelligence agencies, aspects relating to

security, especially national security, play a major role within the EU. On account of the conferral principle, the Member States remaining the masters of the Treaties and the lack of 'competence-competence' as defined in the consistent past decisions of the German Federal Constitutional Court, the EU's primary law in particular plays a key role and secondary-legislation requirements and limits cannot be explained by taking recourse to secondary legislation alone.[1] Beyond the normal hierarchy of EU norms, Treaty law and its limits must be thoroughly investigated in addition in order to accurately understand the extent of the binding force of secondary legislation.

II. Focus on intelligence agencies in the following examination of national security and intelligence agencies

The term 'security' is used in manifold ways in both the EU Treaties and in national laws (Leino Sandberg counts 212 uses → § 8 mn. 3.). The terms 'security' and 'public policy' are also used in various contexts and with various meanings in primary EU legislation.[2] The term 'security' alone is used more than 200 times with a wide variety of different adjectives in the TFEU – often without reference to security in the military or police sense. 6

Where this contribution to the debate addresses the question of what secondary legislation requirements and limits apply to intelligence agencies, the focus is on an uncontroversial core area of national security, that is those agencies that are engaged in intelligence work. This focus permits an exposition of the fundamental consequences of the primary-legislative particularities of national security between the EU and Member States. This also allows conclusions to be drawn in relation to other areas of national security without it being necessary to examine all the possible areas of application of Art. 4(2) sent. 3 TEU.[3] That is why it is not necessary to provide a definitive definition of the – not uncontroversial – scope of the possible areas of application of Art. 4(2) sent. 3 TEU here. 7

III. Binding nature of laws and values on the intelligence services of the Member States in the community of laws and values

It goes without saying that the intelligence agencies in the states that constitute the community of values, that is the European Union, are embedded within the regulatory framework of their state's democratic structures and legitimation processes.[4] They must remain well within the value and legal framework in all that they do. They are subject to democratic oversight and the right to give instructions of the executive, which has responsibility therefor and is accountable to parliament. The intelligence agencies have special powers that derive from their tasks in relation to the protection of national 8

[1] See the fundamental analysis by Sule in Dietrich/Sule, Intelligence Law and Policies in Europe, p. 335 et seqq., though it also assumes the primacy of Union law in relation to aspects that are exempted under the Treaty.

[2] See the overview in Schill/Krenn in Grabitz/Hilf/Nettesheim, EUV Art. 4 mn. 39–42.

[3] Civil and military spheres are also mentioned, e.g., see Karpenstein/Sangi, GSZ 2020, 162 (167); for detailed derivations, comparisons and an approximation to an understanding of the concept of 'national security', see Sule in Dietrich/Sule, Intelligence Law and Policies in Europe, mn. 28 et seqq.

[4] For a detailed description of the legal framework and oversight of the intelligence services, see the report by the European Union Agency for Fundamental Rights, 'Surveillance by intelligence services: fundamental rights safeguards and remedies in the EU. Mapping Member States' legal frameworks', 2015.

security from internal and external threats and they are – specifically as regards their remit – bound by law and justice and subject to specific supervision and control – be it by parliament or the judiciary. It is beyond debate that national parliaments are empowered to introduce rules that apply to the intelligence agencies and by which the intelligence agencies are bound. The matter is, however, more complex at EU level.

IV. Scope of concrete primary legislation requirements

1. Lack of powers to establish a European intelligence agency

9 There have been repeated calls both at the political and technical level for the establishment of a European Intelligence Agency.[5] Whilst Art. 88 TFEU creates an explicit rule establishing the powers of the police, there is no comparable rule pertaining to the intelligence services. Art. 88 TFEU establishes, at the primary legislative level, an EU agency responsible for law enforcement cooperation (Europol) and includes the authorization to enact secondary legislation to determine its structure, operation, field of action and tasks.[6] There is no such provision of primary legislation pertaining to an EU intelligence agency. There is no primary legislation that makes explicit provision for the establishment of such an agency, nor is there any explicit legal basis for the establishment and structure of such an agency under secondary legislation. It is, however, not a fundamental requirement for the establishment of EU agencies that they be explicitly provided for under primary legislation.[7] However, the EU must have the relevant powers and competences in order to be able to establish such agencies.[8]

10 The EU itself has no intelligence agency. The EU Intelligence Situation Centre (INTCEN), which is sometimes described both by politicians and in the literature[9] as such, is not an intelligence agency. Unlike national intelligence agencies, INTCEN does not have its own operational capacities. It has neither operational capabilities nor its own powers to collect data, and it cannot implement any intelligence measures.[10] It works neither with direct intelligence (only with assessed information) nor person-related.[11]

---

[5] For further details concerning calls within the European area and the discussion, see, e.g., Palacios, IJIC 2020, 483.

[6] Röben in Grabitz/Hilf/Nettesheim, AEUV Art. 88 mn. 2.

[7] See, on the question regarding the power of establishment, Kirchof in Dürig/Herzog/Scholz, GG Art. 83 mn. 104 et seq., with further references.

[8] For details and ECJ case law, see Kirchof in Dürig/Herzog/Scholz, GG Art. 83 mn. 105.

[9] For instance Bergmann in Bergmann, Handlexikon der Europäischen Union, p. 597. For an open assessment, see Sule in Dietrich/Sule, Intelligence Law and Policies in Europe, mn. 151 ('an intelligence analysis centre'). For *Sule*, Europol und FRONTEX are also two EU agencies with 'genuine powers of intelligence collection as well as analysis and evaluation […]' (mn. 152). However, a distinction must be drawn between 'intelligence' as used in relation to the intelligence services and 'criminal intelligence', which would be more precise in relation to police information, see Rüß in Dietrich/Eiffler, Handbuch des Rechts der Nachrichtendienste, p. 453 et seqq.

[10] The Hague Programme explains that strategic analyses are to be 'based on intelligence from Member States' intelligence and security services and, where appropriate, on information provided by Europol.' See also Bundestag, 'Response by the Federal Government to Question 15 in the Minor Interpellation by the Member of the Bundestag Andrej Hunko et al. and The Left Party Parliamentary Group', 9.12.2013, Printed Paper 18/146 and Bundestag, 'Response of the Federal Government to Question 10 of the Minor Interpellation by the Member of the Bundestag Andrej Hunko et al. and The Left Party Parliamentary Group',16.3.2005, Printed Paper 18/737. See also Nomikos, IJIC 2007, 191 (193), which laments the absence of HUMINT and SIGINT in the gathering of 'all-source' information.

[11] Storbeck in Jäger/Daun, Geheimdienste in Europa, p. 160; on the work of INTCEN and its Intelligence Circle, see Jäger/Daun in Jäger/Daun, Geheimdienste in Europa, p. 220 et seqq.

It is, thus, also misleading to say that INTCEN forms the nucleus of an EU intelligence agency. And, as yet, it has not been expanded into an actual intelligence service.[12] 11

In view of the limited level of integration and the reservation set out in Art. 4(2) sent. 3 TEU, there is not seen to be any such power to establish such an agency and it is the widely held belief that applicable EU Treaties do not allow for the establishment of an EU intelligence agency.[13] 12

An EU legislative act that either establishes such an EU agency or the powers to perform such tasks or the oversight over such an agency at EU level is, therefore, inconceivable. 13

2. Lack of explicit primary-legislative powers to regulate Member States' intelligence services

If the EU is not empowered to set up or flesh out an EU intelligence service, then the question arises of whether, and if so what, powers exists under Union law for the sector-specific regulation of the Member States' intelligence services. 14

It should be pointed out that, irrespective of the absence of any concrete basis for establishing an EU intelligence agency, the EU Treaties are also silent on this about the work of the intelligence services. Whilst the police get their own chapter (Chapter 5, Police Cooperation), intelligence cooperation is mentioned neither in the area of national and judicial cooperation (Title V, Area of Freedom, Security and Justice) nor in relation to the Common Security and Foreign Policy (CSFP), with its external dimension. Nor can any sector-specific provisions be made out. The term 'intelligence' is not used in the Treaties. 15

The solidarity clause in Art. 222 TFEU also creates no such basis and has nothing to say about how the work of the intelligence services is to be structured within the EU.[14] The clause primarily refers to the EU level.[15] As regards the security of the Union, it states that it is to 16

> mobilise all the instruments at its disposal, including the military resources made available by the Member States, to: (a) prevent the terrorist threat in the territory of the Member States; protect democratic institutions and the civilian population from any terrorist attack; assist a Member State in its territory, at the request of its political authorities, in the event of a terrorist attack.

Solidarity obligations are thus primarily limited to instruments at the Union's disposal. That does not encompass the intelligence services' or the Member States' instruments.[16] This is reflected in the secondary legislation *implementation arrange-* 17

---

[12] Cross Perspectives on European Politics and Society 2013, 388 (esp. 389 and 400), does not regard INTCEN as an EU intelligence agency, but places it at the centre of a transnational network.

[13] Geiger in Jäger/Daun, Geheimdienste in Europa, p. 244 et seqq.; Rüß in Dietrich/Eiffler, Handbuch des Rechts der Nachrichtendienste, mn. 5 et seqq.; Scheren in Jäger/Daun, Geheimdienste in Europa, p. 180. On the concept of 'national security offices', see also Röben in Grabitz/Hilf/Nettesheim, AEUV Art. 73 mn. 9. The German Federal Government has also regularly pointed out that the EU does not have competence for national security, see, e.g., Bundestag, 'Response of the Federal Government to Question 3 of the Minor Interpellation by the Member of the Bundestag Andrej Hunko et al. and The Left Party Parliamentary Group', 3.6.2015, BT-Drs. 18/5048. For another perspective with detailed explanations, see Sule in Dietrich/Sule, Intelligence Law and Policies in Europe, mn. 158 et seqq., who wishes to draw a distinction between the activities of the intelligence services at national and at EU level and therefore does not see any contradiction, on principle, to primary legislation.

[14] Thym in Grabitz/Hilf/Nettesheim, AEUV Art. 222 mn. 25 also negates this. Rüß in Dietrich/Eiffler, Handbuch des Rechts der Nachrichtendienste, with further references, mn. 12 et seqq.

[15] Calliess in Calliess/Ruffert, AEUV Art. 222 mn. 23.

[16] Thym in Grabitz/Hilf/Nettesheim, AEUV Art. 222 mn. 30 also emphasize the fact that this does not establish any EU powers in relation to the intelligence services.

ments.[17] Art. 222(4) TFEU and the requirement to 'regularly assess threats facing the Union' do not provide the basis for any competence and legislative powers either.[18]

3. Interim findings

18 There is no evidence of any concrete provision laying down the powers to set up an EU intelligence agency. No explicit mention is made of any intelligence powers or competences on the part of the EU that would justify the establishment of an EU intelligence agency. The EU has not enacted a specific EU regulation in this regard. There is also no evidence of any specific rule concerning the regulation of national security specifically under secondary legislation.

19 Therefore, since there are no concrete requirements, the possibilities for secondary-legislation regulation and its limits must be considered in the light of the relevant primary-legislation requirement, the extent of integration to date and the sovereignty reservations, or rather the limits to conferral. These issues will all be considered in more depth in the following.

V. Art. 4(2) sent. 3 TEU

20 Some of the Member States have agencies that perform both police and intelligence service tasks and that may, thus, be covered pro rata by the existing legal framework on police cooperation under Title V, Chapter 5 TFEU.[19] The following observations would then only be relevant to their intelligence activities in relation to protecting national security.

21 The examination that follows thus focuses solely on the intelligence sector. Art. 4(2) sent. 3 TEU will only be considered in relation to the national security dimension, not in relation to the military or other matters that might also be subsumed under the provision (on the question of what could also be encompassed by the term 'national security', → § 8 mn. 2). And it is also this specific clause in the TEU that actually raises the question of the role of secondary EU legislation in relation to the intelligence services. It is especially on account of this provision that the EU Treaties and the framework on competences and constitutional law determine the scope and interpretation of secondary EU legislation in relation to the intelligence services.

22 The significance of this provision is not uncontroversial, and there is no consensus as to its character and legal nature.[20] Even if one does not wish to go so far as to refute the regulatory nature of an assertion that is so centrally placed within the 'common provisions' of primary EU legislation (for different interpretations → § 6 mn. 21 and → § 8 mn. 2 et seqq.), it still has a clear impact on the relevance of secondary legislation for the Member States' intelligence services, since '*[…] national security remains the sole responsibility of each Member State*'. As already mentioned in the above, the term 'security' is used frequently in the EU Treaties and in secondary legislation – besides

---

[17] Council of the European Union, 'Council Decision on the arrangements for the implementation by the Union of the solidarity clause', 7.1.2014, 2014/415/EU.

[18] On the interpretation of Art. 222 of the TFEU, see Rüß in Dietrich/Eiffler, Handbuch des Rechts der Nachrichtendienste, mn. 12 et seqq., esp. mn. 14.

[19] See, in that regard, also the report of the European Union Agency for Fundamental Rights, 'Surveillance by intelligence services: fundamental rights safeguards and remedies in the EU. Mapping Member States' legal frameworks', 2015, 13 et seqq. on intelligence services in EU Member States.

[20] Sule in Dietrich/Sule, Intelligence Law and Policies in Europe, mn. 342 also laments the fact that the clause leaves key questions unanswered. For a summary re Art. 4(2) sent. 3 TEU, see, e.g., Karpenstein/Sangi, GSZ 2020, 162 (163) (esp. footnote 18).

other aspects such as social security and health security. That in particular applies to national security under Title V TFEU, which is regarded as coming close to the area under investigation here in terms of its content. However, national security is only singled out in primary legislation, namely in Art. 4 TEU, which, being a 'basic EU treaty',[21] regulates the foundations of the EU. It is not – thus consistently – used in the implementing provisions, that is the TFEU: It is not the subject of the 'functioning' but regulates what remains outside of Union law.

Whether one interprets this provision of primary legislation broadly or narrowly has **23** direct consequences as regards the question of the formal application and scope of secondary legislation and its requirements and limits. In the most extreme case, it diverges by 180 degrees. One possible interpretation would be that secondary legislation makes no requirements or has no limits whatsoever in relation to the intelligence services. Ultimately, that would raise numerous questions concerning repercussions for the interaction between the EU level and the Member States, between the Member States, as well as regarding the possibility of pro rata funding from EU resources (→ mn. 63 et seqq.) or access to EU databases (→ mn. 59 et seqq.). This would be a very categorical stance, and one would then have to ask whether it actually corresponds to the status of EU integration and of cooperation, including at EU level, and, last but not least, the Member States' intent. A stance that would be diametrically opposite would be the comprehensive application of all Union law – except where there are concrete reservations or special secondary legislation rules – and comprehensive EU jurisdiction.

Solutions ranging between these two polar opposites are presented in the following **24** based on the legal framework and specialist powers.

C. Impact of the absence of sector-specific powers of regulation at EU level

I. Availability of a national security reservation and consequences of the Member States' involvement in EU lawmaking?

1. Indirect assumption of Member States' 'responsibility' within the meaning of Art. 4(2) sent. 3 TEU?

Is secondary legislation (in the sense of an undivided legal sphere and legal **25** uniformity) fully applicable – even to national security and thus to the performance of all intelligence service tasks? What speaks against this is the fact that the Member States, the Treaty makers, decided not to extend the EU's competences to include this area. The aim was to counter what some people refer to as the 'competence creep',[22] including on account of the case law of the Court of Justice of the European Union.[23]

---

[21] Nettesheim in Grabitz/Hilf/Nettesheim, EUV Art. 1 mn. 44: There is no hierarchy among the Treaties.

[22] Karpenstein/Sangi, GSZ 2020, 162 (165) refer to 'extensive competence creep', see also Hillgruber, JZ 2022, 584.

[23] Karpenstein/Sangi, GSZ 2020, 162 (165) refer to 'travaeux preparatoire'; Hillgruber, JZ 2022, 584.

26 One could argue that the Member States were involved in adopting the secondary legislation and thus meet their 'responsibility' within the meaning of Art. 4(2) sent. 3 TEU. That might not perhaps rule out targeted, sector-specific regulation that determines the tasks of the intelligence services.

27 The Council of the Member States was involved in enacting the secondary legislation (Art. 289 TFEU), delegated legislative acts (Art. 290 TFEU) and conferred implementing powers (Art. 291 TFEU). It could, thus, be argued that the Member States are themselves complying with the reservation set out in Art. 4(2) sent. 3 TEU in the context of EU lawmaking, that they are shaping and defining it. They may have met their responsibility and their needs through the Council. The enacted secondary legislation could thus to a large extent be applicable. But is that in line with the legal taxonomy, and do the Member States' representatives in the Council have the relevant legitimacy, thereby obviating the need for a review of Art. 4(2) sent. 3o TEU? In this context, 'responsibility' is not solely to be understood as political responsibility, but includes the allocation of rights and obligations, in the spirit of the sovereignty debate, which also encompasses the distribution of powers and thus also the power to legislate.[24]

28 What speaks against that is the fact that the Member States are not acting in the same capacity as they were when Art. 4(2) TEU was enacted, that is as the masters of the Treaties, i.e. outside the EU framework. By contrast, the Council of the European Union, a party to lawmaking, is an EU institution. It is not constituent in the sense of possibly shaping the EU Treaties in a manner that changes their content. The Council is not the master of the Treaties, it does not amend the Treaties or produce a constitution. The same goes for the European Parliament. That is already clear from Art. 48 TEU, which makes concrete provision for Treaty amendments. Some Member States require a referendum before they can agree to any Treaty amendments. A distinction needs to be drawn between the Member States' representatives acting within the EU institutions – be it in the Council or through their elected representatives (who are elected and legitimized within the EU framework) – and the *pouvoir constituant*.[25]

29 Further, Art. 4(2) sent. 3 TEU also refers to the responsibility of the *individual* Member States. In the Council, though, the Member States act as a whole, as an EU organ.[26] One cannot, thus, derive from the fact that the Member States are involved in the legislative process that they have thereby exercised their 'responsibility' within the meaning of Art. 4(2) sent. 3 TEU.

30 Art. 4(2) sent. 3 TEU is not a provision that the Member States could renounce in another manner, that is without a Treaty amendment: it is not disposable.[27] The effect of the reservation is that the Union has not had competence for national security conferred upon it.[28] Nor can a Member State unilaterally waive it. As already explained in the above in relation to the question of responsibility, this would be tantamount to competence creep and to circumventing established procedures relating to Treaty amendments, which are explicitly regulated in the Treaties.[29]

---

[24] See, for details, Karpenstein/Sangi, GSZ 2020, 162 (164), with further references.

[25] Calliess in Calliess/Ruffert, EUV Art. 1 mn. 56 et seqq. deal extensively with the question of 'pouvoir constituant' and the establishment of the EU and the interplay between the Member States and the EU.

[26] On the role of the Council and the Member States' respresentatives working within it, see Ziegenhorn in Grabitz/Hilf/Nettesheim, EUV Art. 16 mn. 18–24.

[27] Karpenstein/Sangi, GSZ 2020, 162 (167).

[28] ibid.

[29] ibid.

2. Interim findings

Sector-specific regulation as defined in the above is thus definitely ruled out. This is also reflected in the sector-specific exceptions introduced under secondary legislation.[30] The fact that the Member States cannot relinquish their competence without a formal amendment also has an impact on generally applicable secondary legislation. The extent of that impact will be addressed in the following. 31

II. Application of secondary legislation not specifically enacted to regulate it also in relation to the intelligence services?

1. Possible conflict scenarios

If there is also no sector-specific legislative competence, then the question arises of to what extent general secondary EU legislation applies fully to the intelligence services. There are various possible scenarios, for instance provisions of secondary legislation that overlap with tasks performed by the intelligence services, because there are no exceptions in relation to the protection of national security, or these have only been partially enacted. Or secondary legislation rules limit the work, measures or possibilities of the intelligence services when it comes to the (legitimate) protection of national security, for instance in the area of data protection or as part of technical regulations, such as when it comes to developing or using artificial intelligence (AI) or encryption. 32

2. General primacy of EU law including in the case of Art. 4(2) sent. 3 TEU?

It would be easy to give a decision on the above-mentioned scenarios in those cases where the general primacy of EU law applies. In such cases, secondary EU legislation would – regardless of its content – always take precedence and be superimposed over any national legislation that runs counter to it.[31] In the case of such unlimited primacy, national legislation would cede to EU law, granting the intelligence agencies certain powers when it comes to protecting national security that is contrary to secondary legislation. Measures taken by the intelligence services could also violate Union law, that is to the extent that it applies and such measures are contrary to established rules. 33

Even if it is not legally permissible to introduce sector-specific rules, the question nevertheless arises of whether general secondary legislation – ranging from data protection to competition law – is fully applicable to the intelligence services. What is decisive here is the impact of the reservation and how far that impact goes. That influences whether and to what extent secondary legislation applies to the intelligence services. Formally speaking, the primacy of Union law could be asserted here. If Union law exists that, possibly, limits the national powers of the intelligence services under the 34

---

[30] Directive (EU) 2016/680 on the protection of natural persons with regard to the processing of personal data by competent authorities for the purposes of the prevention, investigation, detection or prosecution of criminal offences or the execution of criminal penalties, and on the free movement of such data, and repealing Council Framework Decision 2008/977/JHA; Recital 24 of Directive (EU) 2019/1937 of the European Parliament and of the Council of 23 October 2019 on the protection of persons who report breaches of Union law and Directive (EU) 2016/679 on the protection of natural persons with regard to the processing of personal data and on the free movement of such data, and repealing Directive 95/46/EC (General Data Protection Regulation) (GDPR).

[31] As regards the non-extension of EU law on the basis of the Charter of Fundamental Rights pursuant to Art. 51(2) CFR, see Cameron, Common Market Law Review 2021, 1433 (1457 et seq.).

Member States' own legislation, then national legislation would always be subordinate.[32] EU law would then take precedence. It would, thus, again be possible to comprehensively regulate the intelligence agencies' competences under Union law.

35 However, the objection must be raised that legislation can only take precedence if it actually applies.[33] The precondition for Union law to be applicable is that the Member States have conferred on the Union the comprehensive power to legislate relevant substantive issues.[34] In view of the Member States' reservation that is so clearly postulated in Art. 4(2) sent. 3 TEU, doubts must be raised as to whether that is in fact the case. There has been no constitutional conferral of sovereignty in the sense of a competence-competence.[35] Nor can it arise from the further evolution of and developments in relation to secondary legislation. Otherwise, the reservation would be without effect.[36]

36 Regardless of the question of the extent to which that is to be assessed on the basis of Union law or of the conferral of powers under international law, this question can be answered substantively in the negative. Art. 4(2) sent. 3 TEU already rules out such an effect under the EU Treaties. The requirements of the EU Treaties must be complied with by all, that is by the Member States and the EU legislature in equal measure, by the European Commission, the guardian of the Treaties, and by legal practitioners and the judiciary.[37] They are bound by the relevant requirements – in the legislative process relating to secondary legislation and when it comes to developing the legal framework.

III. Scope of the reservation

1. Special status of Art. 4(2) sent. 3 TEU compared to the exemption clauses to the EU fundamental freedoms

37 What is decisive when it comes to determining the relevant requirements and limits is the scope of the reservation set out in Art. 4(2) sent. 3 TEU.[38] It is not only the extent of its factual scope that must be considered here, but also who gets to define its scope of application. The question arises of whether Art. 4(2) sent. 3 TEU is comparable to the public security clauses. In that case it would be a concept of Union law, would have to be interpreted accordingly and would also be comprehensively justiciable at EU level.

38 However, the situation as regards Art. 4(2) sent. 3 TEU is different than, for instance, it is in relation to Art. 36, Art. 45(3), Art. 52(1) and Art. 65(1)(b) TFEU, which provide

[32] On the question of the primacy of Union law over national legislation with a decidedly pro-EU perspective, see Skouris, EuR 2021, 3–27.

[33] Kirchhof, NJW 2020, 2057.

[34] ibid.

[35] According to the consistent past decisions of, e.g., the German Federal Constitutional Court, see, specifically regarding the case in hand, Hillgruber, JZ 2022, 584. See also Polzin, AöR 2021, 1 (24).

[36] For further details, Karpenstein/Sangi, GSZ 2020, 162.

[37] On the approach adopted by the French *Conseil d'État*, see, e.g., Stepanek, EuZW 2021, 701–707, which analyses the decision (Conseil d'État, 21.4.2021, No, 393039.20210421). The *Conseil d'État* does not argue in favour of *ultra vires* use, but focuses on the French constitution, more in the sense of an identity check (see, esp. 703 and 705). That creates a sunset clause for secondary legislation, too, Stepanek EuZW 2021, 701 (702). On the decision, see also Friess EuR 2022, 504. On the German approach and on vertical balance of powers between national and international levels see in detail: Polzin, AöR 2021, 1.

[38] Regarding the conflicting interests when it comes to defining 'national secruity' narrowly (the EU institutions) and keeping their intelligence services outside (the Member States), see Cameron, IJIC 2020, 452 (455).

for the limitation of fundamental freedoms on the grounds of public security.[39] They do not represent a sovereignty reservation.[40] The Treaty makers clearly expressed their will to integrate here. The clauses only serve the purpose of limiting EU fundamental freedoms by way of exception. Full EU competence was conferred on the EU here in line with the Treaty provisions. Accordingly, they are, in principle, subject to interpretation by the CJEU. The Member States are not empowered to freely define 'public security' as they wish. Its application is interpreted restrictively.[41]

The situation in relation to national security is somewhat different. In this instance, the **39**
Treaty makers clearly imposed limitations to integration and conferred *no* powers on the EU, but, as described in the above, they did include a full competence reservation. Account also needs to be taken of this when interpreting and applying Art. 4(2) sent. 3 TEU. That is why it cannot be assumed that it only represents an exemption clause that must be interpreted as narrowly as possible. Rather, it applies fully and cross-sectionally across all legal areas.[42] This also justifies its placement right at the start of the TEU.

What limits apply when interpreting primary legislation concerning the extent of the **40**
EU's conferral principle and distinct from the Member States' remaining competences is a controversial issue, both in academic circles and in the assessments of the highest courts, such as the CJEU and national constitutional courts.[43] The constitutional stance that is adopted is that, on account of the special nature of the EU, a community of nations, the application and interpretation of EU law is limited both in terms of legitimacy and constitutionally and that acts by any of the Union's institutions can, by way of exception, also be ultra vires (on the ultra vires problem, → § 10).[44] They do not have the power to extend the scope of application of primary legislation beyond that which is set out in the Treaties,[45] nor to enact secondary legislation outside of their own competence or beyond the limits of their competence.

2. Competence reservation and secondary legislation: significance of the derogation for the intelligence services

The particularity of the competence reservation means any interpretation of Art. 4(2) **41**
sent. 3 TEU lies outside the sphere of a definition reserve under EU law (for detail → § 10).[46] Unfortunately, this limits the usability of the term 'security' and of secondary

---

[39] Sule in Dietrich/Sule, Intelligence Law and Policies in Europe, mn. 44 also emphasizes the fact that 'public security' and 'national security' are not identical concepts.

[40] Streinz in Grabitz/Hilf/Nettesheim, AEUV Art. 36 mn. 4, referring to consistent past decisions, such as ECJ 12.6.1979 – case C-153/78, ECLI:EU:C:1979:194, para. 5 – *Commission v. Germany*, with references, ECJ 26.11.1985 – case C-182/84, ECLI:EU:C:1985:470 – *Miro*.

[41] *CJEU* case law, see Streinz in Grabitz/Hilf/Nettesheim, AEUV Art. 36 mn. 2 with further references to judgments.

[42] Karpenstein/Sangi, GSZ 2020, 162 (164).

[43] For details re the relationship between the CJEU and the national courts, esp. the German Federal Constitutional Court, see Hillgruber, JZ 2022, 584. On the French *Conseil d'État's* sunset clause, see Stepanek, EuZW 2021, 701–707. With a specific focus view on Germany see Polzin, AöR 2021, 1.

[44] See Hillgruber, JZ 2022, 584 (589), who explains, in relation to Germany, that it is 'impossible to give up the Constitutional Court's right of final decision'. On the other Member States' supreme courts, see Mayer in Grabitz/Hilf/Nettesheim, EUV Art. 19 mn. 92 et seqq. On the French approach, which avoids the ultra vires issue but also conflicts with adopted provisions of national constitutional law in the field of guaranteeing security, see Stepanek, EuZW 2021, 701 (707). Polzin, AöR 2021, 1 (25 et seq.) develops a concrete scheme for legitimate ultra-vires objections.

[45] See, in this regard, details regarding the CJEU, Kirchhof, NJW 2020, 2057, and Polzin AöR 2021 (146), 1.

[46] Sule in Dietrich/Sule, Intelligence Law and Policies in Europe, p. 343, despite the reservation, regards Art. 4(2) sent. 3 TEU as comprehensibly 'actionable before the CJEU'. See also mn. 46 et seqq. on the evolution of CJEU decisions.

legislation when it comes to interpreting national security and its scope of application from the point of view of constitutional doctrine. Without competence, it is not possible to shape competence – which is not in fact conferrable – under secondary legislation. That leads to a legally complicated situation that requires close cooperation between lawmakers, the judiciary and those interpreting the law.[47]

42 On account of the aforementioned lack of competence, Union law enacted as secondary legislation can only to a limited extent be used to define that for which the EU is not competent. At the same time, the extent of the reservation cannot and must not be placed at the discretion of the Member States. That already applied to the above-mentioned exemption clause concerning fundamental freedoms, and it must also apply to the reservation given ongoing EU integration and cooperation. That also has an impact on mechanisms that have been enacted to counter objections relating to the lack of competence on account of the reservation. For instance, the EU legislature has created explicit exceptions when it comes to security issues, including Art. 23(1)(a) GDPR[48], exemptions from Directive 2016/680[49], or Art. 3(a)(i) of the E-Commerce Directive[50]. This also applies to the ongoing legislative procedure to regulate AI in the EU. Here, too, exceptions are being discussed in the field of national security.[51] Sector-specific exemptions to the application of secondary legislation are, from the legal doctrine perspective, a good way for legal practice to meet any conflicts that may arise around the scope of application with technical means. However, this can still leave some questions unanswered and cannot clearly delineate each and every conflict.

43 Since the EU is not empowered to regulate matters relating to national security under secondary legislation, the question arises of whether relevant provisions in secondary legislation are constitutive or, on account of the reservation. are solely declaratory.[52] That does not, in principle, pose a problem if and to the extent that the exemptions map Art. 4(2) sent. 3 TEU. However, where rules are concretized or limits are imposed, the rules conflict with Art. 4(2) sent. 3 TEU. That means that when the question arises of whether secondary legislation does not take sufficient account of Art. 4(2) sent. 3 TEU, this cannot, in the worst case, simply be brought into line with possibly legitimate Member State rules or measures relating to national security. Hence, even sector-specific exemptions in favour of Art. 4(2) sent. 3 TEU may possibly be insufficient or, rather, their absence in a provision of secondary legislation does not, in and of itself, mean that the EU legislature was able to decide that Art. 4(2) sent. 3 TEU was irrelevant. As a result, they ought not to stand in the way of the aforementioned legitimate Member States' interests.

---

[47] On the need for dialogue between the national and EU level, see Cameron, IJIC 2020, 452 (452 et seqq., esp. 460 et seq), the focus being on the CJEU.

[48] Regulation (EU) 2016/679 on the protection of natural persons with regard to the processing of personal data and on the free movement of such data, and repealing Directive 95/46/EC, 1–88, see also mn. 16 of the Recitals.

[49] Directive (EU) 2016/680 on the protection of natural persons with regard to the processing of personal data by competent authorities for the purposes of the prevention, investigation, detection or prosecution of criminal offences or the execution of criminal penalties, and on the free movement of such data, and repealing Council Framework Decision 2008/977/JHA, 89–131.

[50] Directive 2000/31/EC on certain legal aspects of information society services, in particular electronic commerce, in the Internal Market, 1–16.

[51] The General Approach contains an exemption, see Council of the European Union, 'Artificial Intelligence Act: Council calls for promoting safe AI that respects fundamental rights' (6.12.2022) <https://www.consilium.europa.eu/de/press/press-releases/2022/12/06/artificial-intelligence-act-council-calls-for-promoting-safe-ai-that-respects-fundamental-rights/> (last accessed: 26.9.2023).

[52] On the question of the clarifying impact of exceptions, see also Sandhu, EuZW 2012, 209 and Wollenschläger/Krönke, NJW 2016, 906 (908).

That is why this complex and hardly cut-and-dried situation calls for close cooperation and attention in order to resolve such difficult legal scenarios and questions. Unfortunately, there is no clear hierarchy between the national level and the EU level in this matter. Just as the EU is not permitted to define Member States' intelligence services, it cannot, in principle, limit their tasks by introducing an exemption clause that may possibly not be sufficiently covered by Art. 4(2) sent. 3 TEU. **44**

At the same time, there cannot and must not be full arbitrariness when it comes to defining what 'national security' actually is[53] – and thus also not what the scope and application of secondary legislation is beyond the actual guaranteeing of national security and thus beyond the scope of the regular tasks of the Member States' intelligence services. When drafting the Treaties the Member States set the EU clear objectives as regards cooperation within the EU, for instance in the area of economic cooperation or competition law.[54] **45**

That is why – drawing on existing national and international terminology, general practice and a common understanding, for instance as part of non-Treaty-based cooperation between the Member States' intelligence services – a decision will have to be taken on a case-by-case basis for each scenario, even if the intelligence services' tasks and focuses are very different.[55] **46**

However, if the intelligence agencies were not bound or limited in any way whatsoever under secondary legislation that would be tantamount to a wide-ranging exemption from applying Union law,[56] which would impact secondary EU legislation as a whole. Value decisions, the interaction between legal and policy areas,[57] which could not be foreseen in the early stages of integration, set limits to that. For instance, recourse can and must be taken to Member States' understanding, since they have adopted national security concepts both under their national legislation and in their cooperation beyond the EU framework.[58] There is, by tradition, a core area of the work of the intelligence services, that is the analysis and handling of sources (HUMINT), etc. Fewer overlaps with EU regulation are to be expected here. Things get more complicated in areas that, in a liberal, modern Europe, are non-governmental and interact with the business and private sector,[59] where critical infrastructure or telecommunications are neither governed nor operated by the state, especially in the field of technical reconnaissance (signals intelligence, or SIGINT). **47**

The typical remit of modern intelligence services calls for support and cooperation even beyond their own specific area, especially in relation to technical matters such as the internet, telecommunications, encryption or AI research and development.[60] The Lisbon Treaty is a piece of recent primary legislation into which the Treaty makers incorporated a provision like Art. 4(2) sent. 3 TEU based on their experience of the **48**

---

[53] Which is also the conclusion drawn in Sule in Dietrich/Sule, Intelligence Law and Policies in Europe, mn. 70 et seqq.

[54] However, Karpenstein/Sangi, GSZ 2020, 162 (166) also highlight, with regard to these areas, the fact that Art. 4(2) sent. 3 TEU can also, in principle, be applied to such cross-cutting competences. As *Sule* also emphasizes, this cannot, however, be regarded as a false justification for misuse.

[55] See the key findings on 'objectives and structures of intelligence services', in Report of the European Union Agency for Fundamental Rights, 'Surveillance by intelligence services: fundamental rights safeguards and remedies in the EU. Mapping Member States' legal frameworks', 2015, 27.

[56] Karpenstein/Sangi, GSZ 2020, 162 (166).

[57] For further details, see Sule in Dietrich/Sule, Intelligence Law and Policies in Europe, mn. 15 et seqq.

[58] On the problems of providing definitions at different national levels and for individual Member States, ibid., mn. 62 et seqq.

[59] For further details re this problem, see Cameron, Common Market Law Review 2021, 1433.

[60] ibid., 1458–1459.

information age. Departing from the CJEU's more restrictive interpretation of the law and decision practice, its scope cannot, thus, be limited to the fact that the intelligence services act alone and independently.[61] The clause is not directed at those who apply it (the intelligence services) and their staff; it is task- and target-oriented. Instead, it must also encompass – as regards the protection of national security – areas in which others are active in systemically relevant areas that used to be only within the purview of the state.[62] And thus Art. 4(2) sent. 3 TEU can, for instance, also have an impact on and must be taken into account in relation to EU regulation on technology, communications or development.[63]

49 On the other hand, though, Art. 4(2) sent. 3 TEU cannot be misused to circumvent primary EU legislation and its goals as set out in secondary legislation – for instance by means of interpreting it broadly.[64] There are areas in which intelligence services may possibly perform tasks in the same way as others – or areas in which they can act in accordance with their Member State's national legislation that do not belong to national security.

50 And so we come to the question of the extent to which certain intelligence service activities are not permitted in the area of economic freedoms. Examples worth mentioning include competition law and industrial espionage.[65] This is less a question of secondary legislation and chiefly one of primary legislation, and must be considered on the basis of the principle set out in Art. 4(3) of the TEU, that is sincere cooperation, in accordance with which the Union and the Member States are to assist each other in carrying out tasks that flow from the Treaties.

51 Here, too, the Member States are in particular to facilitate the achievement of the Union's tasks and refrain from any measure that could jeopardize the attainment of the Union's objectives.

3. Specific fields

a) Data protection

52 In terms of its impact on EU citizens, data protection is of elementary importance specifically in relation to the limits of measures taken to protect national security and the work of the intelligence services. That is why the central questions that arise at the intersection between EU and national security and the Member States' reservation revolve around the issue of the scope of data protection.

53 EU data protection regulations are exemplary the world over. Data protection has been regulated in secondary legislation and is also the subject of an ambitious, groundbreaking and intensive judicature. It has numerous objectives but serves the central objective of citizens' right to determine what happens to their personal data (also referred to as 'informational self-determination'). In terms of its impact and objective, data protection is closely linked to fundamental rights objectives.

54 Fundamental rights and data protection set important limits and are key elements when considering proportionality when setting secondary legislation or when it

[61] For further details, see, with reference to the case law, ibid. On the development of CJEU case law and the problem of third-party action, see also Sandhus, EuZW 2012, 209, comment 220–222.

[62] Cameron, Common Market Law Review 2021, 1433 (1458–1459).

[63] ibid.

[64] For a detailed description of the debate around intelligence service activities in the Member States and EU law restraints on intelligence activities, see Sule in Dietrich/Sule, Intelligence Law and Policies in Europe, p. 335.

[65] See, in much more detail, ibid., p. 375 et seqq.

comes to issues around the EU's international treaties. That was revealed in the course of the decision-making on the Privacy Shield and telecommunications data retention.[66]

As it is a cross-cutting competence, it has an important, an exceptional status and function within EU law. All the actors involved in EU legislative processes are aware of the debates and the importance attached to it. That is why the need to strengthen data protection and its drafting paved the way for the recast of the Europol Regulation in 2022. **55**

As it is a cross-cutting EU competence, data protection can only be regulated if and to the extent that the EU has competence and jurisdiction.[67] Accordingly, Art. 16(2) TFEU states that, acting in accordance with the ordinary legislative procedure, the European Parliament and the Council may **56**

> lay down the rules relating to the protection of individuals with regard to the processing of personal data by Union institutions, bodies, offices and agencies, and by the Member States *when carrying out activities which fall within the scope of Union law*, and the rules relating to the free movement of such data. (emphasis added)

In conjunction with Art. 4(2) sent. 3 TEU, the scope of application of Art. 16 TFEU narrows (comparable with the particularities of Art. 39 TFEU in relation to the CSFP). **57**

However, that cannot mean that any limitation whatsoever within the meaning of this fundamental principle is ruled out.[68] When performing their tasks to benefit national security, the Member States' intelligence services have no right of unlimited access and are not exempt from complying with any data protection principles whatsoever. Where intelligence services are not bound by any rules whatsoever, that conflicts with the values that the EU and its Member States share. Art. 2 TEU is very clear on that: 'The Union is founded on the values of respect for human dignity, freedom, democracy, equality, the rule of law and respect for human rights, including the rights of persons belonging to minorities.' The absence of secondary EU legislation does not create an area in which fundamental rights do not apply, since both national and constitution law and international law apply.[69] There is no legal vacuum either here or in other areas for which the Union is not competent. It is simply not an area that is regulated under Union law that is subject to the CJEU's data protection monitoring tools or its evaluation. Therefore, there are not and ought not to be two contradictory worlds, a regulated one and an unregulated one. **58**

b) Binding force in the context of use of the JHA databases and legal consequences

The databases used in the area of Justice and Home Affairs (JHA) both technically and legally represent an important information interface between national security and secondary EU legislation. Within the common Area of Freedom, Justice and Security, the intelligence services need information about people and processes in order to be able **59**

---

[66] For an example of a comprehensive review, see Wollenschläger/Krönke, NJW 2016, 906.

[67] See Gärditz, EuGRZ 2018, 6 (14 et seq.), with further references to the debate.

[68] On the question of the binding nature of fundamental rights between the EU and national fundamental rights especially in the field of telecommunications surveillance and traffic data retention, see Wollenschläger/Krönke, NJW 2016, 906.

[69] See also the European Commission's response to the European Parliament's questions '[…]Member States are bound by their national constitutions to ensure that their national intelligence systems are used in a proportionate and responsible manner, respecting the rights of their citizens […]', cited in Sule in Dietrich/Sule, Intelligence Law and Policies in Europe, p. 343, mn. 22.

to protect national security and for the work and functioning of the intelligence services. The territory covered by the intelligence services is no longer ringfenced by means of the relevant limits and controls, and external borders, residency and movement are not exclusively subject to national control. That is why the intelligence services are reliant on European information in the performance of tasks relating to the guaranteeing of national security. On account of their relevance for fundamental rights and data protection, these databases, which are used in security- and migration-relevant areas, are shaped by secondary legislation. It would have to be examined whether the references to national security and to the intelligence services have consequences under Union law.

60 These references consist, first and foremost, in opportunities to access the relevant data as part of statutory tasks related to the guaranteeing of national security. Whilst, in the past, security-relevant areas in the sense of state territory used to be limited and controlled nationally, they have now been Europeanized within the common European space. Sometimes, it is only an EU database that can reliably depict the current state of play since, for instance, entries by those requiring a visa are not limited to a Member State's territory or because information on the entire Schengen Area is needed on account of the freedom of control. Examples include the following:

- The Schengen Information System (SIS), which first and foremost serves the EU Member States' police authorities as an investigation tool. It can, however, be used by the intelligence services, too. It allows for open as well as undercover searches of both persons and things. An example of an issue that concerned the intelligence services was the prosecution of 'foreign terrorist fighters', in relation to which the SIS is also a key national security tool. Legislation was specifically updated to improve information-sharing on alleged terrorists and to support the Member States in invalidating suspects' travel documents. This is thus an example of secondary legislation that is also of relevance to the scope of areas relating to national security.
- The Visa Information System (VIS), which enables the Schengen countries to share data about visa applications for short-term stays. Its aim is to simplify visa application procedures, facilitate control and contribute to threat prevention. The VIS comprises both a centralized system and independent national systems. National implementing legislation determines which police and prosecution authorities as well as intelligence services are given access to the VIS. This means that the intelligence services can also access the VIS.[70]

61 It is, however, questionable whether that has an impact on the EU's competence in the area of national security or whether any secondary-legislation requirements and limits flow from it. Could this be referred to, for instance, as the start of a communitization creep?

62 Taking a closer look at the content level shows that some informational deficits are only partially balanced out – in some cases directly, in some cases indirectly – following the abolition of former border control at internal borders. The databases are primarily tools used by the police and for migration-related purposes. No requirements have been made in relation to the intelligence services, nor can any fundamental realignment of the work of the intelligence services be made out. Legally, too, access and potential uses are set by national legislation. Everything else is regulated by the Member States and based on national requirements. Thus, no specific competences in relation to the

[70] See § 2(1) of Germany's VIS Access Act (*VIS-Zugangsgesetz*, VISZG) from 6 May 2009 (BGBl. I p. 1034; 2013 I p. 3212), according to which the Federation and federal states determine which police and prosecution authorities and intelligence services are authorized to access the VIS.

evaluation, regulation and oversight of the intelligence services arise as a result. These points of contact between national and EU databases, which compensate for national deficits, do not reverse the allocation of competences in relation to the intelligence services.

c) EU funding for intelligence service interfaces and legal consequences

The question of secondary-legislation requirements and limits is also relevant in relation to EU funding. Sufficient funding is regularly a challenge even when it comes to guaranteeing security. If the EU is active in this area, then it will, where there are references to national security, always be necessary to examine whether and to what extent the EU has any competence that justifies the provision of funding. **63**

At the same time, account will have to be taken of whether the rights of control, transparency and oversight associated with such financing are proportionate to the Member States' reservation under Art. 4(2) sent. 3 TEU. That is why practitioners are quite reticent. For example, the Recitals in Regulation 2021/1149 establishing the Internal Security Fund also refer to types of cooperation among the intelligence services. Recital 16 calls for the exploration and examination of **64**

> [n]ew approaches to cooperation and exchanging information, including in relation to threat analysis […] taking into account existing frameworks within and outside the Union framework, such as the EU Intelligence and Situation Centre (INTCEN), Europol's European Counter Terrorism Centre (ECTC), the European Counter Terrorism Coordinator and the Counter Terrorism Group.

However, as regards the scope of support from the Fund, reference is made to Member State's 'competent authorities responsible for the prevention, detection and investigation of criminal offences, as referred to in Art. 87 TFEU', the article concerning 'police cooperation'. This appears to limit the scope of police cooperation. And so secondary legislation ought to have done justice to the requirements under Art. 4(2) sent. 3 TEU, namely that funding must also refer to competences and objectives under EU competence. **65**

D. Summary

The answer to the question of the interdependency between the competence reservation laid down in Art. 4(2) sent. 3 TEU and secondary-legislation requirements and limits for Member States' intelligence agencies is not merely a black and white one. However, on account of this specific provision, it must take account of the following: **66**

Secondary EU legislation reaches its limits owing to the lack of conferral of powers under primary legislation. **67**

The possibility of dispensing with applying Union law[71] can also encompass secondary EU legislation when it concerns the Member States' intelligence services' powers if it falls within the sphere of legitimate protection of national security. **68**

Secondary EU legislation provisions on national security and on the powers of the intelligence services can assist in creating an understanding of this concept and in interpreting Art. 4(2) sent. 3 TEU, but its binding nature is, ultimately, limited by the fact that EU institutions have no Treaty and constitutional legitimacy when it comes to finally enacting legislation on national security or defining the concept. **69**

---

[71] Karpenstein/Sangi, GSZ 2020, 162 (166).

70 This complex situation makes high demands of all those involved – at both national and EU level. It requires the EU and the Member States and their intelligence services to make efforts to cooperate. The relevant forums and dialogue processes are still in their infancy, but will contribute to doing justice to the particular importance of cooperation when it comes to guaranteeing national security whilst at the same time safeguarding common EU values.[72]

---

[72] See, regarding developments, e.g., Lledo-Ferrer/Dietrich, IJIC 2020, 440–451.

§ 8
The non-integrable core area of national security? On the function and scope of Art. 4(2) sent. 3 TEU*

Päivi Leino-Sandberg

Bibliography: Bonelli, 'National Identity and European Integration Beyond "Limited Fields"', EPL 2021 (27), 537; Boucon, 'EU Law and Retained Powers of Member States' in Azoulai (ed.), The Question of Competence in the European Union, Oxford/New York 2014, p. 168; Cameron, 'Metadata retention and national security: Privacy International and La Quadrature du Net', Common Market Law Review 2021 (58:5), 1433; de Witte, 'Exclusive Member State Competences: Is There Such a Thing?' in Garben/Govaere (eds), The Division of Competences between the EU and the Member States. Reflections on the Past, the Present and the Future, Oxford/Portland 2017, p. 59; de Witte, 'Guest Editorial: EU emergency law and its impact on the EU legal order', Common Market Law Review 2022 (59), 3; Garben, 'Collective Identity as a Legal Limit to European Integration in Areas of Core State Powers', JCMS 2020 (58), 41; Leino-Sandberg, 'The Institutional Politics of Objective Choice: Competence as a Framework for Argumentation' in Garben/Govaere (eds), The Division of Competences between the EU and the Member States. Reflections on the Past, the Present and the Future, London 2017, p. 210; Leino-Sandberg, The Politics of Legal Expertise in EU Policy-Making, Cambridge 2021; Lenaerts, 'Constitutionalism and the Many Faces of Federalism', AJCL 1990 (38), 205; Lindseth, 'The Perils of "As If" European Constitutionalism', EPL 2016 (22), 696; Randazzo, 'Article 346 and the qualified application of EU law to defence', European Union Institute for Security Studies Brief 2014 (22); Schütze, From Dual to Cooperative Federalism: The Changing Structure of European Law, Oxford 2009; Tsourdi, 'Relocation blues – Refugee protection backsliding, division of competences, and the purpose of infringement proceedings: Commission v Poland, Hungary and the Czech Republic', Common Market Law Review 2021 (58), 1819; Weiler, 'The Transformation of Europe', Yale Law Journal 1991 (100), 2403.

A. Introduction

In many EU Member States, including my own (Finland), Russia's war in Ukraine has quickly escalated a debate about the impact of EU competence and legislation on the possibilities of a Member State taking national decisions to safeguard its internal and external security. At the heart of the debate is the question of the room for manoeuvre left to a Member State when it comes to defining and protecting national security: Is there a core of national security that the EU cannot intervene in? After all, under Art. 4(2) TEU, 1

> [t]he Union shall respect the equality of Member States before the Treaties as well as their national identities, inherent in their fundamental structures, political and constitutional, inclusive of regional and local self-government. It shall respect their essential State functions, including ensuring the territorial integrity of the State, maintaining law and order and safeguarding national security. *In particular, national security remains the sole responsibility of each Member State.*[1]

* I would like to thank the organizers and participants of the Conference 'European Security – Responsibility of Member States in the European Security Union' for their comments, Martti Koskenniemi, Timo Makkonen, Tuomas Pöysti and Milka Sormunen for discussions around this topic and Katarina Flinck for helpful research assistance.

[1] Emphasis added.

2 But what legal or political significance does this provision actually have, and who gets to define its meaning? The sentence has its background in the debates leading to the approval of the Lisbon Treaty and the growing concern about the interference of EU law in areas traditionally reserved to the Member States. Art. 4(2) TEU was seen as a way to better shield 'retained competences' in areas where EU institutions have not been conferred legislative competences, and to possibly create no-go areas for EU law.[2] The provision is often explained as a Member State competence reserve – but is it really?

3 'Security' is not an EU-free zone. A search in the EU Treaties for the word 'security' provides 212 hits. The Treaties approach 'security' from various different angles and place it in several 'frames' while also remaining silent on many aspects of 'security'. Yet, the Court of Justice of the European Union (CJEU) has repeatedly stressed that the concept of 'public security' is a broad concept that

> covers both the internal security of a Member State and its external security and that, consequently, a threat to the functioning of institutions and essential public services and the survival of the population, as well as the risk of a serious disturbance to foreign relations or to peaceful coexistence of nations, or a risk to military interests, may affect public security.[3]

4 The Court's line of argumentation indicates that even military threats are situations that do not entirely rule out the need to apply EU legislation. The mutual assistance clause in Art. 42(7) TEU refers to a situation where 'a Member State is the victim of armed aggression on its territory', and Art. 222 TFEU speaks of solidarity in the face of a terrorist attack or a natural or man-made disaster. Art. 326 and 327 TFEU strike a balance between internal market considerations and exceptional security needs. Otherwise, more existential crises causing significant harm to national security are largely absent from the Treaties. Nor do the Treaties include provisions on a state of emergency in the EU or provide for the possibility of a state of emergency declared in a Member State and its effects in the EU legal order. Instead, the EU Treaty rules must be used in good and bad times.[4]

5 In this contribution I examine how the EU Treaties approach 'security'; what general issues figure in legislation in key policy fields that are relevant for 'security'; and how Art. 4(2) TEU has figured in Court jurisprudence since its introduction through the different frames in which it has been used. I look at the provision from the perspective of my own earlier research, which sees competence constraints in the EU as largely political constraints[5] that the CJEU supervises only to a very limited extent. More specifically, I find it highly unlikely that the Court would establish that the EU legislature has exceeded its mandate at the expense of national sovereignty.[6] This leaves a great deal of leeway for the EU's legislative and executive institutions to interpret competence constraints in any manner that finds sufficient political support. This flexibility is particularly visible when the EU operates to tackle a crisis – as it has repeatedly done in recent years. In these contexts, competence constraints constrain strikingly little.[7] The EU legislature has also approved legislation in many areas that are relevant for the application of Art. 4(2) TEU.

6 Case law involving security considerations in general, and Art. 4(2) TEU in particular, typically involves many intervening governments, irrespective of whether the cases

---

[2] Bonelli, EPL 2021, 537.

[3] ECJ 2.7.2020 – case C-18/19, ECLI:EU:C:2020:511 para. 44 – *WM v Stadt Frankfurt am Main.*

[4] De Witte, Common Market Law Review 2020, 3.

[5] Leino-Sandberg in Garben/Govaere, The Division of Competences between the EU and the Member States, p. 210–231.

[6] Leino-Sandberg, p. 1 et seqq.

[7] ibid.

are preliminary references or infringement actions brought by the Commission against a Member State. In other words, a typical feature in these cases is teaming up to defend Member State scope for action. This demonstrates that, for the Member States, the provision has both political and legal significance – but they have seldom been successful in claiming it before the Court. Does the provision have any use and, if so, where does it find its usefulness? Finally, how does action by the EU legislature (that of course involves all Member State governments) affect our understanding of what it means when 'national security remains the sole responsibility of each Member State'?

B. The backdrop to Art. 4(2) TEU

I. National security and horizontal principles

When tracing the historical origins of Art. 4(2) TEU, it is best to start with its predecessor. The earlier EU Treaty included an Art. 6(3), which established that '[t]he Union shall respect the national identities of its Member States.' Ex-Art. 5 of the Treaty Establishing the European Community (TEC) also specified that the 'Community shall act within the limits of the powers conferred upon it by this Treaty and of the objectives assigned to it therein.' These provisions were not considered strong enough to control the greatest challenge to the legitimacy of European integration: the competence creep.[8] As *Koen Lenaerts* argued in his classic piece back in 1990, residual powers of the Member States have no reserved status. For him, the EU could 'exercise its specific, implied or non-specific powers in the fullest way possible, without running into any inherent limitation set to these powers as a result of the sovereignty that the Member States retain as subjects of international law. There simply is no nucleus of sovereignty that the Member States can invoke, as such, against the Community.'[9] 7

The EU differs from most federations where the division of competences between the federal and state levels is sacred, protected by the constitution and established jurisprudence. In the EU, hardly any policy area is immune from Union action. *Schütze* has argued that the EU legal order reflects that of 'cooperative federalism' as opposed to 'dual federalism'[10]: Instead of being autonomous in their own, strictly demarcated spheres, the EU and national level are to some degree involved in the governance of most matters. Despite certain questions being 'reserved for the Member States' in one way or another, they can often be regulated through horizontally applicable provisions. Classic examples of this include *Bosman*, a football player whose situation was framed as an internal market rather than sports issue,[11] and access to education by the children of migrant workers, which was framed as a question of non-discrimination rather than education policy.[12] The advance of integration into areas where direct Treaty compe- 8

[8] Garben, JCMS 2020, 41 (53).

[9] Lenaerts, AJCL 1990, 205 (220).

[10] Schütze, p. 1 et seqq.

[11] ECJ 15.12.1995 – case C-415/93, ECLI:EU:C:1995:463 para. 104 – *ASBL v Bosman*: 'Consequently, the transfer rules constitute an obstacle to freedom of movement for workers prohibited in principle by Article 48 of the Treaty. It could only be otherwise if those rules pursued a legitimate aim compatible with the Treaty and were justified by pressing reasons of public interest. But even if that were so, application of those rules would still have to be such as to ensure achievement of the aim in question and not go beyond what is necessary for that purpose.'

[12] ECJ 3.7.1974 – case 9/74, ECLI:EU:C:1974:74 para. 12 – *Donato Casagrande v Landeshauptstadt München*: 'Although educational and training policy is not as such included in the spheres which the

tence is absent often creates tension with the conferral principle[13] and the role of Member States as the masters of the Treaties. This creates an inherent and unstable tension between state policies and the European level,[14] which is often accentuated by the EU's political and judicial institutions. This has remained largely unchanged.

9 Before Lisbon, the relevance of horizontal principles was also debated in the context of security. The ECJ addressed preliminary references concerning alleged gender discrimination in the armed forces and military service. While the EU has not regulated these questions directly, even here horizontally applicable EU legislation could become applicable 'through the back door'. One example is a case where the UK had refused to employ a woman as a chef in the Royal Marines. The French, Portuguese and UK governments argued that 'decisions concerning the organization and administration of the armed forces, particularly those taken for the purpose of ensuring combat effectiveness in preparation for war, fall outside the scope of the Treaty.' The UK explained that chefs in the Royal Marines are also required to serve as front-line commandos in their unit, which acts as the 'point of the arrow head. They are a small force and are intended to be the first line of attack.' For the Commission, not all decisions affecting armed forces fell entirely outside the scope of EU law and the Treaty did not establish a general exception covering all measures taken for reasons of public security.[15] The Court accepted the Member State justification: The exclusion of women from service in special combat units such as the Royal Marines may be justified by reason of the nature of the activities in question and the context in which they are carried out.[16]

10 In another preliminary reference some years later, the ECJ addressed the question of whether EU law precludes compulsory military service being reserved to men.[17] Germany explained how compulsory military service was of great importance politically and

> that the institution of such service makes a contribution to the democratic transparency of the military, national integration, the link between the armed forces and the population, and the mobilisation of the manpower needed by the armed forces in the event of a conflict.

For Germany, such a choice, enshrined in its *Grundgesetz*, the Basic Law, consists of imposing an obligation to serve the interests of territorial security, albeit in many cases to the detriment of young people's access to the labour market.[18] Here, too, the ECJ accepted that while the principle of equal treatment, including access to military posts, was relevant for the application of EU law, it did not follow that EU law governs the Member States' choices of military organization for the defence of their territory or of their essential interests.[19] The delay in career progress

---

Treaty has entrusted to the Community institutions, it does not follow that the exercise of powers transferred to the Community is in some way limited if it is of such a nature as to affect the measures taken […] although the determination of the conditions referred to there is a matter for the authorities competent under national law, they must however be applied without discrimination between the children of national workers and those of workers who are nationals of another Member State who reside in the territory.'

[13] Garben, JCMS 2020, 41 (53).

[14] See Weiler, Yale Law Journal 1991, 2403.

[15] ECJ 26.10.1999 – case C-273/97, ECLI:EU:C:1999:523 para. 15 – *Angela Maria Sirdar v The Army Board.*

[16] ibid. para. 32

[17] ECJ 11.3.2003 – case C-186/01, ECLI:EU:C:2002:718 – *Alexander Dory v Bundesrepublik Deutschland.*

[18] ibid., para. 37 et seq.

[19] ibid., para. 35.

of persons called up for military service is an inevitable consequence of the choice made by the Member State regarding military organisation and does not mean that that choice comes within the scope of Community law. The existence of adverse consequences for access to employment cannot, without encroaching on the competences of the Member States, have the effect of compelling the Member State in question either to extend the obligation of military service to women, thus imposing on them the same disadvantages with regard to access to employment, or to abolish compulsory military service.[20]

In this case, the ECJ thus recognized choices relating to military organization as a Member State competence. These two cases are also exceptional in that the Court actually ruled in favour of Member State choice. However, even here the ECJ stressed that the Member States must comply with EU law even in areas outside the scope of EU competence.[21] The scope of EU law is not conditional on the existence of Treaty provisions empowering the EU but is broader than the scope of EU powers.[22] While the EU has not assumed full control of such fields, the law that it creates may **11**

intervene in any area in sometimes unpredictable and unforeseen ways, with potentially important disruptive effects, and there is no single policy area or issue that can a priori be shielded from these dynamics. In other words, from the viewpoint of EU law, there are no core state powers or, in any event, they are not for that reason carved out of the scope of application of the treaties. While EU integration in these areas is not unlimited, it is not limited by virtue of these powers being considered core to the state or essential for self-determination and collective identity on the national and subnational level.[23]

II. 'In particular, national security remains the sole responsibility of each Member State.'

What was the final sentence in Art. 4(2) TEU as introduced by the Treaty of Lisbon meant to change then? It is placed in the 'common provisions' of Title I TEU and therefore concerns EU action in general. Its emphasis is on *national* security, which is repeated twice, first as a need to 'respect essential state functions' that include 'safeguarding national security', after which the article goes on: 'In particular, national security remains the sole responsibility of each Member State.' **12**

Preparatory materials in EU law are often difficult to find, but some are available for this particular provision. The Constitutional Convention that drafted the Constitutional Treaty considered enlisting pure Member State competences.[24] In its final report, the relevant Working Group considered that the principle of allocated powers **13**

is a basic principle of Union law. In a narrow sense it establishes a fundamental condition for the exercise of any Union activity. In a wider sense the principle is a vital safeguard for the Member States ensuring that powers not allocated to the Union remain with the Member States. In the opinion of the working group the latter aspect of the principle of allocated powers ought to be expressly stated in the Treaty. Such an amendment would in itself establish an assumption in favour of national competence.

---

[20] ibid., para. 40 et seq. – *Alexander Dory v Bundesrepublik Deutschland* (emphasis added).

[21] ECJ 11.12.2007 – case C- 438/05, ECLI:EU:C:2007:772, paras. 39 et seq. – *International Transport Worker's Federation and Finnish Seamen's Union v Viking Line ABP and OÜ Viking Line Eesti.*

[22] Boucon in Azoulai, The Question of Competence in the European Union, p. 174.

[23] Garben, JCMS 2020, 41 (44).

[24] See Christophersen, 'Option paper: Highlighting the Limits of EU Competence' (Working group V "Complementary Competencies", 11.7.2002) available from https://dorie.ecu.europa.eu (last accessed: 25.6.2024) which explains that '[t]he desire for clarification of EU competence vis-à-vis Member States' competence in a way likely to be understood by the citizens may raise the question, whether the essence of these principles might be better understood if expressed also partly by way of referring to the rights and competences remaining with the Member States.'

14 The considerations of the Working Group V 'Complementary Competencies' resulted in no listing of Member State competence. Instead, the result was Art. 4(2) TEU. The Working Group aimed to safeguard

> the role and importance of the Member States in the Treaty while at the same time allowing the necessary margin of flexibility. In the latter respect it was noted that the provision was *not a derogation clause.* The Member States will remain under a duty to respect the provisions of the Treaties. The article would therefore *not constitute a definition of Member State competence, thereby wrongly conveying the message that it is the Union that grants competence to the Member States, or that Union action may never impact on these fields.* The purpose would be to render more visible and more operational the existing principle that the Union, in the exercise of its competence, is under an obligation to respect the national identities of the Members States. The clause would send an important message to the citizens as well as provide useful guidance for the Union institutions in the fulfilment of its tasks.[25]

15 While clarifying the EU's competence structure in various ways, the Treaty of Lisbon allows for several ways in which Member State competence may be retained. *Bruno de Witte* speaks about 'retained competence' and 'reserved competence'.[26] The former builds on the principle of allocated competence and refers to competence not allocated to the EU. Such areas include social security, laws on nationality, name-giving, civil status of persons, registration of ships and recovery of debts.[27] The latter refers to matters where the Treaty sets limits to what the EU can do.[28] The Working Group discussed ways to clarify that the Union respects certain core responsibilities of the Member States with a view to providing 'added transparency of what constitutes essential elements of national identity, which the EU must respect in the exercise of its competence', in particular as regards two areas of core national responsibilities:

- Fundamental structures and essential functions of a Member State e.g., (a) political and constitutional structure, including regional and local self-government; (b) national citizenship; (c) *territory*; (d) the legal status of churches and religious societies; (e) *national defence and the organisation of armed forces;* (g) choice of languages.
- Basic public policy choices and social values of a Member State e.g., (a) policy for distribution of income; (b) imposition and collection of personal taxes; (c) system of social welfare benefits; (d) educational system; (e) public health care system; (f) cultural preservation and development; (g) *compulsory military or community service.*[29]

16 Therefore, while referring to 'national security' in rather broad terms, the ideas behind the provision were more confined to questions involving territory and choices relevant for national defence.

---

[25] See Christophersen, 'Option paper: Highlighting the Limits of EU Competence' (Working group V "Complementary Competencies", 11.7.2002) (emphasis added).

[26] De Witte in Garben/Govaere, The Division of Competences between the EU and the Member States, p. 59.

[27] ECJ 29.4.2004 – case C-224/02, ECLI:EU:C:2004:273, para 22 – *Heikki Antero Pusa v Osuuspankkien Keskinäinen Vakuutusyhtiö*. This particular case concerned the area of freedom, security and justice.

[28] Art. 345 TFEU establishes that '[t]he Treaties shall in no way prejudice the rules in Member States governing the system of property ownership.' See Art. 153(4) and (5) of the TFEU on social policy. See Art. 2(5) of the TFEU, where the EU has 'competence to carry out actions to support, coordinate or supplement the actions of the Member States,' its competence does not supersede their competence, and '[l]egally binding acts of the Union adopted on the basis of the provisions of the Treaties relating to these areas shall not entail harmonisation of Member States' laws or regulations.' Under Art. 6 TFEU, such areas include (a) protection and improvement of human health; (b) industry; (c) culture; (d) tourism; (e) education, vocational training, youth and sport; (f) civil protection; (g) administrative cooperation.

[29] Emphasis added. European Convention, 'Final Report of Working Group V', 4.11.2002, CONV 375/1/02 REV 1 <https://data.consilium.europa.eu/doc/document/CV-375-2002-REV-1/en/pdf> (last accessed: 18.1.2024).

In my own country, the Finnish government explained the new provision as specifying the provision of national identity, which also includes state identity and the basic functions of a state. The government saw this as a political principle, which is given legal significance through the special provisions relating to the core functions of the state. Keeping in mind the general formulation of the provision, its significance was seen as being *political* but aiming to *guide* the use of Union competence, and with significance placed on the interpretation of various other Treaty provisions, in particular Art. 72 TFEU.[30] Other states may have read more into the provision, as is visible in the case law. **17**

De Witte argues that Art. 4(2) TEU **18**

> recognises the primary responsibility of the states in this respect, and directs the EU institutions to respect that responsibility, but it does not define policy areas as being 'off-limits' for the EU. Only the final sentence [...] strikes a different note, mainly due to the word 'sole', which could be interpreted as guaranteeing the exclusive competence of the Member States for national security.[31]

Yet, he notes that this is not how the Court has interpreted the provision when governments have chosen to refer to it. Therefore, 'the little phrase of Art. 4(2) TEU, despite its sharp wording, is not a genuine competence reservation clause either'.[32] However, as *de Witte* also observes, this may not be the reading of Member States and their constitutional bodies.[33] *Azoulai* notes how the interpretation of the article involves striking a difficult balance because allowing the Member States to block competence areas would hamper the effectiveness of EU law. At the same time, constantly extending competence also produces a legitimacy problem, 'a problem of boundaries'.[34] The jurisprudence – that is discussed further in the following section – demonstrates this tension, as it involves a broad spectrum of Member States arguing for a strong reading of Art. 4(2) TEU as a limitation clause on EU competence. In practice, the whole of Art. 4(2) TEU has been invoked in various different contexts, such as religion, family and nationality. Overall, the national identity clause has not worked as a limit to EU competences and the scope of EU law, but has sometimes contributed to deference being shown to national preferences. As such, *Bonelli* argues, the Article should be read as 'one of the many clauses that stand for, and guarantee, national diversity'.[35] **19**

The focus of the following analysis is on the national security aspects of Art. 4(2) TEU. It is often invoked in connection with other Treaty provisions that refer to security, which appears in various different frames in EU Treaties, and the interpretation and scope given to security-related arguments may be affected by which of these frames is chosen. My own search in Curia gave 49 post-Lisbon hits in which Art. 4(2) **20**

---

[30] Finish Government, 'Hallituksen esitys Eduskunnalle Euroopan unionista tehdyn sopimuksen ja Euroopan yhteisön perustamissopimuksen muuttamisesta tehdyn Lissabonin sopimuksen hyväksymisestä ja laiksi sen lainsäädännön alaan kuuluvien määräysten voimaansaattamisesta [Government proposal concerning the approval of the Lisbon Treaty.]', HE 23/2008 <https://www.finlex.fi/fi/esitykset/he/2008/20080023> (last accessed: 26.9.2023).

[31] De Witte in Garben/Govaere, The Division of Competences between the EU and the Member States, p. 71.

[32] ibid. p. 72.

[33] ibid., p. 73.

[34] Boucon in Azoulai, The Question of Competence in the European Union, p. 175.

[35] Bonelli, EPL 2021, 537.

TEU was referred to, five of them being orders.[36] However, six cases seem to be of some interest when it comes to discussing the concept of 'national security' and will be discussed in the relevant context below, thus underlining the reading that Member States have argued for the provision and how the EU institutions (Commission and Court) have responded to them.

C. Security in the EU Treaties: it's all about framing?

I. Freedom, security and justice

21 The first frame of 'security' is that of an area of freedom, security and justice. This section of the Treaty is geared towards internal security: 'law and order'. The EU has considerable shared competence for realising this objective (Art. 67(1) TFEU). Despite explicit EU competence, Art. 72 TFEU specifies that '[t]his Title shall not affect the exercise of the responsibilities incumbent upon Member States with regard to the maintenance of law and order and the safeguarding of *internal security*' (emphasis added).

22 When reading the case law, the Member States seem to make reference to Art. 72 TFEU as a more specific exception, sometimes in connection with Art. 4(2) TEU. The *ZZ case*, for example, concerned the relevance of State security considerations for assessing whether the principle of effective judicial protection requires an EU citizen to be informed about his exclusion grounds when such disclosure would be considered contrary to State security. Italy stressed that 'it is clear from Art. 4(2) TEU and Art. 346(1)(a) TFEU that State security remains the responsibility of solely the Member States. The question referred thus relates to an area governed by national law and, for that reason, does not fall within European Union competence.'[37] Austria emphasized that it is for the Member States to define their essential security interests and to define the necessary measures for protecting public security (in the context of the printing of identity documents and other official documents), a point that was accepted by the ECJ. However, the Court established that while 'it is for Member States to take the appropriate measures to ensure their internal and external security, the mere fact that a decision concerns State security cannot result in European Union law being inapplicable.'[38] Therefore, Member State measures taken in the frame of public security are not automatically excluded in their entirety from the application of EU law.[39]

23 Art. 72 TFEU has served as justification for various arguments that resemble those brought under Art. 4(2) TEU, many of them recently in the context of cases relating to migration law and relocation schemes. In one of the recent cases, Poland and Hungary

---

[36] Six of the rulings concern the position of the judiciary, eight concern citizenship or free movement, and another two social and health care. Data protection and privacy are at the core of four rulings, and the conferral and position of noble titles are discussed in two. In addition, there are ten cases in various different policy fields ranging from customs to the environment, taxation, European citizen initiatives and two opinions concerning accession to international treaties without a clear connection to 'national security'.

[37] ECJ 4.6.2013 – case C-300/11, ECLI:EU:C:2013:363 para. 35, *ZZ v Secretary of State for the Home Department.*

[38] ibid., para. 38.

[39] ibid., para. 75 et seq.

argued that Art. 72 TFEU allowed them to disapply EU decisions.[40] The Court, however, stressed that

> according to settled case-law of the Court of Justice, although it is for the Member States to adopt appropriate measures to ensure law and order on their territory and their internal and external security, it does not follow that such measures fall entirely outside the scope of European Union law. As the Court has already held, the only articles in which the Treaty expressly provides for derogations applicable in situations which may affect law and order or public security are Articles 36, 45, 52, 65, 72, 346 and 347 TFEU, which deal with exceptional and clearly defined cases. It cannot be inferred that the Treaty contains an inherent general exception excluding all measures taken for reasons of law and order or public security from the scope of European Union law. The recognition of the existence of such an exception, regardless of the specific requirements laid down by the Treaty, might impair the binding nature of European Union law and its uniform application.[41]

The Court then argued that, like all exceptions, the derogation provided for in Art. 72 TFEU must be interpreted strictly. It follows that the provision **24**

> cannot be read in such a way as to confer on Member States the power to depart from the provisions of the Treaty based on no more than reliance on those responsibilities. The scope of the requirements relating to the maintenance of law and order or national security *cannot therefore be determined unilaterally by each Member State, without any control by the institutions of the European Union.* It is for the Member State which seeks to take advantage of Article 72 TFEU *to prove that it is necessary* to have recourse to that derogation in order to exercise its responsibilities in terms of the maintenance of law and order and the safeguarding of internal security.[42]

The above quote refers to how EU legislation in this area provides room for emergency measures to be taken swiftly by individual Member States to address concerns in non-legislative procedures.[43] The flexibility needed to tackle emergencies is not a free space for Member States to act in, but is created by EU legislation, and the actors are EU institutions that take measures to react to unexpected situations affecting Member States and their national security. The effective safeguarding of essential State functions should thus be carried out by applying the leeway provided by the EU legislature.[44] After all, the EU legislature has taken 'due account of the exercise of the Member States" responsibilities under Art. 72 TFEU and laid down provisions that 'allow Member States to derogate from a number of rules laid down by that directive if required for the protection of public order or public or national security.'[45] **25**

The most recent case concerns restrictions in relation to the right to apply for international protection due to a great flux of immigrants approaching Lithuania from Belarus, which had led Lithuania to apply legislation based on the justification of a **26**

[40] ECJ 2.4.2020 – joined cases C-715/17, C-718/17 and C-719/17, ECLI:EU:C:2020:257, *European Commission v Poland, Hungary and the Czech Republic.*

[41] ibid., para. 143.

[42] ibid., para. 143–147. Cf. Tsourdi Common Market Law Review 2021, 1819.

[43] The Treaty sets an objective to 'develop a common policy on asylum, subsidiary protection and temporary protection with a view to offering appropriate status to any third-country national requiring international protection and ensuring compliance with the principle of non-refoulement.' Art. 78(3) TFEU sets a procedure relating to 'the event of one or more Member States being confronted by an emergency situation characterised by a sudden inflow of nationals of third countries.' It is for the Council, acting on a proposal from the Commission and after consulting the European Parliament, to 'adopt provisional measures for the benefit of the Member State(s) concerned.'

[44] ECJ 2.4.2020 – joined cases C-715/17, C-718/17 and C-719/17, ECLI:EU:C:2020:257 para. 170 et seq., *European Commission v Poland, Hungary and the Czech Republic.*

[45] ECJ 17.12.2020 – case C-808/18, ECLI:EU:C:2020:1029 para. 263 – *European Commission v Hungary.*

martial war or state of exception.[46] The ECJ stressed again that Art. 72 TFEU must be interpreted strictly.[47] The Court found that invoking a general threat caused by the mass influx of third-country nationals could not justify the provisions Lithuania had introduced, as EU legislation already provided for special procedures for specific circumstances that make recourse to Art. 72 TFEU unnecessary. In this context the Court also referred to its own earlier interpretations of 'national security' and 'public order'.[48] The former presumes the existence of a genuine, present and sufficiently serious threat affecting one of the fundamental interests of society or the internal or external security of the Member State concerned.[49]

27 As Art. 78 TFEU indicates, EU law is closely intertwined with international human rights law. EU law establishes a procedure for reacting to exceptional situations, but such measures need to comply with basic human rights standards. Yet, it seems that States easily feel that national action is more reliable in responding to threats and feel that in threatening circumstances even basic human rights should be negotiable. In anticipation of possible hybrid interference, the Finnish Parliament has also recently approved legislation that enables the temporary closure of an external border, the limitation of border crossings and the centralized handling of applications for international protection. When handling the proposal, the *Constitutional Law Committee* of the Parliament (the Finnish equivalent of a constitutional court) pointed out that both international law and EU law allow a broader spectrum of measures when a state's security is seriously and suddenly threatened. It also referred to international customary law, which allows international obligations to be breached on the grounds of necessity with a view to safeguarding an essential interest against a grave and imminent peril if no alternative way of addressing the threat exists.[50] The Act empowers the government to close the external border in case of a mass influx of immigrants or cases (or suspected cases) of hybrid influencing by a third state to the extent necessary to counter the threat to public order, national security or national health, while the rights of persons protected under EU law or the right to international protection still need to be protected.[51] While there is no public information concerning a possible Commission reaction to the new legislation, the Council of Europe Commissioner for Human Rights has called for clear safeguards to ensure that recently adopted amendments to the Border Guard Act would not lead to human rights violations.[52]

28 These cases are examples of the instrumentalization of migration addressed in Art. 78 (3) TFEU, which puts the EU institutions in the driving seat. However, the situations debated in the context of the Finnish Act described above also involve scenarios that may escalate to more of an existential threat where migrants are counted in hundreds of thousands, actively transported by a third state with a view to destabilising a society and perhaps aiming at creating disorder and disagreement in the EU institutions that are supposed to respond swiftly to the situation. In such cases, the migrants will likely be

---

[46] ECJ 30.6.2022 – case C-72/22, ECLI:EU:C:2022:505 – *M.A. v alstybės sienos apsaugos tarnyba.*

[47] ibid., para. 2015.

[48] ECJ 15.2.2016 – case C-601/15, ECLI:EU:C:2016:84 para. 66 – *J. N. v Staatssecretaris van Veiligheid en Justitie*; ECJ 23.11.2010 – case C-145/09, ECLI:EU:C:2010:708 para. 43 et seq., *Land Baden-Württemberg v Panagiotis Tsakouridis.*

[49] ECJ 15.2.2016 – case C-601/15, ECLI:EU:C:2016:84 para. 65 and 67 – *J. N. v Staatssecretaris van Veiligheid en Justitie.*

[50] Statement by the Constitutional Law Committee, PeVL 37/2022 vp. See also United Nations, Responsibility of States for Internationally Wrongful Acts (International Law Commission, 2001), Art. 25.

[51] Parliament of Finland, 'Eduskunnan vastaus EV 100/2022 vp', HE 94/2022 vp.

[52] Council of Europe Commissioner for Human Rights, 'Letter to the Finnish Minister of Interior', 27.7.2022, CommHR/DM/sf 022-2022.

met by defence forces rather than border guards acting under their ordinary competences. Then it may well be the case that the 'migration' frame is not the correct one for addressing the situation, but it would actually need to be addressed in a frame directed specifically at external security and territorial integrity described below.

II. Internal market and (public) security

Second, various internal market provisions make reference to 'public security' as a ground for exemption, as they allow a Member State to diverge from internal market regulation on public interest grounds, including public security.[53] Unlike Art. 4(2) TEU, these provisions do not refer to 'national security' but to *'public security'* – a concept that 'covers both a Member State's internal and its external security'.[54] These derogation provisions have produced a great deal of case law when Member State governments have used them to argue that the derogations entail 'the matters to which it refers to be dealt with by Member States under their sovereign powers'.[55] Such claims have been rejected by the Court with reference to how these clauses are 'not designed to reserve certain matters to the exclusive jurisdiction of Member States' but instead allow national legislation that can be justified on public interest grounds.[56] Therefore, 'it cannot be inferred that the Treaty contains an inherent general exception excluding all measures taken for reasons of public security from the scope of Community law.'[57] In interpreting secondary legislation, the Court has emphasized that while EU law does not impose a uniform scale of values to be used to assess what kind of conduct is contrary to public security, those requirements – like the measures justified by Member States under Art. 72 TFEU discussed above – must be interpreted strictly and cannot be determined unilaterally by each Member State without any control by the EU institutions.[58] The logic is thus the same. **29**

The internal market provisions that indicate most clearly that Member States may have some independent scope for security-related measures are not found in the internal market part of the Treaties but in some of the final provisions of the TFEU. Art. 346 and 347 TFEU include provisions that can be invoked when Member State measures taken for security purposes may affect the functioning of the internal market. Both are formulated in a manner that underlines the role of the Member State concerned when defining its own security interests. Their relationship to Art. 4(2) TEU is visible in how Art. 4(2) TEU and Art. 346 TFEU have figured jointly in recent legislative action on Regulation 2019/452 establishing a framework for the screening of foreign direct investments into the Union,[59] which reflects on an 'Europeanization of security concerns'. Its preamble stresses how **30**

> [i]t is important to provide legal certainty for Member States' screening mechanisms on the grounds of security and public order, and to ensure Union-wide coordination and cooperation

---

[53] See, for example, Art. 36, 45(3), 52, 65, 202 TFEU.

[54] See, for example, ECJ 23.11.2010 – case C-145/09, ECLI:EU:C:2010:708 para. 43 – *Land Baden-Württemberg v Panagiotis Tsakouridis,* (emphasis added).

[55] See, for example, ECJ 15.12.1976 – case 35–76, ECLI:EU:C:1976:180 para. 13 et seq. – *Simmenthal SpA v Ministero delle Finanze italianopara.* In this case the claim was made by Italy.

[56] ibid., para. 13 et seq.

[57] ECJ 15.12.2009 – case C-387/05, ECLI:EU:C:2009:781 para. 45 – *European Commission v Italian Republic.*

[58] ECJ 22.5.2012 – case C-348/09, ECLI:EU:C:2012:300 para. 21 and 23 – *P.I. v Oberbürgermeisterin der Stadt Remscheid.*

[59] Regulation (EU) 2019/452 establishing a framework for the screening of foreign direct investments into the Union.

> on the screening of foreign direct investments likely to affect security or public order. That common framework is without prejudice to sole responsibility of Member States for safeguarding their national security, as provided for in Article 4(2) TEU. It is also without prejudice to the protection of their essential security interests in accordance with Article 346 TFEU.[60]

31 Art. 346(1) TFEU establishes that the Treaties do not preclude the possibility of Member States refusing to 'supply information the disclosure of which it considers contrary to the essential interests of its security'. The formulation suggests that it is the Member State *itself* that defines what information is included in such a category. The following subparagraph enables the Member States to 'take such measures as it considers necessary for the protection of the essential interests of its security which are connected with the production of or trade in arms, munitions and war material.' However, the measures are not to 'adversely affect the conditions of competition in the internal market regarding products which are not intended for specifically military purposes.' The article was long read as excluding the whole defence sector from the remit of EU law, and discussions primarily focused on what kind of military products are covered by it.[61] Art. 347 TFEU is a rare Treaty article, in that it directly refers to the possibility of serious security challenges demanding Member State action. It sets up a consultation procedure *among Member States* that is to be used if the internal market is

> affected by measures which a *Member State may be called upon* to take in the event of serious internal disturbances affecting the maintenance of law and order, in the event of war, serious international tension constituting a threat of war, or in order to carry out obligations it has accepted for the purpose of maintaining peace and international security. (emphasis added)

Both Art. 346(1) and 347 TFEU mirror the possibility of a Member State taking measures with a view to safeguarding its own security interests and, interestingly, the latter article makes no reference to the EU institutions or their role. It simply places the Member States under an obligation to 'consult each other with a view to taking together the steps needed to prevent the functioning of the internal market being affected by measures which a Member State may be called upon to take […].'

32 A search in Curia for Art. 347 TFEU does not provide any hits, but it seems that Member States have attempted to invoke Art. 346 TFEU many times. There is, thus, in particular, case law on its interpretation in matters involving state aid and public procurement. The ECJ has stressed that

> it is for the Member State which seeks to rely on [Art. 296 TEC] to furnish evidence that the exemptions in question do not go beyond the limits of such [clearly defined] cases' and to demonstrate 'that the exemptions […] are necessary for the protection of the essential interests of its security.[62]

33 Jurisprudence has clarified that the article has a highly limited scope of application. The provision came to be applied in a series of nine cases against various Member States around the same time, which also touched upon its application on dual-use products. In one of these cases Italy claimed that the purchases of Agusta and Agusta Bell helicopters fell under the provision as dual-use items that could serve both civilian and military purposes.[63] The Court, however, refused to accept this and stressed that in order for the provision to apply the products 'must be intended for specifically military purposes.'[64]

---

[60] Regulation (EU) 2019/452, Recital 7.

[61] Randazzo, European Union Institute for Security Studies Brief 2014 (22).

[62] ECJ 16.9.1999 – case C-414/97, ECLI:EU:C:1999:417 para. 22 – *European Commission v Kingdom of Spain.*

[63] ECJ 8.4.2008 – case C-337/05, ECLI:EU:C:2008:203 – *Commission of the European Communities v Italian Republic.*

[64] ibid., para. 47

In another case brought by the Commission against Finland[65] (supported by the governments of Denmark, Germany, Greece, Italy, Portugal and Sweden), the Grand Chamber addressed a situation where Finland had exempted imports of military equipment from customs duties in 1998–2002, claiming that 'the imports related to equipment exclusively intended for military purposes, for the protection of its essential security interests.'[66] Finland argued that 'the Member States have a wide discretion in relation to measures which they may take for the protection of the essential interests of their security' and that 34

> it is for it to assess what measures are required for the defence of its essential security interests and considers that, before the Court can review whether the exercise of its rights by the Republic of Finland is improper, it is for it to specify the essential security interests on which it relies and to demonstrate that it has taken the measures concerned in the firm belief that they were necessary for the safeguarding of those interests.[67]

The ECJ repeated its case law on how there is no 'inherent general exception excluding all measures taken for reasons of public security from the scope of Community law' and that the derogations must be interpreted strictly, rejecting the arguments put forward by Finland.[68] The question here was framed as one that interprets the common customs tariffs rather than security, and the Court pointed out that a failure to collect customs duties would lead to an avoidance of the obligations to finance the EU budget at the expense of those States that collect and pay the customs duties on such imports. Instead, the Member State must prove that it is necessary to have recourse to the exception to protect its essential security interests.[69] Several of the cases also addressed the question of *who* gets to define a State's essential security interest. In one of the cases, Sweden (supported by Denmark, Finland and Germany) argued that the Article

> permits it to take measures for the protection of the essential interests of its security. […] The *purpose of that article is to ensure that Member States have freedom of action in certain areas affecting national defence and security.* The fact that Article 296 EC is among the general and final provisions of the EC Treaty confirms its general scope and its effect on all provisions of general scope within the Treaty and within secondary Community law.[70]

The Court rejected this and held that

> although that Article refers to measures which a Member State may consider necessary for the protection of the essential interests of its security or of information the disclosure of which it considers contrary to those interests, that Article cannot however be read in such a way as to confer on Member States a power to depart from the provisions of the Treaty based on no more than reliance on those interests. […] Consequently it is for the Member State which seeks to take advantage of Article 296 EC to prove that it is necessary to have recourse to that derogation in order to protect its essential security interests.[71]

---

[65] ECJ 15.12.2009 – case C-284/05, ECLI:EU:C:2009:778 – *European Commission v Republic of Finland.*

[66] ibid., para. 20.

[67] ibid., para. 35 (emphasis added).

[68] ibid., para. 47.

[69] ibid., para. 50 – *European Commission v Republic of Finland.* Here the Court referred to an earlier case, ECJ 16.9.1999 – case C-414/97, ECLI:EU:C:1999:417 – *Commission v Spain,* and to the fact that there had been a failure to fulfil obligations on the ground that the Kingdom of Spain had not shown that the exemption from that tax on imports and acquisitions of arms, ammunition and equipment exclusively for military use, an exemption provided for by Spanish legislation, was justified, under Art. 296(1)(b) EC Treaty, by the need to protect the essential interests of the security of that Member State. Consequently, it is for the Member State that seeks to take advantage of Art. 296 EC Treaty to prove that it is necessary to have recourse to that derogation in order to protect its essential security interests.

[70] ECJ 15.12.2009 – case C-294/05, ECLI:EU:C:2009:779 para. 35 – *European Commission v Kingdom of Sweden* (emphasis added).

[71] ibid., para. 45 and 47.

35 In 2006, the Commission adopted an interpretative communication on this provision 'to prevent possible misinterpretation and misuse' even though the Communication acknowledges that it 'can neither give an interpretation of Member States' essential security interests nor determine ex ante to which procurement contracts the exemption under Art. 296 TEC applies or not.'[72] For the Commission,

> [i]t is Member States' responsibility to define and protect their security interests. Article 296 TEC recognises this prerogative and provides a derogation for cases where compliance with European law would undermine Member States' essential security interests. [...] any derogation under Article 296 TEC touches the core of the European Community and is, by its very nature, a legally and politically serious matter. The Treaty therefore contains strict conditions for the use of this derogation, *balancing Member States' interests in the field of defence and security against the fundamental principles and objectives of the Community.* The aim of these conditions is to prevent possible misuse and to ensure that *the derogation remains an exception limited to cases where Member States have no other choice than to protect their security interests nationally.*[73]

36 Finally, in 2009 the EU legislature approved a specific Defence Procurement Directive,[74] which applies to contracts awarded in the fields of defence and security for the supply of military and sensitive equipment. While the preamble of the Directive starts by acknowledging that '[n]ational security remains the sole responsibility of each Member State, in the fields of both defence and security', the specific aim of the EU institutions seems to be making extensive recourse to Art. 346 TFEU unnecessary as specific rules and safeguards are now laid down in EU legislation. The logic is the same as regarding the application of Art. 72 TFEU in the area of migration control as discussed above.

37 As noted above, Art. 346 TFEU has also been applied in the area of state aid control. Earlier, the Commission focused on controlling spill-over effects that could impact on the non-military sector.[75] Even here the logic has changed: The Commission highlighted, in a Communication from July 2013, how the frame of security challenges has changed. They are now 'numerous, complex, interrelated and difficult to foresee' and thus require a 'comprehensive approach combining different policies and instruments, short and long-term measures', 'underpinned by a large range of civil and military capabilities', which makes it 'increasingly unlikely that Member States can bear this burden in isolation'.[76] The Commission emphasizes the Member States' duty to notify all state aid measures, including those in the military sector. They

> may only derogate from that obligation if they can prove that non-notification is necessary for reasons of essential security interests under Article 346 TFEU. Therefore, if a Member State intends to rely on Article 346, it must be able to demonstrate that the concrete measures in the military sector are necessary and proportionate for the protection of their essential security interests and that they do not go beyond what is strictly necessary for that purpose. The burden of proof that these conditions are fulfilled lies upon Member States.[77]

---

[72] Commission of the European Communities, 'Interpretative Communication on the Application of Article 296 of the Treaty in the Field of Defence Procurement', 7.12.2006, COM(2006) 779 final.

[73] ibid. (emphasis added).

[74] Directive 2009/81/EC on the coordination of procedures for the award of certain works contracts, supply contracts and service contracts by contracting authorities or entities in the fields of defence and security, and amending Directives 2004/17/EC and 2004/18/EC.

[75] Randazzo, European Union Institute for Security Studies Brief 2014 (22).

[76] European Commission, 'Communication from the Commission to the European Parliament, the Council, the European Economic and Social Committee and the Committee of the Regions: Towards a more competitive and efficient defence and security sector', 24.7.2013, COM(2013) 542 final.

[77] ibid., 6–7.

Recently the Court has addressed these questions in the context of state aid given to shipbuilding,[78] the EU–Russia Partnership and Cooperation Agreement and restrictive measures adopted to respond to the situation in Ukraine, where it repeated that it is 'for the Member State which seeks to rely on Art. 346 TFEU to prove that it is necessary to have recourse to that derogation in order to protect its essential security interests.'[79] **38**

In conclusion, even in the internal market the conditions under which public security claims can be made are diminishing. It is increasingly covered by EU legislation and carefully monitored by EU institutions. Member States have only objected to this to a limited extent, since I have only come across one Court case where a Member State has objected to EU legislative action on the basis of Art. 4(2) TEU, and that is the annulment action brought by the Czech Republic against Directive 2017/853 on control of the acquisition and possession of weapons.[80] For the Czech Republic, **39**

> [i]ndeed, in the field of prevention of crime and terrorism, harmonisation is specifically excluded by Article 84 TFEU. That echoes Article 4(2) TEU, pursuant to which Member States are solely responsible for national security in their territory and must have the possibility of maintaining law and order in that territory. In adopting the contested directive, therefore, the EU legislature exceeded its powers and infringed Article 5(2) TEU.

The Court remained unresponsive to the claims about a lack of competence on the grounds that 'the fight against international terrorism in order to maintain international peace and security constitutes an objective of general interest. The same is true of the fight against serious crime in order to ensure public security.'[81]

III. When security crosses boxes: horizontal matters

There are also various security-related matters that cross policy fields and engage various kinds of security authorities, such as terrorism. One example is the new Regulation on terrorist content online, the preamble to which stresses its aim 'to ensure the smooth functioning of the digital single market in an open and democratic society, by addressing the misuse of hosting services for terrorist purposes and contributing to *public security across the Union*.'[82] Public security concerns can also be found in new policy fields. Recently 'security of energy supply' has been recognized as 'an essential element of public security'. Therefore, '[f]unctioning electricity markets and, in particular, the networks and other assets associated with electricity supply are essential for public security.'[83] This indicates how security measures may cross 'boxes', and such EU measures clearly indicate that the EU assures a role across the competence and policy borders. **40**

Public security concerns have also come up in several data protection–related cases. The processing of personal data in the electronic communications sector in relation to **41**

[78] ECJ 28.2.2013 – case C-246/12 P, ECLI:EU:C:2013:133 – *Ellinika Nafpigeia AE v European Commission.*

[79] ECJ 17.9.2020 – case T-715/14, ECLI:EU:C:2020:727 para. 174 – *PAO Rosneft Oil Company and Others v Council of the European Union.*

[80] ECJ 3.12.2019 – case C-482/17, ECLI:EU:C:2019:1035 – *Czech Republic v European Parliament and Council of the European Union.*

[81] ibid., para. 40.

[82] Regulation (EU) 2021/784 on addressing the dissemination of terrorist content online, Recital 1 (emphasis added).

[83] Directive 2009/72/EC concerning Common Rules for the Internal Market in Electricity and Repealing Directive 2003/54/EC. See also ECJ 22.10.2013 – case C-105/12, ECLI:EU:C:2013:677 para. 59 – *Staat der Nederlanden v Essent NV.*

national security and combating terrorism[84] and the application of Directive 2002/58 have been subject to a preliminary ruling on intelligence measures implemented directly by French authorities.[85] Eight intervening governments submitted that Directive 2002/58 does not apply to national legislation that aims to safeguard national security:

> The intelligence services' activities, in so far as they relate to the maintenance of public order and to the safeguarding of internal security and territorial integrity, are part of the essential functions of the Member States and, consequently, are within their exclusive competence, as evidenced, in particular, by the third sentence of Article 4(2) TEU.

42 This example is different from other EU legislation discussed in the previous sections for the reason that Art. 1(3) Directive 2002/58 *specifically excludes from its scope* activities concerning public security, defence and State security. However, despite this specific exclusion, the Court found that 'all operations processing personal data carried out by providers of electronic communications services fall within the scope of that directive […] which covers all processing operations concerning public security, defence, or State security, regardless of the person carrying out those operations.'[86] The Court further stressed that the 'objective of safeguarding national security […] has not yet been specifically examined by the Court in its judgments interpreting Directive 2002/58' and that

> Article 4(2) TEU provides that national security remains the sole responsibility of each Member State. That responsibility corresponds to the primary interest in protecting the essential functions of the State and the fundamental interests of society and encompasses the prevention and punishment of activities capable of seriously destabilising the fundamental constitutional, political, economic or social structures of a country and, in particular, of directly threatening society, the population or the State itself, such as terrorist activities.[87]

Such threats 'can be distinguished, by their nature and particular seriousness, from the general risk that tensions or disturbances, even of a serious nature, affecting public security will arise.'[88] As *Cameron* argues,

> in these judgments the Court has left very little outside the scope of EU law (and its own jurisdiction). […] it considers that as soon as a national legislature enacts powers requiring natural or legal persons to cooperate with national security agencies in some way, and such an obligation in some way involves a limitation of a natural or legal person's rights under primary or secondary EU law, then the exclusion in Article 4(2) TEU does not apply. This seems clearly at odds with the text of the provision.[89]

Cameron also points out that while determining the intentions of Treaty framers is often difficult, 'it is hardly contentious to say that the number of Member States intervening in the case, and their arguments, show a broad level of resistance to the policy outcome which the Court has now imposed.'[90] It is evident that, unlike in the various fields discussed in the above, in this case the legislature specifically aimed at limiting the scope of the legislation with a view to leaving certain matters to the national domain. Therefore, *Cameron* continues, while it is one thing to be concerned about the

---

[84] ECJ 6.10.2020 – Case C-511/18, ECLI:EU:C:2020:791 – *La Quadrature du Net and Others v Premier ministre and Others.*

[85] The same question was also at the forefront of Case C-623/17 *privacy international* and resolved in the same way. See ECJ 6.10.2020 – case C-623/17, ECLI:EU:C:2020:790 – *Privacy International v Secretary of State for Foreign and Commonwealth Affairs and Others.*

[86] ECJ 6.10.2020 – Case C-511/18, ECLI:EU:C:2020:791 para. 101 – *La Quadrature du Net and Others v Premier ministre and Others.*

[87] ibid., para. 134 et seq.

[88] ibid.

[89] Cameron, Common Market Law Review 2021, 1433 (1458).

[90] ibid.

risk of States abusing national security concerns, 'whether or not the result is seen as a good thing is a separate issue from the question of how this result has been achieved.'[91]

IV. Common foreign and security policy

Finally, the EU Treaties include a number of provisions on common foreign and security policy, even though they have been long treated as a rather theoretical piece in the overall puzzle of the Union's external role.[92] Yet, under these provisions, the 'Union's competence in matters of common foreign and security policy shall cover all areas of foreign policy and *all questions relating to the Union's security*, including the progressive framing of a common defence policy that might lead to a common defence' (Art. 24(1) TEU; emphasis added). Art. 42(2) TEU is even more specific: It establishes that the 'common security and defence policy shall include the progressive framing of a common Union defence policy. This will lead to a common defence, when the European Council, acting unanimously, so decides.' In addition to making reference the 'specific character of the security and defence policy of certain Member States' and the NATO obligations of other States, the Article largely refers to Member States' civilian and military capacities and their obligation to progressively improve their military capabilities. 43

The provision includes a commitment to progress in the direction of common defence, even though its exact structure and timing is left open. The provision would enable a significant development of Union operational and institutional capacity, which would enter into force without Treaty reform, after approval by the Member States in accordance with their constitutional requirements. The Treaties thus provide a clear legal basis for more independent EU defence policy. Yet, no decision by the European Council is in sight. The debate about exercising this EU competence is not legal but (security) political, as any development by the EU towards such capacity has been opposed by NATO and its members. However, the war in Ukraine heightens the awareness of the need for military tools and coordination. The Common Foreign and Security Policy (CFSP) thus remains underdeveloped. Finally, Art. 42(7) TEU includes a mutual assistance clause to be activated in case a Member State is the victim of armed aggression on its territory. It mirrors the uneven degrees of integration within the Union: Military assistance or collective defence is left to an inter-state level, so far without assigning specific procedures or a role to the EU institutions. The physical security of the Member States' territory is also a matter of common interest. 44

The Treaties leave the relationship between the CFSP and national defence policy largely undefined. Under Art. 2(4) TFEU, '[t]he Union shall have competence, in accordance with the provisions of the Treaty on European Union, to define and implement a common foreign and security policy, including the progressive framing of a common defence policy.' This provision is separate from the general provisions on EU exclusive, shared and supportive competence. Thus, what the effect of a European Council decision on shifting to common defence on national competence would be is not defined, as this is not an area of exclusive or shared competence. 45

Art. 40 TEU further underlines that the implementation of the CFSP 'shall not affect the application of the procedures and the extent of the powers of the institutions laid down by the Treaties for the exercise of the Union competences' referred to in Art. 3–6 46

---

[91] ibid.

[92] See Leino-Sandberg/Ojanen, 'Time for Military Integration in the EU? Armed aggression and the scope of Article 42 TEU' (Verfassungsblog, 3.3.2022) <https://verfassungsblog.de/time-for-military-integration-in-the-eu/> (last accessed: 26.9.2023).

TFEU, nor does implementation of these Articles 'affect the application of the procedures and the extent of the powers of the institutions laid down by the Treaties for the exercise of the Union competences under this Chapter.' As a result, there is little institutional and judicial practice relating to these provisions. After all, under the second subparagraph of Art. 24(1) TEU, the CFSP is 'subject to specific rules and procedures'. The atypical role of the Commission is 'defined by the Treaties', and the European Court of Justice 'shall not have jurisdiction with respect to these provisions', with certain limited exceptions. This means that there are no infringement actions or jurisprudence on these provisions and their effect on Member State action specifically.

47 The case law discussed above suggested that the organization of military forces and national defence has been one of the few cases where the Court has actually occasionally accepted Member States' justifications for diverging from horizontally applicable EU legislation. This area also provides the only example where Art. 4(2) TEU has been successfully used by a Member State, namely in a Grand Chamber ruling involving working time in armed forces in the context of Directive 2003/88.[93] The national court wondered whether the Directive applies to 'workers employed in the defence sector and to military personnel who perform guard duty in peacetime' and whether 'it precludes legislation that enables the time spent by defence sector workers at a place other than their home on stand-by, and time when military personnel performs guard duty in barracks but not actually working not to be counted as their "working time"'. The French and Spanish governments stressed that EU law does not govern the organization of the working time of military personnel on the ground that that organization falls within the organizational arrangements of the armed forces of the Member States, which, under Art. 4(2) of the TEU, are excluded from the scope of that legislation.

48 The Court pointed out that the principal tasks of the armed forces of the Member States are the preservation of territorial integrity and safeguarding of national security, which are expressly included in the essential functions of the State under Art. 4(2) of the TEU. Previous case law establishes that Member States' choices of military organization for the defence of their territory or of their essential interests are not, as such, governed by EU law. However, decisions on the organization of their armed forces do not fall entirely outside the scope of EU law, in particular where the rules at issue relate to the organization of working time, as even measures taken to protect national security must comply with EU law. This also applies to national measures adopted for the protection of the territorial integrity of a Member State. The harmonized rules on working time do not 'prevent the armed forces from fulfilling their tasks and, consequently, so as adversely to affect the essential functions of the State, namely the preservation of its territorial integrity and the safeguarding of national security.'[94] Therefore,

> [i]t follows that the *specific features which each Member State imposes on the functioning of its armed forces must be duly taken into consideration by EU law, whether those specific features result, inter alia, from the particular international responsibilities assumed by that Member State, from the conflicts or threats with which it is confronted, or from the geopolitical context in which that State evolves.* The application of the provisions of EU law and, specifically, those relating to the organisation of working time must not prevent the performance *of the specific tasks which each Member State entrusts, in the light of its own constraints and responsibilities, to its armed forces with a view to preserving its territorial integrity or safeguarding its national security.*[95]

[93] ECJ 15.7.2021 – case C-742/19, ECLI:EU:C:2021:597 – *B. K. v Republika Slovenija (Ministrstvo za obrambo).*

[94] ibid., para. 43.

[95] ibid., para. 43 et seq. (emphasis added).

However, the Court pointed out that Directive 89/391/EEC provides specific exceptions that relate to certain specific public service activities, such as the armed forces. For the Court,

> in order to ensure the operational efficiency of the armed forces, it must be possible to expose military personnel, during their initial and operational training, to situations which reproduce as accurately as possible the conditions, including the most extreme of conditions, in which actual military operations take place. [...]The armed forces must be entirely able to carry out the tasks which they undertake in order to preserve national security and territorial integrity, including during peacetime. It should be added that *it is the exclusive responsibility of each of the Member States [...] to carry out the military operations which it considers appropriate and to determine the intensity of the initial and operational training which it deems necessary for the proper performance of those operations, without any review by the Court being possible in that regard, since such questions must be regarded as falling outside the scope of EU law.*[96]

As a result, the ECJ accepted that a number of security activities performed by a member of military personnel could be excluded from the scope of that Directive.

D. 'No other choice'

Based on the above analysis, the core function of the final sentence of Art. 4(2) TEU as read by the EU institutions may in fact be close to what the Treaty drafters had in mind. While referring to 'national security' in rather broad terms, the ideas behind the provision were more confined to questions involving territory and choices relevant for national defence – in a narrow sense, as, for example, purchases that are relevant for serving those purposes are excluded, as the jurisprudence on Art. 346 TFEU suggests. The organization of defence forces seems to be the only question that the Court has recognized as falling outside the scope of EU law. Legislative action by the EU legislature has often fed into such an outcome, as EU legislation has been used to accommodate Art. 4(2) TEU-related concerns instead of excluding such questions from the scope of EU legislative agendas. By doing so, the EU legislature has laid down an institutional and legislative framework for observing the requirements of Art. 4(2) TEU. In the rare cases where it has attempted to leave such questions outside the scope of EU legislation, the solution has been subsequently rejected by the Court. In areas regulated by the EU, national security considerations are primarily accommodated by the EU legislature. With every exception comes the risk of misuse, which the Court generally counters by adopting the approach of *'no other choice'*, and it has generally been difficult to convince of the lack of alternatives to autonomous national actions. **49**

Therefore, while some more sensitive areas exist, Member States are never free to operate quite as they please, but they act within a frame established by EU law, under the supervision of EU institutions, which have the right to approve or reject national measures. *Koen Lenaerts* argued back in 1990 that the EU may exercise its specific, implied or non-specific powers in the fullest way possible without running into any inherent limitation of these powers as a result of the sovereignty of Member States.[97] This has not changed. **50**

The above analysis of case law demonstrates how Art. 4(2) TEU – based arguments hardly ever work as a trump card but simply enable a Member State to argue and justify a measure – subject to approval by the EU institutions. Such measures require **51**

[96] para. 81–84 (emphasis added).
[97] Lenaerts, AJCL 1990, 205 (220).

convincing reasoning that demonstrates that discretion has not been misused. These situations often witness a tension between a larger group of Member States that then get beaten in the European Court of Justice. Yet, the competence of the EU legislature to engage in legislative activities in this field has seldom been challenged, and when it has, the ECJ has not been favourable to arguments defending Member State sovereignty. This pattern is familiar from other areas of EU law, and it is not without its problems. *Lindseth* reminds us of the need to ask 'legitimate for what?', referring to a link between the nature of a legal or political order and the scope of power that it can successfully exercise. The potential of the EU in this respect remains highly limited when compared with 'the socio-political and socio-cultural demos-based legitimacy that supports compulsory mobilization powers in national constitutional law.'[98]

52 There may be more room for independent Member State measures in the case of genuine and more existential threats to national security – but it is difficult to think of cases where this room could so far have been legitimately claimed. In such a case, it is conceivable that both the legal and political framework would be read as allowing a Member State to react to a situation that threatens the State directly and acutely through defence, with a view to protecting territorial integrity. In these questions, the EU has so far claimed a modest role – but could of course develop it further, since the EU Treaties provide for far-reaching competence to deepen and even replace national defence policies by EU policy. In cases of existential threat, a question of national security would also likely have a dimension of Union security. But even this is not a 'non-integrable core area of national security' as the title of this contribution suggests.

---

[98] Lindseth, ELJ 2016, 696 (709).

§ 9
Sovereigns in chains? Art. 4(2) sent. 3 TEU and EU law constraints on the use of AI in national security contexts*

Johannes Buchheim

Bibliography: Abiri, 'Moderating from Nowhere', BYU L. Rev. 2022 (47), 757; Anders, 'Europäische Integration als Ausdruck einer Strategie zur Ausweitung exekutiver Handlungsspielräume?', ZPol 2018 (28), 343; Azoulai, 'The Complex Weave of Harmonization' in Arnull/Chalmers (eds), The Oxford Handbook of European Union Law, Oxford 2015, p. 589; Benn, 'The Uses of Sovereignty' Political Studies 1955 (3), 109; Benrath, Die Konkretisierung von Loyalitätspflichten, Tübingen 2019; von Bogdandy/Bast, 'The Federal Order of Competences' in von Bogdandy/Bast, Principles of European Constitutional Law, 2nd edn, Oxford/Munich/Baden-Baden 2010, p. 275; von Bogdandy/Hering, 'Die Informationsbeziehungen im europäischen Verwaltungsverbund' in Voßkuhle/Eifert/Möllers (eds), Gundlagen des Verwaltungsrechts I, Munich 2022, p. 1799; Botta, 'Die Förderung Innovativer KI-Systeme in der EU zum Kommissionsvorschlag der KI-Reallabore', ZfDR 2022, 391; Bumke/Voßkuhle, German Constitutional Law, Oxford 2019; Calliess/Ruffert (eds), EUV/AEUV – Das Verfassungsrecht der Europäischen Union mit Europäischer Grundrechtecharta, 6th edn, Munich 2022; Cohen, 'Regulating Manipulative Artificial Intelligence', Journal of Law, Technology and Society 2023 (20), 203; Craig/de Búrca, EU Law – Text, Cases, and Materials, 7th edn, Oxford 2020; Dieter, 'The new raison d'état as a problem for democracy in world society', Eur. J. Int. Relat. 1999 (5), 333; Djeffal, 'The Normative Potential of the European Rule on Automated Decisions: A New Reading for Art. 22 GDPR', ZaöRV 2020 (80), 847; Ebers/Hoch/Rosenkranz/Ruschemeier/Steinrötter, 'The European Commission's Proposal for an Artificial Intelligence Act – A Critical Assessment by Members of the Robotics and AI Law Society (RAILS)', J 2021 (4) 589; Egbert/Krasmann 'Predictive policing: not yet, but soon preemptive?', Policing and Society 2020 (30), 905; Fabbrini, 'The Principle of Subsidiarity' in Schütze/Tridimas (eds), Oxford Principles of European Union Law I, Oxford 2018, p. 221; Galetta/Hofmann/Schneider 'Information Exchange in the European Administrative Union: An Introduction', EPL 2014 (20), 65; Geiger/Khan/Kotzur (eds), European Union Treaties, Portland/Munich 2014; Gerstner, 'Predictive Policing to Prevent Residential Burglary – Findings from the Pilot Project P4 in Baden-Württemberg, Germany', Eur. J. Secur. Res. 2019 (3), 115; Guastaferro, 'Sincere Cooperation and Respect for National Identities' in Schütze/Tridimas (eds), Oxford Principles of European Union Law I, Oxford 2018, p. 350; Hills, 'Against Preemption: How Federalism Can Improve the National Legislative Process', N.Y.U. L. Rev. 2007 (82), 1; Höffler/Meyer/Möller, 'Risk-Assessment–the Key to More Security? Factors, Tools, and Practices in Dealing with Extremist Individuals', Eur. J. Crim. Policy Res. 2022 (28), 269; Isensee, Das Volk als Grund der Verfassung, Opladen 1995; Kahn, Sovereignty – Four New Chapters on the Concept of Sovereignty, New York 2012; Karpenstein/Sangi, 'Nationale Sicherheit im Unionsrecht: Zur Bedeutung von Art. 4 II 3 EUV', GSZ 2020, 162; Klamert, The Principle of Loyalty in EU Law, Oxford 2014; Korzenov, 'The New Format of the *Acte Claire* Doctrine and its Consequences', Common Market Law Review 2016 (53), 1317; Kramer, 'Understanding Federalism', Va. L. Rev. 1994 (47), 1485; Krommendjik, National Courts and Preliminary References to the Court of Justice, Cheltenham 2021; Kuner/Bygrave/Docksey (eds), The EU General Data Protection Regulation (GDPR) – A Commentary, Oxford 2020; Kühling/Buchner, DS-GVO/BDSG Kommentar, 3rd edn, Munich 2020; Lenaerts, 'Constitutionalism and the Many Faces of Federalism', AJCL 1990 (38), 205; Lenartes/Maselis/Gutman, EU Procedural Law, Oxford 2014; von Lewinski, 'Europäisierung des Datenschutzrechts', DuD 2012 (36), 564; Lisken/Denninger, Handbuch des Polizeirechts, 7th edn, Munich 2021; Mahler, 'Between risk management and proportionality: The risk-based approach in the EU's Artificial Intelligence Act Proposal' in Colona/Greenstein (eds), Nordic Yearbook of Law and Informatics 2020-2021. Law in the Era of Artificial Intelligence, Sweden 2021, p. 247; Marsch, 'Artificial Intelligence and the Fundamental Right to Data Protection' in Wischmeyer/Rademacher (eds), Regulating Artificial Intelligence,

* I very much thank *Jannik Kellermann, Yohanna Villablanca, Milad Schubart* and *Nele Sprunk* for their valuable comments, research and their support in formally editing and finalising this article.

Heidelberg/New York/Dordrecht/London 2020, p. 33; Masing, 'Verfassung im internationalen Mehrebenensystem' in Herdegen/Masing/Poscher/Gärditz (eds), Handbuch des Verfassungsrechts, Munich 2021, p. 61; Mendoza/Bygrave, 'The Right not to be Subject to Automated Decisions based on Profiling', University of Oslo Faculty of Law Research Paper 2017 (20), 1; Mitsilegas/Guild/Kuskonmaz/Vavoula, 'Data retention and the future of large-scale surveillance: The evolution and contestation of judicial benchmarks', ELJ 2022, 1; Nettesheim, 'Kompetenzen' in von Bogdandy/Bast, Europäisches Verfassungsrecht, 2nd edn, Berlin/Heidelberg 2009, p. 389; Nettesheim, 'Kompetenzkonflikte zwischen EuGH und Mitgliedsstaaten', ZRP 2021, 222; Nguyen, 'Die Subsidiaritätsrüge des Deutschen Bundesrates gegen den Vorschlag der EU-Kommission für eine Datenschutz-Grundverordnung', ZEuS 2012, 277; Ortlep and Verhoeven, 'The principle of primacy versus the principle of national procedural autonomy', NALL 2012, 1; Pechstein/Nowak/Häde (eds), Frankfurter Kommentar zu EUV, GRC und AEUV I, Tübingen 2017; Peers/Hervey/Kenner/Ward (eds), The EU Charter of Fundamental Rights, 1st edn, Oxford/Munich/Baden-Baden 2014; Peuker/Ruffert, Inhalte und Grenzen unionsrechtlicher Regelungskompetenzen im Bereich nationaler Sicherheit, 2023, Gutachten für das Bundesministerium des Inneren und für Heimat, (manuscript on file with author); Rademacher, Realakte im Rechtsschutzsystem der Europäischen Union, Tübingen 2014; Rademacher, 'Artificial Intelligence and Law Enforcement' in Wischmeyer/Rademacher (eds), Regulating Artificial Intelligence, Heidelberg/New York/Dordrecht/London 2020, p. 225; Raposo, 'Ex machina: preliminary critical assessment of the European Draft Act on artificial intelligence', Int. J. Law Inf. Technol. 2022 (30), 88; Schmitt, Political Theology – Four Chapters on the Concept of Sovereignty, transl. by Georg Schwab, Chicago 2005; Schneider, 'Stand und Perspektiven des Europäischen Datenverkehrs- und Datenschutzrechts', Die Verwaltung 2011, 499; Schneider, 'Informationssysteme als Bausteine des Europäischen Verwaltungsverbunds', NVwZ 2012, 65; Schneider, 'Information exchange and its problems' in Harlow/Leino/della Cananea (eds), Research Handbook on EU Administrative Law, UK 2017; Schneider, Die Durchsetzung von Normenkontrollentscheidungen, Tübingen 2022; Schoch/Schneider (eds.), Verwaltungsrecht, Munich 2022; Schulze, Verschränkung von europäischem Verordnungsrecht und nationalen Normen, Tübingen 2022; Schütze, From dual to cooperative federalism: the changing structure of European law, Oxford 2009; Schütze, 'EU Competences: Existence and Exercise' in Arnull/Chalmers (eds), The Oxford Handbook of European Union Law, Oxford 2015, p. 75; Slaughter, 'Global Government Networks, Global Information Agencies, and Disaggregated Democracy', MJIL2003 (24), 1041; Sommerer, Self-imposed Algorithmic Thoughtlessness and the Automation of Crime Control, Baden-Baden 2022; Sonka/Meier/Rossegger/Endrass/Profes/Witt/Sadowski, 'RADAR-iTE 2.0: Ein Instrument des polizeilichen Staatsschutzes', Kriminalistik 2020 (6), 386; Spiecker gen. Döhmann/Eisenbarth, 'Kommt das "Volkszählungsurteil" nun durch den EuGH? – Der Europäische Datenschutz nach Inkrafttreten des Vertrags von Lissabon', JZ 2011, 169; Stone Sweet/Brunell, 'The European Court and the national courts: a statistical analysis of preliminary references, 1961–95', JEEP 1998 (5), 66; Sydow/Marsch, DS-GVO/BDSG Handkommentar, 3rd edn, Baden-Baden 2022; Szpunar, 'Procedural Autonomy and Private Law', ZEuP 2018, 1; Tomada, 'Start-ups and the Proposed EU AI Act: Bridges or Barriers in the path from Invention to Innovation?', J. Intellect. Prop. Inf. Technol. E-Commer. Law 2022 (13), 53; Tridimas, 'The Principle of Proportionality' in Schütze/Tridimas (eds), Oxford Principles of European Union Law I, Oxford 2018, p. 243; Trute, 'Die demokratische Legitimation der Verwaltung' in Voßkuhle/Eifert/Möllers (eds), Grundlagen des Verwaltungsrechts, Munich 2022, p. 551; White, 'Constitutionalizing the EU in an Age of Emergencies', JCMS 2023 (61), 781; de Witte, 'Non-market values in internal market legislation' in Shuibhne (eds), Regulating the Internal Market, Cheltenham,/Northampton 2006, p. 61; Wolff/Brink/v. Ungern-Sternberg, BeckOK Datenschutzrecht, 44th edn, Munich 2023; Zarza, Exchange of Information and Data Protection in Cross-border Criminal Proceedings in Europe, Heidelberg/New York/Dordrecht/London 2015.

A. Giving content to Member States' national security reserve

1 Almost 15 years after the entry into force of the Lisbon Treaty, the meaning and content of Art. 4(2) sent. 3 TEU remain largely unchartered territory.[1] This may well have something to do with the provision having been prompted by Member States'

[1] For rare exceptions prior to writing, see Karpenstein/Sangi, GSZ 2020, 162; ECJ 6.10.2020 – case C-151/73, ECLI:EU:C:2020:791 para. 135 – *La Quadrature du Net and Others v. Premier minstre and Others.*

sovereignty concerns,[2] since the demands of sovereignty are notoriously elusive and disputed.[3] To shed more light on the issue, it may help to leave this abstract question aside for a moment and turn to the more concrete.

In the following, I discuss the Union law boundaries imposed on Member State policy and action concerning the use of artificial intelligence (AI) by their security agencies. After getting a sharper picture of the restrictions EU law imposes on Member States' AI-related toolkits and security policies, we will be able to judge more reliably whether and to what extent it conflicts with Member States' 'sole responsibility' for national security. 2

B. Art. 4(2) sent. 3 TEU in a nutshell: overlapping powers, duties to coordinate, instruments of coordination

Before taking this inductive approach, I must begin by roughly sketching out my (preliminary) understanding of the meaning, function and legal requirements that derive from Art. 4(2) sent. 3 TEU. 3

I. Art. 4(2) sent. 3 TEU in the context of the treaties' conception of competitive federalism

In my opinion, the origin of the provision, the regulatory context and its wording argue against an understanding that establishes exclusive competence to regulate the specific subject matter or field of 'national security' in which only one authority – in this case the respective Member State – may act. 4

1. General functioning of Union competences

Such an understanding of the order of competences as a system of mutually exclusive spheres of regulation, which, wherever possible, do not overlap, does not generally correspond to the way in which competence titles function in EU law.[4] Instead, EU law requires a sufficient basis for Union action in one of the regulatory titles listed in the Treaties. Based on those competence titles, EU action can often have regulatory effects on the same subjects and areas of life that Member States also regulate. The two competing claims to competence then need to be reconciled on the basis of the rules set out in the Treaties. 5

If this were any different, many titles of EU competence, such as those relating to data protection and internal market regulation, would make no sense at all. That is 6

[2] The UK government pushed for the adoption of Art. 4(2) sent. 3 TEU; see, e.g., Peuker/Ruffert, p. 34 (manuscript on file with author). Art. 4(2) sent. 3 TEU has been characterized as a new attempt to create a robust guarantee of Member State powers in the domain of national security; see Schütze in Arnull/Chalmers, The Oxford Handbook of European Union Law, p. 81 et seqq.

[3] See, notoriously, Schmitt, p. 1 et seqq; for a critical appraisal of Schmitt's obscure and inscrutable text, see Kahn, p. 1; see also Benn, Political Studies 1955, 109 (122): 'there would seem to be a strong case for giving up so Protean a word.' Similarly, the use of popular sovereignty as a legal standard has been described by Isensee, p. 73 as a fairytale for lawyers (*'Klapperstorchmärchen für Volljuristen'*).

[4] This certainly holds for shared competences. The Member States are only pre-empted to the extent that the EU has decided to exercise its competence. On the limited extent of pre-emption in shared competences, see Craig/de Búrca, p. 114 et seq.

because regulating these issues will inevitably affect countless areas of law, politics and life on a cross-sectional basis.[5] Therefore, the competence rules and practices set out in the Treaties stay close to the political origins of any federal division of competences in conflicts between several actors who compete for (regulatory) powers. Of course, this way of conceptualising and operationalising the federal division of powers is dependent on moderation as well as mutual restraint and respect in the exercise of structurally overlapping powers.[6] Consequently, the moderating principles of proportionality and subsidiarity[7] are clear evidence of the Treaties' leaning towards an understanding of the federal division of powers that focuses on mutual coordination rather than on the sharp delineation of regulatory powers.[8]

2. Specific reasons that support this reading of Art. 4(2) sent. 3 TEU

7 This general understanding of the division of EU regulatory powers is confirmed by the specific context of Art. 4(2) sent. 3 TEU. Its close textual connection to the principle of loyal cooperation (Art. 4(3) TEU)[9] speaks to understanding Art. 4(2) sent. 3 TEU as a rule on how to coordinate and harmonize overlapping competences, not as a rule that constitutes a reserved and completely separate area or sphere of regulation.[10] The same results from the systematic connection to the other content of Art. 4 TEU: The provision sets the ground rules and lays the foundations for the relationship between the EU and Member States, but it does not enumerate and demarcate concrete regulatory spheres and powers on both sides. The concrete regulatory competences of the EU – and some specific domains that are reserved to the Member States (e.g. securing their energy supply (Art. 194(2) TFEU)) – are set out in various provisions throughout the TFEU. Delineating and enumerating concrete powers in a directly operational way is not the function of the TEU, which only establishes general principles and institutions. Finally, the wording of Art. 4(2) sent. 3 TEU also speaks

---

[5] The EU's competence as regards harmonising the internal market has been defined very broadly and has often been used to achieve non-market goals; see Azoulai in Arnull/Chalmers, The Oxford Handbook of European Union Law, p. 602; see, generally, regarding non-economic objectives being pursued based on the EU internal market competences, de Witte in Shuibhne, Regulating the Internal Market, p. 61.

[6] For an extensive account of this reading of EU federalism, see Schütze, p. 1 et seqq. Strictly delineating spheres of legislation is a dualist approach that one can find in US and German constitutional law. Even in the United States, the dual federalism approach is not uncontested; see, e.g., Hills, N.Y.U. L. Rev. 2007, 1. As regards the EU, it has been argued that a clear division of competences is not feasible (Nettesheim in Bogdandy/Bast, Europäisches Verfassungsrecht, p. 400).

[7] See, e.g., Craig/de Búrca, p. 125 et seqq.; Fabbrini in Schütze/Tridimas, Oxford Principles of European Union Law I, p. 221; Tridimas in Schütze/Tridimas, Oxford Principles of European Union Law I, p. 243.

[8] Schütze, p. 241 et seqq.

[9] On the principle of loyal cooperation, see Klamert, p. 1 et seqq.; Benrath, esp. p. 129 et seqq.; this principle presupposes overlap and cooperation, not sharp delineation and separation. In this respect, the principle of loyalty is similar to the principle of good faith in international law and to federal fidelity in federal states or unitary regional states; see Guastaferro in Schütze/Tridimas, Oxford Principles of European Union Law I, p. 351, 359 et seqq.

[10] Whether sole responsibility for national security is an independent feature or just an annex to and aspect of respect for national identities in Art. 4(2) TEU is a disputed matter; see Calliess in Calliess/Ruffert, EUV Art. 4 mn. 40. In any case, Art. 4(2) TEU calls for respect for the Member States and their fundamental features, which ultimately means that the EU cannot encroach disproportionately on them; see Franzius in Pechstein/Nowak/Häde, EUV Art. 4 mn. 55. Consequently, in its jurisprudence on national identity, the ECJ has not determined what encompasses national identity but treats the claims on a case-by-case basis. It attempts to harmonise conflicting interests by reviewing whether a Member State can substantiate its claim of national identity (see, e.g., ECJ 22.12.2010 – case C-208/09, ECLI:EU:C:2010:806 para. 81 et seqq. – *Sayn-Wittgenstein v. Landeshauptmann von Wien*, in which the Court holds that the abolition of nobility is part of the Austrian national identity that is a justifiable obstacle to freedom of movement).

against understanding it as a true competence reserve, i.e. as a substantive area or 'sphere' that is to be completely exempt from EU intervention. The term 'competence' is not used in the provision, rather Member States are said to have 'sole responsibility' for national security. The fact that Member States bear this responsibility 'alone' does not necessarily mean that only they may lay down rules that may in some situations also affect the task of ensuring national security.

In view of this, I do not think there are any good reasons to regard Art. 4(2) sent. 3 TEU as an exception to the general functioning of competing and overlapping competences under the Treaties.[11] On the contrary, it is more appropriate to understand the provision in line with its position in the Treaties (the TEU, not the TFEU; general coordination rules, not enumeration of concrete regulatory powers) as well as with the general logic according to which the Treaties imagine and operationalize the federal division of powers. 8

II. Functions and normative demands of Art. 4(2) sent. 3 TEU

According to this interpretation, Art. 4(2) sent. 3 TEU is primarily a rule that addresses moments and institutions of lawmaking and the political negotiation processes involved in that.[12] Acknowledging the Member States' sole responsibility for their national security functions as an additional political asset. Member States can and should use this asset against EU regulatory projects that are within the general purview of EU competences but which are deemed to be too far-reaching. Moreover, Member States can invoke the provision to better shield their own national security measures from Union challenges. For example, Art. 4(2) sent. 3 TEU may provide a reason, based in EU primary law, not to problematize certain national policies for being incompatible with EU law, to interpret Union law in a way that respects Member State sovereignty in the field of national security[13] or to refrain from initiating infringement proceedings (Art. 258 et seq. TFEU).[14] Member States may invoke this reason at all stages of the legislative process and whenever EU law is being applied and put into action. This way of using and invoking Art. 4(2) sent. 3 TEU is standard procedure, as seen, for example, in each of the referral decisions leading up to the judgment of the Court of Justice of the European Union (CJEU) in the *Quadrature du Net* case.[15] Given this universal applicability in the processes of forming and applying EU law, Art. 4(2) sent. 3 TEU to some extent counterbalances an inbuilt centripetal tendency of the EU federal division of 9

[11] For the contrary view that interprets Art. 4(2) sent. 3 TEU as constituting and delineating a sphere of exclusive Member State competence, see Peuker/Ruffert, p. 35 (manuscript on file with author); Karpenstein/Sangi. GSZ 2020, 162 (164).

[12] For a similar interpretation of Art. 4(2) sent. 3 TEU → 8.

[13] Peuker and Ruffert stress that Art. 4(2) sent. 3 TEU is a rule that guides legal interpretation in national security contexts; see Peuker/Ruffert, p. 52 (manuscript on file with author); Karpenstein/Sangi. GSZ 2020, 162 (166).

[14] For the Treaties' infringement proceedings, see Lenaerts et al., p. 159 et seqq.; the political element and large room for manoeuvre when it comes to implementing these proceedings are illustrated in Schneider, p. 54 et seqq.; this political dimension of infringement proceedings became particularly clear after the German Federal Constitutional Court's PSPP decision, BVerfG 5.5.2020 – 2 BvR 859/15, NJW 2020, 1647. The European Commission chose to initiate, but not go through with, the proceedings (see European Commission <https://ec.europa.eu/commission/presscorner/detail/en/inf_21_6201> (last accessed: 18.9.2023)), which has been acknowledged as a sound decision to resolve the issue in the political arena; see Nettesheim, ZRP 2021, 222 (224).

[15] Conseil d'État 26.7.2018 – case no. 393099, ECLI:FR:CECHR:2018:393099.20180726, para. 6; *Privacy International v. Secretary of State for Foreign and Commonwealth Affairs* [2017] IPT/15/110/CH, para. 4.

powers. This tendency arises in many federations on account of the fact that the federal level can regularly refer to a list of enumerated powers, while the Member States can only claim the unspecified 'remainder' for themselves.[16] Titles explicitly reserved to the Member States may thus help to re-establish balance in the competition between opposing or overlapping regulatory pretensions.

10 In addition to these effects on the making and application of EU law, Art. 4(2) sent. 3 TEU establishes a legal duty of consideration on the part of the Union when exercising its competences. In accordance with Art. 4(2) sent. 3 TEU, the EU is required to exercise its regulatory powers in such a way that Member States can still fulfil their responsibility to guarantee national security. This legal obligation is, of course, limited in terms of its justiciability. However, the same is true of other legal duties of consideration and respect – such as the principle of loyal cooperation (Art. 4(3) TEU) [17] and the German principle of federal loyalty.[18] Violation of such duties of respect cannot be determined in the abstract based on given EU rules or activity alone. Instead, the possibility that a violation may have occurred only arises against the background of concrete regulatory projects and other measures[19] that a given Member State regards as central to guaranteeing its national security. This results in the strong proceduralization and situational dependence of the standard established by Art. 4(2) sent. 3 TEU.[20] Moreover, the content of this legal standard is so limited and specific that it will hardly ever be successfully invoked.[21]

III. Instruments for managing competence overlap: the example of the GDPR

11 Given this limited role as a legal standard that is operational in its own right, it seems more interesting to analyse the role and functioning of Art. 4(2) sent. 3 TEU under normal circumstances. Rather than looking at its immediate legal effects in the theoretical case of mutual incompatibility, I would like to take a closer look at the moderating techniques and strategies by which EU secondary law tries to avoid and reduce in practice the power conflict that is inherent in the provision. To that end, I will first illustrate these instruments of moderation using the example of the EU General Data Protection Regulation (GDPR). Based on this example, I will consider

[16] Kramer, Va. L. Rev 1994, 1485 (1488): 'The Court tells us, for example, that states are protected by the limitation of federal powers to those enumerated in Art. I, stunningly ignoring that the practical effect has been all but obliterated in the years since the New Deal.'

[17] Klamert, p. 1 et seqq.; Benrath, esp. p. 129 et seqq.; Guastaferro in Schütze/Tridimas, Oxford Principles of European Union Law I, p. 351, 359 et seqq.

[18] The principle of federal loyalty obligates the German federal states and the federation to execute their competences in a federalism-friendly manner. It creates no self-standing obligations, but has an accessory character that moderates the exercise of existing rights and powers; for the relevant case law, see Bumke/Voßkuhle, p. 341 et seqq.

[19] For this perspective, which does not focus on the duty, but on the instances of its breach, see Benrath, p. 283 et seqq.

[20] The Treaties reference the Member States' security concerns multiple times. The case law of the CJEU is quite clear in that security exemptions, such as Art. 36, 45, 52, 65, 72, 346 and 347 TFEU require more than simply invoking security concerns. The Member States have the burden of proof; ECJ 2.4.2020 – case C-715/17 (joined with C-718/17 and C-719/17), ECLI:EU:C:2020:257 para. 43–147 – *Commission v. Poland*. This procedural approach could be adopted in Art. 4(2) sent. 3 TEU, see Peuker/Ruffert, p. 49 (manuscript on file with author).

[21] For a more categorical approach (though before the Treaties of Maastricht and Lisbon), see Lenaerts, AJCL 1990, 205 (220): 'The residual powers of the Member States have no reserved status. […] There simply is no nucleus of sovereignty that the Member States can invoke, as such, against the Community.'

how EU law uses these instruments in relation to Member States' AI practices in the context of national security.

1. Choice of instrument: regulation v directive

As a first instrument of moderation, EU law can deflate conflicts of competence by **12**
choosing between directives and regulations as regulatory instruments (Art. 288 TFEU). If the EU restricts itself to a directive,[22] this already rules out many serious conflicts between EU policy and design and Member States' national security reserve. The exemption of criminal prosecution and crime prevention from the scope of the GDPR (Art. 2(2)(d) GDPR)[23] must thus be understood as a means of respecting Member States' special claim to sovereignty in this field. This choice brings these issues under the more flexible regulatory framework of the JHA Directive,[24] thus deflating possible conflicts. Depending on which instrument is chosen, Member States keep considerable legislative latitude to adopt measures in line with their understanding of public interests, especially regarding national security.

2. Determining the scope of EU legislation (scope exceptions)

Carving out the scope of application of EU secondary legislation is another means of **13**
managing power conflicts. Art. 2(2)(a) and (b) GDPR is an example of this. It exempts from the GDPR activities outside the scope of Union law and within the framework of the EU Common Foreign and Security Policy.[25]

3. Opening clauses

Opening clauses in EU regulations are another instrument of moderation. For **14**
example, Art. 85 GDPR (media privilege) entrusts to national political processes the difficult task of reconciling journalistic freedom with general data protection and privacy interests.[26] In this way, the provision leaves room for Member State policies and political culture in relation to a crucial question that is no less important for and characteristic of their political identity[27] than the ways in which Member States understand and enforce their 'national security'.

---

[22] See Art. 288(3) TFEU; on the heuristic character of the choice of instrument for Member States' remaining legislative latitude, see BVerfG 6.11.2019 – 1 BvR 276/16, NJW 2020, 314 (315 para. 38).

[23] Regulation (EU) 2016/679 on the protection of natural persons with regard to the processing of personal data and on the free movement of such data, and repealing Directive 95/46/EC (General Data Protection Regulation), OJ L 119, 4.5.2016, 1.

[24] Directive (EU) 2017/541 on combating terrorism and replacing Council Framework Decision 2002/475/JHA and amending Council Decision 2005/671/JHA, OJ L 88, 31.3.2017, 6.

[25] See Recital 16 GDPR. The ECJ has found that the exceptions to the material scope of the GDPR in Art. 2(2)(a) and (b) and Recital 16 are partly a continuation of the former Directive 95/46, which had equally exempted from its scope Member State action outside the scope of Community law and operations concerning public security, defence and state security, ECJ 22.6.2021 – case C-439/19, ECLI:EU:C:2021:504 paras. 63–67 – *Latvijas Republikas Saeima*. On the adoption of this understanding, see OVG Münster 28.7.2021 – 16 B 1733/19, ZD 2022, 67 (67 para. 7), a ruling that states that security vetting is part of national security concerns and, therefore, falls under the scope exception in Art. 2(2)(a) GDPR.

[26] Kranenborg in Kuner/Bygrave/Docksey, GDPR Art. 85 mn. 1202 (1204): 'The reconciliation of the rights of privacy and data protection with the right to freedom of expression and to receive and impart information is a matter which the Union legislator has basically preferred to leave to Member States.'

[27] On the importance of speech norms to a political community and its identity, see Abiri, BYU L. Rev. 2022, 757. *Abiri* highlights the importance of social norms regulating speech in a political community. Prior to the Internet, the mass media were able to practically exclude most forms of hurtful speech from

4. Permissive standards

15 Another means of managing the conflict inherent in Art. 4(2) sent. 3 TEU is using techniques of permissive or generous EU standard-setting. There are EU regulations and policies whose regulatory content is so open-ended and permissive that it cannot seriously impair Member States' performance of their tasks. An example of this are the legal bases of the 'fulfilment of a legal obligation' (Art. 6(1)(c) GDPR) or the 'performance of public services' (Art. 6(1)(c), (2) and (3) GDPR) required to process personal data. This is because, in these cases, the substantive reasons for data processing are ultimately defined by the Member States.[28] By prompting the EU legislator to set permissive or delegatory standards such as these, the national security reserve in Art. 4 (2) sent. 3 TEU can become operational even within the scope of application of EU secondary legislation. This is the case wherever the EU law frameworks to be applied are such that the Member States retain sufficient options for action.

5. Enhancing national security policy

16 Last but not least, EU law can avoid conflicts in relation to Art. 4(2) sent. 3 TEU by reinforcing Member State policies and task fulfilment in the field of national security. In these cases, the thrust of EU activities coincides with the objectives of the national security reserve that the Member States claim. Due to such goal alignment, EU measures such as the EU Data Retention Directive[29] cannot come into conflict with Art. 4(2) sent. 3 TEU. Of course, some Member States might object to such 'enhancing' EU measures as overly intrusive and imbalanced in their pursuit of national security interests. However, the type of arguments levelled against such EU interventions would revolve around fundamental rights or other foundational normative commitments on the part of the Member States. Given the origins, context and current argumentative use of Art. 4(2) sent. 3 TEU, few people would cite the national security reserve as an argument *against* such security-affirming EU measures.[30]

C. The case of AI regulation: EU law constraints on Member States' use of AI in the context of national security policy

17 Against this background, let us look at the EU law pertaining to the Member States' development and use of AI systems in the context of national security. In my view, the relevant EU law meets the requirements to be derived from Art. 4(2) sent. 3 TEU. In a nuanced manner and through a mix of moderating instruments, EU secondary law

---

reaching a wide audience. *Abiri* is sceptical that global platforms can perform a similar function, since they are not rooted in a particular society and its speech norms (at 762–765).

[28] Kotschy in Kuner/Bygrave/Docksey, GDPR Art. 6 mn. 321 (340).

[29] Directive 2006/24/EC on the retention of data generated or processed in connection with the provision of publicly available electronic communications services or of public communications networks and amending Directive 2002/58/EC, OJ L 105, 13.4.2006, 54. The ECJ held that the Directive was invalid in ECJ 8.4.2014 – cases C-293/12 and C-594/12, ECLI:EU:C:2014:238 – *Digital Rights Ireland Ltd. v. Ireland.*

[30] This one-sided, security-centred interpretive practice is another argument against understanding Art. 4(2) sent. 3 TEU as constituting a sphere that is exempted from any kind of EU intervention: If this were so, the competence reserve would have to go both ways, i.e. would have to block both EU enhancement/support and restrictions on national security measures.

gives the Member States more than sufficient leeway in order for them to pursue and safeguard their national security using AI technology.

It should first be noted that EU law pertaining to the development, marketing and use of AI cannot be easily determined and certainly not derived from a single body of law. Instead, EU law requirements as regards AI development and use follow from a patchwork of different European legal acts. The applicable rules and restrictions differ in various scenarios and contexts in which AI is used. Nevertheless, I will hopefully provide at least general orientation with regard to national security contexts in the following. 18

I define AI broadly, as is the case in the draft AI Act that is currently facing its last step of the EU legislative process.[31] This definition, most importantly, includes deterministic algorithms.[32] At this point in time, such deterministic algorithms – rather than dynamic and opaque AI – are likely to be the predominant type of instruments being used in security agency practice – for example in the context of strategic telecommunications data analysis[33] or predictive policing (e.g. RADAR iTe[34]). 19

Based on this broad definition of AI, two areas of EU regulation are particularly relevant to the question of Member States' discretion and leeway in the development and use of AI: the EU's (general and specific) data protection law framework (i.), which functions as an indirect form of AI regulation,[35] and direct EU AI regulation (ii.), set out in the – soon to be finalized – EU AI Act.[36] 20

I. EU data protection law frameworks as indirect AI regulation

1. General data protection law: ample discretion in security matters

In the field of national security, the EU's general data protection framework creates a first layer of flexibility for Member States through *instrumental restraint*. It does so in part by choosing *a directive as its main legal instrument*, in part by altogether abstaining from setting data protection rules. For, regardless of how the term 'national 21

[31] See Art. 3(1) and Annex I, European Parliament legislative resolution of 13 March 2024 on the proposal for a regulation of the European Parliament and of the Council on laying down harmonised rules on Artificial Intelligence (Artificial Intelligence Act) and amending certain Union Legislative Acts (COM(2021)0206 – C9-0146/2021 – 2021/0106(COD)) (hereinafter: The European Parliament legislative resolution (2024)).

[32] Some scholars highlight problems that arise from this broad definition; see, e.g., Ebers et al. J 2021, 589 (590); Botta, ZfDR 2022, 391 (397).

[33] For an outline of these practices, see, e.g., ECtHR 25.5.2021 – App. Nos. 58170/13, 62322/14 and 24960/15, para. 341 et seq., *Big Brother Watch and Others v. The United Kingdom*.

[34] On practices of predictive policing in Germany, see Rademacher in Wischmeyer/Rademacher, Regulating Artificial Intelligence, p. 229; Gerstner, Eur. J. Secur. Res. 2019, 115; Sommerer, p. 1 et seqq.; on the specific instrument of RADAR-iTE, see Sonka et al., Kriminalistik 2020, 386; Lisken/Denninger, p. 1210 et seq.

[35] On the AI-regulating effect of data protection law, see Marsch in Wischmeyer/Rademacher, Regulating Artificial Intelligence, p. 33 mn. 5 et seq.: 'the conventional objective of the current data protection law is to rationalise data processing by only allowing the personal data to be processed on a statutory basis, for specified purposes and in a transparent manner. […] It is obvious that AI conflicts with this objective of data protection law'.

[36] European Commission, 'Proposal for a regulation laying down harmonised rules on artificial intelligence (artificial intelligence act) and amending certain union legislative acts', 21.4.2021, COM (2021) 206 final; Council of the European Union, 'Presidency options paper for the policy orientation debate on the Artificial Intelligence Act', 17.6.2022, WK 8862/2022 (INIT); European Parliament, 'Amendments adopted by the European Parliament on 14 June 2023 on the proposal for a regulation of the European Parliament and of the Council on laying down harmonised rules on artificial intelligence (Artificial Intelligence Act) and amending certain Union legislative acts (COM(2021) 0206 – C9-0146/2021-2021/0106(COD))', 14.6.2023, P9_TA(2023)0236; The European Parliament legislative resolution (2024).

security' is to be understood,[37] it does not include more than two types of situations that are both excluded from the directly applicable GDPR. Many of the situations relating to Member States' national security are covered by the JHA Directive, thus exempting them from the GDPR (Art. 2(2)(d) GDPR). Others are entirely excluded from the scope of EU data protection law through Art. 2(2)(a) GDPR and Art. 2(3)(a) of the JHA Directive.[38] This instrumental choice already creates considerable leeway for Member States to develop and/or use AI systems in the context of ensuring their national security. In the case of AI systems developed exclusively for use by state (security) agencies, one could argue that, for lack of reference to the scope of application of Union law, the data protection standards set out in the JHA Directive do not apply at all (scope exception (Art. 2(2)(a)).[39] For the same reason, EU data protection law also does not apply to AI systems developed and used solely in the area of national defence – such as AI-supported weapons systems.[40]

22 Given that the JHA Directive does apply to at least some situations that touch on Member States' national security, Art. 11 JHA Directive – that is especially relevant in AI matters – is an example of *permissive regulation* coupled with an *opening clause*. AI use in the mere preparation of a decision or in support of human decision-making ('analytical'/'preparatory' AI use) is not covered by its prohibition.[41] Thus, depending on one's understanding of the scope and meaning of Art. 11 JHA Directive,[42] many or most cases in which Member States' security authorities could want to make use of AI systems in the course of investigations and surveillance activities[43] are not covered by the prohibition. This concerns, for example, the real-time analysis of large telecommunication data streams[44] or non-conclusive statistical risk assessments of individuals in the context of predictive policing.[45]

---

[37] For some elements that could be considered to be part of national security, see Sule in Dietrich/Sule, Intelligence Law and Policies, mn. 28 and 72; Peuker/Ruffert, p. 37 et seqq. (manuscript on file with author) – they offer an overview of different approaches to defining the term 'national security'.

[38] See recital 16 of the GDPR and recital 14 of the JHA Directive.

[39] On the equivalent scope exception in the GDPR, see Kühling/Raab in Kühling/Buchner, DSGVO Art. 2 mn. 22; Bäcker in Wolff/Brink/v. Ungern-Sternberg, DSGVO Art. 2 mn. 10 et seq.; Ennöckel in Sydow/Marsch, DSGVO, Art. 2 mn. 9; regarding the strict interpretation of Art. 2(2)(b) TEU see ECJ 22.6.2021 – case C-439/19, ECLI:EU:C:2021:504, para. 62 – *Latvijas Republikas Saeima (Points de pénalité)*; ECJ 16.7.2020 – case C-311/18, ECLI:EU:C:2020:559, para. 84 – *Facebook Ireland and Schrems.*

[40] National security is the main example of activities outside the scope of Union law in Art. 2(2) (a) of the GDPR. How far-reaching this exception is a matter for debate. However, none of the commentaries raises doubts that national security does not encompass military defence, see, e.g., Kranenborg in Kuner/Bygrave/Docksey, GDPR Art. 2 mn. 60 (69) (who only debate whether private activities in the context of national security fall outside the scope of application); Bäcker in Wolff/Brink/v. Ungern-Sternberg, DSGVO Art. 2 mn. 9a–9d (who question whether every counterterrorism measure or whether intelligence agencies in general are exempted on account of their connection with national security).

[41] Regarding this limitation, see Mendoza/Bygrave, University of Oslo Faculty of Law Research Paper 2017, 1; Djeffal, ZaöRV 2020, 847 (esp. 862).

[42] For a case that turns on the understanding of Art. 22 GDPR, see AG Pikamäe 16.3.2023 – case C-634/21, ECLI:EU:C:2023:220, para. 36 et seqq. – *SCHUFA Holding and Others (Scoring)* and AG Pikamäe 16.3.2023 – joint cases C-26/22 and C-64/22, ECLI:EU:C:2023:222 – *SCHUFA Holding and Others (Discharge from remaining debts)*.

[43] For some such AI uses, Rademacher in Wischmeyer/Rademacher, Regulating Artificial Intelligence, p. 227 et seq.

[44] For this type of practice in France, see Conseil d'État 26.7.2018 – case no. 394922, ECLI:FR:CECHR:2018:394922.20180726, para. 15; ECJ 6.10.2020 – case C-151/73, ECLI:EU:C:2020:791 – *La Quadrature du Net and Others v. Premier minstre and Others.*

[45] As regards crime prediction software in German-speaking countries, see Egbert/Krasmann, Policing and Society 2020, 905; other risk assessment instruments are described in Höffler et al., Eur. J. Crim. Policy Res. 2022, 269 (270).

Where Art. 11 JHA Directive does apply, the opening clause in Art. 11(1) enables Member States to permit fully-automated AI decision-making in their legislation. Such legislation must, of course, comply with the general requirements and limits of EU data protection law (Art. 11(1) JHA Directive). However, this does not constitute a serious additional obstacle that stands in the way of security agencies using AI. For, at least from the German perspective, EU data protection law in security matters is not more stringent and demanding than the domestic constitutional limits imposed on security agencies. This impression is corroborated if one compares the regular and detailed interventions of the German Federal Constitutional Court in this field[46] with the occasional and more restrained judicial oversight exerted by the CJEU.[47] Therefore, general EU data protection rules do not appear to reduce any of the leeway and discretion that Member States do in fact enjoy under their own constitutional law. 23

However, it should be noted that the general EU data protection framework may substantially burden the development and training of new AI systems – whether these are to be used in national security contexts or otherwise. This is because development and training data as well as their usability are in most cases subject to European data protection law. Since this legal framework curbs and limits the pooling and use of large data sets, it may also become a hindrance or nuisance in the development and testing of new AI systems.[48] However, these effects of the general EU data protection framework are quite speculative, indirect and unpredictable in detail. Therefore, it would seem rather far-fetched to claim that these effects restrict the Member States' irreducible discretion and responsibility in matters of their national security in a legally relevant way. 24

2. Specific EU data protection frameworks

a) The data processing side of Member States' procedural autonomy

The more specific EU data protection frameworks likewise afford Member States ample discretion to use AI systems in pursuit of their national security. Based on the principle of national procedural autonomy,[49] the procedures and measures applied by the Member States' police authorities, intelligence services, criminal prosecution, etc., are generally subject to regulation by the respective Member State. This overall procedural autonomy also extends to the personal data processing these procedures entail. Member State agencies must, of course, abide by applicable European data 25

---

[46] As regards the use of algorithms in policing, see BVerfG 16.2.2023 – 1 BvR 1547/19, 1 BvR 2634/20, NJW 2023, 1196, para. 71 et seqq. – *Hessen-Palanthir*; for a ruling on data sharing by domestic intelligence services, see BVerfG 28.9.2022 – 1 BvR 2354/13, NVwZ-*RR* 2023, 1, para. 117 et seqq. – *Bundesverfassungsschutzgesetz – Übermittlungsbefugnisse*; for a ruling on counter-terrorism databases, see BVerfG 10.11.2020 – 1 BvR 3214/15, NVwZ 2021, 226, para. 83 et seqq. – ATDG II; for a ruling on foreign surveillance powers, see BVerfG 19.5.2020 – 1 BvR 2835/17, NJW 2020, 2235, para. 136 – *BNDG*; for a similar overall assessment, see Rademacher in Wischmeyer/Rademacher (eds), Regulating Artificial Intelligence, p. 225 (232 et seqq.): 'The German Constitutional Court's jurisprudence on automated systems of surveillance (sometimes) seems contradictory and (most of the times) excessively fine-tuned. This judicial fine-tuning roots in the 1983 "census judgement" (*Volkszählungsurteil*).' (233).

[47] Rademacher in Wischmeyer/Rademacher (eds), Regulating Artificial Intelligence, p. 238. 'However, even if we take into account the casuistic nature of its proportionality approach, it appears from Opinion No. 1/15 that the CJEU might actually be more open than its German counterpart for EU and Member State legislators to deploy smart surveillance technology.'

[48] On the relevance of data protection law for the use of AI, see Marsch in Wischmeyer/Rademacher, Regulating Artificial Intelligence, p. 35 et seqq.; Spiecker gen. Döhmann in DiMatteo/Poncibò/Cannarsa, Artificial Intelligence. Global Perspectives on Law and Ethics, p. 132.

[49] Regarding the principle's normative foundations, see Szpunar, ZEuP 2018, 1 (1); see also Ortlep/Verhoeven, NALL 2012, 1 (1 et seqq.).

protection principles and more specific EU law frameworks. However, the tasks, powers and activities of Member States' public authorities are not even close to being determined by these standards either in terms of the details or more generally.[50] Instead, the public authorities' tasks, procedures and measures – as well as the legal boundaries – tend to be as diverse as Member States' political and administrative institutions and cultures. The same holds true for the informational or data protection side of this procedural diversity.

b) The case of telecommunications data

26 One example of this pluralist structure under the umbrella of EU data protection frameworks is the ePrivacy Directive.[51] This piece of legislation sets EU-wide standards for the data-intensive and highly AI-relevant potentials brought about by the storage and structured analysis of telecommunications data. Here, too, secondary EU law offers a large amount of leeway for Member State action in the context of national security, including the use of AI. It does so through instrumental choice (a directive as opposed to a regulation), permissive standards and an opening clause in favour of Member State security purposes (Art. 15 ePrivacy Directive).[52] According to recent ECJ decisions, the ePrivacy Directive does regulate whether and to what extent Member States may make use of telecommunications providers for algorithm-based analyses of telecommunications data.[53] However, it does not rule out the comprehensive algorithm-based analysis of all telecommunications data, as the ECJ's ruling in the *Quadrature du Net* case shows. It is true that Union law only permits such widespread user-independent traffic data analyses under narrow conditions that practically exclude them as a regular practice of the security authorities.[54] But this is owed more to EU primary law (Art. 7 and 8 Charter of Fundamental Rights) than to the rules set out in the ePrivacy Directive. That is because the standard applied by the ECJ in the *Quadrature du Net* case clearly originates in the first data retention ruling that vacated the EU Data Retention Directive on account of its violating the Treaties.[55] This rare categorical limitation of Member States' powers to make use of telecommunications data for security purposes, therefore, stands on the same normative level as Art. 4(2) sent. 3 TEU itself. Given this equal rank, it cannot easily be claimed that the national security reserve should trump the limitations on state surveillance powers to be derived from the Charter of Fundamental Rights. What is more, the conditions under which the ECJ does allow comprehensive and user-independent algorithmic traffic data analyses in real time[56] do in fact refer to the Member States' task of ensuring their national security. In this regard, the case law on communications data analyses is thus an example of the normative restraint of EU

---

[50] → mn. 21 et seqq.

[51] Directive 2002/58/EC concerning the processing of personal data and the protection of privacy in the electronic communications sector (Directive on privacy and electronic communications), OJ L 201, 31.7.2002, 37.

[52] ECJ 6.10.2020 – case C-151/73, ECLI:EU:C:2020:791, para. 91–99, 136 – *La Quadrature du Net and Others v. Premier minstre and Others*; AG (Collins) 8.06.2023 – case C-178/22, ECLI:EU:C:2023:463, para. 21–27 – *Procura della Pepubblica presso il Tribunale di Bolzano.*

[53] ECJ 6.10.2020 – case C-151/73, ECLI:EU:C:2020:791, para. 96 – *La Quadrature du Net and Others v. Premier minstre and Others*: 'The scope of that directive extends not only to a legislative measure that requires providers of electronic communications services to retain traffic and location data, but also to a legislative measure requiring them to grant the competent national authorities access to that data.'

[54] ibid. para. 177 et seqq.

[55] ECJ 8.4.2014 – case C-293/12 and C-594/12, ECLI:EU:C:2014:238, para. 37 et seqq. – *Digital Rights Ireland Ltd.*

[56] ECJ 6.10.2020 – case C-151/73, ECLI:EU:C:2020:791, para. 177 et seqq. – *La Quadrature du Net and Others v. Premier minstre and Others.*

law, which is tailored so as to respect and accommodate the Member States' sole responsibility for ensuring their national security.

The final assessment of how far this national security exception extends is not, of course, up to the Member State in question.[57] But the moderating mechanisms of the Treaties also prove to be resilient in the face of possible conflicts of interpretation around what counts as a threat to national security:[58] Preliminary reference proceedings pursuant to Art. 267 TFEU leave adjudication of a specific case to the referring Member State court.[59] This enables Member States to at least provisionally assert their own understanding of when and by what events their national security is actually threatened. This is precisely what the French *Conseil d'État* (Council of State) did following the ECJ's decision in the *Quadrature du Net* case.[60] It is true that such judicial resistance can lead to infringement proceedings under Art. 258 and 259 TFEU against a Member State.[61] However, especially in their preliminary stages, such proceedings offer ample room for political negotiation and bargaining.[62] Member States' sovereignty claims concerning their national security can be accounted for during these more flexible, political stages of the infringement proceedings. Thus, the procedural law of the Treaties also facilitates the moderation of conflicting claims to competence. 27

c) Tighter EU interventions in the field of security cooperation and networks

Despite this overall restraint vis-à-vis Member States' procedural autonomy, EU interventions in some specific areas and contexts of data processing are more intensive and detailed, especially in the context of cross-border, security-related information cooperation between EU Member States.[63] Very specific requirements of Union law apply, for example, to data processing within the framework of Europol,[64] on the basis of the Air Passenger Data Directive[65] or in the Travel Information System (ETIAS).[66] In each of these cases, requirements are also made in terms of the use and limits of 28

---

[57] ECJ 7.9.2022 – case C-624/20, ECLI:EU:C:2022:639, para. 19 – *E.K. v Staatssecretaris van Justitie en Veiligheid*: 'The terms of a provision of EU law which makes no express reference to the law of the Member States for the purpose of determining its meaning and scope must normally be given an independent and uniform interpretation throughout the European Union.' AG Collins 8.6.2023 – case C-178/22, ECLI:EU:C:2023:463, para. 24 – *Procura della Pepubblica presso il Tribunale di Bolzano*.

[58] As regards the scenario of such conflicts between the CJEU and the Member State courts, see Peuker/Ruffert, p. 50 (manuscript on file with author).

[59] For an analysis of how this power of implementation is exercised by referring courts, see Krommendjik, p. 5 et seq., 142 et seqq.; see also Stone Sweet/Brunell, JEEP 1998 (5), 66.

[60] Mitsilegas, et al., Eur. Law J. 2022, 1 (23 et seq.).

[61] On the very rare complaint of judicial violations of Union law in infringement proceedings, see Korzenov, Common Market Law Review 2016 (53), 1317 (1332): 'The second available remedy is the infringement proceeding under Article 258 TFEU. Its potential has however been left largely unexplored.'

[62] Craig/De Búrca, p. 469.

[63] Schneider in Harlow/Leino/della Cananea, Research Handbook on EU Administrative Law, p. 81; Schneider, NVwZ 2012, 65; Rademacher, p. 100 et seqq.; see also Galetta/Hofmann/Schneider, EPL 2014, 65; Bogdandy/Hering in Voßkuhle/Eifert/Möllers, Grundlagen des Verwaltungsrechts, § 25, specifically mn. 78 et seq.; see also Gutiérrez, p. 1 et seqq.

[64] See Regulation 2016/794/EU on the European Union Agency for Law Enforcement Cooperation (Europol), OJ L 135, 24.5.2016, 53, esp. Art. 17 et seqq.

[65] Directive 2016/681/EU on the use of passenger name record (PNR) data for the prevention, detection investigation and prosecution of terrorist offences and serious crime, OJ L 119, 4.5.2016, 132.

[66] Regulation 2018/1240/EU establishing a European Travel Information and Authorisation System (ETIAS) and amending Regulations (EU) No 1077/2011, (EU) No 515/2014, (EU) 2016/399, (EU) 2016/1624 and (EU) 2017/2226, OJ L 236, 19.9.2018, 1. While the Regulation has been in force since 2018, the ETIAS system is not set to become operational until 2024; see also Rankin, 'Introduction of €7 visa-waiver forms for travellers to EU delayed' (The Guardian, 10.08.2021) <https://www.theguardian.com/world/2022/aug/10/introduction-of-7-euro-visa-waiver-forms-for-travellers-to-eu-delayed> (last accessed: 18.9.2023).

algorithmic data analyses,[67] which the ECJ further tightened, for instance in its PNR ruling.[68] However, such legislative and judicial interventions by EU actors only serve to contain and structure new informational resources, networks and practices that were created by the EU in the first place. The fact that EU law keeps at bay new informational capacities that are brought about by EU networking and coordination of Member States' security efforts cannot affect the Member States' national security reserve. On the contrary, it is inevitable that Member States that deepen their police and judicial cooperation, in this context, also lose some of their autonomy to decide on the scope and nature of permissible information processing.

29 Beyond their direct effects, it is foreseeable that the sometimes quite detailed interventions of the European legislator and the ECJ in the field of EU security networks and cooperation may have indirect effects on Member States. For example, they can lead to spill-over effects in those areas in which Member States still act on their own to safeguard their national security. EU decisions in the field of security cooperation regarding fundamental rights restrictions on permissible data analysis and use of AI can take on a life of their own. This can create a certain dynamic to adopt these principles sooner or later in purely domestic security contexts. However, such effects of EU interventions are too indirect and unforeseeable to be regarded as legally relevant constraints on Member States' discretion in the area of their domestic national security activities. Ultimately, the Member States are always left with the option of determining their domestic legal boundaries in a different way, i.e. to develop their own approaches to fundamental and human rights protection in the security context.[69] Beyond the realm of EU law obligations, it is up to each Member State as to whether and to what extent it will bow to EU-induced peer pressure.

d) Overall security-focused thrust of EU interventions

30 All in all, the EU's legislative activity in the vast field of data processing by security agencies seems – at least from a German perspective – to expand rather than limit Member States' options for using AI in national security contexts. It is precisely because they are primarily limited to networking transnational security activities, information exchange and analysis[70] that EU interventions and activities will often involve new forms of data collection and analysis. Many of these EU-induced practices would not be realistic without any EU intervention due to more stringent constitutional limits or inert and change-averse administrative structures in the Member States. For example, the extensive data collection and processing powers in the context of detecting and fighting money laundering[71] or airline passenger data[72] can only pass constitutional muster in Member States such as Germany precisely because they are of European provenance. Complaints about undue European restrictions of Member State discretion in the area of national security, therefore, tend to ignore the overall thrust of EU interventions in

---

[67] See Art. 33(1) Regulation (EU) 2018/1240/EU.

[68] ECJ 21.6.2022 – case C-817/19, ECLI:EU:C:2022:491, para. 58 – *Ligue des droits humains v Conseil des ministres*.

[69] See BVerfG 6.11.2019 – 1 BvR 16/13, NJW 2020, 300, para. 50–54 – *Recht auf Vergessen I*, see also Masing in Herdegen et al., Handbuch des Verfassungsrechts, § 2, mn. 26.

[70] For a general account of this phenomenon, see Galetta/Hofmann/Schneider, EPL 2014, 65; Bogdandy/Hering in Voßkuhle/Eifert/Möllers, Grundlagen des Verwaltungsrechts, § 25, specifically mn. 78 et seq.; see also Gutiérrez, p. 1 et seqq.

[71] Art. 40 and 41 of Directive 2015/849/EU on the prevention of the use of the financial system for the purposes of money laundering or terrorist financing (Money Laundering Directive) OJ L 156, 19.6.2018, 43.

[72] Art. 6–13 of Directive 2016/681/EU on the use of passenger name record (PNR) data for the prevention, detection, investigation and prosecution of terrorist offences and serious crime (Air Passenger Data Directive) OJ L 119, 4.5.2016, 132.

security matters. This may have something to do both with greater EU judicial restraint in regard to constitutional issues of security law[73] and a more clearly developed political preference for security. This pro-security preference may have very deep roots: A political entity such as the EU that bases itself strongly on bureaucratic, output-type legitimation will tend to exhibit a preference for efficiency and security over political liberty.[74] The same follows from the typical executive leaning of intergovernmental and inter-administrative cooperation structures.[75]

II. Direct AI regulation: constraints on Member States' security policy imposed by the proposed AI Act

The picture is very similar when one considers the proposed AI Act, the main piece 31
of direct EU AI Regulation.[76] Judging from the various drafts, most importantly according to the recent European Parliament legislative resolution (2024), Member States will enjoy ample possibilities and discretion to use AI in national security contexts.

1. Instrumental choice: direct regulation of Member State procedure

A first significant constraint imposed by the proposed AI Act on Member State 32
discretion follows from the chosen legislative instrument: The proposed regulation sets out to directly govern certain technologies and their use throughout the EU. The drafts do not exclude from their scope AI development and use by state agencies but, on the contrary, specifically address certain types of such use.[77] By regulating forms and instruments of data analysis, the AI Act thus directly regulates a relevant section of Member States' administrative, criminal and civil procedure. By doing so, the proposed AI Act deviates considerably from the principle of national procedural autonomy. Member States' concerns regarding the choice of legislative instrument (a regulation) have not been addressed in the legislative arena. This is unfortunate, as they could have easily been accommodated. As in the case of the JHA Directive, the EU could have used a directive to set substantive standards for the use of AI by the Member States' security authorities without departing from its regulatory objective. For, even if a general AI Regulation applies directly in all Member States, the very sensitive use of AI by security authorities will ultimately have to be more closely regulated and contained in national procedural law. Here, the coexistence of several directly applicable pieces of legislation

[73] *Schmidt-Aßmann* and *Schenk* claim there is a more restrained degree of judicial scrutiny (*Kontrolldichte*) at the level of European courts; see Schmidt-Aßmann/Schenk in Schoch/Schneider, VwGO Einleitung mn. 131, 143.

[74] On the connection between the EU's technocratic outlook and executive appetites, see White, JCMS 2021, 781 (785): 'A second structural vulnerability to emergency politics lies in what can be called the EU's instrumentalist orientation. Note the prominent role accorded to technocracy.'

[75] See Dieter, Eur. J. Int. Relat. 1999, 333; for an extensive review of the literature on this question, see Anders, ZPol 2018 (28), 343; White, JCMS 2021, 781; on the democratic accountability risks of administrative networks, see Slaughter, MJIL 2003, 1041 (1053 et seqq.); Trute in Voßkuhle/Eifert/Möllers, Grundlagen des Verwaltungsrechts, § 9, p. 551.

[76] This evaluation is based on the legislative documents elaborated in the light of Procedure 2021/0106/COD: Proposal COM(2021) 206 final, the Member States' Common Position (General Approach) on the AI Act of 6 December 2022, the European Parliament's Draft Compromise Amendments on the Draft Report of 16 May 2023 and the European Parliament legislative resolution (2024).

[77] Title II Art. 5 establishes a list of prohibited AI practices, some of which are AI uses by state actors. Annex III lists high-risk AI systems to which the most stringent legal regime applies. The list includes many types of AI use by state actors and can be adjusted by delegated legislation.

at both levels (the EU and the Member States) will only cause a host of practical problems, as is the case under the framework of the GDPR.[78]

2. Broad definition of AI as a constraint on Member States' national security policy

33 The broad definition of AI in the proposed Act[79] also has the potential to affect Member States' discretion in the area of national security. It is especially the inclusion of deterministic algorithms that multiplies the possible points of friction between direct EU AI regulation and the Member States' use of new analytical tools in the context of national security. In doing so, the broad definition of AI expands the 'zone of conflict' with regard to Art. 4(2) sent. 3 TEU.

3. Scope I: exception for military AI use

34 The definition of the scope of the AI Regulation throughout the main part of legislative proceedings presented a mixed picture regarding the Member States' discretion to use AI for national security purposes. According to all the drafts, AI systems that are developed and employed exclusively for military use – such as semi-autonomous weapons systems – were to be excluded from the Regulation.[80] From the very outset of the AI Act, a substantial part of 'national security' tasks, i.e. national military defence, therefore was to be exempt from the new rules governing AI.[81]

4. Scope II: general exception for national security matters

35 On the other hand and in contrast to data protection law, the Commission's draft did not exclude from its scope the use of AI by Member States beyond the scope of application of Union law. Consequently, the Commission's explanatory memorandum explicitly addresses the lack of internal market relevance of some elements of the proposed Regulation. However, the memorandum points out that the EU is competent to regulate data protection (Art. 16 TFEU) in order to justify these elements.[82] Since this competence title covers data protection vis-à-vis Member States only within the scope of application of Union law,[83] this argument was not very persuasive. Given this questionable competence basis, there thus were strong arguments especially in the light of Art. 4(2) sent. 3 TEU, to include in the AI Act a scope exception for AI systems that are developed and used solely within government agencies and without any reference to the EU single market. Such an exception could cover many situations in which AI is used in national security contexts and exempt them from the Regulation. This is not without precedent, as data protection law exempts these types of situations under Art. 2(3) JHA Directive and under Art. 2(2) and Recital 16 GDPR.[84] Accordingly, in their consolidated

[78] On the challenges arising from this, see Schulze, p. 1 et seqq.

[79] For a critical appraisal, see Raposo, Int. J. Law Inf. Technol. 2022, 88 (91); scholars highlight problems that arise from this broad definition; see, e.g., Ebers et al., J 2021, 589 (590); Botta, ZfDR 2022, 391 (397) and Tomada, J. Intellect. Prop. Inf. Technol. E-Commer. Law 2022, 53 (54).

[80] Art. 2 no. 3 related to military purposes has remained throughout the drafts, including the European Parliament legislative resolution (2024).

[81] Dual-use AI research and development will, of course, be affected by the new Regulation.

[82] Recital 2 of Proposal European Commission, 'Proposal for a regulation laying down harmonised rules on artificial intelligence (artificial intelligence act) and amending certain union legislative acts', 21.4.2021, COM(2021) 206 final.

[83] See Art. 16 TFEU: '[…] by the Member States when carrying out activities which fall within the scope of Union law'; see, e.g., Kotzur in Geiger/Khan/Kotzur TFEU Art. 16.

[84] Kranenborg in Kuner/Bygrave/Docksey, GDPR Art. 2 mn. 60 (70 et seq.).

position,[85] the Member States called for an exemption for 'national security' that goes beyond military AI usage.

Despite the intention of the Commission and Parliament to regulate certain types of AI use by security agencies, Member States have fully prevailed in this respect: Art. 2 (3) of the European Parliament legislative resolution (2024) now includes a scope exception for AI use outside of the scope of EU law. The provision explicitly exempts the use of AI in national security contexts as long as these systems and their output are not meant to be placed on the EU market. This sweeping change in the rules governing the AI Act's field of application is clearly motivated by reasons of limited EU competence, especially in the field of national security. As such, it is a perfect example of the political – not legal – mechanics through which Art. 4(2) TEU does its work: The national security reserve clearly shifted the balance of arguments in the trilogue negotiations, leading to a result that accommodates any national security concerns. **36**

Although such concern for the Treaties' distribution of competences should be welcomed, this result is not without problems. Exempting Member States' AI activities 'beyond the scope of EU law' may seem like a good solution, since such clauses are firmly rooted in the practice of EU law and thereby promise ease of application. However, this may well be an empty promise given the notoriously unclear meaning of the term. One prominent case in point is the consistent practice of EU institutions to understand Art. 16(2) TFEU – despite its limitation to the scope of EU law – as a more or less unlimited title for regulating Member State and private data protection practices throughout the EU.[86] **37**

What is more, the provision's reference to questions of 'national security' simply mirrors, at the secondary law level, the extremely vague national security reserve in Art. 4(2) sent. 3 TEU. Therefore, the same problems when it comes to interpreting this vague exception are likely to reappear when applying the AI Act in practice. From a regulatory point of view, it would have been preferable to carve out a more specific scope exception tailored to the goals, risks and contexts of regulating AI. One means of this could have been an opening clause permitting Member State legislation to exempt AI use by certain public authorities for national security purposes. Such an opening clause would have forced Member States to explicitly designate in their legislation the areas and situations they understand as pertaining to their 'national security' – such as intelligence activities. It is precisely through such more concrete legislation that secondary EU law, in concert with Member State legislation, could have translated the vague terms and requirements in Art. 4(2) sent. 3 TEU, thereby fulfilling its moderating task as set out in the provision. **38**

5. Discretion in virtue of classification

Even disregarding the rather sweeping but vague scope exception, the content of the proposed AI Act leaves the Member States substantive leeway to develop and use AI in the area of national security. **39**

---

[85] The Member States suggested clarifying Art. 2 in relation to national security by explicitly stating that AI systems for national security purposes should be excluded from the scope of regulation. They wished to add this exemption to Art. 2 no. 3 of European Commission, 'Proposal for a regulation laying down harmonised rules on artificial intelligence (artificial intelligence act) and amending certain union legislative acts', 21.4.2021, COM(2021) 206 final. See Council of the European Union, 25.11.2022, Interinstitutional File: 2021/0106(COD), 70.

[86] It thus remains to be seen if the scope exception in Art. 2(3) AI Act (The European Parliament legislative resolution (2024)) will make any difference in practice – which it does not seem to make in the case of the GDPR and the JHA.

40 A first element of discretion is introduced at the level of the classification of AI applications and practices based on their risk.[87] High-risk systems are subject to special, primarily procedural, requirements as regards certification and human oversight and are listed in an Annex to the proposed AI Act.[88] According to this list, the vast majority of situations in which public authorities could use AI systems in order to ensure national security would be considered high-risk practices.[89] However, this classification is subject to amendment through delegated legislation by the Commission based on the review procedure in the Comitology Regulation.[90] In virtue of their rights to participate in the Comitology proceedings, Member States enjoy some discretion and powers when it comes to risk classifications.

6. Discretion in virtue of implementation

41 Even if it were applicable, the supervisory and conformity assessment regime of the proposed AI Act would not decisively limit Member States' discretion to develop and use AI in national security contexts. The overall lack of substantive requirements in the proposed AI Regulation as well as the Member States' authority regarding the details and implementation of these procedures will likely mean that the Member States retain a large degree of leeway. This leeway all but guarantees that AI applications to be used in the context of national security activities will not be subject to legal requirements they cannot fulfil. In addition, the proposed AI Act[91] allows for temporary exemptions from conformity assessment procedures, among other things for exceptional reasons of public security. Here, too, the draft AI Act takes into consideration the Member States' responsibility to ensure their national security.

42 The large degree of Member State discretion in virtue of their implementation powers is likely to be somewhat relativized on account of the independent status of AI supervisory authorities. However, EU data protection practice shows that serious conflicts between independent data protection authorities and security agencies that are co-regulated by them are quite rare. Moreover, this practice also shows that security agencies continue to be much less receptive to interventions by independent data protection authorities than to judicial decisions. Despite the independence of AI supervisory authorities, the procedural dominance of the Member States and their powers and irreducible role in implementing the EU AI framework will thus remain decisive factors in securing the Member States' ability to act and use AI in the context of their national security.

43 In addition to this discretion in virtue of implementation, the proposed AI Act, through its provisions on regulatory sandboxes,[92] opens up spaces to experiment with

---

[87] On the proposal's risk-based approach, see Mahler in Colona/Greenstein, Nordic Yearbook of Law and Informatics 2020-2021, p. 247; Cohen, Journal of Law, Technology and Society 2023 (20), 203 (208 et seqq.); see also Raposo, Int. J. Law Inf. Technol. 2022, 88.

[88] See Arts 8–15 of the European Parliament legislative resolution (2024) on the AI Act. (Chapter 2: Requirements for high-risk AI Systems) and Annex III; see also Kranenborg in Peers et al., CFR Art. 8 mn. 08.15 et seqq.; Kingreen in Calliess/Ruffert, AEUV Art. 16 mn. 6; Schneider, Die Verwaltung 2011, 499 (506 et seq.); Spiecker gen. Döhmann/Eisenbarth, JZ 2011, 169 (172); von Lewinski, DuD 2012, 564 (565); Nguyen, ZEuS 2012, 277 (286 et seq.).

[89] See the European Parliament legislative resolution (2024), Annex III.

[90] The European Parliament legislative resolution (2024), Art. 7(1).

[91] COM(2021) 206 final, Art. 7(1); Art. 47 of the Member States' Common Position (General Approach) on the AI Act of 6 December 2022; Art. 47 of the European Parliament´s Draft Compromise Amendments on the Draft Report of 16 May 2023; Art. 46 of the European Parliament legislative resolution (2024).

[92] The European Parliament legislative resolution (2024), Art. 57.

new AI applications. According to the proposal, this will include a more forgiving data protection regime, especially for AI applications with security relevance. Here, too, the proposed AI Act, therefore, accommodates Member States' responsibilities vis-à-vis their public security.

7. Forbidden AI practices: permissive standard-setting

In contrast to the rather inflationary classification as 'high-risk systems', the AI Act's list of forbidden practices (Art. 5 of the European Parliament legislative resolution (2024)) is quite restrained. In this list, only the prohibitions of some types of racial, political or other discriminatory profiling (1(g)), of some forms of predictive policing (1(d)) and of real-time biometric identification of individuals for law enforcement purposes seem relevant to the issues relating to Art. 4(2) sent. 3 TEU before us. The ban on racial and other discriminatory racial profiling does not cover practices of 'labelling or filtering of lawfully acquired biometric datasets … in the area of law enforcement'. The prohibition on predictive policing only includes those cases where AI-driven analysis is the sole instrument of prediction, thus excluding all cases where the AI system is used to support the human assessment of existing evidence. Both prohibitions thus are clearly tailored not to stand in the way of any law enforcement practices assumed to be legitmate and realistic. The general prohibition of real-time biometric identification in publicly accessible places (1(h)), in turn, only covers very few types of conceivable security agency practices. Among other things, any other form of algorithmic real-time identification and detection of individuals – for example based on online behavioural patterns – remains unaffected by the prohibition. Most predictive policing techniques, too, are not subject to any ban as long as they stay within the boundaries mentioned above and do not constitute general social scoring (1(c)). Since there are no powers of delegated legislation with regard to prohibited AI practices, the *numerus clausus* laid down in the AI Act will be around for a while. Member States' room for manoeuvre and experimentation in the field of security-relevant AI will therefore remain. 44

To the extent that the general ban on real-time biometric identification in public spaces applies, it is anything but unconditional. Instead, the proposed AI Act contains an opening clause for Member States to permit such types of AI use under specific legislation. The corresponding Member State legislation is subject to a specified procedural framework and substantive limits. However, real-time biometric identification in public spaces may be permitted when searching for criminal suspects, for example. The criminal offences in relation to which the use of real-time biometric identification is permitted are all those that could justify the issuing of a European arrest warrant and that are punishable by a maximum sentence of at least four years' imprisonment. In the German context, this would include, for example, tracing a person charged with embezzlement (§ 266 German Criminal Code (*Strafgesetzbuch*, StGB)). Obviously, such lenient standards – even if applicable in such contexts – would not constitute a serious limitation of Member States' national security action. 45

Limitations of real-time biometric identification in public spaces are more relevant when such technology is used for preventive purposes. Where these can be classed as 'law enforcement purposes', such biometric AI use is only permissible to prevent the genuine and present or foreseeable threat of a terrorist attack or a specific, substantial, and imminent danger to life or limb. Given these restrictive conditions, the question of defining 'law enforcement purposes' is crucial. It remains to be seen 46 whether this will be understood to encompass intelligence gathering or counter-terrorism activities at a stage way before any imminent threats arise.[93] Depending on whether that is the case, the general prohibition of real-time biometric detection in public spaces may become a relevant constraint on the Member States' use of AI in national security contexts. However, this presupposes that such intelligence practices will not be entirely discarded from the scope of the AI Act under the above-mentioned national security-exception (Art. 2(3) of the European Parliament legislative resolution (2024)).

8. Summary: not anything goes, but everything's possible in the field of AI

47 The results of the overview presented in the above are mixed, but still rather clear-cut as far as the proposed AI Act currently in the final stages is concerned. In terms of its instrumental choice, its general scope of application, the definition of AI and the classification as high-risk systems, EU law ventures into areas that it usually leaves to national procedural autonomy. Nevertheless, the scope exception for AI use in national security contexts,[94] a degree of normative leeway (security exemption from conformity assessment procedures;[95] de-classification via delegated legislation[96]) and their concretization and implementation powers[97] afford Member States ample possibilities and discretion to use AI for national security purposes. This will enable Member States to deploy those AI systems they deem necessary to safeguard their national security.

48 At the substantive level, the AI Act is an instance of permissive standard-setting: It prohibits hardly anything and creates opening clauses for Member State legislation where it does introduce prohibitions. The AI Act essentially limits itself to classifying many uses of AI by security agencies as 'high-risk' practices. This mainly results in subjecting these practices to an elaborate but mostly procedural and open-ended testing and oversight regime. This will certainly lead to the bureaucratization and formalization of AI use. In the case of the security agencies, this promises a confrontation with a generally applicable legal regime that is not specifically tailored to the tasks and contexts of public, let alone security, authorities. Although this will likely lead to a certain degree of irritation and pose some obstacles to current practice, it seems unlikely that the procedural regime will give rise to significant hurdles to AI use by security agencies. After all, government agencies already follow a much more bureaucratic procedure and apply stricter standards than private individuals or businesses are accustomed to doing, especially regarding the sensitive use of AI. A security agency making use of an algorithm whose functions have neither been understood nor tested would – even if no specific AI legislation had been enacted – be acting in an extremely questionable manner from a rule-of-law and democratic point of view. Similar constitutional requirements do not apply to private AI use. While the AI Act's overall regulatory approach, which relies heavily on procedur-

[93] Given the English version and the explicit danger threshold in point (b), this interpretation seems very likely. This, in turn, explains the Member States' wish to exempt AI use by intelligence services and other agencies associated with national security concerns from the scope of the AI Act altogether (→ mn. 35 et seq.).

[94] → mn. 34 et seqq.

[95] → mn. 39 et seqq.

[96] → mn. 37 et seqq.

[97] → mn. 39 et seqq.

alization and certification, could become a real hindrance for the private sector,[98] it is therefore unlikely to impose any serious burdens on the Member States' use of AI when it comes to ensuring their national security.

D. EU AI Regulation and Art. 4(2) sent. 3 TEU: sovereigns in sovereignty-respecting chains

To conclude, EU secondary law has at its disposal and makes use of a broad array of tools to moderate the fundamental conflict of competences inherent in Art. 4(2) sent. 3 TEU. Mediated by EU secondary law, the national security reserve ensures the Member States have the necessary instruments and leeway to realize their responsibility to ensure their national security. On the other hand, Art. 4(2) sent. 3 TEU does not seem to have any relevance as a directly operational exception from the primacy of EU law or as a true competence reserve for a defined and delineated field or sphere of regulation. **49**

An analysis of EU law constraints on Member States' discretion when it comes to developing and using AI systems in national security contexts confirms this theoretical picture: Ultimately, EU secondary law strikes very few AI instruments from the hands of Member States. Instead, it permits the use of almost any algorithmic tool that Member States might deem necessary for their security purposes. EU legislation creates this room for manoeuvre through a mix of instrumental choice, scope exceptions, opening clauses, permissive standard-setting and own support work to benefit Member States' national security. The main effect of the national security reserve seems to be that AI-relevant EU lawmaking is held to permanently reflect the question of Member States' sovereignty over their national security. As a result, the Member States' room for discretion and manoeuvre in the field of AI receives its shapes and contours from EU secondary law. The national security reserve, in turn, negatively determines the legitimate scope and content of the EU's AI-related regulatory claims. Art. 4(2) sent. 3 TEU thus establishes the permanent task of coordination and reconciliation of competing regulatory claims regarding the use of AI and its limits. However, it does not itself provide the solution to this task by being directly inferable from EU primary law. **50**

---

98 Regarding the challenges the proposed AI Act may pose for small and micro enterprises, see Tomada, J. Intellect. Prop. Inf. Technol. E-Commer. Law 2022, 53; some in the private sector highlight barriers in the light of this proposal, more specifically the fragmentation of certifications and obstacles for SMEs; see BSA-The Software Alliance, 'BSA Recommendations on the EU Artificial Intelligence Act, *Position Paper* (BSA-The Software Alliance, August 2023) <https://www.bsa.org/files/policy-filings/08062021aiactreccpospaper.pdf> (last accessed: 18.9.2023); Intellera Consulting, 'The AI Act: Help or Hindrance for SMEs? An analysis of the cost of compliance with the AI Act for SMEs' (Intellera Consulting, August 2023) available from <https://www.intelleraconsulting.com> (last accessed: 18.9.2023).

§ 10
ECJ in the *ultra vires* trap? French perspectives after the *Quadrature du Net* ruling

A. Introduction

Bertrand Warusfel

The ECJ judgments of 6 October 2020 regarding *Quadrature du Net* and *Privacy International*[1] have been extensively commented on with regard to the protection of personal data, but are also highly significant in terms of the national security law of the various Member States. 1

We can now focus on the impact had by these rulings on the law of the Member States, and in particular on French law, more than two years after they were handed down, given that one of the preliminary questions underlying the *Quadrature du Net* judgment had been posed by the *Conseil d'État* (French Council of State) following a court action filed against certain French statutory provisions granting the intelligence services access to connection data previously stored by operators in a general way. 2

It was therefore via the *French Data Network* judgment of 21 April 2021 that the highest French administrative court finally drew the initial conclusions from the ECJ's judgments of October 2020.[2] This ruling had been all the more anticipated given that the representative of the French Government had submitted in Luxembourg that the Court of Justice would overstep the boundaries of its jurisdiction if it were to agree to have European law take precedence in an area impacting on Member States' national security, and that the representative had taken up a similar line of argument before the *Conseil d'État* in order to dissuade the French administrative judge from following the course set by the Union judge. 3

The *Conseil d'État* therefore had little room for manoeuvre due to the threat of an *ultra vires* review and the reference to objectives that have constitutional status which are amenable to justify setting European Union law aside. However, although the ECJ had affirmed that it had jurisdiction in spite of the provisions contained in Art. 4(2) TEU regarding national security (B.), the French judge interpreted its case-law in such a way as to permit the preservation of a large part of the domestic French margin of appreciation related to electronic intelligence (C.). On the other hand, the disagreement which continues to prevail concerning the use of connection data in the fight against serious crime has not yet been entirely resolved, and might force French judges to seek to have their interpretation of the French Constitution take precedence over the ECJ's interpretation of European law in this regard (D.). 4

---

[1] ECJ 6.10.2020 – case C-623/17, ECLI:EU:C:2020:790 – *Privacy International*; ECJ 6.10.2020 – joined cases C-511/18, C-512/18 and C-520/18, ECLI:EU:C:2020:791 – *La Quadrature du Net*.

[2] Conseil d'État, 21.4.2021 – 393099.

B. ECJ jurisdiction to assess national security for the purposes of EU law

5 To justify the data collection capabilities of their intelligence and judicial police services, France – followed by the United Kingdom, the Czech Republic, Estonia, Ireland, Cyprus, Hungary, Poland and Sweden – cited Art. 4(2) TEU, which provides that 'national security remains the sole responsibility of each Member State'. The ECJ however rejected this argument, and preferred to introduce its own interpretation of the scope of national security.

I. Art. 4(2) TEU cited to justify potential lack of jurisdiction on the part of the Court of Justice

6 The French Government, and those Member States which concurred with it in this regard, opined that legislation organising the general retention of connection data with a view to permitting their security services to carry out retroactive investigations on crime suspects should be considered as a national security measure to which European law does not apply, so that the implementation of the latter was not subject to adjudication by a European judge.

7 The argument was amplified by the fact that this legal provision had only recently been introduced (as part of the Treaty of Lisbon), and that the understanding of national security had not yet been interpreted by the Court of Justice based on this more detailed foundation.

8 This type of stance on the part of these Member States was highly significant in political terms, in particular in the wake of the '*PSPP' judgment* of the German Federal Constitutional Court of 5 May 2020[3] (which compared German constitutional law to the provisions of European law relating to the European Central Bank), and even more so in the post-Brexit context of challenges to the primacy of EU law in various Eastern European countries[4].

9 This interpretation moreover ran counter to the manner in which the ECJ had previously applied other provisions affecting the 'essential security interests' of each Member State. The *ECJ* has therefore always interpreted Art. 346 TFEU (formerly Art. 223 of the Treaty of Rome) restrictively, given that this safeguard clause did not constitute a general exemption from the application of European law, but instead included a simple derogation, the scope of which fell within its sovereign discretion. This was particularly stressed in the Court's *Johnston* judgment of 15 May 1986, in which it expounded that the derogations provided for by the Treaties for security reasons

> which deal with exceptional and clearly defined cases. Because of their limited character those articles do not lend themselves to a wide interpretation and it is not possible to infer from them that there is inherent in the treaty a general proviso covering all measures taken for reasons of public safety.[5.]

[3] BVerfG 5.5.2020 – 2 BvR 859/15, NJW 2020, 1647.

[4] With specific reference to the ruling of the Polish Constitutional Court (*Trybunał Konstytucyjny*) 7.10.2021 – K 3/21.

[5] ECJ 15.5.1986 – case C-222/84, ECLI:EU:C:1986:206 para. 26 – *Johnston*. By the same token: ECJ 16.9.1999 – case C-414/97, ECLI:EU:C:1999:417 – *Commission v Kingdom of Spain*,. And to a lesser

The Court has also stated more recently that, although it is up to the Member States to adopt their own measures relating to homeland security, or to external security, the mere fact that a ruling relates to national security cannot render European law inapplicable.[6] **10**

II. Recognition of national security subject to review by an EU judge

It comes as no surprise that the ECJ judges refused to entertain any lack of jurisdiction for them to assess the manner in which national security imperatives were to dovetail with the provisions contained in the 1995 Directive on the protection of individuals with regard to the processing of personal data[7], if we also bear in mind that the two judgments of 6 October 2020[8] follow on from two other rulings which prohibited the preventive, general storage of collection data (the *Digital Rights Ireland judgments* from 2014[9] and *Tele2 Sverige* from 2016[10]). **11**

Contrary to Art. 4(2) TEU, the ECJ found as follows: **12**

> although it is for the Member States to define their essential security interests and to adopt appropriate measures to ensure their internal and external security, the mere fact that a national measure has been taken for the purpose of protecting national security cannot render EU law inapplicable and exempt the Member States from their obligation to comply with that law.[11]

That having been said, by declaring the relevant European data law to be applicable, the supreme court case-law within the European court system did not as such disregard the need for the Member States to adopt measures essential to the preservation of their security. **13**

The *Quadrature du Net* and *Privacy International* rulings in fact lent judicial acknowledgement to, and defined in operational terms, that very thing which the Treaty of Lisbon referred to as the 'national security' of each Member State. **14**

The Court has effectively acknowledged that responsibility for national security, as referred to in Art. 4(2) TEU: **15**

> corresponds to the primary interest in protecting the essential functions of the State and the fundamental interests of society and encompasses the prevention and punishment of activities capable of seriously destabilising the fundamental constitutional, political, economic or social structures of a country and, in particular, of directly threatening society, the population or the State itself, such as terrorist activities.[12]

---

degree: ECJ 17.10.1995 – case C-83/94, ECLI:EU:C:1995:329 – *Leifer and Others*; ECJ 17.10.1995 – case C-70/94, ECLI:EU:C:1995:328 – *Fritz Werner.*

[6] ECJ 4.06.2013 – case C-300/11, ECLI:EU:C:2013:363 para. 38 – *ZZ*; similarly, ECJ 5.12.2009 – case C-239/06, ECLI:EU:C:2009:784 para. 46 – *Commission v Italy.*

[7] Directive 95/46/EC on the protection of individuals with regard to the processing of personal data and on the free movement of such data.

[8] ECJ 6.10.2020 – case C-623/17, ECLI:EU:C:2020:790 – *Privacy International*; ECJ 6.10.2020 – joined cases C-511/18, C-512/18 and C-520/18, ECLI:EU:C:2020:791 – *La Quadrature du Net.*

[9] ECJ 8.4.2014 – joined cases C-293/12 & C-594/12, ECLI:EU:C:2014:238 – *Digital Rights Ireland and Seitlinger and Others.*

[10] ECJ 21.12.2016 – case C-203/15, ECLI:EU:C:2016:970 – *Tele2 Sverige.*

[11] ECJ 6.10.2020 – joined cases C-511/18, C-512/18 and C-520/18, ECLI:EU:C:2020:791 para. 99 – *La Quadrature du Net.* By the same token: ECJ 6.10.2020 – case C-623/17, ECLI:EU:C:2020:790 para. 49 – *Privacy International.*

[12] ibid.

16 Having thus provided a definition of what the ECJ regards as falling within the scope of national security (and thus capable of being used in derogation from the application of provisions of EU common law), the Court has thereby concluded that safeguarding said national security constituted a higher-ranking objective than did other security-related objectives:

> The importance of the objective of safeguarding national security, read in the light of Article 4(2) TEU, goes beyond that of the other objectives referred to in Article 15(1) of Directive 2002/58, inter alia the objectives of combating crime in general, even serious crime, and of safeguarding public security. Threats such as those referred to in paragraph 74 above can be distinguished, by their nature and particular seriousness, from the general risk that tensions or disturbances, even of a serious nature, affecting public security will arise. Subject to meeting the other requirements laid down in Article 52(1) of the Charter, the objective of safeguarding national security is therefore capable of justifying measures entailing more serious interferences with fundamental rights than those which might be justified by those other objectives.[13]

17 We can therefore observe that these rulings seek to strike a subtle balance: On the one hand, national security is not considered in itself as grounds to derogate from European law, but this same level of national security is conversely accepted in the European case-law as being able to justify the most extensive derogations from the application of provisions of common law.

18 This made it relatively straightforward for the *Conseil d'État* to refuse to carry out the *ultra vires* review, even though this was precisely what the French Government was asking it to do, and to reach a sufficiently broad interpretation of the Court's case-law so that any legal framework for the implementation of intelligence techniques could not be disrupted too severely. This constructive dialogue with the European judge however reached its boundaries when it came to collecting connection data for judicial police purposes, instead of for intelligence purposes.

II. The constructive echo of European case-law by the *Conseil d'État*

19 The *Conseil d'État*, which had to settle a dispute relating to the conformity of French law regarding intelligence techniques (authorising the collection of connection data by intelligence services from electronic communication operators), and having on this occasion raised one of the preliminary questions underlying the *Quadrature du Net judgment*, then had to draw the appropriate legal consequences in French law from this new European case-law.

1. Refusal to carry out an *ultra vires* review

20 Once again, the French Prime Minister was asking the *Conseil d'État* to disregard the lessons of the ECJ judgments on grounds that, by declaring itself to have jurisdiction, the ECJ was said to have violated the provisions contained in Art. 4(2) TEU, and thus to submit said Court to an *ultra vires* review:

> (The Prime Minister) maintains (…) that the response given by the Court of Justice of the European Union to the preliminary questions asked of the Court manifestly disregarded the principle of conferral provided for in Article 5 of the Treaty on European Union by encroaching on the competences conferred upon the Member States by virtue of Article 4(2) of this Treaty.[14]

---

[13] ECJ 6.10.2020 – joined cases C-511/18, C-512/18 and C-520/18, ECLI:EU:C:2020:791 para. 136 – *La Quadrature du Net*. By the same token: CJECJ 6.10.2020 – case C-623/17, ECLI:EU:C:2020:790 para. 75 – *Privacy International*.

[14] Conseil d'État, 21.4.2021 – 39309.

This is the reasoning with which the *Conseil d'État* refused to concur, instead maintaining that: 21

> contrary to what the Prime Minister maintains, it is not for the administrative court judge to make sure that the secondary law of the European Union, or indeed the Court of Justice itself, adheres to the division of powers between the European Union and the Member States. He or she cannot therefore exercise any control over the compliance with European law of rulings handed down by the Court of Justice, and nor may he or she, in particular, divest such rulings of the binding nature with which they are invested, as recalled by Article 91 of its Rules of Procedure, on the basis of that Court having overstepped the boundaries of its jurisdiction by conferring on a principle or a European legal act any scope over and above that provided for by the Treaties.[15]

Considerable significance attaches to this assertion on the part of the highest French administrative court, not only with regard to the question of the law on intelligence and national security that the Council had to address in this case, but more generally for the preservation of the founding principle of the primacy of European law (and what French lawyers call 'systemic relations' between European law and national law). This did not however prevent that court from taking into consideration a second argument expounded by the French Government concerning the preservation of French constitutional identity. 22

2. The reservation regarding the constitutional identity of France

The Prime Minister did not content himself with citing Art. 4(2) TEU, but in fact went on to argue as follows: 23

> on the other hand, this response does not per se serve to guarantee the effectiveness of the objectives of constitutional status when it comes to safeguarding the fundamental interests of the Nation, of preventing crimes and of pursuing criminal offenders, as well as combatting terrorism, the latter itself forming part of the objective of safeguarding public order, to which constitutional status attaches.[16]

It was by citing the French Constitution here (similar to the German Federal Constitutional Court in its *PSPP judgment* from 2020[17]) that the French authorities expressed their desire for the *Conseil d'État* to potentially permit said Constitution to take precedence over the application of a provision of European law. 24

In response, the *Conseil d'État* therefore had to verify whether the limits set by the ECJ[18] for retention of and access to connection data still provided adequate protection of the imperatives enshrined in the French Constitution, namely of maintaining national security and combating serious crime. Were this not to be the case, the Council was to refuse to abide by these limits. 25

The *Conseil d'État* recalled the ECJ's definition of national security and its scope given in this case, and considered that the Court had indeed provided for the possibility for a State to continue to prescribe that data be preserved when the level of threat to its national security could so justify. The *Conseil d'État* held that this was consistent with the situation pertaining in France: 26

---

[15] ibid., para. 8.
[16] Conseil d'État, 21.4.2021 – 39309.
[17] BVerfG 5.5.2020 – 2 BvR 859/15, NJW 2020, 1647.
[18] Conseil d'État, 21.4.2021 – 39309, para. 42.

> which was faced with a threat to its national security as assessed on the grounds of the overall fundamental interests of the Nation listed in article L.811-3 regarding the Code of Homeland Security (*Code de la sécurité intérieure*[19]) cited in no. 19 which, by its intensity, was of a serious and genuine nature. As per the date of the present ruling, the threat was not only predictable, but was also present.[20]

27 This assessment carried out by the judges of the *Conseil d'État* was subsequently confirmed by the adoption of a decree by the Prime Minister imposing on operators an obligation to retain data for a period of one year 'in view of the genuine and present threat to national security'[21], which enabled the intelligence services to continue to gain access to connection data that had been stored.

28 The *Conseil d'État* also upheld an interpretation of the *Quadrature du Net* judgment which it considered to meet the requirements of the French Constitution in terms of preventing serious crime and criminal activity when it came to combatting serious crime (wording of European law covering more or less exactly what French law defines as 'organised crime'). According to the French administrative court judges, the ECJ's judgment would indeed not prohibit an obligation for the expedited preservation of stored computer data (within the meaning of Art. 16 of the 2001 Convention on Cybercrime – Budapest-Convention) being imposed on service-providers[22], and would not prohibit such an injunction from relating to 'data initially retained for the purposes of safeguarding national security'[23].

29 That having been said, and certainly aware of the fact that criticism could be levelled at the conformity of its interpretation of the ECJ's case-law (in particular with regard to the use of data for the purposes of combatting serious crime), the *Conseil d'État* hoped to hedge its bets by maintaining that:

30 on the one hand, the requirements enshrined in the French Constitution for safeguarding the fundamental interests of the Nation, preventing any adverse effects on public order, and pursuing criminal offenders, 'cannot be regarded as enjoying, under European law, protection equivalent to that guaranteed by the Constitution'[24], and, on the other hand,

> in the event of the application of a European directive or regulation, as interpreted by the Court of Justice of the European Union, having the effect of depriving one of these constitutional requirements of effective guarantees, so that such requirements did not enjoy equivalent protection under European law, the administrative court judge, when seized of such directive or regulation, must set it aside to the extent absolutely necessitated by adherence to the Constitution.[25]

31 The policy formula put forward in this judgment is by no means gratuitous, even though the *Conseil d'État* considered in the present case that there was no reason to rule out the application of Union law. It does actually refer to the case-law of the French Constitutional Council (*Conseil constitutionnel*), which has accepted since 2004 that it is possible to derogate from the application of Union law in rare cases in the event that

[19] Art. L.811-3 of the Code of Homeland Security (*Code de la sécurité intérieure*) from 24.7.2015 (JORF 0171 26.7.2015, 2).

[20] Conseil d'État, 21.4.2021 – 39309, para. 44.

[21] Decree no. 2021-1363 of 20.10.2021, handed down in application of Art. L. 34-1 of the Code of Post and Electronic Communication (*Code des postes et communications éléctroniques*) from 27.2.1952 (JORF 56 4.3.1952, 2515).

[22] Conseil d'État, 21.4.2021 – 39309, para. 55.

[23] ibid., para. 57.

[24] ibid., para. 10.

[25] ibid., para. 5.

this law comes into conflict with French constitutional law.[26] After initially asserting that 'the transposition into domestic law of a community directive could only be impeded by a mandatory provision of the Constitution to the contrary'[27], the *Conseil constitutionnel* confirmed even more clearly that

> the transposition of a directive, or the adaptation of domestic law in line with a regulation, must not be at variance with a rule or principle inherent in the constitutional identity of France, unless the Parliament adopting the Constitution has consented thereto;[28]

and this was concurred with in this regard by the *Conseil d'État*.[29] **32**

This could be interpreted as a reserve of last resort, or indeed as a veiled threat aimed **33** at the ECJ, giving him to understand that any more extensive intervention by European law in these areas of sovereignty constituted by national security intelligence, or activities to combat serious crime, would of necessity encounter considerable resistance on the part of the national judge, forcing the latter to use the French Constitution as a legal shield between European case-law and national legal provisions touching on criminal proceedings or national security.

This veiled threat in the form of a reserve must be taken all the more seriously, given **34** that the dispute regarding the retention and use of connection data for the purpose of combating serious crime has resurfaced more recently, which risks calling the constructive but somewhat risky interpretation into question, and which the judgment of the *Conseil d'État* had established in 2021.

III. A persistent disagreement regarding the use of data in action to combat serious crime

Even though they relate more specifically to electronic intelligence practices, the **35** judgments of 6 October 2020[30] have nevertheless engendered an unexpected difficulty which lies in the possibility for the judiciary and the police services to use the same connection data for judicial purposes. This discrepancy was further heightened by a new judgment that was handed down in 2022.

1. A theoretical divergence regarding the scope of national security

The difficulty stems from a somewhat restrictive understanding of national security, **36** as defined within these rulings. True, they cite the fight against terrorism amongst other objectives related to the protection of the 'fundamental interests of society', whilst at the same time omitting to touch on the fight against the various forms of serious crime.[31] That having been said, doctrine in France has always taken a broader view of security which 'encompasses internal security policy for everything that does not touch on the individual security of both individuals and property on a day-to-day basis.'[32] By the

---

[26] Conseil constitutionnel, 10.5.2004 – 2004-496 DC.

[27] Conseil constitutionnel, 27.6.2006 – 2006-540 DC. For an initial application: Conseil constitutionnel, 15.10.2021 – 2021-940 QPC.

[28] ibid.

[29] Conseil d'État, 8.2.2007 – 287110.

[30] ECJ 6.10.2020 – case C-623/17, ECLI:EU:C:2020:790 – *Privacy International*; ECJ 6.10.2020 – joined cases C-511/18, C-512/18 and C-520/18, ECLI:EU:C:2020:791 – *La Quadrature du Net*.

[31] ECJ 6.10.2020 – joined cases C-511/18, C-512/18 and C-520/18, ECLI:EU:C:2020:791 para 135 – *La Quadrature du Net*.

[32] Cf. Commission sur le Livre blanc sur la défense et la sécurité nationale, 'Livre blanc sur la défense et la sécurité nationale', Vol. I, 2008, 62.

same token, the object of 'preventing (organised) crime' is officially within the aegis of the intelligence services.[33]

37 It is easy to understand in terms of this French logic that measures taken to combat the various forms of organised crime extend well beyond the basic day-to-day security of individuals and property, and that they are integral to national security because of the major risks that serious crime can pose to public order and to the rule of law, and of the scale of the resources that must be brought to bear in order to combat such crime. The *Conseil constitutionnel* therefore recently confirmed the possibility of using special technical intelligence service methods (dedicated to national security missions) in order to help police investigations engaged in combatting (organised) crime recover computer data remotely.[34]

38 This conceptual controversy could have remained minor had the ECJ not concluded from it that there was a need to deny access to connection data previously preserved by digital operators in judicial inquiries, whilst authorising such access, subject to pre-conditions, for investigations carried out by the intelligence services relating to national security. In order to prevent such discrimination, the *Conseil d'État* considered a mechanism to be in compliance with European case-law such that it would be possible for the judicial police services to issue an order for expedited preservation in order to gain access to said data that had already previously been preserved for national security purposes, and to do so without it being able to directly justify any prior preservation of data for reasons given by the judicial police.

39 Pursuant to a law dated 30 July 2021, para. III b) of Art. L. 3 4-1 of the Post and Electronic Communications Code[35] therefore provides as follows:

> data preserved by the operators pursuant to the present Article may remain subject to an expedited preservation order from the authorities having access to data in application of the law relating to electronic communications for the purpose of preventing and reducing (serious) crime and other serious breaches of the rules with which they are to ensure compliance in order to access this data.

40 But this so-called conformity was once again seriously weakened by the new *Dwyer judgment* handed down by the ECJ on 5 April 2022[36], which confirmed the Court's uncompromising position on the matter in question. This verdict relating to Irish criminal procedure law, in which the ECJ first reaffirmed that there must be a hierarchy between the grounds of general interest that can justify encroachments on privacy in terms of the principle of proportionality, and that in this case:

> the objective pursued by the access request proposed, namely the fight against serious crime, is of lesser importance in the hierarchy of objectives of public interest than that which justified the retention, namely the safeguarding of national security. To authorise, in that situation, access to retained data would be contrary to that hierarchy of public interest objectives.[37]

---

[33] Art. L. 811-(6) of the Homeland Security Code (*Code de la sécurité intérieure*) from 24.7.2015 (JORF 0171 26.7.2015, 2).

[34] French Constitutional Council 8.4.2022 – 2021-987 QPC – (which confirms Art. 706-102-1 of the Code of Criminal Procedure [*Code de procedure pénale*] amended by the Law 2019-222 from 23.3.2019 (JORF 0071 24.3.2019).

[35] Post and Electronic Communications Code (*Code des postes et communications éléctroniques*) from 27.2.1952 (JORF 56 4.3.1952, 2515).

[36] ECJ 5.4.2022 – case C-140/20, ECLI:EU:C:2022:258 – *Dwyer.*

[37] ibid. para. 99.

2. A subsequent questioning of the compromise approved by the *Conseil d'État*

But the Dwyer ruling did not stop there. It also rejected a mechanism similar to the one endorsed by the *Conseil d'État* the previous year, which allowed the police to continue to access connection data as long as it has been collected and retained beforehand for national security purposes: **41**

> traffic and location data cannot be the object of general and indiscriminate retention for the purpose of combating serious crime and, therefore, access to those data cannot be justified for that same purpose. Where those data have exceptionally been retained in a general and indiscriminate way for the purpose of the safeguarding of national security against a genuine and present or foreseeable threat, in the circumstances referred to in paragraph 58 of this judgment, the national authorities competent to undertake criminal investigations cannot access those data in the context of criminal proceedings, without depriving of any effectiveness the prohibition on such retention for the purpose of combating serious crime, recalled in paragraph 65.[38]

Finally, it should also be added that this very *Dwyer* judgment also rejected any possibility of adjusting the effects of its ruling over a period of time, at the risk of retroactively invalidating any judicial investigations based on the use of connection data retained previously in a general way which had been justified by reasons of national security. This new European case-law therefore potentially places French criminal procedure at risk, and will force the various courts to draw the appropriate conclusions from it regarding the permissibility of judicial investigations seeking to combat organised crime. **42**

The first French court to react was the *Cour de cassation* (which is the supreme court within the criminal court system) with its four judgments of 12 July 2022[39]. The *Cour de cassation* first recognised in these judgments that the use of connection data to seek evidence on organised crime (particularly drug trafficking related) had led to 'access irregularities with regard to connection data' from the standpoint of the applicable European law where the impact on the validity of the investigative acts had to be ascertained. **43**

The Court went on to restrict the impact of this irregularity by considering that an individual under investigation can only invoke it 'if he or she claims to be the holder or user of an identified line, or if he or she demonstrates that his or her private life was infringed upon' on the one hand, and, on the other hand, that the procedural acts could only be nullified if 'the data could not be subject to expedited preservation', or that access to any retained connection data had not been 'limited to what was strictly required for the investigation in question to be carried out correctly'. **44**

It is however possible to foresee that the implementation by French investigators of new methods to access connection data for the benefit of investigations into serious crime will once again be challenged before the French courts for reasons of conformity with the Treaties. The French judges might be enticed at such a juncture to exercise the reservation implemented in 2021 by the *Conseil d'État*, and to consider the fact that, if the judicial police were to be denied the possibility of using any connection data previously retained, Union law would not grant levels of protection of the objective of preventing breaches of public order and tracking criminal offenders equivalent to that guaranteed by the Constitution. **45**

---

[38] ibid., para. 100.

[39] Cour de cassation, 12.7.2022 – 21-83.710, 21-83.820, 21-84.096 and 20-86.652.

46 Under such circumstances, there therefore continues to be a risk that the French judge will set aside the application of a European legal provision in order to maintain the French constitutional identity, and the French Constitution's understanding of national security. The *Conseil d'État* had recently considered the principle in litigation concerning the application of European working hours arrangements for officers from the French National *Gendarmerie*, only to then abandon it.[40]

47 The Conseil d'Etat has also maintained its position on the application of the Quadrature judgment by considering valid the renewal in October 2022 of the Prime Minister's injunction requiring electronic communications operators to generalize the retention of their connection data. subscribers for reasons of national security.[41]

48 In that judgment of 30 June 2023, the *Conseil d'État* considered that France was indeed the subject of 'a serious threat, not only foreseeable but current, to national security' and detailed the main components: high terrorist risk (of Islamist origin or linked to instability in the Sahel), risk of interference and espionage, particularly linked to the war in Ukraine, activity of radical groups of the ultra-right and ultra-left that could seriously threaten public peace and a high cyber threat, particularly against operators of vital importance.

49 By carrying out this detailed analysis and validating the classification of threat to French national security, the Supreme Administrative Court exercises an independent judicial review, as required by the Court of Justice, and which goes beyond the limited control generally exercised by the administrative judge in the areas of security and defence and which was limited to sanctioning 'manifest error of assessment' thus leaving the State a large margin of appreciation.

50 It must therefore be concluded that the French judges have not given up defending the French understanding of national security, and possibly seeing to it that its fundamental interests take precedence over European law, by refusing to carry out the *ultra vires* review of the jurisdiction of the Court of Justice. They have so far favoured a subtle 'dialogue between judges', and compromise solutions. The constitutional weapon is however already set for deployment in the event that the ECJ does not take sufficient account of French interpretations of national security law.

---

[40] Conseil d'État, 17.12.2021 – 437125.

[41] Conseil d'État, 30.6.2023 – 468361.

PART IV
COOPERATION IN THE EUROPEAN SECURITY UNION

§ 11
Dynamics of cooperation, soft ways to legal harmonization – an introduction

Markus Sehl

Bibliography: Bellanova/Glouftsios, 'Formatting European security integration through database interoperability', European Security 2022 (31), 454; Bossong/Rhinard, 'Alternative Perspectives on Internal Security Cooperation in the European Union: Setting the Scene' in Bossong/Rhinard (eds), Theorizing Internal Security in the European Union, Oxford 2016, p. 3; Calliess/Ruffert (eds), EUV/AEUV, 6th edn, Munich 2022; Cameron, 'The problem of oversight' in Dietrich/Sule (eds), Intelligence Law and Policies in Europe, Munich/Oxford/Baden-Baden 2019, p. 388; Cross, 'The Merits of Informality: The European Transgovernmental Intelligence Network' in Dietrich/Sule (eds), Intelligence Law and Policies in Europe, Munich/Oxford/Baden-Baden 2019, p. 235; Custers/Dechesne/Sears/Tani/Van der Hof, 'A comparison of data protection legislation and policies across the EU', Computer Law & Security Review 2018 (34:2), 234; Giegerich, 'Zwischen Europafreundlichkeit und Europaskepsis', ZEuS 2016, 3; Karpenstein/Sangi, 'Nationale Sicherheit im Unionsrecht', GSZ 2020, 162; Masing, 'Nachrichtendienste im freiheitlichen Rechtsstaat' in Dietrich/Gärditz/Graulich/Gusy/Warg, Nachrichtendienste im demokratischen Rechtsstaat, Tübingen 2018, p. 3; Mitsilegas, 'Rule of Law: Theorizing EU Internal Security Cooperation from a Legal Perspective' in Bossong/Rhinard (eds), Theorizing Internal Security in the European Union, p. 109; Mitsilegas, 'The Constitutional Implications of Mutual Recognition in Criminal Matters in the EU', Common Market Law Review 2006 (43), 1277; Monar, 'EU Internal Security Cooperation After Four Decades: Observations and Reflections' in Bossong/Rhinard (eds), Theorizing Internal Security in the European Union, Oxford 2016, p. 28; Palacios, 'EU intelligence: On the road to a European Intelligence Agency?' in Dietrich/Sule (eds), Intelligence Law and Policies in Europe, Munich/Oxford/Baden-Baden 2019, p. 201; Pernice, 'Der Schutz nationaler Identität in der Europäischen Union', AöR 2011 (136), 185; Rojszczak, 'The uncertain future of data retention laws in the EU: Is a legislative reset possible?', Computer Law & Security Review 2021 (41) 105572, 1; Sule, 'National Security and EU law restraints on Intelligence Activities' in Dietrich/Sule (eds), Intelligence Law and Policies in Europe, Munich/Oxford/Baden-Baden 2019, p. 335.

A. When it comes to national security… sensitive issues in relation to Member States' sovereignty and EU integration

The narrative of progress and the dynamics of integration[1] that are associated with continually adding new policy areas into European Union (EU) law sometimes almost make one forget that it all began with the limited transfer of sovereignty in individual regulatory areas. This principle of conferral continues to determine the relationship between the Member States and the EU. It marks the boundaries of regulatory power, the legal primacy of application and judicial final decision – ultimately everything that constitutes the project of EU integration. 1

[1] Giegerich, ZEuS 2016, 3 (7).

I. Reserved power and different security cultures

2 In no other area are the Member States so hesitant and sceptical when it comes to transferring sovereignty than in the area of national security.[2] Ultimately, what is at stake for constitutional states is the balancing of effective security measures against the protection of their citizens' fundamental rights. The term 'national security' alone, which can be found in Art. 4(2) TEU, implies that this is an area the Member States primarily associate with their own sovereignty. It is no coincidence that the wording used in Art. 4(2) sent. 3 TEU – 'In particular, national security remains the sole responsibility of each Member State' – stands out from the other regulatory systems of the Lisbon Treaty, as it does not transfer competence to the EU but clarifies what Member States' area of responsibility is.[3]

3 In a phase of EU integration in which the Member States are also moving closer together in the area of security, attention is increasingly being focused on Art. 4(2) TEU. The provision has so far been the subject of surprisingly little debate.[4] Even where the CJEU would have been invited to discuss the scope, it has not paid any particular attention to the provision. In its decision on data retention, the ECJ succeeds in a remarkable way in briefly invoking the Article but then making it disappear again, so to speak, in its further explanations.[5]

4 Scholars, even the commentary in the literature, have so far hardly dealt with the provision, even though it is enshrined in law in a prominent place.[6] Significantly, some courts in the Member States in particular have invoked Art. 4(2) sent. 3 TEU in their submissions in an attempt to justify why security measures fall under national competence.[7]

5 What remains is uncertainty about the scope of the provision. Although it has received little attention for a long time, it can ignite sensitive conflicts in the area of national security between the Member States and the EU that can even go as far as constitutional crises (→ § 10).

6 Data retention is a subject of regulation that is ideal for arguing about the scope of competence in the area of security.[8] The political emphasis with which a Member State wants to use the instrument of data retention, and to what extent, may also be an expression of a country's specific experience of (in)security and its security culture. As a countervailing interest with a fundamental rights basis, data protection is a matter that is also to a large extent culturally influenced in the Member States.[9] On the other hand, data retention – actually a key instrument of national security – falls within the EU's

---

[2] Cameron in Dietrich/Sule, Intelligence Law and Policies in Europe, p. 415; according to *Monar*, an indicator of the fate of the EU integration process, see Monar in Bossong/Rhinard, Theorizing Internal Security in the European Union, p. 32.

[3] Which is closely linked to the state's monopoly on the use of force; see Pernice, AöR 2011, 185 (193).

[4] See Karpenstein/Sangi, GSZ 2020, 162.

[5] ECJ 6.10.2000– case C-511/18, ECLI:EU:C:2020:791 para. 135 et seqq. – *Quadrature du Net.* Probably also in the knowledge of the potential for conflict its decision would unleash in France with regard to Art. 4(2) TEU.

[6] But see Karpenstein/Sangi, GSZ 2020, 162 et seqq.; that appears to be changing, though, see the detailed and instructive remarks by Sule in Dietrich/Sule, Intelligence Law and Policies in Europe, p. 335 et seqq.

[7] Karpenstein/Sangi, GSZ 2020, 162 (163).

[8] See Cameron in Dietrich/Sule, Intelligence Law and Policies in Europe, p. 388 et seqq., 415.

[9] Custers et al., Computer Law & Security Review 2018, 234 et seqq.

harmonising competence EU and the jurisdiction of the *CJEU* on account of its relation to data protection.[10]

In its decision on the *La Quadratur du Net* case, the ECJ in 2020 set narrow limits as regards the retention of data.[11] Private communication providers may only be required to store connection data in the case of serious forms of crime and terrorism. By imposing this obligation, the ECJ created the potential for conflict with France's security interests.[12] Within the framework of 'national security' as set out in Art. 4(2) TEU, France also sees itself as ultimately responsible for combating numerous facets of crime and therefore does not want to be dictated to by the ECJ as to whether or not it may retain data.[13] In the end, the *Conseil d'État* (French Council of State) avoided open confrontation with the ECJ but formulated remarkable reservations. 7

First, the ECJ defined threats to 'national security' very broadly.[14] Not only does the *Conseil d'État* assume a persistently high terrorist threat it also perceives the risk of military and economic espionage, as well as foreign interference, up to and including sabotage, loss of reputation and the poaching of experts.[15] And, last but not least, the *Conseil d'État* mentioned the threat of activities by radical and extremist groups in the country. 8

Second, the *Conseil d'État* combined defence against these threats to 'national security' with France's constitutional identity: 9

> La sauvegarde des intérêts fondamentaux de la Nation, la prévention des atteintes à l'ordre public, notamment celle des atteintes à la sécurité des personnes et des biens, la lutte contre le terrorisme, ainsi que la recherche des auteurs d'infractions pénales constituent des objectifs de valeur constitutionnelle, nécessaires à la sauvegarde de droits et de principes de même valeur, qui doivent être conciliés avec l'exercice des libertés constitutionnellement garanties, au nombre desquelles figurent la liberté individuelle, la liberté d'aller et venir et le respect de la vie privée.[16]

Critical observers analysed the situation as follows: 'With such a definition of public order and national security, France can oppose virtually any piece of European legislation.'[17] 10

Third, as long as there is no amendment to primary law, France reserves the right to retain data on the basis of its own interpretation of 'national security'. And even if primary law were to be amended, the amendments would still have to be measured against French security standards.[18] At the EU legislative level, France is endeavouring to remove the instrument of data retention from the grasp of the CJEU in the course of the revision of ePrivacy Directive.[19] 11

---

[10] An area of regulation of which the ECJ makes extensive use to advance integration in the field of internal security, see, e.g., ECJ 6.10.2020 – case C-623/17, ECLI:EU:C:2020:790 – *Privacy International.*

[11] ECJ 6.10.2020– case C-511/18, ECLI:EU:C:2020:791 – *Quadrature du Net.*

[12] As an expression of the different security cultures: Belgium's Constitutional Court put up no resistance to the ECJ decision in its ruling of 22.4.2021 (Cour Constitutionnelle 22.4.2021 – arrêt no. 57/2021).

[13] In what must have been an unprecedented letter to the *Conseil d'État*, the French government invoked the principle of delegation of powers and the ECJ disregard for Art. 4(2) TEU and argued that the ECJ's ruling was *ultra vires.*

[14] Conseil d'État Assemblée 21.4.2021 – 393099, para. 44.

[15] ibid., para. 44.

[16] ibid., para 9.

[17] Vallée/Genevoix, 'A Securitarian Solange: France has launched a cluster bomb on the EU's legal and political order' (Verfassungsblog, 25.4.2021) <https://verfassungsblog.de/a-securitarian-solange/> (last accessed: 27.9.2023).

[18] ibid.

[19] Rojszczak, Computer Law & Security Review 2021, 2; Kayali, 'France seeks to bypass EU top court on data retention' (Politico, 3.3.2021) <https://www.politico.eu/article/france-data-retention-bypass-eu-top-court/> (last accessed: 27.9.2023).

12 For the time being, the *Conseil d'État* has thus defused the open constitutional conflict with the ECJ, but it clearly expressed the challenges that EU integration has to overcome in the area of internal security law. Here, political needs, previous experience and legal cultures diverge. Remarkably, the Belgian Constitutional Court, for example, did not hesitate to fully implement the ECJ's 2020 ruling.[20]

II. Transnational threats from outside and inside the EU

13 The constitutional struggle to find a fitting solution to data retention reveals the potential for conflict regarding state reservations in the field of 'national security'. At the same time, it is becoming apparent that threats to national security can no longer be dealt with by means of national measures. Threats to one state also present as threats to other states, just as, conversely, threats can be decentralised in origin. And it is not least since the dissolution of internal borders within the EU that security can hardly be thought of in terms of nation-states.[21]

14 Looking at the core elements of 'national security' as the *Conseil d'État* also put them, it is striking that current threats to these elements are systematic and all are transnational in nature: terrorism, cyberattacks, espionage. And so it is obvious that the responses to such threats must also be transnational in nature.[22]

15 A summary of the elements of 'national security' that the CJEU and the European Court of Human Rights (ECtHR) occasionally invoke also points to the foundations of (national) statehood:[23] protection of territorial integrity against internal and external threats; protection of the constitutional order, i.e. democracy, the rule of law and the separation of powers; protection of the function of political governance and the economic system; protection of critical infrastructure.[24] However, these elements are typically exposed to unbounded threats: The protection of national territoriality is now inextricably linked to issues around the EU territory and its external borders; combating terrorist threats is a transnational task; the EU calls on some of its Member States to uphold key rule-of-law principles. Crises outside the EU call for joint political and economic capacities in order to be able to act internally, for example the strict enforcement of sanctions in the face of Russia's war of aggression in Ukraine. The protection of critical infrastructure in the areas of energy, cyber, mobile networks, and supply chains cannot be implemented by nation-states alone.

III. Modes of cooperation: a question of trust

16 Where Member States are reluctant to transfer competences in the area of 'internal security',[25] although they at the same time recognise that effective resilience primarily needs to be established across borders, the focus inevitably shifts to cooperation (→ § 12 mn. 38 et seqq.). Cooperation has developed in different areas, in different forms and between different actors – what they have in common is that they are all dependent on mutual trust.

---

[20] Cour Constitutionnelle 22.4.2021 – arrêt no. 57/2021.

[21] Calliess in Calliess/Ruffert, TEU Art. 4 mn. 47.

[22] See European Commission, 'EU Security Union Strategy', 24.7.2020, COM(2020) 605 final, 1 et seqq.

[23] See Sule in Dietrich/Sule, Intelligence Law and Policies in Europe, p. 358.

[24] ibid.

[25] On the term as used in the European context, see Bossong/Rhinard in Bossong/Rhinard, Theorizing Internal Security in the European Union, p. 5.

In the aftermath of 9/11, the EU created a remarkable instrument for cooperation in the form of the European arrest warrant. It provides States with a fast and uncomplicated cross-border criminal prosecution tool without the need to harmonise the substantive criminal law system – the core of state sovereignty.[26] *Mitsilegas* aptly states: 'The executing authority is in principle obliged to execute a decision emanating from a different legal system whose rules must be respected extraterritorially, leading thus to a journey into the unknown.'[27] It is a system that – as the ECJ has repeatedly emphasised – depends on a 'high degree of trust'.[28] The same holds for the European investigation order, which was based on the model of the arrest warrant. In addition, law enforcement authorities can join together to cooperate across borders in Joint Investigation Teams.[29] However, the instruments of cooperation that are based on trust are in jeopardy when Member States weaken the rule of law and dismantle safeguards.[30] **17**

IV. Information sharing: a boost for security cooperation

The essential substance that drives cooperation between the EU Member States is data. **18** Member States have a particular interest in data exchange and interoperable databases in law enforcement, border control and migration. Numerous database formats have emerged in these areas.[31] Most cooperation is geared to information exchange; ambitious cooperations also take it as the starting point for developing structures up to operational capacities. Thus, what used to take the form of informational cooperation between state security agencies has gradually evolved into the EU's own security agencies, such as Europol and Frontex, on the basis of equipment, institutionalization and supranationalization.[32]

B. Dynamics of cooperation: soft ways to harmonization?

Cooperation gives EU Member States an approach in the security field that addresses **19** the need for cross-border exchange and concerns about the loss of sovereignty. The EU is currently using cooperation to open up new areas, ranging from security data networks to operational administration (→ § 13).

EU agencies such as Europol or Frontex already represent institutionalized models **20** of cooperation. In adopting these models, Member States also accept the political risks of overlapping competences and responsibility.[33] In the recent past, the gradual

---

[26] Mitsilegas in Bossong/Rhinard, Theorizing Internal Security in the European Union, p. 118.

[27] Mitsilegas, Common Market Law Review 2006, 1277 (1309); on the limits of the Charter of Fundamental Rights, see, e.g., ECJ 5.4.2016 – case C-404/15, ECLI:EU:C:2016:198 – *Aranyosi.*

[28] ECJ 27.5.2019 – case C-508/18, ECLI:EU:C:2019:456 para. 5, with further references.

[29] See Council Resolution 2017/C 18/01 on a Model Agreement for setting up a Joint Investigation Team, 19.1.2017.

[30] See, e.g., ECJ 22.2.2022 – joined cases C-562/21 PPU and C-563/21 PPU, ECLI:EU:C:2022:100 – *Openbaar Ministerie.*

[31] For an overview of recent developments, see Bellanova/Glouftsios, European Security 2022, 454 et seqq.

[32] → § 13 Schöndorf-Haubold also critically describes the agencies' evolution, and that accountability, oversight and legal protection is decreasing with increasing legal and operational independence.

[33] Which framework conditions and obligations apply if, for example, an agency wants to carry out an operation on site with joint teams, → § 13 mn. 84 et seqq.

institutionalization of these forms of cooperation has also set in motion the legalisation of cooperation. As institutionalization progresses through cooperation, the result will inevitably be a certain degree of legal harmonization (→ § 9 mn. 28 et seqq.; → § 12 mn. 18 et seqq.). In the case of data exchange, this may include the following basic building blocks: determination of a specific purpose, thresholds, the protection of core areas of private life, protection of relationships of trust, oversight and legal protection. Where there are regulations governing the exchange of information between States, there is the potential not only to exchange data in individual cases but also to agree, more generally, on mutual standards for dealing with this information.

I. Sharing intelligence as an endurance test

21 The exchange of intelligence is a particularly sensitive area within EU security cooperation. This field can be seen as an endurance test for cooperation on the road to harmonization.[34] The tension between a State's interests in sharing information on matters of 'national security' and concerns about the loss of sovereignty is becoming ever more acute.[35] Where information is shared, the challenge in terms of building mutual trust is to safeguard certain expectations about how data that leave a State's sphere of access are handled. Information transfers are, therefore, subject to purpose limitation and the obligation to delete data, for example, including so as to comply with their own constitutional requirements.[36] Conversely, mutual coordination – which is also always constitutionally charged – creates a certain pressure to standardise. Despite all the restraint shown by the Member States, coordination should at least lead to shared minimum rule-of-law standards, not least because the ECJ, which is itself involved in the process of harmonization, claims legal access to the area of data processing and transfer, and thus to the intelligence services' core business (→ § 14 mn. 2 and 33).[37]

II. How a new type of threat to fundamental rights could lead to a European security benchmark on surveillance

22 This minimal harmonization[38] may ultimately also lead to the creation of a common European standard.[39] It would represent a new benchmark that the EU could get behind in its external relations, for example in negotiations with the United States on

---

[34] See Cross in Dietrich/Sule, Intelligence Law and Policies in Europe, p. 236 et seq.; for an overview of EU cooperation structures, see Palacios in Dietrich/Sule, Intelligence Law and Policies in Europe, p. 201 et seqq.

[35] Cross in Dietrich/Sule, Intelligence Law and Policies in Europe, p. 237.

[36] On international intelligence sharing, see BVerfG 19.5.2020 – 1 BvR 2835/17, NJW 2020, 2235 mn. 236, 243 et seqq.

[37] The ECtHR 25.5.2021 – App. No. 58170/13, 25/05/2021 – *Big Brother Watch* has intervened and developed benchmarks for, among other things, cooperation on data exchange.

[38] Reflections on international harmonization in surveillance protection to some extent go back to a joint series of events with *Sebastian Thess* at Humboldt University in the summer of 2021.

[39] *Masing* already thought in this way; see Masing in Dietrich et al., Nachrichtendienste im demokratischen Rechtsstaat, p. 3 (15). *Masing* was also the rapporteur on a subsequent ruling by the German Federal Constitutional Court, BVerfG 19.5.2020 – 1 BvR 2835/17, NJW 2020, 2235 mn. 236, 243 et seqq.

transatlantic data traffic.[40] The dynamic of harmonization will gain momentum when nation-states and their constitutional courts realise that they can no longer protect the fundamental rights of their citizens if they alone are responsible for monitoring international movements of data. This is due to a new type of threat to fundamental rights that strategic surveillance of communications poses. Typically, threats that trigger fundamental rights protection occur within the spatial sphere, and exclusively within that sphere. The physical presence of a legal asset and the danger to it have typically been strongly linked to where it is located. National fundamental rights are good at protecting territorially delimited legal threats.

The surveillance of international data flows, on the other hand, poses an unbounded **23**
threat to fundamental rights and constitutes a new challenge for constitutional regimes. Communicating via e-mail, a messenger service or phone app means that data packets 'pass through' cables and servers outside a territorial fundamental rights regime.[41] Constitutional courts that impose requirements within a territorially limited sphere can no longer deliver on the promise of fundamental rights protection in regard to these communications. Even if an ambitious standard of surveillance protection is created for domestic security authorities (determining the specific purpose, thresholds, protection of core areas of private life, protection of relationships of trust, oversight, legal protection), the level of protection can no longer safeguard the same communication process along its route as soon as it triggers other legal systems and their – possibly lower-threshold – surveillance rights regimes at international level.[42]

This assessment seems to be shared by the German Federal Constitutional Court, **24**
which adopted a similar a position in its decision on the binding effect of fundamental rights outside of Germany. And it turned a challenge into an opportunity. The standards developed by the Federal Constitutional Court can be 'exported', as it were, by setting rules for cooperation and data exchange with other intelligence services.[43] The dynamic of cooperation can thus also become a dynamic of harmonization.

C. Cooperation as a pathway in sensitive areas of common EU policy fields

Member States are especially sensitive when it comes to European standardization in **25**
the area of 'national security'. They have gone through different security experiences and have different cultures. The Member States are caught in the tension between

[40] Sehl, 'Internationale Überwachungsregeln made in Karlsruhe?' (Legal Tribune Online, 21.10.2020) <https://www.lto.de/recht/hintergruende/h/bverfg-bnd-gesetzgeber-ueberwachung-geheimdienst-ausland-grundrechte-international-europa-eugh-schrems/> (last accessed: 27.9.2023). Even after the latest agreement between the EU and the USA, which included elements such as a proportionality assessment and legal protection, a review by the ECJ is likely to be forthcoming, see Satariano/Pronczuk/McCabe, 'U.S. and E.U. Complete Long-Awaited Deal on Sharing Data' (New York Times, 10.7.2023) <https://www.nytimes.com/2023/07/10/technology/us-eu-data-privacy-deal.html< (last accessed: 27.9.2023).

[41] Such a case is also described by the ECtHR 25.5.2021 – App. No. 58170/13, 25/05/2021 para. 52 – *Big Brother Watch and Others*, with a partly concurring and partly dissenting opinion of judge *Pinto de Albuquerque*.

[42] This is particularly true in view of the fact that strong rule-of-law and fundamental rights safeguards are likely to be seen by the intelligence services as a locational disadvantage in an international comparison.

[43] BVerfG 19.5.2020 – 1 BvR 2835/17, NJW 2020, 2235 mn. 320 et seqq; also taken up by ECtHR 25.5.2021 – App. No. 58170/13 para. 247 et seqq., 251 – *Big Brother Watch*.

fundamental sovereignty interests in 'national security' and basic restrictions on citizens' fundamental rights that are at stake on the one hand and cross-border threats in the guise of current crises that call for exchange and cooperation on the other.

26 Cooperation gives the EU Member States a means to deal with this tension in the security sphere. At present, the EU is using cooperation to open up new areas with structures reaching from sharing information up to enforcement capacities. The starting point for such cooperation and its institutionalization is generally data exchange formats. To ensure that account is taken of the Member States' political expectations, institutional trust and constitutional requirements, these formats are legalized. Thus, cooperation dynamics are also accompanied by juridification, which in turn leads to a certain degree of harmonization in a sensitive area. The ECJ's case law on data retention, for example, opens up access to facets of the legal field of 'national security', thus contributing to a trend towards harmonization. However, that trend is also likely to trigger conflicts with the Member States.

27 The exchange of intelligence represents a particularly sensitive area within EU security cooperation. Expectations of thoroughgoing legalization in this (foreign) policy area are not too high. Nevertheless, the Member States' constitutional courts, the CJEU and the ECtHR are now developing benchmarks and minimum standards. The courts may also be driven by the fact that they see themselves confronted with a new type of fundamental rights threat in the guise of communications surveillance. The surveillance of international data flows poses an unbounded threat to fundamental rights; individual constitutional systems and their courts can no longer guarantee an established level of protection on their own if a communication process flows through extraterritorial cables and servers and triggers surveillance law regimes there that are designed quite differently. The response to this dissolution of the boundaries of threats to fundamental rights need not be resignation, but can, conversely, also lead to the self-confident elaboration of European standards.

§ 12
Between coordination, harmonization and centralization – modes of (inter)action in the European Security Union*

Carolyn Moser

Bibliography: Armada/Weyembergh, 'The Mutual Recognition Principle and EU Criminal Law' in Fletcher/Herlin-Karnell/Matera (eds), The mutual recognition principle and EU criminal law, Abingdon/New York 2017, Ch. 5; Brandsma/Heidbreder/Mastenbroek, 'Accountability in the Post-Lisbon European Union', International Review of Administrative Sciences 2016 (82), 621; Brandsma/Moser, 'Accountability in a Multi-Jurisdictional Field' in Scholten/Brenninkmeijer (eds), Controlling EU Agencies, Cheltenham/Northampton 2021, p. 60; Brants, 'What Limits to Harmonising Justice?' in Colson/Field (eds), EU Criminal Justice and the Challenges of Diversity. Legal Cultures in the Area of Freedom, Security and Justice, Cambridge/New York 2016, p. 221; Calderoni, Organized Crime Legislation in the European Union: Harmonization and Approximation of Criminal Law, National Legislations and the EU Framework Decision on the Fight Against Organized Crime, Heidelberg 2010; Calliess/Ruffert (eds), EUV/AEUV. Das Verfassungsrecht der Europäischen Union mit Europäischer Grundrechtscharta, 6th edn, Munich 2022; Carrera, 'The 20 Years Anniversary of the Tampere Programme: Securitization, Intergovernmentalism and Informalization', Maastricht Journal of European and Comparative Law 2020 (27), 3; Carrera/Mitsilegas/Stefan, Criminal Justice, Fundamental Rights and the Rule of Law in the Digital Age, Brussels 2021; Catanzariti/Türk, EU Agencies and the Rise of a Mixed Administration in the EU Multi-Jurisdictional Setting: Facing the Challenges of the Rule of Law, Cheltenham/Northampton 2020; Colson/Field, 'Legal Cultures in Europe: Brakes, Motors, and the Rise of EU Criminal Justice' in Colson/Field (eds), EU Criminal Justice and the Challenges of Diversity. Legal Cultures in the Area of Freedom, Security and Justice, Cambridge/New York 2016, p. 1; Coman-Kund, 'Holding Europol Accountable. The Promise and Challenges of (Hybrid) Multilevel Accountability' in Arcuri/Coman-Kund (eds), Technocracy and the Law. Accountability, Governance and Expertise, London 2021, chap 12; Craig, EU Administrative Law, 3rd edn, Oxford/New York 2018; Curtin, 'Holding (Quasi-)Autonomous EU Administrative Actors to Public Account', ELJ 2007 (13), 523; de Waele, 'Entrenching the Area of Freedom, Security and Justice. Questions of Institutional Governance and Judicial Control' in Fletcher/Herlin-Karnell/Matera (eds), The European Union as an Area of Freedom, Security and Justice, Abingdon/New York 2017, p. 485; Eliantonio, 'Judicial Review in an Integrated Administration: The Case of "Composite Procedures"', Review of European Administrative Law 2014 (7), 65; Fink, Frontex and Human Rights. Responsibility in 'Multi-Actor Situations' under the ECHR and EU Public Liability Law, Oxford 2018; Hofmann, 'Mapping the European Administrative Space', West European Politics 2008 (31), 662; Hofmann, 'Decisionmaking in EU Administrative Law – The Problem of Composite Procedures', Administrative Law Review 2009 (61), 199; Holland/Holland-Kunkel/Röhl/Zachau, European Security Union. On the Dichotomy of Liberty and Security in the Area of Freedom, Security and Justice, Frankfurt 2022; Kohler, 'The EU Cybersecurity Act and European Standards: An Introduction to the Role of European Standardization', International Cybersecurity Law Review 2020 (1), 7; Mégie, 'Eurojust in Action: An Institutionalisation of European Legal Culture?' in Colson/Field (eds), EU Criminal Justice and the Challenges of Diversity. Legal Cultures in the Area of Freedom, Security and Justice, Cambridge/New York 2016, p. 87; Monar, 'The Area of Freedom, Security and Justice' in von Bogdandy/Bast (eds), Principles of European Constitutional Law, 2nd edn, Oxford 2009, chap 15; Moser, Accountability in EU Security and Defence. The Law and Practice of Peacebuilding, Oxford/New York 2020; Paine, Rights of Man (edited with an introduction and notes by Gregory Claeys), Indianapolis/Cambridge 1992; Papadopoulos, 'Problems of Democratic Accountability in Network and Multilevel Governance', ELJ 2007 (13), 469; Paul, 'Harmonisation by Risk

* The author would like to thank *Effi Spiegel* and *Finn Preiß* for their valuable assistance in finalizing this chapter.

Analysis? Frontex and the Risk-Based Governance of European Border Control', Journal of European Integration 2017 (39), 689; Peers, EU Justice and Home Affairs Law II, 4th edn, Oxford/New York 2016; Peers, 'The Rise and Fall of EU Justice and Home Affairs Law' in Fletcher/Herlin-Karnell/Matera (eds), The European Union as an Area of Freedom, Security and Justice, Abingdon/New York 2017, p. 11; Rosenau, 'Change, Complexity, and Governance in Globalizing Space' in Pierre (ed.), Debating Governance: Authority, Steering, and Democracy, Oxford/New York 2000, p. 167; Stein, 'Assimilation of National Laws as a Function of European Integration', American Journal of International Law 1964 (58), 1; Stein, 'Harmonization of European Company Laws', Law and Contemporary Problems 1972 (37), 318; Streinz (ed.), EUV/AEUV, 3rd edn, Munich 2018; Thompson, 'Harmonization of Laws', JCMS 1965 (3), 302; von Bogdandy/Bast (eds), Unionsverfassungsrecht, Baden-Baden forthcoming (cited in its manuscript version); Voss, 'The Concept of Accountability in the Context of the Evolving Role of ENISA in Data Protection, EPrivacy and Cybersecurity' in Arcuri/Coman-Kund (eds), Technocracy and the Law. Accountability, Governance and Expertise, Abingdon/New York 2021, p. 247; Xanthopoulou, 'Mutual Trust and Rights in EU Criminal and Asylum Law: Three Phases of Evolution and the Uncharted Territory beyond Blind Trust', Common Market Law Review 2018 (55), 489.

A. Introduction

1 Ensuring security is an increasingly complex and sometimes unpredictable endeavour. The reasons for this are manifold. On the one hand, (seemingly) clear-cut security categories – such as internal vs. external and online vs. offline – are eroding due to globalization, digitalization and other transformative phenomena, including climate change.[1] On the other hand, the scope of potential security threats and challenges is constantly broadening – one only need call to mind the ever-expanding opportunities for transboundary criminal activities in cyberspace.[2] Thus, for security policies to be and remain effective, they need to be comprehensive enough to tackle the rapidly-evolving and borderless security realities of our times.

2 This already difficult security setting is compounded by intricate governance structures in the European Union (EU) context. Indeed, efforts by the Union and its Member States to ensure security within the EU unfold in a multilevel governance environment within which there are horizontally and vertically interlaced competences and in which national, transnational and supranational entities with overlapping mandates interact. Apart from the almost inevitable tensions relating to the division of competences and labour, this multilevel setup also raises broader governance questions, in particular as regards political and legal accountability (i.e. democratic scrutiny, judicial review) and transparency.[3]

3 With a view to solving this dual problem of (i) evolving security threats and (ii) fragmented security realities in the EU, the European Commission coined the concept of the European Security Union in 2016.[4] The European Security Union is not a legal scheme, but serves as a conceptual umbrella under which various cross-cutting security threats and phenomena – such as counterterrorism, border management,

[1] European Commission, 'Communication on the EU Security Union Strategy', 24.7.2020, COM(2020) 605 final; Council of the European Union, 'A Strategic Compass for the Union', 21.3.2022, Council Doc. 7371/22.

[2] ENISA, 'ENISA Threat Landscape Report 2022' (November 2022), DOI: 10.2824/764318.

[3] On the difficulties of accountability in multilevel settings, see Papadopoulos, EPL 2007, 469; Brandsma/Moser in Scholten/Brenninkmeijer, Controlling EU Agencies, p. 60. On the Area of Freedom, Security and Justice (AFSJ) more specifically, see de Waele in Fletcher/Herlin-Karnell/Matera, The European Union as an Area of Freedom, Security and Justice, p. 485.

[4] European Commission, 'Communication on delivering on the European Agenda on Security to fight against terrorism and pave the way towards an effective and genuine Security Union', 20.4.2016, COM (2016) 230 final, 2.

cybersecurity or crisis response – can be addressed more holistically and, thus, more effectively.[5] The underlying rationale is primarily to foster systematic cooperation and information sharing so as to facilitate joint action in the Area of Freedom, Security and Justice (AFSJ) that draws together several of the Union's security-related policies (border control, asylum and immigration; judicial cooperation in civil and criminal matters; cooperation in law enforcement).[6] The overall objective of the Security Union framework is as broad as it is ambitious: it is to contribute to ensuring the security of EU citizens, protecting critical infrastructure, combating terrorism, defending against cyber threats and improving overall resilience, including in relation to hybrid threats.[7] To achieve these manifold objectives comprehensive approaches need to be adopted that reflect the complexity and interconnectedness of different security phenomena while being mindful of the delicate competence arrangements regarding security matters in the EU. This is because, in principle, national governments retain their security policy prerogatives, even though at the EU level the incremental Europeanization and supranationalization of numerous security dossiers is rampant both in law and practice.[8]

Against this backdrop, this chapter examines three modes of (inter)action that exist 4
within the policy framework of the European Security Union, namely (i) coordination, (ii) harmonization and (iii) centralization. Coordination, harmonization and centralization have indeed emerged as key courses of action in the pursuit of shaping and operationalizing a European Security Union. Coordination involves the establishment of mechanisms and platforms for information sharing, joint operations and crisis management. Harmonization seeks to align the applicable legal framework as well as operational standards across Member States. Centralization refers to the concentration of decisional, regulatory or operational functions in specific institutions or bodies, usually situated at the EU level, to streamline processes and increase effectiveness.

By analysing and comparing coordination, harmonization and centralization as 5
modes of action within the European Security Union, this chapter pursues a threefold objective. First, we seek to understand how these three modes of (inter)action unfold within the current law and governance framework of the European Security Union. Second, we want to gauge the functions, challenges and limits of these different modes of action in addressing current and future security challenges. Finally, we will reflect on possible future developments regarding the interplay of these modes of action.

To achieve this threefold objective, this chapter is organized as follows: Section B 6
provides a brief overview of the purposes and objectives as well as the law and governance features of the European Security Union. Next, Section C introduces the three modes of action – coordination, harmonization and centralization – and their respective applications, challenges and implications for cooperation and coherence, both for the EU and the Member States. With a view to enriching the analysis with in-depth insights, section D is dedicated to two case studies that deal with border management and cybersecurity, respectively, with a focus on the agencies that chiefly operate in these fields, namely Frontex (border control) and ENISA (cybersecurity). Finally, section E offers some reflections on future decisional and operational developments within the European Security Union.

---

[5] ibid., 2: see, in particular, the introductory paragraphs on p. 2 and 3.

[6] Part 3 Title V TFEU deals with the AFSJ. General provisions on the AFSJ are contained in Art. 67–76 TFEU. Art. 77–80 TFEU cover asylum, migration and border management. Art. 81 TFEU deals with judicial cooperation in civil matters, while Art. 82–86 address judicial cooperation in criminal matters. Law enforcement cooperation is the focus of Art. 87–89.

[7] Hybrid threats are attracting increasing attention in strategy documents on both internal and external security. See, inter alia, COM(2020) 605 final; Council Doc. 7371/22.

[8] Farahat in von Bogdandy/Bast, EUV Art. 3(2) sent. 2 (forthcoming (cited in its manuscript version)).

B. The European Security Union in a nutshell

7 The European Security Union's frame of reference was set relatively recently. It was introduced in 2016 by the European Commission to provide an overarching framework for a raft of security-related policies and measures carried out by the EU and its Member States in parallel or jointly in the AFSJ.[9] The AFSJ is both an objective (Art. 3 (2) TEU) and an EU policy area set out in Title V of Part Three of the TFEU that covers four fields of action: (i) border control, asylum and migration; (ii) judicial cooperation in civil matters; (iii) judicial cooperation in criminal matters; and (iv) law enforcement cooperation. The Security Union is thus a conceptual framework that helps to understand the different objectives and (operational) branches of the AFSJ as a whole.[10]

I. Policy context

8 Driven by the need to provide a collective and coordinated response to intensifying cross-border security phenomena, such as transboundary crimes or migratory flows, Member States started to integrate internal security matters (e.g. border management, judicial cooperation, law enforcement cooperation) under the EU umbrella in the early 1990s.[11] Initially codified as an intergovernmental policy area under the so-called Third Pillar dedicated to Justice and Home Affairs (JHA), the different branches of the policy field subsequently underwent an incremental (partly separate) process of Europeanization as well as supranationalization.[12] This process culminated in the abolition of the pillar structure under the Treaty of Lisbon, paving the way for the AFSJ in its entirety to be governed by the so-called Community method, although with certain exceptions (→ mn. 11 et seqq.).

9 This incremental Europeanization, or even supranationalization, of the AFSJ is, however, not without friction. This is because the AFSJ touches upon essential functions and prerogatives of Member States by aiming to ensure the security of citizens, control access to territory and administer justice across the Union – all key functions of the modern nation-state that are at the core of national sovereignty.[13] Thus, the integration of the AFSJ or, in other words, the construction of a European Security Union, raises questions of sovereignty.[14] It is, therefore, hardly surprising that Member States have been reticent to agree to integrate security matters and have ultimately put in place arrangements to ensure that key security competences remain formally at the national level.[15] This becomes clear when one looks at the EU Treaties: the relevant primary law provisions unequivocally state that ensuring territorial integrity, maintaining law and

---

[9] COM(2016) 230 final, 2 et seq.

[10] Holland et al., p. 43.

[11] For a concise overview of JHA developments up until the entry into force of the Lisbon Treaty in 2009, see Peers in Fletcher/Herlin-Karnell/Matera, The European Union as an Area of Freedom, Security and Justice, p. 11.

[12] Weiß/Satzger in Streinz, AEUV Art. 67 mn. 835.

[13] Monar in von Bogdandy/Bast, Principles of European Constitutional Law, p. 552 et seq.; Farahat in von Bogdandy/Bast EUV Art. 3(2) (forthcoming (cited in its manuscript version)).

[14] Weiß/Satzger in Streinz, AEUV Art. 67 mn. 835, 841 et seq.; Suhr in Calliess/Ruffert, AEUV Art. 67 mn. 1041, 1042 et seq.

[15] In a similar vein, see Peers, p. 1, 4; Colson/Field in Colson/Field, EU Criminal Justice and the Challenges of Diversity. Legal Cultures in the Area of Freedom, Security and Justice, p. 5 et seqq.

order and safeguarding national security *is a national prerogative only* (as expressly mentioned in Art. 4(2) TEU and Art. 72 TFEU).

This setup, in turn, implies a collective effort imperative: as security competences remain nationally fragmented even though they have become horizontally and vertically interlaced, systematic cooperation and information sharing across Member States are pivotal to actually ensuring security in a border-free Union. Yet, despite several programmatic documents aiming at overcoming structural and operational obstacles to effective security cooperation across Member States in the face of (increasingly) serious threats,[16] there was and still is room for improvement.[17] Consequently, the European Commission came up with the idea of the European Security Union to give cooperation and coordination efforts new impetus and a new look. The motivation for subsuming a variety of security-related activities and measures under the Security Union was to substantially improve security cooperation and response capabilities across the Union given, not least, the drastically increasing complexity and interconnectedness of different security phenomena. Although with slight variations over time, the Security Union's main objectives include protecting EU citizens, securing critical infrastructure, combating terrorism, ensuring cybersecurity and responding effectively to different types of crises.[18] As reports have regularly emphasized, the European Security Union has evolved and matured over the years, with various legislative and policy measures being implemented to achieve its goals.[19] However, it remains a work in progress, and several important challenges persist.[20] **10**

II. Law and governance

As mentioned above, the Security Union does not create a new legal scheme or category under EU law. It is (so far) an aspirational frame of reference that helps to understand and tackle the EU's various security-related policies as a whole. Thus, the Security Union project is based on a kaleidoscopic legal framework that includes EU treaties, directives, regulations and administrative agreements. The Security Union is legally anchored in primary law. Art. 67 TFEU sets out the AFSJ, in which the Union shall endeavour to ensure a high level of security (para. 3) by different means (i.e. prevention; coordination and cooperation; recognition of judicial decisions and alignment of laws). Furthermore, secondary law plays a crucial role in shaping the security landscape in the EU. There is indeed an impressive corpus of legislative acts **11**

---

[16] See, e.g., Tampere European Council 15 and 16 October 1999, 'Presidency Conclusions'; European Commission, 'Area of Freedom, Security and Justice: Assessment of the Tampere programme and future orientations', 2.6.2004, COM(2004) 401 final; European Council, 'The Hague Programme–Strengthening freedom, security and justice in the European Union', 3.3.2005; European Commission, 'The Hague Programme: Ten priorities for the next five years The Partnership for European renewal in the field of Freedom, Security and Justice', 10.5.2005, COM(2005) 184 final; European Council, 'The Stockholm Programme – An open and secure Europe serving and protecting citizens', 4.5.2010; European Commission, 'Delivering an area of freedom, security and justice for Europe's citizens – Action Plan Implementing the Stockholm Programme', 20.4.2010, COM(2010) 171 final.

[17] European Commission, 'Communication on delivering on the European Agenda on Security to fight against terrorism and pave the way towards an effective and genuine Security Union', 20.4.2016, COM (2016) 230 final, 2 et seq.

[18] ibid., 2; COM(2020) 605 final.

[19] The latest Commission report on the matter was published in December 2022. See European Commission, 'Communication on the Fifth Progress Report on the implementation of the EU Security Union Strategy', 13.12.2022, COM(2022) 745 final.

[20] ibid.

that brings the somewhat abstract concept of the AFSJ to life. In addition, decisions by the Court of Justice of the European Union (CJEU) and by national courts have shaped key features of the Security Union, notably by corroborating the mutual recognition requirement and its (potential) limits.[21] Finally, policy documents provide guidance. Noteworthy in this context are, inter alia, the Commission's European Agenda on Security of 2015,[22] which was replaced in 2020 by the European Security Union Strategy[23] together with a raft of additional strategies and agendas.[24] The New Strategic Agenda adopted by the European Council in 2019 is also notable.[25]

12 Despite this density of legal provisions, court decisions and policy documents relating to security in the EU, one should not forget that ensuring security remains a fundamentally national prerogative. Indeed, Treaty provisions leave national security within the Member States' remit (Art. 4(2) TEU, Art. 67(1) TFEU, Art. 69 TFEU and Art. 72 and 73 TFEU) and seem to attribute EU institutions rather a subordinate role, even though, in accordance with Art. 4(2)(j) of the TFEU, the AFSJ belongs to the category of shared competences. In other words, the primary actors that ought to be ensuring security across Member States are the Member States themselves. Consequently, no law enforcement competences have been transferred to the EU. At the same time, Treaty provisions also stipulate that the Union 'shall endeavour to ensure a high level of security' by adopting a variety of measures (Art. 67(3) TFEU). This means that Treaty law provides for Union activity in this policy field, even though national actors remain central. This idiosyncratic division of competences and labour, which has been described as a codified requirement of pluralism (in terms of actors and their priorities),[26] has important implications for institutional and operational realities. It leaves us with a somewhat fragmented administrative space[27] in which cooperation among Member States and with EU entities is imperative to ensure security across the Union. This cooperation can take many different forms, including the exchange of public officials, the establishment of contact points, the creation of networks or agencies, the alignment of rules and practices or joint activities.[28] One can subsume these cooperation efforts under the labels of coordination, harmonization and centralization.

13 As stated above, the so-called Community method prevails in the Security Union. In terms of law-making, this means that, in principle, the ordinary legislative procedure set out in Art. 294 of the TFEU applies.[29] Likewise, in terms of judicial review, it implies that the CJEU has jurisdiction over AFSJ dossiers.[30] Yet, the AFSJ (i.e. the Security

---

[21] A very informative account of the principle of mutual recognition and the evolution of judicial cooperation in criminal matters in the EU can be found in Armada/Weyembergh in Fletcher/Herlin-Karnell/Matera, The European Union as an Area of Freedom, Security and Justice, p. 111.

[22] European Commission, 'Communication on the European Agenda on Security', 28.4.2015, COM (2015) 185 final.

[23] COM(2020) 605 final.

[24] For example, EU Strategy to tackle Organized Crime; EU Drugs Strategy; EU Drugs Agenda and Action Plan; EU action plan on firearms trafficking; EU Strategy on Combating Trafficking in Human Brings; EU strategy for a more effective fight against child sexual abuse; Counter-Terrorism Agenda. For an overview, see <https://home-affairs.ec.europa.eu/policies/internal-security/new-way-forward-internal-security_en> (last accessed: 5.10.2023).

[25] European Council, 'Conclusions', 20.6.2019, EUCO 9/19, Annex: A New Strategic Agenda (2019–2024).

[26] Farahat in von Bogdandy/Bast, EUV Art. 3(2) (forthcoming (cited in its manuscript version)).

[27] Others have labelled the phenomenon of EU-wide administrative arrangements as multilevel, mixed, shared, composite or integrated administration. For an overview, see Catanzariti/Türk in Scholten/Brenninkmeijer, Controlling EU Agencies, p. 20.

[28] Weiß/Satzger in Streinz AEUV Art. 75 mn. 862.

[29] Peers, p. 4.

[30] ibid.

Union) also presents some notable exceptions. First, it offers Member States many avenues for differentiated participation, notably because they can decide to opt out,[31] as did Ireland and Denmark (and, formerly, the United Kingdom). While Denmark settled for a strict opt-out (no participation in the AFSJ),[32] Ireland chose a more flexible opt-out (it can decide to opt in to legislation on a case-by-case basis).[33] Second, national parliaments have a privileged role, in that subsidiary issues fall under a special procedure.[34] What is more, national parliaments are involved in the evaluation of policies carried out under the AFSJ, including the performance of Eurojust and Europol (Art. 70 TFEU, Art. 85(1) TFEU, Art. 88(2) TFEU). And, third, some branches of the AFSJ have retained specific features as regards law-making. When it comes to both police cooperation and judicial cooperation in criminal matters, the Commission shares its right of initiative with the Member States, provided they represent a quarter of the members of the Council (Art. 76(b) TFEU). The Council also takes the legislative lead when it comes to measures concerning family law with cross-border implications (Art. 81(3) TFEU) and the establishment of a European Public Prosecutor's Office (EPPO; Art. 86 TFEU). As regards parliamentary involvement, the European Parliament is merely consulted when it comes to operational matters, which are adopted unanimously by the Council (Art. 74 TFEU). Family law with cross-border implications is also adopted according to a special legislative procedure that only involves parliamentary consultation followed by a unanimous vote in the Council (Art. 81(3) TFEU). And, as regards the establishment of minimum standards in matters of criminal justice, Member States can pull the 'emergency brake' and (momentarily) pause the ordinary legislative procedure (Art. 82(3) and 83(3) TFEU). While these intergovernmental reminiscences underscore how difficult it can be to find a compromise in the AFSJ area, which is concerned with core state prerogatives, they also emphasize that these are exceptions to the general rule that the ordinary legislative procedure applies.[35]

C. Modes of (inter)action

As previously mentioned, the EU and its Member States face multifaceted security challenges that require flexible and adaptive responses. Indeed, a one-size-fits-all approach to various security threats and challenges cannot adequately address the intricate security realities of our times. What is more, responsibilities in relation to security matters sit somewhat uneasily between the EU and its Member States. Indeed, current primary law mirrors the drafters' emphasis on cooperation rather than integration: instead of putting in place a set of common rules and institutions with transnational decisional and operational powers, Treaty law favours cooperation between national actors and systems.[36] As a result of these external and internal factors, coordination, harmonization and centralization have emerged as the dominant modes of action within the European Security Union. Coordination, harmonization and centralization each have different strengths and benefits as well as weaknesses and challenges. We will address the different modes and their features and implications in 14

[31] Monar in von Bogdandy/Bast, Principles of European Constitutional Law, p. 552 et seq., 569.
[32] Protocol 22 TFEU. For further details, see Weiß/Satzger in Streinz AEUV Art. 67 mn. 850.
[33] Protocol 21 TFEU. For further details, see ibid., mn. 849–850.
[34] Protocol 2 TFEU.
[35] Farahat in von Bogdandy/Bast, EUV Art. 3(2) (forthcoming (cited in its manuscript version)).
[36] Monar in von Bogdandy/Bast, Principles of European Constitutional Law, p. 552 et seq., 574.

turn. Before doing so, it is important to stress that they are not mutually exclusive. On the contrary, they often overlap and complement each other in practice.

I. Coordination

15 Within the European Security Union, coordination is the basic and thus the most widespread mode of action.[37] By facilitating information sharing, joint operations and crisis management, coordination is intended to promote a collective response to security challenges, harness expertise and resources, and to enable the pooling of efforts to achieve more effective results. Ideally, coordination also fosters a sense of solidarity and shared responsibility among Member States. When it comes to sovereignty concerns, it is the least invasive mode of action, as it leaves the distribution of competences intact. Yet, coordination may be difficult in terms of information sharing, in particular in respect of confidential or classified material, particularly in an increasingly digitalized world.[38] Differences in national priorities (which can sometimes go as far as nationalism), resource allocation and operational capacity may also hinder effective coordination.[39]

16 Several coordination arrangements and mechanisms among Member States have emerged in relation to internal security dossiers (i.e. in the Security Union). On the law enforcement front, one can, for instance, mention Europol, the EU's law enforcement agency.[40] Europol is mandated to support and strengthen law enforcement authorities across Member States in their efforts to prevent and combat serious crime (such as organized crime, drug trafficking, money laundering and human trafficking), terrorism and other forms of transnational crime, such as cybercrime.[41] Furthermore, it serves as a hub for information sharing, strategic analysis and operational coordination, not least because it coordinates and supports joint operations and investigations involving multiple Member States. Still, Europol is above all a 'non-operational support organization'[42] that helps national law enforcement authorities to do their job. Eurojust, the EU's judicial cooperation agency, is another important coordination actor.[43] By coordinating the joint investigation and prosecution of serious cross-border crimes, Eurojust helps overcome some of the legal obstacles and promotes cooperation between national judicial authorities.[44] In the past, joint investigations and operations by Europol, Eurojust and national law enforcement authorities have led to the dismantling of international criminal networks, the disruption of terrorist activities and the recovery of illicit assets. A prominent example of successful

[37] ibid., p. 573 et seq.

[38] For an intriguing account of the EU's increasingly digitalized criminal justice domain, including its challenges and risks, see Carrera/Mitsilegas/Stefan, p. 1 et seqq.

[39] A critical view can be found in Carrera, Maastricht Journal of European and Comparative Law 2020, 3.

[40] Europol was based on a multilateral Convention signed in 1995 before it was established as an EU agency by a Council Decision in 2009. Convention based on Art. K.3 of the Treaty on European Union, on the establishment of a European Police Office (Europol Convention), 27.11.1995; Council Decision (2009/371/JHA) of 6 April 2009 establishing the European Police Office (Europol).

[41] Regulation (EU) 2022/991 of 8 June 2022 amending Regulation (EU) 2016/794, as regards Europol's cooperation with private parties, the processing of personal data by Europol in support of criminal investigations, and Europol's role in research and innovation.

[42] Coman-Kund in Arcuri/Coman-Kund, Technocracy and the Law. Accountability, Governance and Expertise, p. 292.

[43] Regulation (EU) 2018/1727 of 14 November 2018 on the European Union Agency for Criminal Justice Cooperation (Eurojust).

[44] Craig, p. 167. On the remaining obstacles to coordination, for instance due to asymmetrical judicial prerogatives, see Mégie in Colson/Field, EU Criminal Justice and the Challenges of Diversity, p. 87.

cooperation between Europol, Eurojust and national authorities (including from third states) is Operation Avalanche, which, in 2016, led to the dismantling of a massive international cybercriminal network – the 'Avalanche' botnet – that was responsible for launching and managing global malware attacks and money mule recruiting campaigns.[45] The network operated as a delivery platform (cybercrime-as-a-service), enabling criminals from around the world to carry out their illegal activities. The operation, which was said to have a significant impact on the cybercriminal underground, resulted in five people being arrested, 37 premises being searched and 39 servers being seized.[46] Another case that exemplifies the added value of multilevel cooperation was Operation Pollino, a large-scale international investigation carried out in 2018 aimed at dismantling the 'Ndrangheta, a powerful and notorious Italian organized crime group involved in various criminal activities, including drug trafficking, money laundering, corruption and violence.[47] The joint investigation under Eurojust's auspices led to the arrest of more than 70 individuals in the Netherlands, Italy, Germany, Belgium and Luxembourg and the seizure of almost 4,000 kg of cocaine and other drugs.[48]

While coordination can yield efficiency and effectiveness gains, as the success stories mentioned above show, it also comes with potential governance problems. When many entities interact in a fragmented administrative space, it is quite difficult to figure out which actor actually has the leadership role, that is to attribute responsibility for decisions or actions.[49] Indeed, composite administrative structures are known for leading to blurry lines of accountability, and they often lack transparency. Besides potentially impeding proper political oversight, this situation can also create obstacles to judicial review, with potentially severe consequences for fundamental rights protection.[50] 17

II. Harmonization

Harmonization is another crucial tool of EU law and governance, and this also holds for the European Security Union. While some see harmonization as an objective, others conceive it as a process or method.[51] Regardless of one's reading, there is agreement that harmonization is about crafting a coherent legal framework across all Member States that will allow for both legal coherence and operational consistency. In essence, harmonization is about the alignment of laws, regulations, administrative arrangements and eventually also practice to achieve a common (legal) approach to specific policy matters and to increase legal certainty. It aims to eliminate major discrepancies, differences and inconsistencies among Member States and to establish minimum requirements or standards.[52] It has, therefore, also been dubbed assimilation.[53] As 18

[45] For a detailed description of the operation, see Wainwright/Cilluffo, Europol Issue Brief 2017.

[46] Information drawn from Europol's webpage https://www.europol.europa.eu/media-press/newsroom/ (last accessed: 5.10.2023).

[47] Eurojust, 'Coordinated crackdown on 'Ndrangheta mafia in Europe, Joint Press Release', 3.12.2018 <https://www.eurojust.europa.eu/news/coordinated-crackdown-ndrangheta-mafia-europe> (last accessed: 5.10.2023).

[48] ibid.

[49] Hofmann, Administrative Law Review 2009, 199.

[50] Curtin, ELJ 2007, 523; Eliantonio, Review of European Administrative Law 2014, 65.

[51] Calderoni, p. 1.

[52] This definition is inspired by Calderoni, p. 3.

[53] Stein, American Journal of International Law 1964, 1.

writings on harmonization in the early phases of the European Communities show, harmonization is generally a multi-layered endeavour: besides reform efforts at the national level, in the course of which laws and regulations are aligned to meet EU standards, there is also legislative or regulatory activity at the EU level with the objective of fostering and steering further harmonization.[54] Harmonization should not be confused with unification, though, which would suppose the introduction of the same law in the legal orders of all the involved countries.[55] In addition to setting common minimum (and potentially also maximum) standards, harmonization can entail the approximation of laws, which is a narrower concept that denotes the elimination of national norms that are incompatible with the applicable EU standard.[56]

19 In the EU, harmonization is mostly referred to in the context of the common market. Indeed, since the early days of integration it has been a key tool to facilitate the establishment and enhance the functioning of the internal market,[57] the current core primary law point of reference for initiating legal harmonization for market reasons being Art. 114 TFEU. But harmonization goes beyond market dossiers. Its ability to promote legal coherence and legal certainty is essential in the AFSJ domain, too, where it mostly finds its expression in the establishment of (minimum) common standards.[58] Importantly, Treaty provisions relating to the AFSJ mark the distinction between harmonization on the one hand and approximation of laws on the other: relevant Treaty provisions distinguish between the establishment of minimum rules (i.e. harmonization) and the approximation of laws, and in certain circumstance expressly exclude harmonization. This explicit exclusion applies to incentive measures relating to the integration of third-country nationals residing legally in Member States (Art. 79(4) TFEU) and crime prevention (Art. 84 TFEU). This means that, in the European Security Union, we encounter different manifestations of both harmonization and approximation of laws.

20 That said, significant efforts have been made to align legal frameworks in several key areas of the Security Union, a handful of which will be highlighted in the following. One prominent example of harmonization is the EU's counter-terrorism legislation. The 2017 Counter-Terrorism Directive establishes common definitions of terrorist offences and criminalizes certain terrorist acts (e.g. directing a terrorist group, recruitment for terrorism, providing or receiving training for terrorism).[59] Another instance of harmonization is the Cybercrime Directive of 2013, which establishes minimum rules concerning the definition of criminal offences, designates activities that Member States are to criminalize and sets out benchmarks for penalties.[60] In addition, harmonization of border controls and management is one of the cornerstones of the European Security Union. The Schengen Borders Code lays down uniform external border management rules, allowing the free movement of persons within the Schengen Area while main-

---

[54] Stein, Law and Contemporary Problems 1972, 318.

[55] Thompson, JCMS 1965, 302 (304).

[56] Calderoni, p. 1, 5.

[57] See also Stein, Law and Contemporary Problems 1972, 318.

[58] The establishment of minimum rules relates to the mutual recognition of judgments and judicial decisions in criminal matters (Art. 82(2) TFEU) as well as to the definition of criminal offences and sanctions by way of directives for the following areas of crime: terrorism; trafficking in human beings and sexual exploitation of women and children; illicit drug trafficking; illicit arms trafficking; money laundering; corruption; counterfeiting of means of payment; computer crime; and organized crime (Art. 83(1) TFEU).

[59] Directive (EU) 2017/541 of 15 March 2017 on combating terrorism.

[60] Directive 2013/40/EU of 12 August 2013 on attacks against information systems.

taining a harmonized set of security measures at the EU's external borders.[61] It mandates that Member States conduct systematic checks, including against relevant databases, on all individuals crossing the external borders, regardless of their right to free movement under EU law (i.e. EU citizens and their non-EU family members). Finally, there is also harmonization in the field of cybersecurity. The second Network and Information Systems Directive (NIS II Directive) of 2022 in particular has a strong streamlining dimension, in that it aims to harmonize rules on cybersecurity risk management and incident reporting across Member States.[62]

Despite its merits, harmonization (including the approximation of laws) within the **21**
European Security Union faces several challenges. Even though the adoption of legislative acts at the EU level can foster harmonization in the AFSJ, the diversity of legal systems, cultural differences and differing threat perceptions among Member States present obstacles to full harmonization, as does the Member States' propensity to preserve their unique legal traditions and systems.[63] Finding the right balance between harmonization on the one hand and respect for national sovereignty and legal distinctiveness on the other is a delicate endeavour. This particularly holds true in respect of the sensitive area of security, which concerns core state prerogatives that national governments are generally wary of delegating or integrating. Therefore, harmonization may require trade-offs and adjustments to accommodate the Member States' different legal systems and traditions, not least because the pursuit of full harmonization may result in the dilution of certain national approaches and practices, which some deem important from a legal diversity point of view, though.[64] Another criticism of harmonization concerns the fact that differences in national priorities, political will and implementation capacity can delay the adoption and implementation of harmonized measures, meaning that harmonization may turn out to be a lengthy process.[65] Last but not least, when harmonization is not brought about via legislation – which implies parliamentary involvement and, thus, democratic control – but via technocratic rule-making (e.g. standardization, certification), this can create problems of unchecked law-making and democratic legitimacy,[66] with potentially detrimental consequences for the protection of fundamental rights.

III. Centralization

Centralization as a mode of action focuses on the concentration of functions – be **22**
they decisional, regulatory or operational – within specific units or bodies. In the EU context, it mostly means that powers are concentrated in the hands of EU actors (institutions, agencies, etc.) and thus implies a certain level of delegation by the Member States to a designated EU entity. Yet, it is important to note that centralization is not uniform across all EU policy areas. The EU operates according to the principle of

---

[61] Regulation (EU) 2016/399 of 9 March 2016 on a Union Code on the rules governing the movement of persons across borders (Schengen Borders Code).

[62] Directive (EU) 2022/2555 of 14 December 2022 on measures for a high common level of cybersecurity across the Union (NIS II Directive).

[63] Colson/Field in Colson/Field, EU Criminal Justice and the Challenges of Diversity, p. 1, 5 et seqq.

[64] Mégie in Colson/Field, EU Criminal Justice and the Challenges of Diversity, p. 87.

[65] On the different legal cultures and socio-legal contexts at the national level that may pose limits to harmonization and their potential consequences, see Brants in Colson/Field, EU Criminal Justice and the Challenges of Diversity, p. 221.

[66] The fact that lawmakers were not accountable to anyone was one of the major criticisms of the Enlightenment. See Paine, p. 53. Similarly, see Curtin, ELJ 2007, 523.

subsidiarity, which means that decisions are to be taken at the most appropriate level – either at the EU, national or local level, depending on the nature and scope of the matter (Art. 5(3) TEU). Therefore, some policy areas remain closer to the control of national governments, thus preserving a certain degree of national sovereignty. This also holds for the sensitive matters of the European Security Union, where subsidiarity is an important feature (Art. 69 TFEU).[67] Therefore, instances of centralization are rather less common than instances of coordination or harmonization, even though the different modes cannot always be neatly separated in practice. What is more, centralized and decentralized modes of action co-exist in the functionally (partly) integrated but decentralized administrative space that the AFSJ represents.[68]

23 That said, one can distinguish between at least two types of centralization in the Security Union. First, there is a certain degree of normative centralization. One example of this is the legislative definition of minimum rules for certain criminal offences and sanctions and the recognition of judgments in criminal matters at the EU level (Art. 82 and 83 TFEU). In addition, the Council can adopt measures to ensure administrative cooperation between Member States (Art. 74 TFEU). Importantly, external border control, immigration and asylum matters are subject to common rules defined by the EU legislator (Art. 77(2), 78(2) and 79(2) TFEU). Second, there are instances of operational centralization. The creation of the EPPO, for instance, contributes to the centralization of the investigation and prosecution of financial crimes that are detrimental to the EU's budget, such as fraud, corruption and money laundering in relation to EU funds.[69] The EPPO is an independent body, operational since 2021, which was established by way of enhanced cooperation (Art. 20 TEU in conjunction with Art. 86 TFEU). The EPPO consists of a central level (based in Luxembourg) and decentralized offices (in the participating Member States).[70] At the central level, the EPPO has a European Chief Prosecutor, who heads the office and is assisted by a College of Prosecutors. The College comprises European Delegated Prosecutors from each participating Member State, who are responsible for investigations and prosecutions in their respective countries. The EPPO operates across participating EU Member States (currently 22), and its jurisdiction in principle supersedes that of national authorities in relevant cases.[71] Data processing (in relation to potential security threats and risks) is also increasingly centralized, for instance within Frontex or the European Union Agency for Cybersecurity (ENISA). Indeed, the data processing and information analysis functions of these entities give them a key role when it comes to overseeing activities and providing input to policy processes and thus (de facto) involve a certain degree of centralization.

24 Centralization within the European Security Union has both advantages and challenges. Pooling powers and functions can help streamline processes, increase efficiency and ensure a coherent approach to security issues. However, centralization also comes with costs: It raises concerns about the potential erosion of Member States' sovereignty and democratic control. Striking the right balance between centralizing certain functions and respect for national sovereignty and autonomy remains a challenge. For

[67] Suhr in Calliess/Ruffert, AEUV Art. 69 mn. 1073; Mégie in Colson/Field, EU Criminal Justice and the Challenges of Diversity, p. 87.

[68] On the centralized/decentralized nature of the EU administrative space, see Catanzariti/Türk in Scholten/Brenninkmeijer, Controlling EU Agencies, p. 20 et seqq.; Hofmann, West European Politics 2008, 662 (668 et seqq.).

[69] Council Regulation (EU) 2017/1939 of 12 October 2017 implementing enhanced cooperation on the establishment of the European Public Prosecutor's Office ('the EPPO').

[70] Art. 8–13 Regulation (EU) 2017/1939.

[71] Art. 25(1) and 27(5) Regulation (EU) 2017/1939.

centralization to be in line with the standards of good governance, it is crucial to ensure transparency and to establish robust mechanisms for accountability. Indeed, when functions are lifted from the national to the international – or, as in our case, the supranational EU – level, accountability mechanisms need to follow if the exercise of these functions is to be legitimate from a democratic governance point of view.[72] In other words, increased centralization as a mode of action implies the creation of political, legal and administrative accountability arrangements that mirror centralized decision-making, rule-setting or implementation.[73]

D. Case studies: navigating modes of action in border management and cybersecurity

As the following case studies on border management (with a focus on Frontex) and cybersecurity (with a focus on ENISA) show, the different modes of action in the European Security Union – coordination, harmonization and centralization – do not occur in isolation from each other. Rather, they interlace, overlap and often complement each other in the real world of the European Security Union. 25

I. Frontex

Frontex, the EU agency responsible for external border control, has undergone a transformative trajectory over the last two decades that reflects the evolving realities of the European Security Union and its modes of action. Initially serving as a support agency, Frontex provided assistance, training and expertise to enhance operational cooperation among Member States in external border management. However, successive mandate amendments continuously expanded the agency's responsibilities and capabilities, propelling it into a pivotal, centralized hub for integrated border management. The Frontex Regulation currently in place lists more than 30 tasks, among them various executive responsibilities, including joint return operations and search and rescue missions.[74] Despite Frontex having outgrown its mere support role, it formally continues to operate alongside national authorities that retain primary responsibility for border control, raising crucial accountability questions, especially concerning activities in third countries and return operations during which human right violations allegedly frequently occur. 26

Frontex gained prominence with the progressive abolition of borders within the EU, which culminated in the AFSJ without internal frontiers being elevated to one of the core aims of the Union under the Treaty of Lisbon (Art. 3(2) TEU).[75] The process of gradually eliminating checks at internal borders in Europe was initiated in the 1980s 27

---

[72] Moser, p. 96 et seqq. In global governance, this minimalist democratic governance standard is rarely met, however. See Rosenau in Pierre, Debating Governance, p. 192.

[73] Brandsma/Moser in Scholten/Brenninkmeijer, Controlling EU Agencies, p. 60.

[74] See the long list of the agency's tasks according to its current mandate, as listed in Art. 10 of Regulation (EU) 2019/1896 of 13 November 2019 on the European Border and Coast Guard.

[75] Treaty of Lisbon amending the Treaty on European Union and the Treaty establishing the European Community, signed at Lisbon, 13.12.2007.

with the establishment of the Schengen Area.[76] In 1997, the Treaty of Amsterdam further solidified this process by incorporating the Schengen *acquis* into the EU legal framework.[77] While national governments agreed on common rules governing external border control, such as the Schengen Borders Code, they preferred a decentralized and informal implementation mode based on a network of national contact points. Indeed, for many years Member States displayed little enthusiasm for sharing their prerogative of controlling who entered and left their territory – an act considered a fundamental aspect of sovereignty – with an EU structure. However, this decentralized approach proved ineffective.[78] The mid-2000s enlargement towards the Eastern neighbourhood compelled national governments to eventually overcome their reluctance and agree to partially Europeanize external border management by creating a permanent EU structure tasked with coordinating the implementation of common rules.[79]

28 This is why and how, in October 2004, the European Agency for the Management of Operational Cooperation at the External Borders, better known as Frontex, was established through Council Regulation (EC) 2007/2004.[80] Initially designed to complement national efforts, the Warsaw-based agency focused on coordinating the Schengen *acquis* implementation, particularly the Schengen Borders Code,[81] helping Member States to control their external borders.[82] Yet, over time, this initial *cahier de charges* was complemented by a whole raft of new tasks that were successively added to the agency's to-do list. In 2007, the RABIT Regulation added operational tasks to Frontex's portfolio, granting it the authority to temporarily deploy Rapid Border Intervention Teams (RABIT) to Member States facing an exceptional upsurge in illegal border crossings.[83] In 2011, further enhancement of operational capacities occurred when Frontex was permitted to establish European Border Guard Teams, enabling participation in joint operations alongside national contingents.[84] Prompted by the surge in migration in 2015, Frontex's legal framework underwent a comprehensive overhaul in 2016.[85] The revised mandate led to the agency being renamed the European Border and Coast Guard Agency (while retaining its Frontex acronym) and significantly expanded its operational

[76] The Schengen acquis – Agreement between the Governments of the States of the Benelux Economic Union, the Federal Republic of Germany and the French Republic on the gradual abolition of checks at their common borders signed at Schengen 14 June 1985 [2000]; The Schengen acquis – Convention implementing the Schengen Agreement of 14 June 1985 between the Governments of the States of the Benelux Economic Union, the Federal Republic of Germany and the French Republic on the gradual abolition of checks at their common borders signed at Schengen 19 June 1990 [2000].

[77] Treaty of Amsterdam amending the Treaty on European Union, the Treaties establishing the European Communities and certain related acts signed at Amsterdam, 2 October 1997, Protocol integrating the Schengen acquis into the framework of the European Union [1997].

[78] House of Lords, 'European Union Committee, Proposals for a European Border Guard', 1.7.2003, Twenty-ninth Report (2002–3), paras. 19–30.

[79] For a concise overview of the discussions that took place in the early 2000s on the establishment of a permanent EU body to support national border management efforts, see ibid.; Fink, p. 25 et seq.

[80] Council Regulation (EC) No 2007/2004 of 26 October 2004 establishing a European Agency for the Management of Operational Cooperation at the External Borders of the Member States of the European Union.

[81] In its current version: Regulation (EU) 2016/399 of 9 March 2016 on a Union Code on the rules governing the movement of persons across borders (Schengen Borders Code).

[82] Art. 2(1)(a) Council Regulation (EC) No 2007/2004.

[83] Regulation (EC) No 863/2007 of 11 July 2007 establishing a mechanism for the creation of Rapid Border Intervention Teams and amending Council Regulation (EC) No 2007/2004 as regards that mechanism and regulating the tasks and powers of guest officers.

[84] Regulation (EU) No 1168/2011 of 25 October 2011 amending Council Regulation (EC) No 2007/2004 establishing a European Agency for the Management of Operational Cooperation at the External Borders of the Member States of the European Union.

[85] Regulation (EU) 2016/1624 of 14 September 2016 on the European Border and Coast Guard.

powers. Indeed, on account of the 2016 amendments, Frontex transcended its previous support role and unequivocally transformed into a supervisory and operational player.[86] The agency's expansion continued with the most recent mandate amendment in 2019, when its powers related to organizing, coordinating and conducting return operations of irregular migrants were further strengthened.[87] Moreover, the latest reform entailed a substantial increase in the agency's human resources and financial means.[88] Yet, the expansion of Frontex is not confined to its remit, budget and staff growth alone. It also entails the significant geographical enlargement of its operational reach.[89]

Prior to delving into Frontex's different modes of action, it is judicious to mention that the agency's amplified role has attracted heightened scrutiny and continues to spark criticism. The growing number of (quasi-)judicial proceedings at the EU level that address accountability concerns and alleged human rights violations (e.g. to the European Ombudsman, the CJEU and the European Parliament) are, not least, indicative of this. Thus, the agency's accountability and human rights track record remains a contentious issue.[90] 29

That said, coordination is still at the core of the agency's tasks, despite important mandate amendments. Indeed, Frontex continues to act as a supporting coordinator that helps Member States address challenges related to external border control and migration management. Frontex facilitates cooperation and information exchange among Member States and relevant stakeholders, for instance, with a view to contributing to a coordinated response to migration and security issues. Joint operations are an important manifestation of the agency's coordination efforts. They involve the pooling of resources and expertise from multiple Member States to tackle specific border challenges.[91] What is more, Frontex also collaborates with other EU agencies, for instance Europol and the European Asylum Support Office (EASO), to foster information sharing and, potentially, also streamline activities.[92] 30

Frontex also performs activities that aim at harmonizing external border control practices across EU Member States. For instance, the agency develops common operational standards, guidelines and best practices to foster a uniform approach to border management. It also conducts specialized training courses for Member States' border guards and other law enforcement personnel (e.g. customs staff), which effect some level of harmonization. Yet, it is important to underline at this juncture that, even though the agency contributes to harmonization via operational practice, it is not a legislative or regulatory harmonization actor. 31

---

[86] Moser, 'A Very Short Introduction to Frontex–Unravelling the Trajectory of One of the EU's Key Actors' (Verfassungsblog, 3.2.2020) <https://verfassungsblog.de/a-very-short-introduction-to-frontex-unravelling-the-trajectory-of-one-of-the-eus-key-actors/> (last accesed: 5.10.2023).

[87] See, e.g., Art. 1 and 7(2) Regulation (EU) 2019/1896.

[88] See, e.g., Art. 54 Regulation (EU) 2019/1896 (on the agency's staff).

[89] For a concise overview of this geographical expansion, see Coman-Kund, 'The Territorial Expansion of Frontex Operations to Third Countries: On the Recently Concluded Status Agreements in the Western Balkans and Beyond…' (Verfassungsblog, 6.2.2020) <https://verfassungsblog.de/the-territorial-expansion-of-frontex-operations-to-third-countries-on-the-recently-concluded-status-agreements-in-the-western-balkans-and-beyond/> (last accessed: 5.10.2023); Moser/Ferahkaya/Märtin, 'Frontex Goes Africa: On Pre-Emptive Border Control and Migration Management' (Verfassungsblog, 6.2.2020) <https://verfassungsblog.de/frontex-goes-africa-on-pre-emptive-border-control-and-migration-management/> (last accessed: 5.10.2023).

[90] On the intricacies of holding Frontex to account, see the in-depth study by Fink, p. 25 et seq. (n 78).

[91] On the different types of joint operations, ibid., p. 35–45.

[92] Art. 10(r) and (q) Regulation (EU) 2019/1896. Furthermore, explicit provision is made for cooperation with the Fundamental Rights Agency and the European Fisheries Control Agency (Art. 10(s) and (t), respectively).

32 Finally, the centralization dimension of the agency's portfolio has increased, notably as data analysis and exchange have become central components of the agency's remit. As Frontex monitors migratory flows, assesses risks, identifies potential threats and evaluates potential vulnerabilities at the EU's external border, it has become a crucial information and expertise hub that, in turn, fosters harmonization.[93] Frontex is, for instance, situated at the apex of the European Border Surveillance System (EUROSUR) pyramid of data exchange and situational awareness in EUROSUR.[94] This means that Frontex conducts centralized situational awareness and risk analysis, which, in turn, leads to a certain streamlining of policies and activities, as the agency's output guides border control agents on the ground. The agency's Risk Analysis Unit is an example of this centralization: it analyses data and intelligence related to migratory flows and border security and produces actionable risk assessments that guide the allocation of resources and the development of operational strategies at the EU level and also has repercussions at the national level.[95]

33 The evolution of Frontex underscores four things. First, context matters. In other words, evolving circumstances prompt changes in relation to responsibilities and capabilities, as the wide-ranging revisions of the agency's mandate show. Second, by adapting tasks and modes of action to changing circumstances there is a certain propensity to move from 'coordination only' to a more densely integrated, though still composite (and thus fragmented), administrative space in the EU's external border management and the European Security Union more broadly. Third, different modes of action are often superposed: they operate simultaneously (in the best case complementarily) and regularly reinforce each other. Frontex's task of fostering information sharing across Member States (coordination) overlaps with its risk analysis role (centralization), streamlining operational practices (harmonization) and improving joint operations (coordination). Fourth, adjusting Frontex's modes of action to new border control and migration management realities poses governance challenges in that the agency's increasingly complex mandate is not (yet) necessarily complemented by appropriate accountability arrangements. This is not unusual within European integration, though. There tends to be a significant link between the novelty of a governance arrangement and its level of accountability. In other words, accountability measures tend to be established later on once a governance system has been in place for some time.[96]

34 In summary, Frontex's trajectory showcases the intricacies of coordination, harmonization and centralization within the European Security Union. While Frontex has evolved from a coordinating body into a comprehensive operational agency, the complex interplay of coordination, harmonization and centralization continues to change in response to dynamic contexts.

II. ENISA

35 ENISA, the EU's Agency for Cybersecurity, plays a pivotal role in the Union's efforts to strengthen cybersecurity and protect digital assets. It is tasked to promote cybersecurity cooperation, provide technical expertise and coordinate responses to cyber

93 On risk analysis by Frontex as a means of harmonization, see Paul, Journal of European Integration 2017, 689.

94 See, e.g., Art. 26 and 28 Regulation (EU) 2019/1896.

95 Art. 26 and 28 Regulation (EU) 2019/1896.

96 Brandsma/Heidbreder/Mastenbroek, International Review of Administrative Sciences 2016, 621.

incidents.[97] With the growing significance of the digital domain to economic and social development and the steady increase of cyber threats and their intensity, the EU legislator has become aware of the urgent need to provide for robust cybersecurity measures across Member States.[98] Indeed, with a view to safeguarding its digital infrastructure, data and citizens from cyber threats, the EU in 2004 established ENISA as the Union's specialized agency for cybersecurity through Regulation (EC) No 460/2004.[99]

Originally set up as a temporary body, ENISA became a permanent EU agency in 2019, and its mandate and responsibilities have evolved over time to reflect the changing cybersecurity landscape. At its outset, it was tasked with supporting Member States develop and implement effective cybersecurity measures while at the same time fostering cross-border collaboration. Its core modus of action was coordination.[100] In the meantime, though, harmonization and centralization aspects have gained more prominence in the agency's work. Thus, ENISA's current operational realities involve manifold activities that reflect a multifaceted approach to cybersecurity and are tailored to address diverse cyber threats and vulnerabilities. This means that, nowadays, ENISA fulfils complementary coordination, harmonization and centralization tasks. **36**

When ENISA came into being in 2004, it was mandated to provide expert advice, undertake awareness campaigns and promote best practices in cybersecurity among Member States.[101] However, recognizing the need for a more comprehensive approach given the rapidly-evolving cyberrealities, the agency's initial mandate was reinforced in 2013 by Regulation (EU) No 526/2013.[102] The Regulation solidified ENISA's role as the key facilitator of cooperation and coordination in the field of cybersecurity across the EU. In 2016, the adoption of the Network and Information Systems Directive (NIS I Directive) also bolstered ENISA's role in the European Security Union.[103] Among other things, the Directive introduced the obligation on the part of the Member States to adopt a national strategy on the security of network and information systems and mandated ENISA to help national authorities, upon their request, with elaborating these strategies.[104] In 2019, ENISA's mandate was made permanent by the Cybersecurity Act.[105] Not least with the steep rise of cyberattacks during the COVID-19 pandemic and in the wake of Russia's aggression towards Ukraine,[106] it became obvious that cybersecurity at the EU level needed another boost. Consequently, the revised version of the NIS II Directive, which entered into force in January 2023, significantly deepened and widened ENISA's mandate.[107] Importantly, ENISA was designated to host the secretar- **37**

---

[97] On the tasks of ENISA, see Art. 5–12 Regulation (EU) 2019/881.

[98] Craig, p. 166.

[99] Regulation (EC) No 460/2004 of 10 March 2004 establishing the European Network and Information Security Agency.

[100] Craig, p. 166.

[101] Art. 3 Regulation (EC) No 460/2004.

[102] Regulation (EU) No 526/2013 of 21 May 2013 concerning the European Union Agency for Network and Information Security (ENISA).

[103] Directive (EU) 2016/1148 of 6 July 2016 concerning measures for a high common level of security of network and information systems across the Union. Member States were required to incorporate this directive into national law by 9 May 2018 (NIS I Directive).

[104] Art. 7 NIS I Directive.

[105] Regulation (EU) No 2019/881 of 17 April 2019 on ENISA (the European Union Agency for Cybersecurity) and on information and communications technology cybersecurity certification and repealing Regulation (EU) No 526/2013 (Cybersecurity Act).

[106] ENISA, 'ENISA Threat Landscape Report 2021' (October 2021), DOI: 10.2824/324797; ENISA, 'ENISA Threat Landscape Report 2022' (November 2022), DOI: 10.2824/764318.

[107] See the long list of (additional) tasks ENISA is to carry out in the context of the NIS II Directive according to its preamble. Tasks include coordination in the event of incidents (Recital 40), monitoring

iat of the newly created European Cyber Crises Liaison Organisation Network (CyCLONe) and mandated to develop and maintain a European vulnerability registry.[108] What is more, the NIS II Directive makes ENISA a core cybersecurity certification actor and thus a key driver of standardization in relation to information and communications technology products, services and processes.[109] This underscores the fact that the harmonization as well as the centralization dimension of ENISA's work is increasing. Thus, there are features that are similar to Frontex's development, in that – in response to new security realities – ENISA is progressively outgrowing its mere support (i.e. coordination) role and is taking on more and more harmonization and, lately, also centralization tasks.

38 That said, coordination still lies at the core of ENISA's role. The agency acts as a focal point for collaboration and information exchange among Member States, EU institutions and other relevant (including private) stakeholders. It also acts as a central platform for the sharing of knowledge, best practices and threat intelligence. By organizing forums, workshops and exercises, ENISA promotes information exchange and the development of joint strategies to counter cyber threats. What is more, through its secretarial role in the Computer Security Incident Response Teams (CSIRTs) network,[110] ENISA enhances coordination among national cybersecurity teams and fosters a harmonized response to cyber incidents across the EU.[111]

39 This brings us to the agency's harmonization portfolio. As the EU's cybersecurity landscape became increasingly complex, ENISA's harmonization role also expanded. Thus, ENISA assists in the development of national cybersecurity strategies, (de facto) aligning them with the EU's broader cybersecurity framework. Additionally, the agency actively contributes to the development of cybersecurity guidelines and recommendations. The agency's work thus contributes to streamlining cybersecurity capabilities across Member States, reducing fragmentation and enhancing the EU's collective resilience against cyber threats in areas such as risk management, incident reporting and security certification. Importantly, the agency works towards standardizing cybersecurity practices and frameworks across Member States to ensure a consistent and coherent approach to cybersecurity. ENISA plays a crucial role in developing and promoting European Union cybersecurity certification schemes, for instance.[112] These schemes aim to establish a common framework for certifying the security and resilience of digital products, services and processes within the EU. By harmonizing certification standards, ENISA works to facilitate the free flow of secure digital products and services across EU borders, bolstering cybersecurity across the Union. It has also been argued that ENISA played a certain role in the shaping and development of uniform EU law relating to data protection, electronic primacy and cybersecurity.[113]

40 And so we come to centralization. ENISA serves as the EU's repository of cybersecurity expertise and knowledge. It thus acts as a central knowledge hub, pooling cybersecurity intelligence and insights from various sources, which are then shared

---

and analysis of national cyber hygiene policies (Recital 49), tracing vulnerability (Recital 62) and security risk assessment regarding supply chains (Recital 90).

[108] Art. 12(2) and 16 (2) NIS II Directive.

[109] On this issue, see Kohler, International Cybersecurity Law Review 2020, 7.

[110] Art. 7(3) Regulation (EU) 2019/881 and Art. 12(2) NIS I Directive.

[111] Recital 46 Regulation (EU) 2019/881; see also Art. 15(2) NIS II Directive.

[112] Art. 8 Regulation (EU) 2019/881; see also Art. 24 NIS II Directive; see also Kohler, International Cybersecurity Law Review 2020, 7.

[113] Gregory in Arcuri/Coman-Kund, Technocracy and the Law, p. 254 et seqq.

with Member States to improve their capabilities.[114] By centralizing such expertise, ENISA acts as a valuable resource for both Member States and EU institutions, providing them with actionable recommendations and technical assistance to address emerging cyber challenges effectively.[115] In addition, as previously mentioned, ENISA supports the elaboration of national cybersecurity strategies that, besides entailing a harmonization dimension, also leads to a certain degree of centralization, as ENISA has accumulated knowledge about how to draft an appropriate national cyber strategy, and can then feed that centralized expertise into national documents. If the Commission's legislative proposal on cyber solidarity were to be adopted, that would give an important boost to centralization.[116] If that were to happen, ENISA would, inter alia, also be mandated to (i) operate and administer the new EU cybersecurity reserve and (ii) review and assess threats and mitigation actions with respect to a specific significant or large-scale cybersecurity incident.[117]

At this juncture, it is important to once more stress that the different modes of **41**
action are neither mutually exclusive nor neatly separate, but often interlace or overlap in practice. As in other security-related policy fields, cybersecurity is also composed of centralized and decentralized structures. Certification is an important instance of interlaced modes of action. It entails harmonization with a view to facilitating cooperation and also has an element of centralization, as the certification standards are defined under the leadership of ENISA. The CSIRTs network, which aims to foster cooperation, information sharing and trust with regard to cross-border incidents, is another example of superposed modes of action.[118] ENISA supports incident coordination, upon request, and provides the network's secretariat. The network is thus a means of effective cross-border coordination that operates within a harmonized framework with centralized elements. Cross-border cybersecurity exercises are another example of interwoven modes of action. ENISA organizes and coordinates cybersecurity exercises, such as Cyber Europe 2022,[119] which aim to foster Member States' preparedness to adequately respond to crisis situations.[120] In doing so, the cyber exercises also entail a harmonization dimension, as they promote a common approach to cybersecurity preparedness.

ENISA's significance in the European cybersecurity landscape should not be **42**
understated. Through coordination, harmonization and centralization, it fosters collective resilience to cyber threats across the EU. As digitalization continues to shape the world, ENISA's role as a facilitator and expert cybersecurity hub remains crucial to ensuring cybersecurity in the EU, and its role – notably in relation to harmonization and centralization – is likely to grow in the (digital) future. ENISA's broadening portfolio will, in turn, increase the need for appropriate accountability and transparency arrangements to be (put) in place.

---

[114] Art. 9 Regulation (EU) 2019/881.

[115] Gregory in Arcuri/Coman-Kund, Technocracy and the Law, p. 251 et seqq.

[116] European Commission, 'Proposal for a Regulation of the European Parliament and of the Council laying down measures to strengthen solidarity and capacities in the Union to detect, prepare for and respond to cybersecurity threats and incidents', 18.4.2023, COM(2023) 209 final.

[117] ibid., Art. 12(6) and 18(1).

[118] Art. 15(1) NIS II Directive.

[119] Cyber Europe 2022 (CE2022) is a pan-European cyber crisis exercise involving more than 1,000 participants from across Europe. ENISA organizes the exercise. For more information, see <https://www.enisa.europa.eu/topics/training-and-exercises/cyber-exercises/cyber-europe-programme/cyber-europe-2022> (last accessed: 5.10.2023).

[120] Recital 47 Regulation (EU) 2019/881.

E. Conclusions

43 As we have seen, the European Security Union is a fragmented administrative space within which there are different modes of action, namely coordination, harmonization and centralization. These modes are not mutually exclusive, though. On the contrary, they often overlap and tend to mutually reinforce each other in practice.

44 Despite the clear benefits of cooperation in terms of effectiveness, it is important to note that collaboration in the European Security Union – be it in the form of coordination, harmonization or centralization – is not without its challenges and complexities. Immigration, asylum, justice cooperation as well as law enforcement are sensitive issues that touch on national sovereignty and cultural differences between EU Member States. Balancing the need for collective action with respect for national prerogatives and identities remains an ongoing challenge.

45 In some cases, harmonization and, in particular, centralization face resistance from certain Member States that prioritize national autonomy in these areas or that are wary that the ongoing rule-of-law crisis in some central Eastern European Member States undermines the validity of the mutual recognition principle, as mutual trust is diminishing.[121] As a result, certain aspects of the AFSJ are subject to advanced intergovernmental cooperation rather than full harmonization or centralization.

46 Cooperation, harmonization and centralization as modes of action in the Security Union also pose governance challenges. Interweaving the mandates of national and EU actors in a fragmented administrative space through coordination, harmonization and centralization risks undermining transparency and impeding effective political, legal and administrative accountability. This, in turn, can have potentially serious consequences for democratic legitimacy and the protection of fundamental rights. Therefore, it is crucial to set up effective transparency and accountability arrangements that cover the involved actors and their different modes of (inter)action.

47 That said, developments in relation to the European Security Union have involved continuous negotiations and compromises between the Union and its Member States to strike the right balance between effective joint action and common rules on the one hand and preserve national sovereignty in matters related to justice, security and immigration on the other. As the Security Union evolves and attempts to cope with new challenges, the need for more coordination, harmonization and centralization is likely to increase. It will be interesting to see how security realities in the coming decades will impact the different modes of action and their interplay in the construction of the European Security Union.

[121] On the past, present and possible future jurisdictional developments regarding mutual trust in criminal cooperation in the EU, see Xanthopoulou, Common Market Law Review 2018, 489.

§ 13
The institutional dimension of the EU Security Union: the EU agencies*

Bettina Schöndorf-Haubold

Bibliography: Aden, 'Europäische Rechtsgrundlagen und Institutionen des Polizeihandelns' in Lisken/Denninger (eds), Handbuch des Polizeirechts, 7th edn, Munich 2021, p. 1809; Aden, 'Interoperability Between EU Policing and Migration Databases: Risks for Privacy', EPL 2020 (26), 93; Allegrezza, 'The European Public Prosecutor's Office (EPPO): A Milestone for the EU Integration Process' in Ambos/Rackow (eds), The Cambridge Companion to European Criminal Law, Cambridge 2023, p. 413; Augsberg, 'Europäisches Verwaltungsorganisationsrecht und Vollzugsformen' in Terhechte (ed.), Verwaltungsrecht der Europäischen Union, 2nd edn, Baden-Baden 2022, § 6; Blasi Casagran, 'The New Europol Legal Framework' in O'Neill/Swinton (eds), Challenges and Critiques of the EU Internal Security Strategy: Rights, Power and Security, Cambridge 2017, p. 149; Böse, 'Die europäische Staatsanwaltschaft "als" nationale Strafverfolgungsbehörde – Kritik eines neuen Rechtsschutzmodells', JZ 2017, 82; Bossong, 'Die Weiterentwicklung von Schengen und der europäischen Migrations- und Asylpolitik', SWP-Studie 2022 (3); Bossong, 'Intelligente Grenzen und interoperable Datenbanken für die innere Sicherheit der EU, Umsetzungsrisiken und rechtsstaatliche Anforderungen', SWP-Studie 2018 (4); Chamon, EU agencies, Oxford 2017; Cooper, 'A New Form of Democratic Oversight in the EU: The Joint Parliamentary Scrutiny Group for Europol', Perspectives on Federalism 2018 (10), 184; Freudlsperger/Maricut-Akbik/Migliorati, 'Opening Pandora's Box? Joint Sovereignty and the Rise of EU Agencies with Operational Tasks', Comparative Political Studies 2022 (55), 1983; Gkliati, 'The EU Returns Agency: The Commissions' Ambitious Plans and Their Human Rights Implications', European Journal of Migration and Law 2022 (24), 545; Goldner Lang/Nagy, 'External Border Control Techniques in the EU as a Challenge to the Principle of Non-Refoulement', ECLR 2021 (17), 442; Groß, 'Defizite des Grundrechtsschutzes bei FRONTEX-Einsätzen', ZAR 2020, 51; Groß, Die Legitimation der polyzentralen EU-Verwaltung, Tübingen 2015; Hecker, Europäisches Strafrecht, 6th edn, Berlin 2021; Hernández López/Jiménez-Villarejo Fernández, 'Eurojust' in Ambos/Rackow (eds), The Cambridge Companion to European Criminal Law, Cambridge 2023, p. 387; Herrnfeld, 'The EPPO's Hybrid Structure and Legal Framework: Issues of Implementation – a Perspective from Germany', eucrim 2018, 117; Herrnfeld/Brodowski/Burchard (eds), European Public Prosecutor's Office, Baden-Baden 2023; Hruschka, 'Grenzkontrollen an den Grenzen des Rechts', APuZ 2022 (42), 35; Jansen/Schöndorf-Haubold (eds), European Composite Administration, Antwerp 2011; Karpenstein/Sangi, 'Nationale Sicherheit im Unionsrecht: Zur Bedeutung von Art. 4 II 3 EUV', GSZ 2020, 162; König, The Rise of EU Police Cooperation: Governing Differentiated Integration, London 2023; Krämer, Der Einsatz gemeinsamer Teams im Europäischen Verwaltungsverbund, University of Gießen 2023 (doctoral thesis, manuscript); Ligeti/Giuffrida, 'Europol', in Ambos/Rackow (eds), The Cambridge Companion to European Criminal Law, Cambridge 2023, p. 361; Orator, Möglichkeiten und Grenzen der Einrichtung von Unionsagenturen, Tübingen 2017; Peers, EU Justice and Home Affairs Law II, 4th edn, Oxford 2016; Peuker, Bürokratie und Demokratie in Europa, Tübingen 2011; Pfeffer, 'Stille Europäisierung – Wie europäisch wird das deutsche Polizeirecht?', NVwZ 2022, 294; Pilniok, Governance im europäischen Forschungsförderverbund, Tübingen 2011; Priebe, 'Europol – neue Regeln für die Zusammenarbeit auf dem Gebiet der Strafverfolgung', EuZW 2016, 894; Riedel, 'Grenzschutz, Migration und Asyl: Wege der Europäischen Union aus der Politikverflechtungsfalle', SWP-Studie 2020 (23); Rijpma, 'Frontex and the European System of Border Guards: the Future of European Border Management' in Fletcher/Herlin-Karnell/Matera (eds), The European Union as an Area of Freedom, Security and Justice, London 2017, p. 217; Schmidt-Aßmann/Schöndorf-Haubold (eds), Der Europäische Verwaltungsverbund, Tübingen 2005; Schmidt-Aßmann/Schöndorf-Haubold, 'Verfassungsprinzipien

* This chapter draws on findings from previous publications, to which reference is made throughout.

für den Europäischen Verwaltungsverbund' in Voßkuhle/Eifert/Möllers (eds), Grundlagen des Verwaltungsrechts I, 3rd edn, Munich 2022, § 5; Schöndorf-Haubold, 'Europäisches Polizei- und Sicherheitsrecht' in Terhechte (ed), Verwaltungsrecht der Europäischen Union, 2nd edn, Baden-Baden 2022, § 35; Schöndorf-Haubold, 'Europäisches Sicherheitsrecht' in Ehlers/Fehling/Pünder (eds), Besonderes Verwaltungsrecht III, 4th edn, Heidelberg 2021, § 68; Schöndorf-Haubold, 'Legitimationsfragen der Verbundverwaltung' in Kahl/Mager (eds), Verwaltungsaufgaben und Legitimation der Verwaltung, Baden-Baden 2022, p. 219; Schoppa, Europol im Verbund der europäischen Sicherheitsagenturen, Berlin 2013; Siegel, Entscheidungsfindung im Verwaltungsverbund, Tübingen 2009; Simantiras, Netzwerke im Europäischen Verwaltungsverbund, Tübingen 2016; Vos, 'EU agencies on the move: challenges ahead', SIEPS 2018 (1); Yolaçan, Verteidigung in grenzüberschreitenden Ermittlungen der Europäischen Staatsanwaltschaft, Berlin 2023.

A. The EU security architecture: introductory remarks on its process of differentiation

1 Notwithstanding the fact that Member States are responsible for ensuring their own internal security, an overarching security architecture has gradually evolved at the European Union level that is becoming ever more firmly entrenched and more highly differentiated.[1] The European Union Agency for Law Enforcement Cooperation (Europol), the European Border and Coast Guard Agency (Frontex) and the European Union's Agency for Criminal Justice Cooperation (Eurojust) are constituent parts of that security architecture, as are the European Union Agency for Law Enforcement Training (CEPOL), the European Public Prosecutor's Office (EPPO) and the European Union Agency for the Operational Management of Large-Scale IT Systems in the Area of Freedom, Security and Justice (eu-LISA).[2] Provision was made for some of these EU security agencies under the Treaties, whilst others, such as Europol, were subsequently provided with a basis in primary EU legislation.[3]

2 The EU's security agencies are organizationally separate from the Member States' police and security authorities. Nevertheless, the two levels are both interconnected in manifold ways and reliant on and aligned to cooperate with each other to fulfil their respective information, coordinating and supporting tasks. That cooperation does not only occur procedurally on an ad-hoc basis by way of bilateral and multilateral exchange or practical cooperation, but is becoming firmly established and institutionally consolidated primarily on account of personnel overlaps within joint bodies and facilities as well as in the context of ongoing, reciprocal information sharing in common network infrastructures.

3 In terms of their history and organizational structure, the EU agencies are themselves characteristic of cooperation at the interface between Member States' sovereignty, supranatural oversight and international integration. They are being

[1] For an overview, see Aden in Lisken/Denninger, Handbuch des Polizeirechts, M., p. 1809; Schöndorf-Haubold in Ehlers/Fehling/Pünder, Besonderes Verwaltungsrecht III, § 68; regarding developments, see Ehlers/Fehling/Pünder, Europäisches Sicherheitsverwaltungsrecht, 2010.

[2] The European Monitoring Centre for Drugs and Drug Addiction (EMCDDA), the European Union Aviation Safety Agency (EASA), the European Maritime Safety Agency (EMSA), the European Union Agency for Railways (ERA), the European Union Agency for Cybersecurity (ENISA) and the European Academic Exchange Service also implement tasks within the EU Security Union, but will not be made discussed in the following. On the Common Security and Defence Policy (CSDP), see, e.g., European Parliament, 'Resolution of 18.1.2023 on the implementation of the common security and defence policy – annual report 2022', OJ C 214, 16.6.2023, 54.

[3] See, in particular, Art. 85, 86 and 88 TFEU.

increasingly augmented by information networks and information-related facilities that make available permanent structures within a bewildering overarching security-related information network.

All the EU's security agencies are built on cooperation mechanisms between national security authorities that often developed out of what were initially informal networks and were subsequently institutionalized or even supranationalized under the umbrella of the European Community and then the European Union. What all the institutions have in common is their claim to be constantly evolving, expanding and being given legal legitimacy. Most of the many legal adjustments, for instance to the Europol and Frontex regimes, have, therefore, gone along with expanding mandates as well as expanding personnel, budgetary and infrastructural capacities that comes with the agencies' gradual emancipation and their growing into genuine Union security agencies. For legal and factual reasons, the EU's agencies are nevertheless always dependent on cooperating with national security agencies, which operate across their respective territories and – at least thus far – have the necessary operative powers of intervention and compulsion.[4] 4

The Member States' decentralized and the EU's centralized (usually deconcentrated) security agencies are intertwined within policy programmes, such as the Security Strategy the European Commission put forward in 2020 and called the 'Security Union'[5] – that appears to go beyond the Area of Freedom, Security and Justice (AFSJ) as set out in Title V of Part 3 TFEU, melds internal security concerns with and external security concerns, and also encompasses issues around resilience and the 'security ecosystem'. The following analysis shows that behind significant intertwining at the EU level there is always a strong intention to steer a particular policy area at the central, supranational level, which thus generally fosters further centralization.[6] That trend can be made out for the area of EU security provision, too.[7] The fundamentally altered security situation following Russia's war of aggression against Ukraine is also giving a further boost to this Unionization process in the area of internal security.[8] Its increased relevance is in part associated with an increase in legal and social scrutiny as well as the call for legitimation, greater accountability (e.g. as regards issues around the binding nature of fundamental rights) and the in-depth oversight of legal ties.[9] 5

---

[4] For an outlook on overarching forms of cooperation in the grey areas of EU, supranational and national competences, see Commission Recommendation (EU) 2021/1086 of 23.6.2021 on building a Joint Cyber Unit, OJ L 237, 5.7.2021, 1. On the evolution and limits of Europeanization and harmonization of Member States' police and security legislation, see Pfeffer, NVwZ 2022, 294 et seqq.

[5] European Commission, 'Communication on the EU Security Union Strategy', 24.7.2020, COM(2020) 605 final; see also the periodical progress reports, most recently European Commission, 'Communication on the Fifth Progress Report on the implementation of the EU Security Union Strategy', 13.12.2022, COM (2022) 745 final, following the 'Fourth Progress Report on the EU Security Union Strategy', 25.5.2022, COM(2022) 252 final.

[6] On the general direction of travel, see, e.g., Augsberg in Terhechte, Verwaltungsrecht der Europäischen Union, § 6 mn. 77.

[7] Schöndorf-Haubold in Terhechte, Verwaltungsrecht der Europäischen Union, § 35 mn. 32, 100, 136 et seqq.

[8] On the EU's structured security cooperation with Ukraine as well as with Europol and Frontex, see, COM(2022) 745 final, 22 et seq.; see European Commission, 'Joint Communication EU Policy on Cyber Defence', 10.11.2022, JOIN(2022) 49 final.

[9] Progress is not always an entirely seamless process. Examples include the debate around Europol's recently extended mandate – not only, but also in response to objections raised by the European Data Protection Supervisor (EDPS), who required Europol to delete large amounts of data; see, most recently, the EDPS's action aimed at getting Art. 74a and 74b of the Europol Regulation deleted on account of the impermissible retroactive effect of legalizing the processing of large amounts of data without any concrete reference to specific criminal offences (European Data Protection Supervisor, 'EDPS takes legal action as new Europol Regulation puts rule of law and EDPS independence under threat', 22.9.2022, Press Release EDPS/2022/23. The resignation of *Fabrice Leggeri*, the then Executive Director of Frontex, in April 2022

6 Besides the 'classic' security agencies, first and foremost Europol and Frontex, the investigation that follows covers centralized infrastructures, including their institutional link to eu-LISA, and networks backed by the EU agencies. However, the group of agencies and authorities that the European Commission itself categorizes as belonging to the Security Union goes well beyond the scope of this chapter (→ mn. 12 et seq.).[10]

7 Three examples serve to illustrate the processes of emancipation and becoming independent that are characteristic of the EU security architecture (→ mn. 82 et seq.):

8 Operational cooperation at the EU's external borders is the key point of reference for the continuous expansion of the operative powers of EU security agencies. In the coming years, Frontex, the Union's border management agency, will be expanded to stand alongside existing structures and become a genuine border police force that, in addition to having its own border guards, will in particular have its own powers and equipment. The increasing criminalization of migration and the ever more vigorous approach being taken to illegal migration[11] mean that the issue of border protection is turning into one of the main issues of the Union's security provision being addressed under secondary EU legislation (→ mn. 86 et seq.).

9 The other two examples relate to the sharing of information between the security agencies, which forms the basis of all security cooperation. The main reason for the recent amendment to the Europol Regulation[12] was to enable the agency to take direct receipt of personal data on private individuals and process large amounts of data without the need for any concrete reference to a criminal offence.[13] The amendment, which refers to this as 'cooperation with private parties', appears to seek to rhetorically obscure the fact that even when Europol directly receives data on a voluntary basis that means it is independently collecting data. Regardless of the fact that the authority to take receipt of data without the corresponding obligation on the part of private platform operators and service providers to transfer data will likely hardly be effective, this amendment is also evidence of the general and ongoing evolution of the EU security agencies' own security-related powers (→ mn. 89 et seq.).

---

was also a consequence of a number of weak spots in the structure of the European security architecture. *Leggeri*, not least, resigned in response to continuing criticism of his time in office because the Europol was very likely involved in illegal pushbacks and other potential fundamental rights violations. Criticism was first raised by his own staff within the Agency, because they were unable to properly investigate fundamental rights violations, and Frontex was also facing investigations by other EU bodies and oversight bodies, such as the European Court of Auditors and the European Anti-Fraud Office (OLAF). The European Parliament had also refused to discharge Frontex's budget for 2020 on account of the ongoing investigations; regarding the accusations made, see European Parliament, 'Briefing for the European Parliament – European Parliament scrutiny of Frontex', 26.9.2022, PE 698.816; European Parliament, 'Decision (EU) 2023/325 on discharge in respect of the implementation of the budget of the European Border and Coast Guard Agency (Frontex) for the financial year 2020', 18.10.2022, OJ L 45, 14.2.2023, 13.

[10] The authorities responsible for air safety, railways and maritime traffic, the MCDDA and the European External Action Service (EEAS) will not be included in the following analysis; see European Commission, 'European Security Union' <https://ec.europa.eu/info/strategy/priorities-2019-2024/promoting-our-european-way-life/european-security-union_de> (last accessed: 27.3.2024) and European Parliament, 'Resolution of 18.1.2023 on the implementation of the common security and defence policy – annual report 2022', OJ C 214, 16.6.2023, 54.

[11] See, in this regard, Schöndorf-Haubold in Ehlers/Fehling/Pünder, Besonderes Verwaltungsrecht III, § 68 mn. 90 et seqq.

[12] Regulation (EU) 2016/794 on the Agency of the European Union for Law Enforcement Cooperation (Europol) […], OJ L 135, 24.5.2016, 53, as last amended by Regulation (EU) 2022/991 amending Regulation (EU) 2016/794, as regards Europol's cooperation with private parties, the processing of personal data by Europol in support of criminal investigations, and Europol's role in research and innovation, OJ L 169, 27.6.2022, 1 (Europol Regulation).

[13] See Art. 26(2) Europol Regulation, as last amended by Regulation (EU) 2022/991.

Alongside and with these powers, institutionalized information structures are also taking on a life of their own, as can be seen from the example of eu-LISA (→ mn. 93 et seq.). 10

In view of this manifold interleaving of agencies and bodies, the question arises of the relationship between the EU security architecture and the Treaty competences as well as the distribution of responsibilities between the Union and the Member States. There are rule-of-law limits to the recourse to and the instrumentalization of Member States' fundamental responsibilities (→ mn. 97 et seq.). 11

B. The EU security architecture: stocktaking

The key components of the EU's security architecture are its internal security agencies, authorities and facilities, that is Europol, Frontex, Eurojust, the EPPO, CEPOL and eu-LISA (→ mn. 15 et seq.). On account of the complexity of assigned competences and the Member States' basic responsibilities, they are also part of the common European security architecture. The Union's agencies form a superstructure that originally enabled national and international agencies to interconnect but that is now itself increasingly fulfilling security tasks without, though, simultaneously taking an institutional/hierarchical position in relation to the Member States' agencies. The EU agencies are all characterized by the fact that the Member States are, on the one hand, represented within their administrative structures, i.e. the board or a governing body, and that, on the other hand, the work of the Union agency generally relates to the work of a national authority, i.e. it supports cooperation, facilitates the exchange of information and, in some cases, assists in operational security provision. 12

Being a relatively new agency, eu-LISA, the central operator of large IT systems in the AFSJ, has held a special position since 2012. It has no security-related powers of its own, but takes on key interface functions in relation to the other security agencies. eu-LISA's status and mission relate to data networks and data infrastructure, a second key element of the institutional dimension of the European Security Union that is both legally intertwined through the relevant legal acts and technically entwined through eu-LISA. Operational networks and corresponding legislation regularly make large amounts of data accessible to a number of Union and sometimes even national security agencies, which can be illustrated using the example of the ETIAS travel information system (→ mn. 72 et seq.). 13

The agencies as well as the information systems they operate are typical of the administrative structure within the 'European composite administration'.[14] They are evidence of institutionalized cooperation structures that either already existed or are being newly established and that link the different security agencies within that 'composite administration' at the organizational and procedural level.[15] Taking recourse 14

[14] Regarding terminology and constitutional requirements, see Schmidt-Aßmann/Schöndorf-Haubold in Voßkuhle/Eifert/Möllers, Grundlagen des Verwaltungsrechts I, § 5 mn. 22 et seqq., with further references; on the features, references and issues around legitimation, see only Peuker, p. 7 et seqq.; Siegel, p. 223 et seqq., 273 et seqq.; Pilniok, p. 15 et seqq.; Simantiras, esp. p. 19 et seqq.; with different terminology and a focus on the EU administration Groß, p. 1 et seqq.; see also the contributions in Jansen/Schöndorf-Haubold as well as in Schmidt-Aßmann/Schöndorf-Haubold.

[15] As already in Schöndorf-Haubold in Terhechte, Verwaltungsrecht der Europäischen Union, § 35 mn. 30 et seqq. Describing it as 'EU self-administration' or 'direct implementation' would be misleading, since these terms cannot express the specific characteristics of a centralized, cooperative administration in contrast to a purely EU self-administration in the strict sense; see Aden in Lisken/Denninger, Handbuch des Polizeirechts, M. mn. 98, with further references.

to 'agencies' as specialized, mostly independent bodies follows the general trend within European administrative structures towards a highly differentiated administration that is not integrated into the hierarchies and oversight structures of either the Member States or the EU, for example vis-à-vis the European Commission[16]; however, the Commission and the Member States are generally represented on the governing boards of these bodies. Each of these agencies embodies, in a subject-related specific way, the characteristic structures of 'composite administration', which are situated between the separation of competences and cooperation, overarching intertwinedness and the remaining basic responsibilities and competences of the Member States.

I. Security agencies

1. European Union Agency for Law Enforcement Cooperation (Europol)

a) Legal bases and structure

15 Europol was established as the European Police Office in The Hague back in 1999 on the basis of the then applicable intergovernmental European Convention (Europol Convention)[17].[18] Since the signing of the Lisbon Treaty, Art. 88 TFEU has provided its primary law basis, significantly strengthening the agency's mandate. In addition to information processing, that mandate now also encompasses the coordination, organization and implementation of joint investigations and operational measures, for example in the context of Joint Investigation Teams (JITs; Art. 88(2) subpara. 1 sent. 2(b) TFEU).

16 The Europol Regulation (EU) 2016/794 currently provides the secondary EU legislative basis for the establishment of today's European Union Agency for Law Enforcement Cooperation (Europol), the earlier agency's legal successor; the most recent amendments in the Europol Regulation of 2022 extended and strengthened the Agency's powers in regard to data processing and big data.[19]

---

[16] See only Groß, p. 56 et seqq.; on agencies, see Vos, SIEPS 2018; Chamon, p. 1 et seqq.; Orator, p. 1 et seqq.

[17] Council of the European Union, 'Council Act drawing up the Convention based on Art. K.3 of the Treaty on European Union, on the establishment of a European Police Office', 26.7.1995, OJ C 316, 27.11.1995, 1.

[18] For details on the Agency and its history, see Aden in Lisken/Denninger, Handbuch des Polizeirechts, M. mn. 99 et seqq.; Ligeti/Giuffrida in Ambos/Rackow, The Cambridge Companion to European Criminal Law, p. 361 et seqq.; for a social sciences perspective, see König, p. 1 et seqq.; also, Peers, p. 325 et seqq.; Priebe, EuZW 2016, 894 et seqq.; Blasi Casagran in O'Neill/Swinton, Challenges and Critiques of the EU Internal Security Strategy: Rights, Power and Security, p. 149 et seqq.; Schoppa, p. 1 et seqq.; Schöndorf-Haubold in Ehlers/Fehling/Pünder, Besonderes Verwaltungsrecht III, § 68 mn. 54 et seqq.

[19] See Regulation (EU) 2022/991 amending Regulation (EU) 2016/794, as regards Europol's cooperation with private parties, the processing of personal data by Europol in support of criminal investigations, and Europol's role in research and innovation, which entered into force on 28 June 2022; the EDPS has raised considerable privacy concerns about the most recent amendment and recently brought an action before the Court of Justice of the European Union (CJEU): see European Data Protection Supervisor 'Opinion 4/2021 on the Proposal for Amendment of the Europol Regulation' (for a summary, see OJ C 143, 23.4.2021, p. 6, for the full text <https://edps.europa.eu/system/files/2021-03/21-03-08_opinion_europol_reform_en.pdf> (last accessed: 27.3.2024), the decision on the basis of which Europol was obliged to delete large databases (European Data Protection Supervisor, 'EDPS orders Europol to erase data concerning individuals with no established link to a criminal activity', 10.1.2022, Press Release EDPS/2022/01 and the action brought against individual provisions of the amended Regulation (European Data Protection Supervisor, 'EDPS takes legal action as new Europol Regulation puts rule of law and EDPS independence under threat', 22.9.2022, Press Release EDPS/2022/23, the aim of which was to prevent the amended Regulation being used to circumvent an order issued by the EDPS to delete data (see European

Europol is structured in a similar way to the other agencies: Pursuant to Art. 9 Europol Regulation, the administrative and management structure comprises a Management Board and an Executive Director. The Management Board is composed of one representative of each of the Member States and one representative of the Commission. It is responsible for long-term and key decision-making for the Agency, for instance as regards adopting its multiannual programming, annual budget, annual activity report and internal rules.[20] **17**

The actual management of the Agency is the responsibility of the independent Executive Director, its legal representative, who is accountable to the Management Board and manages Europol's day-to-day business.[21] The Agency, in turn, is accountable to the Justice and Home Affairs Council (JHA), which in accordance with Art. 54 Europol Regulation also appoints the Executive Director (*Catherine De Bolle* at the time of writing). **18**

Cooperation with the national security agencies, which pursuant to Art. 88(3) sent. 2 TFEU have exclusive responsibility for the application of coercive measures, is firstly organized via Europol National Units[22] in the Member States and, secondly, via Europol liaison officers, who are seconded to the Agency by the Europol National Units to assist in the exchange of information and support operational cooperation.[23] **19**

At the same time as expanding Europol's mandate, the Treaty of Lisbon also laid the foundation for stronger parliamentary oversight, which is exercised by the European Parliament in cooperation with the national parliaments in a special Joint Parliamentary Scrutiny Group (JPSG).[24] In contrast, mirroring its administrative structures, the administrative oversight functions are divided between the Agency and the Member States: Consequently, depending on the origin of the data in question, data protection supervision is either the responsibility of the Member States or Europol.[25] **20**

Europol currently employs more than 1,400 staff in addition to the 264 liaison officers who are seconded by the Member States;[26] 170 members of staff are what are known as 'analysis specialists'. The Agency's spending under the general budget has been rising on an annual basis. The final budget for 2024 totalled 219m EUR (compared to just under 159m EUR in 2020 and 179m EUR in 2022).[27] The biggest shares of the budget are earmarked for staff, operational activities and technical equipment. Through the creation of a differentiated substructure and the establishment of thematic centres (e.g. for counter-terrorism, cybercrime and migrant smuggling), the agency is becoming increasingly specialized and thematically focused.[28] **21**

Data Protection Supervisor, 'Amended Europol Regulation weakens data protection supervision Press Release', 27.6.2022 EDPS/2022/16).

[20] See Art. 10 et seqq. Europol Regulation.

[21] Art. 16 Europol Regulation.

[22] The Europol National Units act as the interface to the domestic agencies – in Germany's case the Federal Criminal Police Office (*Bundeskriminalamt*, BKA) (§ 1 of the Europol Act (*Europolgesetz*, EuropolG)).

[23] See Art. 7 and 8 Europol Regulation.

[24] See Art. 51 Europol Regulation; in that regard, see Cooper, Perspectives on Federalism 2018, E-184 et seqq.

[25] See, in particular, Art. 38, 42–45 and 47 Europol Regulation.

[26] Data from <www.europol.europa.eu/about-europol:de> (last accessed: 27.3.2024).

[27] See Europol, 'The Statement of revenue and expenditure for the 2024 financial year – European Union Agency for Law Enforcement Cooperation (Europol)', 28.2.2023, OJ C 73, 25.3.2024, OJ C 2024, 1735.

[28] See, in this regard, Schöndorf-Haubold in Ehlers/Fehling/Pünder, Besonderes Verwaltungsrecht III, § 68 mn. 60, with further references.

b) Tasks

22 **aa) Limited competence and prioritization.** From the start, Europol was tasked with assisting and strengthening police activities in the Member States in relation to certain serious crimes with a cross-border dimension. Its remit is thus limited and, based on its mandate as defined in Art. 88(1) TFEU[29] and Art. 3(1) in conjunction with Annex I of the Europol Regulation,[30] covers an inventory of specific types of serious crimes that includes terrorism, money laundering, trafficking in human beings and immigrant smuggling, drug trafficking, cybercrime, organized crime, and crimes against humanity. It is in the Council of the European Union that the Member States decide (at least formally) in the context of the EMPACT cycle established in 2021[31] which criminal offences Europol is to attach priority to, which means the Member States are responsible for setting the Agency's priorities.[32] This prioritization is based on Europol's periodical Serious and Organized Crime Threat Assessment (EU SOCTA) updates.[33]

23 **bb) Information collection point.** Pursuant to Art. 88(2) sent. 2(a) and (b) TFEU, Europol is responsible for the collection and processing of information in the relevant areas and for the 'coordination, organisation and implementation of investigative and operational action carried out jointly with the Member States' competent authorities or in the context of joint investigative teams, where appropriate in liaison with Eurojust.'

24 By setting up its own computer system (TECS) and database (the Europol Information System, EIS), Europol initially had an information and service function as an information collection and forwarding agency. Under the new Europol regime and as

---

[29] 'Europol's mission shall be to support and strengthen action by the Member States' police authorities and other law enforcement services and their mutual cooperation in preventing and combating serious crime affecting two or more Member States, terrorism and forms of crime which affect a common interest covered by a Union policy.'

[30] See Europol-Regulation (EU) 2016/794, as last amended by Regulation (EU) 2022/991.

[31] See Council of the European Union, 'Conclusions on the permanent continuation of the EU Policy Cycle for organised and serious international crime: EMPACT 2022+', 9.3.2022, Doc. 6481/21. The abbreviation 'EMPACT' (European Multidisciplinary Platform Against Criminal Threats) replaced the earlier designation 'EU Policy Cycle for organised and serious international crime'; see also the EMPACT mandate as elaborated by the Standing Committee on Operational Cooperation on Internal Security (COSI) and approved by the Council, Doc. 9921/21, as updated by the Council of the European Union on 17.5.2023, EMPACT Terms of Reference (Doc. 8975/23). On EMPACT, see also Ligeti/Giuffrida in Ambos/Rackow, The Cambridge Companion to European Criminal Law, p. 374 et seq. On COSI, which was established on the basis of Art. 71 of the TFEU, see Schöndorf-Haubold in Terhechte, Verwaltungsrecht der Europäischen Union, § 35 mn. 103, with further references.

[32] See Council of the European Union, 'Conclusions setting the EU's priorities for the fight against serious and organised crime for EMPACT 2022–2025', 9.3.2023, Doc. 7101/23. On the coordinating, impetus-giving and financing role of the European Commission, see European Commission, 'Communication on the EU Strategy to tackle Organised Crime 2021–2025', 14.4.2021, COM(2021) 170 final, 8 et seq.; the EMPACT mechanism is to be permanently embedded within secondary EU law as an 'EU flagship instrument' (COM(2021) 170 final, 7 and 10), as well as the supporting working document European Commission, 'EMPACT, the flagship EU instrument for cooperation to fight organised and serious international crime', 14.4.2021, SWD(2021) 74 final. EMPACT represents both a policy-shaping process and a platform for concrete operational horizontal and diagonal police cooperation on the relevant crimes. The European Fund for Internal Security, which was set up on the basis of Regulation (EU) 2021/1149 establishing the Internal Security Fund, OJ L 251, 15.7.2021, 94, also contributes to financing operational measures taken in the context of EMPACT.

[33] COM(2021) 170 final, 7 at footnote 20: 'The EU SOCTA is produced every four years by Europol, on the basis of extensive input provided by Member States and other relevant stakeholders. It identifies key crime threats in the EU and proposes EU crime priorities for the next four years. The EU SOCTA is the first step of each EMPACT cycle, and is used as a basis upon which the Council adopts EU crime priorities to concentrate on in the next four years.' See Europol's most recent EU SOCTA report of 2021, 'A corrupting influence: the infiltration and undermining of Europe's economy and society by organised crime' <www.europol.europa.eu/cms/sites/default/files/documents/socta2021_1.pdf> (last accessed: 27.3.2024).

part of an overarching data networking strategy within the AFSJ, the old Europol information system was replaced by a new system in which data are assigned solely on the basis of their purpose, access to that data has been made easier and Europol has been linked to other data and information systems such as, specifically, the ETIAS travel information system.[34]

cc) Operational functions, specifically participation in JITs. In operational terms, Europol primarily has a supportive function. However, given its growing powers of coordination, initiation and instruction, which are changing in qualitative terms, Europol may, in certain circumstances, grant targeted access to the coercive powers reserved to the Member States. Under Art. 5 Europol Regulation, Europol may participate in investigations conducted in the Member States in JITs and may itself propose the setting up of such JITs.[35] Pursuant to Art. 6 Europol Regulation, Europol may request the Member States to initiate a concrete criminal investigation, which the Member States must comply with and may only decide not to accede to where they have justified reason to do so.[36] **25**

JITs are tasked to conduct criminal investigations in two or more Member States. The legal basis for cooperation within a JIT is set out in Art. 13 of the European Convention on Mutual Assistance in Criminal Matters[37] and Art. 1 of Council Framework Decision on joint investigation teams.[38] Based on an agreement between the participating authorities, the activities of a JIT are then governed by the law of the State of operation.[39] The European legislature has now created a legal basis in secondary EU law[40] for information exchange, which is intended to give JITs access to a central information system within eu-LISA and a uniform communication software for information sharing purposes, although that also requires putting in place a complex administrative structure. **26**

Some JITs have achieved astounding successes. One such example was the outcome of joint investigations conducted by French and Dutch law enforcement and judicial authorities together with Europol and Eurojust, presented in the summer of 2020, which led to the breaking up of an encrypted network (EncroChat) used by criminal groups.[41] The authorities gained access to criminal networks using an anonymous encrypted **27**

---

[34] For details on issues around information processing and data protection, see Aden in Lisken/Denninger, Handbuch des Polizeirechts, M. mn. 108, 121 et seq., 139 et seqq.; also, Schöndorf-Haubold in Terhechte, Verwaltungsrecht der Europäischen Union, § 35 mn. 79 et seqq.; on the data protection issues raised on account of the policy of interoperability and interconnectivity that is increasingly being pursued, Schöndorf-Haubold in Ehlers/Fehling/Pünder, Besonderes Verwaltungsrecht III, Europäisches Sicherheitsrecht, § 68 mn. 118 et seqq., with further references.

[35] On JITs, see Schöndorf-Haubold in Terhechte, Verwaltungsrecht der Europäischen Union, § 35 mn. 120 et seqq.

[36] Art. 6 Europol Regulation.

[37] See Council, 'Act establishing in accordance with Art. 34 of the Treaty on European Union the Convention on Mutual Assistance in Criminal Matters between the Member States of the European Union' 29.5.2000, OJ C 197, 12.7.2000, 1 and the Convention on Mutual Assistance in Criminal Matters between the Member States of the European Union included in the Annex, 29.5.2000, OJ C 197, 12.7.2000,3.

[38] Council Framework Decision on joint investigation teams, OJ L 162, 20.6.2002, 1, as last amended by Directive (EU) 2022/211 amending Council 'Framework Decision 2002/465/JHA as regards its alignment with Union rules on the protection of personal data', OJ L 37, 18.2.2022, 1.

[39] See consolidated text of the model agreement on the establishment of a Joint Investigation Team, following the approval of the Council Resolution of 22 December 2021 on a revised Appendix I, OJ C 44, 28.1.2022, 6.

[40] Regulation (EU) 2023/969 establishing a collaboration platform to support the functioning of joint investigation teams and amending Regulation (EU) 2018/1726, OJ L 132, 17.5.2023, 1.

[41] Cited in COM(2021) 170 final, 1; also in COM(2022) 745 final, 18.

smartphone and were then able to solve drug- and money laundering-related crimes.[42] It was not least the horizontal and diagonal cooperation between the Member States' and the EU's security authorities that led to the concrete success of these investigations.

28 **dd) Data evaluation and analysis.** Another of Europol's priority areas of action is the analysis of data collated by the Agency and the production of analyses and situation reports, such as EU SOCTA, on the basis of which the Member States' and EU's security agencies plan and jointly implement, at short notice, their medium-term operational activities.[43]

2. European Border and Coast Guard Agency (Frontex)

a) Legal bases and structure

29 Frontex was founded in 2004, based on the Schengen *acquis*, as a Community body with legal personality.[44] The objective was to develop and implement European integrated border management at national and Union level.[45] The border agency was to act as a corrective to the opening of internal borders within the Schengen Area and to safeguard the joint monitoring and control of the Union's external borders whilst at the same time guaranteeing internal security. From 2007 onwards, the foundations were gradually laid for joint operational units and thus for an EU police force[46] whose actions are, however, based on the law applicable in the respective State of operation and subordinate to its leadership.

30 In 2016 and 2019 the legal regime underpinning Frontex was fundamentally revised.[47] The new Frontex Regulation[48] regards the Agency as part of an overarching European border and coast guard that also encompasses national entities responsible for borders and coast guards as well as those responsible for returns; it is thus a good sectoral example of administrative structures within the European 'composite administration'.

---

[42] On the background and consequences, see Eurojust, 'Annual Report 2020', 28 et seqq. <www.eurojust.europa.eu/ar2020 resp. www.eurojust.europa.eu/sites/default/files/assets/ar2020-de.pdf> (last accessed: 27.3.2024) and the Eurojust press release on the EncroChat case dated 27.6.2023 (www.eurojust.europa.eu/news/dismantling-encrypted-criminal-encrochat-communications-6-500-arrests-900-eur-seized> last accessed: 27.3.2024).

[43] See Europol's most recent EU SOCTA report of 2021, 'A corrupting influence: the infiltration and undermining of Europe's economy and society by organised crime' <www.europol.europa.eu/cms/sites/default/files/documents/socta2021_1.pdf> (last accessed: 27.3.2024).

[44] Council Regulation (EC) No 2007/2004 establishing a European Agency for the Management of Operational Cooperation at the External Borders of the Member States, OJ L 349, 25.11.2004, 1, as amended by Regulation (EC) No 863/2007 on establishing a mechanism for the creation of Rapid Border Intervention Teams […] as regards that mechanism and regulating the tasks and powers of guest officers, OJ L 199, 31.7.2007, 30 (RABIT Regulation) and by Regulation (EU) No 1168/2011 amending Council Regulation (EC) No 2007/2004, OJ L 304, 22.11.2011, 1. On Frontex, see Rijpma in Fletcher/Herlin-Karnell/Matera, The European Union as an Area of Freedom, Security and Justice, p. 217 et seqq.; Groß, ZAR 2020, 51 et seqq.; Schöndorf-Haubold in Ehlers/Fehling/Pünder, Besonderes Verwaltungsrecht III, § 68 mn. 64 et seqq.

[45] Regulation (EU) 2019/1896 on the European Border and Coast Guard, OJ L 295, 14.11.2019, 1 (the new Frontex Regulation).

[46] Sometimes also misleadingly referred to as the 'EU's first uniformed law-enforcement service'; on p. 5 of its Social Media Guidelines one reads that 'Frontex is a law enforcement agency <https://frontex.europa.eu/assets/Key_Documents/Social_Media_Guidelines/0020.0025_DE_04.pdf> (only the German version is still available, last accessed: 27.3.2024); see also European Court of Auditors, 'Special Report 08/2021: Frontex's support to external border management: not sufficiently effective to date', 7.6.2021, 9.

[47] See Regulation (EU) 2016/1624 on the European Border and Coast Guard […], OJ L 251, 16.9.2016, 1.

[48] Regulation (EU) 2019/1896 on the European Border and Coast Guard […], OJ L 295, 14.11.2019, 1) (Frontex Regulation) (Art. 59(1) sent. 1 was corrected in OJ L 251, 29.9.2022, 18), as amended by Regulation (EU) 2021/1134 for the purposes of reforming the Visa Information System, OJ L 248, 13.7.2021, 11.

Frontex is based in Warsaw and is directed by a Management Board and an Executive Director. Following *Fabrice Leggeri's* resignation and the acting director *Aija Kalnaja's* term of office, *Hans Leijtens* from the Netherlands took over responsibility for managing the Agency and its day-to-day business on 1 March 2023.[49] The Management Board is responsible for the Agency's key and/or long-term decision-making; its decisions on the vulnerability assessment and any measures associated with it are taken by qualified majority vote.[50] The Board comprises one representative of each Member State and two representatives of the Commission; representatives of Schengen-associated states have a limited voting right on the Management Board.[51] To guarantee sufficient fundamental rights protection, the Management Board and the Executive Director are supplemented by an independent consultative committee, which assists in fundamental rights issues, and a fundamental rights officer.[52] **31**

Despite all the criticism levelled against it, Frontex is becoming one of the EU's most important security agencies. The most recent reform of November 2019, which is based on Art. 77(2)(b) and (d) and Art. 79(2)(c) TFEU, for the first time creates a genuine supranational border reserve.[53]A standing corps of 6,500 EU officers from 2021 and 10,000 officers from 2027 will no longer only comprise seconded officers from the Member States but will also include EU staff who will be hired by the Agency itself. **32**

The Agency's staffing level and total budget illustrate how it has evolved: From a staff of 400 in 2016 it grew to more than 1,000 in 2020 and more than 2,100 in 2023; its budget has increased more than hundredfold, from around 6m EUR in 2005 to more than 543m EUR in 2021 and 845.4m EUR in 2023.[54] Owing to ongoing investigations into possible fundamental rights violations by the Agency, the Parliament has, however, refused to approve parts of the budget.[55] Investigations carried out by the European Anti-Fraud Office (OLAF),[56] the Court of Auditors[57] and the European Parliament bear **33**

---

49 See <https://frontex.europa.eu/about-frontex/who-we-are/structure> (last accessed: 27.3.2024).

50 Art. 100 in conjunction with Art. 32 Frontex Regulation.

51 Art. 101(1) and (3), Art. 105(4) Frontex Regulation; in accordance with Art. 101(2), members must have experience of operational border management.

52 Art. 99 Frontex Regulation.

53 See the Frontex Regulation.

54 See <https://european-union.europa.eu/institutions-law-budget/institutions-and-bodies/search-all-eu-institutions-and-bodies/frontex_en> (last accessed: 27.3.2024); the European Court of Auditors is critical of the justification used for budgetary developments: European Court of Auditors, 'Press release on the Special Report 08/2021, 7.6.2021.

55 On the deferral of discharge, see European Parliament, 'Decision on discharge in respect of the implementation of the budget of the European Border and Coast Guard Agency for the financial year 2020' 18.10.2022, 2021/2146(DEC); see also in this regard the informative Briefing by the European Parliamentary Research Service, 'European Parliament scrutiny of Frontex', 26.9.2022, EPRS_BRI(2021)698816_EN <www.europarl.europa.eu/RegData/etudes/BRIE/2021/698816/EPRS_BRI(2021)698816_EN.pdf> (last accessed: 27.3.2024); the Parliament expresses its deep concern about fundamental rights violations and criticized the lack of transparency in relation to Frontex activities (as does the European Parliament decision 'on the Annual Report on the functioning of the Schengen area', 8.7.2021, 2019/2196(INI).

56 OLAF had already found that Frontex staff had engaged in misconduct back in 2020 in connection with potential fundamental rights violations by the Agency; a confidential report has to date only been published unofficially online – see an article by Christides/Lüdke, 'Warum der SPIEGEL den Frontex-Untersuchungsbericht veröffentlicht (English: Why DER SPIEGEL is publishing the Frontex Report)' (Der SPIEGEL, 13.10.2022) which includes parts of the confidential report that had been made available to the authors; OLAF's 23rd Annual Report for 2022 also refers to concrete investigations and the finding of similar misconduct within Frontex, OLAF, 'On the front line against misconduct' <https://ec.europa.eu/olaf-report/2022/index_en.html> (last accessed: 27.3.2024). See the Agency's Anti-fraud Strategy 2022–2024, CO/IRBA/10152021, <https://frontex.europa.eu/assets/Key_Documents/Anti_fraud_strategy/2022/22.0009_Anti-Fraud_Strategy_EN_F2.pdf> (last accessed: 27.3.2024).

57 See European Court of Auditors, 'Frontex's support to external border management: not sufficiently effective to date', 7.6.2021, Special Report 08/2021.

witness both to the fully functional oversight mechanisms and to the fact that the administrative structures required for a future EU police force are not yet fit for purpose.[58]

b) Objectives and tasks

34 **aa) Mandate.** Frontex's objective and mission is to establish an integrated European border management at the EU's external borders. Under the currently applicable Frontex Regulation, that border management and the protection of the external borders is assigned, as a shared responsibility,[59] to the 'European Border and Coast Guard' and the Member States' authorities, in order, not least, to guarantee a high level of internal security within the Union in situations involving high migration pressure and, pursuant to Art. 1 of the Frontex Regulation, to contribute to the detection, prevention and combating of cross-border crime at the external borders. Notwithstanding this shared responsibility, the Member States retain primary operational territorial responsibility, though.[60]

35 **bb) Basic responsibilities.** Under the Frontex Regulation, the Agency's core tasks include ongoing situational monitoring in order to be able to draw up a European situational picture, general annual risk analyses to monitor migratory flows and flows into the EU, concrete vulnerability assessments in relation to individual Member States' capacities and readiness, joint operational activities organized by Frontex, rapid border and return interventions, and intensive information sharing with the Member State authorities and other EU security agencies. It was to that end that the European Border Surveillance System (EUROSUR) was incorporated into the new Frontex Regulation.

36 **cc) Border management and return teams.** One of Frontex's main tasks is to organize and participate in the operational activities of various teams.[61] In accordance with Art. 2 nos. 18, 19 and 29 Frontex Regulation, there are three different types of teams in which the Agency's staff, Union assets and the Member States' border guards cooperate: 'border management teams', which are primarily deployed for joint operations at the external borders and rapid border interventions to protect the borders where national assets are exposed to particular challenges; 'migration management support teams', which are formed of EU and national experts and especially provide technical and administrative support, including at hotspots, when there are particularly strong migration flows; and 'return teams', which carry out return interventions and operations in the Member States.

---

[58] In an answer to a parliamentary question, the Commission provided no information whatsoever about the results of OLAF's investigation; see European Commission, 28.7.2022, E-000861/2022(ASW). In a statement regarding the confidential OLAF report that was published in the media, Frontex called the accusations only the wrongs of the past and referred to the strengthening of fundamental rights protection under the new legal regime (Statement by the Frontex Executive Management following publication of OLAF report <https://frontex.europa.eu/media-centre/news/news-release/statement-of-frontex-executive-management-following-publication-of-olaf-report-amARYy> (last accessed: 27.3.2024)); an in-depth analysis of the fundamental rights regime set out in the Frontex Regulation, by contrast, justifies adopting a very sceptical approach, see Schöndorf-Haubold in Ehlers/Fehling/Pünder, Besonderes Verwaltungsrecht III, § 68 mn. 67 et seqq. and 84 et seqq.); see also Gkliati, European Journal of Migration and Law 2022, 545 et seqq. (on the OLAF report: 562); Groß, ZAR 2020, 51 et seqq.

[59] Art. 7 Frontex Regulation.

[60] Art.7(1) sent. 2 Frontex Regulation.

[61] For details regarding teams as a specific form of action and organization, see Krämer, in particular p. 75 et seqq. (of the manuscript); on Frontex teams, see also Schöndorf-Haubold in Ehlers/Fehling/Pünder, Besonderes Verwaltungsrecht III, § 68 mn. 123 et seqq.

What all three teams have in common is a cooperative deployment mechanism, which is generally triggered when Frontex receives a request from a State of operation. In special crisis situations, the Executive Director may also propose measures to eliminate vulnerabilities at the external borders or to support return interventions; by way of exception, the Agency may also invoke the sovereignty clause.[62] 37

Operations are subject to the law of the State of operation, although they must also comply with requirements set out in operational plans for joint operations agreed between Frontex and a State of operation. Compliance with these plans is guaranteed by the Frontex liaison officers on the ground.[63] That creates formal uncertainty as regards the Agency's and the State of operation's respective accountability. The serious accusations of fundamental rights violations in the Mediterranean that Frontex was supposedly involved in illustrate the need for robust, supranational responsibility that guarantees that Frontex itself complies with minimum rule-of-law standards, despite the fact that the legal framework does not yet sufficiently guarantee that.[64] 38

dd) New operational powers. The amended Frontex Regulation for the first time grants the Agency its own operational powers, permits it to take coercive measures and gives it the right to use arms and other weapons, as well as to make use of police surveillance tools, such as facial recognition technology – a matter that is by no means uncontroversial.[65] This means that Frontex is being gradually expanded from what was initially a purely supportive agency into a genuine EU (border) police force with its own personnel, equipment and operational coercive powers, including through the use of armed force. It is the first real European police force with a comparable mandate. 39

c) Fundamental rights protection

The main purpose of the Frontex Regulation is to set the framework for efficient border management and expand the EU's returns policy. The Agency focuses neither on guaranteeing asylum nor even on providing access to a procedure for reviewing asylum applications, since its main task is to direct and participate in border controls, prevent – by definition illegal – migration, combating cross-border crime and implementing return operations.[66] 40

---

[62] See Art. 42 Frontex Regulation.

[63] In this regard and on 'soft instruction mechanisms', see Schöndorf-Haubold in Ehlers/Fehling/Pünder, Besonderes Verwaltungsrecht III, § 68 mn. 128.

[64] On the problem of accountability, see Schöndorf-Haubold in Terhechte, Verwaltungsrecht der Europäischen Union, § 35 mn. 132 et seq.

[65] ibid., § 35 mn. 126 et seqq.

[66] If and to the extent to which Frontex is integrated into practical border management, such activities must also safeguard the requisite asylum procedures; on the reform of the current law of asylum procedure, see European Commission, Proposals on the New Pact on Migration and Asylum; for a critical take, see Bossong, SWP-Studie 2022, 27 et seqq.; see also the critical Opinion 9/2020 of the European Data Protection Supervisor on the New Pact on Migration and Asylum. The EDPS admits, resignedly, that 'as stated in the EDPS Strategy 2020–2024, data protection is one of the last lines of defence for vulnerable individuals, such as migrants and asylum seekers approaching the EU external borders', adding that '[t]herefore, the EDPS considers that the proposed comprehensive approach must be based on full respect to the fundamental rights of persons who seek international protection and other migrants, including their right to data protection and privacy'; finally, the EDSP notes that the legislative proposals made in the Pact 'either lack entirely any substantive legal provisions on personal data protection, or the proposed texts are not fully in line with the relevant Union law' (for a summary, see OJ C 99, 23.3.2021, p. 9; full text <https://edps.europa.eu/system/files/2021-03/21-03-08_opinion_europol_reform_en.pdf> (last accessed: 27.3.2024); for a nuanced fundamental rights perspective, see Kasparek, 'Zugang zum Europäischen Asylsystem, Neues Migrations- und Asylpaket, Stellungnahme für den Innenausschuss des Deutschen Bundestages', BT-Drs. 19/22125 and 19/18680, Committee Printed Paper 19(4)615 E.

41 Each action directed against refugees who – rightly or wrongly – invoke their refugee status is not only relevant to that status and to existing obligations under international law in relation to *non-refoulement*,[67] but also very specifically to those refugees' life and health in the context of their concrete situation. That applies in particular to children and other vulnerable individuals. Turning these people into criminals – which is what, according to secondary EU legislation, they are assumed to be, contrary to fundamental rights – must not serve as justification for not conducting a review of their cases (which is justified by fundamental rights) and to guarantee them the minimum level of protection afforded them under international law.

42 The 2019 Frontex Regulation (sometimes repeatedly and redundantly) recognizes the importance of fundamental rights as well as (merely declaratorily) the application of fundamental rights to the Agency's operational activities. By creating the post of 'fundamental rights officer' as well as an advisory consultative forum, a fundamental rights strategy, a large number of fundamental rights monitors and a complaints mechanism, it also sets an institutional framework, though that still needs to prove its worth in the course of practical implementation.[68] In no way does the fact that a Member State takes the formal operational lead for joint operational measures exculpate Frontex from its responsibilities. An EU institution's even subordinate participation leads to supranationalization, which at any rate triggers the need for the Agency in question to take responsibility for the EU.[69]

43 Serious accusations have been levelled against Frontex that have led to personal consequences at the management level. Although the accusations have still not been transparently investigated,[70] it is hoped they will ensure that minimum fundamental rights standards are upheld going forward.[71] Nevertheless, the system and structure of the Regulation make it clear that Frontex's primary responsibility is not to protect the individual and subjective legal fundamental rights of each person but to ensure the effective performance of the Agency's tasks whilst formally complying with minimum standards of fundamental rights. The Regulation very precisely defines the Agency's mandate in relation to returns and deportations, but it fails to set out any concrete practical procedural measures for complying with fundamental rights when return measures are carried out.[72] This legal regime is the product of a policy dilemma that is resolved – despite the invocations of fundamental rights – to the detriment of refugees arriving at the EU's external borders. It is doubtful whether this meets the requirements set in the Charter of Fundamental Rights of the European Union and the European Convention on the Protection of Human Rights (ECHR), which also apply to Frontex.

---

[67] See, e.g., Goldner Lang/Nagy, ECLR 2021, 442 et seqq., who comes to a devastating conclusion as regards the fundamental rights situation.

[68] See the detailed analysis by Groß, ZAR 2020, 51 et seqq., who reaches a similar overall conclusion; see also Schöndorf-Haubold in Ehlers/Fehling/Pünder, Besonderes Verwaltungsrecht III, § 68 mn. 84 et seqq.; for a sceptical approach, see also Hruschka, APuZ 2022, 35 et seqq.

[69] Thus, unravelling shared competences, the solution backed by some in the social sciences (see Riedel, SWP-Studie 2020, cannot mean being released from fundamental rights commitments.

[70] See <https://european-union.europa.eu/institutions-law-budget/institutions-and-bodies/search-all-eu-institutions-and-bodies/frontex_en> (last accessed: 27.3.2024); the European Court of Auditors is critical of the justification used for budgetary developments: European Court of Auditors, 'Press release on the Special Report 08/2021, 7.6.2021.

[71] See also a claim for damages filed against Frontex before the General Court by the Syrian national *Omar B.*; the General Court recently rejected the agency's responsibility in principle, referring to its exclusively supportive function, GC 6.9.2023 – case T-600/21, ECLI:EU:T:2023:492.

[72] On the relevance of fundamental rights, in particular return operations by Frontex, including statistics, see Gkliati, European Journal of Migration and Law 2022, 545 (552 et seqq., 556, with further references).

3. European Union Agency for Criminal Justice Cooperation (Eurojust)

a) Legal bases and structure

Eurojust, which was set up in 2003 as the 'coordination centre for criminal justice',[73] was also initially created as an intergovernmental body under the third pillar but was then transformed on the basis of Art. 85 TFEU and most recently Regulation (EU) 2018/1727[74] into an EU agency. In contrast to Europol, Eurojust's activities exclusively relate to cooperation between law enforcement and judicial authorities, whose actions are repressive rather than preventive. Eurojust now also cooperates closely with the EPPO.[75] It is based in The Hague and focuses on facilitating and coordinating cooperation between the judicial authorities in the fight against serious, organized cross-border crime. To that end it supports the use and enforcement of European arrest warrants,[76] European Investigation Orders (EIOs)[77] and JITs (→ mn. 25 et seq.), which the Agency itself participates in. **44**

Unlike the other agencies, Eurojust also comprises one National Member per Member State, who must be a qualified criminal judge or public prosecutor, and is managed by a College comprising all the National Members and a representative of the Commission, which is – sometimes solely – responsible for its operational decision-making.[78] More than is the case with Europol and Frontex, this structure also better reflects, at the institutional level, the Member States' remaining basic responsibilities. The National Members must be able to exercise certain powers under their domestic law and to order investigatory measures, request these or carry them out.[79] Cooperation with the Member States' authorities is channelled through what are called National Correspondents for Eurojust in the Member States.[80] Eurojust itself had only 265 own **45**

---

[73] For details about Eurojust, see Aden in Lisken/Denninger, Handbuch des Polizeirechts, M. mn. 14 and 148, with further references; Hernández López/Jiménez-Villarejo Fernández in Ambos/Rackow, The Cambridge Companion to European Criminal Law, p. 387 et seqq.; Hecker, p. 177 et seqq.

[74] Regulation (EU) 2018/1727 on the European Union Agency for Criminal Justice Cooperation (Eurojust) and replacing and repealing Council Decision 2002/187/JHA, OJ L 295, 21.11.2018, 138, as amended by Regulation (EU) 2022/838 amending Regulation (EU) 2018/1727 as regards the preservation, analysis and storage at Eurojust of evidence relating to genocide, crimes against humanity, war crimes and related criminal offences, OJ L 148, 31.5.2022, 1 (Eurojust Regulation); see also the Commission Proposal for a Regulation amending Regulation (EU) 2018/1727 […] as regards the digital information exchange in terrorism cases, 1.12.2021, COM(2021) 757 final.

[75] See Art. 3(1), Art. 4(1) point I and Art. 50 Eurojust Regulation and Art. 3(3) and Art. 100 of Regulation (EU) 2017/1939 implementing enhanced cooperation on the establishment of the European Public Prosecutor's Office (EPPO), OJ L 283, 31.10.2017, 1 (EPPO Regulation), as amended by Commission Delegated Regulation 2020/2153 amending Council Regulation (EU) 2017/1939 as regards the categories of operational personal data and the categories of data subjects whose operational personal data may be processed in the index of case files by the European Public Prosecutor's Office, OJ L 431, 21.12.2020, 1, which was, in turn, corrected by OJ L 433, 21.12.2020, 80; see also the Working Arrangement between the EPPO and Eurojust on strategic, operational and administrative cooperation between the two agencies.

[76] European arrest warrants were introduced on the basis of Council Framework Decision 2002/584/JHA on the European arrest warrant and the surrender procedures between Member States, OJ L 190, 18.7.2002, 1, as amended by Council Framework Decision, OJ L 81, 27.3.2009, 24.

[77] European Investigation Orders (EIOs) facilitate and simplify cross-border criminal investigations. They can be issued by national judicial authorities to get another Member State to collect and transmit evidence; Member States must recognize and execute EIOs issued to them. The legal basis for this recognition mechanism is set out in Directive 2014/41/EU regarding the European Investigation Order in criminal matters, OJ L 130, 1.5.2014, 1, as amended by Directive (EU) 2022/228, OJ L 39, 21.2.2022, 1.

[78] See Art. 6–15 and Art. 5(2) Eurojust Regulation.

[79] Art. 7–9 Eurojust Regulation, which also include other powers.

[80] Known as the Eurojust National Coordination System (ENCS; Art. 20 of the Eurojust Regulation).

members of staff in 2022 in addition to the 78 National Members and their Deputies who are employed by the Member States.[81]

46 In contrast to the Eurojust College, the smaller Executive Board is not involved in the Agency's operational tasks, but is responsible for programme planning, decision-making in relation to the Anti-Fraud Strategy, as well as for administrative procedures and structures. The Administrative Director, who is appointed by the College on the proposal of the Executive Board, has administrative tasks and is responsible for managing Eurojust's day-to-day business.[82]

b) Objectives and tasks

47 Pursuant to Art. 85 TFEU and Art. 2 Eurojust Regulation 2018/1727, Eurojust supports and strengthens coordination and cooperation measures between the national authorities that are responsible for investigating and prosecuting serious crimes, that is when two or more Member States are affected by a crime or a crime requires prosecution on a common basis. Eurojust bases its work on operations conducted and information delivered by the national and other EU security authorities, such as Europol, the EPPO and OLAF.

48 In contrast to Europol, Eurojust's task is limited to the prosecution of criminal offences, which is a repressive rather than a preventive task. Like Europol, Eurojust's responsibilities are defined in a list of particularly serious crimes, including terrorism, organized crime, drug trafficking, money laundering, immigrant smuggling and trafficking in human beings, murder and grievous bodily harm, vehicle crime, racism and xenophobia, insider dealing, illegal trafficking in endangered plant species and varieties, and corruption.[83]

49 In addition to its information and supporting tasks, Eurojust can, in particular, request the competent national authorities to carry out specific investigations or to set up a JIT as well as, in conflict situations, to issue written opinions to the authorities concerned, which those authorities may only refuse to follow up if doing so would harm essential national security interests or jeopardize the success of an ongoing investigation or a person's safety.[84] The Eurojust Regulation makes provision for wide-ranging exchanges of information and a case management system composed of temporary work files and an index containing personal information.[85]

50 Eurojust also supports and finances (sometimes jointly with Europol) the setting up of JITs, which it may also participate in.[86] The JITs Network Secretariat[87] belongs to the

[81] Eurojust, 'Consolidated Annual Activity Report 2022, Criminal justice across borders', 13.6.2023, 4 et seq. <www.eurojust.europa.eu/sites/default/files/assets/eurojust-consolidated-annual-activity-report-2022.pdf> (last accessed: 27.3.2024); the Report also sets out the annual budget, which totalled around 50m EUR in 2022 (p. 50).

[82] Art. 16–18 Eurojust Regulation.

[83] Art. 2(1) and Art. 3(1) and (3) in conjunction with Annex I of the Eurojust Regulation; if prosecution of a crime falls within the EPPO's jurisdiction, then, in accordance with Art. 3(1) sent. 2 of the Eurojust Regulation, Eurojust only exercises its competence at the request of the EPPO or individual Member States if the Member States involved did not participate in enhanced cooperation to establish the EPPO. See, for further exceptions and special cases, Art. 3(2)–(6) Eurojust Regulation.

[84] Art. 4–5 Eurojust Regulation.

[85] Art. 21 et seqq. Eurojust Regulation; privacy protections are set out in Art. 26 et seqq. Eurojust Regulation; for a critical stance, see Aden in Lisken/Denninger, Handbuch des Polizeirechts, M. mn. 161 et seq.

[86] In 2022, Eurojust provided support to 265 JITs and 78 JITs were newly established; see Eurojust, 'Consolidated Annual Activity Report 2022', 13.6.2023, 13.

[87] As well as this network, the Secretariat of the European Judicial Network, the Genocide Network Secretariat and the European Judicial Cybercrime Network are also based in Eurojust's offices. They use National Contact Points or connected national experts for the purposes of judicial cooperation and

Agency's staff. JITs are used to conduct criminal investigations in two or more Member States and/or third countries on the basis of Art. 13 of the European Convention on Mutual Assistance in Criminal Matters and Art. 1 of Council Framework Decision on joint investigation teams (→ mn. 25 et seq.). Coordination centres, which are used in support of simultaneous operational activities in large-scale cross-border proceedings, are another tool created by Eurojust. Even beyond those successful investigations that have gained wide media attention, such as the EncroChat case,[88] JITs have achieved other notable successes in the fight against organized crime, drug trafficking and immigrant smuggling.[89]

4. EPPO

Going forward, increasing importance will also be attached to the European Public Prosecutor's Office,[90] which was established in late 2020 on the basis of Art. 86 TFEU as part of enhanced cooperation between initially 22 States.[91] The EPPO, which has its offices in Luxembourg and was at the time of writing headed by Chief Prosecutor *Laura Codruța Kövesi*,[92] is continuously being expanded. It currently has an annual budget of approx. 50m EUR and employed 221 staff (as at late 2022).[93] The EPPO is tasked with prosecuting, before the Member States' courts and in accordance with uniform EU standards, large-scale cross-border crimes against the financial interests of the EU.[94] 51

a) Jurisdiction

Pursuant to Art. 4 EPPO Regulation 2017/1939, the EPPO is responsible for 'inves- 52
tigating, prosecuting and bringing to judgment the perpetrators of, and accomplices to, criminal offences affecting the financial interests of the Union which are provided for in

information sharing, and illustrate Eurojust's function as a nexus for Member State cooperation in the field of law enforcement.

[88] See Eurojust, 'Annual Report 2020'. <www.eurojust.europa.eu/ar2020, www.eurojust.europa.eu/sites/default/files/assets/ar2020-de.pdf> (last accessed: 27.3.2024), 28 et seqq and the joint Eurojust-Europol press release on the EncroChat case dated 27 June 2023. See Europol's most recent EU SOCTA report of 2021, 'A corrupting influence: the infiltration and undermining of Europe's economy and society by organised crime' <www.europol.europa.eu/cms/sites/default/files/documents/socta2021_1.pdf> (last accessed: 27.3.2024).

[89] See, e.g., EPPO, 'Press release of 29.6.2023 on successful investigations against 'Ndrangheta'; on successes and case numbers, see Eurojust, 'Consolidated Annual Activity Report 2022', 13.6.2023, 8 et seqq.

[90] See the unanimously adopted EPPO Regulation (EU) 2017/1939 as amended by Commission Delegated Regulation 2020/2153 as regards the categories of operational personal data and the categories of data subjects whose operational personal data may be processed in the index of case files by the European Public Prosecutor's Office, OJ L 431, 21.12.2020, 1, which was, in turn, corrected by OJ L 433, 21.12.2020, 80; on the EPPO, see Aden in Lisken/Denninger, Handbuch des Polizeirechts, M. mn. 163 et seqq.; Hecker, p. 500 et seqq.; Allegrezza in Ambos/Rackow, The Cambridge Companion to European Criminal Law, p. 413 et seqq.; Yolaçan, p. 25 et seqq.; critical Böse, JZ 2017, 82 et seqq. For a commentary on the EPPO Regulation, see Herrnfeld/Brodowski/Burchard, p. 1 et seqq.

[91] Austria, Belgium, Bulgaria, Croatia, Cyprus, Czech Republic, Estonia, Finland, France, Germany, Greece, Italy, Latvia, Lithuania, Luxembourg, Malta, Netherlands, Portugal, Romania, Slovakia, Slovenia and Spain.

[92] See Decision (EU) 2019/1798 appointing the European Chief Prosecutor of the European Public Prosecutor's Office, OJ L 274, 28.10.2019, 1. Pursuant to Art. 11(1) of the EPPO Regulation, the European Chief Prosecutor is Head of the EPPO, organizes the work of the EPPO, directs its activities and takes decisions in accordance with the EPPO Regulation and the internal rules of procedure of the EPPO.

[93] EPPO, 'Consolidated Annual Activity Report 2022', <www.eppo.europa.eu/sites/default/files/2023-06/EPPO_Consolidated_Annual_Activity_Report_2022.pdf> (last accessed: 27.3.2024), 24 et seqq.

[94] The Agency recorded more than 1,100 investigations in 2022 with 14.1bn EUR worth of damages; see EPPO, 'Annual Report for 2023', 1.3.2023, 4 <www.eppo.europa.eu/en/news/annual-report-2022-eppo-puts-spotlight-revenue-fraud> (last accessed: 27.3.2024).

Directive 2017/1371 and determined by this Regulation. In that respect the EPPO shall undertake investigations, and carry out acts of prosecution and exercise the functions of prosecutor in the competent courts of the Member States, until the case has been finally disposed of.' Its substantive jurisdiction is determined under the 'PIF Directive' 2017/1371[95] and the EPPO Regulation. The EPPO generally only gets involved in cases of serious criminal conduct that jeopardizes the financial interests of the EU once a minimum threshold has been exceeded.[96]

53 In addition to prosecuting cases of VAT fraud to the detriment of the financial interests of the EU totalling billions of euros, the EPPO in particular gets involved in cases involving the misuse of Structural Funds resources and of Recovery and Resilience Facility (RRF) funding. Provision was explicitly made under Art. 86(4) TFEU for its mandate to be extended to fighting serious cross-border crime, which thus does not in principle rule out the prosecution of terrorist offences, although that needs to be based on a unanimous Council decision.

b) Organization and structure

54 Pursuant to Art. 8 EPPO Regulation, the EPPO is an indivisible Union body with a decentralized structure that is organized at both a central and a decentral level. The central level comprises a Central Office in Luxembourg, and the decentral level is formed of the (to date) 140 European Delegated Prosecutors in the Member States (in whose service they remain).[97] In Art. 3(1) and (2) EPPO Regulation the EPPO is not referred to as an agency, but as a 'body' with special legal personality that is independent and cooperates in particular with Eurojust. Its administrative structure therefore to some extent differs from that of the 'classic' agencies in that it is managed by its College, there is no board and the Administrative Director is only responsible for carrying out administrative tasks, including running the EPPO's day-to-day business.

55 The Chief Prosecutor, the two Deputy Chief Prosecutors as well as 22 European Prosecutors from the participating States, the College they constitute, the Permanent Chambers and the Administrative Director are all based in the EPPO's Central Office in Luxembourg. Like Eurojust, the EPPO is managed by a College that comprises one European Prosecutor from each of the involved Member States. However, the College does not take any operational decisions in individual cases, but is responsible for decisions on strategic matters and dealing with general issues, especially with a view to ensuring coherency, efficiency and consistency of the EPPO's prosecution policy in the EU, as well as for general oversight of the activities of the EPPO.[98]

56 Besides the European Chief Prosecutor, the Council appoints one European Prosecutor for each participating Member State.[99] In accordance with Art. 12 EPPO Regulation, the European Prosecutors are explicitly tasked with supervising their Member State's European Delegated Prosecutors and 'function as liaisons and information channels between the Permanent Chambers and the European Delegated Prosecutors in their respective Member States of origin.'

---

[95] Directive (EU) 2017/1371 on the fight against fraud to the Union's financial interests by means of criminal law, OJ L 198, 28.7.2017, 29, (PIF Directive; PIF = *protection des intérêts financiers*).

[96] Art. 22(1) sent. 2 and Art. 25(2) EPPO Regulation in conjunction with Art. 3(2)(d) PIF Directive: at least 10m EUR in cases of VAT fraud and no less than 10,000 EUR worth of damages in all other cases.

[97] Regarding its structure, see Art. 8 et seqq. EPPO Regulation; for a critical approach from the perspective of a federal state, see Herrnfeld, eucrim 2018, 117 et seqq.

[98] See Art. 9(2) EPPO Regulation.

[99] Art. 14 and 16 EPPO Regulation; see, e.g., Council Decision (EU) 2023/1539 appointing the European Prosecutors of the European Public Prosecutor's Office, OJ L 187, 26.7.2023, 74.

European Delegated Prosecutors are appointed by the College upon the proposal of the Chief Prosecutor after being nominated by the participating Member States. Pursuant to Art. 13(1) EPPO Regulation, they 'act on behalf of the EPPO in their respective Member States'; they are in the service of the national courts and public prosecution offices and can exercise the same powers as national prosecutors. In particular, they are responsible for opening proceedings within the EPPO's jurisdiction, for preferring charges and conducting investigations (right of evocation under Art. 13(1) second subparagraph in conjunction with Art. 27(6) and Art. 28 EPPO Regulation). 57

c) Performance of tasks

Basic operational decisions[100] are taken by 15 Permanent Chambers set up by the College on the proposal of the European Chief Prosecutor; each Permanent Chamber comprises three European Prosecutors, who in accordance with Art. 10(3), (4) and (5) EPPO Regulation, monitor and direct the investigations and prosecutorial measures carried out by the European Delegated Prosecutors. They also safeguard the coordination of investigations and prosecutorial measures in cross-border cases and the implementation of the decisions taken by the College pursuant to Art. 9(2) EPPO Regulation. 58

Pursuant to Art. 25(1) EPPO Regulation, the EPPO exercises its competence 'either by initiating an investigation under Art. 26', i.e. by means of corresponding decisions taken by the responsible European Delegated Prosecutor, or 'by deciding to use its right of evocation under Art. 27. If the EPPO decides to exercise its competence, the competent national authorities shall not exercise their own competence in respect of the same criminal conduct'. In accordance with Art. 27 EPPO Regulation, the EPPO may exercise its right of evocation in ongoing proceedings within its jurisdiction by taking a decision or by a decision of the European Delegated Prosecutors. 59

The way in which the EPPO is structured shows that the organizational structures of facilities and agencies within the European 'composite administration' are not limited to administrative competences in the strict sense; rather, they form typical patterns under the EU's organizational law in relation to cooperation and the balancing of shared competences within the multilevel EU system.[101] 60

5. European Police College/European Union Agency for Law Enforcement Training (CEPOL)

The European Union Agency for Law Enforcement Training (CEPOL),[102] which is based in Budapest, is of only indirect operational relevance. It is the legal successor to the former European Police College (for which the abbreviation 'CEPOL'[103] was also used).[104] 61

---

[100] See Art. 10(3) and (4) EPPO Regulation, in particular as regards bringing cases to judgment and dismissing cases or instructing European Delegated Prosecutors to act.

[101] On the complex interplay between the EPPO and national public prosecution offices, see Aden/Sanchez-Barrueco/Stephenson, 'The European Public Prosecutor's Office: strategies for coping with complexity', 15.5.2019, IPOL_STU(2019)621806_EN <www.europarl.europa.eu/RegData/etudes/STUD/2019/621806/IPOL_STU(2019)621806_EN.pdf> (last accessed: 27.3.2024).

[102] The United Kingdom had requested back in 2014 that its former seat in Bramshill, UK be relinquished.

[103] The abbreviation derives from the agency's former official name in French: *Collège européen de police*.

[104] On CEPOL, see Aden in Lisken/Denninger, Handbuch des Polizeirechts, M. mn. 194 et seqq.; Schöndorf-Haubold in Terhechte, Verwaltungsrecht der Europäischen Union, § 35 mn. 56 et seqq.

In accordance with Recital 1 CEPOL Regulation,[105] the European Police College was originally established on the basis of Council Decision 2005/681/JHA[106] as 'an entity of the Union with the aim of training senior police officers of the Member States and facilitating cooperation between national police forces by organising and coordinating training activities with a European policing dimension.' That remit is fleshed out in Art. 3 CEPOL Regulation:

> CEPOL shall support, develop, implement and coordinate training for law enforcement officials, whilst putting particular emphasis on the protection of human rights and fundamental freedoms in the context of law enforcement, in particular in the areas of prevention of and fight against serious crime affecting two or more Member States and terrorism, maintenance of public order, in particular international policing of major events, and planning and command of Union missions, which may also include training on law enforcement leadership and language skills.

62 The Agency is responsible for knowledge transfer and knowledge sharing between police officers in the EU Member States as well as with third countries, networking purposes and training and strategic cooperation in relation to joint activities in the case of serious security threats.

63 CEPOL had a budget of almost 11m EUR in 2024 and a very limited staffing level.[107] Its structure mirrors that of the 'classic' agencies: Its main decision-making body is its Management Board; the Agency itself is managed by the Executive Director. The Management Board is composed of one representative per Member State and the Commission, with each representative having one vote. The Chairperson and Deputy Chairperson of the Management Board are elected by the Management Board from 'among its members representing the group of three Member States that have jointly prepared the Council's 18-month programme'.[108] The Management Board also has the option of setting up further advisory committees.[109] Communications and exchange with the Member States is primarily conducted via the National Units, which form a network of their own and meet regularly either on their own initiative or at the request of the Management Board or Executive Director.[110]

64 CEPOL is tasked with implementing training activities, that is (in-person or online) seminars, courses and conferences on security priorities, police cooperation and information sharing as well as with elaborating curricula, learning and teaching tools,

---

[105] Recital 1 Regulation (EU) 2015/2219 on the European Union Agency for Law Enforcement Training (CEPOL) and replacing and repealing Council Decision 2005/681/JHA, OJ L 319, 4.12.2015, 1 (CEPOL Regulation).

[106] CEPOL was originally established on the initiative of the Tampere European Council based on existing cooperation between and networks of national police academies by means of Council Decision 2000/820/JHA establishing a European Police College (CEPOL), OJ L 336, 30.12.2000, 1 and Council Decision 2005/681/JHA, OJ L 356, 1.10.2005, 63, as amended by Regulation (EU) No 543/2014, OJ L 163, 29.5.2014, 5 establishing the European Police College (CEPOL). As explicitly stated in Art. 3(3) of the CEPOL Regulation, the establishment of this agency institutionalizes at central level an existing informal network of national facilities: 'CEPOL shall bring together a network of Member State training institutes for law enforcement officials and shall liaise with a single national unit in each Member State functioning within the network.'

[107] See Consolidated Annual Activity Report (CAAR) of the European Union Agency for Law Enforcement Training (CEPOL) for financial year 2024, OJ C/2024/1331 <www.cepol.europa.eu/about/key-documents> (last accessed: 27.3.2024).

[108] Art. 11(1) Regulation (EU) 2015/2219; on the troika, see Council Decision (EU) 2016/1316 amending Decision 2009/908/EU laying down measures for the implementation of the European Council Decision on the exercise of the Presidency of the Council, and on the chairmanship of preparatory bodies of the Council, OJ L 208, 2.8.2016, 42.

[109] Art. 7(c) and (d) in conjunction with Art. 9(1)(q), Art. 15 and Art. 16 Regulation (EU) 2015/2219.

[110] Art. 6 Regulation (EU) 2015/2219.

preparing multiannual training programmes and exchange programmes, and conducting own research projects. The objective is to develop a 'genuine European law enforcement culture' by drawing up common concepts for combating and preventing crime and by promoting cross-border cooperation in these areas. The CEPOL Regulation abandoned the original idea of only granting access to high-ranking police officers in favour of adopting a broad-based concept that draws in all service levels.[111]

6. European Union Agency for the Operational Management of Large-Scale IT Systems in the Area of Freedom, Security and Justice (eu-LISA)[112]

eu-LISA is not an EU security agency as such.[113] Nevertheless, it stands for an important institutional trend within EU security policy. The Agency, which was established in 2011 and is based in Tallin, has a decentralized technical infrastructure for data management and data backup in Strasbourg, France and St. Johann, Austria. It draws together numerous security-related technical information systems and functions, some of which are technically intertwined.[114] The Agency's current legal basis rests on numerous provisions of primary EU legislation in Title V of Part 3 TFEU[115] and in the eu-LISA Regulation,[116] which has been amended multiple times. 65

a) Large-scale IT systems

eu-LISA was tasked with the management of various police information systems as of 1 December 2012. The second generation of the Schengen Information System (SIS II)[117] 66

[111] See Recitals 2 and 3 and Art. 4 Regulation (EU) 2015/2219.

[112] European Union Agency for the Operational Management of Large-Scale IT Systems in the Area of Freedom, Security and Justice (eu-LISA).

[113] On eu-LISA, see Aden in Lisken/Denninger, Handbuch des Polizeirechts, M. mn. 190 et seqq.; Schöndorf-Haubold in Terhechte, Verwaltungsrecht der Europäischen Union, § 35 60 et seqq.

[114] On its status and history and for statistics relating to individual systems as well as information on their interconnectivity and interoperability, see eu-Lisa Management Board, 'Consolidated Annual Activity Report 2022', 22.6.2023, Document 2023-182 REV 3, 11 et seq. available from <www.eulisa.europa.eu> (last accessed: 27.3.2024).

[115] Based on Art. 74, Art. 77(2)(a) and (b), Art. 78(2)(c), Art. 79(2)(c), Art. 82(1) (d), Art. 85(1), Art. 87 (2)(a) and Art. 88(2) TFEU.

[116] Regulation (EU) 2018/1726 on the European Union Agency for the Operational Management of Large-Scale IT Systems in the Area of Freedom, Security and Justice (eu-LISA) [...], OJ L 295, 21.11.2018, 99 (eu-LISA Regulation), amended, inter alia, to add further information systems (ECRIS-TCN-Regulation (EU) 2019/816 [establishing a centralised system for the identification of Member States holding conviction information on third-country nationals and stateless persons (ECRIS-TCN) to supplement the European Criminal Records Information System and amending Regulation (EU) 2018/1726, OJ L 135, 22.5.2019, 1], e-Codex-Regulation (EU) 2022/850 [on a computerised system for the cross-border electronic exchange of data in the area of judicial cooperation in civil and criminal matters (e-CODEX system), and amending Regulation (EU) 2018/1726, OJ L 150, 1.6.2022, 1] and JIT-Regulation (EU) 2023/969 [establishing a collaboration platform to support the functioning of joint investigation teams and amending Regulation (EU) 2018/1726, OJ L 132, 17.5.2023, 1] and to establish interoperability by Regulation (EU) 2019/817 on establishing a framework for interoperability between EU information systems in the field of borders and visa [...], OJ L 135, 22.5.2019, 27 (which in turn has been amended several times), as well as the parallel Regulation (EU) 2019/818 on establishing a framework for interoperability between EU information systems in the field of police and judicial cooperation, asylum and migration [...], OJ L 135, 22.5.2019, 85 (which has also been amended several times).

[117] Recital 1 and Art. 1(3) and Art. 3 eu-LISA Regulation. The legal bases for the SIS are set out in Regulation (EU) 2018/1861 on the establishment, operation and use of the Schengen Information System (SIS) in the field of border checks [...], OJ J L 312, 7.12.2018, 14 and Regulation (EU) 2018/1862 on the establishment, operation and use of the Schengen Information System (SIS) in the field of police cooperation and judicial cooperation in criminal matters [...], OJ L 312, 7.12.2018, 56; both Regulations were amended by the Interoperability Regulations (EU) 2019/817 and (EU) 2019/818, subsequently by Regulations (EU) 2021/1150 and (EU) 2021/1152 [...] as regards the establishment of the conditions for accessing other EU information systems for the purposes of the European Travel Information and

was originally transferred to its remit, as was the Visa Information System (VIS)[118] and the Asylum Fingerprint Database (Eurodac).[119] The European travel information and authorization system (ETIAS),[120] the Entry/Exit System (EES)[121] and the DubliNet[122] were added under the eu-LISA Regulation.

Authorisation System, OJ L 249, 7.7.2021, 1, 15 and (only Regulation (EU) 2018/1862) by Regulation (EU) 2022/1190 amending Regulation (EU) 2018/1862 as regards the entry of information alerts into the Schengen Information System (SIS) on third-country nationals in the interest of the Union, OJ L 185, 12.7.2022, 1. Regulation (EU) 2018/1860 on the use of the Schengen Information System for the return of illegally staying third-country nationals, OJ L 312, 7.12.2018, 1 is of particular relevance to security law (and was, in turn, amended by Regulation (EU) 2021/1134 and Regulation (EU) 2021/1152). On 7 March 2023 the SIS began operations based on new Regulations that were adopted in 2019; see the relevant Commission Implementing Decision (EU) 2023/201 setting the date on which operations of the Schengen Information Systems start pursuant to Regulation (EU) 1861 and Regulation (EU) 2018/1862, OJ L 27, 31.1.2023, 29. On the complex system of Schengen-related regulations, see Schöndorf-Haubold in Terhechte, Verwaltungsrecht der Europäischen Union, § 35 mn. 72 et seqq.

118 Recital 2 and Art. 1(3) and Art. 4 eu-LISA Regulation. On the VIS, see Regulation (EC) No 767/2008 concerning the Visa Information System (VIS) and the exchange of data between the Member States on short-stay visas, OJ L 218, 13.8.2008, 60 (VIS Regulation), in particular amended by Regulation (EU) 2021/1134 […] for the purpose of reforming the Visa Information System, OJ L 248, 13.7.2021, 11; further amendments were proposed in the European Commission, 'Proposal for a Regulation […] as regards the digitalisation of the visa procedure', 27.4.2022, (COM(2022) 658 final).

119 Recital 3, Art. 1(3) and Art. 5 eu-LISA Regulation. On Eurodac, see Regulation (EU) No 603/2013 on the establishment of 'Eurodac' for the comparison of fingerprints for the effective application of Regulation (EU) No 604/2013 establishing the criteria and mechanisms for determining the Member State responsible for examining an application for international protection lodged in one of the Member States by a third-country national or a stateless person and on requests for the comparison with Eurodac data […] (recast), OJ L 180, 29.6.2013, 1, as last amended by Regulation 2021/1133 […] as regards the establishment of the conditions for accessing other EU information systems for the purposes of the Visa Information System, OJ L 248, 13.7.2021, 1.

120 Art. 1(4) and Art. 7 of the eu-LISA Regulation (EU) 2018/1726 in conjunction with Regulation (EU) 2018/1240 establishing a European Travel Information and Authorisation System (ETIAS) […], OJ L 236, 19.9.2018, 1, amended by, e.g., the Interoperability Regulation (EU) 2019/817, Regulation (EU) 2021/1134 […] for the purpose of reforming the Visa Information System and, in particular, Regulation (EU) 2021/1152 […] as regards the establishment of the conditions for accessing other EU information systems for the purposes of the European Travel Information and Authorisation System, OJ L 249, 14.7.2021, 15; further amendments were proposed in the Commission, 'Proposal for a Regulation introducing a screening of third country nationals at the external borders […]', 23.9.2020, COM(2020) 612 final.

121 Art. 1(4) and Art. 6 eu-LISA Regulation in conjunction with Regulation (EU) 2017/2226 establishing an Entry/Exit System (EES) to register entry and exit data and refusal of entry data of third-country nationals crossing the external borders of the Member States and determining the conditions for access to the EES for law enforcement purposes […], OJ L 327, 9.12.2017, 20, as amended by the ETIAS Regulation (EU) 2018/1240, the eu-LISA Regulation, the Interoperability Regulation, VIS-Regulation (EU) 2021/1134 […] for the purpose of reforming the Visa Information System and by the ETIAS Access Regulation (EU). Further amendments were proposed in COM(2020) 612 final and in COM(2022) 658 final.

122 Art. 1(4) and Art. 8 eu-LISA Regulation in conjunction with Art. 18 Regulation (EC) No 1560/2003 for the purposes of the application of Art. 31, 32 and 34 of Regulation (EU) No 604/2013 establishing the criteria and mechanisms for determining the Member State responsible for examining an application for international protection lodged in one of the Member States by a third-country national or a stateless person (recast), OJ L 180, 29.6.2013, p. 31.

67 Further, the European Criminal Records Information System (ECRIS-TCN),[123] the JITs collaboration platform[124] and the e-CODEX System[125] are also intended to form part of the Agency's operations, although provision has not yet been for them under the eu-LISA Regulation and they are all still at the development stage. Pursuant to Art. 1(5) and Art. 9 eu-LISA Regulation, the Agency can also be entrusted with the preparation and operational management of other large-scale IT systems.

68 Further proposals for expanding the eu-LISA mandate are in the legislative pipeline: eu-LISA has been tasked with making available a router and with putting in place a European Police Records Index System ('Prüm II' und EPRIS)[126] to facilitate information sharing between the authorities responsible for the prevention, detection and investigation of crimes. It is also to set up a second router to enable airlines to transmit Advanced Passenger Information (API) data relating to EU inbound flights to the relevant border authorities and to the central Passenger Information Unit (PIU).[127]

b) Organization and structure

69 In 2022 the Agency employed a total of 310 staff at its three locations.[128] Its 2023 budget totalled 327m EUR.[129] The Agency's fundamental, key decisions are taken by its Management Board, which is composed of one representative of each Member State and two representatives of the Commission.[130] The Executive Director, who is appointed by the Management Board based on a proposal by the Commission, directs the Agency and manages its day-to-day business.[131] Each of the information systems established and/or managed by eu-LISA is supported by an Advisory Group comprising one member of each of the involved Member States and the Commission as well as, optionally, of any associated third country and/or other EU security agency.[132]

c) Objective: to establish an overarching security agency data network

70 The declared political and legally binding objective is to bring together the various databases for security-policy and security-law purposes under an overall and over-

---

[123] ECRIS-TCN-Regulation (EU) 2019/816 establishing a centralised system for the identification of Member States holding conviction information on third-country nationals and stateless persons (ECRIS-TCN) to supplement the European Criminal Records Information System and amending Regulation (EU) 2018/1726, OJ L 135, 22.5.2019, 1, which was amended by, amongst other regulations, Regulation (EU) 2021/1151 amending Regulations (EU) 2019/816 and (EU) 2019/818 as regards the establishment of the conditions for accessing other EU information systems for the purposes of the European Travel Information and Authorisation System, OJ L 249, 14.7.2021, 7; further amendments were proposed in European Commission, 'Proposal for a Regulation […] for the purpose of introducing a screening of third country nationals at the external borders'. 2.3.2021, COM(2021) 96 final.

[124] Art. 7 JIT-Regulation (EU) 2023/969: optional use of the platform through the creation of what are referred to as 'JIT collaboration spaces' (Art. 13); automatic deletion of operational data after four weeks at the latest (Art. 21).

[125] Regulation (EU) 2022/850 on a computerised system for the cross-border electronic exchange of data in the area of judicial cooperation in civil and criminal matters (e-CODEX system), and amending Regulation (EU) 2018/1726, OJ L 150, 1.6.2022, 1.

[126] See the corrected European Commission, 'Proposal for a Regulation on automated data exchange for police cooperation ('Prüm II') […]', 8.12.2021, COM(2021) 784 final/2.

[127] See European Commission, 'Proposal for a Regulation on the collection and transfer of advance passenger information (API) for enhancing and facilitating external border controls […]', 13.12.2022, COM(2022) 729 final.

[128] For statistics and the Agency's history to date, see eu-LISA, '10-Year Anniversary', available from <www.eulisa.europa.eu> (last accessed: 27.3.2024).

[129] See eu-LISA <www.eulisa.europa.eu/AboutUs/Finance> (last accessed: 27.3.2024).

[130] Art. 18 et seqq. eu-LISA Regulation.

[131] Art. 18 and 24 eu-LISA Regulation; *Agnès Diallo* was appointed Executive Director on 16.3.2023.

[132] Art. 27 eu-LISA Regulation.

arching EU border management concept. An integrated search function will provide access to the various databases that were originally conceived of as legally separate. A European Search Portal (ESP)[133] developed and operated by eu-LISA will act as an interface and provide simultaneous access to the various different information systems. Interoperability of the systems is based on the relevant Union legal acts[134] and joint technical operational management. eu-LISA's key concern is not only the administration of technical systems but, specifically, the provision of data to the competent authorities, that is the risk prevention and prosecution authorities as well as asylum and border protection authorities. The result will be an overarching police data network. The objective is technical efficiency, which will lead to a visible increase in site visits.[135] However, the explosive nature of data protection issues has not yet been sufficiently registered, nor is it even possible to gauge how extensive they will be.[136] The European Data Protection Supervisor (EDPS) notes in an Opinion on the Interoperability Regulations (which provide the legal basis for the ESP) that

> interoperability is not primarily a technical choice, it is first and foremost a political choice to be made, with significant legal and societal implications in the years to come. Against the backdrop of the clear trend to mix distinct EU law and policy objectives (i.e. border checks, asylum and immigration, police cooperation and now also judicial cooperation in criminal matters), as well as granting law enforcement routine access to non-law enforcement databases, the decision of the EU legislator to make large-scale IT systems interoperable would not only permanently and profoundly affect their structure and their way of operating, but would also change the way legal principles have been interpreted in this area so far and would as such mark a 'point of no return'. For these reasons, the EDPS calls for a wider debate on the future of the EU information exchange, their governance and the ways to safeguard fundamental rights in this context.[137]

---

[133] Art. 6 et seqq. of both Interoperability Regulations ((EU) 2019/817 and (EU) 2019/818), which were issued on different primary EU legislative bases, according to which a 'European search portal (ESP) is established for the purposes of facilitating the fast, seamless, efficient, systematic and controlled access of Member State authorities and Union agencies to the EU information systems, to Europol data and to the Interpol databases for the performance of their tasks and in accordance with their access rights and the objectives and purposes of the EES, VIS, ETIAS, Eurodac, SIS and ECRIS-TCN.' Pursuant to Art. 6(2) of both Regulations, the ESP is composed of '(a) a central infrastructure, including a search portal enabling the simultaneous querying of the EES, VIS, ETIAS, Eurodac, SIS, ECRIS-TCN as well as of Europol data and the Interpol databases; (b) a secure communication channel between the ESP, Member States and Union agencies that are entitled to use the ESP; (c) a secure communication infrastructure between the ESP and the EES, VIS, ETIAS, Eurodac, Central SIS, ECRIS-TCN, Europol data and the Interpol databases as well as between the ESP and the central infrastructures of the CIR and the MID.'

[134] See Art. 13 eu-LISA Regulation.

[135] See eu-LISA, 'Consolidated Annual Activity Report 2022', 22.6.2023, Document 2023-182 REV.

[136] See European Data Protection Supervisor, 'Opinion 4/2018 on the Proposals for two Regulations establishing a framework for interoperability between EU large-scale information systems', 16.4.2018 (for a summary, see OJ C 162, 23.5.2017, 9; full text <https://edps.europa.eu/sites/edp/files/publication/2018-04-16_interoperability_opinion_en.pdf> (last accessed: 27.3.2024): The EDPS stresses that 'both in legal and technical terms, the Proposals add another layer of complexity to the existing systems, as well as those that are still in the pipeline with precise implications that are difficult to assess at this stage. This complexity will have implications not only for data protection, but also for governance and supervision of the systems. The precise implications for the rights and freedoms which are at the core of the EU project are difficult to fully assess at this stage. For these reasons, the EDPS calls for a wider debate on the future of the EU information exchange, their governance and the ways to safeguard fundamental rights in this context.' For a critical approach, see Aden in Lisken/Denninger, Handbuch des Polizeirechts, M. mn. 193.

[137] European Data Protection Supervisor, 'Opinion 4/2018 on the Proposals for two Regulations establishing a framework for interoperability between EU large-scale information systems', 16.4.2018, mn. 143.; mn 144 reads as follows: 'Although the Proposals as presented could give the impression of interoperability as the final component of already fully functioning information systems (or at least systems the legal founding acts of which are already "stable" and in the final stages of the legislative process), the EDPS wishes to recall that this is not the case. In reality, three of the six EU information

The EDPS understands the need for 'law enforcement authorities to benefit from the best possible tools to quickly identify the perpetrators of terrorist acts as other serious crimes'. However, 'removing genuine safeguards introduced to preserve fundamental rights mainly in the interest of speeding up a procedure would not be acceptable.'[138] 71

II. Security networks and communications infrastructure: the example of ETIAS

The example of eu-LISA is proof, firstly, of the fact that centralized databases are an important basis for cooperation between national and EU security authorities because they contain large amounts of relevant data that can be accessed via various mechanisms. They generally have a central database, decentral access points and a communications infrastructure with technical back-up. Such large-scale IT systems represent institutionalized cooperation instruments and, thus, along with the agencies, they form part of the supranational EU security architecture. Consolidation of a data processing and communications infrastructure is frequently the first step in a supranationalization process, which can at any rate also act as the point of reference for the subsequent establishment of an agency.[139] 72

1. Information systems used in EU security law: an overview

Databases that are of security-policy relevance include the SIS,[140] VIS, Eurodac,[141] ECRIS-TCN,[142] the EES (primarily in relation to third-country nationals),[143] ETIAS[144] and the JITs collaboration platform.[145] They all have a central network function; as they 73

---

systems the Proposals seek to interconnect do not exist at the moment (ETIAS, ECRIS-TCN and EES), two are currently under revision (SIS and Eurodac) and one is to be revised later this year (VIS). Assessing the precise implications for privacy and data protection of a very complex system with so many "moving parts" is all but impossible. The EDPS recalls the importance to ensure consistency between the legal texts already under negotiation (or upcoming) and the Proposals in order to ensure a unified legal, organizational and technical environment for all data processing activities within the Union.'

138 ibid., mn. 148.

139 On the individual information systems and their interoperability, see Schöndorf-Haubold in Terhechte, Verwaltungsrecht der Europäischen Union, § 35 mn. 64 et seqq.

140 On the SIS, its legal bases and the complex system of the Schengen-related regulations, see the references in footnote 122.

141 On the VIS and Eurodac, see footnotes 123 and 124.

142 See ECRIS-TCN-Regulation (EU) 2019/816 establishing a centralised system for the identification of Member States holding conviction information on third-country nationals and stateless persons (ECRIS-TCN) to supplement the European Criminal Records Information System and amending Regulation (EU) 2018/1726, OJ L 135, 22.5.2019, 1, which was amended by, amongst other regulations, Regulation (EU) 2021/1151 amending Regulations (EU) 2019/816 and (EU) 2019/818 as regards the establishment of the conditions for accessing other EU information systems for the purposes of the European Travel Information and Authorisation System, OJ L 249, 14.7.2021, 7; further amendments were proposed in European Commission, 'Proposal for a Regulation […] for the purpose of introducing a screening of third country nationals at the external borders'. 2.3.2021, COM(2021) 96 final.

143 Regulation (EU) 2017/2226 establishing an Entry/Exit System (EES) to register entry and exit data and refusal of entry data of third-country nationals crossing the external borders of the Member States and determining the conditions for access to the EES for law enforcement purposes […], OJ L 327, 9.12.2017, 20, amended several times: Introduction of an Entry/Exit System (EES) as an electronic alternative to passport stamping.

144 Regulation (EU) 2018/1240 establishing a European Travel Information and Authorisation System (ETIAS) […], OJ L 236, 19.9.2018, 1, amended several times.

145 Regulation (EU) 2023/969 [establishing a collaboration platform to support the functioning of joint investigation teams and amending Regulation (EU) 2018/1726, OJ L 132, 17.5.2023, 1.

are information platforms used for the purpose of horizontal and vertical cooperation between the security agencies, they each have their own specific relevance. At the same time, recent developments – such as the steady expansion of eu-LISA's tasks and the adoption of specific regulations like the ETIAS Regulation – are preparing the way for specific security-related, overarching data spaces.

2. Wide-ranging networks: the example of ETIAS

74 In accordance with the ETIAS Regulation (EU) 2018/1240,[146] ETIAS relates only to the entry and stay of visa-exempt third-country nationals. Its purposes is, in combination with other existing databases, to facilitate the wide-ranging decentralized monitoring of the entry into and stay in the EU of third-country nationals and to establish the required centralized databases.[147]

75 In addition to preventing illegal migration and protecting against high epidemic risks, 'security provision' is one of the declared objectives of the ETIAS Regulation[148] that cannot merely be achieved by denying entry to anyone posing a security risk, but in addition, and independently of that, requires that the security authorities be given access to the ETIAS databases.[149] The ETIAS Regulation seeks to establish wide-ranging information networks among the security authorities within the 'European composite administration' and it creates the legal and technical conditions for an overarching data space, which Europol and Frontex are involved, into which the SIS, VIS, EES, Eurodac, ECRIS-TCN and Europol data are incorporated[150] and to which the border control and security authorities have access. The applicable use limitations are, by comparison. quite general.

76 The ETIAS Regulation makes provision for the pooling of security-relevant databases within the 'EU Information System' in order to facilitate the granting and control of travel authorizations and the more far-reaching use of data for security purposes.

---

[146] ETIAS Regulation (, amended by, e.g., the Interoperability Regulation (EU) 2019/817, Regulation (EU) 2021/1134 […] for the purpose of reforming the Visa Information System and, in particular, Regulation (EU) 2021/1152 […] as regards the establishment of the conditions for accessing other EU information systems for the purposes of the European Travel Information and Authorisation System, OJ L 249, 14.7.2021, 15; further amendments were proposed in COM(2020) 612 final; for details, see Schöndorf-Haubold in Terhechte, Verwaltungsrecht der Europäischen Union, § 35 mn. 91 et seqq.

[147] See, in particular, regarding the privacy concerns, the summary of the EDPS's Opinion 4/2018, which includes the following in regard to jointly addressing security and migration management purposes: 'With the ETIAS Proposal, the EU legislator appears to follow the increasing trend of addressing security and migration management purposes jointly, without taking into account the substantial distinctions between these two policy areas', OJ C 162, 23.5.2017, 9.

[148] Art. 4 ETIAS Regulation.

[149] Authorization is granted, based on an algorithm generated by Frontex using specific risk indicators, either automatically by the centralized ETIAS system or manually following a risk assessment by a Member State's ETIAS unit. Pursuant to Art. 40 et seq. of the ETIAS Regulation, authorization can be annulled or revoked by any Member State that is in possession of the necessary evidence; see Art. 21(1), Art. 26 in conjunction with Art. 36(1) ETIAS Regulation.

[150] See Regulation (EU) 2018/1241 amending the Europol Regulation (EU) 2016/794 for the purpose of establishing a European Travel Information and Authorisation System (ETIAS), OJ L 236, 19.9.2018, 72; see, in particular, Regulations (EU) 2021/1150, (EU) 2021/1151 and (EU) 2021/1152 as regards the establishment of the conditions for accessing other EU information systems for the purposes of the European Travel Information and Authorisation System, OJ L 249, 14.7.2021, 1, 7, 15 as regards the SIS, VIS, Eurodac, EES, ECRIS-TCN and Europol. The aim is also to create a further link to the API data and PNR data; the definition of 'PNR data' is provided in Directive (EU) 2016/681 on the use of passenger name record (PNR) data for the prevention, detection, investigation and prosecution of terrorist offences and serious crime, OJ L 119, 4.5.2016, 132; see COM(2022) 729 final.

Europol data[151] and various Interpol databases[152] are listed in the Regulation and likewise form part of the network. The databases are linked based on a legal/technical access regime: The ETIAS is first linked up to the information systems in question, after which the security authorities are granted access to them via ETIAS.[153] Provision has not yet been made for automatic access to the data.

3. The role of the agencies in the ETIAS information network

eu-LISA (which is responsible for technical systems and data quality), the Border Agency Frontex (the ETIAS Central Unit) and Europol contribute in different ways and have different responsibilities within a complex institutional structure in relation to the use, operation and administration of ETIAS.[154] The already complex vertical and diagonal interconnections between the security authorities within the 'European composite administration' are also becoming more opaque and abandoning clear-cut allocations of responsibilities. The confusing and ramified referencing technique used in the likewise confusingly large number of relevant legal acts increases the level of complexity. 77

No provision has been made, at the system level, for ETIAS to have any of its own bodies with decision-making powers; a number of broadly composed committees do undertake different advisory tasks, though: Whilst it was being established and shaped, a Programme Management Board was established within eu-LISA that is composed of members of the eu-LISA Management Board, the Chair of the EES–ETAIS Advisory Group and of one representative appointed by the eu-LISA Executive Director, by Frontex and by the Commission; the Programme Management Board is required to guarantee proper management throughout the development phase and has no decision-making or representative powers.[155] 78

The EES–ETIAS Advisory Group, by contrast, has a general advisory function, especially in the context of the preparation of the annual work programme and annual 79

---

151 In accordance with Art. 34 et seq. of the ETIAS Regulation (EU) 2018/1240 and Art. 4(1) points (n) and (o) of the Europol-Regulation in the version as amended by Regulation (EU) 2018/1241, Europol keeps an ETIAS watchlist consisting of 'data relating to persons related to persons who are suspected of having committed or taken part in a terrorist offence or other serious criminal offence or persons regarding whom there are factual indications or reasonable grounds, based on an overall assessment of the person, to believe that they will commit a terrorist offence or other serious criminal offence.'

152 Recital 4 Regulation (EU) 2021/1150 [establishing the conditions for accessing other EU information systems for the purposes of the European Travel Information and Authorisation System, OJ L 249, 14.7.2021, 1] reads as follows: 'This Regulation, together with Regulations (EU) 2021/1151 and (EU) 2021/1152 of the European Parliament and of the Council, lays down rules on the implementation of interoperability between the ETIAS Information System, on the one hand, and other EU information systems and Europol data, on the other hand, and the conditions for the consultation of data stored in other EU information systems and Europol data by ETIAS for the purpose of automatically identifying hits. As a result, it is necessary to amend SIS-Regulation (EU) 2018/1862 and Interoperability-Regulation (EU) 2019/818 of the European Parliament and of the Council in order to connect the ETIAS Central System to other EU information systems and to Europol data and to specify the data that will be sent between those EU information systems and Europol data.

153 Access authorization is granted to the ETIAS units as well as to the border management and immigration authorities, which are appointed and authorized by the Member States. The national security authorities and Europol also have access authorization for the purpose of tackling terrorist and other serious crimes. See Art. 13 and Art. 50 et seqq. ETIAS Regulation; as regards access authorization to the SIS, see the almost 300-page list in the List of competent authorities, OJ C 85, 7.3.2023, 1.

154 On the internal structure of ETIAS, which in accordance with Art. 5 ETIAS Regulation, comprises the ETIAS Information System pursuant to Art. 6, the ETIAS Central Office pursuant to Art. 7 and the ETIAS National Units pursuant to Art. 8, as well as the individual elements of the ETIAS Information System, see Schöndorf-Haubold in Terhechte, Verwaltungsrecht der Europäischen Union, § 35 mn. 94.

155 Art. 73(4) ETIAS Regulation.

activity report.[156] The ETIAS Screening Board, which also only acts in an advisory capacity, is composed of one representative of each of the ETIAS National Units, of Frontex and of Europol. It must be consulted on specific risk indicators and on the implementation of the ETIAS watchlist referred to in Art. 34 TIAS Regulation; it may issue general guidelines and recommendations, too.[157]

80 The ETIAS Fundamental Rights Guidance Board is based in Frontex's offices. It is administered by the Agency and also has a special, overarching role. Established as an independent ETIAS Advisory Group with an advisory and appraisal function, it is composed of the Fundamental Rights Officer of the European Border and Coast Guard Agency, a representative of the consultative forum on fundamental rights of the European Border and Coast Guard Agency, a representative of the EDPS, a representative of the European Data Protection Board established by Regulation (EU) 2016/679 and a representative of the European Union Agency for Fundamental Rights. Even though it has no decision-making powers of its own, the ETIAS Fundamental Rights Guidance Board is designed as a (soft) supervisory body that primarily supports the ETIAS Screening Board (which also only has an advisory function) by making recommendations and regularly performing appraisals of the impact on fundamental rights, in particular with regard to privacy, personal data protection and non-discrimination.[158]

81 All these bodies are part of a soft, informal administrative substructure that is neither tasked nor legally empowered to conduct binding fundamental, legality or data protection audits. In view of the considerable sensitivity of the data in question from the point of view of fundamental rights, it appears doubtful whether that substructure will be sufficient to reliably guarantee minimum rule-of-law standards.

C. The law relating to the EU security agencies: the direction of development

82 At its basis, European security law remains cooperation law.[159] Operational and informational cooperation mechanisms are a manifestation of the Member States' ongoing basic responsibility for ensuring internal security. The agencies also tie their evolution, functions and structure to this important structural principle, namely of a polycentric security architecture. More than a few of the agencies were founded upon existing network structures and cooperation mechanisms; the mandate of all the security agencies encompasses close cooperation with the Member States and/or the coordination and support of cooperation among the Member States; finally, the security agencies' organizational structures evidence a distribution of competences between the Member States and the EU, that is in the interplay between centralized and decentralized offices and, in terms of their internal structure, between management boards, advisory bodies and networks, even though the boundaries of that division of compe-

[156] Art. 18(1)(c) and Art. 27(1)(d) eu-LISA Regulation in conjunction with Art. 91 ETIAS Regulation. The Advisory Groups are each composed of one representative of all the participating Member States, the Commission and, optionally, of Europol and Frontex.

[157] Art. 9 ETIAS Regulation.

[158] Art. 10 in conjunction with Art. 7(2)(e) and Art. 33 ETIAS Regulation.

[159] See Schöndorf-Haubold in Ehlers/Fehling/Pünder, Besonderes Verwaltungsrecht III, § 68 mn. 52 et seqq. and mn. 109 et seqq.

tences are by no means clear-cut and the direction of the Union's security agencies' travel is being given an unbounded supranationalization boost.

The continuous expansion of the EU's security architecture testifies to the political will, backed by the majority in the Council and Parliament, to strengthen supranational security provision.[160] Even though the EPPO is definitely not an agency in the strict sense, as a non-judicial public EU facility it is at any rate comparable to the security agencies and can be described as an 'EU security authority'. Whilst new offices are being set up, existing offices are subject to permanent change, the momentum of which is not always easy to understand and regularly leads to the strengthening of mandates and the extension of functions. Frontex, Europol and even eu-LISA are notable examples that fit this trend. **83**

These agencies can also be used to illustrate their characteristically functional and organizational nature on account of the multilevel structure of the 'composite administration', which is reflected in joint bodies, network structures and an intensive level of cooperation. The instruments of this horizontal, vertical, and diagonal cooperation are, in turn, enabled, simplified, and directed by the agencies, thus decentrally and supranationally. It is not always possible to clearly distinguish between the targeted commissioning of the Member States' security authorities and the mere provision of support during their operations. The ever more complex level of interconnectedness of operations and information sharing is clear evidence of the attempt to grant the EU the broadest steering capabilities whilst maintaining existing competences. Those capabilities in part reflect the division of competences very well, but they in part also attempt to hide the lack of operational competence and/or authority at the EU level, and they lack a sufficiently clear-cut counterpart in the division of competences between the EU and the Member States. **84**

Three examples serve to illustrate the security agencies' ongoing tendency to break free of existing structures: the expansion of Frontex into a genuine EU border police force with its own operational powers of intervention; the strengthening of Europol's own data processing functions; and the establishment of an overarching information sharing environment administered by eu-LISA with central access via the ESP. **85**

I. Establishing a genuine European border police force

Frontex (→ mn. 29 et seq.) by tradition has a supportive function. As it has no border guards, police powers and equipment of its own, the Agency has so far always been reliant on commissioning Member States' resources. In the past, JITs could only draw on a staff and an equipment pool, and these were then deployed to joint border operations, with the agreement of the State of operation, under its leadership and in accordance with its law.[161] **86**

[160] That is also the direction taken in strategic policy programmes on strengthening the Security Union; see, in particular, COM(2020) 605 final; European Commission, 'Communication, A Counter-Terrorism Agenda for the EU: Anticipate, Prevent, Protect, Respond', 9.12.2020, COM(2020) 795 final, as well as European Commission, 'Communication, Stronger and Smarter Information Systems for Border Management and Security', 6.4.2016, COM(2016) 205 final; European Commission, 'Communication, delivering on the European Agenda on Security to fight against terrorism and pave the way towards an effective and genuine Security Union', 20.4.2016, COM(2016) 230 final, which makes reference to European Commission, 'The European Agenda on Security', 28.4.2015, COM(2015) 185 final.

[161] On this development, see Schöndorf-Haubold in Ehlers/Fehling/Pünder, Besonderes Verwaltungsrecht III, § 68 mn. 64 et seqq.

87 The creation of a Frontex standing corps of 10,000 officers will change all that. Even though it will initially be very limited in scope,[162] it will, for the first time, have its own coercive powers.[163] From being an instrument that is used to lend out administrative bodies to other public authorities on account of a lack of its own infrastructure under applicable law, deployable personnel and the necessary powers of intervention, these teams are thus evolving into an EU instrument with police powers, even though, under the provisions of the regulations, formal operational management is still ascribed to the State of operation.[164]

88 Strengthening the Agency's legal as well as actual means of influence goes along with a weakening of its accountability.[165] The soft instruments that have primarily been used in the past, such as operational plans, opinions, and the sovereignty clause – which can nevertheless still lead to a significant shift in decision-making powers – appear to be being consciously used as a means to sidestep the issue of sovereignty. The complicated references to a State of operation's obligation to comply with the Agency's operational plans, opinions and invocation of the sovereignty clause are also evidence of that. They make it more difficult to clearly assign joint operations and, based on the current CJEU case law, are also likely to preclude the review of the Agency's legal act in accordance with Art. 263(1) sent. 2 TFEU, although it is undoubtedly subject to the Court's jurisdiction.[166]

II. Expanding Europol's mandate on information processing

89 It is not only since the entry into force of the most recent amendment of the Europol regime in 2022[167] that that regime has included wide-ranging privacy rules on, in particular, the handling of personal data and the conditions under which Europol may transmit and receive such data. For want of its own coercive powers, which are explicitly precluded under Art. 88(3) TFEU, as well as its own service facility for the Member States' police authorities,[168] the Agency has so far had no police powers that enable it to collect information itself.

---

[162] The German Federal Criminal Police Office employs over 8,100 staff (see <https://www.bka.de/EN/TheBKA/FactsAndFigures/factsandfigures_node.html> (last accessed: 27.3.2024)); the German Federal Police has a total of 30,000 officers and 40,000 employees (see <www.bmi.bund.de/DE/ministerium/behoerden-und-einrichtungen/behoerden-und-einrichtungen-node.html> (last accessed: 27.3.2024) (German only)).

[163] See Art: 54 and Annex I Frontex Regulation.

[164] Art: 43 Frontex Regulation.

[165] On this, specifically in relation to joint Frontex operations, see Schöndorf-Haubold in Kahl/Mager, Verwaltungsaufgaben und Legitimation der Verwaltung, p. 243 et seqq.

[166] See the General Court's recent judgment of 6.9.2023, rejecting the agency's responsibility in principle by reference to its exclusively supporting function, GC 6.9.2023 – case T-600/21, ECLI:EU:T:2023:492 para. 57 and 66: 'More specifically, they argue that, if Frontex had not infringed its obligations relating to the protection of fundamental rights in the context of joint operations, in particular the principle of non-refoulement, the right to asylum, the prohibition of collective expulsion, the rights of the child, the prohibition of degrading treatment, the right to good administration and to an effective remedy, they would not have been unlawfully returned to Türkiye and they would have obtained the international protection to which they were entitled, given their Syrian nationality and the situation in Syria at the material time' vs. 'Consequently, and since Frontex has no competence either as regards the assessment of the merits of the return decisions or as regards applications for international protection, the direct causal link alleged by the applicants between the damage allegedly suffered and the conduct of which Frontex is accused cannot be established.'

[167] See the Europol Regulation (EU) 2016/794, as last amended by Regulation (EU) 2022/991.

[168] Aden in Lisken/Denninger, Handbuch des Polizeirechts, M. mn. 135.

One of the key aspects of the most recent Regulation amending the Europol Regulation[169] is that it permits the Agency to directly take receipt of personal information on private individuals.[170] This innovation (referred to as 'cooperation with private parties') on the one hand ensures that Europol is permitted to receive data on private parties in order to determine the competent national authority. Nevertheless, the new Art. 26a also releases the Agency from that obligation in online crisis situations and permits the – apparently exclusively voluntary – receipt and processing of such data in order, for example, to prevent the dissemination of online content related to terrorism or violent extremism.[171] In accordance with Art. 26a of the amended Europol Regulation, the Agency may also request the Member States, via their National Units, to obtain personal data from private parties in their territory that are necessary for its work by collecting those data from the private parties under their applicable laws. 90

Regardless of the fact that the authority to receive such data alone without the corresponding obligation on the part of private platform operators and service providers to transmit data is likely to be hardly effective and that the request made to the Member States will likely be decisive. This new rule, which has been adopted by the Parliament and Council and has entered into force, is likewise an expression of the gradual and ongoing evolution of the EU security agencies' own powers. However, the wording of the amended provisions is too vague to mean that Europol's direct receipt of data on a voluntary basis will lead to independent data collection on its part. The fact that private parties voluntarily reveal personal data does not cancel out the lack of consent by non-identical data subjects. 91

This, too, raises the question of whether the apparent recourse to the Member States' powers (an option that avoids the sovereignty issue) does not in fact shift responsibility for the fundamental rights interference and it thus becomes difficult for the data subject affected by such interference to have Europol's actions reviewed.[172] 92

III. Establishing a security information architecture

The attempt to follow the complicated references in and ramifications of the eu-LISA regime (→ mn. 65 et seq.) clearly indicate that information structures have emerged in relation to the issue of security provision that are breaking free and consolidating into a large, legally and factually quite opaque security information system. 93

This is evidenced in the creation of overarching infrastructures such as eu-LISA itself[173] as well as in legal acts that seek to establish technical and legal interoperability between the various systems.[174] It is the Commission's declared aim to facilitate exchange between and access to the systems – which it has given the title 94

[169] Europol Regulation(EU) 2016/794 , as last amended by Regulation (EU) 2022/991 amending Regulation (EU) 2016/794 as regards Europol's cooperation with private parties, the processing of personal data by Europol in support of criminal investigations, and Europol's role in research and innovation, OJ L 169, 27.6.2022, 1.

[170] Art. 26(2) Europol Regulation (EU) 2016/794, as last amended by Regulation (EU) 2022/991.

[171] Art. 26a of the European Commission, 'Proposal for a Regulation as regards Europol's cooperation with private parties, the processing of personal data by Europol in support of criminal investigations, and Europol's role on research and innovation', 9.12.2020, COM(2020) 796 final and the Europol Regulation (EU) 2016/794, as last amended by Regulation (EU) 2022/991.

[172] For a sceptical approach to the extension of Frontex's and Europol's operational mandate, see Freudlsperger/Maricut-Akbik/Migliorati, Comparative Political Studies 2022 , 1983 et seqq.

[173] See the eu-LISA Regulation.

[174] See the Interoperability Regulations 2019/817 and 2019/818 on establishing a framework for interoperability between EU information systems in the field of borders and visa respectively in the field

'Stronger and Smarter Information Systems for Borders and Security'.[175] ETIAS and the creation of an overarching information system, is another example of this trend (→ mn. 72 et seq.).

95 eu-LISA administers the SIS, VIS and Eurodac databases, for which a specific structure has been established. In future, ETIAS, the EES and the ECRIS-TCN are also to be incorporated into that structure and administered by eu-LISA. Although data are not consolidated in a large data cloud – which would anyway be impermissible from a privacy perspective – the data are administered in such a way that access by security agencies such as, in particular, Europol, is easier and cross-checking is at any rate possible. The ESP is to act as the interface and to provide easier and simultaneous access to various information systems (→ mn. 65 et seq.).

96 The more data become interconnected within a single infrastructure, the more important data-protection supervision not only of the operation but specifically of access to and the use of data collated in that way becomes. It is not yet clear, though, whether the establishment and interconnection of the systems has created sufficient clarity on fundamental rights and privacy issues, including with regard to the CJEU case law[176].[177] Standards have not yet been set on to the division of powers and competences in relation to information. Effective cooperation between the security agencies and effective joint security provision as such are not likely to be sufficient in and of themselves to justify the additional centralization. Limitations imposed on individual systems, the reference to Regulation (EU) 2018/1725[178] and the general purpose limitation of data processing[179] – whose purpose, though, is not sufficient precisely delimited but is broadly defined and task-based – are also not sufficient, even in combination with non-binding working arrangements between the involved facilities,[180] to capture the added value and greater data-protection and fundamental-rights relevance of overarching information sharing under police law.

D. Outlook and evaluation

97 In view of the manifold interconnections described in the above, the question arises of the relationship between this EU security architecture on the one hand and the Treaty competences and the distribution of responsibilities between the Union and the Member Staes on the other. The rule of law sets limits to the institutionalization of and

---

of police and judicial cooperation, asylum and migration […], OJ L 135, 22.5.2019, 27 resp. 85 (both amended several times); for a critical take, see Aden, EPL 2020 (26), 93 et seqq.

[175] COM(2016) 205 final.

[176] On data retention, e.g., see ECJ 8.4.2014 – case C-293/12 and C-594/12, ECLI:EU:C:2014:238 – *Digital Rights Ireland Ltd and Others*.; on confirmation of the ban on data retention, see ECJ 12.12.2016 – case C-203/15 and C-698/15, ECLI:EU:C:2016:970 – *Tele2 Sverige AB*.

[177] See the critique by Bossong, SWP-Studie 2018 (4); Aden in Lisken/Denninger, Handbuch des Polizeirechts, M. mn. 193; see also → mn. 65 et seq., with references to the European Data Protection Supervisor's sceptical Opinions.

[178] Art. 35 eu-LISA Regulation, with reference to Regulation (EU) 2018/1725 on the protection of natural persons with regard to the processing of personal data by the Union institutions, bodies, offices and agencies and on the free movement of such data, and repealing Regulation (EC) No 45/2001 and Decision No 1247/2002/EC, OJ L 295, 21.11.2018, 39 (General Data Protection Regulation).

[179] Art. 36 eu-LISA Regulation.

[180] Art. 41 eu-LISA Regulation.

recourse to the Member States' basic responsibilities.[181] Nevertheless, general developments as regards the security architecture are likely to still be within the bounds of the division of competences defined under primary EU legislation, although the concrete shape the Security Union and the security architecture are taking on is less of an issue than the political attempt to seemingly continually align both existing institutions and rules and their future development to Member States' sovereignty, as the example of Frontex in particular shows, if the deployment of joint teams is primarily oriented to the relevant Member State's domestic law despite the Union taking on a steering function.

By contrast, the bases provided in primary EU law do not in principle preclude **98** developing the EU security agencies further and giving them their own powers. Although there is a certain amount of tension between the high level of European security that is to be ensured in accordance with Art. 67(3) TFEU and the Member States' primary, and in some cases sole, competence for security, Art. 4(2) TEU must be interpreted narrowly and limited to national security as the genuine core of a State's security concerns, especially those of an intelligence and political nature. On the other hand, Art. 72 TFEU is broader and guarantees that the Member States retain competence for maintaining public security and protecting internal security.[182]

However, exercising that basic competence in the territory of each Member State **99** affected in a specific case is not even called into question where EU agencies themselves gain increasing powers to guarantee operational and informational security in order to ensure European security with a cross-border reference. Instead, the European security architecture is polycentric, not hierarchical, and pursues its own goals vis-à-vis the national security authorities, even if they sometimes go beyond cooperating on and supporting national security provision. National competences are neither transferred nor replaced. Rather, they are supplemented by additional EU tasks and powers.

In the case of Europol, too, Art. 88(3) subpara. 2 TFEU rules out any coercive powers **100** whatsoever – in order not to circumvent existing Member State competences. However, this on the one hand presupposes that such competences can in fact be made out, which is not always possible in the case of cyber threats. On the other hand, the provision can also be read to mean that coercive powers, and thus enforcement powers, but not any types of intervention whatsoever, are ruled out *vis-à-vis* third parties. The fact that Europol can participate in JITs, an option that was also expanded as part of the amendment of the Europol Regulation, also speaks to that (→ mn. 15 et seq.).[183]

Pressing legal questions relating to further developing an EU security architecture are **101** therefore do not primarily only arise in relation to competences, but more decisively in relation to the rule-of-law and democratic disciplining of activities, which are becoming ever broader.

Where they are not absolutely essential, efforts to maintain sovereignty must not run **102** counter to the development of a rule-of-law-based, disciplined, fundamental rights-based and democratically responsible security law by avoiding clear-cut structures of intervention and strictly ruling out fundamental rights interference by definition (because that which is not permitted is forbidden), thereby excluding rule-of-law oversight, for instance by the CJEU and democratic oversight by other EU bodies, or at least making it more difficult.

---

[181] See also Schöndorf-Haubold in Kahl/Mager, Verwaltungsaufgaben und Legitimation der Verwaltung, p. 219 et seqq.

[182] Regarding the interpretation of Art. 4(2) sent. 3 TEU, see Karpenstein/Sangi, GSZ 2020, 162 et seqq.

[183] See the Europol Regulation (EU) 2016/794, as last amended by Regulation (EU) 2022/991.

§ 14
Towards EU standards on control and oversight of intelligence agencies

Iain Cameron

Bibliography: Cameron, 'European Union Law Restraints on Intelligence Activities', IJICI 2020 (33), 452; Cameron, 'Metadata retention and national security: Privacy International and La Quadrature du Net', Common Market Law Review 2021 (58), 1; Cameron, National Security and the European Convention on Human Rights, Uppsala/Dordrecht 2000; Cameron, 'The Problem of Oversight' in Dietrich/Sule (eds), Intelligence Law and Policies in Europe, Munich/Baden-Baden/Oxford 2019, p. 388; Sule, 'National Security and EU law restraints on Intelligence Activities' in Dietrich/Sule (eds), Intelligence Law and Policies in Europe, Munich/Baden-Baden/Oxford 2019, p. 335.

A. Introduction

This chapter examines the EU dimension to oversight of intelligence and security agencies. National security is – not surprisingly – a national responsibility. How security and intelligence agencies are organized, controlled, and overseen are thus matters primarily for each EU Member State. Still, at least since the end of the Cold War, there has been a European dimension to oversight in the form of the case law of the European Court of Human Rights (ECtHR) dealing, directly and indirectly, with the issue of intelligence accountability.[1] This case law is binding, though how much attention states actually pay to it has varied considerably, depending largely upon their level of commitment to democracy and the rule of law. Other Council of Europe bodies have also contributed to oversight 'best practices' through soft-law standard setting, which has interacted in different ways with the binding case law of the ECtHR. In particular, the Venice Commission reports on oversight, together with its more general 'rule of law checklist', provide a framework for states to critically analyse their own systems of control and oversight of security and intelligence agencies.[2] 1

However, the entry of EU institutions to the field of intelligence oversight is a relatively new phenomenon. This has been because the Member States have given EU institutions only limited competence in issues of national security. Art. 4(2) TEU provides that '[the Union] shall respect [the Member States] essential State functions, including [...] safeguarding national security. [...] National security remains the sole responsibility of each Member State.'[3] This is further buttressed by Art. 72 TFEU, which provides that the EU's competence in justice and security 'shall not affect the exercise of the responsibilities incumbent upon Member States with regard to the maintenance of law and order and the safeguarding of internal security.'[4] Much of the doctrinal discussion in the past has 2

---

[1] Cameron, National Security and the European Convention on Human Rights, p. 1 et seqq.

[2] Venice Commission, 'Report on the Democratic Oversight of Signals Intelligence Agencies (2015)', CDL-AD(2015)011-e; Venice Commission, 'Report (revised) on the Democratic Oversight of Internal Security Services (2015)', CDL-AD(2015)010; Venice Commission, 'Rule of Law Checklist (2016)', CDL-AD(2016)007.

[3] Art. 4(2) TEU.

[4] Art. 72 TFEU.

concerned this issue of competence, with opposing lines being drawn up over the issue of what falls within Member States' exclusive competence and what could be said to be shared with the EU.[5] However, it is the European Court of Justice which has the 'last word' on the interpretation of the treaties. And the ECJ has a restrictive view on what is still within Member-States' exclusive competence as regards national security. The ECJ has long asserted that it can determine whether a Member State may invoke national security to justify making an exception to an EU right, such as freedom of movement – e. g., denying admission to a person based on national security grounds.[6] What is newer is the ECJ's moving away from the principle of institutional autonomy, and instead emphatically asserting of its jurisdiction over how Member States' institutions handle issues of data retention, data processing and data transfer – all of which are central to any security and intelligence agency. As is well known, this process began with the ECJ's preliminary ruling in the Digital Rights case[7] that the Data Retention Directive,[8] dealing with retention of telecommunications metadata, was invalid. This was then followed by two different sets of case law. The first set of cases deal with the obligations states have before a transfer of data to a third state can be made, in particular *Schrems v Data Protection Commissioner*[9] and *Schrems II*.[10] The second set of cases deal with states' obligations under the e-Privacy Directive[11] as regards retention of telecommunications metadata for the purpose of law enforcement (*Tele2* and *Watson*)[12] and national security (*Quadrature du Net*).[13] The ECJ's findings in the preliminary ruling in *Quadrature du Net* in particular can be seen as the beginning of what may become a corpus of EU law standards on control and oversight over intelligence agencies. The ECJ in this case (concerning the e-Privacy Directive) drew a distinction between the 'activities' of security and intelligence agencies to protect national security and national legislation enacted for the protection of national security that involves imposing obligations on individuals which affects their EU rights. What was outside the scope of EU law was 'where the Member States directly implement measures that derogate from the rule that electronic communications are to be confidential, without imposing processing obligations on providers of electronic communications services.'[14] The case is thus a bold assertion of the ECJ's jurisdiction, and competence, to govern issues at the heart of the work of security and intelligence agencies.

---

[5] See, e.g. Sule in Dietrich/Sule, Intelligence Law and Policies in Europe, p. 335.

[6] See, e.g., ECJ 4.6.2013 – case C-300/11, ECLI:EU:C:2013:363 – *ZZ v. Secretary of State for Home Dept.*

[7] ECJ 8.4.2014 – joined cases C-293 and 594/12, ECLI:EU:C:2014:238 – *Digital Rights Ireland and Seitlinger and others.*

[8] Directive 2006/24/EC on the retention of data generated or processed in connection with the provision of publicly available electronic communications services or of public communications networks and amending Directive 2002/58/EC.

[9] ECJ 6.10.2015 – case C-362/14, ECLI:EU:C:2015:650 – *Maximillian Schrems v Data Protection Commissioner (Schrems I).*

[10] ECJ 16.7.2020 – case C-311/18, ECLI:EU:C:2020:559 – *Data Protection Commissioner v Facebook Ireland Ltd and Maximillian Schrems (Schrems II).*

[11] Directive 2002/58/EC concerning the processing of personal data and the protection of privacy in the electronic communications sector.

[12] ECJ 21.12.2016 – joined cases C-203 and 698/15, ECLI:EU:C:2016:970 – *Tele2 Sverige AB v Post- och telestyrelsen*; and *Secretary of State for the Home Department v Tom Watson, Peter Brice and Geoffrey Lewis.*

[13] ECJ 6.10.2020 – case C-623/17, ECLI:EU:C:2020:790 – *Privacy International v Secretary of State for Foreign and Commonwealth Affairs, Secretary of State for the Home Department, Government Communications Headquarters, Security Service, Secret Intelligence Service*; and ECJ 6.10.2020 – joined cases C-511/18, C-512/18 and C-520/18, ECLI:EU:C:2020:791 – *La Quadrature du Net and others.*

[14] ECJ 6.10.2020 – joined cases C-511/18, C-512/18 and C-520/18, ECLI:EU:C:2020:791 para. 102 – *La Quadrature du Net and others*, emphasis added.

What are the implications of the *Quadrature du Net* judgment for control and oversight requirements generally? The case ostensibly only concerned the retention and accessing of telecommunications metadata, not the other things which security and intelligence agencies do: running informers, subjecting the content of emails and internet sites to analysis, different forms of targeted surveillance (data hacking, bugging, telecommunications interception), data processing by security and intelligence agencies of their own data stores, or other 'bulk' data sets from the public or private sector (insurance, banking transactions etc.). The ECJ had earlier accepted in *Parliament v Council and Commission*[15] that processing of personal data by companies (but on national security grounds) fell outside the scope of the directive at issue in that case, i.e. Directive 95/46/EC[16]. That case concerned the transmission from airline companies to police and security authorities of sensitive personal data, namely passenger name records (PNR). However, as noted in *Quadrature du Net*, it took a different approach. Of course, security and intelligence agencies have a lot of data of their own, but it needs to be continually supplemented by data from private sources. It is unclear how much the exclusions routinely made in relevant directives for security and intelligence agencies are nowadays worth, e.g. as regards data processing in the Law Enforcement Directive[17]. At least where security and intelligence agencies are processing data for the investigation of security crime, they would appear to fall within the scope of this Directive. So, even if, formally speaking, several powers of security and intelligence agencies are (and are likely to remain) largely outside the scope of EU law, it is very significant that an essential part of the work of security and intelligence agencies is now to be seen as within the scope of EU law. Security and intelligence agencies can no longer claim a blanket exemption from ECJ case law on the basis of Art. 4(2) TEU, even if the article will continue to be invoked by states to limit the scope of new EU legislation. National legislatures will now have to take account of EU law, and ECJ case law, in devising control and oversight arrangements. But what ECJ case law apart from *Quadrature du Net* is, or can be, relevant? The present chapter is a first attempt to sketch out that case law. As such it has an element of speculation. To set the boundaries of what should be seen as within oversight and control, I use the two Venice Commission reports as a framework of reference, looking in turn at courts, prosecutors and data protection authorities. I will close with a number of concluding remarks. 3

B. The control and oversight 'landscape'

Oversight tracks, or should track, control. One is, after all, being held accountable for what one has done, or what one should have done. You cannot devise sensible oversight arrangements without knowing how the intelligence and security agencies are structured in a particular state (How many are they? What are their respective mandates? How are they controlled on paper, and in practice?) Every European state has its own particular 4

[15] ECJ 30.5.2006 – joined cases C-317 and 318/04, ECLI:EU:C:2006:346 – *Parliament v Council and Commission (PNR)*.

[16] Directive 95/46/EC on the protection of individuals with regard to the processing of personal data and on the free movement of such data.

[17] Directive 2016/680, on the protection of natural persons with regard to the processing of personal data by competent authorities for the purposes of the prevention, investigation, detection or prosecution of criminal offences or the execution of criminal penalties, and on the free movement of such data, and repealing Council Framework Decision 2008/977/JHA.

control system, strongly influenced by the state's history and political and legal culture. The control system for security and intelligence agencies obviously depends on certain basic constitutional choices a country makes (or is made for it) between presidentialism and parliamentarism, or something in between, and between centralized power or a federal system. But other choices relating to public administration, not necessarily at the constitutional level, are also relevant. In the area of public security, a basic choice is whether or not you want to separate the internal agency from the police (as e.g. in the Netherlands, Slovenia, the Czech Republic, and Germany) and in which case, which of the two are to be given primacy over what issues which straddle security and crime (e.g. terrorism, corruption, certain types of organized crime and cyber crime). In some countries, the prohibition on exercising police powers is taken particularly strictly.[18] Other countries instead have security police which – ostensibly at least – only investigate security offences, e.g. Denmark, Finland, France, Ireland, and Sweden. In the latter group of states, offences are simultaneously 'threats to national security' and 'serious crime', making a distinction between them difficult in practice. Foreign intelligence agencies, including signals intelligence agencies, have traditionally been subject to less in the way of controls, primarily due to the fact that they interfere with foreigners rights. However, for a variety of reasons, the line between 'foreign' and 'domestic' intelligence is now increasingly difficult to draw, quite apart from the fact that for EU states the EU principles of loyal cooperation and non-discrimination have created a new, third category of people, foreigners who are citizens of another EU Member State.

5 In every state, the 'front line' of oversight are the 'internal' controls for the agency itself, often combined with controls at the top bureaucratic (permanent secretary) level. The Venice Commission recognized that in practice these controls are often the most important, with the goal being that the staff of the agency have internalized respect for democracy and the rule of law (and thus attempt to minimize the abuse of power). The level of political control over an agency and its operations, i.e. the control capable of being exercised by, and actually exercised by government ministers, is likely to vary from state to state and from time to time. The two main dangers in the field are 'political policing' and the 'state within the state': both have to be avoided, and states have different approaches as regards which problem is seen as worst. Several states have thus deliberately attempted to limit the control political appointees exercise over security and intelligence agencies, and, for that matter, the police. However, in all states, the secrecy surrounding the work of the agency, the complexity of the threats it tries to predict and combined with, the complexity of its investigative methods, mean that amateurs will usually experience difficulty in exercising meaningful control, quite apart from the problem ministers tend to have of having enough time to cope with all their other duties. Permanent civil servants have more time to develop the necessary experience and expertise, although even they can find themselves at a disadvantage if the agency has a monopoly of knowledge and sources. Still, the 'executive' (meaning the top bureaucracy and the politicians together) should usually have the power to direct the work and priorities of the agency in general, or even in specific operations.

6 The fact that security and intelligence agencies engage in activities which limit constitutional rights means that judiciary are invariably requested to 'authorize' the use of special powers by the agency, i.e. that permission must be sought before a particular power, such as electronic surveillance, is employed against an individual.

[18] For example in Germany, the *Trennungsgebot* is set out in the Act on the Federal Office for the Protection of the Constitution (*Bundesverfassungsschutzgesetz* – BVerfSchG), BGBl. I, 2954, 2970, as amended, § 2(1) sentence 3; § 8(3).

Where an internal security agency investigates security crime, prosecutors are likely to be involved in monitoring the use of special powers. They might also be given a more general supervisory power over the agency. There are two basic constitutional models applied by European states as regards prosecutors: these are either part of the judiciary, or they are controlled by the executive. The parliament or an independent expert body may have a power of 'post hoc review' or 'oversight' of the work of the agency, meaning a power to supervise the work of the agency, either in general or in relation to specific activities, usually subject to a proviso that this should not interfere overmuch with ongoing operations. Depending upon how the oversight task is formulated, as a control of legality, or as a general control, including efficiency and effectiveness, an independent expert body may be a mix of different types of expert: serving or former judges, historians, political scientists, IT specialists, and economists. The independent body may be a 'hybrid' body, consisting both of serving or former politicians and other experts, in particular judges, combining the functions of political and legal oversight. Such a body might exist in addition to the general data protection body which EU Member States are obliged to have under EU law. The mandate and powers of the oversight body may be formulated in different ways. As well as a power to publish an annual report, it may have a power to make special investigations and special reports. It may only make recommendations, or it can have some type of power to bind the agency, e.g. by authorizing certain types of operation. In addition to this function, it may be given the power to hear complaints of wrongdoing by the agency, or complaints in relation to security vetting. Finally, audit issues can be entrusted to a separate audit body, or a specialist chamber of the general Audit office.

The Venice Commission noted that, while oversight was a public function, the **7**
situation as regards media (publicly or privately owned) was a significant part of the national context. The ability of the media to investigate this area effectively is dependent on rules on freedom of information/official secrecy, whistleblowing,[19] responsibility of editors (rather than individual journalists) for what is published etc. but also on the 'tolerance' of the political and legal culture: are prosecutions of journalists actually threatened or brought?

The Venice Commission took a holistic and results-based approach to oversight and **8**
control, meaning that one has to look at the whole system of control and oversight, and assess it, not on the basis of formal factors (such as: is there an oversight body, is it parliamentary in nature, does it have meetings etc.) but on the basis of its results: does it deliver a satisfactory level of control and oversight? As to what is 'satisfactory', the level of parliamentary and press criticism in a state is one indication of how satisfactory its system of oversight is. A more objective indication is whether a state has been found by the ECtHR to have violated the ECHR. Of course, the accident of litigation determines which cases get to the ECtHR, so an absence of negative judgments is not a guarantee that everything is fine. But it seems clear from a number of judgments that there are major failings in the systems of control and oversight in several EU states.[20]

---

[19] As regards whistleblowers, Directive (EU) 2019/1937 on the protection of persons who report breaches of Union law contains the usual exclusion clause for intelligence agencies (Art. 3(2)) as well as excludes the application of the directive to the protection of classified information (Art. 3(3)).

[20] See, e.g. ECtHR 20.6.2002 – App. No. 50963/99 – *Al-Nashif and others v. Bulgaria*; ECtHR 24.6.2011 – App. Nos 3381/07 and 18817/08 *Association '21 December 1989' and Others v. Romania*; ECtHR (Grand Chamber) 8.1.2013 – App. No. 40238/02 – *Bucur and Toma v. Romania*; ECtHR (Grand Chamber) 13.12.2012 – App. No. 39630/09 – *El-Masri v. Macedonia*; ECtHR 24.7.2014 – App. Nos 28761/11 and 7511/13 – *Al Nashiri and Husayn (Abu Zubaydah) v. Poland*; ECtHR 21.1.2016 – App. No. 37138/14 – *Szabó and Vissy v. Hungary*; ECtHR 26.2.2016 – App. No. 44883/09 – *Nasr and Ghali v. Italy*; ECtHR 31.5.2018 – App No. 46454/11 – *Abu Zubaydah v. Lithuania;* ECtHR 31.5.2018 – App No. 33234/12 –

9 The above very brief sketch of the control and oversight 'landscape' shows the type of issues which need to be covered in each state. I will content myself here with making two points. First, different functions, control, authorization, oversight and remedies can be mixed in different ways, in different bodies. Functionally, oversight and remedies on the one hand should be separated from authorization/control, as otherwise the same body is being asked to 'oversee' itself. Nonetheless, it is not unusual for a primarily oversight body to have been given some authorization functions. Secondly, it seems clear that whatever European oversight standards which can be formulated are at the level of principles rather than more concrete rules. Otherwise, insufficient room will be left for national peculiarities. In the next section I sketch out the ECJ case law which can be relevant.

C. Judicial and independent bodies

I. General comments

10 As noted above (→ mn. 6), one of the main roles for courts is to authorize special powers that can infringe constitutional rights. Courts can also play a role in other areas relevant to security, most obviously in criminal trials, or administrative proceedings, where material gathered by an intelligence agency is submitted in evidence,[21] or as regards subsequent administrative or civil proceedings (claims for damages, etc.) after an individual has been notified that s/he has been subjected to security measures. In all of these roles, courts obviously have to be independent and impartial. Authorization proceedings in particular are confidential and *ex parte*, and it is therefore particularly important that the public feels it can trust the judges to ensure that the law is being followed and executive powers of surveillance are not being abused and overused. In this respect it can be noted that is not unusual for states to apply special forum rules to limit the courts (and within particular courts, the judges) competent to issue national security surveillance warrants. Security vetting of judges is also common in EU states.[22] The rule of law crisis in Poland has led the ECJ increasingly to emphasize the role national courts play, and must play, as guardians of the EU legal order. Consequently, it now has extensive case law on what is a 'court', and on the requirements of judicial independence.[23] Judicial independence is both an institutional framework and an attitude of mind. In particular, the appointment process must not give the Executive a predominant role in substance. The ECJ's case law on the disciplinary chamber of the Polish Supreme Court indicates that there is potential for the ECJ to rule on such matters as specialist national security chambers, forum rules and security vetting.

Al Nashiri v. Romania; ECtHR 11.1.2022 –App. No. 70078/12 – *Ekimdzhiev and Others v. Bulgaria*; ECtHR 23.6.2022 – App Nos. 58359/12, 27787/16 and 67667/16 – *Haščák v. Slovakia*.

[21] The Romanian constitutional court's controversial blanket exclusion of evidence in corruption cases which had been gathered with the assistance of the intelligence services was the subject of ECJ 21.12.2021 – joined cases C-357/19, C-379/19, C-547/19, C-811/19, C-840/19, ECLI:EU:C:2021:1034 – *DNA-Serviciul Teritorial Oradea*. The *ECJ* avoided ruling on this issue in the case. See, however, the Opinion of Advocate-General *Brobek* in AG Brobek 4.3.2021 – case C-379/19, ECLI:EU:C:2021:174 – *DNA-Serviciul Teritorial Oradea*.

[22] See e.g. Venice Commission, 'Croatia, Opinion on the Introduction of the Procedure of Renewal of Security Vetting Through Amendments to the Courts Act (2022)', CDL-AD(2022)005.

[23] See the many cases regarding Poland, in particular ECJ 19.11.2019 – joined cases C-585/18, C-624/18 and C-625/18, ECLI:EU:C:2019:982 – *Independence of the disciplinary chamber of the Supreme Court* and ECJ 29.3.2022 – case C 132/20, ECLI:EU:C:2022:235 – *BN and Others v Getin Noble Bank S.A.*

II. Authorization

As regards the issue of judicial authorization, the ECJ in *Quadrature du net* had differential standards depending upon how great the interference in protected rights was adjudged to be. The first power at issue in the case entails a duty on telecommunications providers to retain data and allow the authorities to access it where a national security threat (situation) exists. Here, as regards authorization/oversight, the ECJ simply stated that 11

> it is essential that decisions giving an instruction to providers of electronic communications services to carry out such data retention be subject to effective review, either by a court or by an independent administrative body whose decision is binding, the aim of that review being to verify that one of those situations exists and that the conditions and safeguards which must be laid down are observed.[24]

The use of 'words situation' (and 'threat') by the ECJ can cause some confusion. It makes most sense to interpret 'situation' as being about security investigations, either into security offences, or legally defined national security threats. Here the national court, or independent body, is to check whether the legal basis for allowing the security agency to access the retained data is fulfilled. In states which follow the model of security crime, this will mean that there is concrete indications and reasonable suspicion, against a particular person, or group of persons, of engaging in a particular security offence, or at least, criminal activity dangerous to security. In states where security agencies are not limited to investigating security crime, but have a more general investigative competence, it will mean that the legal conditions for this more general investigative competence are fulfilled (which will usually also include some form of concrete indications). In both cases the review must also check that whatever conditions and safeguards the law contains to try avoid the risk of misuse, or overuse, are also fulfilled. 12

By way of comment here, I would also say that experience shows that the risks for human rights can be different depending upon which model the state follows. A more general investigative competence, not linked to security crime, can undoubtedly open for abuse or overuse. On the other hand, even the security crime model can be abused, where judicial, or prosecutorial, authorization of the investigation only assesses the initial suspicions, and there is no 'follow-up' control of the investigation and what sort of intelligence it produced. 13

The second and third powers at issue in *Quadrature du Net* are more within the area of signals intelligence. The second power entails a requirement which could be issued to telecommunications providers to enable the police and intelligence agencies to follow, in real time, the metadata trail of people suspected of involvement in terrorism. This also includes a power to monitor the metadata trail of other people belonging to the circle of the suspect where there are 'substantial grounds' for believing that they are capable of providing information on the suspect. The third power required telecommunication providers to install devices on their networks, permitting the intelligence services to 'detect links that might constitute a terrorist threat'. The search or registration parameters are issued by the intelligence services for renewable periods of two months. Applications for renewal must include a record of the number of identifiers flagged by the automated processing and an analysis of the 14

[24] ECJ 6.10.2020 – joined cases C-511/18, C-512/18 and C-520/18, ECLI:EU:C:2020:791 para. 139 – *La Quadrature du Net and others.*

relevance of that flagging. This third power is thus proactive, allowing the use of algorithms to detect as yet unknown terrorist suspects, as well as their links with existing known threats.

15 As regards this second French system, the Court went into some detail in setting out different types of regulation and safeguard that are to be put in place. For real-time tracking of traffic and/or location data, this can only be permissible for people in respect of whom there was a valid reason to suspect that they are involved in one way or another in terrorist activities. The Court also insists on a prior review by a court or independent administrative body, whose decision is binding. For other people whose data would be useful in investigating terrorism, (the Court formulates this category vaguely – 'any sort of contribution to terrorism in some way') only historical traffic and/or location data can be collected, and only where there is objective evidence from which it can be deduced that that data might, in a specific case, make an effective contribution to combating terrorism (or another national security purpose).

16 When it came to the third system, the ECJ emphasizes the need for the algorithms to be non-discriminatory and that the reliability (specificity) of these be subject to a continuous (follow-up) control. Moreover, the Court emphasized the need for manual reassessment of the data generated. It did not expressly state that there had to be judicial/independent authorization of the search parameters, but that there had to be judicial/independent review of the process, and that the decisions by this body or bodies must be binding.[25]

17 The ECJ does not specify what it means by an independent administrative body. As well as data protection, examined further below (→mn. 26), there is other ECJ case law in other areas, such as supervision of anti-trust, telecommunications, or railways where the ECJ requires independent regulatory agencies.[26] In such areas, there is usually a cross-border aspect (potential discrimination of foreign actors), which is not present as regards oversight of security and intelligence agencies. The purpose is different: it is not corporations who need to be reassured that there is a 'level playing field' but the public who needs to be reassured that someone trustworthy, and seen as outside of the arcane intelligence community, is keeping the agency within the bounds of what is acceptable behaviour. For these reasons, it is common for oversight bodies to be parliamentary, or 'hybrid' (i.e. mixing lawyers with former politicians), thus combining political insight and experience with respect for the law. Here I can note that in a recent ruling on the regulation of the German energy market, the ECJ specified not simply that the regulatory body not simply had to be independent from the executive, but also from the legislature.[27] However, an oversight body is not just for the protection of individual rights: it can also be to reassure the parliamentary opposition in a state that a security agency is not being used by the government for party political purposes.

18 It is also interesting to compare these standards with those of the Venice Commission and the ECtHR. When it studied the issue of controlling signals intelligence agencies, the Venice Commission noted that there are several stages in an algorithmic-based search process. On the basis of broad intelligence needs assessments, bulk metadata is

---

[25] ECJ 6.10.2020 – joined cases C-511/18, C-512/18 and C-520/18, ECLI:EU:C:2020:791 para. 179-182 – *La Quadrature du Net and others.*

[26] See, as regards telecommunications, Art. 6 et seq. of Directive (EU) 2018/1972 establishing the European Electronic Communications Code, railways, Art. 55(1) Directive (EU) 2012/34 establishing a single European railway area and anti-trust, Art. 4 Directive (EU) 2019/1 to empower the competition authorities of the Member States to be more effective enforcers and to ensure the proper functioning of the internal market.

[27] ECJ 2.9.2021 – case C-34/20, ECLI:EU:C:2021:677 – *Telekom Deutschland GmbH v Bundesrepublik Deutschland.*

acquired, usually already filtered by certain criteria (search paths, etc.), processed by means of search terms (often cumulative), collated with other intelligence (including other bulk intelligence sets, such as records of financial transfers), before being analysed. A decision is then taken whether to retain the finished product, and/or transfer it to government or other agencies (national or foreign).

While the process as described above is sequential, in reality it is presumably more of a continuous, heuristic process. In any event, the Venice Commission identified the authorization/processing phase and the phase where a decision is taken to retain/transfer data (follow-up) as being particularly important from the perspective of privacy rights. These two types of decision call for two different types of control/oversight; judicial/quasi-judicial and administrative/data-protection. It noted that both forms of control must be performed, that both legality and proportionality issues must be examined, that the control functions must be performed by an independent body, or bodies, and that this body or bodies must have sufficient resources and technical know-how to act as a proper safeguard.[28] **19**

The ECtHR followed a similar line when it spoke about the need for 'end to end' controls, i.e. at all stages of the process.[29] The ECtHR also stressed the principle that controls should be stronger, the greater the potential for damage to privacy etc. rights. It considered that heightened safeguards should accompany algorithmic searches involving 'strong' identifiers (names, email addresses, etc.). **20**

III. Post hoc functions of courts

When it comes to the question of post-hoc challenges in the courts to executive (ab) uses of security powers, this presupposes that alleged abuses have come to light. Courts cannot normally act *proprio motu* and so must usually wait for an appropriate case to present itself. Notification of potential victims is thus a crucial element in ensuring effective remedies. The ECJ was prepared to in *Quadrature du Net* to accept non notification to people affected by security and intelligence agencies' retention and accessing of telecommunications metadata. It may not be so understanding in other areas, where secrecy is not so important.[30] **21**

Even where a case has been brought, as the Venice Commission has noted,[31] courts may lack the procedural competence (e.g. constitutional or jurisdictional obstacles) to intervene. Even if there are no formal obstacles, courts may consider that the policy element looms large in national security decision making, outweighing the adjudicative element. Or they may reason that they have neither the access to all the relevant information nor the training and experience necessary to evaluate this information properly, if they had it. Or they may feel that the public nature of the judicial process is inappropriate for matters which should be kept secret. National security considerations are already relevant in many areas of administrative decision-making, and one can question how effective judicial remedies actually are. These areas have expanded in recent years. For example, after a long period of (naïve) belief in relatively unrestricted foreign investment, EU rules have recently been introduced to protect critical infra- **22**

[28] CDL-AD(2015)011-e.

[29] ECtHR (Grand Chamber) 25.5.2021 – App. No. 35252/08 – *Centrum för Rättvisa v. Sweden*; ECtHR (Grand Chamber) – App. No. 58170/13 – *Big Brother Watch and others v. UK.*

[30] Particularly bearing in mind the distinction the ECtHR has drawn between open and secret measures in ECtHR20.6.2002 – App. No. 50963/99 – *Al Nasif and others v. Bulgaria.*

[31] CDL-AD(2015)010, para 88.

structure. Many of the limitations which exist in judicial review, legal and practical, can come under the scrutiny of the ECJ. The ECJ has a built-in interest in expanding national courts' jurisdiction, in that this also expands its own jurisdiction and the principle of effective protection of EU rights provides the ECJ, and national courts, with a mechanism for doing so.[32]

D. Prosecutors

23 The role of prosecutors can be difficult to categorize. Most often they can be seen as a control/authorization body for specific security operations (when these involve security offences), rather than a general 'oversight' body, but it depends upon what competence they have been given under national law. Are they 'independent' or not? One could argue that in states following the executive model of control over prosecutors, they are a part of the executive, and therefore not independent, whereas in states where the prosecutors are part of the judiciary, then they are independent. But this may be too simplistic. In some states following the executive model, prosecutors have in practice a large element of independence from the Executive, as well as 'internal' independence from hierarchically superior prosecutors.

24 The ECJ has examined several times the role of prosecutors, not in security issues, but in the context of the European Arrest Warrant (EAW). The ECJ has stated that

> issuing judicial authority' is capable of including authorities of a Member State which, although not necessarily judges or courts, participate in the administration of criminal justice and act independently. The latter condition presupposes the existence of statutory rules and an institutional framework capable of guaranteeing that the authorities concerned are not exposed, when issuing a European arrest warrant, to any risk of being subject to directions or instructions in a specific case from the executive.[33]

25 The Court here is referring to 'internal' prosecutorial independence, i.e. the need to protect the objective[34] decision-making competence of junior prosecutors in different ways, while maintaining the 'quality control' function of more senior prosecutors in the hierarchy, with the (usually government-appointed) chief public prosecutor at the top. Internal prosecutorial independence is deficient in many EU states. Although limited to the EAW, the same requirements are equally relevant in surveillance matters, where prosecutors, often specially selected, act as 'gate-keepers' in national security warrants.

E. Data protection authorities

26 State approaches to exactly what measures are regarded as sufficiently serious to require judicial approval tend to vary somewhat, depending on the scope and strength

[32] See, e.g. ECJ 6.3.2018 – case C-284/16, ECLI:EU:C:2018:158 – *Achmea*.

[33] ECJ 12.12.2019 – joined cases C-566/19 PPU and C-626/19 PPU, ECLI:EU:C:2019:1077 – *Parquet général du Grand-Duché de Luxembourg and Openbaar Ministerie (Public Prosecutor, Lyon/Tour)*; and in ECJ 12.12.2019 – cases C-625/19 PPU, ECLI:EU:C:2019:1078 – *Openbaar Ministerie (Swedish Public Prosecutor's Office)* and ECJ 12.12.2019 – C-627/19 PPU, ECLI:EU:C:2019:1079 – *Openbaar Ministerie (Public Prosecutor, Brussels)*.

[34] See also ECJ 27.5.2019 – joined cases C-508/18 OG, ECLI:EU:C:2019:456 para. 73 – *Public Prosecutor's Office Lübeck*.

of the constitutional rights recognized in the State in question, in particular, the scope of the right of privacy. Much security work may not be regarded as affecting a person's constitutional rights, or his or her rights under the relevant rules of criminal procedure (e.g. gathering information on individuals from databanks or public sources or opening a thematic, or organizational file).

Processing personal data in 'activities concerning national security [as well as] activities of agencies or units dealing with national security issues' falls outside the scope of the Law Enforcement Directive.[35] On the other hand, the extensive interpretation the ECJ has of the concept of 'public security' means that the Directive will probably be regarded as applicable when national security agencies investigate security crime. Under EU law, states must establish a data protection authority. Article 51(2) and 52(2) GDPR set particularly high standards of independence. The ECJ has clarified that these bodies must be independent, **27**

> allowing them to perform their duties free from external influence in whatever form, whether direct or indirect, which may have an effect on their decisions and which could call into question the performance by those authorities of their task of striking a fair balance between the protection of the right to private life and the free movement of personal data.[36]

Thus, supervisory authorities must have a degree of security of tenure during their periods of office. Independence can largely be seen as a requirement of result: how each state chooses to get there may reasonably vary. Having said this, and although the ECJ has not specifically set out any requirements in this respect, it is reasonable to suppose that there must be some form of appointment process which avoids giving the sole, or even predominant, role to the government of the day. There are various different ways of doing this, e.g. allowing some members to be appointed by the opposition in parliament, making the whole membership subject to confirmation by qualified majority in parliament, or giving the political opposition, at least if it is united, a power of veto over appointments. **28**

A data protection authority must also have sufficient powers and resources to be able to perform its role (cf. Article 52(4) GDPR). The ECJ has clarified that this means, in particular, investigative powers, such as the power to collect all the information necessary for the performance of their supervisory duties, effective powers of intervention, such as that of imposing a temporary or definitive ban on processing of data, and the power to engage in legal proceedings.[37] It must have a degree of financial independence (Article 56(6) GDPR). Transfer of data outside the jurisdiction must also be subject to the review of an independent data protection body.[38] One should note the differences between the expertise necessary to monitor compliance with good practices in filing etc. factual data, and in filing etc. speculative ('soft') data. **29**

One model for supervising security and intelligence agencies' data processing is to give such a mandate to the general data protection body, presumably a specially security cleared part of it. A Fundamental Rights Agency (FRA) study showed that in only seven EU states the general data protection bodies had jurisdiction over national security data processing.[39] Another model is to create one or more specialist bodies. There are advantages and disadvantages with both approaches. **30**

---

[35] Recital 14 Law Enforcement Directive.

[36] ECJ 8.4.2014 – case C-288/12, EU:C:2014:237 para. 51 – *Commission v Hungary*.

[37] ECJ 6.10.2015 – case C-362/14, ECLI:EU:C:2015:650 para. 43 – *Maximillian Schrems v Data Protection Commissioner (Schrems I)*.

[38] ECJ 16.7.2020 – case C-311/18, ECLI:EU:C:2020:559 para. 195 – *Data Protection Commissioner v. Facebook Ireland Ltd and Maximillian Schrems (Schrems II)*.

[39] FRA, 'Fundamental Rights Report' (2017).

F. Concluding remarks

31 It is not enough that an issue falls partially within the scope of EU law: to develop the EU law of security oversight suitable cases must present themselves before the ECJ. In these concluding remarks, I make a number of tentative remarks on this issue. As is well known, any court in an EU state may ask for a preliminary ruling, and a lower court does not have to seek permission from a higher court before making a referral. Under Art. 267 TFEU, a court from which there is no appeal and that has a case where EU law is central to its outcome, is obliged to ask for a preliminary ruling. However, there is a crucial difference between a national legislature, which can frame general rules governing all aspects of control and oversight (even if it must now take account of ECtHR and ECJ case law) and the ECJ. The ECJ has to wait for a case, either in the form of an infringement proceeding, brought by the Commission, or a request for a preliminary ruling. The procedural restraints on the ECJ moreover mean that it is limited to examining systems of control and oversight through the lens of the EU law, which to a large extent repeats ECHR requirements, i.e. that a limitation on a given human right be for the 'protection of national security,' 'in accordance with the law,' proportional ('necessary in a democratic society') and accompanied by 'effective remedies' at the national level.

32 Having said this, the case law on metadata illustrates how telecommunications corporations, but also individuals and human rights interest groups (nongovernmental organizations), have been provided with a potent weapon to challenge, in a supranational court, national laws that have been agreed on in democratically elected legislatures. Nonetheless, outside metadata retention, the ECJ may struggle to find relevant EU secondary legislation which is central to the case. Having said this, the Law Enforcement Directive, if the concept of 'public security' is interpreted widely and the concept of 'national security' is interpreted narrowly, will provide a basis for partial ECJ jurisdiction in the field of data protection. The same applies as regards whatever data transfer arrangements are made with third states in treaties (where inter alia the European Parliament can be expected to be eager to show it is defending individual rights). The different EU legislation on terrorism, and conceivably, on sanctions (restrictive measures), might also provide bases for suitable cases, as security and intelligence agencies are often involved in such cases at the national level.

33 The EU Commission clearly takes the view that control and oversight of security and intelligence agencies are now issues to be regarded as at least partially within EU competence. Several of the headings in the EU Commission's first annual Rule of Law report have potential relevance in this respect. In particular, 'Justice systems' includes the subheading 'independence/autonomy of the prosecution service '. The heading 'Other Institutional Issues related to Checks and Balances' includes (v) independent authorities, (vi) accessibility, judicial review of administrative decisions and (vii) enabling framework for civil society. The heading 'Media Pluralism and Media Freedom' is also relevant. The first report, in 2022, notes the problem of a lack of meaningful oversight of national security surveillance in Hungary, referring to the (as yet) unimplemented ECtHR judgment in *Szabó* and *Vissy v. Hungary*[40] and the apparently widespread use of surveillance technology against the press and defence lawyers.[41] Similar criticisms were also noted as

[40] ECtHR 12.1.2016 – App. No. 37138/14 – *Szabó and Vissy v. Hungary*.

[41] European Commission, 'Rule of Law report, Hungary', 13.7.2022, SWD(2022) 517 final, 26.

regards Poland.[42] While it is understandable that the Commission takes up these two states in particular, being the most obvious examples of rule of law backsliding, there are other states with problems, both 'political policing' and 'state within the state', as well as problems of corruption or low state capacity (ineffectiveness, etc.).

On the issue of corruption, there are potential overlaps between this and control and oversight issues. The mechanism for protection of the EU budget[43] has now been approved by the ECJ.[44] In some states security and intelligence agencies have primary competence to investigate corruption allegations, where there is a risk to national security, or generally to assist the police or a specialist anti-corruption agency in doing so. A corrupt government will obviously want to exert control over security and intelligence agencies in different ways, to ensure that its own corruption can continue unimpeded,[45] while using state agencies to harass political opponents, and elements of the media who are reporting on government corruption. Security and intelligence agencies may not be seen as 'low-hanging fruit' by the Commission in corruption cases, but you never know. **34**

---

42 European Commission, 'Rule of Law report, Poland', 13.7.2022, SWD(2022) 521 final, 17, 26.

43 EU Regulation (EU, Euratom) 2020/2092 on a general regime of conditionality for the protection of the Union budget.

44 ECJ 16.2.2022 – case C 157/21, ECLI:EU:C:2022:98 – *Republic of Poland v European Parliament and Council of the European Union.*

45 Which was part of the backdrop to the *DNA – Serviciul Teritorial Oradea* case, ECJ 21.12.2021 – joined cases C-357/19, C-379/19, C-547/19, C-811/19, C-840/19, ECLI:EU:C:2021:1034 – *DNA – Serviciul Teritorial Oradea.*

PART V
OPERATIONALIZING THE EUROPEAN SECURITY UNION

§ 15
Operationalizing the European Security Union – an introduction

Gerhard Conrad

Bibliography: Aden, 'Interoperability Between EU Policing and Migration Databases: Risks for Privacy', EPL 2020 (26:1), 93; Adler-Nissen, 'Symbolic power in European diplomacy: the struggle between national foreign services and the EU's External Action Service', Review of International Studies 2014 (40:1), 657; Amato, 'Exploring the Legal Requirements for Cross Border Judicial Cooperation: The Case of the Service of Documents', European Quarterly of Political Attitudes and Mentalities 2019 (8:2), 36; Bachmann/Paphiti, 'Mass Migration as a Hybrid Threat? – A Legal Perspective', Polish Political Science Yearbook 2021 (50:1), 119; Bellanova/Glouftsios, 'Formatting European security integration through database interoperability', European Security 2022 (31:3), 454; Bendiek/Bossong, '"Hybride Bedrohungen": Vom Strategischen Kompass zur Nationalen Sicherheitsstrategie', SWP-Aktuell 2022 A40; Bendiek/Kettemann, 'Revisiting the EU Cybersecurity Strategy: A Call for EU Cyber Diplomacy', SWP Comment 2021 (16); Bicchi/Schade, 'Whither European diplomacy? Long-term trends and the impact of the Lisbon Treaty', Cooperation and Conflict 2022 (57:1), 3; Bossong, 'Intelligence Support for EU Security Policy', SWP Comment 2018 (51); Bossong, 'Intelligente Grenzen und interoperable Datenbanken für die innere Sicherheit der EU. Umsetzungsrisiken und rechtsstaatliche Anforderungen', SWP-Studie 2018 S 04; Bossong, 'Policy Networks for European Internal Security governance: toward a more systematic empirical and normative assessment', Journal of Transatlantic Studies 2020 (18), 190; Bossong, 'The Expansion of Frontex. Symbolic Measures and Long-term Changes in EU Border Management', SWP Comment 2019 C 47; Casagran, 'Fundamental Rights Implications of Interconnecting Migration and Policing Databases in the EU', Human Rights Law Review 2021 (21:2), 433; Cirdei/Ispas, 'A Possible Answer of the European Union to Hybrid Threats', Scientific Bulletin 2017 (22:2), 71; Conrad, 'Emerging Terrorism Threats: European Counterterrorism Structure' in CEP-Report (ed.), The Taliban's Takeover in Afghanistan – Effects on Global Terrorism, Berlin 2022, p. 85; Conrad, 'Europäische Nachrichtendienstkooperation – Entwicklungen, Erwartungen und Perspektiven' in Dietrich/Gärditz/Graulich/Gusy/Warg (eds), Reform der Nachrichtendienste zwischen Vergesetzlichung und Internationalisierung, Tübingen 2019, p. 161; Conrad, 'Lessons learned and still to be learned. The case of the European Union' in Meyer/Michaels/Ikani/Guttmann/Goodman (eds), Estimative Intelligence in European Foreign Policymaking, Edinburgh 2022, p. 220; Conrad, 'Situational Awareness for EU Decision-making: The Next Decade', European Foreign Affairs Review 2021 (26:1), 55–70; Craig/De Búrca, EU Law, 7th edn, Oxford 2020; de Kerchove/Höhn, 'The EU and International Terrorism. Promoting Free Movement of Persons, the Right to Privacy and Security' in Bignami (ed.) EU Law in Populist Times, Cambridge 2020, p. 269; Derave/Genicot/Hetmanska, 'The Risks of Trustworthy Artificial Intelligence: The Case of the European Travel Information and Authorisation System (ETIAS)', European Journal of Risk Regulation 2022 (13:3), 389; Frunzeti, 'Individual Security and Critical Infrastructure Security – Relationships and Interrelations', Journal: Annals – Series on Military Sciences 2013 (5), 3; Gerbaudo, 'The European Commission's Instrumentalization Strategy: Normalizing Border Procedures and De Facto Detention', European Papers 2022 (7:2), 615; Gruszczak, 'Intelligence Fusion for the European Union's Common Security and Defence Policy', Politeja 2022 (79), 131; Jagdhuber, Sharing Sovereignty in the EU's Area of Freedom, Security and Justice. The Integration Trajectories of Judicial Cooperation and Migration Policies in the European Union, Munich 2021; Kietz/von Ondarza, 'Sicherheit delegieren. EU-Agenturen in der inneren und äußeren Sicherheit', SWP-Studie 2016 S 06; Klaus, 'ESTA, ETA und bald ETIAS: das europäische Modell der elektronischen Reisegenehmigung', NJOZ 2023, 544; Kruse, Der Europäische Auswärtige Dienst zwischen intergouvernementaler Koordination und supranationaler Repräsentation, Berlin 2014; Ladenburger, 'The Principle of Mutual

Trust between Member States in the Area of Freedom, Security and Justice', Zeitschrift für europarechtliche Studien 2022 (23:3), 373; Lauer, Informationshilfe im Rahmen der polizeilichen und justiziellen Zusammenarbeit in Strafsachen, Baden-Baden 2018; Leese, 'Fixing State Vision: Interoperability, Biometrics, and Identity Management in the EU', Geopolitics 2022 (27:1); 113; Lonardo, 'EU Law Against Hybrid Threats: A First Assessment', European Papers 2021 (6:2), 1075; Mesko, 'Police Cooperation in the European Union, Supported by Strengthening the EU Internal Security's External Dimension', European Journal of Crime Criminal Law and Criminal Justice 2017 (25:2), 109; Miadzvetskaya/Wessel, 'The Externalisation of the EU's Cybersecurity Regime: The Cyber Diplomacy Toolbox', European Paper 2021 (7:1), 413; Mohamed/Alegria, 'Cooperation as an Essential Component of European Integrated Border Management (EIBM)', Romanian Journal of European Affairs 2022 (22), 46; Niedernhuber (eds), Die neue Europäische Staatsanwaltschaft. Bedeutung, Herausforderungen und erste Erfahrungen, Baden-Baden 2023; Noori, 'Suspicious Infrastructures: Automating Border Control and the Multiplication of Mistrust through Biometric E-Gates', Geopolitics 2022 (27:4), 1117; Nuñez-Belda, 'How Intelligence Supports EU Security. Given the resurgence of great power competition, intelligence has a decisive role to play in strengthening the European Union's security', IP Quarterly 2023 (4); Neiva, 'Big Data applied to criminal investigations: expectations of professionals of police cooperation in the European Union', Policing and Society. An International Journal of Research and Policy 2022 (32:10); Ozkul, Automating Immigration and Asylum: The Uses of New Technologies in Migration and Asylum Governance in Europe, Oxford 2023; Palacios, 'EU intelligence: On the road to a European Intelligence Agency?' in Dietrich/Sule (eds), Intelligence Law and Policies in Europe, Munich/Oxford/Baden-Baden 2019, p. 201; Ryder, 'European Criminal Intelligence' in Dietrich/Sule (eds), Intelligence Law and Policies in Europe, Munich/Oxford/Baden-Baden 2019, p. 249; Sachetti, 'The EU Response to Terrorist Content Online: Too Little, (Maybe not) Too Late?', European Papers 2021 (6:2), 967; Thörner, 'Der Nexus von innerer und äußerer Sicherheit. Zur horizontalen Kompetenzabgrenzung im Lichte von Art. 40 EUV', Tübingen 2022; Trauner/Servent, 'The Communitarization on the Area of Freedom, Security and Justice: Why Institutional Change does not Translate into Policy Change', JCMS 2016 (54:6), 1417; Tereszkiewicz, 'The role of COSI in the European Union's internal security area: the initial years of activity', Studia i Materiały. Miscellaneo Oeconomica 2016 (4), 245; Ucarer, 'EU Asylum Governance and E(xc)lusive Solidarity: Insights From Germany', Social Inclusion – Open Access Journal 2022 (10:3); Van Vooren, 'A legal-institutional perspective on the European External Action Service', CLEER Working Papers 2010 (7).

A. Introduction

1 For more than two decades, the European Union and its Member States have been confronted with a multitude of severe, if not critical, challenges in the fields of external and internal security. Wide-ranging legislative, political and administrative initiatives have been implemented, or at least initiated, to create adequate frameworks for mitigating threats and risks. A broad and complex array of regulations, provisions, structures and practices has emerged, known since 2016 as the 'Security Union'. The sheer complexity of the involved subject matters, the legal framework of the European Treaties, as well as the underlying diversity of Member States' laws, interests, structures and procedures have not always facilitated the creation of a meaningful, pertinent EU security environment. From the outset and throughout the years, operationalizing the European Security Union has therefore been a major task and challenge.

2 A short initial overview of the main features of today's Security Union in this introductory chapter recalls the scope and complexity of the steps to be taken and the multitude of actors that need to be involved in that process. The fundamentals of citizens' rights and freedoms should, however, not be glossed over. This backdrop provides a wider context within which to elaborate the particular significance of the chapters that follow.

B. The Union's security has an intergovernmental and an institutional dimension

The scope, nature and pertinence of the European Security Union is determined by the Treaties. The EU can only act within the competences granted to it through them, either as a supranational body through the Commission or as a confederation that relies on intergovernmental agreement. EU action in the field of security has to fit into these two dimensions and has to adapt to their respective specificities and preconditions. Art. 4(1) TEU sets out the inherently accessory nature of the Union: 'competences not conferred upon the Union in the Treaties remain with the Member States.' Art. 4(2) TEU is even more explicit, stating that 'the Union shall respect [the Member States'] essential State functions, including ensuring the territorial integrity of the State, maintaining law and order and safeguarding national security. In particular, national security remains the sole responsibility of each Member State.' Hence, creating a 'Europe that protects'[1] is a major political and legislative project that largely depends on Member States' readiness and ability to cooperate in creating and empowering viable common structures and procedures. 3

I. Intergovernmental cooperation to ensure external security and support internal security

Over the years, instruments and procedures based on primary EU law were put in place for a Common Foreign and Security Policy (CFSP) and a Common Security and Defence Policy (CSDP), leading to Council structures such as the Political and Security Committee (PSC), a preparatory body in the fields of foreign, security and defence policies, which are to be agreed on by Member States' governments in the Council of Foreign and Defence Ministers (FAC/FAC Defence). A similar Council structure was put in place for internal security, namely the Council of Ministers for Justice and Home Affairs (JHA), which has a Standing Committee for Operational Cooperation (COSI) as its preparatory body.[2] 4

Under Art. 4(2) TEU, the EU's foreign, security and defence policies are necessarily the result of intergovernmental discussion and decision-making, though facilitated, structured and managed within the European Council. Since 2010, the respective Council structures relating to foreign and defence affairs have been supported by the European External Action Service (EEAS) established on the basis of Council Decision 2010/427/EU.[3] 5

---

[1] European Commission President, 'The State of the Union 2016: Towards a Better Europe – A Europe that Protects, Empowers and Defends', 14.9.2016; Molthof, '"A Europe that protects": what does that actually mean?' (euobserver 7.6.2019) <https://euobserver.com/opinion/145065> (last accessed: 28.9.2023).

[2] Craig/De Búrca, p. 12. See also the EEAS's webpage on the Common Security and Defence Policy, <https://www.eeas.europa.eu/eeas/common-security-and-defence-policy_en> (last accessed: 28.9.2023) and the following webpage on the Common Foreign and Security Policy: <https://fpi.ec.europa.eu/what-we-do/common-foreign-and-security-policy_en> (last accessed: 28.9.2023). Tereszkiewicz Studia i Materiały. Miscellaneo Oeconomica 2016, 245; Mesko, European Journal of Crime, Criminal Law and Criminal Justice, 109–121.

[3] Council Decision 2010/427/EU establishing the organisation and functioning of the European External Action Service. Bicchi/Schade/Whither, Cooperation and Conflict 2022, 3 et seqq.; Van Vooren, CLEER Working Papers 2010; on the reluctance of Member States to engage in the EEAS, see Adler-Nissen, Review of International Studies 2014, 657 et seqq. 681, and in a comprehensive systematic approach Kruse, p. 1 et seqq.

6 It is within this framework that the EU Member States' intelligence services have found their agreed, though clearly limited, space for voluntarily supporting EU decision-making in the various fields of foreign, security and defence policies, with strategic intelligence contributions to the European Union Intelligence Analysis Centre (EU INTCEN) and the Intelligence Directorate of the European Military Staff (EUMS.INT).[4] In 2006, INTCEN was accorded the additional competence of receiving and assessing strategic intelligence 'on all aspects of the terrorist threat'.[5] For that purpose, EU Member States' security services provided counter-terrorism experts (CT experts) to INTCEN, within which a specialized CT section was created that managed incoming reports, drafted assessments for their 'customers' in the institutions and contributed to INTCEN's geopolitical analysis in general. The relevant voluntary contributions are provided by Member States' security services, which have since 2001 cooperated outside the EU on a strictly intergovernmental basis within the Counter-Terrorism Group (CTG).[6] Ten years later, it was again INTCEN, being the single point of entry for strategic intelligence, that had to build a 'Hybrid Fusion Cell' (HFC) whose mission was to inform decision-makers in the EU and Member States about the nature, pertinence and origin of hybrid threats to security emanating from state and non-state actors.[7] In all these fields, INTCEN and EUMS.INT provide strategic intelligence to EU decision-makers and decision-making structures well beyond the EEAS. They are to support and facilitate policy decisions and legislative action by providing timely and pertinent situational awareness, analysis and foresight, which are continuously introduced into the respective consultation and decision-making processes of the Commission (DG HOME and others) and Council Bodies (Working Party on Terrorism (TWP), Standing Committee on Operational Cooperation (COSI)). These contributions are neither case-related nor directly actionable in a strictly operational sense. CSFP and CSDP action 'in the field' therefore still has to be based on specific Member State authorization via a Council decision.

7 Over two decades, EU Member States have been developing a large diplomatic and military toolbox for CFSP action, including decision-making processes relating to implementation. On account of Member States' reluctance to confer elements of national security and, hence, sovereignty to an international body, these steps have mostly been taken in response to major external shocks and challenges such as the major terrorist attacks of 2001, 2004 and 2005, Russia's invasion of Ukraine in 2014 and 2022, and war, turmoil, deprivation and migration in the EU's neighbourhood and beyond. Implementation has always been subject to unanimity and thus limited or even hampered by a complex process of reaching compromises between national prerogatives and the best interests of the community.

II. Supranational dimension of an 'EU Security Union' based on Treaty competences

8 From the outset, the concept of an Area of Freedom, Security and Justice (AFSJ) was defined in the Treaties as one of the EU's key objectives, and it has been developed and

[4] Bossong, SWP Comment 2018; Palacios in Dietrich/Sule, Intelligence Law and Policies in Europe, p. 201–234; Conrad, European Foreign Affairs Review 2021, 55–70. Gruszczak, Politeja 2022, 131–150.

[5] De Kerchove/Höhn in Bignami, EU Law in Populist Times, p. 269–300.

[6] France 24, 'European spy agency to boost intel-sharing on potential terrorists' (France 24, 19.2.2016) <https://www.france24.com/en/20160219-europe-counter-terrorism-intelligence-sharing> (last accessed: 29.9.2023); Speech by Intervention Director-General AIVD, 'Global Counterterrorism Forum – The Netherlands' (AIVD, 11.12016) <https://english.aivd.nl/publications/speeches/2016/january/11/director-general-speaks-at-international-counterterrorism-meeting-the-hague> (last accessed: 29.9.2023).

[7] European Commission, 'Joint Framework on countering hybrid threats', 6.4.2016.

promoted in considerable breadth and detail.[8] Based on Art. 3(2) TEU and Arts. 67–89 TFEU, and with specific regard to the Schengen Agreement of 1995, particular emphasis has been placed on the following:

- Policies on border checks, asylum and immigration,
- Judicial cooperation in civil matters,
- Judicial cooperation in criminal matters,
- Police cooperation.

Once again, in areas that relate to domestic policies and legislation, external shocks that have immediate relevance for internal security have had a strong impact on the Union and its Member States and have triggered policies and legislation. The following should be called to mind: **9**

- The terrorist threat since 2001, with major attacks in Madrid (2004), London (2005) and a wave of European terrorist fighters that flocked to the self-proclaimed 'Caliphate of ISIS' in Syria and Iraq, eventually culminating in atrocities in Paris (2015) and Brussels (2016), with shared origins abroad and in the Union.
- Novel hybrid dimensions of war and conflict such as have become manifest in Russia's war against Ukraine since 2014, particularly threats to cybersecurity and a new, cyber-induced information warfare.
- New dimensions of irregular migration since 2015, emanating from major existential paradigm shifts, such as that caused by Russia's invasion of Ukraine.

Back in June 2014, the Member States, united in the European Council, called on the Commission to review the 2010 EU Internal Security Strategy and to update it by mid-2015. The December 2014 Justice & Home Affairs Council set out its priorities for renewing the Strategy. On 28 April 2015, the Commission presented its European Agenda on Security for the period 2015–2020, whose objective was to support Member States' cooperation on tackling security threats and to step up common efforts in the fight against terrorism, organized crime and cybercrime.[9] **10**

Finally, in the wake of the Brussels terror attacks, Commission President *Jean-Claude Juncker* on 23 March 2016 introduced the concept of a 'Security Union' to effectively face the threat of terrorism,[10] and he later appointed *Sir Julian King* as Commissioner for the Security Union[11] tasked with supporting implementation of the 2015 European Agenda on Security, mainly by coordinating and invigorating CT-related Member State legislation and improving EU institutions' administrative and budgetary support for such efforts. The Commissioner was to be assisted by a task force that was to draw on the expertise of the entire European Commission. **11**

---

[8] An area of freedom, security and justice: for general aspects, see the EP's webpage on the AFSJ, <https://www.europarl.europa.eu/factsheets/en/sheet/150/an-area-of-freedom-security-and-justice-general-aspects> (last accessed: 28.9.2023); for a valuable overview, also with regard to Europol and other structures within the AFSJ, see Ryder in Dietrich/Sule, Intelligence Law and Policies in Europe, p. 249–289, for further details, see Ladenburger, Zeitschrift für europarechtliche Studien 2022, 373–408; for two comprehensive recent legal studies on the concept, see Thörner, p. 1 et seqq.; Jagdhuber, p. 1 et seqq.

[9] European Commission, 'Press Release: Commission takes steps to strengthen EU cooperation in the fight against terrorism, organised crime and cybercrime', 28.4.2015 <https://ec.europa.eu/commission/presscorner/detail/en/IP_15_4865> (last accessed: 28.9.2023).

[10] ibid. However, see Trauner/Ripoll Servent, JCMS 2016, 1417–1432, on the drivers and limitations of this process.

[11] Eder, 'Juncker makes UK Commissioner Julian King EU's anti-terror tsar' (Politico, 2.8.2016) <https://www.politico.eu/article/jean-claude-juncker-makes-sir-julian-king-security-commissioner/> (last accessed: 28.9.2023).

12 In 2019, the new Commission entrusted the Security Union portfolio to the 'Vice-President for promoting our European way of life',[12] and a follow-up to the EU Security Union Strategy covering the period 2020–2024 was set out.[13]

13 It is this strategy that lays the foundation and sets the current broad systematic framework for EU and Member State action on security matters. It proposes the tools and measures to be developed to ensure security in both the physical and digital environments. It is composed of the following four strategic priorities for action at EU level and will draw heavily on the work of the EU agencies by making use of their findings as well as supporting them in their further work:[14]

- *A future-proof security environment* focussing on the protection of public spaces and critical infrastructure, be it physical or digital. This includes addressing cybersecurity threats (*key action fields:* critical infrastructure, cybersecurity, protecting public spaces).
- *Tackling evolving threats* by equipping national authorities with the right tools to detect and combat hybrid threats, cybercrimes and illegal content online, taking account of technological developments (*key action fields*: hybrid threats, illegal content online, cybercrime, modern law enforcement).
- *Fighting terrorism and organized crime*, by strengthening existing instruments and providing new tools for effective law enforcement (*key action fields*: organized crime, terrorism, and radicalization).
- *Building a strong security ecosystem*, by improving the exchange of information between national authorities and EU agencies and using research and innovation to counter current and future threats (*key action fields*: strengthening research and innovation, cooperation and information exchange, skills and awareness-raising, strong external borders).

14 The European Commission regularly publishes progress reports on the implementation of the 2020 EU Security Union Strategy, the most recent one on 13 December 2022.[15] These reports continuously cover and update work in the aforementioned action fields.

III. The European Security Union: no executive powers, but initiation, support and coordination of Member States' policies and action

15 It is important to emphasize that the European Security Union follows a comprehensive approach that covers internal and external aspects of security policy and thus also involves the predominantly intergovernmental, Council-led areas of CFSP and, in particular, CSDP insofar as they reflect on issues of internal security.

16 The Security Strategy's aim is to focus on priority areas in which the EU can help Member States when it comes to fostering security for all those living in Europe while respecting European values and principles. In particular, it is to

- ensure that EU security policy reflects the changing threat landscape,
- build long-term, sustainable resilience,

[12] See European Commission's webpage on the European Security Union Background <https://commission.europa.eu/strategy-and-policy/priorities-2019-2024/promoting-our-european-way-life/european-security-union_en#background> (last accessed: 28.9.2023).

[13] ibid.

[14] ibid.

[15] European Commission, 'Fifth Progress Report on the implementation of the EU Security Union Strategy', 13.12.2022, COM(2022) 745 final. The Sixth Progess Record was issued on 18 October 2023.

- engage the EU institutions and agencies, governments, private sector and individuals in a whole-of-society approach and
- bring together the many policy areas with a direct impact on security.[16]

Again, it should be noted that the European Security Union can only be tasked to 'help' Member States in their activities. It is not authorized to make use of policy-making and, in particular, executive powers. These powers remain largely under the reservation of national sovereignty, unless they are conferred, mostly on a case-by-case basis and in close cooperation with the respective national authorities, to an EU body, generally one of the following agencies providing support and services in security matters,[17] as mentioned in the relevant chapters of the Strategy:[18] **17**

- European Union Law Enforcement Agency (Europol)
- European Union Agency for Law Enforcement Training (CEPOL)
- European Union Agency for the Operational Management of Large-Scale IT Systems (eu-LISA)
- European Union Aviation Security Agency (EASA)
- European Union Agency for Railways (ERA)
- European Union Agency for Criminal Justice Cooperation (Eurojust)
- European Union Border and Coast Guard Agency (Frontex)
- European Monitoring Centre for Drugs and Drug Addiction (EMCDDA)
- European Maritime Safety Agency (EMSA)
- European Union External Action Service (EEAS).

The remit and powers of EU agencies are set out in their respective founding regulations. **18** They are subject to the ongoing oversight of the Member States through the national representatives, who have a seat on the respective management boards.[19] EU Member States are frequently involved in the agencies' institutional design and operation, which have been expressly designed to be dependent on various institutions, mainly the European Commission, and to act within networks that rely heavily on their national counterparts in terms of staff, expertise and funding. This demonstrates the delicate nature of the relationship between EU agencies on the one hand and EU institutions and the Member States on the other.[20] The core EU agencies relating to the AFSJ, such as Europol and Frontex, are thus authorized to collect information (though not secret intelligence), to analyse it, share it with Member States' authorities and to use it to support and advise EU organs within their respective remits.[21] They are also permitted to coordinate national authorities' operational action, though, again, only by asking not tasking their counterparts to act in a specific way.[22] Training and research is a more independent field of action in which agencies can proactively support Member States by offering and organizing programmes on their own or in collaboration with individual supporting and participating Member States.[23]

Thus, operationalizing the Security Union mainly revolves around the fields of **19** legislative, regulatory, advisory, supporting and coordinating action, which is meant to

[16] On this important feature of the EU Security Strategy, see Bossong, Journal of Transatlantic Studies 2020, 190–208.

[17] See the comprehensive study by EPRS, 'EU Agencies, Common Approach and Parliamentary Scrutiny. European Implementation Assessment', 21.11.2018, PE 627.131.

[18] See <https://commission.europa.eu/strategy-and-policy/priorities-2019-2024/promoting-our-european-way-life/european-security-union_en> (last accessed: 30.9.2023).

[19] Kietz/von Ondarza, SWP-Studie 2016 S06.

[20] EPRS, 'EU Agencies, Common Approach and Parliamentary Scrutiny. European Implementation Assessment', 21.11.2018, PE 627.131, 7

[21] Kietz/von Ondarza, SWP-Studie 2016, 14–15.

[22] ibid., 15–16.

[23] ibid., 16.

empower Member States to engage in common action. EU action, therefore, by design and the will of the EU Member States, remains on the meta level.

C. The Fifth Progress Report on the implementation of the EU Security Union Strategy – the framework for this chapter

20 In adopting the comprehensive Security Union Strategy, the Commission committed to regularly report to the Member States and institutions on steps taken, mainly in terms of proposed legislation and action plans that have to be adopted by the European Parliament, transformed into national legislation and subsequently operationalized by Member States in a concerted and harmonized manner. Five Progress Reports have been issued to date. They convey quite a detailed picture of developments and ambitions in the various fields of action.

21 The Fifth Progress Report on the implementation of the EU Security Union Strategy, published on 13 December 2022,[24] states that the 'overwhelming majority of the actions itemised in the Strategy have been addressed', but it has to concede that 'work remains to be done to achieve the full impact of the Security Union Strategy […] in particular, the adoption of outstanding legislative proposals by the European Parliament and the Council and the implementation by Member States of agreed legislation'.[25] The Progress Report then follows the respective chapters and action items of the 2020 Security Union Strategy. It will be quoted extensively in the following so as to provide a first-hand overview of the subject matters involved as they are presented by the Commission. To enable further scrutiny, reference is made in the footnotes to comments and remarks by academics.

I. Protecting critical infrastructure in the EU against physical and digital attacks[26]

22 The Progress Report presents two linked initiatives that provide the framework for resilience-building: the revised Directive on measures for a high common level of cybersecurity across the Union (Network Infrastructure Security Directive (NIS2 Directive))[27] and a new Critical Entities Resilience Directive (CER Directive).[28] Both Directives entered into force on 16 January 2023; Member States are expected to implement them by the end of 2024.

23 'The NIS2 Directive [is to] increase the coverage for medium and large entities in a range of key sectors'[29] such as '[strengthening] security requirements' (incident response, crisis management, supply chain security, vulnerability handling and disclosure, cybersecurity testing and encryption). '[t]he physical resilience of critical entities' against hazards is covered by the CER Directive, which aims to improve the physical and procedural resilience of entities that provide essential services.[30]

---

[24] COM(2022) 745 final.

[25] ibid., 1.

[26] ibid., 1–7. See already in 2013: Frunzeti, Journal: Annals – Series on Military Sciences 2013, 3–10.

[27] Directive (EU) 2022/2555 on measures for a high common level of cybersecurity across the Union (NIS 2 Directive).

[28] Directive (EU) 2022/2557 on the resilience of critical entities.

[29] COM(2022) 745 final, 2.

[30] ibid., 2.

Beyond that, 'the Commission, the High Representative and the NIS Cooperation Group are developing cyber security risk scenarios [...] in the energy, telecoms, transport sectors as well as space systems and services'.[31] In addition '[t]argeted cybersecurity risk assessments for communications infrastructure' are under way as well as a scenario-building initiative covering 'natural disasters linked to security-related threats like cyberattacks or terrorism'.[32] **24**

The threat to EU critical infrastructure was further highlighted on account of the sabotage of the Nord Stream pipelines in September 2022.[33] The Progress Report therefore suggests a Council Recommendation that should allow further acceleration of implementation of the NIS2 and CER Directives: A common approach should be prepared 'to conducting stress tests on entities operating critical infrastructure, starting in the energy sector, drawing on agreed common principles.'[34] Stress tests should be completed before the end of 2023.[35] A Blueprint should be prepared by the Commission in cooperation with the Council, that should help ensure a coordinated response at EU level to significant disruptions of critical infrastructure.[36] **25**

In the *energy sector*,[37] the Commission points to its work on a 'network code on cybersecurity for cross-border electricity flows,[38] including rules on risk assessments, common minimum requirements, planning, monitoring, reporting and crisis management'. In view of Russia's aggression against Ukraine, 'the electricity grids of Ukraine and the Republic of Moldova were synchronized with the Continental Europe Grid in March 2022'.[39] **26**

In the *transport sector*,[40] **27**

> the Commission works with Member States, the European Union Aviation Safety Agency (EASA) and the EU Intelligence and Situation Centre (EU INTCEN) to regularly assess the level of threat and risk to EU civil aviation from conflict zones.[41] The EU Conflict Zone Alerting System is referenced as a best practice at the international level.[42]

Maritime critical infrastructure[43] is also mentioned as a field of action: A 'Common Information Sharing Environment for the maritime domain[44] is currently being developed and will be fully operational by the end of 2023'.[45] It is intended to interconnect **28**

---

[31] Council conclusions on the development of the European Union's cyber posture, 23.5.2022, 9364/2.

[32] COM(2022) 745 final, 3.

[33] ibid., 2.

[34] ibid.

[35] ibid.

[36] ibid., 2–3.

[37] ibid., 3.

[38] Network Code on Cybersecurity <https://www.entsoe.eu/network_codes/nccs/> (last accessed: 28.9.2023); ACER, 'ACER submits to the European Commission the revised Network Code on electricity cybersecurity' (Acer, 14.7.2022) <https://acer.europa.eu/news-and-events/news/acer-submits-european-commission-revised-network-code-electricity-cybersecurity> (last accessed: 28.9.2023).

[39] COM(2022) 745 final, 3.

[40] ibid.

[41] European Commission, 'Working towards an enhanced and more resilient aviation security policy: A stocktaking', 2.2.2023, SWD(2023) 37 final.

[42] International Civil Aviation Organisation, 'Risk Assessment Manual for Civil Aircraft Operations Over or Near Conflict Zones', 2018, Doc. 10084.

[43] COM(2022) 745 final, 3.

[44] See the EMSA's webpage on the Common Information Sharing Environment (CISE) <https://www.emsa.europa.eu/cise.html> (last accessed: 28.9.2023); the European Commission's webpage on the CISE <https://oceans-and-fisheries.ec.europa.eu/ocean/blue-economy/other-sectors/common-information-sharing-environment-cise_en> (last accessed: 28.9.2023).

[45] COM(2022) 745 final, 3.

'maritime surveillance authorities on a voluntary basis'. In addition, the European Coast Guard Functions Forum[46] has improved 'its capacity to guard against cyberattacks.'[47]

29 Most of the initiatives mentioned in the above show that the Commission cannot act on its own. It already needs to engage Member States as necessary partners in the complex process of conceptualization and elaboration. Furthermore, implementation of the proposed measures to a large extent depends on the capability and political will of the Member States. Major drivers in this process will again be urgent security concerns that arise on account of incidents like the sabotage of the Nord Stream pipelines.

II. Enhancing the EU's cybersecurity[48]

30 Here, reference can be made to the EU Cybersecurity Strategy for the Digital Decade[49] presented on 16 December 2020 by the Commission and the High Representative. According to the Progress Report, the Strategy has been 'almost fully implemented'.[50]

31 Based on the NIS2 Directive, a European Cyber Crisis Liaison Organisation Network (EU-CyCLONe)[51] is under development that is meant to support the coordinated management of large-scale cybersecurity incidents and crises at operational level. For internal purposes, the Commission is developing a cybersecurity situation and analysis centre.[52] On 9 May 2023, the European Cybersecurity Competence Centre (ECCC), aimed at supporting innovation and industrial policy in cybersecurity, inaugurated its new headquarters in Bucharest.[53] Reference is also made to the Commission working with Member States to ensure an EU-wide coordinated response to large-scale cyber incidents in a follow-up to its Recommendation on building a Joint Cyber Unit. The Member States, Commission and High Representative were also involved in cyber exercises in 2022.[54]

32 In September 2022, the Commission proposed the Cyber Resilience Act[55] in order to mitigate the increasing exposure of hardware and software products to cyberattacks that exploit software vulnerabilities.[56] Products with digital elements (both hardware and soft-

---

[46] See the European Commission's webpage on the European Coast Guard Functions Forum (ECGFF) <https://oceans-and-fisheries.ec.europa.eu/news/european-coast-guard-functions-forum-ecgff-ten-years-fruitful-co-operation-address-security-2019-11-20_en> (last accessed: 28.9.2023).

[47] COM(2022) 745 final, 4.

[48] ibid., 3–6.

[49] Joint Communication, 'The EU's Cybersecurity Strategy for the Digital Decade', 16.12.2020, JOIN(2020) 18 final; Annexes to JOIN(2020) 18; Wahl, 'Council Conclusions on Cybersecurity Strategy' (eucrim 9.4.2021) <https://eucrim.eu/news/council-conclusions-on-cybersecurity-strategy/> (last accessed: 28.9.2023).

[50] COM(2022) 745 final, 3.

[51] EU CyCLONe (European cyber crisis liaison organisation network) <https://www.enisa.europa.eu/topics/incident-response/cyclone> (last accessed: 30.9.2023).

[52] See the ECCC's webpage on the European Cybersecurity Competence Centre and Network <https://cybersecurity-centre.europa.eu/index_en> (last accessed: 28.9.2023).

[53] ECCC, 'The European Cybersecurity Competence Centre (ECCC) opens its doors in Bucharest' (ECCC, 9.5.2023) <https://cybersecurity-centre.europa.eu/news/eccc-opens-its-doors-bucharest-2023-05-09_en> (last accessed: 28.9.2023).

[54] ENISA supports and organizes cyber exercises. See ENISA's webpage, <https://www.enisa.europa.eu/topics/training-and-exercises/cyber-exercises> (28.9.2023). ENISA also manages the programme of pan-European exercises. Cyber Europe 2022, see ENISA's webpage <https://www.enisa.europa.eu/topics/training-and-exercises/cyber-exercises/cyber-europe-programme> (last accessed: 28.9.2023).

[55] European Commission, 'Proposal for a regulation on cybersecurity requirements for products with digital elements (Cyber Resilience Act)', 15.9.2022, COM/2022/454 final.

[56] For a definition of products with digital elements, see the lawinsider website <https://www.lawinsider.com/dictionary/goods-with-digital-elements> (last accessed: 28.9.2023): 'goods with digital ele-

ware) are only to enter the market if they meet specific essential cybersecurity requirements.[57] The proposal is still under deliberation by Parliament and Member States.[58] By 19 July 2023, both Council and Parliament had adopted their positions. Unless MEPs formally request a vote in plenary, trilogue negotiations could start in the autumn of 2023.[59]

In that context it should be noted, however, that the Progress Report fails to even 33
mention cases in which governments and other actors applied the Pegasus spyware[60] to mobile devices within the EU.[61] The European Parliament installed a Committee of Inquiry to investigate the use of Pegasus and equivalent surveillance spyware (PEGA). The Committee adopted its final report and recommendations on 8 May 2023 following a year-long inquiry into the abuse of spyware in the EU.[62] In the report, MEPs condemn spyware abuses that aim to intimidate the political opposition, silence critical media and manipulate elections. They note that EU governance structures cannot effectively deal with such attacks and say reforms are needed.[63]

III. Countering hybrid threats, fighting foreign interference and enhancing EU cyber defence[64]

Hybrid threats as part of hostile foreign and security policies below the threshold of 34
war have been an issue for action and coordination in the EU as well as within NATO

ments: any tangible movable items that incorporate, or are inter-connected with, digital content or a digital service in such a way that the absence of that digital content or digital service would prevent the goods from performing their functions.'

[57] For example,. ENISA Minimum Security Measures for Operators of Essentials Services, see ENISA's webpage <https://www.enisa.europa.eu/topics/cybersecurity-policy/nis-directive-new/minimum-security-measures-for-operators-of-essentials-services> (last accessed: 28.9.223).

[58] See the European Commission's webpage on the EU Cyber Resilience Act <https://digital-strategy.ec.europa.eu/en/policies/cyber-resilience-act> (last accessed: 28.9.2023).

[59] Publyon, 'European Cyber Resilience Act: can new requirements for products strengthen your organization's cybersecurity resilience?' (Publyon, 19.7.2023) <https://publyon.com/european-cyber-resilience-act/> (last accessed: 28.9.2023).

[60] Pegasus is spyware developed by the Israeli cyberarms company NSO Group that can be covertly installed on mobile phones (and other devices) running most versions of iOS and Android. Pegasus exploits iOS versions up to 14.7 through a zero-click exploit. As of 2022, Pegasus was capable of reading text messages, tracking calls, collecting passwords, location tracking, accessing the target device's microphone and camera, and harvesting information from apps. In August 2016, Pegasus was discovered on the iPhone of a human rights activist; an investigation revealed details about the spyware, its abilities, as well as the security vulnerabilities it exploits. News of the spyware led to significant media coverage. The spyware has been used for the surveillance of anti-regime activists, journalists and political leaders from several nations around the world. In July 2021, both the Pegasus Project investigative initiative and an in-depth analysis by the human rights group Amnesty International reported that Pegasus was still being widely used against high-profile targets. See <https://en.wikipedia.org/wiki/Pegasus_(spyware)> (last accessed: 28.9.2023).

[61] Think Tank European Parliament, 'The use of Pegasus and equivalent surveillance spyware – The existing legal framework in EU Member States for the acquisition and use of Pegasus and equivalent surveillance spyware', 5.12.2022; European Parliament Think Tank, 'Europe's PegasusGate: Countering spyware abuse', 6.7.2022.

[62] European Parliament, 'Press Release: Spyware: MEPs sound alarm on threat to democracy and demand reforms', 8.5.2023, <https://www.europarl.europa.eu/news/en/press-room/20230505IPR84901/spyware-meps-sound-alarm-on-threat-to-democracy-and-demand-reforms> (last accessed: 19.9.2023).

[63] For further details, see European Agency for Fundamental Rights, 'Surveillance by intelligence services: Fundamental rights safeguards and remedies in the EU – 2023 update', 23.5.2023; European Parliament, 'Press Release: Spyware: MEPs call for full investigations and safeguards to prevent abuse', 15.6.2023, <https://www.europarl.europa.eu/news/en/press-room/20230609IPR96217/spyware-meps-call-for-full-investigations-and-safeguards-to-prevent-abuse> (last accessed: 30.9.2023).

[64] COM(2022) 745 final, 6 et seq.

since Russia's invasion of Ukraine in 2014.[65] Countering them touches upon Member States' responsibility under Art. 4(2) TEU.

35 In that context, the Council of EU Member States in March 2022 approved the EU Strategic Compass for Security and Defence,[66] which sets out an ambitious plan of action for the EU to increase its capabilities as a global actor in security and defence, to strengthen its resilience and to invest better in its defence capabilities. A first Annual Progress Report on its implementation was issued by the High Representative/Vice President on 20 March 2023.[67] It complements the Commission's Fifth Progress Report on the Security Union with regard to aspects that affect Member States' competences.

36 In turn, the Commission's Progress Report[68] states, with regard to hybrid threats, that 'the EU's role and remit lie in complementing national action by supporting coordination, enhancing situational awareness, promoting cooperation with like-minded countries and international organizations, and providing joint response options',[69] and it recalls that 'more than 200 measures have been put in place to enhance resilience and counter hybrid threats at EU level'.[70] In that regard the Report highlights the Hybrid Fusion Cell[71] that was created in 2016 as part of the EU Intelligence Assessment and Situation Centre (EU INTCEN) at the EEAS, which is meant to contribute to EU decision-making and to be 'the central body providing comprehensive situational awareness and strategic foresight by aggregating all-source information and conducting intelligence assessments on hybrid threats'.[72] Of the other projects that are also mentioned in the Strategic Compass, the Commission mentions EU Hybrid Rapid Response Teams,[73] and the development of an EU Hybrid Toolbox[74] is in preparation and is meant to provide a framework for a coordinated response to hybrid campaigns. A more Commission-related initiative that involves the Joint Research Centre (JRC) is the

[65] See the Hybrid CoE webpage, 'Hybrid threats as a concept' <https://www.hybridcoe.fi/hybrid-threats-as-a-phenomenon/> (last accessed: 30.9.2023); NATO's webpage on 'Countering hybrid threats' <https://www.nato.int/cps/en/natohq/topics_156338.htm> (last accessed: 30.9.2023) and the EEAS's webpage on 'Countering hybrid threats', 31.3.3.2022 <https://www.eeas.europa.eu/eeas/countering-hybrid-threats_en> (last accessed:30.9.2023).

[66] See the EEAS's webpage on 'A Strategic Compass for Security and Defence' <https://www.eeas.europa.eu/eeas/strategic-compass-security-and-defence-1_en> (last accessed: 30.9.2023).

[67] EEAS, '2023 Annual Progress Report on the Implementation of the Strategic Compass for Security and Defence' (March 2023) <https://www.eeas.europa.eu/eeas/2023-annual-progress-report-implementation-strategic-compass-security-and-defence_en> (last accessed: 30.9.2023).

[68] COM(2022) 745 final, 6–7; for legal dimensions in countering hybrid threats, see Lonardo, European Papers 2021, 1075–1096; on the scope of possible counter measures, see Cirdei, Scientific Bulletin 2017, 71–78.

[69] COM(2022) 745 final, 6.

[70] ibid.

[71] Kert-Saint Aubyn, 'EU Policy on Fighting Hybrid Threats' (CCDCOE) <https://ccdcoe.org/incyder-articles/eu-policy-on-fighting-hybrid-threats/> (last accessed: 30.9.2023) ; Gruszczak, Politeja 2022 (79), 131–150; Joint Staff Working Document, 'Report on the implementation of the 2016 Joint Framework on countering hybrid threats and the 2018 Joint Communication on increasing resilience and bolstering capabilities to address hybrid threats', 31.7.2020, SWD(2021) 729 final.

[72] COM(2022) 745 final, 6.

[73] See ENISA's webpage <https://www.enisa.europa.eu/topics/cybersecurity-policy/nis-directive-new/minimum-security-measures-for-operators-of-essentials-services> (last accessed: 39.9.2023), 11; Lasoen, 'Realising the EU Hybrid Toolbox: opportunities and pitfalls' (Clingendael Policy Brief, December 2022) < https://www.clingendael.org/sites/default/files/2022-12/Policy_brief_EU_Hybrid_Toolbox.pdf> (last accessed: 30.9.2023).

[74] See Council conclusions on a Framework for a coordinated EU response to hybrid campaigns, 21.6.2022; Bendiek/Bossong, SWP-Aktuell 2022 A40.

'identification of existing sectoral resilience baselines'[75,76] as well as further 'analytical research on building resilience to hybrid threats'.[77]

Based on numerous examples during the COVID-19 pandemic and Russia's war against Ukraine, the threat of 'manipulating [...] the information environment'[78] of the EU and partners around the globe has become a matter of major concern. The Report hence puts strong emphasis on countering foreign information manipulation and interference (FIMI).[79] 'Building on the European Democracy Action Plan,[80] [...] a set of tangible measures and structures' has been put in place, 'including the revised Code of Practice on Disinformation,[81] the Digital Services Act,[82] and the proposal on transparency of political advertising[83] currently in inter-institutional negotiations.[84]'[85] The result of such a regulation 'would be new obligations on platforms and, for the first time, a legally binding oversight framework'.[86, 87] The Commission Progress Report also mentions the EEAS's Toolbox to tackle Foreign Information Manipulation and Interference (FIMI **37**

---

75 COM(2022) 745 final, 6.

76 The European Commission's webpage on the Joint Research Centre, 'A new method to help policymakers defend democracy against hybrid threats', 20.4.2023 <https://joint-research-centre.ec.europa.eu/jrc-news-and-updates/new-method-help-policymakers-defend-democracy-against-hybrid-threats-2023-04-20_en> (last accessed: 30.9.2023).

77 COM(2022) 745 final, 6.

78 ibid.

79 EEAS, 'Tackling Disinformation, Foreign Information Manipulation & Interference (FIMI)', 27.10.2021 <https://www.eeas.europa.eu/eeas/tackling-disinformation-foreign-information-manipulation-interference_en> (last accessed: 30.9.2023); ENISA, 'Foreign Information Manipulation Interference (FIMI) and Cybersecurity – Threat Landscape', 8.12.2022 <https://www.enisa.europa.eu/publications/foreign-information-manipulation-interference-fimi-and-cybersecurity-threat-landscape> (last accessed: 30.9.2023).

80 See the European Commission's webpage on the European Democracy Action Plan 2019–2024, <https://commission.europa.eu/strategy-and-policy/priorities-2019-2024/new-push-european-democracy/european-democracy-action-plan_en> (last accessed: 30.9.2023); EEAS, 'European Democracy Action Plan: making EU democracies stronger', 3.12.2020 <https://ec.europa.eu/commission/presscorner/detail/en/ip_20_2250> (last accessed: 30.9.2023).

81 European Commission, 'The 2022 Code of Practice on Disinformation', 16.6.2022 <https://digital-strategy.ec.europa.eu/en/policies/code-practice-disinformation> (last accessed: 30.9.2023).

82 Bertuzzi, 'Commission announces first platforms to fall under EU digital rulebook's stricter regime' (Euractiv, 25.4.2023) <https://www.euractiv.com/section/platforms/news/commission-announces-first-platforms-to-fall-under-eu-digital-rulebooks-stricter-regime/> (last accessed: 30.9.2023); Bertuzzi, 'EU institutions reach agreement on Digital Services Act' (Euractiv, 23.4.2022) <https://www.euractiv.com/section/digital/news/eu-institutions-reach-agreement-on-digital-services-act/> (last accessed: 30.9.2023).

83 European Commission, 'Proposal for a regulation of the European Parliament and the Council on the transparency and targeting of political advertising', 25.11.2021, COM(2021) 731 final.

84 Barata, 'Regulation of online political advertising in Europe and potential threats to freedom of expression' (LSE blog, 9.3.2023) <https://blogs.lse.ac.uk/medialse/2023/03/09/regulation-of-online-political-advertising-in-europe-and-potential-threats-to-freedom-of-expression/> (last accessed: 30.9.2023).

85 COM(2022) 745 final, 6 et seq.

86 European Commission, 'Europe fit for the Digital Age: New online rules for platforms' <https://commission.europa.eu/strategy-and-policy/priorities-2019-2024/europe-fit-digital-age/digital-services-act-ensuring-safe-and-accountable-online-environment/europe-fit-digital-age-new-online-rules-platforms_en> (last accessed: 30.9.2023).

87 COM(2022) 745 final, 6 et seq.

Toolbox)[88] as well as the EEAS's outreach to international partners like the G7 Rapid Response Mechanism (RRM) and NATO.[89]

38 As a project of major ambition the Progress Report highlights the new EU Policy on Cyber Defence,[90] which was presented in November 2022 by the Commission and the High Representative. Its objective is 'to defend EU interests in cyberspace by increased cooperation among EU's cyber defence actors'[91] by establishing an EU Cyber Defence Coordination Centre (EUCDCC), which has links to EU INTCEN and EUMS.INT, further developing the EU Cyber Commanders Conference, establishing an operational network for milCERTs (MICNET), exploring options for collaboration with the Computer Security Incident Response Teams (CSIRT) network, etc.[92] and 'developing mechanisms for leveraging capabilities at the EU level, including in the context of CSDP missions and operations.'[93]

39 The Strategy is meant to

> […] boost development of full spectrum cyber defence capabilities and strengthen cooperation between the EU military and civilian cyber communities, enhancing situational awareness, crisis coordination and training, including with the private sector. It will also help reduce strategic dependencies in critical cyber technologies, by developing a strategic roadmap for critical cybersecurity and cyber defence technologies, and strengthen the European Defence Technological Industrial Base.[94]

40 The Commission Progress Report does not make explicit mention of the EEAS-based Cyber Diplomacy Toolbox developed back in 2017[95] that is now part of a wider EU Policy on Cyber Defence.[96] It is a joint EU diplomatic response to malicious cyber activities and part of the EU's approach to CFSP. Toolbox action focusses on coordinated restrictive measures by Member States within the CFSP, denying the EU access to individuals connected with illicit and malicious cyber activities or freezing their EU-based assets and accounts.[97] The aim in defining and communicating this set of countermeasures is to have at least some influence on the behaviour of potential aggressors. Hence, cyber diplomacy is enhancing Commission-led cyber defence measures.

41 Inevitably, space has had to be defined as a new dimension for the Security Union. Space is identified in the EEAS Strategic Compass as 'the fifth operational domain of warfare (alongside land, sea, air and cyber)'.[98] Member States have thus asked the

---

[88] EEAS, 'Tackling Disinformation, Foreign Information Manipulation & Interference (FIMI)', 27.10.2021 <https://www.eeas.europa.eu/eeas/tackling-disinformation-foreign-information-manipulation-interference_en> (last accessed: 30.9.2023); ENISA, 'Foreign Information Manipulation Interference (FIMI) and Cybersecurity – Threat Landscape', 8.12.2022 <https://www.enisa.europa.eu/publications/foreign-information-manipulation-interference-fimi-and-cybersecurity-threat-landscape> (last accessed: 30.9.2023).

[89] G7, 'G7 Rapid Response Mechanism Annual Report 2021' <https://www.international.gc.ca/transparency-transparence/rapid-response-mechanism-mecanisme-reponse-rapide/2021-annual-report-rapport-annuel.aspx?lang=eng> (last accessed: 30.9.2023).

[90] European Commission, 'Cyber Defence: EU boosts action against cyber threats', 10.11.2022 <https://ec.europa.eu/commission/presscorner/detail/en/ip_22_6642> (last accessed: 30.9.2023).

[91] COM(2022) 745 final, 7.

[92] Joint Communication, 'EU Policy on Cyber Defence', 11.11.2022, JOIN(2022) 49 final, 4–7.

[93] COM(2022) 745 final, 7.

[94] ibid.

[95] See the Cyber Diplomacy Toolbox <https://www.cyber-diplomacy-toolbox.com/> (last accessed: 30.9.2023); Miadzvetskaya/Wessel, European Papers 2021 (7:1), 413–438; Bendiek/Kettemann, SWP Comment 2021; European Institute for Public Administration, 'EU Cyber Diplomacy 101', 1.7.2021 <https://www.eipa.eu/de/blog-de/eu-cyber-diplomacy-101/> (30.9.2023).

[96] See also EEAS, '2023 Annual Progress Report on the Implementation of the Strategic Compass for Security and Defence' (March 2023), 12.

[97] Council Decision 2019/797 concerning restrictive measures against cyber-attacks threatening the Union or its Member States.

[98] COM(2022) 745 final, 8.

Commission and High Representative to develop the first Space Strategy for Security and Defence.[99] The Strategy proposed in March 2023 with first steps to be taken by late 2024, includes proposals to improve situational awareness of threats inside the institutions as well as to EU industries, to reduce strategic technological dependencies and to build a viable space defence infrastructure.

IV. Fighting terrorism and radicalization[100]

The Commission Progress Report states that 'nearly all the key initiatives presented in the EU Security Strategy to support Member States in the fight against terrorism and radicalization have been adopted. [...] The next step is to ensure that these initiatives achieve their full impact.'[101] 42

1. The fight against terrorism

The EU Agenda on Counter-Terrorism[102] of 2020 provided the EU with a wide range of means to better anticipate, prevent, protect and respond to terrorist threats. Specific geographical initiatives have also helped respond to the evolving threat situation. In view of the Taliban takeover in Afghanistan, the EU Counter-Terrorism Coordinator, in coordination with the Commission, the High Representative, the Presidency and key EU agencies, drew up a specific Counter-Terrorism Action Plan on Afghanistan,[103] which was endorsed by Member States in October 2021. A voluntary procedure for enhanced security checks of people coming from Afghanistan was implemented in line with proposals in the plan.[104] 43

Besides that, the Progress Report is clear that addressing the 'threat posed by returning Foreign Terrorist Fighters in Syria and Iraq is a priority.'[105] 'While primary responsibility lies with the Member States', common challenges can be better mitigated with EU support, such as ' prosecution of those who have committed terrorist crimes, prevention of undetected entry into the Schengen Area and the reintegration and rehabilitation'[106] of returnees. A key operational and legal challenge in that regard is still to ensure that 'battlefield evidence is entered into EU databases and information systems'.[107] In addition, new ways 44

[99] See the European Commission's webpage on the EU Space Strategy for Security and Defence – For a stronger and more resilient European Union <https://defence-industry-space.ec.europa.eu/eu-space-strategy-security-and-defence_en> (last accessed: 30.9.2023); Joint Communication, 'European Union Space Strategy for Security and Defence', 10.3.2023, JOIN(2023) 9 final.

[100] COM(2022) 745 final, 7–10.

[101] ibid., 7.

[102] European Commission, 'A Counter-Terrorism Agenda for the EU: Anticipate, Prevent, Protect, Respond', 9.12.2020, COM(2020) 795 final.

[103] Council of the European Union/Counter-Terrorism Coordinator, 'Afghanistan: Counter-Terrorism Action Plan', 29.9.2021, 12315/21.

[104] General Secretariat of the Council, 'Voluntary procedure for enhanced security checks on people coming from Afghanistan', 17.9.2021, WK 10904, Limité; also see Statewatch, 'EU ropes in intelligence agencies for enhanced border checks targeting Afghan nationals' (Statewatch, 18.11.2021) <https://www.statewatch.org/news/2021/november/eu-ropes-in-intelligence-agencies-for-enhanced-border-checks-targeting-afghan-nationals/> (last accessed: 30.9.2023).

[105] COM(2022) 745 final, 9.

[106] ibid.

[107] ibid. See also Council of the European Union/EU Counter-Terrorism Coordinator, 'The EU's work on battlefield information. Stocktaking and possible next steps. Developments on Battlefield Information since July 2019', 14.6.2021, 9481/21; on the legal challenges, see Eurojust, 'Memorandum on Battlefield Evidence', September 2020 <https://www.eurojust.europa.eu/sites/default/files/2020-09/2020-09-14-Eurojust-Memorandum-on-Battlefield-Evidence.pdf> (last accessed: 30.9.2023).

are being explored within the framework of CSDP to improve living conditions in prisons and camps in North-East Syria to mitigate or at least reduce the risk of radicalization.[108]

45 Although the Directive on combating terrorism adopted in 2017 has since been implemented by all the Member States to criminalize training and travelling for terrorism as well as terrorist financing,[109] the Commission still remarks that 'incorrect transposition of the Directive in a number of Member States is a matter that still needs to be addressed.'[110]

46 Disrupting terrorist financing remains a major challenge both at the EU and the global level. Again, the Commission can state that '[n]early all Member States have now adopted the updated legislation on firearms in their national law.'[111] New legislation on explosive precursors came into force in February 2021.[112] A similar legislative approach is currently being studied by the Commission to restrict access to dangerous chemicals.[113]

2. Combatting radicalization that leads to violent extremism and terrorism online and offline

47 Since 2011 the Commission has been supporting Member States through the Radicalisation Awareness Network (RAN),[114] which about 6,000 experts are involved in. Activities include 'countering violent extremist ideologies and polarisation […]; radicalisation online and misuse of new technologies [as well as] managing and preparing the reintegration of offenders released from prison.'[115] Hate speech as a precursor for radicalization and violent action can be addressed with the support of the EU Code of Conduct on countering illegal hate speech online.[116]

48 The Progress Report states that '[t]he Regulation to address the dissemination of terrorist content online[117] became applicable in June 2022.'[118] With the support of the EU, national authorities can now 'require terrorist content to be removed by online platforms within one hour of an official removal order.'[119] 'Online service providers exposed to terrorist content have to take specific measures to protect their platforms against misuse.'[120] The 'EU Internet Forum (EUIF),[121] launched by the Commission to bring together Member States, internet companies and civil society'[122] further contri-

---

[108] European Commission, 'Gender-sensitive responses to returnees from foreign terrorist organisations: insights for practitioners', 2021 <https://home-affairs.ec.europa.eu/system/files/2021-12/ran_ad-hoc_gender_sensitive_response_ftfs_122021_en.pdf> (last accessed: 30.9.2023).

[109] Directive (EU) 2017/541 on combating terrorism.

[110] COM(2022) 745 final, 8.

[111] ibid.

[112] Regulation (EU) 2019/1148 on the marketing and use of explosives precursors.

[113] See COM(2020) 795 final; for a critical overview, see Sacchetti, European Papers 2021, 967–986.

[114] Since it was founded in 2011, the RAN has attracted over 6,000 practitioners who collectively represent all the EU Member States, see <https://home-affairs.ec.europa.eu/networks/radicalisation-awareness-network-ran/about-ran_en> (last accessed: 30.9.2023).

[115] COM(2022) 745 final, 10.

[116] European Commission, 'The EU Code of conduct on countering illegal hate speech online' <https://commission.europa.eu/strategy-and-policy/policies/justice-and-fundamental-rights/combatting-discrimination/racism-and-xenophobia/eu-code-conduct-countering-illegal-hate-speech-online_en> (last accessed: 30.9.2023); EU Monitor, 'High Level Group on combating hate speech and hate crime' (EU Monitor) <https://www.eumonitor.eu/9353000/1/j9vvik7m1c3gyxp/vk66hki61cxo> (last accessed: 30.9.2023).

[117] Regulation (EU) 2021/784 on addressing the dissemination of terrorist content online.

[118] COM(2022) 745 final, 9.

[119] ibid.

[120] ibid.

[121] European Commission, 'European Union Internet Forum (EUIF)' <https://home-affairs.ec.europa.eu/networks/european-union-internet-forum-euif_en> (last accessed: 30.9.2023).

[122] COM(2022) 745 final, 9.

butes to preventing the dissemination of violent extremist and terrorist content online. 'Recent EUIF support […] include a directory on Terrorist-Operated Websites, and a yearly updated knowledge package of violent right-wing extremist groups [emphasis added], symbols and manifestoes'.[123]

V. Fighting organized crime[124]

Elaborating on that dimension of security threat, the Commission remarks that 49

> [c]riminal networks may be involved in a variety of criminal activities, combining drugs trafficking, organised property crime, fraud, migrant smuggling and trafficking in human beings. Cybercrime and gender-based cyber violence has been further stimulated by the increased use of internet and online services. The increasing use of encrypted communication channels, while protecting privacy and fundamental rights, poses additional challenges for law enforcement. Meanwhile, the disruption caused by the Russian war of aggression against Ukraine has created new openings, swiftly exploited by organised crime groups.[125]

According to the Commission, '[the implementation of the EU Strategy to tackle 50
Organised Crime 2021–2025] is now well underway, with several key actions already adopted or implemented.'[126] Financial support to Member States has also been extended by the Commission to that end.[127]

The Second Additional Protocol to the Budapest Cybercrime Convention was 51
finalized in May 2022[128] and had been signed by 41 states by June 2023. The Protocol provides tools for cross-border cooperation beyond the EU in investigating and prosecuting cybercrime.

VI. Organized crime

Trafficking in human beings is still a major and essentially unresolved security 52
challenge that was again enhanced by the events in Ukraine.[129] A Common Anti-Trafficking Plan[130] has been added to Commission, Member State, EU agency and EEAS

---

[123] ibid. See also European Commission, 'Back to the Future? Twenty-First Century Extremist and Terrorist Websites', 2021 <https://home-affairs.ec.europa.eu/system/files/2022-03/Terrorist%20Operated%20Websites%20Workshop-paper.pdf> (last accessed: 30.9.2023); Directorate-General for Migration and Home Affairs, '7th EU Internet Forum Ministerial: curbing harmful content online through joint efforts', 24.2.2022 <https://home-affairs.ec.europa.eu/news/7th-eu-internet-forum-ministerial-curbing-harmful-content-online-through-joint-efforts-2022-02-24_en> (last accessed: 30.9.2023).

[124] COM(2022) 745 final, 10–14.

[125] ibid., 10. See also Europol, 'A common response to serious and organised crime linked to the war in Ukraine. The EMPACT community gathered at Europol to discuss coordinated operational actions for evolving threats linked to the war in Ukraine', 7.4.2022 <https://www.europol.europa.eu/media-press/newsroom/news/common-response-to-serious-and-organised-crime-linked-to-war-in-ukraine> (30.9.2023).

[126] ibid.10.

[127] ibid., 11. In July 2022, the Commission allocated EUR 15.7 million to Member States via the Internal Security Fund (ISF) to support long-term projects and activities within the European Multidisciplinary Platform Against Criminal Threats (EMPACT), tackling the EU'S 10 crime priorities adopted by the Council for 2022–2025. Europol, '57 Internet Organised Crime Threat Assessment Report (IOCTA)'.

[128] Council of Europe, Second Additional Protocol to the Cybercrime Convention on enhanced co-operation and disclosure of electronic evidence (CETS No. 224).

[129] COM(2022) 745 final, 12.

[130] Pingen, 'Common Anti-Trafficking Plan for Victims of Ukraine War' (eucrim, 25.5.2022) <https://eucrim.eu/news/common-anti-trafficking-plan-for-victims-of-ukraine-war/> (last accessed: 30.9.2023).

efforts. They have at least contributed to limiting the number of confirmed trafficking cases, although the threat remains high.[131]

53 The Commission is to follow up the EU Strategy on Combatting Trafficking in Human Beings 2021–2025[132] with an upcoming proposal amending the Anti-trafficking Directive.[133] 'Shortcomings in the current legal framework and updates'[134] with regard to the online dimension and the means for the reduction of demand are to be developed. The Progress Report commends the results of a first EU-wide hackathon against trafficking in human beings (EMPACT 2022), supported by Europol and Eurojust, with law enforcement authorities from 20 countries that took place in September 2022. Eleven suspected human traffickers and 45 possible victims were identified.[135]

54 In that regard, the Commission also states that

> [...] implementation of the EU Action Plan against Migrant Smuggling 2021–2025[136] is progressing, with Anti-Smuggling Operational Partnerships being developed with Morocco, Niger and the Western Balkans supported by EU institutions, bodies and agencies and EU funding.[137]

55 Another final major challenge for EU action is the illegal drugs market, estimated to have a minimum retail value of EUR 30 billion per year. According to the Progress Report,

> [it] remains the largest criminal market in the EU and a major source of income for organized crime groups, as well as a threat to social stability and health. In 2021, EU action and cooperation led to EUR 7 billion worth of drugs being taken off the streets.[138]

56 The July 2020 EU Agenda and Action Plan on Drugs 2021–2025[139] envisages the transformation of the European Monitoring Centre for Drugs and Drug Addiction (EMCDDA) into the European Union Drugs Agency. The agency's revised mandate, proposed in January 2022, was adopted as a Regulation on 30 June 2023.[140] Commission initiatives regarding cooperation in the EU Internet Forum to address online drugs trafficking and for a specific thematic Schengen evaluation of the smuggling of cocaine into EU ports have been reported[141] as has an increase of Commission support to the Maritime Analysis and Operation Centre – Narcotics. The Commission also held

---

[131] COM(2022) 745 final, 12.

[132] European Commission, 'Press Release: Fighting trafficking in human beings: New strategy to prevent trafficking, break criminal business models, protect and empower victims', 14.4.2021 <https://ec.europa.eu/commission/presscorner/detail/en/ip_21_1663> (last accessed: 30.9.2023).

[133] Directive 2011/36/EU on preventing and combating trafficking in human beings and protecting its victims.

[134] COM(2022) 745 final, 13.

[135] Europol, '20 countries spin a web for human traffickers during a hackathon', 21.9.2022 <https://www.publicnow.com/view/24B8A6671A2F86902E78E86E7CDFFE2BB92CF6AB?1663750642> (last accessed: 30.9.2023). Europol, 'Internet Organised Crime Threat Assessment (IOCTA), Strategic, policy and tactical updates on the fight against cybercrime' <https://www.europol.europa.eu/publications-events/main-reports/iocta-report> (last accessed: 30.9.2023).

[136] European Commission, 'A renewed EU action plan against migrant smuggling (2021–2025)', 29.9.2021, COM(2021) 591 final; on the use of mass migration in hybrid warfare, see Bachmann/Paphiti, Polish Political Science Yearbook 2021, 119–145.

[137] COM(2022) 745 final, 12.

[138] ibid., 12 et seq. with reference to Eurojust, 'Annual report 2021', 21.6.2022.

[139] European Monitoring Centre for Drugs and Drug Addiction, 'EU Drugs Action Plan 2021–2025', 22.6.2021 <https://www.emcdda.europa.eu/drugs-library/eu-drugs-action-plan-2021-2025_en> (last accessed: 30.9.2023).

[140] European Commission, 'Presse Release: Commission proposes stronger mandate for EU Drugs Agency as illicit market proliferates', 12.11.2022 <https://ec.europa.eu/commission/presscorner/detail/en/ip_22_302> (last accessed: 30.9.2023). Regulation (EU) 2023/1322 on the European Union Drugs Agency (EUDA).

[141] European Commission, 'State of Schengen report 2023', 16.5.2023, COM(2023) 274 final, Chapter 4 (Box 5).

political dialogues with third countries regarding drugs, plus a second dialogue with China in July 2022 and a new dialogue with Colombia in June 2022.

VII. Ensuring the security of EU borders and supporting law enforcement and judicial cooperation[142]

'[A] well-functioning Schengen area is key to the EU's security',[143] and it requires effective management of the EU's external borders and enhanced law enforcement cooperation.[144] 'In June 2021, the Commission adopted a Strategy Towards a fully-functioning and resilient Schengen area'[145] and developed a new governance model by creating an annual Schengen cycle. Based on that, a first progress report on the State of Schengen was adopted in May 2022.[146] A key step that provides for enhanced measures and procedures is an amended Schengen Borders Code[147] based on the Commission proposal of December 2021. In a Council general approach dated June 2022, the Commission urges the European Parliament and Council to swiftly conclude negotiations. While this process is still underway,[148] the Commission proposal to include Croatia in the Schengen Area was successful. In December 2022, the Council adopted a decision on the full application of the Schengen *acquis* in Croatia.[149] 57

Progress was also reported in the field of reinforcing law enforcement and judicial cross-border cooperation, albeit against the backdrop of a broad-based legal discussion of the implications and risks for privacy and human rights:[150] 58

---

142 COM(2022) 745 final, 14–18.

143 ibid., 15.

144 ibid., 14 et seq. On legal and practical dimensions of cross border judicial cooperation, see Amato, European Quarterly of Political Attitudes and Mentalities 2019, 36–53; Niedernhuber, p. 1 et seqq.; Lauer, p. 1 et seqq.

145 European Commission, 'A strategy towards a fully functioning and resilient Schengen area', 2.6.2021, COM(2021) 277 final; COM(2022) 745 final, 15.

146 European Commission, 'Press Release: State of Schengen: Commission sets new priorities and new governance model', 24.5.2022 <https://ec.europa.eu/commission/presscorner/detail/en/ip_22_3213> (last accessed: 30.9.2023).

147 European Commission, 'Proposal for a Regulation amending Regulation (EU) 2016/399 on a Union Code on the rules governing the movement of persons across borders', 14.12.2021, COM(2021) 891 final.

148 Agence Europe, 'Schengen Borders Code reform vote in European Parliament Committee on Civil Liberties now expected on 26 April' (Agence Europe, 4.4.2023) <https://agenceurope.eu/en/bulletin/article/13155/6> (last accessed: 30.9.2023).

149 European Parliament, 'Legislative resolution of 10 November 2022 on the draft Council decision on the full application of the provisions of the Schengen acquis in the Republic of Croatia (10624/2022 – C9-0222/2022 – 2022/0806(NLE))', 5.5.2023. European Commission, 'Making Schengen stronger with the full participation of Bulgaria, Romania and Croatia in the area without internal border controls', 16.11.2022, COM(2022) 636 final.

150 Aden, EPL 2020, 93–108; Bossong, SWP-Studie 2018 S 04; Casagran, Human Rights Law Review 2021 (21:2), 433–457; Kilpatrick/Jones, 'A Clear and Present Danger: Missing safeguards on migration and asylum in the EU's AI Act' (Statewatch, 12.5.2022) < https://www.statewatch.org/publications/reports-and-books/a-clear-and-present-danger-missing-safeguards-on-migration-and-asylum-in-the-eu-s-ai-act/> (last accessed: 30.9.2023); Noori, Geopolitics 2022, 1117–1139; Tagliapietra, 'More Connected, Less Protected? How the EU Interoperability Framework Will Affect the European Migration Space' (Robert Bosch Stiftung, Bertelsmann Stiftung and German Marshall Fund, September 2022) <https://www.bosch-stiftung.de/sites/default/files/publications/pdf/2023-02/More%20Connected%2C%20Less%20Protected.pdf> (last accessed: 30.9.2023); Zandstra/Brouwer, 'Fundamental Rights at the Digital Border. ETIAS, the Right to Data Protection, and the CJEU's PNR judgment' (Verfassungsblog, 24.6.2022) <https://verfassungsblog.de/digital-border/> (last accessed: 30.9.2023).

> The police cooperation package in December 2021[151] offered a major enhancement of the tools available. The Directive on information exchange has now found a political agreement between the European Parliament and the Council[152], and a Council recommendation reinforcing operation cross-border police cooperation was adopted by the Council in June 2022.[153] Negotiations continue on a Regulation revising the Prüm framework[154], seeking to allow for more efficient automated exchange of data between law enforcement authorities in specific areas such as DNA, dactyloscopic and vehicle registration data, and adding the categories of police records and facial images.[155]

59 The Commission was able to report that the new Europol mandate[156] entered into force in June 2022,

> […] allowing Europol to step up its expertise and operational capabilities to better support Member States in combating serious and organized crime and terrorism.[157] The mandate also strengthens Europol's data protection framework and the oversight of the European Data Protection Supervisor.[158]

60 Conceptual progress in a related field was made with the adoption of the Digital Justice Package[159] in December 2021. It consists of

> […] practical steps to improve digital information exchange on cross-border terrorism cases, to set up a cooperation platform to support the functioning of Joint Investigation Teams and to enhance the digitalization of cross-border judicial cooperation and access to justice in civil, commercial and criminal matters.[160]

61 Again, the Commission is urging swift adoption by the European Parliament and Council while also lobbying for further promotion of the provisional political agreement

---

[151] Directorate-General for Migration and Home Affairs, 'Boosting police cooperation across borders for enhanced security', 8.12.2021 <https://home-affairs.ec.europa.eu/news/boosting-police-cooperation-across-borders-enhanced-security-2021-12-08_en> (last accessed: 30.9.2023) and Council Recommendation (EU) 2022/915 on operational law enforcement cooperation, 13.6.2022.; see also Neiva, Policing and Society An International Journal of Research and Policy 2022, 1167–1179; Bellanova/Glouftsios, European Security 2022, 454–474.

[152] Directive (EU) 2023/977 on the exchange of information between the law enforcement authorities of Member States.

[153] Council Recommendation on operational law enforcement cooperation, 24.5.2022, 8720/22.

[154] European Commission, 'Proposal for a Regulation of the European Parliament and of the Council on automated data exchange for police cooperation ('Prüm II')', 8.12.2021, COM/2021/784 final; Agence Europe, '"Prüm II" Regulation, several Member States question new objective of automated exchange of information on missing persons' (Agence Europe, 5.2.2022) <https://agenceurope.eu/en/bulletin/article/12884/4> (last accessed: 30.9.2023).

[155] COM(2022) 745 final, 15.

[156] Europol, 'Europol's amended Regulation enters into force', 28.6.2022 <https://www.europol.europa.eu/media-press/newsroom/news/europols-amended-regulation-enters-force> (last accessed: 30.9.2023); European Parliament, 'Strengthening Europol's mandate: entry of alerts in SIS', 27.12.2022, P9_TA (2022)0227.

[157] In the following fields: supporting criminal investigation; research and innovation; SIS: cooperation with private parties; supporting EU Member States in processing data transmitted by third countries or international organizations; own-initiative investigations; establishing a Fundamental Rights Officer (FRO) within Europol; strengthening the European Data Protection Supervisor (EDPS); for a detailed overview, see Europol, 'Europol's amended Regulation enters into force', 28.6.2022 <https://www.europol.europa.eu/media-press/newsroom/news/europols-amended-regulation-enters-force> (last accessed: 30.9.2023).

[158] COM(2022) 745 final, 15.

[159] See the European Commission's webpage on the digitalization of justice <https://commission.europa.eu/strategy-and-policy/policies/justice-and-fundamental-rights/digitalisation-justice_en> (last accessed: 30.9.2023).

[160] COM(2022) 745 final, 16.

reached in November 2022 on e-evidence[161] that is to bring 'secure exchange on evidence of critical value to judicial authorities in the Member State.'[162]

Stating that 'securing the EU's external borders is a common responsibility', the Commission reports that 'the first teams of the European Border and Coast Guard[163] standing corps have been successfully deployed since January 2021, and the standing corps now numbers some 4,800 Frontex and national officers.'[164] **62**

Referring to the recent continuous increase in irregular arrivals across most migratory routes, the Commission underlines the importance of 'systematic identity and security checks of all migrants arriving at external borders of the EU, as well as health checks meeting common standards.'[165] In that context it highlights the importance of the New Pact on Migration and Asylum submitted to Parliament and Member States (Council) back in 2020:[166] 'Channeling migrants quickly to the appropriate procedures under the Screening Proposal would help to ensure that security checks are applied, in full respect of all fundamental rights obligations.'[167] The process is still ongoing, although the Swedish Presidency managed to achieve agreement between EU Member States 'on significant parts of the Pact on Migration and Asylum'[168] in June 2023. Opening negotiations between the Member States (Council) and the European Parliament is the next step.[169] **63**

Yet another complex project of major security importance and urgency is the new EU information systems architecture that is intended to ensure security as well as border and migration management:[170] **64**

> Central to this is the renewed Schengen Information System, which should start its operations in March 2023.[171] Other key tools are the Entry/Exit System (EES) (planned to start work in May

[161] European Commission, 'Press Release: e-Evidence: Commission welcomes political agreement to strengthen cross-border access for criminal investigations', 29.11.2022 <https://ec.europa.eu/commission/presscorner/detail/en/ip_22_7246> (last accessed: 30.09.20230).

[162] COM(2022) 745 final, 16.

[163] See FRONTEX's webpage on the European Border and Coast Guard standing corps <https://frontex.europa.eu/careers/standing-corps/about/> (last accessed: 30.9.2023).

[164] COM(2022) 745 final, 16. See also <https://frontex.europa.eu/careers/standing-corps/about/> (30.9.2023). On FRONTEX's development, see Bossong, SWP Comment 2019/C 47.

[165] COM(2022) 745 final, 16.

[166] European Commission, New Pact on Migration and Asylum <https://commission.europa.eu/strategy-and-policy/priorities-2019-2024/promoting-our-european-way-life/new-pact-migration-and-asylum_en> (last accessed: 30.9.2023), adopted on 23.9.2020. See also Ucarer, Social Inclusion – Open Access Journal 2022, Gerbaudo, European Papers 2022, 615–626; Mohamed/Alegria, Romanian Journal of European Affairs 2022, 46–62.

[167] COM(2022) 745 final, 16.

[168] Government offices of Sweden, 'EU Member States agree on key parts of Pact on Migration and Asylum', 9.6.2023 <https://www.government.se/articles/2023/06/eu-member-states-agree-on-key-parts-of-pact-on-migration-and-asylum/> (last accessed: 30.9.2023).

[169] ibid.

[170] The ambitious legislative and administrative projects are still widely scrutinized and discussed in terms of their legal, administrative and security implications. A very good overview on the subject matter is provided by Dumbrava, EPRS PE 690.706. On individual projects, see Klaus, NJOZ 2023, 544–553; Leese, Geopolitics 2022, 113–133; Ozkul, p. 1 et seqq.; Derave/Genicot/Hetmanska, European Journal of Risk Regulation 2022, 389–420; Eklund,' Frontex and 'Algorithmic Discretion' (Part I). The ETIAS Screening Rules and the Principle of Legality' (Verfassungsblog, 10.9.2022) <https://verfassungsblog.de/frontex-and-algorithmic-discretion-part-i/> (last accessed: 30.9.2023).

[171] European Commission, 'Press Release: Security Union: The renewed Schengen Information Systems enters into operation', 7.3.2023 <https://ec.europa.eu/commission/presscorner/detail/en/ip_23_1505> (last accessed: 30.9.2023).

2023),[172] the European Travel Information and Authorisation System ETIAS (due to enter into operation by the end of 2023)[173] and the update of the Visa Information System (VIS).[174] These will allow more checks and close security information gaps through better information exchange between Member States. Crucial to this work is the interoperability of the systems: it is essential that eu-LISA and Member States take the necessary steps without delay to deliver this ambitious project for full implementation by the end of 2024 [emphasis and footnotes added].[175]

65 The Commission makes similarly critical remarks with regard to the ability of Advance Passenger Information (API)[176] to contribute to security: '[It] is hampered by rules which are outdated and unevenly applied.'[177] The new Commission proposals (submitted in December 2022)

would repeal the current API Directive to clarify and enhance the use of API for both border management and law enforcement. It would expand the use of API to selected intra-EU flights, extending the toolbox available to the Member States law enforcement authorities within the Schengen area. Reflections on the external dimension of the EU's policy on Passenger Name Records (PNR) are ongoing, to reflect the fact that an increasing number of third countries are developing the capability to process this information for law enforcement and border security. The Commission is also preparing a legislative proposal on a framework for reciprocal access to security-related information for front-line officers in the EU and partner third countries, to efficiently detect criminals and terrorists.[178]

VIII. The internal-external security nexus: security in the EU neighbourhood and in partner countries[179]

66 With regard to EU efforts to engage in security cooperation with third countries, the Commission highlights the Council dimension:

The European External Action Service (EEAS) and the Commission services work closely with key partner countries and international organizations through regular counter-terrorism (CT) dialogues. More than 30 CT Dialogues are ongoing with third states and international organizations.[180] In parallel, the network of counter terrorism and security experts in EU delegations[181] in key third countries has been reinforced.[182]

67 That also holds true for the special case of cooperation with Ukraine to mitigate internal security threats stemming from Russia's war of aggression against the country,

---

172 The Entry/Exit system is currently not in operation. See travel-europe's webpage on new requirements for travelling to Europe and the Entry/Exit System (EES) <https://travel-europe.europa.eu/ees_en> (last accessed: 30.9.2023).

173 ETIAS is currently not in operation. The rules for travelling to Europe have changed. From 2024, some 1.4 billion people from more than 60 visa-exempt countries will be required to have travel authorization to enter most European countries, see <https://travel-europe.europa.eu/etias_en> (last accessed: 30.9.2023).

174 See the European Commission's webpage on the Visa Information System (VIS) <https://home-affairs.ec.europa.eu/policies/schengen-borders-and-visa/visa-information-system_en> (last accessed: 30.9.2023).

175 COM(2022) 745 final, 16. The urgent need to overcome delays in relation to these crucial operational questions was again underlined by the Special European Council on 9 February 2023 <https://www.consilium.europa.eu/en/meetings/european-council/2023/02/09/> (last accessed: 30.9.2023).

176 European Commission, 'Press Release: Security Union: Commission proposes new rules on Advance Passenger Information (API) to facilitate external border management and increase internal security', 13.12.2022 <https://ec.europa.eu/commission/presscorner/detail/en/ip_22_7644> (last accessed: 30.9.2023).

177 COM(2022) 745 final, 17.

178 ibid.

179 ibid., 18–21.

180 See the EEAS's webpage on Counter-Terrorism – International partnerships <https://www.eeas.europa.eu/eeas/counter-terrorism_en#15934> (last accessed: 30.9.2023).

181 See <https://www.eeas.europa.eu/eeas/counter-terrorism_en#15934> (last accessed: 30.9.2023).

182 COM(2022) 745 final, 18.

by a 'continuous structured security cooperation'[183] that involves Europol and Frontex and is generally intended to strengthen information exchange on internal security threats. Frontex currently has 277 staff deployed in the region, Europol has 15 and the European Union Asylum Agency has 60.[184]

In the same context the Commission reports that **68**

> Cybersecurity Dialogue between the EU and Ukraine has been stepped up together with coordinated political, financial and material support from the EU to help Ukraine to strengthen its cyber resilience. Overall funding of EUR 29 million to increase Ukraine's cyber and digital resilience has supported cyber security equipment, software and resilient digital transformation.[185]

D. What remains to be done?

Both the Commission's Fifth Progress Report and the first Annual Progress report of **69** the EEAS on the Implementation of the Strategic Compass that have outlined in detail in the above in terms of their aims and action items leave no doubt that, despite major efforts from all sides, the Security Union is still some steps away from being 'fully operational', be it in terms of national legislation or in the sphere of practical implementation and operationalization.

Rather mundane but pertinent factors that are slowing down the intended and very **70** much needed rate of implementation of already agreed and defined action plans continue to be the Member States' budgetary, administrative and logistical constraints. Because of that, the rollout of vital border security systems has had to be postponed several times (now to 2024[186]), leaving core capabilities for safeguarding basic security within the AFSJ in a potentially perilously deficient state.

The same can be said of EEAS structures, in particular the Single Intelligence **71** Analysis Capacity (SIAC) capabilities for providing intelligence-supported situational awareness and strategic foresight to EU decision-makers as well as to EU Member States working together in the Council structures. The 2023 Annual Progress Report remains conspicuously vague on EU INTCEN and EUMS.INT, as the two constituent parts of the SIAC, only mention that 'in order to boost our intelligence-based situational awareness, a proposal for the strengthening of our Single Intelligence Analysis Capacity will be presented in the next months.'[187] In view of the SIAC's major contribution to the Strategic Compass. providing its widely acclaimed basis plus the 360° Threat Analysis,[188] concepts and initiatives to further upgrade their quite nimble capacities should have been a top-priority issue.

---

[183] ibid.

[184] ibid. Frontex, 'Press Release: Frontex stands with Ukraine', 24.2.2023 <https://frontex.europa.eu/media-centre/news/news-release/frontex-stands-with-ukraine-koMhlh> (last accessed: 30.9.2023); Europol, 'Europol's Support to Ukraine: One Year On', 23.2.2023 <https://www.europol.europa.eu/publications-events/publications/europols-support-to-ukraine-one-year> (last accessed: 30.9.2023); EUAA, 'EUAA Response to the War in Ukraine' <https://euaa.europa.eu/euaa-response-war-ukraine> (last accessed: 30.9.2023).

[185] COM(2022) 745 final, 18.

[186] European Commission, 'State of Schengen report 2023', 16.5.2023, COM(2023) 274 final, Chapter 4 (Box 5).

[187] EEAS, '2023 Annual Progress Report on the Implementation of the Strategic Compass for Security and Defence', March 2023, 10.

[188] Council Conclusions on Security and Defence, 17.6.2020, 8910/20, 3 para. 4; Nuñez-Belda IP Quarterly 2022.

E. Subsequent chapters

72 In view of the vast scope of the activities and projects that are covered by the EU Security Strategy, it is of particular merit that the following chapters in this Handbook on the intricacies and implications of operationalizing the Security Union relate to three of the four core strategic priorities mentioned in the above:

73 First, *Cyber security in the European multi-level governance system* (→ § 16), an essential part of any 'future-proof security environment'[189], will be presented and discussed by Thomas Wischmeyer in terms of its vital importance for contemporary societies. The threat to the vital security interests of states, societies, economies and, hence, to the prosperity and stability of the EU and its Member States will be paramount, pervasive and enduring for the foreseeable future. Threats and challenges are transnational both in terms of their origin and their direct and indirect impacts. Incidents involving the malicious use of information and communication technologies (ICTs) by states and non-state actors have increased in scope, scale, severity and sophistication. Prevention and threat mitigation are therefore imperative and need comprehensive approaches throughout the EU, its institutions and Member States, as well as beyond in the context of international cooperation, at least with the G7. Cybersecurity policies – and their absence – therefore have far-reaching consequences for the economy, for prosperity and security, as well as when it comes to safeguarding fundamental rights and democracy and, thus, to protecting and promoting the European way of life. In that context, the EU is emerging as a major cybersecurity player with comprehensive responsibilities for defending EU institutions and Member States against cyber incidents. Cybersecurity can thus be regarded as a 'vehicle' for the EU to position itself as a Security Union.

74 The chapter analyses the emerging EU law of cybersecurity while indicating its specificities, complexities and, in particular, the persistent lack of coordination in legislation and regulatory efforts that will, as a matter of urgency, have to be overcome. At the same time, however, it takes into account the fact that cybersecurity regulation is as complex and transboundary as its subject matter: It 'blurs traditional legal boundaries – between prevention and repression, between internal and external security, between law enforcement and technical security, between private law, criminal law and public law' (→ § 16 mn. 8 et seqq.).

75 Against that backdrop, the author first gives a brief overview of how regulation can address the cybersecurity problem before reconstructing the EU's regulatory response to that cybersecurity problem and pointing out its lack of coherence and the dangerous lacunae in its approach. The author comes to the conclusion that this field is still under-regulated, certainly not over-regulated, and discusses the pertinent underlying question of whether regulatory gaps are mainly the result of cybersecurity competences being divided between the EU and Member States. Based on that, proposals are made for a more stable and coherent regulatory framework shared between the EU and Member States.

76 *Hybrid threats as a challenge to the European Union and the Member States* as presented and discussed in § 17 (→ § 17 mn. 1–64) fall under the Security Union's strategic priority of 'tackling evolving threats'.[190] The broad notion of hybrid warfare

---

[189] European Commission, 'EU Security Strategy', 24.7.2020, COM(2020) 605 final.

[190] ibid., Chapter IV, No. 2; European Commission, 'Press Release: EU Security Union Strategy: connecting the dots in a new security ecosystem', 24.7.2020 <https://ec.europa.eu/commission/presscorner/detail/en/ip_20_1379> (last accessed: 30.9.2023); COM(2022) 745 final, 6–7.

has become familiar in NATO and EU parlance since Russia's invasion of Ukraine in 2014 without having yet become a widely shared and comprehensively operationalized concept across all the Member States. Ultimately, the underlying threat perception derives from a modernized version of the former Soviet concept of 'special measures', that is the concerted and targeted use of coercive means below the threshold of open war and under the cover of deniability. Hybrid warfare aims at weakening the political posture, internal coherence, security, stability and the military defences of an adversary by means of disinformation, subversion, sabotage, cyberattacks and paramilitary action that are organized in a covert way in order to avoid valid attribution for as long as possible. It is a prelude to open war as a final step to bringing down an already weakened adversary or a means of conflict management that is conducive to the desired outcome without the need to use open military force, given the legal, political, economic costs and escalatory risks. First steps in operationalizing or, more correctly, conceptualizing security in this sensitive and complex field to inform and sensitize political decision-makers were devised by the EU as early as 2015, with Foreign Affairs Council (FAC) conclusions inviting the Commission and EEAS to build a Hybrid Fusion Cell (HFC) as part of EU INTCEN that is a single focus of the analysis of hybrid threats.[191] By mid-2016, initial operational capability (IOC) was achieved, and the respective structures and networks within the EU and with the Member States were subject to constant, albeit slow, development, not least, again, due to a marked lack of funds and resolve on all sides despite a sequence of Council Conclusions to date.[192] As early as 2017, the newly formed NATO Joint Intelligence and Security Division (JISD) created a Hybrid Analysis Branch (HAB) that drew its initial inspiration from the EU HFC within the framework of EU–NATO Cooperation inaugurated by the EU–NATO joint declaration of 2016.[193] In 2017, the Hybrid Centre of Excellence (Hybrid CoE) was created by a number of European countries and the United States as an international, autonomous network-based organization promoting a whole-of-government and whole-of-society approach to countering hybrid threats.[194] Much of these bodies' activity, legal and political foundations, and status is covered in § 17 Tiilikaiden, once more emphasizing the major role and relevance of national legislation and administrative practice in security matters that can still only be complemented and coordinated but not overruled by EU supranational approaches.

Finally, *intelligence cooperation in the European Union* (→ § 18) contributes to 'building a strong security ecosystem' as do *'Integrated Border Management'* (→ § 19) and its inherent structures and procedures of *Digital Borders* (→ § 20). 77

Intelligence cooperation remains an issue of particular sensitivity given the prerogatives of national sovereignty underlined by Art. 4(2) TEU. Apart from the strictly legal dimensions as outlined and discussed in § 9 and § 10 of this book, the main challenge will be to create and improve legal frameworks and administrative formats that national governments and their services consider appropriate for intensified cooperation, coordination and possibly even control without encroaching too much on their freedom of discretion and decision. Progress on defence matters, which by definition are also a 78

[191] Joint Communication, 'Joint Framework on countering hybrid threats. A European Union response', 6.4.2016, JOIN/2016/018 final.

[192] EEAS, '2023 Annual Progress Report on the Implementation of the Strategic Compass for Security and Defence', March 2023, 10.

[193] European Council, 'EU-NATO joint declaration by the President of the European Council, Donald Tusk, the President of the European Commission, Jean-Claude Juncker, and the Secretary General of NATO, Jens Stoltenberg', 8.7.2016 <https://www.consilium.europa.eu/en/press/press-releases/2016/07/08/eu-nato-joint-declaration/> (last accessed: 30.9.2023).

[194] See Hybrid CoE's webpage <https://www.hybridcoe.fi/> (last accessed: 30.9.2023).

question of intergovernmental agreement and coordination, may provide blueprints or starting points for further integrative steps, including when it comes to organizing joint secret intelligence. A core prerequisite for meaningful intelligence cooperation will, however, be a framework that ensures sufficient levels of mutual trust among services. Trust is the result of properly shared (and not only declared) concrete interests, shared aims and common standards in relation to operational and security issues. The so-called Five Eyes is a role model for this type of integration, that is the community of US, British, Canadian, Australian and New Zealand intelligence services with a deeply rooted and long-standing common security identity and proven mutual trust that leads to common, highly sensitive collection efforts such as joint analysis, reporting and situational awareness. A similar degree of homogeneity in regard to specific vital aims, interests and procedures is difficult to expect or to create in a community of 27+ Member States. However, intelligence cooperation with quite a high degree of resolution, detail and trust takes place within specific operational, mainly military, environments in which everyone is aware of being 'in the same ditch'. Then, security is as common as it is existential for everyone under these circumstances, mutual trust in the narrower sense becomes vital, behavioural change not only becomes an option but a necessity, on the front lines as well as in the supporting structures at home. In terms of policies and legislation, such special environments might be defined and created by a select group of Member States that genuinely share quasi-identical interests and ambitions within the general framework of EU aims and values. Inspiration could be drawn from the Permanent Structured Cooperation (PESCO) process and possibly adjusted within the framework of Enhanced Cooperation (ENCO) under Art. 328 et seqq. TFEU.[195]

79 The chapters on *border management* (→ § 19) and digital borders (→ § 20) also touch on a core issue of the *third strategic priority of* the Security Union, that is protecting Europe from terrorism and organized crime. In the wake of the Taliban takeover in Afghanistan, the Counter-Terrorism Coordinator (CTC) came up with a Counter-Terrorism Action Plan that was meant to identify areas of action in which the EU and its Member States could prepare and mobilize instruments in a timely fashion to anticipate and address possible risks to EU internal security.[196] Among the most pertinent of the 24 actions that are mentioned, improved and extended checks on the biographical and biometric data of Afghan nationals arriving at the EU's external borders, in particular with regard to the Schengen Information System (SIS), Eurodac, Europol databases, the European Criminal Records Information System – Conviction Information on Third-Country Nationals (ECRIS-TCN), the Visa Information System (VIS), the Entry/Exit System (EES) , the European Travel Information and Authorisation System (ETIAS) and others, were prioritized.[197] This came together with the call to seriously address an all-too-often-overlooked deficiency in the Member States as well as in the EU agencies, namely the lack of sufficient linguistic and socio-cultural competence[198] that is a core prerequisite for the necessary level of data quality, which in turn is essential for the reliability and pertinence of all the aforementioned databases in their

---

[195] Art. 328 TFEU; See, in that context, Conrad in Meyer et al., Estimative Intelligence in European Foreign Policymaking, p. 220–247; Conrad, European Foreign Affairs Review 2021, 55–70; Conrad in Dietrich et al., Reform der Nachrichtendienste zwischen Vergesetzlichung und Internationalisierung, p. 161–177.

[196] EU Counter-Terrorism Coordinator, 'EU counter-terrorism action plan on Afghanistan', 29.9.2021, 12315/21; Conrad in CEP-Report, The Taliban's Takeover in Afghanistan – Effects on Global Terrorism, p. 85–92.

[197] See, in that regard, EPRS, 'The EU's external borders. Key trends and developments' (March 2023), PE 745.696.

[198] EPRS, 'The EU's external borders. Key trends and developments' (March 2023) PE 745.696, 90.

operational as well as their legal dimension. Incorrect and, hence, misleading data are a recipe for disaster in regard to all aspects of preventive and repressive security as well as in law enforcement. That also holds true for all the geographical, linguistic and socio-cultural dimensions of regular or irregular migration to the EU, and will pose an ever-greater challenge in the face of the surge in AI-supported fake data sets.

All these chapters provide ample problem awareness, analysis and proposals that **80** should contribute to providing professional insights and further operational administrative and legislative progress that are urgently needed to implement and operationalize the EU Security Union Strategy in an era of ever-increasing challenges and risks.

§ 16
Cybersecurity in the European multi-level governance system*

Thomas Wischmeyer

Bibliography: Aden, 'Europäische Rechtsgrundlagen und Institutionen des Polizeihandelns' in Lisken/Denninger (eds), Handbuch des Polizeirechts, 7th edn, Munich 2021, p. 1809; Banks, 'State Responsibility and Attribution of Cyber Intrusions After Tallinn 2.0', Texas Law Review 2017 (95:7), 1487; Bannelier/Christakis, Cyber-Attacks – Prevention-Reactions: The Role of States and Private Actors, Les Cahiers de la Revue Défense Nationale, Paris 2017; Bederna/Rajnai, 'Analysis of the cybersecurity ecosystem in the European Union', International Cybersecurity Law Review 2022 (3), 35; Bendiek/Maat, 'The EU's Cybersecurity Policy: Building a Resilient Regulatory Framework' in Siboni/Ezioni (eds), Cybersecurity and Legal-Regulatory Aspects, Singapore 2021, p. 23; Benkler, 'From Consumers to Users: Shifting the Deeper Structures of Regulation Toward Sustainable Commons and User Access', Federal Communications Law Journal 2000 (52:3), 561; Böse, 'Kompetenzen der Union auf dem Gebiet des Straf- und Strafverfahrensrechts' in Böse (ed.), Enzyklopädie Europarecht XI, 2nd edn, Baden-Baden 2021, p. 161; Calliess/Baumgarten, 'Cybersecurity in the EU The Example of the Financial Sector: A Legal Perspective', German Law Journal 2020 (21:6), 1149; Carrapico/Barrinha, 'The EU as a Coherent (Cyber)Security Actor?', JCMS 2017 (55:6), 1254; Cerf/Ryan/Senges, 'Internet Governance is our Shared Responsibility', I/S: A Journal of Law and Policy for the Information Society 2014 (10), 1; Chaudhary/Jordan/Salomone/Baxter, 'Patchwork of Confusion: The Cybersecurity Coordination Problem', Journal of Cybersecurity 2018 (4:1), 1; Christou, Cybersecurity in the European Union, London 2016; Dewar, 'The European Union and Cybersecurity' in O'Neill/Swinton (eds), Challenges and Critiques of the EU Internal Security Strategy: Rights, Power and Security, Newcastle upon Tyne 2017, p. 113; Dewar/Cavelty, 'Die Cybersicherheitspolitik der Europäischen Union' in Schüneman/Kneuer (eds), E-Government und Netzpolitik im europäischen Vergleich, 2nd edn, Baden-Baden 2019, p. 281; Cavelty, 'Europe's cyber-power', European Politics and Society 2018 (19:3), 304; Eichensehr, 'The Law and Politics of Cyberattack Attribution', UCLA Law Review 2020 (67:3), 520; Fahey, 'The EU's Cybercrime and Cyber-Security Rulemaking: Mapping the Internal and External Dimensions of EU Security', European Journal of Risk Regulation 2014 (5:1), 46; Finnemore/Hollis, 'Beyond Naming and Shaming', European Journal of International Law 2020 (31:3), 969; Fischer/Kipker/Voskamp, 'Internationaler Rahmen' in Kipker (ed.), Cybersecurity, Munich 2020, ch. 16; Gehring/Faude, 'The Dynamics of Regime Complexes: Microfoundations and Systemic Effects', Global Governance 2013 (19:1), 119; Goel, 'How Improved Attribution in Cyber Warfare Can Help De-Escalate Cyber Arms Race', Connections 2020 (19:1), 87; Gross/Canetti/Vashdi, 'Cyberterrorism: Its effects on psychological well-being, public confidence and political attitudes', Journal of Cybersecurity 2017 (3:1), 49; Hakimi, 'Introduction to the Symposium on Cyber Attribution', American Journal of International Law Unbound 2019 (113), 189; Kello, 'Cyber Defence' in Meijer/Wyss (eds), The Handbook of European Defence Policies and Armed Forces, Oxford 2018, p. 658; Keohane/Victor, 'Regime Complex for Climate Change', Perspectives on Politics 2011 (9:1), 7; Krämer, 'Europäische Sicherheitsarchitektur' in Brings-Wiesen/Ferreau (eds), 40 Jahre "Deutscher Herbst", Baden-Baden, 2019, p. 39; Lin, 'Attribution of Malicious Cyber Incidents: From Soup to Nuts', Columbia SIPA Journal of International Affairs 2016 (70:1), 75; Lindsay, 'Tipping the scales: the attributiton problem and the feasibility of deterrence against cyberattack', Journal of Cybersecurity 2015 (1:1), 53; Miadzvetskaya/Wessel, 'The Externalisation of the EU's Cybersecurity Regime: The Cyber Diplomacy Toolbox', European Papers 2022 (7:1), 413; Monroy, 'Cybersecurity-Initiativen als Teil einer Technologieoffensive', Vorgänge 2015 (209), 54; Mueller/Grindal/Kuerbis/Badiei, 'Cyber Attribution: Can a New Institution Achieve Transnational Credibility?', The Cyber Defense Review

* The presentation character of the paper has been preserved. The author would like to thank *Emilie Voth* for support in the preparation of the final manuscript. Parts of this chapter are based on Wischmeyer, Informationssicherheit, Tübingen 2023.

2019 (4:1), 107; Müller/Schwabenbauer, 'Unionsgrundrechte und Datenverarbeitung durch nationale Sicherheitsbehörden', NJW 2021, 2079; Odermatt, 'The European Union as a Cybersecurity Actor' in Blockmans/Koutrakos (eds), Research Handbook on the EU's Common Foreign and Security Policy, Cheltenham 2018, p. 354; Repasi, 'Das Recht des Raums der Freiheit, der Sicherheit und des Rechts' in Hatje/Müller-Graff (eds), Enzyklopädie Europarecht I, 2nd edn, Baden-Baden 2022, p. 469; Rid/Buchanan, 'Attributing Cyber Attacks', Journal of Strategic Studies 2015 (38: 1-2), 4; Romanosky, 'Examining the costs and causes of cyber incidents', Journal of Cybersecurity 2016 (2:2), 121; Sauer, 'Die Errichtung von Europäischen Agenturen', DÖV 2014, 549; Schober, Europäische Polizeizusammenarbeit zwischen TREVI und Prüm: Mehr Sicherheit auf Kosten von Freiheit und Recht?, Heidelberg 2017; Schöndorf-Haubold, 'Europäisches Polizei- und Sicherheitsrecht' in Terhechte (ed.), Verwaltungsrecht der Europäischen Union, 2nd edn, Baden-Baden, 2022, p. 1461; Schöndorf-Haubold, 'Europäisches Sicherheitsrecht' in Ehlers/Fehling/Pünder (eds), Besonderes Verwaltungsrecht III, 4th edn, Heidelberg 2021, p. 395; Schucht, 'Safety & Security bei smarten Produkten', NVwZ 2021, 532; Sliwinski, 'Moving beyond the European Union's Weakness as a Cyber-Security Agent', Contemporary Security Policy 2014 (35:3), 468; Solum/Chung, 'The Layers Principle: Internet Architecture and the Law', Notre Dame Law Review 2004 (79), 815; Steffens, Attribution of Advanced Persistent Threats: How to Identify the Actors Behind Cyber-Espionage, Berlin 2020; Taeger/Pohle (eds), Computerrechts-Handbuch, 36th edn, Munich 2021; Tsagourias, 'Cyber attacks, self-defence and the problem of attribution', Journal of Conflict and Security Law 2012 (17:2), 229; Tsagourias/Farrell, 'Cyber Attribution: Technical and Legal Approaches and Challenges', European Journal of International Law 2020, (31:3), 941; Wessel, 'European Law and Cyberspace' in Tsagourias/Buchan (eds), Research Handbook on International Law and Cyberspace, 2nd edn, Cheltenham 2021, p. 491; Wessel, 'Towards EU Cybersecurity Law: Regulating a New Policy Field' in Tsagourias/Buchan (eds), Research Handbook on International Law and Cyberspace, Cheltenham 2015, p. 403; Wiebe, 'IT-sicherheitsbezogene Pflichten von Herstellern smarter Produkte', InTeR 2021 (2), 66; von Wintzingerode/Müllmann/Spiecker gen. Döhmann, 'Ein Netzwerk für Europas Cybersicherheit', NVwZ 2021, 690; Wischmeyer, Informationssicherheit, Tübingen 2023.

A. Introduction

1 Contemporary societies depend on functioning networks and information systems. This dependency manifests itself in a constantly growing number of cyberattacks on government institutions, power utilities, telecommunications providers, hospitals, the military, media companies, etc.[1] It is not only systems and networks that process private data that are at risk: networked industrial robots, power plant turbines and pipelines are also relevant and oftentimes particularly vulnerable targets. The current situation is fragile[2] and individual perceptions of cyber-insecurity is high.[3] According to the United Nations Group of Governmental Experts on Advancing Responsible State Behaviour in Cyberspace in the Context of International Security, rapid improvement is not in sight:

[1] Continuous updates on the cybersecurity situation are provided by the European Network and Information Security Agency (ENISA) <https://www.enisa.europa.eu/topics/threat-risk-management/threats-and-trends> (last accessed: 27.9.2023), Europol <https://www.europol.europa.eu/iocta-report> (last accessed: 27.9.2023) and the German Federal Criminal Police Office <https://www.bka.de/DE/AktuelleInformationen/StatistikenLagebilder/Lagebilder/Cybercrime/cybercrime_node.html> (last accessed: 27.9.2023).

[2] Romanosky, Journal of Cybersecurity 2016, 121; Cybersecurity and Infrastructure Security Agency, 'Cost of a Cyber Incident: Systematic Review and Cross-Validation', 2020.

[3] On the individual perceptions of cybersecurity risks, see the European Commission's Digital Economy and Society Index (DESI) – Panel Cybersecurity <https://ec.europa.eu/newsroom/dae/document.cfm?doc_id=67080> (last accessed: 27.9.2023) and <https://digital-agenda-data.eu/datasets/digital_agenda_scoreboard_key_indicators/indicators#security-and-privacy> (last accessed: 27.9.2023). See also Gross/Canetti/Vashdi Journal of Cybersecurity 2017 (3:1), 49.

> While ICTs [information and communication technologies] and an increasingly digitalized and connected world provide immense opportunities for societies across the globe, the Group reaffirms that the serious ICT threats identified in previous reports persist. Incidents involving the malicious use of ICTs by States and non-State actors have increased in scope, scale, severity and sophistication. While ICT threats manifest themselves differently across regions, their effects can also be global.[4]

In this context, cybersecurity policy matters not only in economic terms, but also affects how fundamental rights and democracy will be protected in the digital age. Consequently, cybersecurity features prominently in the security strategies of governments across the globe.[5] From a legal point of view, this development has two major ramifications. First, we can observe a turn from self-regulation to hard law. Many states no longer trust in market forces alone to solve the cybersecurity problem. Rather, regulators actively engage in the field of cybersecurity.[6] Second, with a growing awareness of the global implications of the matter, states are stepping up regional and international cooperation. The European Union in particular is emerging as a major cybersecurity player and claims comprehensive responsibilities as regards defending EU institutions and Member States against cyber incidents. Like other fields discussed in this book, cybersecurity has become a vehicle for the EU to reinvent itself as a Security Union, which has major implications for the vertical division of power between the Union and its Member States.[7] 2

This chapter analyses emerging EU law on cybersecurity. However, the development outlined in the above should not be understood as a teleological process, nor is the emerging law of cybersecurity a well-structured field. Current regulatory activities on the national, the international and the EU level are as numerous as they are poorly coordinated. They do not follow a 'system' or a set of overarching principles, but form a highly complicated 'regime complex'.[8] 3

---

[4] United Nations General Assembly, 'Group of Governmental Experts on Advancing Responsible State Behaviour in Cyberspace in the Context of International Security', 14.7.2021, A/76/135, mn. 6.

[5] See White House, 'Renewing America's Advantages', 2021, 18; European Commission, 'EU Security Union Strategy', 24.7.2020, COM(2020) 605 final, 1. As regards Germany, see Federal Ministry of the Interior, 'Cybersicherheitsstrategie für Deutschland', 2021; Federal Ministry of the Interior, 'Cybersicherheitsagenda', 2022.

[6] Germany's 1990 Act on the Establishment of the Federal Office for Information Security (*BSI-Errichtungsgesetz*, BSIG) (BGBl. I, p. 2834) was updated in 2009 (Federal Office for Information Security Act (*BSI-Gesetz*) of 14.8.2009 (BGBl. I, p. 2821)), in 2015 (IT Security Act (*Gesetz zur Erhöhung der Sicherheit informationstechnischer Systeme*, IT-Sicherheitsgesetz) of 17.7.2015 (BGBl. I, p. 1324)) and in 2021 (IT Security Act 2.0 (*Zweites Gesetz zur Erhöhung der Sicherheit informationstechnischer Systeme*, IT-SiG 2.0) of 18.5.2021 (BGBl. I, p. 1122)). The German *Länder* have started to enact cybersecurity legislation as well. For an overview of the regulatory activities in various countries across the globe, see <https://css.ethz.ch/en/publications/risk-and-resilience-reports> (last accessed: 27.9.2023).

[7] On the growing role of the EU in this field, see also Fahey, European Journal of Risk Regulation 2014, 46; Sliwinski, Contemporary Security Policy 2014, 468; Wessel in Tsagourias/Buchan, Research Handbook on International Law and Cyberspace, p. 403; Christou, p. 1 et seqq.; Dewar in O'Neill/Swinton, Challenges and Critiques of the EU Internal Security Strategy, p. 113; Carrapico/Barrinha, JCMS 2017, 1254; Kello, in Meijer/Wyss, The Handbook of European Defence Policies and Armed Forces, p. 658; Odermatt in Blockmans/Koutrakos, Research Handbook on the EU's Common Foreign and Security Policy, p. 354; Dunn Cavelty, European Politics and Society 2018, 304; Bendiek/Maat SWP Working Paper 2019; Dewar/Dunn Cavelty in Schüneman/Kneuer, E-Government und Netzpolitik im europäischen Vergleich, p. 281; European Court of Auditors, 'Challenges to effective EU Cybersecurity Policy' (March 2019); Calliess/Baumgarten, German Law Journal 2020, 1149; Bendiek/Pander Maat in Siboni/Ezioni, Cybersecurity and Legal-Regulatory Aspects, p. 23; Wessel in Tsagourias/Buchan, Research Handbook on International Law and Cyberspace, p. 491; Bederna/Rajnai, International Cybersecurity Law Review 2022, 35; Miadzvetskaya/Wessel, European Papers 2022, 413; European Court of Auditors, 'Cybersecurity of EU institutions, bodies and agencies, Special report', May 2022.

[8] On this concept, see Keohane/Victor, Perspectives on Politics 201, 7 and Gehring/Faude, Global Governance 2013, 119.

4 This is to some degree inevitable, because cybersecurity regulation blurs traditional legal boundaries – between prevention and repression, between internal and external security, between law enforcement and technical security, between private law, criminal law and public law. The reasons for this are complex and cannot be discussed here in detail.[9] However, the difficulties regulators face can be quickly understood by considering how different the main authors of cyber-insecurity and their respective goals are: states and their 'proxies' engaging in cyberwarfare; terrorist or criminal groups seeking to further their respective ends; companies pursuing industrial espionage; or individual hackers driven by all kinds of motives.[10] The victims of such attacks are equally diverse: state actors, companies from all sectors and – as collateral damage, or as direct targets – individuals. This creates a spectrum of risks that does not fit into the conventional categories of security law.

5 Things are complicated even more by the fact that in many cases the origins of cyber risks cannot be clearly attributed. The lack of robust identity verification mechanisms on the internet, the complexity and rapid development of the technology involved and the limited resources of victims and investigators often enable attackers to effectively conceal their actions and attack routes. This so-called problem of attribution has received a lot of scholarly attention.[11] For regulators, the problem of attribution makes it necessary to shift the focus from the perpetrators to the potential victims of cyberattacks, i.e. the manufacturers or operators of IT products or services that are then mandated to take appropriate defensive measures. While holding the potential victims of cyberattacks accountable is clearly the second-best solution from a normative point of view, it is oftentimes inevitable under the given circumstances.

6 The EU and its Member States have responded to the situation with a proliferation of cybersecurity laws and agencies. The legal instruments used and the organizational and procedural forms employed to this end are highly diverse, as is the group of actors addressed by law, ranging from the operators of so-called critical infrastructures to manufacturers of IT products and government agencies. Horizontal regulations are complemented by sectoral regulations. The realm of cybersecurity rules is further extended and supplemented by private agreements and technical standards, which oftentimes have a *de facto* binding effect.

7 To analyse and clarify the basic structures of this regulatory 'patchwork of confusion',[12] this chapter approaches the matter as follows: First, a brief overview is provided of how regulation can address the cybersecurity problem (B.). In a second step, the EU's regulatory response to the cybersecurity problem is reconstructed. As will be shown, the existing rules and regulations cover only specific risks, such as the protection of IT systems or the security of IT components, and focus either on prevention or detection or response, while, from a technical perspective, the information security cycle comprises all these phases and requires an integrated approach (→ mn. 25).[13] Besides, some

[9] For a comprehensive analysis, see Wischmeyer, p.1 et seqq.

[10] See Bannelier/Christakis, p. 11.

[11] On the technical background, see Lin, Columbia SIPA Journal of International Affairs 2016, 75; Steffens. On the political and legal implication of the problem of attribution, see Rid/Buchanan, Journal of Strategic Studies 2015, 4; Lindsay, Journal of Cybersecurity 2015, 53; Mueller et al., The Cyber Defense Review 2019, 107; Goel, Connections 2020, 87; Banks, Texas Law Review 2017, 1487; Tsagourias, Journal of conflict and security law 2012, 229; Eichensehr, UCLA Law Review 2020, 520; Finnemore/Hollis, European Journal of International Law 2020, 969; Tsagourias/Farrell, European Journal of International Law 2020, 941. See also the 'Symposium on Cyber Attribution' with introductory remarks by Hakimi, American Journal of International Law Unbound 2019, 189.

[12] Chaudhary et al., Journal of Cybersecurity 2018, 1.

[13] German Federal Government, 'Cyber-Sicherheitsstrategie für Deutschland' 2016, 8 et seq.

types of cybersecurity risk have not been addressed at all by regulators. Overall, therefore, the field is still under-regulated, not over-regulated. This then raises the question of whether the regulatory gaps are due to the fact that competences for cybersecurity are divided between the EU and Member States (C.). The final part of this chapter briefly outlines how the EU and Member States should approach cybersecurity regulation in future in order to develop a more stable and coherent regulatory framework (D.).

B. The cybersecurity problem – and how regulation can fix it

Considering the complexity and heterogeneity of the cybersecurity problem, there is no quick regulatory fix. This raises the question of how cybersecurity can be improved through regulation. In the light of the problem of attribution, this section focuses on ways in which regulation contributes to increasing the resilience of IT systems under attack. Regulations that primarily aim to hold the attackers responsible (e.g. rules on cybercrime or on state responsibility) will not be addressed. **8**

I. From the ends of cybersecurity…

Understanding how regulation can bolster cybersecurity presupposes some working knowledge of what cybersecurity means. A definition can be found in Art. 6(2) NIS 2 Directive,[14] which describes the 'security of network and information systems' as 'the ability of network and information systems to resist, at a given level of confidence, any event that may compromise the availability, authenticity, integrity or confidentiality of stored, transmitted or processed data or of the services offered by, or accessible via, those network and information systems'. This definition mirrors the language of technical standards on information security such as in ISO/IEC 27000:2018. In these standards we find explanations for the different elements of the term. According to ISO/IEC 27000:2018, the 'availability' of a system is ensured if there are no unplanned system failures and if access to its data is possible for authorized users in a reasonable time. 'Authenticity' means that the data processed by a system originates from the specified sources, which presupposes trust in the communication pathways and thus in the established authentication measures. The 'integrity' of data is violated if the data can be or has been changed without authorization, while the integrity of an IT system requires that the system behaves in a logically correct manner. Finally, the 'confidentiality' objective is not met if the rules for authorized access to a system, for the disclosure of information or for communication between IT systems can be violated. **9**

All these definitions are, strictly speaking, technical objectives. They do not in themselves contain any indication of how these objectives are to be achieved., i.e. what (regulatory) means can be employed to make the digital sphere more secure. **10**

[14] Directive (EU) 2022/2555 on measures for a high common level of cybersecurity across the Union (NIS 2 Directive).

II. To the means: three layers of cybersecurity regulation

11 To determine how regulation can contribute to containing the cybersecurity problem, we therefore need to take a closer look at the technical foundations of cybersecurity. The technical structures are obviously highly complex and can be described here only in their most basic terms. To reduce complexity, it is helpful to distinguish between three layers of the cybersecurity problem that each provide distinct pathways for regulation.[15]

12 The first layer is system and network protection. Systems and networks can have numerous different types of vulnerabilities that depend on their respective technical structures and generally increase the more complex they get.[16] Possible attack vectors range from targeted hacks and mass malware distribution to distributed denial of service (DDoS) attacks and social engineering. As the identity, location and motivation of attackers often remain unknown (the above-mentioned problem of attribution), primary responsibility for system and network security lies with the operators, who regularly have (or should have) a high level of self-interest in keeping their system safe and secure. From a regulatory perspective, this means that those operators can and should be approached to take the appropriate defensive measures. This is the traditional approach to cybersecurity regulation and is still reflected in the naming of the 'Network and Information Systems' (NIS) Directives.

13 Second, software and hardware security must be ensured. Every networked system depends on an ecosystem of third-party vendors, including the manufacturers of network and system components. With components, too, complexity is a major risk factor and increases their vulnerability.[17] Here, the manufacturers of the respective components are best placed to invest in the security of their products. At least when it comes to commercially marketed software and hardware components a market has been established in rudimentary form in which security is considered as a quality feature. Where this is not the case, regulators can step in and require manufacturers to adhere to specific technical standards, for example on fault detection and prevention. However, the challenge is huge, because component development involves a high degree of division of labour. In many cases, component manufacturers themselves 'rely on one or more third-party technologies and components such as software modules, libraries or application programming interfaces.'[18] As is well-known, supply chain regulation is

---

[15] As regards the key distinction between the 'physical infrastructure layer', the 'logical layer' and the 'content layer' as a framework for analyzing and guiding internet regulation, see Benkler, Federal Communications Law Journal 2000, 561; Solum/Chung, Notre Dame Law Review 2004, 815; Cerf/Ryan/Senges, I/S 2014, 1. For a different approach that attempts to structure the regulatory space using the categories 'device', 'network', 'system', 'data', 'applications' and 'user', see van der Wees/Dreo/Schmitt, 'Work Package 4: Policy and the European Dimension Deliverable D4.2' <https://www.concordia-h2020.eu/wp-content/uploads/2021/03/Deliverables_D4.4-M24.pdf> (last accessed: 29.9.2023), p. 23.

[16] 'Vulnerability' is defined in Art. 6(15) NIS 2 Directive as a 'weakness, susceptibility or flaw of ICT products or ICT services that can be exploited by a cyber threat'. Similarly, Internet Engineering Task Force, 'Internet Security Glossary RFC 2828', May 2000 <https://datatracker.ietf.org/doc/html/rfc2828> (last accessed: 29.9.2023): 'A flaw or weakness in a system's design, implementation, or operation and management that could be exploited to violate the system's security policy.'

[17] The Common Weakness Enumeration System (CWE) provides a standardized classification of known vulnerabilities <http://cwe.mitre.org/about/index.html> (last accessed: 29.9.2023). Concrete vulnerabilities are classified according to the Common Vulnerabilities and Exposures System (CVE) <https://www.cve.org> (last accessed: 29.9.2023). The severity of vulnerabilities can be determined according to the Common Vulnerability Scoring System (CVSS) <https://www.first.org/cvss/> (last accessed: 29.9.2023).

[18] See Recital 11 Cybersecurity Act.

particularly challenging, not least because market participants are oftentimes not sufficiently aware of the existence and extent of third-party cyber risks.

Finally, the framework for the exchange of information between networks must be secured, i.e. the internet as the 'network of networks'. The internet is not only vulnerable itself: the weaknesses of its architecture can also be used to attack all the systems connected to it. Internet-specific risks are those that exploit the vulnerabilities of the infrastructures, components, protocols or services required for communication via the internet. The complexity of internet technology creates a spectrum of risks that requires equally complex defence mechanisms. One of the distinguishing features of the internet compared to other networks is that it is not managed centrally, thus security cannot be implemented top-down. The operators of internet infrastructure components can thus only be held responsible for the security of their respective operations. Those vulnerabilities arising from the design of key internet protocols, including the Internet Protocol (IP), the Border Gateway Protocol (BGP) and the Domain Name System Protocol (DNS Protocol), are particularly problematic.[19] All these protocols ensure uniquely efficient communication, but – at least in their original versions – did not establish robust security mechanisms. The protocols are defined in technical standards known as Request for Comments (RFCs), which are developed by the Internet Engineering Task Force (IETF) and then subjected to a multi-stakeholder approval process by the Internet Engineering Steering Group (IESG). The IETF recently amended several key protocols in order to close security gaps. However, these new protocol versions are neither universally implemented – in some cases, their implementation would require a profound change in internet usage habits – nor do they fully eliminate the existing vulnerabilities. **14**

The three layers cannot and must not be considered in isolation. Rather, cybersecurity regulation must take a cross-layer perspective. After all, cyberattacks frequently make use of 'interactions' between the layers. For example, social engineering can be used to induce the user of an IT system to install an initial, inconspicuous malware, such as a keylogger. Alternatively, this result can be achieved by manipulating a DNS server, thus enabling a drive-by infection. The knowledge gained during the first attack can then be used to gain access to the targeted IT system and its network and to upload additional malware by exploiting further network security or software vulnerabilities. **15**

C. The European Union's response to the cybersecurity problem

The first major step the EU took in the field of cybersecurity regulation was to enact Regulation (EC) No 460/2004 establishing the European Network and Information Security Agency (ENISA).[20] It then took almost 12 years for the Union to take up the issue again. Since 2016, however, things have moved quickly. This section starts with an overview of important EU legal acts in the field of cybersecurity, again with a focus on regulations that attempt to increase the resilience of IT systems. Then **16**

---

[19] For a comprehensive analysis, see Wischmeyer, p. 198 et seqq.

[20] The agency began operations in September 2005 as the European Network and Information Security Agency. Since 2019, ENISA has operated under the name European Union Agency for Cybersecurity while retaining the old acronym.

the question of whether the prolific activities of the EU legislator address the cybersecurity problem in a comprehensive and coherent way will be analysed. This section concludes with a brief analysis of whether the limited competences conferred upon the Union by the Member States in the treaties prevent the EU from moving beyond the status quo.

I. EU cybersecurity regulation – an overview

17 The number of relevant EU laws on cybersecurity has grown to such an extent that this chapter will have to limit itself to listing the most important acts and leave detailed analysis to the specialized literature. In this respect, the following horizontal regulations are of particular significance:

- Regulation (EU) No 910/2014 on electronic identification and trust services for electronic transactions in the internal market (eIDAS);
- Directive (EU) 2016/1148 concerning measures for a high common level of security of network and information systems across the Union (NIS Directive);
- Regulation (EU) 2016/679 on the protection of natural persons with regard to the processing of personal data and on the free movement of such data (GDPR);
- Regulation (EU) 2019/881 on ENISA and on information and communications technology cybersecurity certification and repealing Regulation (EU) No 526/2013 (Cybersecurity Act) (European Cyber Security Act);
- Directive (EU) 2019/770 on certain aspects concerning contracts for the supply of digital content and digital services;
- Regulation (EU) 2021/887 establishing the European Cybersecurity Industrial, Technology and Research Competence Centre and the Network of National Coordination Centres;
- Directive (EU) 2022/2555 on measures for a high common level of cybersecurity across the Union (NIS 2 Directive).

18 The requirements defined in these horizontal legal acts are further concretized or supplemented by numerous other legal acts relating to specific sectors or entities. They include the following:

- Regulation (EU) 2017/745 on medical devices;
- Commission Delegated Regulation (EU) 2022/30 supplementing Directive 2014/53/EU with regard to the application of the essential requirements referred to in Art. 3 (3)(d), (e) and (f) of that Directive;
- Regulation (EU) 2022/2554 on digital operational resilience for the financial sector;
- Directive (EU) 2022/2557 on the resilience of critical entities.

19 Regulatory developments are by no means at an end. Rather, numerous regulations with cybersecurity implications are currently at various stages of the legislative process, including the following:

- Proposal for a Regulation of the European Parliament and of the Council on horizontal cybersecurity requirements for products with digital elements and amending Regulation (EU) 2019/1020 (Cyber Resilience Act),[21] which will create a horizontal regulation for networked products;

[21] European Commission, 'Proposal for a Regulation on horizontal cybersecurity requirements for products with digital elements and amending Regulation (EU) 2019/1020', 15.9.2022, COM(2022) 454 final.

- Proposal for a Regulation of the European Parliament and of the Council on general product safety;[22]
- Proposal for a Regulation of the European Parliament and of the Council on machinery products;[23]
- Proposal for a Regulation of the European Parliament and of the Council laying down harmonised rules on artificial intelligence (Artificial Intelligence Act) and amending certain union legislative acts,[24] which addresses AI-specific cybersecurity risks such as adversarial examples;
- Proposal for a Regulation of the European Parliament and of the Council establishing a framework of measures for strengthening Europe's semiconductor ecosystem (Chips Act),[25] which contains rules for auditing the design and manufacturing processes of security-relevant hardware;
- 'Network Code' for cybersecurity aspects of cross-border electricity flows under the EU Electricity Regulation and Council Recommendation to improve the resilience of critical infrastructures;[26]
- Joint Communication on an EU Cyber Defence policy and an Action Plan on Military Mobility 2.0.[27]

II. Inconsistencies and gaps in EU cybersecurity regulation

The regulatory programme that the EU has implemented to bolster cybersecurity is extremely ambitious. Nevertheless, the question remains whether the programme meets the regulatory challenge. As already mentioned, the cybersecurity problem necessitates a comprehensive regulatory approach that uses a broad arsenal of instruments to prevent damage both to IT systems and by IT systems and that integrates system, component and internet security. However, current EU regulations far too often follow a piecemeal approach and are not sufficiently integrated. This will be shown here based on three examples. 20

First, Art. 32 GDPR, a key provision of data protection law, requires the controllers and processors of personal data to take into account 'the state of the art, the costs of implementation and the nature, scope, context and purposes of processing as well as the risk of varying likelihood and severity for the rights and freedoms of natural persons' and to 'implement appropriate technical and organisational measures to ensure a level of security appropriate to the risk, including inter alia as appropriate: (a) the pseudonymisation and encryption of personal data; (b) the ability to ensure the ongoing confidentiality, integrity, availability and resilience of processing systems and services; (c) the ability to restore the availability and access to personal data in a timely manner in the event of a physical or technical incident; (d) a process for regularly 21

[22] European Commission, 'Proposal for a Regulation on general product safety', 30.6.2021, COM(2021) 346 final.

[23] European Commission, 'Proposal for a regulation on machinery products', 21.4.2021, COM(2021) 202 final.

[24] European Commission, 'Proposal for a regulation laying down harmonised rules on artificial intelligence (Artificial Intelligence Act)', 21.4.2021, COM(2021) 206 final.

[25] European Commission, 'Proposal for a regulation establishing a framework of measures for strengthening Europe's semiconductor ecosystem (Chips Act)', 8.2.2022, COM(2022) 46 final.

[26] European Commission, 'Digitalising the energy system – EU action plan', 18.10.2022, COM(2022) 552 final.

[27] Joint Communication from the Commission and the High Representative, 'EU Policy on Cyber Defence', 10.10.2022, JOIN(2022) 49 final.

testing, assessing and evaluating the effectiveness of technical and organisational measures for ensuring the security of the processing.' All these measures are obviously important and to the point. A closer look, however, reveals that the provision addresses only the network and system layer of the cybersecurity problem while ignoring the fact that the system operators held responsible are dependent on having secure software and hardware if they want to build secure systems. While the security-by-design principle in Art. 5(1)(f) and Art. 25(1) GDPR controls the controllers' and processors' procurement decisions, the provisions offer little help if sufficiently secure components are not available on the market.

22 Second, the EU legislator has now taken a somewhat broader approach to critical infrastructure regulation. Art. 21(2)(d) and (3) of the new NIS 2 Directive emphasizes the importance of component security and, according to Art. 7(2)(a) and Art. 22 NIS 2 Directive, this aspect must be anchored in the national cybersecurity strategies and supported by the Cooperation Group through risk assessments. Moreover, the EU Cybersecurity Act (CSA), enacted in 2019, directly addresses this issue. Other recent or proposed regulations also attempt to fill this gap and strive to create a more ambitious regime for component security.

23 But while the EU is thus slowly moving towards a more comprehensive regulatory regime, concrete implementation still suffers from inconsistencies. This is demonstrated by the proliferation of cybersecurity certification regimes. The relationship between the CSA and Art. 42 GDPR is unclear. Recital 74 CSA simply refers to the GDPR's certification system and states that this is to remain 'unaffected' by the provisions of the CSA. Similar questions are then raised with regard to the certification programmes established by EU Member States, including Germany.[28] Equally unclear is the question of how the CSA relates to EU product safety law, which originally 'invented' the mechanisms that the CSA is now trying to apply to IT components. So far, the two regimes and their conformity tests do not overlap.[29] However, as part of the regular revision of several sectoral product safety directives, discussions are currently underway as to whether these acts should be expanded to include cybersecurity aspects. For consumers, the large number of competing certification regimes reduces rather than strengthens market transparency. And, for industry, the fragmentation of certification requirements goes along with considerable costs. Therefore, close coordination or even consolidation of the certification regimes is necessary. The question of whether this should be done by integrating the CSA into the New Legislative Framework or by means of a new horizontal legal act on cybersecurity based on the New Legislative Framework will be left open here.[30]

24 Third, and finally, while information security lawmakers have at least begun to address the risks of IT components, internet security is still largely *terra incognita* in regulatory terms. This concerns the risks to the security and stability of the internet itself, for example through BGP highjacking, as well as to those risks that exploit the vulnerabilities of the internet architecture to attack IT systems and networks connected to the internet. In 2020, the issue at least reached the political arena and the Commission announced in its European Cybersecurity Strategy that it would develop plans for dealing with a global DNS routing failure and also intended to participate in

---

[28] See Wischmeyer, p. 262–265.

[29] Schucht, NVwZ 2021, 532; Wiebe, InTeR 2021, 66. For a comparison, see European Commission, 'Report on the safety and liability implications of Artificial Intelligence, the Internet of Things and robotics', 19.2.2020, COM(2020) 64, 7.

[30] Council of the European Union, 'Conclusions on the cybersecurity of connected devices', 2.12.2020, 13629/20.

the development and dissemination of secure internet standards.[31] Additionally, the NIS 2 Directive obliges the operators of central internet infrastructure services, in particular providers of DNS services and Top Level Domain (TLD) registries, to prevent the DNS system being taken over or compromised by imposing due diligence obligations (Art. 3(1)(b), Art. 26(3) and Art. 27(2) NIS 2 Directive).[32] However, these are only very first steps towards a comprehensive internet security regime.

III. The EU Treaties as an obstacle to comprehensive and coherent cybersecurity regulation?

While the Union has established itself as a regulatory pacemaker, in particular in 25 terms of critical infrastructure cybersecurity and IT product certification, the question remains as to how far the EU's powers go and whether they allow the Union to expand and consolidate its regulatory activities in the field of cybersecurity. This raises the question of how the EU treaties distribute competences between the Union and its Member States and whether this is an obstacle to comprehensive and coherent cybersecurity regulation.

Despite its great practical importance, and unlike in the case of data protection, EU 26 primary law does not contain an explicit competence when it comes to cybersecurity. The search for a legal basis for EU activities in the field of cybersecurity is further complicated by the fact that, as already mentioned, the matter is difficult to fit into the traditional categories of security law (→ mn. 4).[33] However, as far as the cyber-resilience of systems and networks or components is concerned, internal market competence allows the EU to establish a uniform level of protection as far as IT security is concerned.[34] Consequently, the EU has based most of the above-mentioned legal acts, including the NIS Directives, the CSA and the eIDAS Regulation, on Art. 114(1) TFEU.[35] The fact that the threat to information security may come from the Member

[31] European Commission, 'The EU's Cybersecurity Strategy for the Digital Decade', 16.12.2020, JOIN (2020) 18 final, 10 et seq.: 'The Commission will also, in liaison with Member States and industry, accelerate the uptake of key internet standards including IPv6 and well-established internet security standards and good practices for DNS, routing, and email security, not excluding regulatory measures like a European sunset clause for IPv4 to steer the market if there is insufficient progress towards their adoption.'

[32] See Recital 32 NIS 2 Directive: 'Upholding and preserving a reliable, resilient and secure domain name system (DNS) are key factors in maintaining the integrity of the internet and are essential for its continuous and stable operation, on which the digital economy and society depend. Therefore, this Directive should apply to top-level domain (TLD) name registries, and DNS service providers that are to be understood as entities providing publicly available recursive domain name resolution services for internet end-users or authoritative domain name resolution services for third-party usage. This Directive should not apply to root name servers.'

[33] For an overview of EU competences in the field of internal security, see Aden in Lisken/Denninger, Handbuch des Polizeirechts, M (p. 98 et seq.); Schöndorf-Haubold in Terhechte, Verwaltungsrecht der Europäischen Union, § 35 mn. 52 et seq.

[34] ECJ 2.5.2006 – case C-217/04, ECLI:EU:C:2006:279 para. 48 et seqq. – *United Kingdom v Parliament and Council*. Cybercrime regulation, which is not discussed here, is based on Art. 83(1) TFEU, see Böse in Böse, Enzyklopädie Europarecht XI, p. 164 et seq.

[35] In Germany, the IT Security Act of 17.7.2015 (BGBl. I, p. 1324), the first federal cybersecurity law, was originally based on 'annex competences' to specific competence titles such as 'telecommunication' or 'energy'. Therefore, only those sectors for which the Basic Law (*Grundgesetz*, GG) granted the Federal Government legislative competences were classified as 'critical' and thus subject to the new rules on cybersecurity. However, the more the Federal Government's approach changed from sectoral regulation addressing a relatively small number of critical infrastructure providers towards horizontal, risk-based regulation, the more plausible it became to use the very broad Art. 74 (1) no. 11 of the Basic Law, which grants the Federation concurrent legislative powers regarding 'the law relating to economic matters' as the

States themselves, as in the case of data retention, does not preclude recourse to Art. 114.[36] Art. 114(1) TFEU also provides the legal basis for most of the EU's administrative agencies dealing with cybersecurity, in particular ENISA.[37] In addition to Art. 114, other provisions in the treaties can be invoked to provide legitimacy to EU cybersecurity regulation. Of particular importance is Art. 16(2) TFEU, that is where the security of personal data is concerned.[38] And Art. 173(3) TFEU grants the EU the power to contribute to strengthening research and development in the field of information security, for instance through the European Cybersecurity Competence Centre (ECCC).[39]

27 As regards cyber-resilience, the EU thus has very broad competences when it comes to regulating private activities and obliging Member States to create and institutionalize administrative structures in the field of cybersecurity. The question remains whether the EU is allowed to integrate Member States' security agencies, namely police and intelligence services, into its governance framework, both as the potential addressees of and as the agencies enforcing EU cybersecurity norms.[40] This also depends on Art. 4(2) TEU, which limits EU activities if Member States' 'essential State functions, including ensuring the territorial integrity of the State, maintaining law and order and safeguarding national security' are affected and which is considered in detail in other chapters in this book (→ § 8) Here, it suffices to say that the Court of Justice of the European Union (CJEU) has in the past interpreted the clause rather narrowly and not precluded the EU from acting, even if this has an impact on the activities of Member States' security or intelligence services.[41] Moreover, the treaties explicitly allow the EU to support security agencies in the Member States and to ensure cross-border coordination (see Art. 67 and 74 TFEU (→ § 13). On this basis, the EU has developed extensive legislative activities in the area of information cooperation between Member States' security authorities, which extend to the field of cybersecurity.[42] The same is true of the EU agencies that are active in the Area of Freedom,

legal basis for cybersecurity regulation. See the Explanatory Memorandum to the IG Security Act 2.0 of 18.5.2021 (BGBl., p. 1122): German Bundestag, 'Gesetzesentwurf der Bundesregierung zum IT-SiG 2.0', 25.01.2021, BT-Drs. 19/26106, 31 et seq.

[36] See ECJ 10.2.2009 – case C-301/06, ECLI:EU:C:2009:68 – *Ireland v European Parliament.*

[37] See ECJ 2.5.2006 – case C-217/04, ECLI:EU:C:2006:279 para. 42 et seq. – *United Kingdom v Parliament and Council,* as regards how far ex-Art. 95 of the Treaty Establishing the European Community (TEC) (now Art. 114 TFEU) covers the establishment of agencies under EU law. See also Sauer, DÖV 2014, 549. Whether Art. 114 TFEU allows the transfer of operational powers to ENISA is discussed by Fischer/Kipker/Voskamp in Kipker, Cybersecurity, ch. 16 (11 et seq.), with a specific focus on Art. 7 of the CSA.

[38] As regards other relevant provisions in EU primary law such as Art. 170 TFEU, see Deusch/Eggenhofer in Taegar/Pohle, Computerrechts-Handbuch, 50.1 mn. 249 et seq.

[39] On Regulation (EU) 2021/887, see von Wintzingerode/Müllmann/Spiecker gen. Döhmann, NVwZ 2021, 690 et seq.

[40] The Directorates-General in the Commission that are mainly responsible for cybersecurity-related issues are Communications Networks, Content and Technology (Connect) and Migration and Home Affairs (HOME), depending on whether the Digital Single Market or the Security Union is concerned.

[41] ECJ 21.12.2016 – case C-203/15, ECLI:EU:C:2016:970 para. 75 et seq. – *Tele2 Sverige AB v Post- och telestyrelsen*; ECJ 2.10.2018 – case C-207/16, ECLI:EU:C:2018:788 para. 29 et seq. – *Ministerio Fiscal*; ECJ 6.10.2020 – case C-623/17, ECLI:EU:C:2020:790 para. 44 et seqq. – *Privacy International v Secretary of State for Foreign and Commonwealth Affairs et al.*; ECJ 6.10.2020 – case C-511/18, ECLI:EU:C:2020:791 para. 99 et seqq. – *La Quadrature et al. v Premier ministre et al.* For a critical perspective, see Müller/Schwabenbauer, NJW 2021, 2079 (2080 et seq.).

[42] See Schober, p. 1 et seqq.; Krämer in Brings-Wiesen/Ferreau, 40 Jahre "Deutscher Herbst", p. 39; Aden in Lisken/Denninger, Handbuch des Polizeirechts, ch. M.; Schöndorf-Haubold in Ehlers/Fehling/Pünder, Besonderes Verwaltungsrecht III, mn. 68; Schöndorf-Haubold in Terhechte, Verwaltungsrecht der Europäischen Union, § 35; Repasi in Hatje/Müller-Graff, Enzyklopädie Europarecht I, p. 469.

Security and Justice (AFSJ), including Europol, Eurojust and eu-LISA, and that currently perform various cooperative or coordinative functions, ranging from cybersecurity research funding to military cooperation.[43] The fact that the agencies do not have the power to directly intervene or implement coercive measures simply reflects the fact that EU agencies can only be authorized to engage in 'operational actions' under specific circumstances (see Art. 88(3) TFEU as regards Europol).[44] Thus, supranational agencies typically only exercise sovereign powers in close cooperation with and subject to the consent of national authorities.

All in all, however, there can be no question of the treaties unduly limiting the Union's competences. A more coherent cybersecurity regulation is thus not dependent on a fundamental overhaul of the treaties, but can be achieved within the existing constitutional framework. **28**

D. Outlook: towards an effective multi-level cybersecurity governance system

Based on the above, I would like to conclude with four very brief remarks on the future of EU cybersecurity regulation and its interplay with the activities of the Member States. **29**

First, cybersecurity is not a clearly defined task, but one dimension of the digital transformation. It is, therefore, not an issue for which a specific competence should be assigned to either the EU or the Member States, and its management should not be entrusted to a single specialized entity. As a global challenge and a cross-cutting issue, the only way to address this matter successfully is through combined and integrated efforts by the relevant actors on all levels. Technical and normative aspects need to be taken into account when choosing the appropriate frame of reference for a regulatory intervention. **30**

Second, internet security is a particularly challenging aspect of cybersecurity. A truly international approach towards internet cybersecurity regulation currently seems out of reach. In this context, it is helpful that the European Commission is developing protection plans to tackle a possible failure of global DNS routing and is participating in the development and dissemination of secure internet standards.[45] In the light of the underlying technological challenges, the EU seems to be in a better position compared to Member States when it comes to pushing this agenda. **31**

Third, regulation that seeks to stimulate innovation or otherwise mitigate the risks of information technology must be intimately familiar with the technical details and the social context of legal intervention. From a regulatory perspective, cybersecurity regulation is thus primarily a knowledge problem. Since legislators and administrators are typically not in possession of the necessary information, their principal aim should be to implement measures that are designed to generate and distribute knowledge. These **32**

[43] For an overview, see Herpig/Rupp, 'Germany's Cybersecurity Architecture' (Stiftung Neue Verantwortung, September 2022) <https://www.stiftung-nv.de/sites/default/files/9thed_cybersecurityarchitecture.pdf> (last accessed: 29.9.2023), p. 70 et seqq.

[44] See Schöndorf-Haubold in Terhechte, Verwaltungsrecht der Europäischen Union, § 35 mn. 123 et seqq. On Europol's European Cybercrime Centre (EC3) and its Joint Cybercrime Action Taskforce, see Monroy, Vorgänge 2015, 54.

[45] European Commission, 'The EU's Cybersecurity for the Digital Decade', 16.12.2020, JOIN(2020) 18 final, 10 et seq.

measures need to encompass the private sector, but also to establish specialized organizational units and sufficiently efficient administrative networks within the administration. Cybersecurity regulation already uses numerous instruments to that end, ranging from research funding to reporting and information obligations. However, little attention is currently being paid to the question of how the quality of the collected data can be increased and its management and distribution improved. Developing such an information system is another important task for the EU.

33 Finally, on the operational level, the diversity of constellations and problems requires decentralized and deconcentrated organization. However, the more differentiated cybersecurity regulation gets, the greater the need for a coordinating framework becomes. Here, again, the European Union must play a leading role. From an institutional perspective, the fact that the EU currently lacks significant operational capacities is therefore less of a problem than the complexity of its administrative arrangements is.[46] Responsibility for coordinating transnational cybersecurity incidents is currently spread across such a large number of EU agencies and networks, meaning that a concentrated response is highly unlikely.[47] To address the shortcomings of the status quo, the Commission is currently pushing ahead with the establishment of a Joint Cyber Unit (JCU), which is supposed to 'ensure a coordinated response to and recovery from large-scale incidents and crises'.[48] Whether this will be successful remains to be seen.[49] What is more important in this context, though, is the fact that the EU and the Member States seem to have recognized that improving cybersecurity within the European multi-level governance system does not require more centralization but better coordination.

[46] See, for example on the unresolved relationship between ENISA and the ECCC, von Wintzingerode/Müllmann/Spiecker gen. Döhmann, NVwZ 2021, 690 (693).

[47] On the EU's ambition, see European Commission, 'Recommendation (EU) 2017/1584 of 13.09.2017 on coordinated response to large-scale cybersecurity incidents and crises', 13.9.2017, COM(2017) 6100 final. Nevertheless, crisis management is still spread across various EU organizations, each with a slightly different focus, including the EU Cyber Crisis Liaison Organisation Network (EU CyCLONe), the European Cybercrime Centre (EC3) with its Joint Cybercrime Action Taskforce (J-CAT), Europol, the NIS Cooperation Group, and the Information Gathering and Analysis Centre (INTCEN EU) based at the European External Action Service.

[48] European Commission, 'Recommendation (EU) 2021/1086 of 23.6.2021 on building a Joint Cyber Unit', 23.6.2021, COM(2021) 4520, III. (4). The JCU involves ENISA, Europol, CERT-EU, INTCEN EU, the CSIRTs network, EU CyCLONe and various other supporting bodies.

[49] The activities of the JCU are not limited to information sharing and technical support but also include an 'operational' level, the scope and details of which do not emerge conclusively from COM (2021) 4520, Recitals 5, 9 and. in particular, point 4: 'Operational participants should be in a position to swiftly and effectively mobilise operational resources for mutual assistance within the Joint Cyber Unit.' The operational resources of Europol (see Art. 88(3) TFEU) and ENISA will probably form the basis for operational activities of the JCU. On the limits of such arrangements, see Schöndorf-Haubold in Terhechte, Verwaltungsrecht der Europäischen Union, § 35 mn. 134 et seq.

§ 17
Hybrid threats as a challenge to the European Union and its Member States

Teija Tiilikainen

Bibliography: Fägersten, 'Forward Resilience in the Age of Hybrid Threats: The Role of European Intelligence' in Hamilton (ed.), Forward Resilience, Protecting Society in an Interconnected World, Washington DC 2017, p. 113; Fiott/Parkes, 'Protecting Europe. The EU's response to hybrid threats', Chaillot Paper 2019 (151), 1; Gruszczak, 'Intelligence Fusion for the European Union's Security and Defence Policy', Politeja 2022 (79:4), 131; Miadzvetskaya/Challet, 'Are EU restrictive measures really targeted, temporary and preventive? – The case of Belarus', Europe and the World – a law review 2022 (6:1), 1; Myrdal/Rhinard, 'The European Union's Solidarity Clause – Empty Letter or Effective Tool?', Occasional UI Papers 2010 (2), 1; Ohlin, 'A Roadmap for Fighting Election Interference', American Journal of International Law Unbound 2021 (115), 69; Pursiainen/Kytömaa, 'From European critical infrastructure protection to the resilience of European critical entities: what does it mean?, Sustainable and Resilient Infrastructure 2022 (8:1), 85; Ringhand, 'Foreign Election Interference: Comparative Approaches to a Global Challenge', Election Law Journal – Rules, Politics, and Policy 2021 (20:1), 1; Sari, 'The Mutual Assistance Clauses of the North Atlantic and EU Treaties: The Challenge of Hybrid Threats', Harvard National Security Journal 2019 (10:2), 405.

A. Introduction

The term 'hybridity', referring to a mixture of known things or concepts, usually reflects something that does not conform to established concepts, conventions or forms of behaviour. By representing something unconventional, hybridity usually requires new approaches, including rules and practices, to incorporate it into society. 1

The discourse on 'hybrid threats' as a particular challenge in current international politics revolves around threats that are seen to emanate from a specific type of power projection. The global competition for leadership of the international order, with its rules and institutions, is the key context for this power projection. Hybrid threats within this framework are also a reflection of the depth of the existing international conflict between the key parties in this rivalry, i.e. the leading great powers. These threats imply that not only the layer of explicit rules and norms but also the underlying implicit understandings and shared practices underpinning global politics and state behaviour are being challenged. 2

Hybridity in the context of international politics refers to a mixture of conventional and unconventional and military and non-military tools used by state or non-state actors in promoting their own broad interests. Usually this takes place by weakening the target state or steering its decision-making in a direction that promotes the interests of the actor behind these measures. Hybridity, however, does not only refer to the character of instruments used – and with the blurring of the line between the target state's foreign and domestic sphere – but also with the tactic of using them. This tactic takes the target state's vulnerabilities as a starting point in selecting the tools and methods. The set of tools used – often to amplify each other's effect – is meant to 3 provide maximum impact and complicate the target state's preparedness and possibilities for taking countermeasures by creating ambiguity and confusion. Hybrid threat activity is also referred to as the 'use of the full spectrum of instruments' or 'measures taken under the threshold of armed conflict', which describes its basic tenets.

4 Recent trends in the global and European security environment and the growing emergence of hostile operations and actions against the European Union that are perceived as hybrid threats have called for new policy approaches from the EU. Better coherence and stronger linkages between the Union's internal and external security have been called for on the one hand. This requires sufficient interaction between policy fields in which the Union's competences vary significantly and a smooth coordination of respective policy instruments. On the other hand, security threats and challenges explicitly targeting different types of vulnerabilities have made varying levels of security practices and societal resilience between the Member States a major challenge for the Union's overall security. This has required new normative frameworks and regulation to set common standards and limit differences in levels of security and protection to the minimum.

5 This chapter focuses on the effects that perceptions about the Union's security environment becoming increasingly hybrid has had as regards the EU's broad security policy tools. What kinds of changes in terms of policies and legislation has the emergence of hybrid threats been seen to demand from the EU and how have they related to the division of competences between the EU and its Member States? The starting point for the EU's role is that the key competences in countering hybrid threats are at the national level, whilst the EU facilitates cooperation and enables the sharing of best practices. It is, however, obvious that the EU has a lot of important legislative tools that can be used to provide more long-term solutions in countering malign foreign interference and preventing their cross-border effects. The EU also needs to properly protect its own policies and political and governance system, which can be targeted by hybrid threat means as well.

6 This chapter starts by outlining the key components of change that the emergence of hybrid threats in the EU's threat perception has given rise to in relation to the Union's policies. These will then be analysed in more detail from the competence point of view and from the point of view of their implications for the Union's institutional system. The time frame of this analysis covers developments up to the adoption of the EU Hybrid Toolbox in late 2022. The concluding part summarizes the implications of the hybrid threat discourse for the EU's overall security policies.

B. The emergence of hybrid threats in the EU's political discourse

7 The topic of hybrid threats entered the EU's political discourse in the context of Russia's annexation of Crimea and the war it launched against Ukraine in 2014. The instruments used by Russia were seen to call for new forms of preparedness from the EU, which initially revolved mainly around cyber security and the better coordination of internal and external security.[1] The need to counter Russian disinformation also came

[1] European Commission, 'The European Agenda on Security', 28.4.2015, COM(2015) 185 final; Council of the European Union, 'Council Conclusions on CSDP', 18.5.2015, 8971/15; Fiott/Parkes, Chaillot Paper 2019 (151), 1 (6).

to the fore in this context.[2] In the Council conclusions on the Common Security and Defence Policy (CSDP) of May 2015, the High Representative for Foreign Affairs and Security Policy, together with the Commission and the European Defence Agency (EDA), were invited to present a joint framework with actionable proposals to help counter hybrid threats and foster the resilience of the EU and its Member States and partners.[3] A month later, the European Council, in its conclusions, added the need to mobilize EU instruments to counter hybrid threats to the list of measures to be taken in the realm of security and defence policy.[4]

The Joint Framework on Countering Hybrid Threats that was published in 2016 (Joint Framework 2016) played an important role in specifying the Union's roles and competences vis-à-vis hybrid threats and defining these threats in the first place.[5] In this document, hybrid threats were linked to the deteriorated security environment in Europe and were seen to consist of a mixture of coercive and subversive activity, conventional or unconventional methods that can be used in a coordinated manner by state or non-state actors to achieve specific objectives whilst remaining below the threshold of formally declared warfare. They were further seen to exploit the target's vulnerabilities and generate ambiguity to hinder decision-making processes. A more precise definition of the actors causing hybrid threats only entered into the official discourse at a later date.[6] 8

Countering hybrid threats was mainly defined as a national responsibility with the Union, however, playing a role in providing a platform for coordinated responses when it comes to common threats, which can also target cross-border networks or infrastructures.[7] Based on the EU's competence, the actions proposed then consisted of concrete measures in support of critical infrastructures such as energy networks, transport and supply change security and space and of measures to improve awareness and study the applicability of certain EU instruments (Art. 222 TFEU and Art. 42(7) TEU) in this context. The EU's role was already at this stage linked to the building of resilience, which has more recently developed into a comprehensive policy tool for the Union.[8] Another thing to note is that the EU's common 9

[2] European Council, 'European Council meeting (19 and 20.3 2015) – Conclusions', 20.3.2015, EUCO 11/15. The High Representative, in cooperation with the Member States and EU institutions, was asked to prepare an action plan on strategic communication with the establishment of a communication team as the first step.

[3] Council of the European Union, 'Council conclusions on the CSDP', 18.5.2015, 8971/15. The geopolitical framework of hybrid threats was still broader and hybrid threats were presented as follows: 'In light of the increasing use of hybrid strategies and operations by state and non-state actors, notably in the immediate and wider EU neighbourhood, the Council invites the High Representative, in close cooperation with Commission services and the European Defence Agency, and in consultation with the Member States, to present by the end of 2015 a joint framework with actionable proposals to help countering hybrid threats and foster the resilience of the EU and its Member States as well as partners. It should take into account relevant work regarding cyber defence, early warning, strategic communications, relevant internal and external policies and assess the implications of capability development. It underlines as well the need for complementarity in this area with relevant partner organizations, including in particular NATO, as well as partner countries, as appropriate.'

[4] European Council, 'European Council meeting (25. and 26.6.2015) – Conclusions', 26.6.2015, EUCO 22/15.

[5] European Commission, 'Joint Framework on countering hybrid threats a European Union response', 6.4.2016, JOIN(2016) 18 final.

[6] Council of the European Union, 'A Strategic Compass for Security and Defence', 21.3.2022, 7371/22, 17–18 linked both Russia and China to hybrid threat activities against the EU.

[7] JOIN(2016) 18 final.

[8] ibid. in which resilience was defined as 'the capacity to withstand stress and recover, strengthened from challenges'.

defence capabilities were also considered to play an important role in the Union's resilience to hybrid threats.

10 The need to consolidate the nexus between internal and external security strongly came to the fore in the Joint Framework 2016, and the themes and findings of the European Agenda for Security of 2015 were also seen to be relevant in this respect.[9] The latter policy document had been built on the idea of security being a shared agenda between the EU and its Member States, where the EU's role, apart from its strict competences, relates to the more overarching tasks of policy coordination, information-sharing and supporting the Member States. Cross-sectoral policy coordination, including the coordination of internal and external policies, was presented as another important task of the EU.

11 When it comes to the EU's external policies in countering hybrid threats, a broader assessment and debate was only to take place later, leaving the approaches still quite vague and generic in the major policy documents of 2016. The Global Strategy for the EU's Foreign and Security Policy (EUGS) of that same year, which set ambitious targets for the Union's overall security and defence policy, presented hybrid threats as one of those multiple security challenges that are targeted at the EU and its citizens, but it hardly identified any specific instruments of external policy to counter them.[10] The related Implementation Plan on Security and Defence 2016 mentioned the continuum between internal and external security, protection of networks such as energy and transport and countering disinformation as important tools.[11] Both the EUGS and the Joint Framework 2016 stressed the role of partner countries in the East and South and the need to support their resilience as an important instrument for the EU's security, including countering hybrid threats. The Implementation Plan on Security and Defence 2016 mentioned strategic communication, cyber security and border security as areas in which partner countries' possibilities for countering hybrid threats could be strengthened.

12 In these early policy documents the EU's approaches to countering hybrid threats were divided into improving situational awareness, building resilience, strengthening the Member States and the EU's ability to prevent and respond to hybrid threats and enhance cooperation with NATO.[12] Six years later, when the early frameworks had been developed into an EU Hybrid Toolbox, the broad approaches had emerged into a set of measures, divided into preventive, cooperative, stability, restrictive and recovery measures and strengthening solidarity and mutual assistance.[13]

13 In the following I study the development of the Union's tools and policies roughly between these two milestones, that is the Joint Framework of 2016 and the more recent establishment of the EU Hybrid Toolbox of 2022, to assess the implications as regards the division of competences between the EU and the Member States and the Union's institutional framework.

[9] COM(2015) 185 final.

[10] European External Action Service, 'Shared Vision, Common Action: A Stronger Europe. A Global Strategy for the European Union's Foreign and Security Policy', June 2016.

[11] Council of the European Union, 'Implementation Plan on Security and Defence', 14.11.2016, 14392/16.

[12] European Commission, 'Joint Report to the European Parliament and the Council on the implementation of the Joint Framework on countering hybrid threats a European Union response', 19.7.2017, JOIN(2017) 30 final.

[13] Council of the European Union, 'Conclusions on a Framework for a coordinated EU response to hybrid campaigns', 21.6.2022, 10016/22 (referred to as 'the EU Hybrid Toolbox 2022').

C. Towards shared control of the information space

One key characteristic of hybrid threats is the way in which they are seen to manipulate the information space and thus hamper any joint assessment of the situation and the flow of events among the targeted actors. By successfully using the information tool, hybrid threats have been seen to target the broader information space and undermine public trust in the government or challenge the core values of target societies.[14] 14

These risks have called for a wide range of policies and measures from the EU in support of its decision-making and the broader public space. In general, an understanding about the fact that the security environment is becoming more instable and unpredictable has not only led to calls for common situational awareness but also more unity at the broader level of strategic culture or in approaches to the common neighbourhood or actors such as Russia and China.[15] The first common public threat assessment conducted by the EU – included in the Strategic Compass of 2022 – was justified, among other things, by the need to adopt a shared assessment of the Union's strategic environment, together with the threats and challenges it implies, and to create greater coherence and a common sense of purpose regarding its actions.[16] 15

The hybrid threat discourse has lent its own support to these calls for better shared control of the European information space. First, some new mechanisms and practices for intelligence cooperation, information-sharing and early warning have been created to ensure common situational awareness among the Member States, and their governments in particular.[17] 16

Gathering intelligence information is part of Member State competence, but the emergence of hybrid threats has created new needs for the EU's bodies to compile and analyse intelligence information for the Union's purposes.[18] The role of the previously established Single Intelligence Analysis Capacity (SIAC), with its civilian and military component, has been further emphasized in an environment where information operations are also widely used to create dividing lines and disunity within the EU.[19] A specific Hybrid Fusion Cell was established in the EU IntCen, in the European External Action Service (EEAS), to act within a broader framework in collecting intelligence information and interacting with national intelligence services and other EU institutions. Its tasks and mandate in providing analyses and reports on long-term trends in regard to hybrid threats is not fully in line with its size, which is still very limited.[20] When it comes to access to intelligence information, it is still dependent on cooperation 17

---

[14] European Commission, 'Joint Report to the European Parliament, the European Council and the Council on the implementation of the Joint Framework on countering hybrid threats' from 07/2017 to 06/2018, 13.6.2018, JOIN(2018) 14 final.

[15] See, e.g., Borrell, 'Why European Strategic Autonomy Matters?' (EEAS Blog, 3.12.2020) <https://www.eeas.europa.eu/eeas/why-european-strategic-autonomy-matters_en> (last accessed: 26.9.2023).

[16] European External Action Service, 'A Strategic Compass for Security and Defence', 24.3.2022, 15.

[17] The establishment of a Hybrid Fusion Cell in the EU Intelligence and Situation Centre (IntCen) in 2016 and the launch of strategic communication task forces in the EEAS in 2015 are early examples of these.

[18] Fägersten in Hamilton, Forward Resilience, Protecting Society in an Interconnected World, p. 113; Gruszczak, Politeja 2022, 131.

[19] The SIAC consists of the EU IntCen and the EUMC Intelligence Directorate.

[20] The need to enlarge the Hybrid Fusion Cell has been regularly confirmed in policy documents (see, e.g., European Commission, 'Joint Staff Working Document – Report on the implementation of the 2016 Joint Framework on countering hybrid threats and the 2018 Joint Communication on increasing resilience and bolstering capabilities to address hybrid threats', 28.5.2019, SWD(2019) 200 final, 2.

with national actors. The need to ensure a common situational awareness has been one important aspect of the EU's strengthened cooperation with NATO within the hybrid threat framework. Whilst the more systematic processes of information-sharing are advancing more slowly, some common practices of cooperation have started to emerge between the two organizations.[21]

18 Apart from protecting decision-makers' access to truthful information, the role of the broader public space has gained increasing attention from the EU. A comprehensive set of tools has gradually been created for the EU since 2015 to address hostile information campaigns that foreign actors have targeted against the broader public space in EU countries. The changing information environment in which social media platforms are playing an increasingly prominent role has been seen to create new and serious vulnerabilities. These vulnerabilities have culminated in democratic elections in many EU countries becoming targets of external interference.[22]

19 The EU's tools in addressing the security concerns related to foreign information campaigns can be divided into information-sharing and early warning mechanisms on the one hand and regulatory mechanisms on the other. Protecting the integrity of democratic elections can still be distinguished as a separate field in this context.[23]

20 Institutionally, the EU's work on foreign information manipulation and interference (FIMI), revolves around the Strategic Communication Division (StratCom) of the EEAS and its task forces.[24] The StratCom Division has been mandated by the Council to conduct proactive communication and awareness raising, to support independent media and to detect, analyse and challenge threat actors' information operations. In 2019 it was also tasked with establishing a Rapid Alert System (RAS) to facilitate the daily exchange of information between EU authorities and the Member States. The growing importance of the use of this information tool in foreign hostile activities has led to the further systematization of the Union's approaches in the form of a specific FIMI Toolbox created in the Strategic Compass of 2022. This toolbox aims at specifying the framework for the StratCom Division's independent activities in concrete information operations – including measures taken to coordinate Member States' corresponding activities – and its role as part of the broader EU toolbox for countering hybrid threats.[25]

21 The EU's regulatory activities aiming to protect its information space from foreign malign interference have grown significantly as a result of the increasing focus on hybrid threats. Social media companies have been one key target of these efforts, with the Commission first urging them to start using self-regulatory instruments to counter the spread of disinformation on their platforms.[26] Recently, two major regulations saw

---

[21] A working-level relationship established between the EU's Hybrid Fusion Cell and NATO's equivalent, the Hybrid Analysis Branch. The European Centre of Excellence for Countering Hybrid Threats (Hybrid CoE) has the mandate to facilitate cooperation between these two organizations in countering hybrid threats and serves as a common platform for sharing and analysing open-source intelligence (see fn. 40 below for more about Hybrid CoE).

[22] Ringhand, Election Law Journal – Rules, Politics, and Policy 2021, 1; Ohlin, American Journal of International Law Unbound 2021, 69.

[23] The EU's Action Plan against Disinformation (2018) is the first broad-based policy document that summarizes these tools and takes them forward (European Commission, 'Action Plan against Disinformation', 5.12.2018, JOIN(2018) 36 final).

[24] The East StratCom Task Force was established in 2015 to address Russian information campaigns and was followed by the emergence of the Western Balkans Task Force and Task Force South in 2017.

[25] The FIMI toolbox includes the establishment of a FIMI Information Sharing and Analysis Centre as a broad-based network of governmental and civil society actors (Council of the European Union, 'Council conclusions on Foreign Information Manipulation and Interference' (FIMI), 18.7.2022, 11429/22).

[26] European Commission, 'Tackling online disinformation: a European Approach', 26.4.2018, COM (2018) 236 final. A self-regulatory Code of Practice was launched in 2018 and was followed by targeted

the light of day – the Digital Services Act (DSA) and the Digital Markets Act (DMA) – to impose new responsibilities on social media companies concerning, among other things, the information that is shared on their platforms.[27] Both regulations build on the rules of the earlier e-Commerce Directive of 2000, which updated and further harmonized the rules for digital markets and services.[28] Whilst the DSA also increases regulatory oversight of social media platforms in particular, the DMA prevents social media companies from unfairly exploiting their market position.

The European Democracy Action Plan of 2020 launched both political and regulatory 22
measures in support of the integrity of European elections. Even though the focus of these measures is on European Parliament elections, there are elements that seek to affect the framework of elections more in general, for instance by referring to national policies relating to the media. A legislative process was launched at the EU level to revise the rules on the statute and funding of European political parties (Regulation No 1141/2014),[29] which aims to increase transparency and tackle indirect funding by foreign actors. A legislative process was also started relating to the transparency of sponsored political content.[30]

Democratic resilience and the integrity of elections were further supported by a set of 23
new forms of cooperation and dialogue established, for instance, between national media regulators and other key stakeholders to strengthen media freedom and pluralism.

When it comes to rules and the control of the common European information 24
space, the hybrid threat discourse has clearly played a significant role in accelerating cooperation and an increased use of both the EU's political and soft-law tools and regulatory competences. By creating new, obvious needs for better information-sharing and intelligence cooperation as well as for a capacity to respond to hostile operations in a more coordinated manner, the hybrid threat discourse has accelerated processes leading to the gradual emergence of a more joint assessment of the threat environment between EU Member States. On the other hand, the discourse has brought to the fore a broad agenda of democratic resilience, where the EU has used its role to identify key vulnerabilities and provide recommendations or best practices for eliminating them. The legislative measures taken to regulate social media companies can be seen as a major decision to prioritize common security needs over the freedoms of the Single Market.

---

monitoring by the Commission and the European Regulators' Group for Audiovisual Media Services (ERGA).

[27] The need for further regulation were already presented in the Action Plan Against Disinformation (European Commission, 'Action Plan against Disinformation', 5.12.2018, COM(2018) 36 final, which adopted a broader approach to the topic. The initiatives developed into the Regulations on the Digital Services Act (Regulation (EU) 2022/2065 on a Single Market For Digital Services and amending Directive 2000/31/EC (Digital Services Act)) and the Digital Markets Act (Regulation (EU) 2022/1925 on contestable and fair markets in the digital sector and amending Directives (EU) 2019/1937 and (EU) 2020/1828 (Digital Markets Act)), which entered into force in August 2022.

[28] Directive 2000/31/EC on certain legal aspects of information society services, in particular electronic commerce, in the Internal Market (Directive on electronic commerce).

[29] Regulation (EU, Euratom) 2018/673 amending Regulation (EU, Euratom) No 1141/2014 on the statute and funding of European political parties and European political foundations and regulation (EU, Euratom) 2019/493 amending Regulation (EU, Euratom) No 1141/2014 as regards a verification procedure related to infringements of rules on the protection of personal data in the context of elections to the European. For a criticism of these measures, see Harth/Kriener/Wolff 'Responding to Foreign Interference in the EU' <https://carnegieeurope.eu/2022/10/12/responding-to-foreign-interference-in-eu-beware-of-unintended-consequences-pub-88101> (last accessed 19.4.2023).

[30] European Commission, 'Proposal for a Regulation of the European Parliament and the Council on the transparency and targeting of political advertising', 25.11.2021, COM(2021) 731 final.

D. Institutional framework for coordinated response

25 The EU's capacity to deal with hybrid threats has also been seen to require some adjustments to its institutional machinery. The aim in creating the set of new institutional bodies and mechanisms in the EU within this framework was originally to ensure a joint understanding among the Member States of the security environment and the emergence of multiple threats. As part of the discussions on the EU's Strategic Compass in 2021/22, which sought to create a more coherent threat perception within the EU, the idea of an EU Hybrid Toolbox took shape. Apart from defining the tools for countering hybrid threats, the Toolbox called for a coordinated response to hybrid campaigns, thus creating new requirements for the decision-making system.[31] Implementation of the EU Hybrid Toolbox thus steers the roles of the new bodies in the direction of more ordinary parts of the EU's decision-making system having a nascent power of their own.[32] Whilst it is too early at this stage to draw any conclusions about the long-term effects of the EU Hybrid Toolbox, some preliminary observations can, however, be made. Thus far, the adjustments made to the EU's institutions and bodies have all been carried out within the existing institutional framework by adding new specialized components.

26 Before going into the details of the elements of the EU Hybrid Toolbox, it should be pointed out that there is a set of other established response models that come very close to the EU Hybrid Toolbox and that might also provide alternatives to it or lead to a major need to coordinate processes. There is, first, the Integrated Political Crisis Response (IPCR) mechanism that gets the key EU actors to share information and coordinate policies in the case of a major internal or external crisis.[33] If a hybrid threat operation is part of such a major crisis in which the IPCR has been activated – or it evolves into such a major crisis – the IPCR mechanisms apply and the bodies central to the EU Hybrid Toolbox can provide their support to this larger framework.[34] More political discretion, again, exists when coordinating the relationship between the Hybrid Toolbox and the Cyber Diplomacy Toolbox established to manage decision-making in the case of a major cyberattack against the EU. The choice of toolbox to be activated is left to the Member States to decide, whilst a crisis with both hybrid and cyber elements can also lead to the activation of both procedures, requiring major coordination between the key preparatory bodies.

27 Countering hybrid threats poses a typical policy coordination challenge for EU institutions, as it not only covers the internal and external aspects of security but also a wide range of policies with quite different divisions of competences at the EU level. This challenge is further exacerbated by the fact that hybrid threats exploit vulnerabilities, including those identified in the decision-making system, in order to harm the target.

---

[31] Lasoen, 'Realizing the EU Hybrid Toolbox: opportunities and pitfalls' (Clingendael Policy Brief, December 2022) <https://www.clingendael.org/sites/default/files/2022-12/Policy_brief_EU_Hybrid_Toolbox.pdf> (last accessed 19.4.2023)

[32] The EU's Strategic Compass for Security and Defence (2022) underlined the need to develop an EU Hybrid Toolbox, for which the implementing guidelines specify the roles of those bodies that had previously been established (Council of the European Union, 'Implementing guidelines for the Framework for a coordinated EU response to hybrid campaigns', 6.12.2022, 15546/22).

[33] Council of the European Union, Council Implementation Decision (EU) 2018/1993 on the EU Integrated Political Crisis Response Arrangements, 11.12.2018, 2018/1993.

[34] Council of the European Union, 'Implementing guidelines for the Framework for a coordinated EU response to hybrid campaigns', 6.12.2022, 15546/22.

As hybrid threats are seen to affect many policy fields and require efficient coordination of policy tools for internal and external security, both the Commission and the EEAS play a key role in policy preparation. The key powers within the Commission that are relevant for countering hybrid threats and building resilience are spread across many Directorate-Generals, with the DG Defence Industry and Space acting as the point of contact. A light coordination mechanism, the so-called Inter-Services Group, is used to bring together the points of view of the Commission, with its Directorate-Generals and the EEAS.[35] **28**

The Hybrid Fusion Cell established within the EEAS's EU Intelligence and Situation Centre (EU IntCen) is to take a key position in the Union's response in the case of hybrid threat operations against the EU. The implementing guidelines of the EU Hybrid Toolbox (2022) envision quite an independent and operative role for the Hybrid Fusion Cell, where this body would assume a leading role in aggregating all-source information, preparing an intelligence-based assessment and providing strategic foresight.[36] When preparing a Council decision on measures taken against a hybrid threat operation, the Hybrid Fusion Cell, together with the Commission and the High Representative, will provide a situational overview for decision-makers. The fact that all the other EU institutions and bodies are expected to make the relevant information available, including to the Hybrid Fusion Cell, is another indication of the role that is planned for this body. **29**

Another new preparatory body that is planned to take an increasingly central role in the EU's decision-making on countering hybrid threats is the Horizontal Working Party on Enhancing Resilience and Countering Hybrid Threats (HWP ERCHT) that was established in the Council in 2019.[37] The HWP ERCHT was created to facilitate a coherent and comprehensive approach vis-à-vis hybrid threats in Council decision-making both with respect to legislative and non-legislative tasks. Even though HWP ERCHT was set to function under the supervision of the Permanent Representatives Committee (Coreper), it was also given tasks that require some level of autonomous agency, such as fostering cooperation with other EU institutions, services and agencies, including the other Council working parties and committees. **30**

The implementing guidelines for a coordinated EU response to hybrid campaigns of 2022 further specify the key role of the HWP ERCHT in preparing a Council decision on invoking measures against hybrid threats and acting as the key platform for internal coordination and information-sharing with other EU bodies. Even though the new coordinated framework is said not to alter existing decision-making procedures, the emergence of a new preparatory body with such a comprehensive mandate both in terms of policy preparation and coordination will very likely affect interinstitutional relations and has already contributed to hybrid threats becoming a permanent part of the policy priorities for the rotating Council presidencies.[38] It is, however, too early to say how the planned centralization of hybrid threat-related policy preparation to HWP ERCHT will function, as it also needs to get its role recognized by the other Council bodies.[39] **31**

---

[35] European Commission, 'The Working Methods of the European Commission', 1.12.2019, P(2019) 2.

[36] Council of the European Union, 'Implementing guidelines for the Framework for a coordinated EU response to hybrid campaigns', 6.12.2022, 15546/22.

[37] Council of the European Union, 'Horizontal Working Party on Enhancing Resilience and Countering Hybrid Threats – Establishment and Adoption of its Terms of Reference', 9.7.2019, 10027/19.

[38] See, e.g., the Trio Presidency Programme for the French, Czech and Swedish EU Presidencies (Council of the European Union, 'Taking forward the Strategic Agenda, 18-month Programme of the Council (1.1.2022 – 30.6.2023)', 10.12.2021, 14441/21).

[39] Lasoen, 'Realizing the EU Hybrid Toolbox: opportunities and pitfalls' (Clingendael Policy Brief, December 2022) <https://www.clingendael.org/sites/default/files/2022-12/Policy_brief_EU_Hybrid_Toolbox.pdf> (last accessed 19.4.2023).

32 The European Parliament addresses hybrid threats as part of its broad legislative mandate. A special committee tasked with ensuring stronger political attention and visibility for hybrid threats was set up in 2020. This special committee on foreign interference in all democratic processes in the EU, including disinformation, was established to identify possible legislative loopholes in fields vulnerable to hybrid threat operations and to make suggestions for remedying them.[40] The EU's institutional resilience prior to the 2024 European Parliament elections is a special task for the committee to contribute to.

33 Apart from these developments in the Union's institutional framework, a specific Centre of Excellence (CoE) was established in Helsinki as an intergovernmental platform of cooperation between EU and NATO members to enhance expertise on hybrid threats and raise common capacity to counter them.[41] Hybrid CoE provides analytical support as well as training courses and exercises to both the Member States and key EU institutions, and it facilitates the creation of a common strategic culture – and strong dialogue and interaction – concerning hybrid threats among EU Member States, but also between the EU and NATO.[42]

34 The hybrid threats discourse seems to have entered the EU's institutional framework at a stage when this framework is affected by multiple new demands stemming from a changing international environment. In many cases these new demands are coherent, such as the need to strengthen interaction between internal and external security or enhance the EU's common intelligence or analytical capability. In other cases, different procedures created for different new threats (based on different institutional responsibilities) – such as creating different frameworks for hybrid threats and cyber threats as well as foreign information manipulation or implementation of Art. 222 TFEU (solidarity clause) – comes with clear risks as regards efficiency and policy coordination.[43]

E. Building resilience

35 The policy of building resilience is the EU's broadest tool for countering hybrid threats. In the initial Joint Framework of 2016 this task was seen to consist of protecting critical infrastructures, protecting public health and food security, cybersecurity, targeting hybrid threat financing, and resilience to radicalization and violent extremism. In addition, increasing cooperation with third countries was considered an important

[40] The first Special Committee on Foreign Interference in all Democratic Processes in the European Union, including Disinformation (INGE) was established in March 2020. Its mandate expired in March 2022, leading to the establishment of the second, so-called ING2 committee, whose mandate expires in March 2023.

[41] According to the initial Joint Framework (2016) (JOIN(2016) 18 final), 'one or a network of multinational institutes could act as a Centre of Excellence addressing hybrid threats'. Within the following months, the idea of a new centre with a mandate of its own gained support and the European Centre of Excellence for Countering Hybrid Threats was established in Helsinki. Its founding document, a Memorandum of Understanding, was signed by nine EU/NATO members in April 2017.

[42] In 2021, a conceptual model for hybrid threats was launched as a joint effort of Hybrid CoE and the Joint Research Centre of the European Commission (Giannopoulos/Smith/Theocharidou, 'The Landscape of Hybrid Threats: A Conceptual Model' (Hybrid CoE, 5.2.2021) <https://www.hybridcoe.fi/publications/the-landscape-of-hybrid-threats-a-conceptual-model/(last accessed> 19.4.2023)). The model has provided support and inspiration for the EU's policies on countering hybrid threats.

[43] Lasoen, 'Realizing the EU Hybrid Toolbox: opportunities and pitfalls' (Clingendael Policy Brief, December 2022) <https://www.clingendael.org/sites/default/files/2022-12/Policy_brief_EU_Hybrid_Toolbox.pdf> (last accessed 19.4.2023).

component of resilience.[44] Since then, the EU's understanding of resilience has been constantly broadened to incorporate new dimensions of broad external dependencies.

The discourse on the EU's strategic autonomy, which first revolved around the Union's defence capabilities and was then expanded to include issues of economic dependence and supply chains, has contributed to the broadening of the notion of resilience. By not being the only driving force behind the need to strengthen the EU's resilience, hybrid threats still stand out as a concrete factor that is seen to require fast responses. The EU's Security Union Strategy, launched in 2020, illustrates well the broadened content of resilience and its connections to hybrid threats.[45] According to the strategy, more needs to be done to engage the whole of society, including governments at all levels, businesses in all sectors and individuals in all Member States, in addressing security policies: 'The increasing awareness of the risks of dependency and the need for a strong European industrial strategy point to an EU with a critical mass of industry, technology production and supply chain resilience.' **36**

The risks of foreign dependence were explicitly mentioned as involving increased exposure to potential threats, from exploitation of the vulnerabilities of IT infrastructures that compromise critical infrastructures (e.g. energy, transport, banking, health), or taking control of industrial control systems, to an increased capacity for data theft or espionage. **37**

This broadened notion of resilience is reflected in the numerous legislative projects that have been launched at the EU level since 2019/20 aiming at enhancing the resilience of the Union and its Member States.[46] These legislative projects extend from the resilience of critical infrastructures, to cyber security, and further to foreign investment screening and space security. **38**

Whilst it will not be possible, here in this chapter, to analyse all the recent political or legislative measures adopted in support of the Union's resilience, motivated by the hybrid threats discourse, a major legislative amendment as regards the protection of critical infrastructures serves as a good example of how the EU's resilience needs in general are conceptualized in a new security environment. **39**

As regards critical infrastructure protection, the needs stemming from the new environment were reflected well in the evaluation of the earlier European Critical Infrastructure Directive (ECI, 2008) and the decision to replace it with the Critical Entities Resilience Directive (CER, 2022).[47] This new directive builds on the needs that are emerging from the new security environment and expands the scope of 'European' critical infrastructures from those covered by the earlier directive, which limited them to transport and energy. This scope proved to be insufficient when assessing it from the point of view of the proper functioning of the Single Market or the possible cross-border effects of critical infrastructures. Ten Critical Infrastructure (CI) sectors were **40**

---

[44] The following definition of resilience was included in the EU's Security Union Strategy (2020): 'Europe needs to be more resilient to prevent, protect and withstand future shocks. We need to build capabilities and capacities for early detection and rapid response to security crises though an integrated and coordinated approach, both globally and through sector-specific initiatives (such as for the financial, energy, judiciary, law enforcement, healthcare, maritime, transport sectors) and building on existing tools and initiatives.', 'EU Security Union Strategy', 24.7.2020, COM(2020) 605 final).

[45] ibidl.

[46] See, e.g., Hindrén, 'Calibrating the compass: Hybrid threats and the EU's Strategic Compass' (Hybrid CoE Working Paper, October 2021) <https://www.hybridcoe.fi/wp-content/uploads/2021/10/Hybrid_CoE_Working_Paper_12_Calibrating_the_compass_WEB.pdf> (last accessed 19.4.2023).

[47] Pursiainen/Kytömaa, Sustainable and Resilient Infrastructure 2022, 85.

included in the scope of the new directive.[48] The sectors are the same as in the related new NIS2 Directive.[49] Also, the NIS2 Directive, which seeks to further increase the Union's level of cyber resilience, has broadened the scope of the previous NIS Directive and the range of actors it applies to.

41 It is obvious that by adopting 'a more common approach' to the resilience of critical entities in a number of sectors across the Union the new CER Directive strengthens the role of the EU in regulating and controlling entities, i.e. companies and bodies in charge of critical functions in the Member States. This is mainly done by regulating the Member States when it comes to their approaches and the requirements made of their critical entities. There are also EU-level mechanisms established in support of policy implementation and identification of critical entities on the basis of common criteria. The related new NIS2 Directive basically equally affects the division of competences by, first, broadening the scope of the directive and imposing more strict requirements on the Member States when it comes to regulating and sanctioning national actors on cyber security requirements.

42 As part of Europe's critical infrastructures, energy networks, transport and supply chain security, and space infrastructures were also referred to more generally in the initial Joint Framework 2016. More recent developments within the global political framework in the light of Russia's war against Ukraine as one culmination have multiplied the vulnerabilities perceived within these domains and have brought them together as part of a larger debate on the EU's economic security. The issue of energy networks, whose initial focus was on risks and hazards against physical networks, has been broadened to cover broader issues of energy security and major concerns in the security of supply. The 2022 Energy Union Report,[50] when assessing the implementation of the Energy Union Policy to reduce dependency on energy imports, to strengthen Europe's resilience and enhance energy security, firmly supports the new policy tool (REPOwerEU) adopted earlier in 2022 to accelerate the multiple new processes for promoting these goals.

F. Tools for preventing hybrid threats and responding to them

43 The list of tools identified in the original Joint Framework 2016 for preventing hybrid threats and responding to them was still short. It included the European Emergency Coordination Centre, the so-called solidarity clause (Art. 222 TFEU), and some training and mentoring capabilities that could take place within the CSDP. Over the following years a wider set of measures was discussed and was affected by developments within the EU's cyber policies as well as by the evolution of the policies of the Union's key partners.

44 The implementing guidelines for a coordinated EU response to hybrid campaigns (2022) summarize what tools are available in the EU Hybrid Toolbox and point out the key perceived gaps. First, the EU's need to tackle the challenge of hybrid threats at the broader international level both by contributing to the international normative framework and cooperating with key partners and like-minded countries comes to the fore.

---

[48] Apart from energy and transport, banking, financial market infrastructure, health, drinking water, wastewater, digital infrastructure, public administration and space are also included in the scope of the directive (Directive (EU) 2022/2557 on the resilience of critical entities).

[49] Directive (EU) 2022/2555 on measures for a high common level of cybersecurity across the Union (NIS Directive).

[50] European Commission, 'State of the Energy Union', 18.10.2022, COM(2022) 547 final.

The political importance of EU–NATO cooperation has been further strengthened due to the constant worsening of the European security environment, including the outbreak of Russia's war against Ukraine without, however, any major new political or institutional openings having taken place.[51]

The other group of instruments outlined deals with the EU's possibilities for supporting its partner countries in countering hybrid threats, with the role of the CSDP missions presented as a key tool. The potential linked to these missions is now at a different level than the tasks referred to in the Joint Framework 2016.[52] It seems obvious that the tasks described as 'assisting, advising, detecting and enhancing the capabilities of partners to withstand hybrid threats as well as being able to detect and respond to hybrid threats' broadens the scope for the use of the CSDP tool beyond traditional crisis management functions.[53] This broadened scope, however, is well in line with the new perspectives envisioned for CSDP operations in the Strategic Compass, which refers to the EU's need to use more robust and flexible CSDP missions to better accompany and support partner countries' security and defence forces. This new role is vindicated by the need to adapt swiftly to new threats and the growing presence of the Union's strategic competitors in operational theatres. **45**

The EU Hybrid Rapid Response Teams are another new EU tool that is to be established to prevent hybrid threats and respond to them and that also originates in the Strategic Compass. This tool, which aims at supporting the Member States as well as CSDP missions and partner countries in countering hybrid threats, has its equivalent in NATO's Counter Hybrid Support Teams, which were established in 2018, as well as in the EU's Cyber Rapid Response teams.[54] The EU's Hybrid Rapid Response Teams are to consist of sectoral experts from the Member States and EU bodies, and their role and tools are to build on existing EU instruments. These instruments could be the Union Civil Protection Mechanism (UCPM) or the EU's civilian crisis management missions, which could provide the legal/institutional framework for the use of the new Hybrid Rapid Response Teams. More precise rules for the Hybrid Rapid Response Teams were still in the making in the spring of 2023. **46**

Countering hybrid threats thus seems to form a broad new task for several EU instruments originally established to manage very different types of conflicts. A common characteristic of these conflicts was that even though they originated in the policies of state actors they were to a lesser extent targeted against the EU itself. Now both the planned new tasks of CSDP operations and the role of the Hybrid Rapid Response Teams pit the Union against state actors whose hostile activities they are **47**

[51] Strong partnership and commitment to common values has been signalled since 2016 with the issuing of joint declarations and related progress reports, the most recent of which is the Joint declaration on EU–NATO cooperation, 10.1.2023. Hybrid threats have been defined as one of the focal areas for cooperation in these declarations.

[52] The Joint Framework 2016 (JOIN(2016) 18 final) referred to tasks such as civilian and military training; mentoring and advisory missions; contingency planning to identify signals of hybrid threats and strengthen early warning capabilities; support to border control management in the case of emergency; and support in specialized areas such as CBRN (chemical, biological, radiological and nuclear) mitigation.

[53] The definition of the CSDP missions in the EU treaties (Art. 42(1) TEU) refers to missions outside the Union for peacekeeping, conflict prevention and strengthening international security in accordance with the UN Charter. Art. 43 TEU further defines these tasks to include joint disarmament operations, humanitarian and rescue tasks, military advice and assistance tasks, conflict prevention and peacekeeping tasks, tasks of combat forces in crisis management including peacekeeping and post-conflict stabilization.

[54] The EU's Cyber Rapid Response Teams have been developed within the framework of a Permanent Structured Cooperation (PESCO) project and have been operational since 2019. The cyber experts pooled within the project are available to assist Member States, EU institutions, CSDP missions and operations as well as partner countries.

supposed to counter or respond to. Even if the individual mandates formulated in relation to the use of these new tools presented their tasks more in the light of building resilience than countering foreign hostilities, the tough geopolitical confrontation in the EU's neighbourhood is likely to affect their role.

48 Whilst the implementing guidelines on EU Hybrid Toolbox refer to the public attribution of hybrid threat operations as a sovereign national prerogative, EU-level coordination of these measures accompanied by strategic communication and different diplomatic responses is presented as a strong collective asset.

49 The use of restrictive measures, or sanctions, against an actor launching hybrid threat operations against the Union is presented as one of the tools for responding to these threats. Decisions on restrictive measures must be taken in accordance with the rules and procedures set out for the use of the instrument, implying, first, unanimity within the Council and, second, implementation either at the national or EU level depending on the character of sanctions applied.[55] The difference between the possibility of imposing sanctions for using hybrid threat instruments and the cyber sanctions regime established in 2019 is that the latter is based on special legislation covering restrictive measures against persons or legal entities but not against state actors.[56] As such, it enables fast reactions from the EU when hostile cyber operations against the Union or one of its Member States fulfil the key defined criteria. A discussion on the legal base that would allow the EU to impose sanctions on Russia and China for hybrid threat activities targeted at the EU or its Member States was still pending in the spring of 2023.

50 The final group of tools identified both in the early policy documents and – in a more specified form – in the implementing guidelines for a coordinated EU response to hybrid campaigns of 2022 deals with the Union's solidarity clause (Art. 222 TFEU) and mutual defence clause (Art. 42(7) TEU). Whilst the applicability of the first seems to be more uncontroversial in a hybrid threat context, the role played by the mutual defence clause has given rise to various interpretations. Current understandings of their potential in relation to the EU's policies for countering hybrid threats forms the final theme to be addressed in this chapter.

51 The EU's solidarity clause (Art. 222 TFEU) has been widely referred to as one of those instruments the Union can use to support one or several of its Member States that have been targeted by hybrid threat operations. The treaty provision originates in a political environment where terrorist attacks constituted the primary security threat for most EU members, with natural disasters providing another obvious context for strengthened solidarity mechanisms in the EU.[57]

52 An interpretation according to which the second field of application of the solidarity clause, with its reference to 'natural or man-made disasters', could also cover different forms of hybrid threats cannot be seen to stretch its scope too far from its original meaning. The solidarity clause was prepared in parallel with the mutual defence clause, which deals with traditional military threats, as a reaction to more modern threats caused by non-state actors and covering less conventional threat forms. Another linkage

---

[55] Miadzvetskaya/Challet, Europe and the World – a law review 2022, 1 (1–2); Council of the European Union, 'Sanctions Guidelines – Update', 4.5.2018, 5664/18.

[56] Council Regulation (EU) 2019/796 concerning restrictive measures against cyber-attacks threatening the Union or its Member States.

[57] The idea and original wording of the solidarity clause came into being in the European Convention in 2002/03. The Working Group on Defence proposed that it be added to the Constitutional Treaty. The clause also entitled the EU to use its military crisis management tools within its own territory, which was seen to be appropriate in the light of the increasing threat of international terrorism (Myrdal/Rhinard, Occasional UI Papers 2010, 1).

to hybrid threat operations could be perceived in the way in which the threats referred to by the solidarity clause were seen to be directed against the whole of society.

The solidarity clause is thus seen, for many reasons, to provide an appropriate tool for the EU to counter hybrid threats. Its reference to 'natural and man-made disaster' is seen to provide a proper legal basis that appears to include sufficient flexibility to address threats as diverse and multidimensional as hybrid threats. The clause first allows for the EU's instruments to be applied in accordance with Council Decision 2014/415.[58] This requires that the Union's measures are to be implemented by means of the IPCR arrangements and defines the set of common instruments that can be used, including CSDP operations. The Council will also act as the coordinating body when it comes to the intergovernmental part of the solidarity clause, i.e. the obligation it creates for the Member States to assist the target state at the request of its political authorities. **53**

In his legal analysis of the applicability of the solidarity clause and mutual defence clause to hybrid threat operations and attacks, Aurel Sari points out that two conditions are important for Art. 222 TFEU to be applicable.[59] Council Decision 2014/15 requires that the disaster 'has or may have a severe impact on people, the environment or property, including cultural heritage.' It also limits the Member States' right to invoke the solidarity clause to a situation where the affected state, after having exploited the possibilities that exist at the national level, considers that the crisis clearly goes beyond its own response capabilities. Whilst the Council Decision limits the application of the solidarity clause to the EU's territory, including territorial sea and airspace, it must be seen as a resilience tool rather than a response to a hybrid threat operation. In this respect, the goals of this treaty provision would not be changed, compared to what was originally envisaged, even if it were now invoked as a response to hostilities caused by state actors. **54**

Also, invoking the EU's mutual defence clause (Art. 42(7) TEU) is referred to as a possible tool for the Union to respond to major hybrid threat operations. The key policy documents on hybrid threats seem to reflect a certain degree of evolution in the legal interpretation of the clause, which has clearly been a divisive topic among the Member States. This controversy revolves around the question of whether a hybrid threat attack could be considered to qualify as an act of 'armed aggression' that is needed to invoke the mutual defence clause (Art. 42(7) TEU). **55**

The original Joint Framework 2016 took a somewhat ambiguous approach to this issue by stating that if multiple, serious hybrid threats constitute armed aggression against the EU, then Art. 42(7) TEU could be invoked to provide an appropriate and timely response. The document might be seen to have left open the decision as to whether these threats could in principle be considered to constitute armed aggression within the meaning of Art. 42(7) TEU. The Council Legal Service adopted a position in 2016, according to which a hybrid threat operation cannot be seen to constitute an armed attack as long as such an enlarged interpretation of Art. 51 of the United Nations Charter does not exist. It refers to the fact that Art. 42(7) TEU is explicitly based on Art. 51 UN Charter, which gives states the right to individual or collective self-defence and defines the necessary conditions for that.[60] **56**

Six years later, in 2022, the clear new demands that had emerged in relation to the EU's security and defence policy were also reflected in the bolder interpretation of the **57**

[58] Council of the European Union, 'Council Decision on the arrangements for the implementation by the Union on the solidarity clause', 24.6.2014, 2014/15.

[59] Sari, Harvard National Security Journal 2019, 405 (405–460).

[60] Council of the European Union, 'Opinion of the Legal Service', 12.7.2016, 11176/16.

scope of the mutual defence clause. Whilst the Strategic Compass, together with the EU Hybrid Toolbox it created, were still quite generic in their wording, the implementation guidelines for the latter of 2022 seemed to suggest a solution to the question that the Member States had earlier been disagreeing on. The implementation guidelines simply stated that serious hybrid campaigns could amount to a use of force or an armed attack within the meaning of the UN Charter. In the latter case, it stated, Member States may choose to exercise their inherent right of individual or collective self-defence as recognized under Art. 51 UN Charter and in accordance with international law, including international humanitarian law.

58 The same document further stated that EU institutions could be called upon to support, through coordination, and/or to facilitate the activities of the Member States if so requested by them.

59 It is still too early to assess how solid and unitary the interpretation of the scope of the mutual defence clause is among the Member States. Also, it remains to be seen to what extent such a new position will accelerate the formulation of clearer guidelines for a situation in which the clause would be invoked in a hybrid threat context, as no specific rules as yet exist when it comes to implementing the clause.

G. Conclusions

60 The discourse on hybrid threats can be seen to have had two types of implications for the EU's overall policies. First, when perceived as an elementary part of the general deterioration of the European security policy environment, hybrid threats have made new types of vulnerabilities visible in the Union's broader societal resilience, including fields such as the information space or control of critical infrastructures or commodities. These new security risks and vulnerabilities have created heavy demand for the EU to manage its internal system of multilevel governance and divided competences to make sure that the system itself does not provide additional vulnerabilities or weak points that can be exploited.

61 The hybrid threat discourse has, thus, not only called for more unity and coherence in the EU's threat assessment or situational awareness but also for a common approach to safeguarding the European democratic space more in general. By fostering a common intelligence and analysis capacity when it comes to monitoring and detecting hybrid threats, and a specific mechanism for policy preparation and decision-making, the EU's leadership wants to ensure that the EU is capable of maintaining its unity and reacting promptly to this set of new threats. Further, by expanding the scope of common security needs and the role of the EU institutions, together with their regulatory frameworks, an effort is being made to diminish the negative consequences that differences in security levels and practices between the Member States may cause.

62 The second implication of the hybrid threat discourse is somewhat different: Instead of creating new tools or solutions, it rather steers the existing policy instruments in a new direction. If the first set of implications approaches the EU in terms of risks and vulnerabilities in the new hybrid threat environment, the latter approach perceives the EU more as a reservoir of unused potential and instruments. However, the effective use of these instruments in the hybrid threat context presupposes new interpretations of existing treaty provisions and other norms. There are also political implications, which cannot necessarily be immediately addressed.

The indications as to the possibilities for using CSDP operations as a tool for countering hybrid threats clearly belongs to this latter group of implications, together with the decisions about the applicability of both the solidarity clause (Art. 222 TFEU) and the mutual defence clause (Art. 42(7) TEU). In both of these cases, as well as in the case of imposing sanctions against an actor that has executed a hybrid threat operation, the benefits of an existing tool are extended into a new context. In all of the above-mentioned cases the instrument needs to be calibrated to meet the demands of the new environment. It is quite obvious that the inability to put these instruments to use owing to legal or political reasons would have been considered a sign of failure and inefficiency. **63**

To conclude, the hybrid threat discourse can be seen to have fostered many types of changes in the EU's overall security policies. By embedding the notion of resilience in the Union's policies it has made visible the internal and external dimensions of security and the need to create a link between them. It has built a security policy role into many policy fields that previously were not seen in this light, thus broadening the notion of security within the Union's policies. And, last but not least, it has paved the way for a much bolder and proactive role for the EU in relation to its general security environment. **64**

§ 18
Intelligence cooperation in the European Union

Jan-Hendrik Dietrich

Bibliography: Aldrich, 'Beyond the vigilant state: globalisation and intelligence', Review of International Studies 2009 (35), 889; Aldrich, 'International Cooperation in Practice' in Born/Leigh/Wills (eds), International Intelligence Cooperation and Accountability, London 2011, p. 18; Bang, 'A Shared Epistemological View Within Military Intelligence Institutions', IJICI 2016 (30), 102; Barczak, 'Wissensabhängigkeit und Wissensgenerierung im Sicherheitsverwaltungsrecht' in Dietrich et al. (eds), Handbuch des Sicherheits- und Staatsschutzrechts, Munich 2022, § 16; Blancke, Private Intelligence, Wiesbaden 2011; Born/Leigh/Wills, Making Intelligence Cooperation Accountable, Geneva 2015; Bossong, 'Intelligence Support for EU Security Policy', SWP Comment 2018 no 51, 1; Calliess/Ruffert (eds), EUV/AEUV, 6th edn, Munich 2022; Cameron, 'Metadata retention and national security: Privacy International and La Quadrature du Net', Common Market Law Review 2021 (58), 1433; Cameron, 'The problem of oversight' in Dietrich/Sule (eds), Intelligence Law and Policies, Munich/Oxford/Baden-Baden 2019, p. 388; Cartmell, 'Long term intelligence sharing: the Five Eyes and the European Union', Journal of Intelligence History 2022; Conrad, 'Europäische Nachrichtendienstkooperation – Entwicklungen, Erwartungen und Perspektiven' in Dietrich et al. (eds), Reform der Nachrichtendienste zwischen Vergesetzlichung und Internationalisierung, Tübingen 2019, p. 161; Conrad, 'Situational Awareness for EU Decision-Making: The Next Decade', European Foreign Affairs Review 2021 (26:1), 55; Cross, 'The Merits of Informality: The European Transgovernmental Intelligence Network' in Dietrich/Sule (eds), Intelligence Law and Policies, Munich/Oxford/Baden-Baden 2019, p. 235; Davies, 'Ideas of Intelligence: Divergent National Concepts and Institutions', Harvard International Review 2002 (24:3), 62; de Kerchove/Höhn, 'The Role of European Intelligence in Countering Terrorism' in Dietrich/Sule (eds), Intelligence Law and Policies, Munich/Oxford/Baden-Baden 2019, p. 82; Dietrich, 'Geheime Mitarbeiter der Nachrichtendienste' in Dietrich/Eiffler (eds), Handbuch des Rechts der Nachrichtendienste, Stuttgart 2017, VI § 2; Dietrich, 'Sicherheitsbegriff und Sicherheitsrecht' in Dietrich/Fahrner/Gazeas/v. Heintschel-Heinegg (eds), Handbuch des Sicherheits- und Staatsschutzrechts, Munich 2022, § 6; Fägersten, 'Bureaucratic Resistance to International Intelligence Cooperation – The Case of Europol', Intelligence and National Security 2010 (25:4), 500; Grabitz/Hilf/Nettesheim (eds), Das Recht der EU, 78th Suppl., Munich 2023; Gruszczak, 'Intelligence Fusion for the European Union's Common Security and Defence Policy', Politeja 2022 (79), 131; Gruszczak, Intelligence Security in the European Union, Building a Strategic Intelligence Community, London 2016; Gruszczak, 'Joint EU Intelligence School – a real asset or an empty shell?', Komentarz ZBN 2018 (40:16), 1; Herman, Intelligence power in peace and war, Cambridge 2008; Jacobs, 'Maximator: European signals intelligence cooperation, from a Dutch perspective', Intelligence and National Security 2020 (35:5), 659; Jensen/McElreath/Graves, Introduction to intelligence studies, 2nd edn, London 2013; Karpenstein/Sangi, 'Nationale Sicherheit im Unionsrecht: Zur Bedeutung von Art. 4 II 3 EUV', GSZ 2020, 162; Labuhn, 'Auf dem Weg zur Europäischen Verteidigungsunion – der PESCO-Prozess in der EU', GSZ 2019, 66; Lledo-Ferrer/Dietrich, 'Building a European Intelligence Community', IJICI 2020 (33:3), 440; ; Maaßen, 'Perspektiven und Grenzen internationaler Zusammenarbeit' in Dietrich et al. (eds), Reform der Nachrichtendienste zwischen Vergesetzlichung und Internationalisierung, Tübingen 2019, p. 179; Myrdal/Rhinard, 'The European Union's Solidarity Clause: Empty Letter or Effective Tool? An Analysis of Article 222 of the Treaty on the Functioning of the European Union', Occasional UI Papers 2010 (2); Omand, 'Means and methods of Modern Intelligence and their wider implications' in Dietrich/Sule (eds), Intelligence Law and Policies, Munich/Oxford 2019, p. 38; Omand, Securing the State, New York 2010; Palacios, 'EU Intelligence: on the road to a European Intelligence Agency?' in Dietrich/Sule (eds), Intelligence Law and Policies, Munich/Oxford/Baden-Baden 2019, p. 201; Pronk/Korteweg, Sharing the Burden, Sharing the Secrets. The Future of European Intelligence Cooperation, Clingdael Report, The Hague 2021; Ramsperger, Die Terrorismusbekämpfung im Rahmen der Europäischen Sicherheits- und Verteidigungspolitik (ESVP),

Berlin 2009; Rauwolf, 'Intelligence in EU-led military missions and operations' in Dietrich/Sule (eds), Intelligence Law and Policies, Munich/Oxford/Baden-Baden 2019, p. 153; Rojszczak, 'National Security and Retention of Telecommunications Data in Light of Recent Case Law of the European Courts', ECLR 2021 (17), 607; Røseth, 'How to classify intelligence relations: partnership types in the intelligence community' in Røseth/Weaver (eds), Intelligence Relations in the 21st Century, Cham 2020, p. 41; Rüß, 'Internationale nachrichtendienstliche Zusammenarbeit' in Dietrich/Eiffler (eds), Handbuch des Rechts der Nachrichtendienste, Stuttgart 2017, IV § 4; Ryder, 'European Criminal Intelligence' in Dietrich/Sule (eds), Intelligence Law and Policies, Munich/Oxford/Baden-Baden 2019, p. 249; Ryngaert/van Eijk, 'International cooperation bay (European) security and intelligence services: reviewing the creation of a joint database in light of data protection guarantees', International Data Privacy Law 2019 (9:1), 61; Scheffler/Dietrich, 'Military Intelligence: Ill-Defined and Understudied', IJICI 2023, 1; Schwarze et al. (eds), EU-Kommentar, 4th edn, Baden-Baden 2019; Sims, 'Foreign Intelligence Liaison: Devils, Deals, and Details', IJICI 2006 (19:2), 195; Sule, 'National Security and EU law restraints on Intelligence Activities' in Dietrich/Sule (eds), Intelligence Law and Policies, Munich/Oxford/Baden-Baden 2019, p. 335; Szép/Sbatino/Wessel, 'Developing Assessment Criteria for Security and Intelligence Cooperation in the EU', ENGAGE Working Paper Series 2022 (10); Walsh, The International Politics of Intelligence Sharing, New York 2010; Warner, 'Wanted: A Definition of "Intelligence"', Studies in Intelligence 2002 (46), 15; Westerfield, 'America and the world of intelligence liaison', Intelligence and National Security 1996 (11:3), 523.

A. Introduction

1 The integration of security provision within the European Union is moving forward apace and has for some years now been underpinned by the ambitious designation of 'Security Union'. The aim of this Security Union is to create a consistent regulatory framework for individual initiatives. In its Communication on the EU Security Union Strategy, dated 24 July 2020, the European Commission sets out its vision for a 'whole-of-society approach to security that can effectively respond to a rapidly-changing threat landscape'.[1] This is accompanied by an extensive process of institutionalization at the Union level on account of the ongoing strengthening of the EU agencies responsible for security provision. While the EU Security Union Strategy primarily focused on internal security in the territory of the Union, the Strategic Compass for Security and Defence was agreed in March 2022 by the Council of the European Union in the face of Russia's war of aggression against Ukraine.[2] It both laid the strategic foundation for the Union's Common Security and Defence Policy (CSDF) and acts as an action plan. The Strategic Compass fleshes out the 2016 Global Security Strategy[3] and precisely defines the EU's ambitions as a global security player.

2 The fact that such an ambitious security policy is highly reliant on knowledge needs no comment.[4] Security-relevant information needs to be generated, facts need to be evaluated by experts and analytical results need to be made available for decision-making in the context of an evidence-based security policy. That is the business the intelligence services are in. They are the key knowledge service providers for decision-makers in politics and the military.[5] Each EU Member State has one or more intelligence services that help guarantee its internal and external security. Unlike the

[1] European Commission, 'EU Security Union Strategy', 24.7.2020, COM(2020) 605 final, 3.

[2] Council of the European Union, 'A Strategic Compass for Security and Defence', 21.3.2022, 7371/22.

[3] European External Action Service, 'Shared Vision, Common Action: A Stronger Europe. A Global Strategy for the European Union's Foreign and Security Policy', June 2016.

[4] For details on security provision's reliance on knowledge, see Barczak in Dietrich et al., Handbuch des Sicherheits- und Staatsschutzrechts, § 16 mn. 4 et seqq.

[5] For details, see Omand in Dietrich/Sule, Intelligence Law and Policies, p. 46 et seqq.

work of the national police authorities, that of the intelligence services has so far largely been done beyond the dense system of EU norms and administrative structures. The prevailing view is that this is because, pursuant to Art 4(2) sent. 3 TEU, 'national security' is excluded from the EU integration process.[6] In fact, there is as yet no EU agency that acts as a 'European Intelligence Service' (similar to Europol, e.g., with the exception of the Commission's 'security service', which is exclusively responsible for the security of the European Administration and part of the DG Human Resources). Nor is there an EU training institution comparable to the European Agency for Law Enforcement Training (*Collège européen de police*, CEPOL).[7] The EU only has what is now called the EU Intelligence and Situation Centre (EU INTCEN) and the Intelligence Directorate in the EU Military Staff (EUMS), a skeleton intelligence framework within the European External Action Service (EEAS). Given recent case law issued in the Member States on the scope of Art 4(2) sent. 3 TEU, there are some indications that the situation is not likely to change any time soon. In 2021, for instance, the French *Conseil d'État* (*Council of State*) made it very clear that the French authorities' intelligence activities – that is strategic foreign signals intelligence conducted by the *Direction Générale de la sécurité extérieure* (General Directorate for External Security, DGSE) – is subject only to national legislation.[8]

The question therefore arises as to whether and to what extent the EU's aforementioned security policy ambitions can be underpinned by the necessary intelligence cooperation structures. To that end, this chapter first investigates what is meant by the term 'intelligence cooperation' (B.). That discussion prepares the ground for a closer look at the legal setting (C. I.) and the types of and limits to EU intelligence cooperation (C. II and III.). Finally, an outlook will be attempted (D.) 3

B. Key terms

I. Intelligence

Before turning to 'intelligence cooperation' it is necessary to have an understanding of what 'intelligence' is. Taking a look at the specialist literature, statutory regulations or official instructions shows that providing a definition of the term is far from straightforward. There are numerous definitions on offer. They vary depending on geographical origin, for instance, or between the scientific disciplines involved or whether they are provided by the scientific community and the military and/or by official practice. Attempting a systematic classification means one can at least draw a distinction between operation-, process-, product- and institution-related approaches. Sometimes these coexist, and sometimes they are combined. Particularly broad attention is given in the political sciences to *Michael Warner*'s operation-related definition in the CIA's own *Studies of Intelligence* journal. His definition of 'intelligence' goes as follows: 'Intelligence is secret, state activity to understand or influence foreign entities.[9]' 4

[6] See, e.g., Sule in Dietrich/Sule, Intelligence Law and Policies, p. 335 et seqq.; Bossong, SWP Comment 2018 no 51, 1.

[7] See Regulation (EU) 2015/2219 on the European Union Agency for Law Enforcement Training (CEPOL).

[8] French Council of State (Conseil d'État), 21 April 2021, French Data Network, nos. 39309 et al., no 95.

[9] Warner, Studies in Intelligence 2002, 15 (21).

5 This oft-cited suggestion has come in for some considerable criticism, especially as regards its focus on foreign matters and the fact that it is limited to 'secret' state activities.[10] Placing the focus on information gathering and processing has met with much broader approval. *Mark Lowenthal's* definition is as follows: 'Intelligence can be thought of as the means by which certain types of information are required and requested, collected, analyzed (…).[11]'

6 *Peter Gill* and *Mark Phythian*, by contrast, prefer a combined definition that links processes and operations and at the same time refers to the function of intelligence:

> (…) the mainly secret activities – targeting, collection, analysis, dissemination and action – intended to enhance security and/or maintain power to competitors by forewarning of threats and opportunities.[12]

7 In some cases, intelligence is (also) understood as being product-related:

> All intelligence is information; not all information is intelligence.[13]
> Intelligence is a subset of the broader category of information.[14]

8 The following detailed description can be found in US military law applicable to the US Armed Forces:

> Intelligence is the product resulting from the collection, processing, integration, evaluation, analysis, and interpretation of available information concerning foreign nations, hostile or potentially hostile forces or elements, or areas of actual or potential operations.[15]

9 Finally, some take an institution-related approach: 'Intelligence can be thought of as the units that carry out its various functions.[16]'

10 It is generally recognized that intelligence is not formally limited to any specific state entities (e.g. civilian or military). How intelligence is organized is one of the subject matters of intelligence studies, not a matter of its definition. Thus, both 'private intelligence'[17] and 'criminal intelligence'[18] are covered by the term 'intelligence'.

11 No uniform jurisprudential definition can be made out among the operation-, process-, product- and institution-related approaches, which can, above all, be attributed to the different national legal systems and legal terminology. The legal terminology used in various countries' domestic legislation cannot simply be transferred by means of a generally accepted English translation. For example, in accordance with German law, the French *Direction Générale de la sécurité intérieure* (Directorate General for Internal Security, DGSI) could only be partially defined as an 'intelligence agency' because, under German legislation, the work of the *Nachrichtendienste* (intelligence services) is characterized by the fact that they do not have any law enforcement powers. § 2(3) sent. 1 of the Federal Intelligence Service Act (*Gesetz über den Bundesnachrichtendienst,*

[10] See, e.g., Gill/Phythian, p. 17 et seq., with further references.
[11] Lowenthal, p. 17.
[12] Gill/Phythian, p. 19.
[13] Lowenthal, p. 2.
[14] Jensen/McElreath/Graves, p. 8.
[15] U.S. Department of Defense, 'The Dictionary of Military and Associated Terms', 2017; U.S. Department of the Army, 'Army Doctrine Reference Publication 2-0 Intelligence (ADRP 2-0)', 31.12.2012.
[16] Lowenthal, p. 116; similarly, U.S. Department of Defense, 'The Dictionary of Military and Associated Terms', 2017.
[17] See, in more detail, Blancke, p. 4 et seqq.
[18] In more detail: Ryder in Dietrich/Sule, Intelligence Law and Policies, p. 255; On 'intelligence-led law enforcement', only Europol, 'Intelligence Analysis' (10.10.2017) < https://www.europol.europa.eu/activities-services/services-support/intelligence-analysis> (last accessed: 11.9.2023).

BNDG), for example, reads as follows: 'Polizeiliche Befugnisse oder Weisungsbefugnisse stehen dem Bundesnachrichtendienst nicht zu.[19]'

Thus, the German intelligence services are not permitted to make arrests or search dwellings. Likewise, they cannot be subordinated to any police administrative/organizational structures. France's understanding of its *services spécialisés de renseignement* (specialized intelligence services) is very different. The following is taken from Art. 1 of the *Décret n° 2014-445 du 30 avril 2014 relatif aux missions et à l'organisation de la Direction Générale de la sécurité intérieure*: 12

> La direction générale de la sécurité intérieure est un service actif de la police nationale. (…) Elle concourt, dans ses domaines de compétence, à l'exercice des missions de police judiciaire sur l'ensemble du territoire dans les conditions prévues à l'article 15-1 du code de procédure pénale.[20]

The DGSI even has its own operational group – known as the *Groupe d'appui opérationnel* (Operations Support Group, GAO) – which is responsible for making arrests, conducting house searches and bringing criminals to justice. It is chiefly made up of police officers. 13

The above example shows that there is no uniform definition of what 'intelligence' is. In particular, there is no international consensus on the matter.[21] National concepts of intelligence deviate too strongly to be able to be subsumed under one term.[22] That has consequences for European intelligence cooperation, the issue being addressed here, because a collaborative approach to cross-border threats to the security of Europe and its citizens will only be successful if 'intelligence' is defined broadly. It must, for example, cover the joint preparation of intelligence products, within the EU, for decision-makers in EU institutions as well as collaboration between individual national authorities on the combating of terrorism. In the following 'intelligence' will therefore be understood as a working concept as proposed by *Lowenthal*: 14

> Intelligence is the process by which specific types of information important to national or European security are requested, collected, analyzed and provided to policy makers; the products of that process; the safeguarding of these processes and this information by counterintelligence activities; and the carrying out of operations as requested by lawful authorities.[23]

II. Intelligence cooperation

It is not surprising that 'intelligence cooperation' is just as multifaceted as our understanding of 'intelligence' itself. There is no generally recognized definition. In the following, specific coordinates will be pegged out to facilitate an understanding of 'intelligence cooperation'. The focus will first and foremost be on international cooperation, since cooperation at the national level plays less of a role in the European dimension. 15

[19] Translation: The federal intelligence services have no police powers or authority to issue orders.

[20] Translation: The DGSI is an active department of the French *police nationale*. (…) Under the conditions set out in Art. 15-1 of the Criminal Code, it contributes, within its remit, to the exercise of the tasks of the criminal police across the entire state territory.

[21] For details, see Bang, IJICI 2016, 102 (106).

[22] Herman, p. 240; Davies, Harvard International Review 2002, 62.

[23] Lowenthal, p. 10

1. Intelligence cooperation as a prerequisite for national security

16 Transnational intelligence cooperation has a long history.[24] The rules on which international relations are based generally also apply to the content and intensity of such cooperation. The closer the diplomatic, military or economic ties a state has with another state, the more comprehensive the intelligence cooperation between the two states will be. 'Information' and 'trust' are the currencies in which business is done.[25] What information a state will need in a specific case will depend on its national policy priorities. An economically strong exporting nation like Germany may, for instance, have a particular interest in safe international trade routes; Estonia, Latvia and Lithuania, by contrast, will want to carefully monitor Russia's and Belarus's troop movements along their borders.

17 National intelligence services' staffing levels and budgets vary depending on a state's size and political significance. Some states have several agencies, while others only have one. In Germany, for example, the Federal Intelligence Service (*Bundesnachrichtendienst*, BND) functions both as a foreign intelligence service and as a military intelligence service. In 2023 it employed around 7,600 staff and had an annual budget of some EUR 1bn.[26] The Netherlands has a General Intelligence and Security Service (*Algemene Inlichtingen- en Veiligheidsdienst*, AIVD), which is responsible for intelligence activities at home as well as abroad. It currently has a staff of approx. 2,000 and an annual budget of some EUR 316m.[27] These statistics alone show that it is hard to avoid cross-border cooperation. For staffing and budgeting reasons, agencies operating in smaller states have fewer sensors of their own. They are grateful for information being provided to them by the intelligence services of larger partner countries. And, vice versa, smaller intelligence services can often bring special regional expertise to the table. On account of their linguistic skills, topographical know-how or ethnic background they can often get their hands on information that would otherwise be beyond the reach of larger agencies. Even very large intelligence services like those in the United States can, thus, be reliant on international cooperation.

18 Within political alliances, intelligence cooperation can also be understood as contributing to burden-sharing. The rise of international Islamist terrorism in particular has shown that cross-border threats can only be tackled by means of close cooperation. The assailants who carried out the awful Bataclan attacks in Paris in 2015 lived in Brussels, acquired their weapons illegally from eastern Europe, via Germany, and took instructions from people based in Syria.[28] It is obvious that such networked organizations, which are highly dynamic and mobile, cannot be dealt with effectively by one single state alone. Cooperation does not always have to involve the exchange of information, though. Where possible on the basis of domestic legislation, cooperation with foreign authorities can also comprise financial or technical support, for instance, or training assistance.[29]

---

[24] See Herman, p. 200.

[25] See Born/Leigh/Wills, p. 16.

[26] See Mascolo, 'Auch Spione strukturieren um' (Süddeutsche Zeitung, 1.12.2022); Gesetz \xFCber die Feststellung des Bundeshaushaltsplans f\xFCr das Haushaltsjahr 2023 vom 19. Dezember 2022, BGBl. I, 2485.

[27] See Ministerie van Binnenlandse Zaken en Koninkrijksrelaties, <https://www.aivd.nl/onderwerpen/werken-bij-de-aivd/vraag-en-antwoord> (last accessed: 11.09.2023); Ministerie van Financiën, 'Rijksbegroting 2020: Artikel 2. Nationale veiligheid'.

[28] See, in that regard, Lledo-Ferrer/Dietrich, IJICI 2020, 440 (442).

[29] See Born/Leigh/Wills, p. 18 et seqq.

2. Intelligence cooperation, intelligence cycle and multi-source intelligence

19 An intelligence product that is delivered to political or military decision-makers is the result of a complex process, often described as the 'intelligence cycle'.[30] Whether the intelligence services' current practice can still be described as a cycle must be viewed sceptically. Rather, there is now a network of interacting processes that places the users of intelligence at its centre.[31] However, the 'intelligence cycle' model still serves very well when it comes to explaining the various facets of intelligence service work, which is why it will also be applied here.

20 Five stages can be roughly made out. At the start of the cycle, political objectives need to be defined, that is what governmental information needs the intelligence services are required to meet. In Germany, for example, the Federal Chancellery, which has lead responsibility in the matter, cooperates with other federal ministries to define 'information requirements' regarding the work of the BND, which sets regional, thematic and political priorities. After these government internal requirements have been delineated, stage two consists of qualitative and quantitative intelligence collection. Incoming raw data regularly need to be classified and processed, analysed and correlated. That is done during the intelligence processing and intelligence analysis phases. Analysis produces knowledge, which has to be tailored to the needs of the specific addressee and turned into an intelligence product. There are various forms that intelligence products can take. Finally, the last stage involves disseminating the intelligence-laden product to the political or military decision-makers and it then being taken into account by them. It is at this stage, at the latest, that a comparison is made as to whether and how much more information is needed; and so the cycle begins again.

21 Intelligence cooperation above all has a key role to play during the intelligence collection and intelligence analysis stages. Intelligence services draw on a variety of sources. Publicly available sources such as speeches given by political leaders at party conferences, press reports and social media posts may be useful. A speech is thus open source intelligence (OSINT). It stands to reason that open sources are not likely to reveal anything about secret missile programmes or planned terrorist attacks. That is why the intelligence services use undercover information-gathering tools, for instance telecommunications surveillance (signals intelligence, SIGINT) and undercover informants (human intelligence, HUMINT). It is only when they are all taken together that these different types of information can provide a meaningful situation report. A single source of information may often not be very productive or may not be very trustworthy. Some terrorist cells, for instance, are already using sophisticated encryption techniques in their telecommunications.[32] As a result, classic telecommunications surveillance comes to nothing. In such cases, recruiting informants is more likely to produce results. During the intelligence analysis stage, the individual pieces of information then act as mutual correctives. It is possible to establish whether, for instance, an informant is telling the truth or merely grandstanding by comparing his or her information with other information. This dovetailing of sources is referred to as 'multi-source intelligence'. It guarantees that the end result is reliable intelligence, that is an intelligence product that can be passed on to decision-makers.

22 Multi-source intelligence is inconceivable without cooperation. Even the most up-to-date satellite monitoring (imagery intelligence, IMINT) cannot get inside people's heads. It cannot overcome barriers such as ethnic origin or exotic languages. That is why large

---

[30] For more details, see Omand, p. 117 et seqq.

[31] See Omand in Dietrich/Sule, Intelligence Law and Policies, p. 55.

[32] See Aldrich, Review of International Studies 2009, 889 (894 et seq.).

agencies are often forced to cooperate with local foreign agencies. And, vice versa, the intelligence services' staffing and finances can sometimes be so limited as to make intelligence cooperation the only means for them to get hold of crucial information.

3. From 'need to know' to 'need to share'

23 The more states, societies and individuals across the world become interconnected on a technical, economic and political level, the more their vulnerabilities will also change. Today, for instance, hate and hate speech can be disseminated in a targeted manner through international networks and thus poison a society's social climate. Right-wing extremist blogs and websites such as *Iron March* and *The Daily Stormer* have long since reached an international audience. The removal of global boundaries is thus a key driver of intelligence cooperation.[33] It has, to a certain extent, led to a paradigm shift as far as administrative practice is concerned: from a 'need-to-know' to a 'need-to-share' basis.[34] During the Cold War only that information was shared that was absolutely essential. However, given the high level of interconnectedness of today's world, it would at times seem almost foolish to keep important information to oneself.

24 However, one should not forget that intelligence cooperation is also a very effective tool of influence.[35] Intelligence services that have only few sensors at their disposal are grateful for information they regularly receive from larger partners. Press reports about foiled terrorist attacks thus often include the following: 'The tip-off came from a foreign intelligence service.'[36] Dangerous political dependencies can arise in such contexts, though. States that give their intelligence services few staff and little funding or only weak legal powers and simultaneously place their trust in international partners run the risk of being exploited.

4. Informal and institutionalized partnerships in bilateral and multilateral cooperation

25 The mode of intelligence cooperation varies fundamentally according to the number of involved partners and the quality of intergovernmental relations. Bilateral cooperation is widespread. States generally have what are known as stations in their diplomatic missions.[37] They act as the interface between a state's own and the foreign authorities. These stations with diplomatic cover are staffed with members of the intelligence service who have diplomatic status and are registered ('accredited') with the foreign authorities.[38] Stations exist regardless of the quality of intergovernmental relations. In difficult times, when communications between political decision-makers have already broken down, they can be used to keep the channels of communication open at the working level. In some cases, though, several authorities are involved in intelligence cooperation. An informal format enables joint undercover operations to be carried out, for example to monitor a suspected terrorist's cross-border movements. Formalized multilateral

---

[33] See Aldrich in Born/Leigh/Wills, International Intelligence Cooperation and Accountability, p. 22 et seq.

[34] For examples, see Cross in Dietrich/Sule, Intelligence Law and Policies, p. 243 et seqq.

[35] Born/Leigh/Wills, p. 17.

[36] In Germany, one in two tip-offs regarding a terrorist attack comes from a foreign entity. See Der Spiegel, 'Ausländische Geheimdienste lieferten jeden zweiten Hinweis' (6.2.2022) <https://www.spiegel.de/politik/deutschland/geplante-terroranschlaege-auslaendische-geheimdienste-lieferten-jeden-zweiten-hinweis-a-d0c347fb-f379-419b-b4bd-47b69c51c306> (last accessed: 11.9.2023).

[37] See Rüß in Dietrich/Eiffler, Handbuch des Rechts der Nachrichtendienste, IV § 4 mn. 105.

[38] See Dietrich in Dietrich/Eiffler, Handbuch des Rechts der Nachrichtendienste, VI § 2 mn. 41 et seqq.

cooperation, on the other hand, can involve the creation of a shared database, for instance.[39]

The quality of intergovernmental relations is an important prerequisite for the chosen 26
mode of intelligence cooperation. Cooperation with foreign states (and their agencies) with which a state has bad or even hostile relations will be very limited. Where, by contrast, states have long-established links at the political level, especially on account of their membership of international alliances, they can in certain circumstances even share sources or technical procurement methods. Typologies of intelligence cooperation have been developed in the political science literature.[40] The model proposed by *Tom Røseth* seems convincing. He distinguishes between different levels of intelligence relations based on how close two states are:

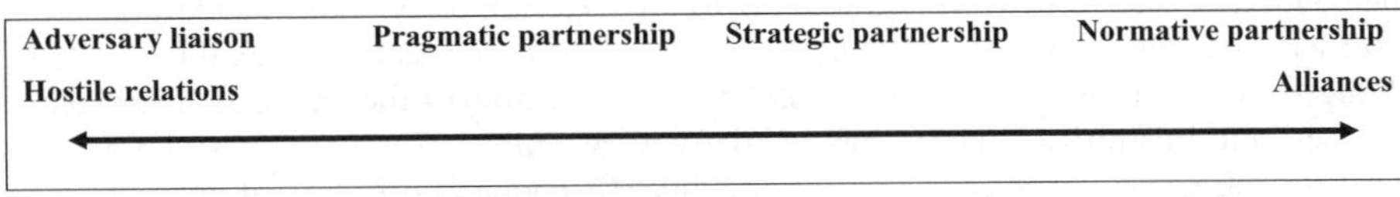

Figure 1: Types of intelligence partnership according to Røseth[41]

According to *Røseth*, a 'normative partnership' is characterized by a common under- 27
standing of norms, values and standards. These include, for instance, respect for human rights, the rule of law and democracy or, specifically, accepting judicial or parliamentary oversight of intelligence activities. A normative partnership is based on a relationship of trust, which may be formalized in security agreements. These are international treaties that take the form of administrative agreements concluded between the governments or individual ministers of two or more states. They regulate the reciprocal exchange and recognition of classified information.[42] Below the threshold of international treaties, non-binding bilateral or multilateral agreements may also be concluded as part of a normative partnership. These are agreed at the intelligence services' management level in the form of Memoranda of Agreement (MoA) or Memoranda of Understanding (MoU), and they represent a basis for doing business in the form of long-term cooperation.[43] According to *Røseth*, a normative partnership is characterized by the pooling of bureaucratic resources to achieve better work results.

By contrast, a 'strategic partnership' – which *Jennifer Sims* calls a 'complex 28
intelligence liaison'[44] – does not necessarily need to be based on shared values and norms. It serves a more or less balanced mutual benefit. *Røseth* is of the opinion that strategic partnerships are planned to be long term and that mechanisms for building mutual trust can be used to offset unilateral vulnerabilities or even setbacks.[45] That can include, for instance, joint fora, training facilities or fusion centres. A 'pragmatic relationship' – sometimes also referred to as a 'simple intelligence liaison'[46] – is, on the other hand, based on more short-term, tactical considerations. It is used to identify common threats that permit (or sometimes even require) a limited amount of

[39] See Maaßen in Dietrich et al., Reform der Nachrichtendienste zwischen Vergesetzlichung und Internationalisierung, p. 185; critical Ryngaert/van Eijk, International Data Privacy Law 2019, 61.

[40] See, e.g., Westerfield, Intelligence and National Security 1996, 523; Røseth in Røseth/Weaver, Intelligence Relations in the 21st Century, p. 41 et seqq.; Sims, IJICI 2006, 195.

[41] Røseth in Røseth/Weaver, Intelligence Relations in the 21st Century, p. 47 et seqq.

[42] See, e.g., Agreement on the Mutual Protection of Classified Information between the Federal Republic of Germany and the United Kingdom of 28.5.2003, BGBl. II 2003, 568.

[43] See Rüß in Dietrich/Eiffler, Handbuch des Rechts der Nachrichtendienste, IV § 4 mn. 108.

[44] See Sims, IJICI 2006, 195 (197).

[45] Røseth in Røseth/Weaver, Intelligence Relations in the 21st Century, p. 51 et seq.

[46] Sims, IJICI 2006, 195 (197).

cooperation, though always at the risk that it will be misused by one of the parties ('asymmetric adversarial liaison'[47]). It goes without saying that it will often not be possible to assign a specific instance of intelligence cooperation to any of the aforementioned categories. In practice, the boundaries are fluid. And it would limit a state's options if the type of cooperation entered into by its intelligence services had to fit into a particular foreign policy model.

29 Regardless of this, however, a trend can be made out as regards the structure of intelligence cooperation. In principle, cooperation between stakeholders is as informal as possible. This provides a maximum amount of flexibility beyond any agreed political, bureaucratic or normative constraints. In such a context, no state and no intelligence service is obliged vis-à-vis any partners to contribute anything in a specific manner to the cooperation or to be held accountable to any steering body. With increasing global interdependencies, however, states', societies' and individuals' vulnerabilities have changed considerably. In consequence, as described above, the mode of intelligence services' administrative practice has in many areas shifted from a need-to-know to a need-to-share basis. The structure of intelligence cooperation has led to increasing institutionalization.

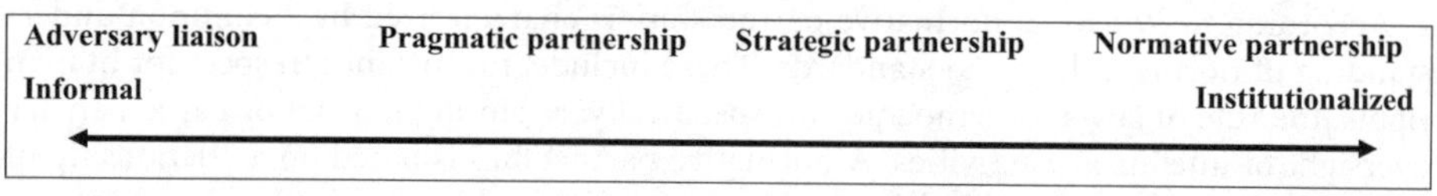

Figure 2: Intelligence partnerships between informality and institutionalization

30 That institutionalization can be manifest in different ways. One possible option is to set up communicative fora in which experts can engage in professional exchange. The Paris Group, for instance, which comprises the national intelligence coordinators of key EU Member States, was set up in 2016 primarily to engage in intergovernmental coordination of policy issues relating to intelligence work.[48] The Counter-Terrorism Group (CTG), which was set up by European domestic intelligence services following the 9/11 attacks, was initially intended to be a dialogue forum. It has since become institutionalized. In 2017 the CTG was expanded to include an operative platform that aims to simplify and accelerate the sharing of operative intelligence between European intelligence services.[49] National authorities can second liaison officers to this operative platform, which is based in The Hague. The creation of shared training structures is another aspect of institutionalization. NATO's HUMINT Centre of Excellence (COE) is one example. It describes its remit as follows:

> HUMINT COE drives the transformation of the HUMINT capability in NATO based on Lessons Learned and Best Practices, coupled with integration of scientific research and modern technologies, innovative standards and effective, quality-based education and training, in order to keep Human Intelligence relevant in NATO and better answer the evolving operational environment requirements and challenges.[50]

31 The institutionalization of intelligence cooperation has progressed the furthest where joint intelligence gathering and analysis capacities are dovetailed. The so-called Five Eyes alliance has garnered international attention. Within the alliance, Australia, New

[47] ibid., 200. See also Walsh, p. 3 et seqq., 11 et seq.; Herman, p. 218.

[48] German Bundestag, BT-Drs. 19/7268. 23.1.2019, 1 et seqq.

[49] See German Bundestag, BT-Drs. 18/9222, 3.8.2016, 1 et seqq.; Rüß in Dietrich/Eiffler, Handbuch des Rechts der Nachrichtendienste, IV § 4 mn. 115.

[50] See also the official website <https://www.natohcoe.org> (last accessed: 12.9.2023).

Zealand, Canada, the United Kingdom and the United States organize their SIGINT capabilities as burden-sharing.[51] Another, less well-known, intelligence alliance is the Maximator project, in which Denmark, France, Germany, Sweden and the Netherlands have joined forces for telecommunications surveillance purposes.[52]

The key advantage of institutionalized cooperation is efficient resource use. Retaining human expertise and maintaining technical sensors is personnel-intensive and costly. A division of labour makes sense from an administrative and financial perspective. The New Zealand Security Intelligence Service (NZSIS) gets to the heart of the matter in one of its annual reports: 32

> (…) the Five-Eyes partnership provides New Zealand with access to systems, technology and information that we would not be able to develop or have access to on our own. The partnership also provides the NZSIS with access to training and skills courses that aren't available in New Zealand.[53]

Despite its undeniable advantages, an institutionalized partnership can also have its disadvantages. The broader the links between the partners, the more susceptible the work of the individual partners is to interference. Where, for instance, one member of a multilateral cooperation uncovers a case of treason, partners' sources or technical capabilities may be put at risk. Another disadvantage of the increasing institutionalization of intelligence cooperation is the concomitant bureaucratization. Multilateral cooperation needs to create a joint basis for doing business that defines how decisions are to be taken, for instance, and by whom. The complicated governance structures within the Intelligence College in Europe (ICE) are an example of such bureaucratization.[54] The ICE's Steering Committee, which comprises representatives of its 24 member countries, is responsible for taking those key decisions that will subsequently be implemented by a Permanent Secretariat, which is based in Paris. ICE business is handled by a Presidency, which a member country holds for a year. The Presidency is supported by troika, which also includes the previous and future Presidencies. The multitude of stakeholders alone indicates that decision-making processes may be time-consuming. 33

C. Intelligence cooperation in Europe

The above remarks have prepared the ground so as to be able to address the various facets of intelligence cooperation among EU Member States. Whether that cooperation takes place within or beyond the supranational construct that is the EU has a big role to play in this and is an issue that will need to be addressed in a nuanced manner in the following. 34

I. EU intelligence cooperation between political ambition and bureaucratic reality

As stated above (→ mn. 1), in adopting its Strategic Compass in March 2022, the EU positioned itself as an international security actor on a level with the 35

[51] See Cartmell, Journal of Intelligence History 2022.

[52] See Jacobs, Intelligence and National Security 2020, 659.

[53] NZSIS, 'Annual Report, For the year Ended', 30.6.2014, p. 18, <https://www.nzsis.govt.nz/assets/NZSIS-Documents/NZSIS-Annual-Reports/NZSIS-Annual-Report-2014.pdf> (last accessed 11.9.2023).

[54] On the ICE, see Lledo-Ferrer/Dietrich, IJICI 2020, 440.

United States and China. There is talk of 'strategic autonomy'.[55] And the Strategy is equally as ambitious when it comes to the Security Union. What is remarkable is that these two policy documents on security policy both make explicit mention of intelligence cooperation within the EU. Previously, the work of the Member States' intelligence services and the EU's intelligence capacities had at most been referred to in the context of counter-terrorism.[56] The Strategic Compass states the following, for instance:

> We will invest more in shared analysis to increase our situational awareness and strategic foresight, building on our Early Warning System and horizon scanning mechanism. We will strengthen our intelligence-based situational awareness and relevant EU capacities, notably in the framework of the EU Single Intelligence Analysis Capacity, as well as the EU Satellite Centre. This will also bring us closer to a common strategic culture and contribute to the EU's credibility as a strategic actor. We need to maintain our excellence in ensuring autonomous EU decision-making, including based on geospatial data. We will reinforce the role of the EU Single Intelligence Analysis Capacity as single entry point for strategic intelligence contributions from Member States' civilian and military intelligence and security services. This will facilitate the exchange of strategic intelligence to better respond to the challenges we are facing and provide improved services to decision-makers across EU Institutions and Member States.[57]

36 And the EU Security Union Strategy states the following as regards fighting hybrid threats:

> The aim should be to ensure that the decision-making process is underpinned by regular, comprehensive intelligence-based reporting on the evolution of hybrid threats. This will rely heavily on Member States' intelligence and on further enhancing intelligence cooperation with Member States' competent services through EU INTCEN.[58]

37 On closer inspection, the objectives that have been set are thus extremely ambitious. Stepping up intelligence cooperation is to contribute to establishing a common strategic culture, which in turn is underpinned by EU foreign and security policy autonomy. The reference to 'autonomous EU decision-making, based on geospatial data' can even be interpreted as an explicit desire to be independent of partners in the United States. Politically, such objectives do in fact appear to be without any alternative. They are practically being foisted on the EU owing to developments in terms of the international balance of powers. The Trump Presidency in the United States made it very clear that even close transatlantic ties can sometimes become volatile. China and Russia have also expressed openly aggressive power political visions of a permanently changed international order. Against this backdrop, European self-assertiveness must be organized at the supranational level, because otherwise individual states' egotisms would be paid for with a loss of importance and wide-ranging dependencies.

38 Nevertheless, security policy ambitions are currently faced with the bureaucratic reality of the inconsequential skeleton structures of EU intelligence capacities. The EU Intelligence and Situation Centre (EU INTCEN), the Union's intelligence nerve centre,

---

[55] Council of the European Union, 'A Strategic Compass for Security and Defence', 21.3.2022, 7371/22, 13.

[56] For instance in European Council, 'The Hague Programme: strengthening freedom, security and justice in the European Union' 3.3.2005, OJ C 53, 3.3.2005, 1, which, in the context of its objective of combating terrorism, explicitly states that the Member States are expected to 'use the powers of their intelligence and security services not only to counter threats to their own security, but also, as the case may be, to protect the internal security of these other Member States, (…)'. See also European Commission, 'A Counter Terrorism for the EU: Anticipate, Prevent, Protect, Respond', 9.12.2020, COM (2020) 795 final, 3.

[57] Council of the European Union, 'A Strategic Compass for Security and Defence', 21.3.2022, 7371/22, 21.

[58] COM(2020) 605 final, 19.

currently only has a relatively small staff of around 80.[59] It has no means of collecting intelligence of its own. Instead, EU INTCEN is reliant on being fed information by the Member States' intelligence services.[60] The principle of voluntary participation applies here, though, and the quality and quantity of information supplied consequently varies significantly. It is thus easy to see where the key problems of intelligence cooperation at the EU level lie. Intelligence collection is not only largely externalized within the European intelligence cycle, it is also based on a certain degree of arbitrariness.[61] *Björn Fägersten* assumes that this is down to the 'bureaucratic resistance' that some intelligence services or their staff have to more intensive cooperation. Their motivation could be a fear of a loss of importance, a divergent bureaucratic culture or secrecy concerns owing to their mistrust of the other partners.[62]

Based on all of the above, it is evident that the EU's global political ambitions cannot be built on its current intelligence capabilities.[63] The EU intelligence infrastructure needs to undergo significant changes in order to be able to meet future needs. This verdict is by no means new, but is in line with the conclusions drawn by many research studies conducted in recent years.[64] The extent to which reforms will be successful will first be determined by the primary legislative setting, to which our attention now turns. 39

II. The primary legislative setting

1. Art. 4(2) sent. 3 TEU – limiting the exercise of powers in the area of 'national security'

Art. 4(2) sent. 3 TEU set the course for EU intelligence cooperation in important ways. Under the provision, 'national security' continues to be the sole responsibility of each Member State. Art. 73 TFEU is the logical extension of that regulatory idea. According to the latter provision, the Member States are free to 'organise between themselves and under their responsibility forms of cooperation and coordination as they deem appropriate between the competent departments of their administrations responsible for safeguarding national security.' Both Art. 73 TFEU and Art. 4(2) sent. 3 TEU were added at the request of the UK Government at the intergovernmental conference on the Treaty of Lisbon.[65] Both provisions establish a competence reservation in matters of national security. The EU's competences may not be interpreted and applied such that the Member States' competence comes to nothing in this area. Conversely, that means that the Member States are free not to apply Union law (e.g. data protection legislation) when they exercise their competence in regard to national security.[66] The Member States' competence reservation, as set out in the primary legislation, is mirrored in EU legislative practice in secondary legislative acts on the scope of specific regulations. The following is taken from Art. 2(2)(a) GDPR[67]: 40

[59] See Conrad in Dietrich et al., Reform der Nachrichtendienste zwischen Vergesetzlichung und Internationalisierung, p. 171.

[60] Palacios is very critical, see Palacios in Dietrich/Sule, Intelligence Law and Policies, p. 217.

[61] See the recent publication by Gruszczak, Politeja 2022, 131 (133).

[62] See Fägersten, Intelligence and National Security 2010, 500 (502 et seqq.).

[63] Szép/Sbatino/Wessel, ENGAGE Working Paper Series 2022, 28.

[64] See, e.g., Pronk/Korteweg; Szép/Sbatino/Wessel, ENGAGE Working Paper Series 2022, 27 et seqq.

[65] See Herrnfeld in Schwarze et al., AEUV Art. 73 mn. 1, with further references.

[66] Karpenstein/Sangi, GSZ 2020, 162 (165), with reference to the *traveaux préparatoires*.

[67] Regulation (EU) 2016/679 on the protection of natural persons with regard to the processing of personal data and on the free movement of such data (General Data Protection Regulation).

> This Regulation does not apply to the processing of personal data:
> a) in the course of an activity which falls outside the scope of Union law (…).

41 Recital 16 GDPR clarifies what is meant by that:

> This Regulation does not apply to issues of protection of fundamental rights and freedoms or the free flow of personal data related to activities which fall outside the scope of Union law, such as activities concerning national security.

42 However, although the regulatory technique is very clear-cut, what is still unclear is what is meant by 'national security'. And it is also still unclear to what extent the Member States' intelligence activities are subsumed under 'national security'. Some in the literature claim that, in the case of 'national security', a blanket exemption from primary and secondary EU law applies, that is as far as regulating the Member States' intelligence activities is concerned.[68] Others express a more nuanced view.[69]

43 On closer inspection, there is little that speaks for a blanket exemption. Although the Court of the Justice of the European Union has so far been quite cautious in its interpretation of the term 'national security',[70] a historical/teleological interpretation makes it clear that the scope of the competence reservation set out in Art. 4(2) sent. 3 TEU must remain extremely limited.[71] Otherwise, the rule would allow Member States to circumvent Union law in certain instances by invoking a threat to security interests, no matter how minor. That at any rate speaks in favour of interpreting 'national security' more narrowly than the term 'public security', which is used elsewhere (e.g. in Art. 36 and 45(3) TFEU). 'National security' thus exclusively refers to concerns relating to a state's fundamental vested interests; in that sense the term is largely congruent with the 'essential interests of its security' within the meaning of Art. 346 TFEU.[72] *Satish Sule* convincingly argues that a Member State's territorial integrity, its constitutional order, political and economic system, and its public supply structures should form part of the core area of its national responsibility.[73]

44 The following conclusion can be drawn for the above: The work of the intelligence services is not in and of itself excluded from the scope of EU law. There is no immunity under EU law. The intelligence services' activities are only exempted from the scope of EU law where they can clearly be defined as matters of national security. Thus, it must be examined in each individual case whether EU law supersedes domestic law. The devil is in the detail.

45 Some of the Member States' intelligence activities can relatively easily be identified as matters of national security. They include, for instance, satellite-based reconnaissance in relation to troop movements in states beyond the EU territory, the monitoring of the activities of violent extremists using undercover informants, uncovering military espionage by foreign powers and the surveillance of terrorist plots by listening in on telephone conversations. However, it is definitely more difficult where agencies have both law enforcement and intelligence powers (→ mn. 11). Arrests and searches are

---

[68] For example, Rüß in Dietrich/Eiffler, Handbuch des Rechts der Nachrichtendienste, IV § 4 mn. 7 et seqq.

[69] See, in that regard, Sule in Dietrich/Sule, Intelligence Law and Policies, p. 358 et seqq.

[70] Latterly without any clear definition of 'national security', ECJ 6.10.2020 – case C-623/17, ECLI:EU:C:2020:790 para. 74 et seq. – *Privacy International* and ECJ 6.10.2020 – joined cases C-511/18, C512/18 and C-520/18, ECLI:EU:C:2020:791, para. 135 – *La Quadrature du Net.* See, in that regard, Cameron, Common Market Law Review 2021, 1433 et seqq.

[71] See Dietrich in Dietrich et al., Handbuch des Sicherheits- und Staatsschutzrechts, § 6 mn. 42.

[72] See Karpenstein/Sangi, GSZ 2020, 162 (167).

[73] Sule in Dietrich/Sule, Intelligence Law and Policies, p. 358.

never a 'national security' matter; they are generally part of protecting 'public security'. And so there may be overlaps between different legal regimes.

How the contradictions that arise in such cases can sensibly be resolved has not yet been sufficiently clarified. It its ruling in the *La Quadrature du Net* case, the ECJ made it clear that 46

> although it is for the Member States to define their essential security interests and to adopt appropriate measures to ensure their internal and external security, the mere fact that a national measure has been taken for the purpose of protecting national security cannot render EU law inapplicable and exempt the Member States from the obligation to comply with that law.[74]

It is not clear what this finding is based on; the ruling contains no reasons. By requiring that when Member States' intelligence services implement measures in the event of a 'serious threat to national security' they at least ensure that 'an effective review' is conducted 'either by a court or by an independent administrative body whose decision is binding', the ECJ is overstepping its competence. The Member States' parliaments and courts face considerable challenges on account of this case law. Although the Member States can easily meet the call for an independent oversight of measures implemented by the intelligence services to protect national security, because most of them already have the relevant bodies, the ECJ has nevertheless ventured into a *domaine réservé* and dangerously shifted the scope of Union law.[75] 47

The *Conseil d'État* hinted at the extent of the problems after the ECJ remitted the *La Quadrature du Net* case back to it. The highest French administrative court was forced to strike a very fine balance in its decision of 21 April 2021 so as to implement the ECJ's ruling under French law.[76] Formally speaking, it resisted the French government's call for the case to be remitted back for being *ultra vires*. In actual fact, though, the *Conseil d'État* has the last word when it comes to reviewing whether the requirements made under French constitutional law to protect public policy and security have been met and whether its national interests so defined are protected when applying Union law as specifically interpreted by the CJEU. As a result, the law enforcement and security authorities can continue to count on it being possible, under French law, to require telecommunications providers to retain data, as the *Conseil d'État* believes that the conditions the ECJ attached to a concrete and ongoing threat are met in France. On closer inspection, a 'permanent state of exception' is here being assumed. This is merely mitigated by the call for additional reviews (an independent review of the Prime Minister's instruction on data use not only *ex post*; regularly reasoned finding by the government of the existence of a threat).[77] 48

The above means two things in relation to the issue of intelligence cooperation that is of interest to us: First, the EU can in fact address regulations to the Member States' intelligence services outside the scope of matters of national security. It would, for instance, be conceivable to introduce a secondary legislative ban on industrial and economic espionage among Member States on the basis of Art. 4(3) TEU.[78] The Member States can, in principle, even be required to cooperate on intelligence matters in areas in which the EU has competence. The setting up of a central intelligence agency, which has 49

---

[74] ECJ 6.10.2020 – joined cases C-511/18, C512/18 and C-520/18, ECLI:EU:C:2020:791 para. 99 – *La Quadrature du Net*.

[75] See, in that regard, Cameron, Common Market Law Review 2021, 1433 (1462).

[76] French Council of State (Conseil d'État) – Assemblée, No. 392099, 21/04/2021, ECLI:FR:CEASS:2021:393099.20210421.

[77] Rojszczak is critical and cautionary: Rojszczak, ECLR 2021, 607 (630).

[78] In detail, Sule in Dietrich/Sule, Intelligence Law and Policies, p. 359 et seqq., 375 et seqq.

been called for on many an occasion,[79] would be possible under primary EU legislation, although its remit would be limited.[80] An own EU agency to protect against espionage targeting EU institutions, for instance, would likewise not be ruled out.[81] Cautious beginnings can be seen in the EU Commission's security service, based at DG HR. Second, the above remarks also clearly show that most binding EU regulations relating to intelligence cooperation would be ruled out by Art. 4(2) sent. 3 TEU. Instead, Art. 73 TFEU emphasizes that the Member States are free to organize forms of cooperation and coordination under their own responsibility, including bilaterally and multilaterally ('between themselves'). Especially in the context of 'national security' – a sensitive issue from the perspective of sovereignty – the Member States are thus to be given the possibility to cooperate at the intergovernmental level. They are thus given a great deal of leeway. If such cooperation is to remain within the framework of the *ECJ*'s (not unproblematical) case law as outlined in the above, then minimum rule-of-law standards must be upheld.

2. Intelligence cooperation on account of the duty to provide assistance in the spirit of solidarity pursuant to Art. 222 TFEU?

50 Whether the Member States should be obliged to step up their intelligence cooperation is being discussed in the context of Art. 222 TFEU.[82] The provision, which regulates a special case in which the Member States are required to act in the spirit of solidarity, has its origins in Art. 3(3) subpara. 3 TEU. The focus is on the Union's and the Member States' obligation to provide assistance in the event of a terrorist attack or a natural or man-made disaster – a typical national emergency. In such cases, assistance in the spirit of solidarity is desirable and necessary in order to ensure that functions of state are maintained and, especially against the backdrop of the state's obligation to protect citizens' fundamental rights, to protect the population against more wide-ranging harm.

51 Sometimes, obligations to step up intelligence cooperation are derived from point (a) of Art. 222(1) sent. 2 and Art. 222(4) TFEU.[83] Under the first of the two, intelligence cooperation is to be brought into position as a preventative measure to counter terrorist threats. Point (a) of Art. 222(1) sent. 2 TFEU reads as follows:

> The Union shall mobilise all the instruments at its disposal, including the military resources made available by the Member States, to:
> (a) – prevent the terrorist threat in the territory of the Member States;

52 The emphasis on the importance of preventative cooperation is not surprising, since the EU sets great store by not only combating terrorism reactively but preventively stopping it happening.[84] However, the reference is specifically to the means that are 'at its disposal'. This primarily refers to EU measures in the area of law enforcement and judicial cooperation in criminal matters right up to the freezing of payments made to

---

[79] See, e.g., Amor, 'Why the EU need access to first-hand intelligence information' (Europe Daily Bulletin No. 13065, 18.11.2022) <https://agenceurope.eu/en/bulletin/article/13065/35> (last accessed: 12.9.2023).

[80] For details, see Sule in Dietrich/Sule, Intelligence Law and Policies, p. 383 et seq.

[81] See, in that regard, Moens, 'The EU has a spy problem – here's why it's so difficult to catch them' (POLITICO, 1.12.2022) <https://www.politico.eu/article/eu-spy-problem-heres-why-its-so-difficult-to-catch-them-espionage-russia-china/> (last accessed: 12.9.2023).

[82] See, in that regard, e.g., Rüß in Dietrich/Eiffler, Handbuch des Rechts der Nachrichtendienste, IV § 4 mn. 12 et seqq.; Sule in Dietrich/Sule, Intelligence Law and Policies, p. 385 et seq.

[83] See Myrdal/Rhinard, Occasional UI Papers 2010, 9.

[84] See, in that regard, COM(2020) 795 final.

terrorist organizations.[85] In relation to intelligence cooperation, Art. 4(2) sent. 3 TEU prevents this rule being extended to matters of national security.[86]

The conclusion is no different in the case of Art. 222(4) TFEU. In order to be prepared to face future threats, paragraph (4) obliges the European Council to 'regularly assess the threats facing the Union'. The aim is to establish an early warning system[87] so that both the Member States and the Union (the addressees of the solidarity clause) are able to meet their obligations as efficiently as possible, that is insofar as there is a risk of such a threat arising.[88] However, Art. 222(4) TFEU explicitly refers to the European Council as the body that is made up of the Member States' heads of state and government. It says nothing about the transfer of competence in order to harmonize the intelligence services' information collection or about the creation of a legal basis on which to build an EU intelligence service.[89] As is clear from the example of the Strategic Compass, existing EU structures are here instead used to conduct the threat analysis referred to in Art. 222(4) TFEU. In the Council Conclusions on Security and Defence of 17 June 2020 the EU foreign and defence ministers called on the High Representative of the Union for Foreign Affairs and Security Policy to put forward, by the end of 2020, a 'threat analysis' that was to form the basis of the Strategic Compass.[90] This was implemented by EU INTCEN and the Intelligence Directorate in the European Union Military Staff (EUMS INT), which are both subordinate to the EEAS and together form the Single Intelligence Analysis Capacity (SIAC).[91] This enabled the processing, on a voluntary basis, of intelligence and analyses from the Member States in connection with the 'perceived threats'. Insofar as policy approaches such as the Strategic Compass or the EU Security Union Strategy are approved by the European Council, they can be regarded as contributing to the implementation of Art. 222(4) TFEU.[92] 53

3. Intelligence cooperation as part of 'Permanent Structured Cooperation' within the meaning of Art. 42(6) and Art. 46 TEU

Stepping up cooperation among the Member States' intelligence services could be facilitated in the context of permanent structured cooperation (PESCO) as established by Art. 42(6) and Art. 46 TEU. The aim of permanent structured cooperation is to close the 'capability gap' of the EU Member States' armed forces and to contribute, by means of a 'coalition of the willing' (that could be expanded at any time), to building those national military capabilities that are needed in the light of the EU's military missions.[93] Art. 42(6) and Art. 46 TEU are thus of decisive importance when it comes to establishing a core security policy Union among those Member States that are more committed in terms of their defence equipment and military. Permanent structured cooperation is reserved to those Member States 'whose military capabilities fulfil higher criteria' and that are prepared to take on 'the most demanding missions' (Art. 42(6) TEU). 54

---

[85] See Thym in Grabitz/Hilf/Nettesheim, AEUV Art. 222 mn. 18.

[86] Rüß also hits the nail on the head, see Rüß in Dietrich/Eiffler, Handbuch des Rechts der Nachrichtendienste, IV § 4 mn. 15.

[87] See Ramsperger, p. 310.

[88] See Calliess in Calliess/Ruffert, AEUV Art. 222 mn. 43.

[89] See Sule in Dietrich/Sule, Intelligence Law and Policies, p. 386.

[90] Council of the European Union, 'Council Conclusions on Security and Defence', 17.6.2020, 8910/20, 4.

[91] See German Bundestag, BT-Drs. 19/28576, 15.4.2021, 1 et seqq.

[92] See Thym in Grabitz/Hilf/Nettesheim, AEUV Art. 222 mn. 30.

[93] See Cremer in Calliess/Ruffert, EUV Art. 46 EUV mn. 1.

55 In Protocol No. 10 to the TEU,[94] the Member States give more concrete expression to the obligations a state must enter into to be able to participate in permanent structured cooperation. The focus is mainly on a Member State's willingness to strengthen its military capabilities as well as its ability, as and when required, to supply both armed forces and logistics within a short space of time and over an extended period. In order that Member States can meet this demand, pursuant to Art. 2 of the Protocol, participating Member States must undertake to cooperate. In particular, the participating States are to ensure interoperability of their defence capabilities, and the identification of military needs is also to be harmonized and means of defence are to be jointly used, too.[95] Permanent structured cooperation is implemented at the project level. A total of 46 PESCO projects have so far been adopted in three previous project rounds. They range from the development of underwater drones to combat naval mines and developing a protective system for harbours and sea routes, to establishing a rapid reaction team to combat cyberattacks.

56 The diversity of the projects referred to in the above clearly shows that the latitude available knows hardly any bounds. It cannot, thus, be ruled out that projects in the field of military intelligence[96] will also be realized.[97] And the Member States have indeed increasingly availed themselves of this opportunity. Some projects address the field of intelligence, surveillance and reconnaissance (ISR) and thus deal with aspects of the military intelligence cycle. Activities in this area include the 'Chemical, Biological, Radiological and Nuclear Surveillance as a Service' (CBRN SaaS), the 'Electronic Warfare Capability/Interoperability Programme for Future Intelligence, Surveillance and Reconnaissance' (JISR) and the 'European Military Space Surveillance Awareness Network' (EU-SSA-N) projects.[98] At the time of writing, all the aforementioned ISR projects were still ongoing. Whether the criticism expressed by some[99] has the desired effect remains to be seen. At any rate, an eye must be kept on whether and to what extent permanent structured cooperation creates any unnecessary doubling of NATO capabilities.

57 Finally, it is doubtful whether individual PESCO projects with links to intelligence can lead to an increase in quality standards. Doubts arise, for example, in the case of the Greek/Cypriot 'Joint European Union Intelligence School' (JEIS) project. The following is taken from the project description:

> The JEIS, in collaboration with member states, NATO CoEs [Centres of Excellence], Intelligence and Security Services, will provide education and training in intelligence disciplines and other specific fields to EU member states intelligence personnel.[100]

58 It is not surprising that only two Member States are currently involved in the project, since it goes well beyond the framework set in Art. 42(6) TEU by addressing 'intelligence and security services' even though permanent structured cooperation, as the law currently stands, is limited to 'military capabilities'. One must agree with *Artur Gruszczak* when he says that there are 'many doubts regarding its [the Joint European Union Intelligence School's] conceptual bases and possibilities of their implementation'.[101]

---

[94] Protocol (No. 10) on permanent structured cooperation established by Art. 42 of the Treaty on European Union, Document 12008M/PRO/10.

[95] For details, see Labuhn, GSZ 2019, 66 (68 et seqq.).

[96] Re this term, see Scheffler/Dietrich, IJICI 2023, 1.

[97] In this regard, see Rauwolf in Dietrich/Sule, Intelligence Law and Policies, p. 173.

[98] For an overview <https://www.pesco.europa.eu/#projects> (last accessed: 12.9.2023).

[99] See, e.g., Labuhn, GSZ 2019, 66 (69 et seqq.).

[100] See <https://www.pesco.europa.eu/project/joint-eu-intelligence-school/> (last accessed: 12.9.2023).

[101] See Gruszczak, Komentarz ZBN 2018, 1.

4. Intelligence cooperation as 'Enhanced Cooperation' in accordance with Art. 326 et seqq. TFEU

Another possibility besides permanent structured cooperation as established by Art. 42(6) and Art. 46 TFEU is intergovernmental intelligence cooperation in the sense of 'enhanced cooperation' as defined in Art. 326 et seqq. TFEU, that is as long as it does not concern 'military capabilities'. Art. 42(6) and Art. 46 TEU are thus *lex specialis* in relation to Art. 326 et seqq. TFEU. Enhanced cooperation means that Member States that have established a greater level of cooperation can avail themselves of the Union's institutional framework. That is why the relevant institutional norms set in the TEU and the TFEU (i.e. rules on organization and procedure) apply to the necessary legislative acts and decisions.[102] 59

Under Art. 329(2) TFEU, enhanced cooperation may be established within the framework of the Common Foreign and Security Policy (CFSP). Member States wishing to establish enhanced cooperation between themselves are not required to submit their proposal to the Commission, but directly to the Council, an indication of the intergovernmental nature of the CFSP. The Council then forwards the request to the High Representative of the Union for Foreign Affairs and Security Policy and to the Commission. The High Representative gives an opinion on whether the proposed enhanced cooperation is consistent with the CFSP. The Commission primarily gives its opinion on whether the proposed enhanced cooperation is consistent with other Union policies. The European Parliament is not required to give its consent. 60

Some have proposed that enhanced cooperation could be used to strengthen intelligence cooperation among Member States.[103] It is conceivable, they claim, that the national intelligence service coordinators, who form a network within the Paris Group could be tasked with examining the possibility of more binding cooperation on the basis of existing EU structures such as EU INTCEN. This could create a solid foundation for future intelligence cooperation at the EU level on the basis of a Council Decision, it is claimed. 61

This proposal is certainly appealing, since the EU intelligence capabilities' biggest weakness is currently their dependency on information being supplied by the Member States' authorities and the simultaneous voluntariness as regards the quality and quantity of that information (→ mn. 38). Establishing enhanced cooperations could lead to the emergence of a core of Member States that undertake to cooperate more closely in certain areas (e.g. Islamist terrorism, hybrid threats), that is specifically to exchange certain types and qualities of information and apply ambitious standards of secrecy and minimum rule-of-law requirements. The established SIAC structures could be enhanced by such new impetus. 62

As desirable as this scenario may be from a global policy perspective, its implementation seems difficult. Under Art. 329(2) TFEU, authorization to proceed with enhanced cooperation is 'granted by a decision of the Council acting unanimously'. That means that a simple veto by an uninvolved Member State could prevent enhanced cooperation among other Member States without the need to provide any reason whatsoever. In the sensitive area of intelligence cooperation it cannot be ruled out that use will be made of the option of entering such a veto. The Member States 63

[102] Ruffert in Calliess/Ruffert, AEUV Art. 330, mn. 2.

[103] See Conrad in Dietrich et al., Reform der Nachrichtendienste zwischen Vergesetzlichung und Internationalisierung, p. 173 et seqq.

would, though, still have the option of cooperating outside the EU framework, as provided for in Art. 73 TEU (→ mn. 49, 85).

III. EU intelligence structures

64 As shown in the above, primary EU legislation permits intelligence cooperation within the EU framework only to a limited extent. Nevertheless, strategic policy decisions taken by EU institutions in regard to the CFSP, in the area of energy policy and cyber security need to be prepared. And those institutions need information to do so, which often includes intelligence. To that end, the EU has put in place support structures, which we will now take a closer look at.

1. Single Intelligence Analysis Capacity (SIAC)

65 EU intelligence is first and foremost organized under the umbrella of the Single Intelligence Analysis Capacity (SIAC), which was set up in 2006.[104] Since then the SIAC has pooled the civilian and military analysis capacities of EU INTCEN (EU Joint Situation Centre, SITCEN, up until 2011) and of EUMS INT. The SIAC is not a separate agency, but more of an alliance of different directorates within the EEAS, which is subordinate to the High Representative of the Union for Foreign Affairs and Security Policy.[105] The SIAC applies the concept of intelligence fusion. It is where information of the most varied provenance is collated to generate all-source intelligence products.[106] EU INTCEN and EUMS INT collaborate within the SIAC alliance defined in this way as and when required and on the basis of an international administrative agreement (SIAC Agreement). Depending on the region or subject matter, staff share information and draw up an integrated situation report based on civilian and military information, which in turn is used to prepare joint intelligence products.[107] One of the two SIAC components takes on lead responsibility in each case.

66 SIAC products are always prepared for EU decision-makers, in particular those in the EEAS, the Commission and the Council. The SIAC is controlled via the Intelligence Support Architecture (ISA) as defined in a proposal made by the High Representative.[108] The Global Strategy, the Strategic Compass and the Security Union Strategy form its political/conceptual basis. ISA has an Intelligence Steering Board (ISB) and an Intelligence Working Group (IWG). Chaired by the High Representative or the EEAS Executive Secretary-General, the ISB comprises senior officials from the relevant Managing Directorates of the EEAS, representatives of the General Secretariat of the Council (GSC), the Commission and the EU Counter-Terrorism Co-ordinator. By comparison, the IWG, co-chaired by the heads of EU INTCEN and EUMS INT, acts as a preparatory body for the ISB. The representatives of the relevant Managing Directorates of the EEAS meet on a monthly basis. The IWG proposes prioritized intelligence requirements (PIR) to the ISB. Once approved by the ISB, priorities, focuses

---

[104] For details on the history of the SIAC, see Palacios in Dietrich/Sule, Intelligence Law and Policies, p. 216 et seq.; Gruszczak, Politeja 2022, 131 (140 et seq.).

[105] See Conrad in Dietrich et al., Reform der Nachrichtendienste zwischen Vergesetzlichung und Internationalisierung, p. 169 et seqq.

[106] Palacios in Dietrich/Sule, Intelligence Law and Policies, p. 216.

[107] See Conrad in Dietrich et al. (eds), Reform der Nachrichtendienste zwischen Vergesetzlichung und Internationalisierung, p. 172.

[108] As regards what follows, see Szép/Sbatino/Wessel, ENGAGE Working Paper Series 2022, 28.

and needs are used to define joint intelligence production. And so the EU intelligence cycle (→ mn. 19 et seqq.) is set in motion.

The importance of the SIAC has steadily increased in recent years, concomitant with the EU's assertiveness in regard to foreign policy. In its Conclusions on Security and Defence in the context of the EU Global Strategy, the Council expressed the following in relation to the SIAC: 67

> The Council welcomes the progress made in promoting EU civil-military intelligence-based situational awareness, notably through the systematic alignment of structures and procedures between EU Intelligence Centre and the Intelligence Directorate of the EU Military Staff, within the EEAS. It supports the gradual approach chosen to enhance the capabilities of the Single Intelligence Analysis Capacity (SIAC) of the EU and the short term needs already defined for additional staffing.[109]

Only a few years later the SIAC prepared the first comprehensive 360-degree analysis of threats to the EU on behalf of the High Representative and in preparation of the Strategic Compass, which was presented to the Member States in November 2020.[110] Against this backdrop it is not surprising that the Strategic Compass also underlines the key role of the SIAC: 68

> We will strengthen our intelligence-based situational awareness and relevant EU capacities, notably in the framework of the EU Single Intelligence Analysis Capacity, as well as the EU Satellite Centre. This will also bring us closer to a common strategic culture and contribute to the EU's credibility as a strategic actor.[111]

It is not difficult to recognize that the SIAC has now become a firmly established structure, and that high hopes are placed in it. However, one should not lose sight of the fact that, in its current format, the SIAC merely represents the lowest common denominator in terms of intelligence cooperation. It is doubtful whether it can be used to deal with the foreign and security policy challenges that are currently being faced, especially since the expansion of the SIAC announced in the Strategic Compass has not yet taken on more concrete form. 69

a) EU Intelligence and Situation Centre (EU INTCEN)

EU INTCEN, the civilian component of SIAC, goes back as far as the late 1990s. Following the entry into force of the Treaty of Amsterdam, the EU Joint Situation Centre (SITCEN) was founded in 2002 within the Policy Unit of the then High Representative of the Union, *Javier Solana*, in order to provide him with regular reports on current events and special analyses of specific incidents.[112] A few years after the entry into force of the Lisbon Treaty, SITCEN was integrated into the EEAS and in 2012 renamed the 'EU Intelligence Analysis Centre'.[113] Since 2015 the abbreviation 'EU INTCEN' has been used to refer to the EU Intelligence and Situation Centre. It was not absolutely essential for it to be incorporated into the EEAS, since the work of EU INTCEN is not limited to foreign affairs. 70

From an administrative and organizational perspective, EU INTCEN is a Directorate of the EEAS that reports directly to the High Representative. It currently has two divisions: Intelligence Analysis and Reporting (INTCEN 1) and Support/Open Sources 71

[109] Council of the European Union, 'Council Conclusions on Security and Defence in the context of the EU Global Strategy', 18.5.2017, 9178/17, 4.

[110] See Szép/Sbatino/Wessel, ENGAGE Working Paper Series 2022, 27et seq.

[111] Council of the European Union, 'A Strategic Compass for Security and Defence', 21.3.2022, 7371/22, 33.

[112] See Rüß in Dietrich/Eiffler, Handbuch des Rechts der Nachrichtendienste, IV § 4 mn. 20 et seqq.

[113] See Palacios in Dietrich/Sule, Intelligence Law and Policies, p. 216.

Research (INTCEN 2).[114] A Hybrid Fusion Cell (HFC), which was added in 2017, processes and prepares information about state-controlled propaganda, disinformation, blackmail and cyberattacks.[115] To date, EU INTCEN has no legal basis. SITCEN is only mentioned in the Council Decision on the Constitution of the EEAS as a precursor to EU INTCEN because it moved from being part of the Council to the EEAS.[116] Since it is not a separate entity, EU INTCEN does not have its own budget. Like EUMS INT, in budgetary terms it is subject to the EEAS; its staff of currently around 80[117] are mainly seconded from the Member States' intelligence services.[118]

72 Independently of the SIAC framework (→ mn. 65), EU INTCEN offers the following products:[119]

- Intelligence assessments: long-term strategic papers, mainly based on intelligence.
- Intelligence reports: follow-up of a crisis or an event, or a thematic paper focusing on a specific topic of current interest.
- Intelligence summaries: focusing on current important events with a short intelligence based analysis.
- Threat assessments: focusing on risks for EU personnel in a given country.

73 When the Hybrid Fusion Cell was created, the breadth and analytical depth of EU INTCEN's products significant increased.[120] Consequently, the Strategic Compass underlines the need to further develop the SIAC and, in particular, the Hybrid Fusion Cell as part of an EU Hybrid Toolbox 'to strengthen the EU's ability to detect, identify and analyse hybrid threats and their source'.[121]

74 EU INTCEN's productivity is controlled via the ISA (→ mn. 66). Since it has no operative sensors of its own, at the intelligence collection stage of the intelligence cycle it is to a significant degree reliant on information from the Member States and other units within the EU (e.g. SATCEN imagery intelligence products). It also draws on open source intelligence. There is a formal procedure that Member States need to follow when passing on information.[122] EU INTCEN sends what are known as requests for information (RFIs) to the more than 80 civilian and military intelligence and security services in the Member States. Information is also shared bilaterally at the working and management level. Information is delivered on voluntary basis (→ mn. 38). Finally, EU INTCEN's analysis units condense incoming information into an overall situation report, which is used to prepare individual intelligence products. Here, too, the intelligence cycle is not perfect, because there is no binding relationship between intelligence collection and intelligence analysis.

75 EU INTCEN's meagre external communications regularly attach importance to the fact that it only obtains finished intelligence from the Member States not personal data.[123]

---

[114] See the EEAS's organizational chart, available at <https://www.eeas.europa.eu/sites/default/files/documents/2023/2023_-_05_-_01_-_EEAS_OrgChart.pdf> (last accessed: 12.9.2023).

[115] See, in more detail, Gruszczak, Politeja 2022, 131 (142 et seqq.).

[116] Council of the European Union, 'Decision of 26 July 2010 establishing the organisation and functioning of the European External Action Service', 26.6.2010, OJ L 201, 3.8.2010, 30.

[117] As at 2019; Conrad in Dietrich et al., Reform der Nachrichtendienste zwischen Vergesetzlichung und Internationalisierung, p. 171.

[118] European External Action Service, 'EU INTCEN, Fact Sheet', 5.2.2015.

[119] ibid.

[120] See Conrad, European Foreign Affairs Review 2021, 55 (61).

[121] Council of the European Union, 'A Strategic Compass for Security and Defence', 21.3.2022, 7371/22, 34 et seq.

[122] See, for more details, Conrad in Dietrich et al., Reform der Nachrichtendienste zwischen Vergesetzlichung und Internationalisierung, p. 169 et seqq.

[123] See European Parliament, 'Answer of 25 April 2017 given by Vice-President Mogherini on the behalf of the Commission to parliamentary question E-000599/2017', 27.2.2018. See also Rüß in Dietrich/Eiffler, Handbuch des Rechts der Nachrichtendienste, IV § 4 mn. 24.

This is an attempt to shift legitimacy to the Member States in order to stave off calls for democratic transparency and rule-of-law oversight. That is hard to reconcile with the fundamental values laid down in Art. 2 TEU, irrespective of whether it is hard to imagine that EU INTCEN's analyses never involve personal data (especially where terrorism is concerned).[124] However, those who, against this backdrop, would like to see the European Parliament exercising greater oversight forget that that body is now filled with not a few members of extremist political parties in the Member States and/or the EU who reject its values as a matter of principle. The political exploitation of and scandal-mongering in relation to intelligence is thus ruled out just as little as is the betrayal of secrets. One must, therefore, agree with *Iain Cameron* when he says that intelligence oversight by the European Parliament would not be a sensible solution to the lack of legitimacy.[125] Should the EU's intelligence capabilities be expanded at some point in the future, then consideration should at least be given to oversight by a panel of experts.

b) EU Military Staff Intelligence Directorate (EUMS INT)

The Intelligence Directorate of the EU Military Staff (EUMS INT, or EUMS B) is the SIAC's military component. It has been part of the EU Military Staff (EUMS), as a Directorate-General of the EEAS, since 2011.[126] The tasks of the Directorate comprise providing early warning and situation assessment, contributing to advanced planning and providing intelligence for crisis response planning, operations and exercises.[127] Compared to EU INTCEN, it still has only a relatively small staff to handle this wide-ranging remit.[128] EUMS INT has no specific legal basis. At least, though, it is based on a Council Decision 2001/80/CFP, in whose Annex reference is made to EUMS INT.[129] **76**

In line with the intelligence cycle (→ mn. 19 et seqq.), EUMS INT is divided into three branches:[130] The Policy Branch is responsible for the design of intelligence concepts and contributes to the planning of EU military operations; the Support Branch is responsible for cooperation with the Member States' military intelligence organizations and serves as information manager; the Production Branch is the key element within the Directorate that fuses all consumer needs at the level of EU institutions. In practice, it often cooperates with EU INTCEN within the SIAC alliance. The Production Branch of EUMS INT regularly takes the lead on joint SIAC products with a military focus (→ mn. 65). **77**

Like EU INTCEN, EUMS INT does not have its own sensors.[131] It is also dependent on being given information by the Member States and other agencies within the EU complex of institutions. There is no obligation to share information, which limits EUMS INT's clout.[132] Cooperation with military and defence intelligence organiza- **78**

[124] On this problem, see Gruszczak, p. 263 et seqq.

[125] On the intelligence oversight of EU institutions, see Cameron in Dietrich/Sule, Intelligence Law and Policies, p. 416 et seqq.

[126] See the EEAS's organizational chart <https://www.eeas.europa.eu/sites/default/files/documents/2023/2023_-_05_-_01_-_EEAS_OrgChart.pdf> (last accessed: 12.9.2023).

[127] See Rauwolf in Dietrich/Sule, Intelligence Law and Policies, p. 169.

[128] According to Conrad in Dietrich et al., Reform der Nachrichtendienste zwischen Vergesetzlichung und Internationalisierung, p. 172; Rauwolf in Dietrich/Sule, Intelligence Law and Policies, p. 172: 'not more than a few dozen'.

[129] Council of the European Union, 'Decision 2001/80/CFSP on the establishment of the Military Staff of the European Union', 30.1.2001, OJ L 27, 7, as last amended by Council Decision 2005/395/CFSP, OJ L 132, 26.5.2005, 17.

[130] See Rauwolf in Dietrich/Sule, Intelligence Law and Policies, p. 169 et seq. and Palacios in Dietrich/Sule, Intelligence Law and Policies, p. 218; Gruszczak, p. 105 et seq.

[131] See Gruszczak, p. 106 et seqq.

[132] Rauwolf is critical: Rauwolf in Dietrich/Sule, Intelligence Law and Policies, p. 172.

tions is based on an informal agreement (Cooperation Framework Arrangement for Intelligence Support to the EU, CFAIS).[133] EUMS INT's production is controlled via ISA (→ mn. 66).

2. European Union Satellite Centre (EU SATCEN)

79 The European Union Satellite Centre (EU SATCEN), initially established in 1992 within the Western European Union (WEU) as the Western European Union Satellite Centre, does not form part of SIAC.[134] It was not turned into an EU agency until 10 years later.[135] In 2014, SATCEN was given its own legal basis in Council Decision 2014/401/CFSP.[136]

80 SATCEN sees itself as the EU's imagery intelligence agency. The term 'intelligence' is nowhere to be found, though, in the agency's profile. Art. 2 of the aforementioned Council Decision merely states that

> SATCEN shall support the decision making and actions of the Union in the field of the CFSP and in particular the CSDP, including European Union crisis management missions and operations, by providing, at the request of the Council or the HR, products and services resulting from the exploitation of relevant space assets and collateral data, including satellite and aerial imagery, and related services, in accordance with Article 3.

81 Based on its own understanding of itself, SATCEN is involved less at the strategic level but above all sees itself as a 'unique operational asset'.[137] Its core competence is interpreting satellite imagery as well as geospatial intelligence in support of EU decision-making.[138] To date, SATCEN does not have its own sensors. In the overwhelming majority of cases, satellite images are purchased from commercial providers.[139] That is a huge advantage, as it means that SATCEN products can be quickly made available to customers.[140] EU INTCEN and EUMS INT are reliant on Member States delivering information. Sometimes SATCEN is also given access to governmental imagery based on individual agreements with specific Member States (e.g. products in the COSMO-SkyMed, SAR-Lupe and HELIOS programmes).[141]

82 SIAC is one of the main consumers of SATCEN products. Within the EU intelligence cycle, SATCEN is responsible for intelligence processing (→ mn. 20) via its cooperation with the SIAC. SATCEN also has customers beyond the EU intelligence community, though, including the European Commission and Frontex. International organizations like the United Nations (UN) and the Organization for Security and Co-operation in Europe (OSCE) also purchase SATCEN products. The Member States without exception all have access to SATCEN products, which is of huge benefit to smaller Member States in particular.

83 Unlike EU INTCEN and EUMS INT, SATCEN has its own website, on which it publishes its annual reports and budget reports. It currently employs around

---

[133] See Palacios in Dietrich/Sule, Intelligence Law and Policies, p. 218.

[134] See Rüß in Dietrich/Eiffler, Handbuch des Rechts der Nachrichtendienste, IV § 4 mn. 30.

[135] Council of the European Union, 'Joint Action 2001/555/CFSP of 20 July 2001 on the establishment of a European Union Satellite Centre', 20.7.2001.

[136] Council Decision, '2014/401/CFSP of 26 June 2014 on the European Union Satellite Centre and repealing Joint Action 2001/555/CFSP on the establishment of a European Union Satellite Centre'.

[137] EU Satellite Centre, 'Annual Report 2021, Luxembourg: Publications Office of the European Union', 2022, 13.

[138] See Palacios in Dietrich/Sule, Intelligence Law and Policies, p. 220.

[139] EU Satellite Centre, 'Annual Report 2021' (2022), p. 40 et seqq.

[140] Palacios in Dietrich/Sule, Intelligence Law and Policies, p. 221.

[141] See EU Satellite Centre, 'Annual Report 2021' (2022), 40 et seqq.

150 people.[142] That is likely to change very soon. The following is taken from the Strategic Compass:

> By 2025, we will strengthen our Single Intelligence Analysis Capacity by enhancing the resources and capacities. By 2025, we will also strengthen the EU Satellite Centre to boost our autonomous geo-spatial intelligence capacity.[143]

SATCEN's success story is thus set to continue. **84**

IV. Intelligence cooperation beyond the EU

All the above has made it clear that although intelligence cooperation within the EU **85** framework is increasing, it has its limits. It is, therefore, not surprising that cooperation between the EU Member States' intelligence services largely occurs outside the EU institutional framework. And, in fact, Art. 73 TFEU does permit that.

Traditionally, bilateral cooperation has occurred between individual entities (for **86** more details, → mn. 25). The intensity of such bilateral cooperation is generally based on foreign policy relations between the involved states for which those entities work. Trust forms the basis of such cooperation. A high level of trust can, for instance, be expressed in administrative agreements (e.g. MoA or MoU), which act as the soft-law basis for long-term cooperation.[144]

Informal networks have existed in parallel at the multilateral level for some time **87** now, and they have become increasingly institutionalized (→ mn. 26 et seqq.). European domestic intelligence services have, for instance, been cooperating since 1971 within the informal Club de Berne.[145] The heads of authorities meet regularly in this format. A special counter-terrorism element (the Counter-Terrorism Group, CTG) was set up within the Club de Berne in the aftermath of the 9/11 attacks. The CTG has evolved into a separate unit and today comprises 30 domestic intelligence services from EU Member States as well as Switzerland and Norway. The CTG is primarily tasked with stepping up cooperation between the EU domestic services, improving information sharing, identifying counter-measures and strengthening cooperation with EU institutions and non-EU services.[146] This work in particular generates regional or thematic threat assessments on aspects of Islamist terrorism.[147] The CTG is therefore linked to EU entities in various ways. For instance, its chair mirrors the Council Presidency, for instance, and it regularly takes part in meetings of the Justice and Home Affairs Council (JHA).[148] Upon request, the CTG also makes its products available to EU INTCEN and other customers within the EU, such as Europol.[149] The CTG is considerably more institutionalized than the Club de Berne (→ mn. 30).

---

[142] ibid., 68.

[143] Council of the European Union, 'A Strategic Compass for Security and Defence', 21.3.2022, 7371/22, 39.

[144] See Rüß in Dietrich/Eiffler, Handbuch des Rechts der Nachrichtendienste, IV § 4 mn. 105 et seqq.

[145] See Cross in Dietrich/Sule, Intelligence Law and Policies, p. 246.

[146] See, in that regard (in German only) <https://www.verfassungsschutz.de/DE/verfassungsschutz/auftrag/zusammenarbeit-im-in-und-ausland/counter-terrorism-group-ctg/counter-terrorism-group-ctg_node.html> (last accessed: 12.9.2023).

[147] See de Kerchove/Höhn in Dietrich/Sule, Intelligence Law and Policies, p. 112.

[148] German Bundestag, BT-Drs. 18/9323, 3.8.2016, 8.

[149] See de Kerchove/Höhn in Dietrich/Sule, Intelligence Law and Policies, p. 112.

88 Finally, the Intelligence College in Europe (ICE), which was put forward in 2019, is a manifestation of multilaterally and institutionally intensified cooperation between EU intelligence services.[150] The ICE was essentially based on a French initiative. In speech given at the Sorbonne in 2017, French President *Emmanuel Macron* called for a common 'strategic intelligence culture' among EU Member States and thus underlined the need to cultivate common values and standards:

> Dans la lutte contre le terrorisme, l'Europe doit assurer le rapprochement de nos capacités de renseignement en créant une Académie européenne du renseignement.[151]

89 That is where the ICE comes into the picture. In accordance with Art. 4(2) sent. 3 TEU, it is not an EU institution, but pursues an intergovernmental approach. It is based on a Letter of Intent that 23 countries in Europe (including the United Kingdom and Norway) signed on 26 February 2020. It states the following as regards its understanding of itself:

> The college is a unique forum where all members of national intelligence communities can get together. It promotes and facilitates strategic dialogue between intelligence communities from participating European Countries, academics, national and European decision-makers to enhance strategic thinking and mutual knowledge on topics of common interest. This process is based on a spirit of openness, common values, voluntariness and collegiality and enhances trust within and between these communities. (…)
> The Intelligence College in Europe is a platform for reflection, engagement and outreach. It fosters mutual understanding through strategic dialogue between:
> – Intelligence communities in participating Countries;
> – European intelligence communities and Academia;
> – European intelligence communities, national and EU decision-makers.[152]

90 To achieve these objectives, the members of the ICE have reached agreement on a governance structure (→ mn. 33). On the one hand, this governance structure is the manifestation of the binding nature of the ICE. On the other hand, though, the ICE's organizational structure is so complicated that cooperation is, in practice, not exactly made any easier. Seven countries (including Poland and Bulgaria) that originally expressed an interest in joining the ICE have since opted for an 'associated partnership' rather than full membership.[153] That impressively demonstrates the high obstacles the ICE still needs to overcome.

91 Nevertheless, the founding of the ICE was an important step, because it is clear that it 'will decisively contribute to the emergence of a European strategic culture by enabling joint reflection about prospective and strategic issues and regular interactions'.[154] It completes the de facto solidarity that already exists at the operational level between the intelligence agencies across Europe and helps build a European intelligence community that is more than the sum of its parts.

---

[150] See Lledo-Ferrer/Dietrich, IJICI 2020, 440 (446 et seqq.).

[151] The speech is available (in French) at <https://www.elysee.fr/emmanuel-macron/2017/09/26/initiative-pour-l-europe-discours-d-emmanuel-macron-pour-une-europe-souveraine-unie-democratique> (last accessed: 12.9.2023).

[152] The ICE Letter of Intent is available at <https://www.intelligence-college-europe.org/wp-content/uploads/2020/03/LoI-English.pdf> (last accessed: 12.9.2023).

[153] See Barigazzi/Momtaz, 'European spies dare to share' (POLITICO, 26.2.2020) <https://www.politico.eu/article/european-spies-dare-to-share-intelligence-college-in-europe-ice/> (last accessed: 12.9.2023); German Bundestag, BT-Drs. 19/19848, 10.6.2020, 2.

[154] See Lledo-Ferrer/Dietrich, IJICI 2020, 440 (448).

C. Conclusions

There is a popular saying in German that expresses a paradox: '*Wasche mir den Pelz, aber mache mich nicht nass*'. Roughly translated, it means 'wash my fur but don't get me wet'. In fact, it conveys the state of European intelligence cooperation rather well, in that current geopolitical developments are forcing EU Member States to step up their foreign and security policy cooperation (→ mn. 37). The EU has grand ambitions. The EU wants to operate at eye level with the United States and China, and intelligence cooperation is key to that. On the other hand, though, European intelligence cooperation faces numerous legal and actual obstacles. It is chiefly based on voluntariness and is non-binding in nature. The Member States and their agencies do not want to be obliged to share a specific quality and quantity of information. **92**

It goes without saying that strategies for bridging the gap are not easy to find. The **93** reality of cooperation by EU INTCEN, the CTG and the ICE shows that robust multilateral cooperation cannot simply be mandated. The European intelligence community is not yet ready for that. The only realistic option appears to be a bottom-up approach.[155] First, though, a common intelligence culture needs to be established, to give intelligence cooperation its own grammar, as it were. The starting point for that is an understanding of common democratic and rule-of-law values and ambitious professional standards. Only then will there be enough trust to make the paradigm shift in relation to information sharing, that is from a 'need-to-know' to 'need-to-share' basis.

---

[155] ibid., 446.

§ 19
Integrated border management: evolving tasks and division of labour between the EU and Member States

Raphael Bossong

Bibliography: Anderson/Apap, Police and Justice Co-operation and the New European Borders, Alphen aan den Rijn 2002; Andreeva, 'The Zerkani Network and the 2015 Paris and 2016 Brussels Attacks: An Illustration of Counter-Terrorism Dysfunction', Europe Studies in Conflict & Terrorism 2023, 1; Argomaniz, 'When the EU is the "Norm-taker": The Passenger Name Records Agreement and the EU's Internalization of US Border Security Norms', Journal of European Integration 2009 (31), 119; Aus, 'Decision-making under Pressure: The Negotiation of the Biometric Passports Regulation in the Council', Arena Working Paper 2006 (11); Bachiller López, 'Border policing at sea: Tactics, routines, and the law in a Frontex patrol boat', British Journal of Criminology 2023 (63), 1; Beduschi, The New European Border and Coast Guard: A failed response to the migration crisis, London 2016; Bellanova/Glouftsios, 'Formatting European security integration through database interoperability' , European Security 2022 (31), 454; Bendiek/Bossong, 'Shifting boundaries of the EU's foreign and security policy', (2019) SWP Research Paper 2019 (12); Bigo/Ewert/Kuşkonmaz, 'The interoperability controversy or how to fail successfully: lessons from Europe', IJMBS 2020 (6), 93; Blasi Casagran, 'Fundamental Rights Implications of Interconnecting Migration and Policing Databases in the EU', Human Rights Law Review 2021 (21), 433; Bossong, 'EU border security in a time of pandemic: Restoring the Schengen regime in the face of old conflicts and new requirements for public health', SWP Comment 2020 (28); Bossong, 'Intelligence Support for EU Security Policy, Options for Enhancing the Flow of Information and Political Oversight', SWP Comment 2018 (51); Bossong, 'Intelligente Grenzen und interoperable Datenbanken für die innere Sicherheit der EU – Umsetzungsrisiken und rechtsstaatliche Anforderungen', SWP-Studie 2018 (4); Bossong, 'The expansion of Frontex, Symbolic Measures and Long-term Changes in EU Border Management', SWP Comment 2019 C 47; Carrera, 'A European Border and Coast Guard, What's in a name?', CEPS Paper in Liberty and Security in Europe 2016 (88); Carrera/Stefan, Fundamental Rights Challenges in Border Controls and Expulsion of Irregular Immigrants in the European Union, Abingdon/Oxon/ New York 2020; Casas/Cobarrubias/Pickles, 'Stretching Borders Beyond Sovereign Territories? Mapping EU and Spain's Border Externalization Policies', Geopolítica 2011 (2), 71; Cortinovis, 'The Evolution of Frontex Governance: Shifting from Soft to Hard Law?', JCER 2015 (11:3), 252; Deleixhe/ Duez, 'The new European border and coast guard agency: pooling sovereignty or giving it up?', Journal of European Integration 2019 (41), 921; Dumbrava, 'Artificial intelligence at EU borders, Overview of applications and key issues', EPRS 2021, PE 690.706; Falkner/Treib/Hartlapp/Treiber, Complying with Europe: EU Harmonisation and Soft Law in the Member States. Themes in European Governance, Cambridge 2005; Gabriel Felbermayr, Jasmin Gröschl and Thomas Steinwachs, 'The Trade Effects of Border Controls: Evidence from the European Schengen Agreement' (2017) ERIA Discussion Paper Series, No. 2; Fernandez-Rojo, 'Regulation 2019/1896 on the European Border and Coast Guard (Frontex): The Supranational Administration of the External Borders?' in Kotzur et al. (eds), The External Dimension of EU Migration and Asylum Policies. Border Management, Human Rights and Development Policies in the Mediterranean Area, Baden-Baden 2020, p. 295; Fink, Frontex and Human Rights, Oxford 2018; Fink, 'The Action for Damages as a Fundamental Rights Remedy: Holding Frontex Liable', German Law Journal 2020 (21), 532; Fletcher, 'Schengen, the European Court of Justice and Flexibility under the Lisbon Treaty: Balancing the United Kingdom's "Ins" and "Outs"', European Constitutional Law Review 2009 (5), 71; Garland, 'The Limits of the Sovereign State: Strategies of Crime Control in Contemporary Society', British Journal of Criminology 1996 (36), 445; Genschel/Jachtenfuchs, 'More integration, less federation: the European integration of core state powers', Journal of European Public Policy 2016 (23), 42; Georgiev, 'Towards a common European border security policy', European Security 2010 (19), 255; Gruszczak, 'The use of force by the Frontex agency – international legal aspects', Studia Prawnicze KUL 2021 (4:88), 73; Grześkowiak, 'The "Guardian of the Treaties" is No More? The European

Commission and the 2021 Humanitarian Crisis on Poland–Belarus Border', Refugee Survey Quarterly 2023 (42), 81; Gülzau, 'A "New Normal" for the Schengen Area. When, Where and Why Member States Reintroduce Temporary Border Controls?', Journal of Borderlands Studies 2021, 1–19; Heinkelmann-Wild/Zangl, 'Multilevel blame games: Blame-shifting in the European Union', Governance 2020 (33), 953–969; Hrabálek/Burianová, 'To Intervene or Not to Intervene? Positions of the Member States Towards the Article 18 of the European Border and Coast Guard Proposal', Slovak Journal of Political Sciences 2019 (19), 43; IBM Global Services, Expanded borders, integrated controls, Achieving national prosperity and protection through integrated border management, 2005; Jo Pesch/Dimitrova/Boehm, 'Data Protection and Machine-Learning-Supported Decision-Making at the EU Border: ETIAS Profiling Under Scrutiny' in Gryszczyńska/Polański/Gruschka (eds), Privacy Technologies and Policy. 10th Annual Privacy Forum, APF 2022, Warsaw, Poland, June 23–24, 2022, Proceedings, Cham 2022, p. 50; Jumbert, 'Control or rescue at sea? Aims and limits of border surveillance technologies in the Mediterranean Sea', Disasters 2018 (42), 674–696; Juszczak/Sason, 'Recalibrating Data Retention in the EU. The Jurisprudence of the Court of Justice of the EU on Data Retention – Is this the End or is this only the Beginning?', eucrim 2021 (4), 238; Karadağ, 'Extraterritoriality of European borders to Turkey: an implementation perspective of counteractive strategies', Comparative Migration Studies 2019 (7), 1; Karamanidou/Kasparek, 'From Exceptional Threats to Normalized Risks: Border Controls in the Schengen Area and the Governance of Secondary Movements of Migration', Journal of Borderlands Studies 2022 (37), 623; Koslowski, Information Technology and Integrated Border Management, Geneva 2003; Koslowski, International Cooperation to Create Smart Borders, Ottawa 2004; Leese, 'Fixing State Vision: Interoperability, Biometrics, and Identity Management in the EU', Geopolitics 2022 (27), 113; Leonard, 'The Creation of FRONTEX and the Politics of Institutionalisation in the EU External Borders Policy', JCER 2009 (5), 371; Lingenfelter/Miettinen, 'Obstacles to supranational operational police powers in the European Union: Europol reform and the construction of trust between national police authorities', Maastricht Journal of European and Comparative Law 2021 (28), 182; Loukinas, 'Drones for Border Surveillance: Multipurpose Use, Uncertainty and Challenges at EU Borders', Geopolitics 2022 (27), 89; Mangold/Kompatscher, Vereinbarkeit kontinuierlicher Kontrollen an der deutsch-dänischen Grenze mit unionsrechtlichen Vorgaben, Kurzgutachten im Auftrag von Rasmus Andresen, Mitglied des Europäischen Parlaments, 2022; Marcus et al., The impact of COVID-19 on the Internal Market. Study requested by the IMCO Committee, 2021; Marin, 'The Cooperation Between Frontex and Third Countries in Information Sharing: Practices, Law and Challenges in Externalizing Border Control Functions', EPL 2020 (26), 157–180; Martins/Jumbert, 'EU Border technologies and the co-production of security "problems" and "solutions"', Journal of Ethnic and Migration Studies 2022 (48), 1430; Mau, Sorting Machines, The reinvention of the border in the 21st century, Cambridge/Hoboken 2023; Mau/Brabandt/Laube, Liberal States and the Freedom of Movement, London 2012; Meissner, 'The European Border and Coast Guard Agency Frontex After the Migration Crisis: Towards a "Superagency"?' in Pollak/Slominski (eds), The Role of EU Agencies in the Eurozone and Migration Crisis. Impact and Future Challenges, Cham 2021, p. 151; Michéa/Rousvoal, 'The Criminal Procedure Out of Itself: A Case Study of the Relationship Between EU Law and Criminal Procedure Using the ETIAS System', EP-JMN 2021 (6), 473; Milivojevic, 'Artificial intelligence, illegalised mobility and lucrative alchemy of border utopia', Criminology & Criminal Justice 2022, 1; Mitsilegas, 'The EU external border as a site of preventive (in)justice', ELJ 2022, 1; Neal, 'Securitization and Risk at the EU Border: The Origins of FRONTEX', JCMS 2009 (47), 333; Niemann/Speyer, 'A Neofunctionalist Perspective on the "European Refugee Crisis": The Case of the European Border and Coast Guard', JCMS 2018 (56), 23; Noori, 'Suspicious Infrastructures: Automating Border Control and the Multiplication of Mistrust through Biometric E-Gates', Geopolitics 2022 (27), 1117; Olwig/Grünenberg/Møhl/Simonsen, The Biometric Border World: Technology, Bodies and Identities on the Move, Oxford/New York 2020; Panebianco, 'The EU and migration in the Mediterranean: EU borders' control by proxy', Journal of Ethnic and Migration Studies 2022 (48), 1398; Paoli, 'How to tackle (organized) crime in Europe? The EU policy cycle on serious and organized crime and the new emphasis on harm', European Journal of Crime, Criminal Law and Criminal Justice 2014 (22), 1; Parusel, 'Should They Stay or Should They Go? Frontex's fundamental rights dilemma', European Policy Analysis, EPA working paper 2022 (22); Buzmaniuk, 'The Union's external borders: a European debate revisited', Schuman Papers 2021 (585), 1; Rudner, 'Intelligence-Led Air Transport Security: Pre-Screening for Watch-Lists, No-Fly Lists to Forestall Terrorist Threats', IJICI 2015 (28), 38; Schaeffer, 'Automated Border Control: Criminalizing the "Hidden Intent" of Migrant Embodiment', Kalfou 2019 (6:2), 177; Schimmelfennig, 'European integration (theory) in times of crisis. A comparison of the euro and Schengen crises', Journal of European Public Policy 2018 (25), 969; Thym, 'The Area of Freedom, Security and Justice in the Treaty establishing a Constitution for Europe', WHI-Paper 2022 (12:4); Thym/Bornemann 'Schengen and Free Movement Law During the First Phase of the Covid-19 Pandemic: Of Symbolism, Law and Politics European Papers', European Papers 2020 (5), 1143; Vavoula, 'The "Puzzle" of EU Large-Scale Information Systems for Third-Country Nationals: Surveillance of Movement and its Challenges for Privacy and Personal Data Protection', European Law Review 2020 (3), 348; Votoupalová, 'Schengen Cooperation: What Scholars Make of It', Journal of Borderlands Studies 2020 (35), 403; Zaiotti (ed.), Externalizing Migration Management, London 2016; Zaiotti, 'Revisiting Schengen: Europe and the emergence of a new culture of border control', Perspectives on European Politics and Society 2007 (8), 31; Zalnieriute, 'A Struggle for Competence: National Security, Surveillance and the Scope of EU Law at the Court of Justice of European Union', Modern Law Review 2020 (85), 198.

A. Introduction

Integrated Border Management (IBM) is a concept that has been widely adopted by the European Union (EU) and its Member States as a means of managing and securing their external borders. Officially, this approach aims to promote efficient border controls while facilitating the movement of people and goods across borders. By working together in a coordinated manner, various agencies responsible for managing national borders, including customs officials, immigration officers as well as law enforcement personnel, are to identify potential risks and threats at the border more effectively. However, in the EU IBM serves additional political purposes and reflects the contested relationship between national and supranational levels of security governance. 1

The EU's competence for border security has developed dynamically over decades. In 1985 the Schengen Convention led to the creation of common rules for short-term visas, external border controls and other flanking measures for security cooperation to lift internal border controls. Since then, the Schengen zone has expanded from 5 to 29 members – that are still not fully identical to the EU's membership – whereas the Schengen *acquis* has been integrated into EU law. Moreover, the understanding that increasing mobility needs to be compensated by intensified cross-border cooperation between security authorities has led to the steady growth of instruments and infrastructures, such as the Schengen Information System (SIS) that currently handles more than 12 billion queries per year and contains more than 86 million entries.[1] These figures underline the density of interactions and the everyday relevance of the EU to the work of national police and border guards. The logic of compensatory measures has, in fact, been central to the EU's overall role in matters of internal security. 2

Art. 3(2) TEU encapsulates this connection, setting out the integration objective of an 'area of freedom, security and justice without internal frontiers, in which the free movement of persons is ensured in conjunction with appropriate measures with respect to external border controls'. EU policymakers regularly stress the vital importance as well as the symbolic dimension of Schengen and personal freedom of movement as one of the most tangible achievements of European integration. To protect this achievement, recent years have seen additional far-reaching reforms and decisions that have pushed the EU's competence in matters of security, most notably the formation of a new category of EU officials with executive roles that are directly recruited by the European 3

[1] eu-LISA, 'SIS II 2022 Annual Statistics', 2023. SIS II has also been repeatedly expanded in terms of its functionalities and obligatory uses by Member State authorities, most recently including the obligation to enter return decisions.

Border and Coast Guard (EBCG)[2] – or Frontex, as the agency is still mainly referred to.[3]

4 Yet Member States also retain primary competence for maintaining internal security, law and order (Art. 72 TFEU) on top of the wider reservation in matters of national security and territorial integrity (Art. 4(2) TFEU). Between this broad set of coordinates, various crises and political confrontations continue to play out. In response to what became known as the migration crisis and a wave of terrorist attacks that were linked to the rise of the so-called Islamic State in Syria, six EU Member States[4] introduced exceptional control measures at internal borders in 2016. In the first half of 2019 decisions to severely limit personal freedom of movement to contain Covid-19 reverted to the national level. Highly divergent practices caused a temporary breakdown of the internal market.[5] While the risks and economic costs of the pandemic were eventually managed collectively by the EU, the episode highlighted the unresolved tension between national reflexes in times of crisis and the gaps in the existing EU legal framework for border control.[6]

5 In 2022 the ECJ stressed that internal border controls may only be introduced as a measure of last resort and should not be prolonged indefinitely.[7] The current Schengen Borders Code allows for exceptional internal border controls for up to six months, which can be renewed three times for up to two years in specific circumstances. In any case, the proportionality of and necessity for internal border controls must be clearly demonstrated, which in the eyes of the Court has not been case with regard to Austria. By implication, this should also apply to five other Schengen states that have similar practices.[8] Such a restrictive reading of national leeway on decision-making is in line with the Court's jurisprudence[9] on the scope of Art. 72 TFEU. The Court has repeatedly argued that binding secondary EU law, specifically on borders and asylum standards, cannot generally be set aside by national authorities with reference to public order. Insofar as EU secondary law already makes provision for partial derogations – as is the case with the Schengen regulation that allows for temporary internal border controls under specific circumstances[10] – these rules take precedence over general derogations or appeals to national reserved areas of competence.

6 A revised Schengen regulation that[11] aims to achieve a new compromise between national emergency measures and a credible and enforceable set of EU rules that guarantee the freedom of movement of Union citizens. Yet this does not justify the

---

[2] Meissner in Pollak/Slominski, The Role of EU Agencies in the Eurozone and Migration Crisis, p. 151. Bossong SWP Comment 2019 C 47.

[3] Recital 3 Regulation (EU) 2019/1896 on the European Border and Coast Guard.

[4] Austria, Denmark, France, Germany, Norway and Sweden.

[5] Marcus et al., p. 1 et seqq. However, the overall economic trade benefits of open borders inside Schengen are estimated to be far lower than the overall benefits of EU membership and so one should not overstress the link between the two. Felbermayr/Gröschl/Steinwachs ERIA Discussion Paper Series 2017 (2).

[6] Bossong SWP Comment 2020 (28). Thym/Bornemann, European Papers – A Journal on Law and Integration 2020, 1143.

[7] ECJ 26.4.2022 – joined cases C-368/20 and C-369/20, ECLI:EU:C:2022:298 – *Landespolizeidirektion Steiermark*.

[8] Mangold/Kompatscher, p. 1 et seqq. Rising migration pressures after the end of the Covid-19 pandemic, the war in Ukraine and the deteriorating security situation in Afghanistan could potentially have provided some factual grounds for new internal border controls since 2022. But no such arguments have been consistently and thoroughly demonstrated. The operational effectiveness and full use of alternative measures to internal border controls in particular remains to be proven.

[9] ECJ 19.7.2012 – case C-278/12 PPU, ECLI:EU:C:2012:508 – *Adil*.

[10] The same argument holds even more strongly for emergency provisions in matters of asylum at the Treaty level, as set out in Art. 78(3) TFEU.

[11] European Commission, 'Proposal for a Regulation of the European Parliament and of the Council amending Regulation (EU) 2016/399 on a Union Code on the rules governing the movement of persons across borders', 14.12.2021, COM(2021) 891 final.

fact that all six Member States that introduced internal border controls in 2016 have maintained them (as at the time of writing). While the overall Schengen regime has withstood several crises and Croatia was accepted as a new full member at the beginning of 2023, this continued deviation from the Schengen regulation and preliminary ruling by the Court of Justice speaks of the wider normalization of emergency or outright illegal practices in response to irregular migration.[12]

On top of the competing legal interpretations of the necessary or appropriate leeway as regards upholding public security, tensions between national and EU-level capacities for border security are also visible when it comes to the role of Frontex. As is elaborated below, one needs to appreciate the dynamic evolution of the agency over the last two decades, which has grown into the best-funded and staffed EU security actor with considerable responsibilities.[13] However, the agency is still far from providing border security on its own. Projected to reach 3,000 staff by 2027, the EU's newly formed border force only supplements the 7,000 national officers who are seconded to Frontex for joint operations. And the overall reserve of 10,000 border guards coordinated by Frontex is dwarfed by the number of national border and coast guards or border police that need to cover an estimated 67,571 km of coastline and 14,647 km of external land borders[14] as well as to conduct supplementary controls within the Schengen zone. The core role of Frontex is still to support and to reform rather than to replace Member State services. 7

Nevertheless, the willingness of Member States to ask Frontex for help at critical border sections is questionable. Since 2021, Poland, Latvia and Lithuania have made highly controversial use of national emergency provisions, have suspended core aspects of EU and international asylum law and have increasingly involved their national military forces in border security in relation to Belarus. The European Commission unsuccessfully sought to channel these emergency measures into a common European framework and failed to exercise a more critical oversight role vis-à-vis systematic violations of fundamental rights.[15] Frontex's contribution in this crisis was small, with comparatively few officers deployed in Lithuania and Latvia.[16] Poland consigned Frontex to limited second-line activities beyond the border and to support forced returns of rejected asylum seekers, irrespective of the fact that the agency is headquartered in Warsaw. 8

External critics, however, underlined their calls for Frontex to terminate various operational missions due to systematic violations of fundamental rights,[17] especially so-called pushbacks of asylum seekers. So far, the decision to withdraw was only taken once with respect to Hungary, but remains a potential option in Greece[18] and other 9

---

12 Karamanidou/Kasparek, Journal of Borderlands Studies 2022, 623. Gülzau, Journal of Borderlands Studies 2021, 1.

13 Fernandez-Rojo in Kotzur et al., The External Dimension of EU Migration and Asylum Policies, p. 295.

14 Pascale, European Issues 2021, 585.

15 Based on Art. 78(3) TFEU, which was used in 2016 to decide Buzmaniuk, 2021, Schumann Papers, on the ultimately unsuccessful relocation of asylum seekers from Greece and Italy. For the wider normative challenges, see Grześkowiak, Refugee Survey Quarterly 2023, 81.

16 Frontex, 'Frontex provides support for Lithuania, Latvia at their borders with Belarus', 1.7.2021, available under <https://www.frontex.europa.eu> (last accessed: 10.10.2023).

17 According to Art. 46 of the current Frontex Regulation (Regulation (EU) 2019/1896 on the European Border and Coast Guard).

18 Sea Watch Legal Aid, 'Campaigning from Samos: a call for Frontex to abide by law and trigger Article 46' (Sea Watch Legal Aid) <https://swla.eu/en/article/frontexadvocacy/> (last accessed: 10.10.2023); Monroy, 'More or less Frontex?' (Monroy, 5.1.2023) <https://digit.site36.net/2023/01/05/more-or-less-frontex-the-eu-border-agencys-fro-wants-more-presence-in-eu-problem-states/> (last accessed:

theatres of operation at southern and eastern external borders. At the time of writing, whether the rights of asylum seekers are more likely to be violated if Frontex – and related European oversight – withdraws or if the agency normalizes and legitimizes illegal practices of Member States is a key political question.[19]

10 The use of EU funds for advanced border control technologies[20] and partnerships with neighbouring countries to contain migration[21] have also been hotly contested. Given daily reports of drownings or other fatalities of irregular migrants and asylum seekers en route to the EU,[22] it, therefore, may seem misplaced to shift the discussion to the administrative concept of 'Integrated Border Management'. Yet this chapter argues that IBM needs to be analysed in more detail to gain a fuller understanding of the EU's role, including its emergence and normative controversies. Standard accounts outline the neo-functionalist dynamic,[23] whereby the primary interest of Member States in completing the Single Market led to the abolition of internal border controls, which in turn spilled over into transnational security integration, including the creation of Frontex.[24] This explanation of integration in matters of border security can be enriched by multiple factors, such as the dynamics of institutionalization, professional socialization[25] and bureaucratic growth.[26] Finally, repeated crises,[27] such as terrorist attacks or large-scale movements of irregular migrants, created significant political pressure to overcome national sovereignty reservations.

11 Something that has been less discussed, though, are the EU's conceptual and legal bases that accompanied and enabled this dynamic integration process in matters of border security. Despite still not being fully congruent with the EU's membership, Schengen remains the most important reference point when it comes to legitimizing the EU's role in border security. In 2022, the European Commission launched a new annual 'State of Schengen Report', which is to feed into a new 'Schengen Forum' that accompanies the Council of Ministers.[28] Policymakers typically justify more investment and integration in matters of border security as a necessary corollary to maintaining freedom of movement within the Schengen zone. In contrast, IBM goes beyond the notion of compensation for prior national border controls. IBM is a fluid aspirational ideal for upgrading or modernizing all aspects of border security at the national and supranational levels. In the European context, IBM may help to sidestep conflicts relating to the division of competences between different levels of governance, but it also raises critical questions concerning accountability and legality.

10.10.2023); LIBE Committee on Civil Liberties, Justice and Home Affairs, 'Report on the fact-finding investigation on Frontex concerning alleged fundamental rights violations', 2021.

[19] Parusel, European Policy Analysis, EPA working paper 2022.

[20] Martins/Jumbert, Journal of Ethnic and Migration Studies 2022, 1430. Most recently, political debates have revolved around the question of whether EU funds can also be used to construct physical border fences, which the European Commission has in the past denied.

[21] Panebianco, Journal of Ethnic and Migration Studies 2022, 1398. Karadağ, CMS 2019.

[22] The International Organization for Migration (IOM) maintains the most authoritative, though still incomplete, complication of cases. The recorded number of fatalities in the Mediterranean and at the EU's external borders between 2014 and spring 2023 surpasses 27,000. See International Organization for Migration, 'Data | Missing Migrants Project'.

[23] Georgiev European Security 2019, 255. Votoupalová, Journal of Borderlands Studies 2020, 403.

[24] Niemann/Speyer, JCMS 2018, 23.

[25] Zaiotti, Perspectives on European Politics and Society 2007, 31.

[26] Leonard, JCER 2009, 371.

[27] Schimmelfennig, Journal of European Public Policy 2018, 969.

[28] Pingen, 'State of Schengen Report 2022' (eucrim, 28.7.2022) <https://eucrim.eu/news/state-of-schengen-report-2022/> (last accessed: 10.10.2023).

The chapter is divided into two parts so as to be able to develop these perspectives. The first part traces the emergence of IBM in the early 2000s and its inclusion as a far-reaching legal provision in the Treaty of Lisbon, which subsequently paved the way for ambition integration, especially with regard to Frontex. The second part discusses a few normative implications and potential future developments of IBM. A genuinely integrated system of border management may obscure who is ultimately accountable if there are violations of irregular migrants' and asylum-seekers' fundamental rights. In addition, contemporary understandings of IBM include the use of sensitive intelligence. In the context of this volume, one may ask to what extent this respects the Member States' reserved competencies. 12

B. The concept of IBM

The concept of IBM originated as an international expert discourse among border professionals.[29] The strategic background was the dynamic growth of globalization since the 1990s – coupled with notions of New Public Management that percolated from business to state governance, including in matters of security.[30] Hence, the main reasons for reforming traditional border control mechanisms were, first, the dynamic increase in international movements of goods and people that could not be handled efficiently by human agents and paper documents and, second, new technologies that enabled more networked, de-territorialized and data-driven forms of authorization, surveillance and tracking. In the aftermath of 9/11, the United States massively accelerated this structural trend. The aim was to detect potential threats to the 'homeland' as early as possible while staying economically competitive and open.[31] In the words of the Bush Administration: 13

> The border of the future must integrate actions abroad to screen goods and people prior to their arrival in sovereign U.S. territory, and inspections at the border and measures within the United States to ensure compliance with entry and import permits. Federal border control agencies must have seamless information-sharing systems that allow for coordinated communication among themselves, and also the broader law enforcement and intelligence gathering communities.[32]

These US reforms to create 'smart borders' quickly became the new global standard in the War on Terror.[33] Border management now meant a shift from the general control of goods or people to more selective, risk-led or 'intelligence-led' checks that facilitated mobility for elites,[34] from the use of human agents to more automated technologies, and from stationary control points to various screening processes before and behind the territorial border. Rather than fixed control routines, border management implied the permanent adaption, optimization and prediction of future trends. IBM also suggested close coordination between different state and private actors that interact with travellers (and goods) at various stages. Aside from 14

---

[29] Koslowski, p. 1 et seqq.

[30] Garland, British Journal of Criminology 1996, 445.

[31] Koslowski, p. 1 et seqq.

[32] The White House, 'Securing America's Borders Fact Sheet' <https://georgewbush-whitehouse.archives.gov/homeland/01.html> (last accessed: 10.10.2023).

[33] Department of State/Department of Homeland Security, 'Western Hemisphere Travel Initiative' <https://www.dhs.gov/western-hemisphere-travel-initiative> (last accessed: 10.10.2023).

[34] Mau et al., p. 1 et seqq.

transport companies and carriers that often carry out checks on behalf of state authorities, a growing security industry, including military and civilian companies, has flourished as a result.[35]

I. European understandings of IBM and the creation of Frontex

15 In Europe, additional factors underlined the need to modernize border control systems. Irregular migration and organized crime, partly driven by the wars in the Former Yugoslavia and the wider dissolution of the former Communist bloc, called for robust and effective cooperation among security authorities. New formats of transnational cooperation among security professionals in the 1990s were driven by the implementation of the Schengen Convention.[36] This process included the swift expansion from the original five Schengen members (Belgium, France, Germany, Luxemburg, the Netherlands) to include most of the EU Member States and, in parallel, the growth of the EU in several rounds of enlargement. By the end of the decade and with signing of the Treaty of Amsterdam, the Schengen *acquis* became integrated into EU law[37] and subsumed under the new integration objective of creating a common 'Area of Freedom, Security and Justice'.[38] In a fuller understanding, the Schengen *acquis* went beyond regulations and soft-law handbooks on the conduct of border controls and police cooperation. The EU also took over responsibility for the SIS for police and border guards, i.e. the technical infrastructure for more networked forms of control.

16 Soon after, European discussions of border security became more acute on account of the fact that a large number of the 9/11 attackers had previously lived in Germany and travelled unhindered from Europe to the United States. The United States accordingly pressed all its international partners to grant access to new forms of information on air travellers[39] and related forms of intelligence to create a new system for tracking and singling out terrorist suspects around the globe. Against this dynamic backdrop in late 2001, the European Council[40] commenced a process to strengthen the EU's external border controls. A few months later, the Commission issued its first communication 'towards integrated border management of the external borders of the member states of the European union'.[41] This landmark communication set out core elements and arguments that continue to define the EU's role in border security to the present day. The starting point was the simple assertion that the conduct of border controls remains with Member States' authorities (in line with Art. 6 Schengen Codex), while operational cooperation between border guards mostly takes place at a regional or bilateral level. In fact, in the early 2000s the EU collectively disposed of no meaningful instruments to ensure coherence, common oversight and solidarity between national measures for

---

[35] IBM Global Services.

[36] Anderson, p. 1 et seqq.

[37] Protocol (No 2) integrating the Schengen acquis into the framework of the European Union (OJ 1997 C 340, 93–96).

[38] This step change in integration was achieved at the price of opt-outs for non-participating EU states (mainly the UK) and flexible legal arrangements for non-EU members of Schengen. Fletcher, European Constitutional Law Review 2009, 71.

[39] Argomaniz, Journal of European Integration 2009, 119.

[40] Council of the European Union, Presidency Conclusions, 'European Council Meeting in Laeken', 14/15.12.2001.

[41] European Commission, 'Towards integrated management of the external borders of the member states of the European Union', 7.5.2002, COM(2002) 233 final.

border security. A 'common policy on management of external borders' had therefore to be built around five pillars:[42]

1. 'A common corpus of legislation', developing the existing Schengen rules;
2. 'A common co-ordination and operation co-operation mechanism', which included 'permanent processes of exchange and processing of data';
3. 'Common integrated risk analysis' among European border professionals;
4. 'Staff trained in the European dimension and interoperable equipment';
5. 'Burden-sharing between Member States in the run-up to a European Corps of Border Guards'.

While all these pillars would be developed in the future, as discussed below, the last aspect of burden-sharing was and remains the most sensitive political question. In October 2001, a core group including Germany, France, Belgium, Spain, Italy and France had already launched a study to explore the options for 'setting up a European Border Police',[43] calling for feedback from security authorities from all other EU Member States. The results were not surprising, namely a rejection of such an option owing to existing competencies, the diversity of national structures and requirements, and the size of external borders. Yet the study also argued for a flexible or pragmatic understanding of the division of labour between Member States and the EU to create a 'unitary notion of secure borders'.[44] This is the origin of the specifically European understanding of IBM as a compromise between the primary responsibilities of national border guards and European needs for common control standards without addressing the question of sovereignty head on. In the eyes of the Member States, an 'integrated system'[45] is to be created between 'community level measures', namely 'external borders control, issue of visas, re-admission and repatriation, illegal entry and residence'; 'intergovernmental level measures', namely 'liaison and coordination between competent authorities for a more efficient fight against criminality, clandestine immigration and illegal trafficking, also for the organizational-management and operative support in the field of control and surveillance of the external borders'; and 'national level' efforts to implement European standards. 17

This may appear to be a straightforward functionalist division of labour, but it needs to be understood in the context of the early 2000s as a decisive opening up to a comprehensive EU policy on border security. Studies on the origins of Frontex have highlighted the fact that, owing to sovereignty concerns, Member States in 2002 opted for a largely ineffective intergovernmental coordination unit on border security before eventually setting up Frontex[46] two years later. But even though the far-reaching ambition of a European border guard could not be realized, Member States' authorities arguably worked around a clear divide between national and European competences. Instead of pitting the creation of Frontex as a zero-sum game in which national authorities lost power to Brussels, IBM was presented as an upgrade to national capacities. 18

It is, therefore, no coincidence that the founding mandate of Frontex[47] started out by referencing the notion of IBM.[48] Approximately one year after the creation of Frontex, 19

[42] ibid., 12.
[43] EBA, 'Feasibility Study for the Setting up of a European Border Police – Final Report' (2002).
[44] ibid., 24.
[45] ibid., 25.
[46] Neal, JCMS 2009, 333. Fernandez-Rojo in Kotzur et al., The External Dimension of EU Migration and Asylum Policies, p. 295.
[47] Recital 1 and Art. 1 of Council Regulation (EC) No 2007/2004 establishing a European Agency for the Management of Operational Cooperation at the External Borders of the Member States of the European Union.
[48] Council Regulation (EC) No 2007/2004.

the Council sought to provide additional guidance on what IBM meant.[49] Despite the reminder that 'the responsibility for the control of external borders remains with the member states' the Council followed the new consensus on IBM, namely to strengthen 'coordination and coherence of activities of Member States, Institutions and other borders of the Community and the Union'.[50] Moreover, the Council added the so-called four-tier accesses model as an explicit element of IBM. This meant that border controls were to take place in countries of origin, countries of transit, at the EU's external border and also within the Schengen zone.[51] This chimed with the wider global technological modernization processes outlined above[52] and the growing legal obligations on transport carriers[53] to support security checks of passengers before they reach their final destination. Finally, it underscored the trend for outsourcing border and migration control to states in the European neighbourhood long before this attracted more systematic critical attention.[54]

20 In sum, in the formative years after the fusion of the Schengen *acquis* with the EU *acquis*, IBM fulfilled a dual function. It followed an international reform agenda for networked and more de-territorialized control mechanisms. At the same time, it set out a technocratic and politically acceptable notion of European integration that foregrounded the incremental alignment of national and European actors rather than a direct transfer of competencies to the supranational level. Formal compliance with EU law, specifically the Schengen regulation, was less important than developing new instruments for operational coordination, supported in the background by Frontex as an administrative agency. This chimed with wider ideas of European multi-level governance in the early 2000s and the priority attached to capacity-building in Member States to bridge a misalignment between national structures and new European requirements over top-down legalistic enforcement.[55]

II. IBM in the Treaty of Lisbon

21 At the time of the adoption of the Lisbon Treaty in 2007, Frontex had just begun to accrue a more substantial profile. 2006 was its first full year of operation and saw first short pilot missions in Greece and the Canary Islands to support Member States at critical sites or border control processes.[56] Soon after, a first addition to the Frontex mandate was adopted to create 'Rapid Border Intervention Teams' and a headquarter capacity for risk analysis.[57] Irrespective of this ongoing reform, the Lisbon Treaty opened a new chapter and provided a new legal basis for the agency's dynamic expansion. The notion of IBM was included in primary law under very permissive conditions.

---

[49] Council of the European Union, 'Integrated Border Management; Strategy deliberations', 21.11.2006, 13926/3/06 REV 3.

[50] ibid., 4.

[51] These internal controls should not be equated with fully fledged internal border controls and target only a sample of travellers (so-called non-systematic checks). For instance, the EURODA system could be used to check asylum seekers who are already in the Union to establish whether they have already crossed external borders into another Member State or applied for asylum elsewhere.

[52] However, the Commission's push to emulate the US programme for smart borders and introduce new a new biometric entry-exit system at all EU external borders was not adopted at the time.

[53] See also Council Directive 2004/82/EC on the obligation of carriers to communicate passenger data.

[54] Casas/Cobarrubias/Pickles, Geopolítica 2011, 71–90. Zaiotti, p. 1 et seqq.

[55] Falkner et al., p. 1 et seqq.

[56] Frontex, 'Frontex Annual Report 2006, Coordination of intelligence driven operational cooperation at EU level to strengthen security at external borders', 2006.

[57] Regulation (EC) No 863/2007 establishing a mechanism for the creation of Rapid Border Intervention Teams

Art. 77(1) TFEU recalls that the primary aim of Union policy is to ensure the 'absence of any controls' when crossing internal borders, while 'carrying out checks on persons and efficient monitoring of the crossing of external borders'. This connection between internal and external borders represents the functionalist rationale for integration since the creation of Schengen. Correspondingly, the main areas of EU action listed in Art. 77 TFEU are a common visa policy, checks of persons at external borders, conditions for free travel within the Union of third-country nationals, or other measures to ensure the absence of internal controls.[58] This list closely corresponds to the previous Art. 73 of the Treaty of Amsterdam.[59] The Lisbon Treaty only added a specific competence in relation to the harmonization of national identity cards, passports and residence permits by a unanimous decision-making procedure (Art. 77(3) TFEU). Common standards for residence permits of third-country nationals had already been regulated in 2002[60] as an area that is closely related to the common visa policy. Biometric standards for passports followed in 2004 after a highly controversial debate and following considerable pressure from the United States.[61] The subsequent consolidation of these steps in the course of the next Treaty revision and its extension to national identity cards under the condition of unanimous decision-making is a typical pattern for cautious integration in sensitive fields.[62] 22

Against this backdrop, it is all the more noteworthy that the Lisbon Treaty included an entirely new integration objective under the regular legislative procedure, namely 'the gradual introduction of an integrated management system for external borders' (Art. 77(2)(c) TFEU). This was the result of the draft Constitutional Treaty that had been rejected in 2005. Members of the preparatory Convention made reference[63] to the 2002 European Council of Seville,[64] which had broadly endorsed the Commission's Communication on integrated border management. While the notion of IBM had barely been introduced at the EU level, the Convention paved the way for the EU's open-ended responsibility in this field. Whereas the consolidated TEU of 2002 spoke more guardedly of 'appropriate measures with respect to external border controls',[65] Art. 77(2)(d) TFEU empowered the EU to take 'any measure necessary for the gradual establishment of an integrated management system for external borders'. 23

This is arguably the most far-reaching formulation in Title V TFEU and the overall Area of Freedom Security and Justice. Even though integration may be slowed down 24

---

[58] A key area where Member States can still take independent action is in their relations with third countries. Despite regular calls for more coordination (currently the so-called Team Europe approach), Member States maintain separate arrangements on border security with third states, such as those between Spain and Morocco. In addition, Art. 77 TFEU underlines the fact that Member States remain solely competent with regard to the demarcation of national borders (Art. 77(4) TFEU, matching the exclusive competence for territorial integrity in Art. 4(2) TEU).

[59] See the Treaty of Amsterdam amending the Treaty on European Union, the Treaties establishing the European Communities and certain related acts, Art. 73.

[60] Publications Office of the European Union, 'EU format for residence permits, Summary of: Regulation (EC) No 1030/2002 – uniform format for residence permits for non-EU nationals', 2020.

[61] Aus, Arena Working Paper 2006.

[62] It took until 2019 for Member States to take the first decision to increase common security standards for national identity cards (Regulation (EU) 2019/1157 on strengthening the security of identity cards of Union citizens and of residence documents issued to Union citizens and their family members exercising their right of free movement).

[63] Thym, WHI-Paper 2022 (12:4), Final Report of Working Group X, and Praesidium of the European Convention, Area of freedom, security and justice – draft Art. 31, Part One and draft articles from Part Two, 14.3.2003, CONV 614/03, 2003, 14.

[64] Council of the European Union, 'Presidency Conclusions – Seville – Revised Version', 21/22.6.2002, DOC/02/13.

[65] Art. 2 TEU (consolidated version 2002). See also the phrase 'flanking measures with respect to external border controls, asylum and immigration' in Art. 73 Treaty of Amsterdam.

by the qualifier 'gradual', there is no fundamental scope limitation to the 'integrated management system for external borders'. Fifteen years after the ratification of the Lisbon Treaty, the potential to use this provision has become clear. Art. 77(2)(d) TFEU serves as the central legal basis for Frontex and other ambitious initiatives in relation to border security. In particular, since 2019 Frontex has been tasked with creating a new EU-own force of border guards. While the state of operation of any Frontex mission always remains in command and holds primary responsibility for any measures,[66] this remains a ground-breaking development and may pave the way to fulfilling the original ambition of a genuine European border police. One needs to recall the historical context from the beginning of the 2000s to understand that this integration process was folded into or hidden in the concept of IBM. The Treaty of Lisbon did not provide any other legal basis for Frontex. An illustrative contrast is provided in Art. 88 TFEU, which defines the competencies of Europol, including the express stipulation that national authorities remain exclusive responsible for coercive measures. This represents a more typical and hesitant attitude on the part of Member States and security professionals towards the creation of strong supranational agencies in sensitive matters.[67]

III. IBM and the subsequent evolution of the European Border and Coast Guard

25 The legal and operational evolution of Frontex since the Treaty of Lisbon cannot be reviewed in detail here.[68] What needs closer attention in the context of this chapter is the shifting understanding of IBM following the migration crisis of 2015, which led to an ever more complex arrangement of enmeshed national and supranational tasks. Compared to its founding mandate,[69] which set out IBM as the core rationale of Frontex yet did not define the meaning of this concept, the first full mandate revision in 2011[70] created additional tasks for Frontex[71] and underlined the importance of fundamental rights.

26 However, the 2016 reform, which officially inaugurated the European Border and Coast Guard,[72] marked a step change with regard to IBM. The new preamble stressed that the European Border and Coast Guard was established in order to ensure the 'effective' implementation of IBM, including the 'requisite financial and human resources and equipment'.[73] This cleared the way for a more distinctly European and supranational provision of border security based on common EU funding and the procurement of border control assets. The new preamble also specified the national

[66] Art. 43 Regulation (EU) 2019/1896 on the European Border and Coast.

[67] Lingenfelter/Miettinen Maastricht Journal of European and Comparative Law 2021, 182

[68] See Bossong, SWP Comment 2019 C 47; Cortinovis, JCER 2015; Carrera, CEPS Paper in Liberty and Security in Europe 2016; Meissner in Pollak/Slominski, The Role of EU Agencies in the Eurozone and Migration Crisis, p. 151; Niemann/Speyer, JCMS 2018, 23.

[69] Recitals 1, 6 and 21 and Art. 1 of Council Regulation (EC) No 2007/2004 establishing a European Agency for the Management of Operational Cooperation at the External Borders of the Member States of the European Union.

[70] Recitals 2, 7 and 31 of Regulation (EU) No 1168/2011 amending Council Regulation (EC) No 2007/2004 establishing a European Agency for the Management of Operational Cooperation at the External Borders of the Member States of the European Union. Art. 1 was not amended with regard to IBM in 2011.

[71] Regulation (EC) No 2007/2004; Art. 2 included six tasks for the agency.

[72] Regulation (EU) 2016/1624 on the European Border and Coast Guard.

[73] Recital 5 Regulation 2016/1624.

authorities' and Frontex's shared responsibility for IBM, which is discussed below. The only explicit limitation to this expanded reading of IBM was the stipulation that 'European integrated border management does not alter the respective competences of the Commission and Member States in the customs area.'[74]

To reiterate, the political dynamic and negotiations that led to the creation of the European Border and Coast Guard in 2016 were clearly driven by external pressures and internal crises in the Schengen zone. Yet it is argued here that one also needs to pay closer attention to the discourse and conceptual framework that enabled and facilitated this reform. Even if an EU-level 'right to intervene' at certain sections of the border was toned down, meaning that the respective Member State still needs to approve an EU mission,[75] it was possible to overcome Member States' sovereignty concerns relating to questions of funding and other new supervisory powers based on a flexible reading of IBM.[76] A completely new article containing a definition of IBM[77] was included and already listed 11 elements, ranging from border control over search and rescue, return of irregular migrants, cooperation with third countries or the use of 'state-of-the-art technology' to 'solidarity measures', among other things. **27**

This centrality of IBM continued to rise with the next Frontex reform, which was already finalized in 2019. Aside from numerous related additions to the preamble, Art. 3(1) of the current mandate officially defines IBM on the basis of 12 core elements[78] and three cross-cutting considerations, most notably respect for fundamental rights. This list could be seen as the main basis for a further extension of the agency's tasks. It goes beyond the scope of this chapter to detail all 33 paragraphs or sub-tasks that are spelled out in Frontex's current mandate (Art. 10).[79] Suffice it to say that the 2016 mandate included 21 sub-tasks (under the then Art. 8), indicating a substantial expansion within the space of only three years. For instance, the EUROSUR (European Border Surveillance System) system for the spatial surveillance of borders and pre-frontier areas (see below) and other new systems for smart border controls have been fully integrated. Frontex has, furthermore, been given more responsibilities in relation to supporting and coordinating the returns of rejected asylum seekers and irregular migrants. **28**

More important than the detailed breakdown of the agency's tasks is the provision of shared responsibility of Member States and Frontex for IBM. Art. 4 of the current mandate states more succinctly than the previous mandate that the European Border and Cost Guard is constituted by the 'Agency' and by 'national authorities of Member States responsible for border management'.[80] In other words, national and EU-level **29**

---

[74] Recital 6 Regulation 2016/1624.

[75] See Art. 19 Regulation 2016/1624, and Deleixhe/Duez, Journal of European Integration 2019, 921; Beduschi, p. 1 et seqq.

[76] Hrabálek/Burianová, Slovak Journal of Political Sciences 2019, 43; Carrera, CEPS Paper in Liberty and Security in Europe 2016.

[77] Art. 4 Regulation 2016/1624.

[78] Art. 3 Regulation 2019/1896. See also the EU's own summary in a recent Communication on IBM: European Commission, 'Policy document developing a multiannual strategic policy for European integrated border management in accordance with Article 8(4) of Regulation (EU) 2019/1896', 24.5.2022, COM(2022) 303 final, 12: '12 thematic components encompass border control, search and rescue in situations that may arise during maritime border surveillance operations, risk analysis, inter-agency cooperation at national and EU level, cooperation between Member States and with the Agency, cooperation with third countries, returns and other measures within the Schengen area, a Schengen quality control mechanism and solidarity mechanisms, in particular EU funding instruments. In addition, three overarching components are identified: fundamental rights; research and innovation; and education and training. Among these, the protection of fundamental rights is of a particular importance.'

[79] Art. 10 Regulation 2019/1896.

[80] Art. 7(1) Regulation 2019/1896.

actors are to share responsibility for IBM to the effect that they functionally act hand in hand as the European Border and Coast Guard. There is no corresponding example in other fields of EU security provision.[81] For instance, Europol and Eurojust have prominent horizontal features and coordination structures for representatives from Member State authorities, yet they are presented as supporting agencies with an independent legal nature that do not fundamentally alter the rationale or mandate of the relevant entities at the national level.

30 Efforts to promote national reforms for close alignment with the European notion of IBM are currently underway. To flesh out its new mandate the agency presented its own strategic vision of IBM in November 2019.[82] This very extensive document underlines the breadth of the intended activities, including in cooperation with both Member States and multiple other EU agencies, such as the European Maritime Safety Agency and Europol. As a strategy, it sets out 14 strategic objectives for improving IBM, bundled under three headings of situational awareness, effective border control standards and sustainability of common European capacities. These strategic objectives are to be pursued by a new High-Level Working Group on IBM with representatives from all Member States. At the time of writing, however, no public record of the activities or the impact of this working group was available.

31 By May 2022 – presumably delayed on account of the pandemic – the European Commission presented another complementary 'multiannual strategic policy cycle for European integrated border management'[83] for the next five years. This Communication is intended to officially fulfil Art. 8 Frontex Regulation, which promises such a policy cycle[84] for IBM. It is not apparent why this stipulation in Art. 8 could not be satisfied by Frontex's own strategy and the High-level Working Group. It is too early to assess whether a complementary dynamic on wider IBM reforms among the Member States may develop between the High-Level Working Group and the proposed policy cycle. The related Commission communication places the main focus on promoting reform processes among all competent national authorities (an estimated 50 to 60), which are to develop and implement corresponding national strategies for IBM.[85] More specifically, the declared strategic aim of the Commission is to promote all 15 aspects of IBM as defined in the current Frontex mandate. At the time of writing in spring 2023, the Council is still to officially endorse this multiannual policy cycle. Member States debated which of the many other aspects of IBM are to be prioritized.[86] In the meantime, the Commission has issued yet another shorter communication underlining the importance of the multiannual policy cycle in IBM.[87] Yet the stress on the 'shared responsibility' and 'duty to cooperate in good

---

[81] One could, potentially, draw an analogy with the European System of Central Banks, Art. 1 of Protocol No. 4 Treaty on the Functioning of the European Union on the Statute of The European System of Central Banks and of the European Central Bank.

[82] Frontex, 'Technical and Operational Strategy for European Integrated Border Management' (2019).

[83] COM(2022) 303 final.

[84] The technocratic expression of a multiannual policy cycle has, in turn, been borrowed from the work of Europol; see Paoli, European Journal of Crime, Criminal Law and Criminal Justice 2014, 1–12.

[85] One of the few Schengen Member States to have published an extensive integrated border management strategy is Switzerland: State Secretariat for Migration, 'Integrated Border Management (IBM)', 2022 <https://www.sem.admin.ch/sem/en/home/themen/einreise/ibm.html> (last accessed: 10.10.2023).

[86] Statewatch, 'EU: Draft Council conclusions and member state comments on the European integrated border management strategy' (Statewatch, 26.9.2022) <https://www.statewatch.org/news/2022/september/eu-draft-council-conclusions-and-member-state-comments-on-the-european-integrated-border-management-strategy/> (last accessed: 10.10.2023).

[87] European Commission, 'Establishing the multiannual strategic policy for European integrated border management', 14.3.2023, COM(2023) 146 final.

faith'[88] rather speaks of the gap between the formal ambition and the implementation of the European Border and Coast Guard.

IV. Additional use of Art. 77(2)(d) TFEU to expand the EU's role in border security

Beyond Frontex, Art. 77(2)(d) TFEU has been invoked to legitimise the EU's **32** expanding investment in new security technologies. As touched upon in the above, the SIS was the first tool to enable the cross-border cooperation of police and border agencies. Subsequently, the EU developed a wide range of additional databases and systems, including systems to register and check the fingerprints of asylum seekers and irregular migrants (EURODAC), to enhance the efficiency and security of visa applications (Visa Information System) or to enable the targeted security screening of air passengers (Advanced Passenger Information (API), Passenger Name Record (PNR)), all with reference to securing the Schengen zone.

Yet more recent border technologies have drawn specifically on IBM for their **33** legitimacy. In line with IBM's four-tier access model and spatial projection beyond the physical external borders of the EU, the EUROSUR system was set up in 2013[89] to fuse situational data from national border guards with 'pre-frontier' information, such as from satellites, aerial assets and shipping tracking systems, to provide a common European and live situational picture.[90] Soon after, the EU passed the sea surveillance regulation[91] having regard to Art. 77(2)(d) TFEU, clarifying the rule of maritime rescue operations of both Member States and Frontex.[92] Finally, Art. 77(2)(d) TFEU provided an important additional legal basis for expanding 'smart borders' that follow the US example. By 2024, the EU is to roll out an electronic entry authorization system for visa-free travellers (ETIAS)[93] and a biometric entry-exit system at external borders for all third-country nationals (EES).[94] These new systems are accompanied by a cross-cutting reform agenda to enable the 'interoperability' of all EU databases for policing and border security.[95] Based on new interfaces (European Search Portal) and infrastructures (biometric matching service), both authorized national actors and EU agencies should be able to crosscheck entries on suspected persons or visa applicants, identify false entries and speed up all relevant database searches.

---

[88] ibid., 3.

[89] Regulation (EU) No 1052/2013 establishing the European Border Surveillance System (EUROSUR).

[90] By 2019, EUROSUR and the EURSUR Regulation had been included in Frontex's current mandate.

[91] Art. 77(2)(d) of Regulation (EU) No 656/2014 establishing rules for the surveillance of the external sea borders in the context of operational cooperation coordinated by the European Agency for the Management of Operational Cooperation at the External Borders of the Member States of the European Union.

[92] European Commission, 'EU will make maritime surveillance more efficient to avoid another Lampedusa', 4.12.2013. Influenced by the 2013 Lampedusa shipwreck, this regulation made prominent reference to fundamental rights and the need to improve common response mechanisms.

[93] Regulation (EU) 2018/1240 establishing a European Travel Information and Authorisation System (ETIAS).

[94] Regulation (EU) 2017/2226 establishing an Entry/Exit System (EES) to register entry and exit data and refusal of entry data of third-country nationals crossing the external borders of the Member States and determining the conditions for access to the EES for law enforcement purposes.

[95] Regulation (EU) 2019/817 on establishing a framework for interoperability between EU information systems in the field of borders and visa. However, in legal terms there is a distinction between interoperability for border control and visas on the one hand and police and criminal justice cooperation on the other hand. The latter is based on a regulation that does not reference Art. 77 TFEU, namely Regulation (EU) 2019/818 on establishing a framework for interoperability between EU information systems in the field of police and judicial cooperation, asylum and migration.

34 The full complexity and historical precedents of this reform agenda cannot be covered in this chapter.[96] The general thrust of including and coordinating a wide range of actors and collecting more data in the context of smart borders and interoperability is fully in line with the global agenda of IBM since the early 2000s.[97] However, the fusion of different databases and the enhanced use of biometrics may have problematic consequences in the EU's legal order.[98] The potential role of intelligence in relation to smart borders and traveller screening is briefly discussed below. Frequent references to the protection of fundamental rights and to the EU Charta of Fundamental Rights, especially to data protection, in EU secondary law on border control systems may block highly intrusive forms of surveillance. It is a notable deficit, however, that aside from the Frontex regulation one cannot find any additional definition or specific cross-referencing of the scope of IBM, even though Art. 77(2)(d) TFEU is invoked in other instances.

35 This critique is not meant to overstate the importance of this Treaty clause on its own. The implementation of smart borders and interoperability has been considerably delayed and is likely to encounter further substantial problems once the systems are rolled out.[99] EU integration and the creation of an integrated system for border management, thus, proceeds more incrementally and cautiously in practice than legislative agreements since 2016 may suggest. Member States remain in charge of the vast majority of operational border control measures and often display a critical or selective attitude towards the EU and its agencies. Nevertheless, without violating the principle of conferral (Art. 5 TEU), the EU may pass 'any measure necessary' to promote IBM. The only definition of IBM in EU secondary law is provided in the Frontex regulation. Given the expansion of Frontex in recent years, it is plausible to assume that additional competencies or tasks may be subsumed under its flexible definition of IBM. IBM is the core mission of Frontex – or rather of the European Border and Coast Guard that functionally includes all the competent national authorities – and the very mandate of Frontex defines the meaning and scope of IBM. In the light of this circular relationship, there is no fundamental limit to the EU's competencies.

C. Additional critique and developments

36 According to the official EU discourse, IBM is to include respect for fundamental rights as a core component.[100] Yet abuse and the extremely high risks for irregular migrants and asylum seekers en route have been critically debated for years.[101] In 2022 Frontex faced credible allegations that it colluded in, or covered up, violations of fundamental rights, specifically systematic pushbacks of asylum seekers.[102] Seen in this light, the technocratic notion of IBM may obscure violent and oppressive practices. Joint missions and other forms of integrated control measures between national authorities and Frontex underline the challenge of ensuring clear lines of accountabil-

[96] Bellanova/Glouftsios, European Security 2022, 454; Leese, Geopolitics 2022, 113; Bigo/Ewert/Kuşkonmaz, IJMBS 2020, 93.
[97] Olwig et al., p. 1 et seqq.
[98] Blasi Casagran, Human Rights Law Review 2021, 433.
[99] Bossong, SWP-Studie 2018.
[100] COM(2022) 303 final.
[101] Carrera/Stefan, p. 1 et seqq.
[102] Mitsilegas, ELJ 2022, 1–18; Bachiller López, British Journal of Criminology 2023, 1.

ity.[103] Court proceedings to make Frontex liable for fundamental rights at EU external borders[104] have not yet been successful, though several cases are still pending.[105] Steady information-sharing and coordination has reached a level of intensity at which it is not sufficient to rely only on national channels of legal redress.

A recent tragic example concerns the shipwreck at Crotone, Italy in March 2023 that claimed more than 80 lives, including many children. A Frontex surveillance plane communicated coordinates and information about the ship to Italian authorities at a comparatively early stage, but did not indicate the need for a rescue operation. While the facts and implications of this disaster remain disputed at the time of writing,[106] other related incidents suggest a pattern of the EU[107] and its Member States avoiding responsibility. An even worse disaster took place in June 2023, when overcrowded vessel with up to 750 irregular migrants – only 104 of which could be rescued – capsized in international waters of the Mediterranean. Frontex claimed that it alerted authorities in due time, but the Greek coast guard failed to intervene in a decisive manner, allegedly due to the migrants' refusal to be disembarked. There are even more serious accusations that the Greek coast guard may be directly responsible for the disaster by trying to tow the vessel to Italian waters.[108] Again, the culpability or failures to act by different actors remain disputed at the time of writing. It is fair to concluded, though, that the integrated 'four-tier access model' of IBM, which is meant to provide for close and continuous monitoring of maritime spaces around the EU, is not used effectively in relation to rescue operations.[109] Communication and coordination between different national and European actors is delayed or delegated to third states, including actors with very questionable standing that are accused of systematic human rights violations.[110] In the light of these well-documented and persistent deficits, the sustainability and legitimacy of the EU's IBM hinges on a more stringent interpretation of fundamental rights, even if this causes friction with various Member State authorities. **37**

The original impetus of IBM as a technological agenda of modernization and data integration raises additional critical questions. The exclusive competence of Member States for national security under Art. 4(2) TEU is understood to encompass intelligence services.[111] While the EU has some analytical units that collate finished intelligence shared voluntarily by the Member States,[112] the EU is not empowered to collect intelligence directly. Insofar as EU police and criminal justice cooperation includes sensitive intelligence on specific persons, such as suspected terrorists, it is handled or **38**

---

[103] Fink, p. 1 et seqq.; Verfassungsblog, 'Frontex and the Rule of Law – Debate (Verfassungsblog, September 2022) <https://verfassungsblog.de/category/debates/frontex-and-the-rule-of-law-debates/> (last accessed: 10.10.2023).

[104] Fink, German Law Journal 2020 (21), 532; Nicolosi, 'Frontex and Migrants' Access to Justice' (Verfassungsblog, 7.9.2022) <https://verfassungsblog.de/frontex-and-migrants-access-to-justice/> (last accessed: 10.10.2023).

[105] Front-lex, Strategic Litigation.

[106] Vasques, 'Seenotrettung: Italien ignorierte Warnungen von Frontex vor Schiffsunglück' (EURACTIV, 1.3.2023) <https://www.euractiv.de/section/innenpolitik/news/seenotrettung-italien-ignorierte-warnungen-von-frontex-vor-schiffsunglueck/> (last accessed: 10.10.2023).

[107] Heinkelmann-Wild/Zangl, Governance 2020, 953.

[108] European Council on Refugees and Exiles, 'Greece: Shipwreck Leaving Hundreds Dead and Missing Sparks National and International Outcry, EU Denounced over Complicity, Conflicting Narratives' (2023).

[109] Jumbert, Disasters 2018, 674; Loukinas, Geopolitics 2022, 89.

[110] Marin, EPL 2020 (26), 157; Bendiek/Bossong SWP Research Paper 2019.

[111] Zalnieriute, Modern Law Review 2022, 198.

[112] Bossong, SWP Comment 2018.

shared by participating national police services, including in horizontal formats and by means of liaison officers under the common roof of Europol.[113] In several EU Member States no categorical distinction is drawn between some police and intelligence services dealing with particularly serious crimes, such as terrorism, while in many others, including Germany, platforms for exchanging information across institutional boundaries were created in the early 2000s.

39 Aside from different domestic arrangements, numerous entries in the SIS originate with the intelligence services of Member States and of third states, most notably the United States. One specific category in the SIS, so-called Art. 36 checks, allows 'discreet' controls of suspects.[114] This is mainly used for counter-terrorism purposes and to support surveillance of travel patterns. A prominent case was the systematic exchange of (biometric) data on suspected 'foreign terrorist travelling fighters' in the context of the US-led international coalition that fought the so-called Islamic State.[115] As EU Member States were also repeatedly attacked at home by associated terrorists since 2013, this cooperation could be considered essential to protect the Schengen zone and to close significant gaps in intelligence-sharing.[116]

40 The next stages of European IBM may nevertheless give rise to concerns that intelligence or other kinds of highly sensitive data are collected on an indiscriminate basis and with insufficient legal safeguards. One reason is the enduring influence of the United States. Its 'no fly list', created after 9/11, has been subject to numerous challenges but remains operative to date[117] and draws extensively on the regular input of various US intelligence agencies or the FBI.[118] In the context of the EU, there is no directly comparable general system beyond entries on terrorist suspects in the SIS. However, given the upcoming expansion of EU databases and smart border systems, Europol will gain additional responsibilities when it comes to managing a 'watch list' of potentially dangerous visa-free travellers to the EU. This watch list will be fed from multiple sources – potentially shadowed by different national watch lists[119] – and will provide the basis for a semi-automated decision on granting electronic travel authorizations (ETIAS). While the legal basis for creating ETIAS and repeated revisions of the Europol mandate emphasize data protection, purpose limitation and legal remedies, it is very challenging to uphold these standards in operational practice,[120] not least since it will include an increasing element of artificial intelligence processing or machine learning.[121]

---

[113] Council of the European Union, 'Manual on Law Enforcement Information Exchange', 25.10.2018, 6727/18.

[114] Monroy, 'Again strong increase for secret searches in Europe's largest police database' (Monroy, 25.1.2019) <https://digit.site36.net/2019/01/25/again-strong-increase-for-secret-searches-in-europes-largest-police-database/> (last accessed: 10.10.2023).

[115] Statewatch, 'EU: Council's internal security committee discusses use of "discreet checks" in the Schengen Information System' (Statewatch, 28.2.2018) <https://www.statewatch.org/news/2018/february/eu-council-s-internal-security-committee-discusses-use-of-discreet-checks-in-the-schengen-information-system/> (last accessed: 10.10.2023).

[116] Andreeva, Europe Studies in Conflict & Terrorism 2023, 1.

[117] Bogaert, 'Are We Entering a No-Fly Zone with the Expansion of the No-Fly List?' (lawblogs, 24.4.2022) <https://lawblogs.uc.edu/ihrlr/2022/04/24/are-we-entering-a-no-fly-zone-with-the-expansion-of-the-no-fly-list/> (last accessed: 10.10.2023).

[118] Rudner, IJICI 2015, 38; Bartiromo, 'No-fly lists' (Fox News, 18.1.2021) <https://www.foxnews.com/lifestyle/no-fly-lists-major-airlines-how-many-passengers-banned> (last accessed: 10.10.2023).

[119] European Data Protection Supervisor, 'EDPS Formal comments on the draft Commission Implementing Decision defining the technical specification of the ETIAS watchlist and of the assessment tool', 22.1.2021, 2.

[120] Michéa/Rousvoal, EP-JMN 2021, 473.

[121] Jo Pesch/Dimitrova/Boehm in Gryszczyńska/Polański/Gruschka, Privacy Technologies and Policy, Proceedings, p. 50.

Current experience of EU border control systems[122] and the practices of other industrialized countries already give reason to doubt this.

Border screening technologies across the world are steadily expanding data collection and automated processing or risk assessment.[123] Many of these instruments are not readily compatible with the EU's legal framework on data protection and fundamental rights, as evidenced in multiple court cases concerning the blanket retention of passenger name records.[124] Much like the long-standing debate on the mandatory retention of telecommunications data, several Member States do not appear to be willing to follow the European Court of Justice's restrictive line on the proportionality of and necessity for such security measures.[125] Rather, both representatives of EU security agencies and national experts seem to prioritize new control technologies. Automated biometric border control gates have been rolled out across European airports.[126] Furthermore, the Future Group on Travel Intelligence and Border Management, with the involvement of Frontex and Europol, discussed further medium-term trends for IBM.[127] The group reviewed options for automatically analysing multiple data sources in order to categorize travellers or expand spatial surveillance of border regions, which have already been pioneered by the United States and Israel.[128] Further, data fusion and the increasing use of artificial intelligence (AI) tools is fully in line with the paradigm of IBM. 41

However, at the time of writing the EU is negotiating a new Artificial Intelligence Act, which may put limits on the use of automated systems to detect, identify, categorize or track people.[129] Several Member States advocate a broad exemption from new EU regulatory standards in the area of public or national security, whereas various representatives from civil society or the European Parliament are calling for wide-ranging bans, such as on AI-driven facial recognition systems that work at a distance and without the express consent or knowledge of those concerned.[130] This debate illustrates the fact that the specific meaning and scope of IBM is far from settled and needs further specification beyond the confines of the Frontex mandate. While Member States may officially refuse to empower the EU in relation to sensitive matters of national security and intelligence, one can observe far more fluid and supportive attitudes towards further integration and supra-nationalization on the technological and operational level of border management. 42

D. Conclusions

Over the last 20 years, IBM has conceptually shifted the agenda beyond compensation for internal border controls within the Schengen zone. In line with the wider global 43

---

122 Vavoula/Niovi, European Law Review 2020, 348–372.

123 Mau, p. 1 et seqq.

124 The Court considers that respect for fundamental rights requires that the powers provided for by the PNR Directive be limited to what is strictly necessary.

125 Juszczak/Sason, eucrim 2021, 238.

126 Noori, Geopolitics 2022, 1117.

127 Statewatch, 'Future Group on Travel Intelligence and Border Management' (Statewatch, 7.9.2021) <https://www.statewatch.org/observatories/frontex/access-to-documents-requests/future-group-on-travel-intelligence-and-border-management/> (last accessed: 10.10.2023).

128 Schaeffer, Kalfou 2019, 177; Milivojevic, Criminology & Criminal Justice 2022, 1.

129 Dumbrava, 'Artificial intelligence at EU borders: Overview of applications and key issues' (2021), EPRS, PE 690.706.

130 Kilpatrick/Jones, p. 1 et seqq.

momentum since the late 1990s, border controls have undergone a process of modernization and de-territorialization. This process has happened at multiple national and international levels of governance, and has also accorded the EU a prominent opportunity to cast itself as a standard-setter and modernizing force among Member States' security agencies. Even more importantly for the European setting, IBM has helped to side step confrontations over sovereignty. Typically, one would expect Member States to block far-reaching integration in matters of 'core state powers',[131] which clearly applies to the area of border security.

44 At the turn of the millennium, hands-on discussions on risk assessments, training, operational burden-sharing among Member States were framed under the heading of IBM. Shortly after, IBM was given a new and unusually permissive legal basis in Art. 77(2)(d) TFEU. By 2016, this enabled the creation of the European Border and Coast Guard, officially constituted by both Member State services and the EU-level agency. Only three years later, Frontex was empowered to recruit a corps of EU-own border guards, still with reference to the aims of IBM. The parallel far-reaching technological project to make all EU databases interoperable for police and border guards drew on the same Treaty provision, which requires the taking of 'any measure necessary for the gradual establishment of an integrated management system for external borders'.

45 The future of Frontex remains contested, as is the practical implementation of interoperability. Crisis-driven decision-making among Member States, such as after the major influx of refugees in 2015/16 and again in 2022, ultimately remains decisive when it comes to the evolution of EU security policy writ large. Yet insofar as crises can be catalysed into political will, IBM has been a critical enabling concept when it comes to deepening integration. The next major question is the actual depth of IBM with regard to Member State actors. If the stated ambition of a joint EU Border and Coast Guard by both Member States and the European agency can be realized – as outlined in the most recent policy cycle on IBM – the relevant competences and legal boundaries, such as in Art. 4(2) TEU, increasingly lose their operational importance.

46 However, the intended fusion of tasks and processes in shared or joint operations for border security can have significant risks. Grave normative problems arise when there is no clear locus of responsibility, a resulting lack of assistance or other failings in rescue operations, which can ultimately result in the death of irregular migrants and asylum seekers. In addition, the use of sensitive intelligence and data-sharing for IBM needs to be closely monitored. While such practices have been helpful for countering concrete terrorist threats, such as is posed by the so-called Islamic State, current technological tools for border security or 'smart borders' tend towards a regularized, expansive and increasingly automated data and intelligence processing. The example of the United States' no-fly lists shows how difficult it can be to ensure meaningful redress for affected third-country nationals.

47 Therefore, IBM needs more codification beyond the existing administrative or soft-law documents issued by Frontex or the European Commission. Closed expert groups, such as the High Level Working Group on IBM, are insufficient to steer and legitimize related reforms, particularly if fundamental rights are genuinely supposed to constitute a core component of IBM. Finally, the use of Art. 77(2) TFEU for further Frontex mandate revisions or new tools of EU border security should be discussed more critically. The next potential revision of EU treaties should consider providing Frontex with an explicit basis comparable to Europol or the European Public Prosecutor.

---

[131] Genschel/Jachtenfuchs, Journal of European Public Policy 2016, 42; Gruszczak, Studia Prawnicze KUL 2021, 73.

§ 20
Paradigm shifts: from siloed databases to interoperability of EU large scale information systems*

Teresa Quintel

Bibliography: Bellanova/Glouftsios, 'Formatting European security integration through database interoperability', European Security 2022 (31:3), 454; Bigo et al., Justice and Home Affairs Databases and a Smart Borders System at EU Borders – An Evaluation of Current and Forthcoming Proposals, Brussels 2012; Craig/de Búrca, EU Law: Text, Cases, and Materials, 5th edn, Oxford 2011; Davis, 'The European Union's Dublin Regulation and the Migrant Crisis Notes', Washington University Global Studies Law Review 2020 (19), 261; de Hert, 'Trends in de Europese politiële en justitiële informatiesamenwerking', Panopticon 2004 (25), 26; de Hert/ Sajfert, 'Regulating Big Data in and out of the data protection policy field: Two scenarios of post-GDPR law-making and the actor perspective', EDPL 2019 (5:3), 338; Demková/Quintel, 'Allocation of Responsibilities in Interoperable Information Exchanges: Effective Review Compromised?', Cahiers Jean Monnet 2020, 589; Ferraro/De Capitani, 'The New European Border and Coast Guard: Yet Another "Half Way" EU Reform?', ERA Forum 2016 (17), 385; Gonzalez Fuster, 'Artificial Intelligence and Law Enforcement – Impact on Fundamental Rights', Study for the LIBE Committee of the European Parliament 2020; Marquenie, 'The Police and Criminal Justice Authorities Directive: Data Protection Standards and Impact on the Legal Framework', CLSR 2017 (33), 324; Melachrinos/Carammia/Wilkin, 'Using big data to estimate migration "push factors" from Africa' in Fargues/Rango (eds), Migration in West and North Africa and across the Mediterranean – Trends, risks, development and governance, Geneva 2020, p. 98; Napierała/Hilton/Forster/Carammia, 'Toward an Early Warning System for Monitoring Asylum-Related Migration Flows in Europe', International Migration Review 2022 (56:1), 33; Niemann/ Speyer, 'A Neofunctionalist Perspective on the "European Refugee Crisis": The Case of the European Border and Coast Guard', JCMS 2018 (56), 23; Quintel, 'Connecting Personal Data of Third Country Nationals: Interoperability of EU Databases in the Light of the CJEU's Case Law on Data Retention, University of Luxembourg Law Working Paper 2018 (2); Quintel, Data Protection, Migration and Border Control. The GDPR, the Law Enforcement Directive and Beyond, Oxford, 2022; Quintel, 'Entry-Exit System' in OUP Encyclopaedia, forthcoming in 2025; Quintel, 'Interoperable Data Exchanges Within Different Data Protection Regimes: The Case of Europol and the European Border and Coast Guard Agency', EPL 2020 (26:1), 205; Quintel, 'The EDPS on Europol's Big Data Challenge in Light of the Recast Europol Regulation. The Question of Legitimizing Unlawful Practices', EDPL 2022 (8:1), 90; Quintel, 'The Commission Proposal on Combatting Child Sexual Abuse – Confidentiality of Communications at Risk?', EDPL 2022 (8:2), 262; Quintel, 'The Impact of Interoperability on the Processing of (Biometric) Data of Third Country Nationals by Europol', KritV 2018, 332; Rijpma, 'The Proposal for a European Border and Coast Guard: Evolution or Revolution in External Border Management?', Study for the LIBE Committee of the European Parliament (2016); Tsourdi, 'Holding the European Asylum Support Office Accountable for Its Role in Asylum Decision-Making: Mission Impossible? Border Justice: Migration and Accountability for Human Rights Violations', German Law Journal 2020 (21), 506; Van Brakel, 'Pre-Emptive Big Data Surveillance and its (Dis)Empowering Consequences: The Case of Predictive Policing' in van der Sloot/Broeders/Schrijvers (eds) Exploring the Boundaries of Big Data, Amsterdam 2016, p. 117; van der Sloot, 'The Quality of Law', JIPITEC 2020 (11), 160; Vavoula, 'Artificial Intelligence (AI) at Schengen Borders: Automated Processing, Algorithmic Profiling and Facial Recognition in the Era of Techno-Solutionism', European Journal of Migration and Law 2021 (23:4), 457; Vavoula, '(Covert)

* This chapter expresses only the personal opinion of the author and does not bind in any way the European Parliament. The author wishes to thank Prof. Dr. Niovi Vavoula for her very insightful comments and devoting her time to providing them.

Surveillance of Foreign Terrorism Fighters (FTFs) via the Schengen Information System (SIS): Towards Maximum Operationalisation of Alerts and an Enhanced Role for Europol', New Journal of European Criminal Law 2023 (14:2), 206; Vavoula, 'Transforming Eurodac from 2016 to the New Pact From the Dublin System's Sidekick to a Database in Support of EU Policies on Asylum, Resettlement and Irregular Migration', ECRE Working Paper 2020 (13); Vavoula, Immigration and Privacy in the Law of the European Union. The Case of Information Systems, Leiden/Boston 2022; Weyembergh/Armada/Briere, 'Competition or Cooperation: State of Play and Future Perspectives on the Relations between Europol, Eurojust and the European Judicial Network', New Journal of European Criminal Law 2015 (6:2), 258.

A. Introduction

1 The Schengen Area, together with the area of freedom, security and justice (AFSJ),[1] could be regarded as one of the clearest manifestations and one of the biggest achievements of European integration. It began as an intergovernmental project among five Member States back in 1985 and has continued growing ever since.[2]

2 However, in recent years, the Schengen Area has been confronted with a series of crises and challenges. The unprecedented 2015 'migration crisis' exposed shortcomings in the Union's management of its external borders and led to the reintroduction of internal border controls in a number of Member States.[3]

3 Since anyone crossing the external borders of one Member State – by air, land or sea – can travel freely to and within the other Member States, the Schengen Area's existence presupposes an integrated and strategic approach to external border management, systematic border surveillance, interconnected databases and increasingly digitalized procedures. This involves the processing of large quantities of personal data of those persons who enter the European Union who are not EU citizens, so-called third-country nationals (TCNs).

4 Over the last 36 years – and especially since 2015 – a comprehensive legal framework and common operational tools have been developed to better protect the Schengen Area. Legislation was introduced, ranging from common visa, asylum and return policies to police and judicial cooperation instruments. In addition, the EU set up various IT and surveillance systems, such as the Schengen Information System (SIS)[4] and the European Border Surveillance System EUROSUR, and granted more powers to EU Agencies, which became more involved in the management of migration flows at the EU's external borders.

---

[1] The creation of the area of freedom, security and justice derives from Title V of the Treaty on the Functioning of the European Union (Art. 67–89 TFEU). The area was created to ensure the absence of border control at internal borders while offering a high level of protection to citizens. According to Art. 3 TEU, which sets out the objectives of the European Union, the EU offers its citizens an area of freedom, security and justice without internal frontiers. The objectives of the AFSJ are laid down in Art. 67 TFEU. See EUR-lex, 'Justice, freedom and security' <https://eur-lex.europa.eu/summary/chapter/justice_freedom_security.html?root_default=SUM_1_CODED%3D23> (last accessed: 12.10.2023).

[2] Craig/de Búrca, p. 31.

[3] For instance at the Austrian, German, French, Danish and Swedish borders, see European Commission, 'Member States' notifications of the temporary reintroduction of border control at internal borders pursuant to Art. 25 and 28 et seq. of the Schengen Borders Code' available from <https://home-affairs.ec.europa.eu/> (last accessed: 12.10.2023). In France, terrorist related events took place at the same time and put a strain on the Schengen Area. See also Brouwer, 'Migration Flows and the Reintroduction of Internal Border Controls' (eumigrationlawblog, 12.11.2015) <https://eumigrationlawblog.eu/migration-flows-and-the-reintroduction-of-internal-border-controls-assessing-necessity-and-proportionality/> (last accessed: 12.10.2023).

[4] European Commission, 'Schengen Information System' <https://home-affairs.ec.europa.eu/policies/schengen-borders-and-visa/schengen-information-system_en> (last accessed: 12.10.2023).

Since 2016, tremendous developments have taken place in terms of large-scale information systems[5] that were set up for internal security, migration and asylum purposes both at the external borders and within the Schengen Area. From what were initially only three databases – the SIS, the Visa Information System (VIS)[6] and Eurodac[7] – the EU legislators created a common European IT architecture with the establishment of three entirely new databases: the Entry/Exit System,[8] the European Travel Information and Authorization System[9] and the European Criminal Records Information System for TCNs and stateless persons.[10] Moreover, all of the founding acts of the existing databases were revised in order to accommodate additional objectives, store further categories of personal data, grant access to additional authorities (both at national and at EU level) and to upgrade the systems in terms of general functionalities. In addition, the AFSJ databases are supposed to increasingly employ algorithmic matching techniques and pre-vetting analyses. In a final step, all of the operational and yet-to-be-established systems are to improve their capacities by inter-exchanging the data they store. 5

While the EU databases were initially established in so-called silos and compartmentalized according to their individual purposes, they are to become interconnected, or interoperable. Full interoperability was to be established by the end of 2023. That initial date, however, was postponed and certain components of the interoperable system are now to be operational in mid-2024.[11] Interoperability will connect all EU databases for borders, migration and security and is to ensure that these underlying systems 'talk' to each other. 6

When issuing a query in the centralized system, end users will be able to access information from all connected databases. This is to ensure that competent authorities have access to all the necessary information and to allow for the timely sharing of information among all the relevant actors. 7

Interoperability streamlines law enforcement access to non-law enforcement databases, including to new datasets that will be generated by the interoperable system itself. The term 'streamlining' is the word used to describe the 'aligning' and 'simplifying' of the conditions for providing access across various systems. 8

In short, more personal data of TCNs will be processed in the form of additional processing operations, more authorities will have access to those data both at national 9

---

[5] Bellanova/Glouftsios, European Security 2022, 454–474.

[6] European Commission, 'Visa Information System (VIS)' <https://home-affairs.ec.europa.eu/policies/schengen-borders-and-visa/visa-information-system_en> (last accessed: 12.10.2023).

[7] eu-LISA, 'Eurodac' <https://www.eulisa.europa.eu/Activities/Large-Scale-It-Systems/Eurodac> (last accessed: 12.10.2023).

[8] European Commission, 'Entry/Exit System (EES)' <https://home-affairs.ec.europa.eu/policies/schengen-borders-and-visa/smart-borders/entry-exit-system_en> (last accessed: 12.10.2023).

[9] European Commission, 'European Travel Information and Authorisation System (ETIAS' <https://home-affairs.ec.europa.eu/policies/schengen-borders-and-visa/smart-borders/european-travel-information-authorisation-system_en> (last accessed: 12.10.2023).

[10] European Union Agency for the Operational Management of Large-Scale IT Systems in the Area of Freedom, Security and Justice, 'ECRIS-TCN' <https://www.eulisa.europa.eu/Activities/Large-Scale-It-Systems/Ecris-Tcn> (last accessed: 12.10.2023).

[11] European Commission, 'Proposal for a Regulation of the European Parliament and of the Council on establishing a framework for interoperability between EU information systems (police and judicial cooperation, asylum and migration)', 12.12.2017, COM(2017) 794 final, 76. It should be noted that the operationalization of the underlying large-scale systems and the interoperability component has been postponed until June 2024, see European Commission, 'Report from the Commission to the European Parliament and the Council on the state of play of preparations for the full implementation of the Interoperability Regulations in accordance with Article 78(5) Regulation (EU) 2019/817 and Article 74(5) Regulation (EU) 2019/818', 13.10.2022, COM(2022) 524 final, 1.

and EU level and more purposes will be added to process these data, including for the prevention, investigation and detection of criminal offences, so-called law enforcement purposes.

10 The complexity that the Interoperability Regulations add to the already complicated system of EU databases, the intertwinedness that new forms of cooperation between authorities at national and EU level will bring and the broadened mandate that EU Agencies have obtained as regards the processing of TCNs' personal data for a variety of purposes are at odds with some of the most important data protection principles.

11 Where personal data from migration and criminal law enforcement databases are interconnected, where such information can be accessed, analysed and exchanged between a multitude of authorities and where large datasets are analysed in order to screen TCNs who end up in these databases, this represents a challenge to the purpose limitation principle. That principle is enshrined in Art. 8 of the EU Charter of Fundamental Rights (CFR) and could, therefore, be seen as one of the most fundamental data protection principles.

12 While, according to that principle, purposes should be strictly defined, most of the legislative texts amending the EU databases transform purposes into objectives that are much wider than envisaged in the original set-up of these EU databases.

13 This widening of the purpose limitation principle will allow law enforcement authorities to access and subsequently process personal data that were initially destined to be processed only for migration-related purposes. It will allow those authorities to exchange this information with their counterparts at the national and EU level and it risks blurring the line between general and law enforcement data protection rules.

14 The EU's data protection reform was adopted in 2016, almost at the same time as all the above measures were proposed and about one year after the migration crisis. It included the General Data Protection Regulation (GDPR)[12] and the Law Enforcement Directive (LED).[13]

15 A mixing of purposes amplifies the unclear delineation between the GDPR (that applies to general or administrative processing) and the LED (that applies to processing that is carried out by competent authorities for law enforcement purposes).

16 This is because it is not always crystal clear what law enforcement processing actually includes. While migration management could be categorized as administrative processing, the boundaries start to become more blurred when it comes to border control. Where border guards are obliged to query law enforcement databases such as the SIS for all entries to the EU, or where national police officers are supposed to check migration databases in the fight against illegal immigration, the distinction between the GDPR and the LED becomes more difficult.

17 Another example where competent authorities could apply the Directive is when it comes to using the more flexible rules on exchanging personal data when they cooperate with EU Agencies.

18 The inclusion of the EU-level Agencies is also relevant because discrepancies may arise in the context of interoperability where systematic data exchanges take place between actors on different levels that apply different data protection regimes.

---

[12] Regulation (EU) 2016/679 on the protection of natural persons with regard to the processing of personal data and on the free movement of such data (General Data Protection Regulation).

[13] Directive (EU) 2016/680 on the protection of natural persons with regard to the processing of personal data by competent authorities for the purposes of the prevention, investigation, detection or prosecution of criminal offences or the execution of criminal penalties, and on the free movement of such data.

Furthermore, certain EU Agencies such as Europol increasingly collect and generate personal data themselves through their own data analyses. Finally, data exchanges between national and EU levels may arise within the framework of EUROSUR, where different national authorities have access to data that were gathered by Frontex, the European Border and Coast Guard Agency.[14] **19**

In addition, shortcomings can be observed regarding the application of the Regulation that governs the processing of personal data by Union institutions, bodies, offices and agencies (EUDPR)[15] and its Chapter IX on the processing of so-called operational personal data. Where EU Agencies such as Frontex apply that Chapter to some of their processing activities, this raises data protection concerns, as Chapter IX remained unfinished. Furthermore, Europol is permitted to disregard some of the rules under the EUDPR due to its tailor-made data protection regime in the recast Europol Regulation,[16] which is to consider the Agency's needs in the performance of its tasks. **20**

This chapter provides a brief synopsis of the operational and soon-to-be EU information systems, assesses the growth of the powers of EU Agencies in terms of processing capabilities and outlines the accompanying data protection concerns. **21**

For that purpose, section B depicts the landscape of existing and anticipated databases and explains the new data flows and generation of new datasets that will emerge with the interoperability of EU information systems. **22**

Section C addresses some of the problems that may emerge with regard to the quality of data and potential biases in algorithmic profiling of individuals whose personal data will be stored in the interoperable system. **23**

Section E briefly outlines the data protection framework applicable at the national and EU level and highlights both the data protection concerns with regard to data flows between the national and EU level and some of the challenges when it comes to data protection rules and supervising the interoperable system. **24**

The conclusion summarizes some of the main concerns raised in the previous sections and sketches a future outlook. **25**

B. The road from separated silos to interconnected systems

I. The underlying databases

Today, the Schengen Information System (SIS)[17] is the most widely used information system within the EU.[18] In the absence of internal border checks after the entry into force of the Schengen Convention, the system was established in order to maintain public policy and public security in the territories of the Member States by using **26**

[14] Regulation (EU) 2019/1896 on the European Border and Coast Guard.

[15] Regulation (EU) 2018/1725 on the protection of natural persons with regard to the processing of personal data by the Union institutions, bodies, offices and agencies and on the free movement of such data.

[16] Regulation (EU) 2022/991 amending Regulation (EU) 2016/794, as regards Europol's cooperation with private parties, the processing of personal data by Europol in support of criminal investigations, and Europol's role in research and innovation.

[17] The rapid growth of the Schengen group, even outside the EU, through association agreements with Norway, Iceland and Switzerland and the prospect of further enlargement of the EU led to the decision to develop a second generation of the system as early as December 1996. See de Hert, Panopticon 2004, 26.

[18] See footnote 4.

information communicated via the SIS.[19] The SIS contains alerts on persons and objects that are available to the authorities that have access to the system. Alert categories include persons wanted for arrest, missing persons, persons sought to assist with a judicial procedure or alerts on refusals of entry or stay.[20]

27 The first generation of the SIS became operational in 1995[21] and has, since then, been updated[22] into a second (SIS II)[23] and a third[24] generation, which is currently used by 25 of the EU Member States and four Schengen Associated Countries, that is Switzerland, Norway, Liechtenstein and Iceland.[25]

28 With the revision of the SIS II in November 2018, three new Regulations were adopted, one on the return of illegally staying TCNs,[26] one in the field of police cooperation and judicial cooperation in criminal matters,[27] and one in the field of border checks.[28] With their entry into force, the SIS was to become *de-pillarized*, meaning that the system would no longer follow the former three-pillar structure. Some of the main changes under the three new SIS Regulations were the storage of new types of alerts and biometrics,[29] additional data on so-called preventive alerts, which are supposed to protect certain categories of vulnerable persons,[30] as well as alerts on return decisions[31] and entry bans.[32]

---

[19] Art. 93 of the Convention implementing the Schengen Agreement (CISA).

[20] European Commission, 'Alerts and data in SIS' <https://home-affairs.ec.europa.eu/policies/schengen-borders-and-visa/schengen-information-system/alerts-and-data-sis_en>.

[21] At that time, the system was used by seven Member States, that is Belgium, the Netherlands, Luxembourg, France, Spain, Portugal and Germany.

[22] On account of the 9/11 terrorist attacks, among other things.

[23] On 31 May 2005, the Commission presented proposals for three legislative instruments governing the SIS II, which were adopted on 12.6.2007: two Regulations (Regulation (EC) 1987/2006 on the development, operation and use of the second generation Schengen Information System (SIS II) (SIS II Regulation) and Regulation (EC) 1986/2006 regarding access to the Second Generation Schengen Information System (SIS II) by the services in the Member States responsible for issuing vehicle registration certificates) and a Council Decision (Council Decision 2007/533/JHA on the establishment, operation and use of the second generation Schengen Information System (SIS II) (SIS II Decision)).

[24] Regulation (EU) 2018/1860 on the use of the Schengen Information System for the return of illegally staying third-country nationals, Regulation (EU) 2018/1861 on the establishment, operation and use of the Schengen Information System (SIS) in the field of border checks and Regulation (EU) 2018/1862 on the establishment, operation and use of the Schengen Information System (SIS) in the field of police cooperation and judicial cooperation in criminal matters.

[25] The second-generation SIS extended its users and allowed for new functions. There are Member States with special arrangements, for instance Bulgaria and Romania are not yet part of the Area without internal border checks. However, in August 2018 Bulgaria and Romania started fully using SIS. Ireland operates SIS, but as it has chosen not to join the Schengen Area, it cannot issue or access Schengen-wide alerts for refusing entry into and stay in the Schengen Area. Cyprus is not yet connected to SIS as it has a temporary derogation from joining the Schengen Area. Croatia has limited access to the SIS. However, since the country joined the Schengen Area in January 2023, it will most likely obtain full access to the system.

[26] Regulation (EU) 2018/1860 on the use of the Schengen Information System for the return of illegally staying third-country nationals.

[27] Regulation (EU) 2018/1862 on the establishment, operation and use of the Schengen Information System (SIS) in the field of police cooperation and judicial cooperation in criminal matters.

[28] Regulation (EU) 2018/1861 on the establishment, operation and use of the Schengen Information System (SIS) in the field of border checks, and amending the Convention implementing the Schengen Agreement.

[29] SIS III stores palm prints (Art. 40 Regulation 2018/1862 regarding alerts on unknown wanted persons for the purposes of identification under national law), fingerprints (Art. 20(3)(y) Regulation 2018/1862), facial images (Art. 20(3)(w) Regulation 2018/1862) and DNA. The latter may only be used to confirm the identity of missing persons. See Art. 20(3)(x), Art. 32(1)(a) and Art. 42(3) Regulation 2018/1862.

[30] Such as missing persons, children at risk of abduction or potential victims of trafficking in human beings or of gender-based violence.

[31] See Art. 4 Regulation 2018/1860.

[32] Art. 4(1)(z) Regulation 2018/1860 and Art. 20(2)(q)(iv) Regulation 2018/1861.

In that vein, the reformed SIS is to facilitate the better enforcement of entry bans and return decisions issued to irregularly staying TCNs.[33] Apart from the creation of crime- and terrorism-related alerts, the SIS will be used for the purpose of effective migration law enforcement. This illustrates that the system is no longer a database that focuses on police cooperation, but that it supplements additional elements of migration management, building upon the already existing alerts on TCNs. **29**

Besides national police forces and other law enforcement authorities (LEAs), the end users of SIS alerts are border guards, customs authorities, consular offices and embassies responsible for the assessment of Schengen visa applications. In several Member States, direct access to the SIS is also granted to asylum authorities.[34] **30**

In addition, Europol and Frontex will be granted additional access opportunities to the SIS for the performance of their tasks.[35] Europol will have access to all SIS alerts and will be permitted to propose that Member States record so-called information alerts in the system.[36] This means that, besides storing new types of personal data and further categories of data subjects, the SIS grants more authorities access for additional purposes. **31**

The primary objective of the currently operational Eurodac database[37] is to determine which Member State is responsible for processing an asylum application. By searching the system using fingerprint data, authorities in the Member States check whether a person has previously applied for international protection in another EU Member State.[38] Eurodac thereby assists in the implementation of the Dublin system to ensure that an individual applies for asylum in the first country of entry and to prevent 'asylum shopping' in different Member States. **32**

Besides asylum seekers' fingerprints, the system stores information on people who are apprehended when attempting to cross an external border illegally. For the moment, Eurodac is the most extensive multi-jurisdictional automated fingerprint identification system (AFIS) globally, with 32 affiliated countries.[39] **33**

In future, Eurodac is to hold data on persons illegally staying in the territory of a Member State for the purpose of their expulsion.[40] The reformed Eurodac aims at **34**

---

[33] Adding an obligation to create an SIS alert for return decisions and alerts on a wider range of stolen and falsified goods and documents. See Art. 3(1) and (4) Regulation (EU) 2018/1860. European Commission, 'Security Union: Technical and Operational Updates of the Schengen Information System – Questions & Answers' <https://ec.europa.eu/commission/presscorner/detail/en/MEMO_16_4427> (last accessed: 12.10.2023).

[34] Please refer to the list of competent authorities that are authorised to search directly the data contained in the second-generation Schengen Information System pursuant to Art. 31(8) Regulation 1987/2006 and Art. 46(8) Council Decision 2007/533/JHA on the establishment, operation and use of the second generation Schengen Information System (2021/C 287/01). See also Bellanova/Glouftsios, Geopolitics 2020, 160–184.

[35] Art. 36 Regulation 2018/1861, Art. 50 Regulation 2018/1862 and Art. 17(3) Regulation 2018/1860.

[36] Pursuant to Regulation (EU) 2022/1190 amending Regulation (EU) 2018/1862 as regards the entry of information alerts into the Schengen Information System (SIS) on third-country nationals in the interest of the Union. See Vavoula, New Journal of European Criminal Law 2023.

[37] Regulation (EU) No 603/2013 on the establishment of 'Eurodac' for the comparison of fingerprints for the effective application of Regulation (EU) No 604/2013 establishing the criteria and mechanisms for determining the Member State responsible for examining an application for international protection lodged in one of the Member States by a third-country national or a stateless person and on requests for the comparison with Eurodac data by Member States' law enforcement authorities and Europol for law enforcement purposes.

[38] Quintel, Luxembourg Law Working Paper 2018, 7.

[39] Thalesgroup, 'The Schengen Entry/Exit System: biometrics to facilitate smart borders' (Thalesgroup) <https://www.thalesgroup.com/en/markets/digital-identity-and-security/government/eborder/entry-exit-system> last accessed: 1.10.2023).

[40] European Commission, 'Proposal for a Regulation of the European Parliament and of the Council on the establishment of 'Eurodac' for the comparison of fingerprints for the effective application of [Regulation (EU) No 604/2013 establishing the criteria and mechanisms for determining the Member

expanding the system's scope to wider objectives of immigration control, such as the monitoring of illegal migration and secondary movements[41] of irregular migrants within the EU.[42] This is to be achieved, among other things, by storing TCNs' personal data for longer periods in order to investigate travel routes and identify unauthorized stays.

35 Following negotiations on the 2016 proposal that ended in deadlock, the Commission, on 23 September 2020,[43] proposed a new Eurodac Regulation[44] amending the 2016 text, among other things to allow Eurodac to function within the interoperability framework between EU large-scale information systems, which is discussed below.[45]

36 The 2020 Eurodac proposal built on the provisional agreement between the Parliament and the Council that was founded on the 2016 proposal. In addition, by making additional changes, the amended proposal sought to transform Eurodac into a common European database to support EU policies on asylum, resettlement and irregular migration.[46] By means of the 2020 Eurodac proposal, the initial purpose of the system was refurbished in order to accommodate all large-scale systems that were amended, adopted and proposed in the meantime.[47] The Eurodac database thus extends its functionalities in order to establish a link between all stages of the pre-entry procedure with those related to the return of TCNs.[48]

37 The Visa Information System (VIS)[49] is a large-scale IT system that seeks to facilitate the administration, issuance and checks of short-stay visas[50] to the Schengen Area by enabling the exchange of visa information and the matching of biometric data to verify

---

State responsible for examining an application for international protection lodged in one of the Member States by a third-country national or a stateless person], for identifying an illegally staying third-country national or stateless person and on requests for the comparison with Eurodac data by Member States' law enforcement authorities and Europol for law enforcement purposes', 4.5.2016, COM(2016) 272 final, 12.

[41] In this context, secondary movements occur when refugees or asylum seekers move from the Member State in which they first arrived to seek asylum in another Member State.

[42] The legal basis for the proposed Eurodac Regulation is Art. 79(2)(c) TFEU. While the legal basis for Regulation 1003/2013 was Art. 78(2)(e), the wider purpose remains immigration.

[43] Because the Eurodac proposal was included as part of a package within which the co-legislators could not agree upon the remaining legislative proposals, the 2016 Eurodac proposal could not go forward on its own and was never adopted.

[44] European Commission, 'Amended proposal for a Regulation of the European Parliament and of the Council on the establishment of 'Eurodac' for the comparison of biometric data for the effective application of Regulation (EU) XXX/XXX [Regulation on Asylum and Migration Management] and of Regulation (EU) XXX/XXX [Resettlement Regulation], for identifying an illegally staying third-country national or stateless person and on requests for the comparison with Eurodac data by Member States' law enforcement authorities and Europol for law enforcement purposes and amending Regulations (EU) 2018/1240 and (EU) 2019/818', 23.9.2020, COM(2020) 614 final. The 2020 Eurodac reform was proposed as part of the New Pact on Migration and Asylum and was put forward together with five additional proposals. These additional proposals included an amended Proposal for Asylum Procedure (COM(2020) 611 final), a Proposal for an Asylum and Migration Management Regulation (COM(2020) 610 final), a Proposal for a Screening Regulation (COM(2020) 612 final) and a Proposal for a Crisis and Force Majeure Regulation (COM(2020) 613 final).

[45] COM(2020) 614 final, 2.

[46] ibid.

[47] Vavoula, ECRE Working Paper 2020, 13.

[48] COM(2020) 614 final, 2.

[49] Council Decision 2004/512/EC establishing the Visa Information System (VIS), Regulation (EC) No 767/2008 concerning the Visa Information System (VIS) and the exchange of data between Member States on short-stay visas (VIS Regulation) and Council Decision 2008/633/JHA concerning access for consultation of the Visa Information System (VIS) by designated authorities of Member States and by Europol for the purposes of the prevention, detection and investigation of terrorist offences and of other serious criminal offences.

[50] For short-stay visas in the Schengen Area normally 90 days within a six-month period (multiple-entry visas).

the authenticity of a visa.[51] For that purpose, the system connects consulates in non-EU countries with all external Schengen border crossing points.[52] Further objectives of the VIS are to prevent 'visa shopping' and to stop individuals from 'overstaying' the authorized duration of their visa in the Schengen Area.[53]

A new legal basis for the VIS was adopted in July 2021.[54] The latter will render the VIS interoperable with the remaining systems, Europol data and two Interpol databases.[55] The data recorded in a visa application file will be matched against a watchlist and specific risk indicators that are supposed to indicate security, illegal immigration or high epidemic risks.[56] The revised VIS extends the personal scope of the system to long-term visa holders and holders of residence permits. In addition, the new Regulation lowers the fingerprinting age from 12 to 6 years.[57] **38**

While the initial purposes of the VIS were maintained, 11 sub-purposes were added under the revised framework, including assistance in identifying people who have gone missing, were abducted or were identified as victims of trafficking in human beings, supporting the objectives of the SIS and facilitating the fight against fraud.[58] With regard to long-stay visas and residence permits, eight purposes were added similar to the ones concerning short-term visas.[59] The revised legal framework and the system's functionalities to automatically verify hits against the other systems rendered the VIS the most complex and difficult to read system next to the ETIAS, which will be discussed below. **39**

Under the revised VIS framework, national LEAs and Europol[60] will have access to additional datasets and Frontex will be granted new access rights, including for law enforcement purposes.[61] While the conditions for accessing the VIS differ from those that allow access to the SIS, the different forms of access may coincide where one authority accesses both systems, or each system for different purposes. This, in turn, could have an impact on the applicable data protection instrument used for any subsequent processing of the personal data consulted.[62] **40**

The legal basis of the Entry/Exit System (EES)[63] is laid down in Art. 77(2)(b) and (d) and in Art. 87(2)(a) TFEU. The system, hence, addresses external border checks, **41**

---

[51] European Commission, 'Visa Information System (VIS)' at footnote 6. See also Quintel, Luxembourg Law Working Paper 2018, 7.

[52] See footnote 6.

[53] Quintel, Luxembourg Law Working Paper 2018, 7.

[54] It needs to be noted that certain provisions under the revised VIS framework require the adoption of additional acts and/or are subject to diverging conditions before entering into application and before specific functionalities of the revised VIS can enter into operation. See: Art. 48 Regulation 767/2008 and Art. 11 and 12 Regulation) 2021/1134.

[55] Art. 9a Regulation 767/2008. See: Regulation (EU) 2021/1134, for the purpose of reforming the Visa Information System.

[56] Art. 9(j) Regulation 2021/1134.

[57] European Parliament 'Legislative Train Schedule, New regulation on the Visa Information System (VIS) in 'Promoting our European Way of Life'', 15.12.2022 <https://www.europarl.europa.eu/legislative-train/theme-towards-a-new-policy-on-migration/file-new-regulation-on-the-visa-information-system-(vis)> (last accessed: 12.10.2023). See Regulation (EU) 2021/1133 as regards the establishment of the conditions for accessing other EU information systems for the purposes of the Visa Information System and Regulation (EU) 2021/1134, for the purpose of reforming the Visa Information System.

[58] Art. 2(1) Regulation (EC) No 767/2008. See: Regulation (EU) 2021/1134.

[59] Art. 2(2) Regulation (EC) No 767/2008. See: Regulation (EU) 2021/1134.

[60] Chap. IIIb Regulation (EC) No 767/2008. See: Regulation (EU) 2021/1134.

[61] Art. 45e Regulation (EU) 2021/1134.

[62] Quintel, Data Protection, p. 35.

[63] Regulation (EU) 2017/2226 establishing an Entry/Exit System (EES) to register entry and exit data and refusal of entry data of third-country nationals crossing the external borders of the Member States and determining the conditions for access to the EES for law enforcement purposes.

the gradual establishment of an integrated management system at the external EU borders and the collection, storage, processing, analysis and exchange of relevant information. Art. 87, which falls within Chapter 5 TFEU on Police Cooperation, provides the legal basis for permitting access to data stored in the EES by national LEAs and Europol.[64]

42 For the time being, the EES will be operated in all Schengen countries, including Denmark, while Bulgaria and Romania will have passive access.[65] Ireland and Cyprus do not participate in the EES. Initially, the EES was to be operational by 2020.[66] However, its implementation met with delays and, according to a new timeline, the system is meant to be operational by 2025.[67]

43 Despite the vast amount of information that was hitherto processed by the operational systems, the SIS, VIS and Eurodac, it was proposed that the EES would cover information on individuals whose personal data were not yet stored in the existing systems. One argument that was put forward in the EES proposal to justify the additional data collection was the need to close the existing information gap.[68]

44 Those individuals who fall neither within the scope of the VIS or Eurodac nor within the provisions of the SIS that cover travellers are TCNs admitted for short stays in the EU Member States who are subject to border checks pursuant to the Schengen Borders Code (SCB).[69] Hence, the personal scope of the EES covers short-term visa holders and visa-exempt travellers crossing the external border into EU Member States that participate in the EES. This includes TCNs who are family members of EU citizens and those who enjoy free movement rights but who do not hold a residence permit.[70] EU citizens and TCNs holding a residence permit or long-stay visa are excluded from the personal scope of the EES.[71]

45 The EES is to improve the management of the EU's external borders and the efficiency of border controls, to facilitate the detection of document and identity fraud and to support the identification of overstayers and undocumented persons in the Schengen Area.[72] To achieve these objectives, the EES will store the date, time and border crossing points of all entries and exits of both, that is TCNs required to obtain a visa and visa-exempted TCNs.[73] The records of entries and exits generated by the

[64] European Commission, 'Proposal for a Regulation of the European parliament and of the Council establishing an Entry/Exit System (EES) to register entry and exit data and refusal of entry data of third country nationals crossing the external borders of the Member States of the European Union and determining the conditions for access to the EES for law enforcement purposes and amending Regulation (EC) No 767/2008 and Regulation (EU) No 1077/2011', 6.4.2016, COM(2016) 194 final, 8.

[65] Recital 57 of the EES Regulation and Council Decision (EU) 2017/1908 on the putting into effect of certain provisions of the Schengen acquis relating to the Visa Information System in the Republic of Bulgaria and Romania.

[66] COM(2016) 194 final, 12.

[67] European Commission, 'Report from the Commission to the European Parliament and the Council on the state of play of preparations for the full implementation of the Interoperability Regulations in accordance with Article 78(5) of Regulation (EU) 2019/817 and Article 74(5) of Regulation (EU) 2019/818', 13.10.2022, COM(2022) 524 final, 1.

[68] Bigo et al., CEPS 2012, 5.

[69] Vavoula, p. 397.

[70] Art. 2(1)(b) Regulation 2017/2226.

[71] See Art. 2(3) Regulation 2017/2226.

[72] European Commission, 'Security Union: Commission Welcomes Adoption of Entry/Exit System for Stronger and Smarter EU Borders', 25.10.2017 <https://ec.europa.eu/commission/presscorner/detail/en/STATEMENT_17_4162> (last accessed: 12.10.2023) . For an analysis of the EES Proposal, please refer to Cole/Quintel, 'Data Retention under the Proposal for an EU Entry/Exit System (EES) Analysis of the Impact on and Limitations for the EES by Opinion 1/15 on the EU/Canada PNR Agreement of the Court of Justice of the European Union (2017)' (October 2017).

[73] Art. 16(2)(a), (b), (3)(a), (b) and Art. 17(2) Regulation 2017/2226.

system will be linked to an individual file on the respective TCN,[74] and, in cases where no exits are recorded in the EES after the duration of his or her authorized stay, the system will flag the person as an overstayer.[75]

The system will be interoperable with the VIS,[76] the European Travel Information and Authorisation System (ETIAS) and Eurodac to complement the information stored on visa applications, rejected visas, visa-exempt travellers and data on asylum applicants. This is the first logical step towards facilitating the exchange of information between the individual systems and achieving full interoperability between all remaining databases in the near future.[77] **46**

In 2008, the Commission issued a plan to establish an Electronic System of Travel Authorization,[78] which was eventually proposed as the ETIAS in 2016.[79] The ETIAS,[80] which will apply to visa-exempt persons[81] travelling to the EU, was adopted in September 2018.[82] According to the ETIAS Regulation, the ETIAS will be an automated system used to determine the eligibility of TCNs to cross the EU's external borders.[83] Similar to the American Electronic System for Travel Authorization (ESTA)[84] and the Canadian and Australian Electronic Travel Authorization (eTA),[85] travellers will have to submit an online travel authorization request prior to their arrival at the border of a Schengen country.[86] Border guards will, however, still have the final say as to whether or not entry to the Schengen Area will be granted.[87] **47**

To remedy the border guards' lack of information about a person entering the EU and to reinforce the internal security of the Union, the ETIAS is supposed to identify people who pose a security, illegal immigration or high epidemic risk before they **48**

---

[74] Council of the European Union, 15-102001, Council Document 12813/01, 3.

[75] Art. 16(4) Regulation 2017/2226.

[76] Art. 8 Regulation 2017/2226.

[77] Quintel, Data protection, p. 37.

[78] European Commission, 'Proposal for a Regulation of the European Parliament and of the Council establishing a European Travel Information and Authorisation System (ETIAS) and amending Regulations (EU) No 515/2014, (EU) 2016/399, (EU) 2016/794 and (EU) 2016/1624', 16.11.2016, COM(2016) 731 final.

[79] ibid.

[80] Regulation (EU) 2018/1240 establishing a European Travel Information and Authorisation System (ETIAS).

[81] Currently, nationals of around 60 countries worldwide do not need a visa to enter the EU.

[82] Council of the European Union, 'European Travel Information and Authorisation System (ETIAS): Council Adopts Regulation', 5.9.2018 <https://www.consilium.europa.eu/en/press/press-releases/2018/09/05/european-travel-information-and-authorisation-system-etias-council-adopts-regulation/> (last accessed: 12.10.2023).

[83] European Commission, Directorate-General for Migration and Home Affairs, and Pricewaterhouse-Coopers, 'Feasibility Study for a European Travel Information and Authorisation System (ETIAS): Final Report (2016)', 12 <http://dx.publications.europa.eu/10.2837/36503> (last accessed: 12.10.2023).

[84] Official ESTA Application Website, U.S. Customs and Border Protection <https://esta.cbp.dhs.gov/> (last accessed: 12.10.2023).

[85] Refugees and Citizenship Canada Immigration, 'Electronic Travel Authorization (ETA)', 15.4.2015 <https://www.canada.ca/en/immigration-refugees-citizenship/services/visit-canada/eta.html> (last accessed: 12.10.2023). Australian Department of Home Affairs, 'Electronic Travel Authority' <https://www.eta.homeaffairs.gov.au/ETAS3/etas.WSA+Winner+2013:+Electronic+Travel+Authority+ETA+and+Integrated+Border+Management+System+IBMSThe> (last accessed: 12.10.2023).

[86] Not having a travel authorization would always result in a refusal of entry.

[87] By checking the relevant databases against the person's travel document. According to Regulation 2016/399 (the 'Schengen Borders Code'), travellers need to comply with the conditions for a short-term stay, which include not posing a threat to public order and security, holding valid travel documents, justifying the purpose and conditions of the intended stay, not being the subject of any alert in the Schengen Information System (SIS) and having sufficient means of subsistence. See Quintel, Luxembourg Law Working Paper 2018, 8.

arrive at the Schengen external border.[88] As a secondary objective, the system will grant access to national LEAs and Europol for the purposes of the prevention, detection and investigation of terrorist offences or of other serious criminal offences falling under their competence.[89]

49 ETIAS applications will be cross-checked against an ETIAS watchlist[90] and against the so-called ETIAS screening rules, an algorithm enabling profiling[91] by comparing data recorded in an ETIAS application file with specific risk indicators. Those risk indicators will be established by the ETIAS Central Unit, which was set up within Frontex and is to define security, illegal immigration or high epidemic risks by way of data combination.[92] Furthermore, ETIAS data will be matched against the other AFSJ databases as well as Europol data, the Interpol Stolen and Lost Travel Document database (SLTD) and the Interpol Travel Documents Associated with Notices database (TDAWN).[93] Such matching will take place in an interoperable manner whenever an entry is created or updated. Like in the case of VIS automated verifications, the datasets in the ETIAS will continuously be matched throughout their retention period against data in the other systems.

50 Arguably, the ETIAS is the most complex system and includes some of the most widely dispersed purposes compared to the other AFSJ databases.[94] This complexity is exacerbated by the numerous implementing acts that lay down the specific procedures applicable, for instance, with regard to the refusal, annulment or revocation of ETIAS travel authorizations, or for the accessing, amending, erasing and advance erasing of data in the ETIAS Central System. Subsequent amendments to the system, the delegated and implementing acts and interoperability between the ETIAS and the remaining systems make it challenging to understand the system.[95]

51 The European Criminal Records Information System for Third Country Nationals and Stateless Persons (ECRIS-TCN)[96] was adopted in April 2019.[97] ECRIS-TCN is a centralized system that, as the name indicates, enables the subsequent exchange of

---

[88] Art. 1(1) Regulation (EU) 2018/1240.

[89] Art. 1(2) Regulation (EU) 2018/1240. See also European Union Agency for Fundamental Rights (FRA), The impact on fundamental rights of the proposed Regulation on the European Travel Information and Authorisation System (ETIAS). Opinion of the European Union Agency for Fundamental Rights (adopted on 30 June 2017) 46, 31.

[90] The ETIAS watchlist will be established for the purpose of identifying connections between data in an application file and information related to suspects or perpetrators of terrorist offences or other serious crime. In addition, the watchlist is meant to identify connections with regard to persons who are believed to commit serious crimes based on factual indications and/or reasonable grounds. The data in the watchlist serving such matching purposes will be entered by Europol. See Art. 34(3) Regulation 2018/1240.

[91] As 'defined by Art. 4(4) Regulation 2016/679.

[92] Art. 33(1) and (4) Regulation 2018/1240. Risk indicators established by the ETIAS Central Unit will also be aligned to serve the analysis of visa applications under the revised VIS.

[93] European Commission, 'Press Release – Security Union: A European Travel Information and Authorisation System – Questions & Answers', 5.6.2018 <https://europa.eu/rapid/press-release_MEMO-18-4362_en.htm> (last accessed: 12.10.2023).

[94] Although it should be noted that the revised versions and additional amendments rendered the remaining systems highly complex.

[95] Quintel, Data protection, p. 39.

[96] European Commission, 'Proposal for a Regulation of the European Parliament and of the Council establishing a centralised system for the identification of Member States holding conviction information on third country nationals and stateless persons (ECRIS-TCN) to supplement and support the European Criminal Records Information System (ECRIS-TCN system) and amending Regulation (EU) No 1077/2011', 29.6.2017, COM(2017) 344 final.

[97] Regulation (EU) 2019/816 establishing a centralised system for the identification of Member States holding conviction information on third-country nationals and stateless persons (ECRIS-TCN) to supplement the European Criminal Records Information System.

criminal records on convicted TCNs and stateless persons who are in the EU.[98] ECRIS-TCN will complement the current ECRIS system that serves facilitating the exchange of criminal records on EU citizens.[99] However, unlike the ECRIS, the updated ECRIS-TCN will store the personal data of TCNs at a centralized location.

The ECRIS-TCN is not a law enforcement database per se.[100] Its purpose – the identification of the Member State(s) holding criminal records on TCNs – should not necessarily be regarded as a law enforcement purpose.[101] Only where a criminal record exists will data be transferred by the convicting Member State to the requesting Member State on a bilateral basis. However, the system includes additional purposes that are clearly of criminal nature.[102] Furthermore, the system will grant national LEAs as well as Europol, Eurojust and the European Public Prosecutor's Office (EPPO) access to consult the retained data.[103] The list of information to be stored in the ECRIS-TCN is long and includes fingerprints and facial images. The ECRIS-TCN will be the only EU system that will be directly connected and primarily store data within the interoperability framework. **52**

II. Interoperability of EU large-scale information systems

On 20 May 2019, the EU co-legislators adopted two Regulations establishing interoperability between the above-mentioned EU information systems.[104] The two Regulations will connect all the underlying systems either directly or indirectly.[105] In addition, interoperability will create three new centralized databases and a search tool that will enable simultaneous queries in all the underlying systems via a connected interface.[106] However, already before the launch of the interoperable system, some of the underlying databases are to be interoperable by automatically matching data against those stored in the other systems.[107] This double-layered interoperability is to allow for the gradual establishment of interconnectivity even before the overall system is finally operational and will eventually serve as an additional fallback procedure.[108] Hence, interoperability **53**

---

[98] Meijers Committee, the Standing Committee of Experts on International Migration, Refugee and Criminal Law, 'CM1710 Note on the Definition of Third-Country Nationals in the Commission's ECRIS-TCN Proposal', 2.10.2017 <https://www.commissie-meijers.nl/sites/all/files/cm1710_note_on_ecris-tcn.pdf> (last accessed: 12.10.2023).

[99] Council Framework Decision 2009/315/JHA of 26 February 2009 on the organisation and content of the exchange of information extracted from the criminal record between Member States.

[100] Nevertheless, the ECRIS-TCN is based on Art. 82(1) of the TFEU, a judicial cooperation in criminal matters legal basis. Thus, the system has law enforcement roots.

[101] Information on a criminal record could be requested where the TCN in question applied for employment in a profession in which such a record is required. On this, see also ECJ 22.6.2021 – case C-439/19, ECLI:EU:C:2021:504 – *B v Latvijas Republikas Saeima*. However, as regards interoperability, the legislator indeed foresees making the ECRIS-TCN a system that primarily serves law enforcement purposes.

[102] See Art. 7 Regulation 2019/816.

[103] Art. 7(3) Regulation 2019/816.

[104] Regulation (EU) 2019/817 on establishing a framework for interoperability between EU information systems in the field of borders and visa and Regulation (EU) 2019/818 on establishing a framework for interoperability between EU information systems in the field of police and judicial cooperation, asylum and migration.

[105] Personal data contained in the SIS III will not be directly linked to the interoperability components, as the SIS III also includes the personal data of EU citizens, while the interoperable system is to only include the personal data of TCNs. Nevertheless, personal data in the SIS III will be searchable via the ESP.

[106] In addition, interoperability will establish a Central Repository for Reporting and Statistics (CRRS), an additional database that will store allegedly anonymized data.

[107] See Vavoula, European Journal of Migration and Law 2021, 457–484.

[108] Vavoula, 'The European Commission Package of ETIAS Consequential Amendments: Substitute Impact Assessment', 2019, PE 642.808.

between the individual systems will be pre-empted even before the operationalization of the entire interoperable framework.

54 Ultimately, the interoperable system is also to be connected to Europol data and certain Interpol databases.[109] A separate international agreement with Interpol is needed before a connection to the Interpol databases can be established and access to Interpol data can be implemented.

55 In July 2021, the Council adopted a mandate for the Commission to enter into negotiations[110] on an international agreement on behalf of the EU that seeks reinforced cooperation with Interpol, including access to its databases. The agreement was expected to be concluded by the end of 2022.[111]

56 The new agreement was to govern cooperation between Interpol and Europol, the EPPO, Eurojust and Frontex and to provide direct access to two of Interpol's databases by these bodies, agencies and Member States for purposes linked to the performance of their tasks, as regulated in their respective basic acts. The two databases are the SLTD and TDAWN databases.[112] However, at the time of writing no such agreement between the EU and Interpol had been adopted.[113]

1. The interoperability components

57 The four main components that will be established under the interoperability regime are a European Search Portal (ESP),[114] a shared Biometric Matching Service (BMS),[115] a Common Identity Repository (CIR)[116] and a Multiple Identity Detector (MID).[117,118]

58 While the ESP will provide a search infrastructure, the BMS, the CIR and the MID are central databases that will store personal data in the underlying systems at EU level. Both the MID and the CIR can be accessed by designated national authorities, Europol and FRONTEX, whereas the BMS, in addition to storing the data centrally, serves as a platform to automatically match the data retrieved from the other two components. Each of the interoperability components have individual purposes and specific capabilities for processing personal data.

59 The ESP, as a central search tool, is to allow authorities at national and EU level to simultaneously query the underlying information systems. In addition, ESP queries will check in Europol data, the CIR and the relevant Interpol databases.[119] ESP end users will

---

[109] The European Search Portal will be composed of a central infrastructure that will enable the simultaneous querying of the underlying AFSJ databases as well as of Europol data and the Interpol databases, see Art. 6(2) Regulation 2019/817 and Regulation (EU) 2019/818.

[110] Council Decision (EU) 2021/1313 authorising the opening of negotiations for a cooperation agreement between the European Union and the International Criminal Police Organization (ICPO-Interpol).

[111] European Parliament, 'Negotiations for a cooperation agreement between the EU and Interpol. European Parliament recommendation of 5 July 2022 to the Council and the Commission on the negotiations for a cooperation agreement between the European Union and the International Criminal Police Organization (ICPO-Interpol)', 5.7.2022, 2022/2025(INI), point C.

[112] ibid., point L.

[113] Remarks by the Interpol Secretary General Jürgen Stock to the Committee on Civil Liberties, Justice and Home Affairs of the European Parliament, 5.12.2022 available from <https://www.Interpol.int> (last accessed: 12.10.2023).

[114] Art. 6 Regulation 2019/817 and Regulation 2019/818.

[115] Art. 12 Regulation 2019/817 and Regulation 2019/818.

[116] Art. 17 Regulation 2019/817 and Regulation 2019/818.

[117] Art. 25 Regulation 2019/817 and Regulation 2019/818.

[118] Art. 1(2) Regulation 2019/817 and Regulation 2019/818.

[119] Art. 6(2)(b) Regulation 2019/817 and Regulation 2019/818. Interpol data, according to Art. 4(1) of the Interoperability Regulations, include the SLTD and TDAWN databases, while Europol data theoretically include all data that the Agency may process in the performance of its tasks. The Interoperability

use travel or ID document data[120] to launch a query in the underlying databases, the CIR, Europol data and the Interpol databases[121] via a direct connection to the ESP. If a search using the input data leads to a match,[122] the end user will be informed in accordance with his or her access rights.[123]

Instead of queries being carried out separately in eight different databases, searches via the ESP will be systematically conducted within all systems in parallel using both alphanumeric and biometric data. The combined results from the data in all the underlying systems will be displayed on a single screen.[124] The ESP results emanating from the underlying databases are to be limited to the information to which the end user is granted access in the underlying systems.[125] **60**

The CIR will create an individual file for each person registered in the underlying systems, including a reference to the information system to which the data belong.[126] The CIR pursues the three main purposes of facilitating and assisting in the correct identification of persons in the underlying systems, supporting the functioning of the MID and facilitating and streamlining access by designated authorities and Europol to the underlying systems where necessary for the prevention, detection or investigation of terrorist offences or other serious criminal offences.[127] **61**

The CIR will be connected to the underlying systems so as to retrieve certain data and store them in one central repository, thereby replacing the underlying databases' central systems.[128] In addition, the CIR will be connected to the ESP, the BMS and the MID[129] and will provide a communication network to allow national and EU authorities access to the repository.[130] **62**

The BMS is to facilitate the identification of persons registered in several information systems in a more reliable manner than alphanumerical data.[131] For that purpose, the BMS will store templates of biometric data retrieved from the SIS[132] and the CIR in one single location, while the original datasets will be retained in the CIR and the SIS.[133] The BMS will serve as a platform to enable the SIS **63**

Regulations refer to Europol data as personal data processed by Europol for the purposes referred to in Art. 18(2)(a), (b) and (c) Regulation 2016/794. The latter Regulation was repealed by Regulation (EU) 2022/991 amending Regulation (EU) 2016/794, as regards Europol's cooperation with private parties, the processing of personal data by Europol in support of criminal investigations, and Europol's role in research and innovation (recast Europol Regulation).

120 Meaning both biographical or alphanumeric data and biometric data.

121 Interpol gives its member states access to 19 databases, with 124 million entries in total and 20 million queries daily, see Monroy, 'Plans for more data exchange: EU agreement with Interpol delayed' (Monroy, 28.9.2022) <https://digit.site36.net/2022/09/28/plans-for-more-data-exchange-eu-agreement-with-Interpol-delayed/> (last accessed: 12.10.2023).

122 Data searched in line with data in one of the systems.

123 Currently, the Framework Decision in place obliges the EU Member States to search and feed the SLTD database, but it requires national implementation.

124 Art. 9(1) Regulation 2019/817 and Regulation 2019/818.

125 Consequently, where the user is not granted access to one or more of the underlying systems, Europol or Interpol data, the ESP will neither indicate whether a person is stored in those systems nor alter their access conditions.

126 Art. 18(2) Regulation (EU) 2019/817 and Regulation (EU) 2019/818.

127 Art. 17(1) Regulation (EU) 2019/817 and Regulation (EU) 2019/818.

128 Art. 17(2)(a) Regulation (EU) 2019/817 and Regulation (EU) 2019/818.

129 Art. 17(2)(c) Regulation (EU) 2019/817 and Regulation (EU) 2019/818.

130 Art. 17(2)(b) Regulation (EU) 2019/817 and Regulation (EU) 2019/818.

131 Recital 18 Regulation (EU) 2019/817 and Regulation (EU) 2019/818.

132 Recital 19 Regulation (EU) 2019/817 and Regulation (EU) 2019/818. Palm prints that are stored in the SIS III are excluded from the BMS as these data are currently not stored in other information systems and therefore cannot be cross-matched. See also Vavoula, p. 613.

133 Recital 18 Regulation (EU) 2019/817 and Regulation (EU) 2019/818.

and the CIR to match the templates in the BMS against the biometric data from the underlying systems.[134]

64 Serving as a technical instrument that allows for the accurate identification of individuals, the MID could be seen as an extension of the BMS.[135] The MID pursues the dual objective of facilitating identity checks of *bona fide* travellers and combating identity fraud by detecting multiple identities. Thus, the MID is to verify whether a person is recorded in a justified or unjustified manner under different identities in different systems, and to clarify that two persons with similar identity data are not the same person.[136]

65 To allow for such detection, the MID will create and retain so-called identity confirmation files, including links on individuals present in more than one EU information system, generated through the automated multiple identity detection.[137] The latter will be triggered whenever an individual file, alert or data record is created or updated by national or EU authorities in the underlying information systems.[138]

66 The MID will automatically create white and yellow links that are to indicate whether the different identities with which a person is stored in different information systems are likely to be lawfully referring to the same person, or whether there could be a case of identity fraud.[139] While white links refer to either the same/similar identity or multiple lawful identities held by one person, yellow links indicate unsolved matches that are to be verified manually in order to ascertain whether a person was registered either lawfully or unlawfully under multiple identities. After such verification, the yellow links would have to be changed into either white, red or green links.[140] While a green link indicates that the linked data refer to two different people who share no biometrics but have similar identity data, red links indicate identity fraud and will have to be followed up in accordance with a separate procedure.[141]

67 Access to the CIR and to the MID by competent authorities will be possible in accordance with different procedures, in line with the purpose of access and the various tasks the Interoperability Regulations foresee. In addition, various provisions under the Interoperability Regulations allow for additional ways to access the system, including data retained in the underlying databases.

2. Development and maintenance of the interoperable system

68 The interoperability components, including their technical functionalities, will be developed by the European Union Agency for the Operational Management of Large-Scale IT Systems in the AFSJ (eu-LISA).[142] The Agency is responsible for defining the

[134] Art. 14 Regulation (EU) 2019/817 and Regulation (EU) 2019/818.

[135] Vavoula, p. 614.

[136] Recital 39 Regulation (EU) 2019/817 and Regulation (EU) 2019/818.

[137] Art. 25 Regulation (EU) 2019/817 and Regulation (EU) 2019/818 and Recital 39 Regulation (EU) 2019/817 and Regulation (EU) 2019/818.

[138] Art. 27 Regulation (EU) 2019/817 and Regulation (EU) 2019/818 and Recital 41 Regulation (EU) 2019/817 and Regulation (EU) 2019/818.

[139] European Commission, 'Proposal for a Regulation of the European Parliament and of the Council on establishing a framework for interoperability between EU information systems (borders and visa) and amending Council Decision 2004/512/EC, Regulation (EC) No 767/2008, Council Decision 2008/633/JHA, Regulation (EU) 2016/399 and Regulation
(EU) 2017/2226', 12.12.2017, COM(2017) 793, and COM(2017) 794 final, 7.

[140] Quintel, p. 48.

[141] In accordance with Art. 32(2) Regulation (EU) 2019/817 and Regulation (EU) 2019/818, a follow-up to a red link is done in accordance with Union and national law.

[142] Established by Regulation (EU) 2018/1726 on the European Union Agency for the Operational Management of Large-Scale IT Systems in the Area of Freedom, Security and Justice (eu-LISA), and

design of the interoperable system's physical architecture and its technical specifications as well as for implementing the necessary adaptations to the underlying systems in relation to their interoperability. In addition, eu-LISA will be responsible for carrying out the necessary testing of the system, including risk assessments and implementation of security, availability, quality and performance.[143]

After the interoperable system starts operations, eu-LISA will host the interoperability components and will be responsible for its technical management, maintenance and implementation of technological developments.[144] In addition, the Agency will carry out data quality checks in the individual components and will train the algorithms used for the data analyses that will be carried out in the system.[145] Finally, it will be responsible for providing training to the end users of the system.[146] Thus, eu-LISA will be charged with a multitude of tasks and will have an enormous amount of responsibility in relation to the interoperability framework, including the underlying databases, which the Agency will likewise develop, maintain and test.[147] 69

According to the Interoperability Regulations, eu-LISA itself will not be granted access to any personal data in the interoperable system unless access serves the purpose of reporting and generating statistics.[148] Hence, eu-LISA will act as a so-called data processor[149] for the individual interoperability components and will only be permitted to act on behalf of the data controllers – primarily the Member State authorities. Thus, it is the respective Member State that owns the data and is ultimately responsible for data quality. 70

Next to eu-LISA, the Member States are responsible for setting up their central access points, arranging for access by authorized staff and connecting their National Uniform Interfaces (NUIs) for the purpose of law enforcement access.[150] Likewise, Europol is responsible for setting up its central access points to the systems and for designating the units that will request and verify access to the data stored in them. In addition, it will be responsible for entering data related to terrorist offences or other serious criminal offences into the ETIAS watchlist.[151] Finally, Frontex will be in charge of operating the ETIAS Central Unit, will be responsible for the automated processing of ETIAS applications, for developing the risk indicators in the ETIAS Screening rules[152] and, in accordance with the Interoperability Regulations, the manual verification of different identities and the carrying out of multiple-identity detection.[153] 71

3. Access to the interoperability components by national authorities

As mentioned above, access to both the underlying databases and to the interoperability components will be granted in accordance with specific user profiles that will be created for each user querying the system and will be based on the purpose of the 72

amending Regulation (EC) No 1987/2006 and Council Decision 2007/533/JHA and repealing Regulation (EU) No 1077/2011.

[143] Art. 54(1) Regulation (EU) 2019/817 and Regulation (EU) 2019/818.

[144] Art. 55(1) Regulation (EU) 2019/817 and Regulation (EU) 2019/818.

[145] Art. 55(3) Regulation (EU) 2019/817 and Regulation (EU) 2019/818.

[146] Art. 55(4) Regulation (EU) 2019/817 and Regulation (EU) 2019/818.

[147] See, for instance, Art. 37(1) Regulation (EU) 2017/2226.

[148] Art. 55(2) Regulation (EU) 2019/817 and Regulation (EU) 2019/818.

[149] Within the meaning of Art. 3(12)(1) Regulation (EU) 2018/1725.

[150] See, for instance, Art. 38(a) and (c) Regulation (EU) 2017/2226 or Art. 76(a) and (c) Regulation (EU) 2018/1240.

[151] Art. 30 Regulation (EU) 2017/2226 and Art. 77 Regulation (EU) 2018/1240.

[152] Art. 75(1) Regulation (EU) 2018/1240.

[153] Art. 57 Regulation (EU) 2019/817 and Regulation (EU) 2019/818.

queries.[154] Generally speaking, the authorities that will be granted access to the system are border, immigration and asylum authorities, coast guards and those offices that are competent to issue visas and residence permits.

73 In the asylum, migration and border control context, a competent authority could, when consulting the interoperable system, obtain vast amounts of information. This could include a person's past travel history,[155] whether visa applications have been submitted, existing re-entry bans or asylum requests. Further, entries and exits would be stored, and both eligible and rejected ETIAS applications would become known. In addition, authorities could gain access to information related to an individual's criminal record or on whether a person is subject to an alert, theoretically all in one search. This information could be acquired by means of one search and the querying authority would be notified by the system if multiple identities were linked to the same person.[156]

4. Access to the interoperability components by national law enforcement authorities

74 In addition to the competent migration, visa and asylum authorities or border guards in the Member States, national LEAs and Europol will also have access to the underlying systems[157] and certain of the interoperability components, subject to certain conditions and different procedures.[158] This includes searches via the ESP and access to data stored in the CIR and the MID. Searches via the ESP will be carried out in accordance with the user's authorization to access the underlying systems. Generally speaking, the ESP may be queried by national authorities and Union agencies that have access to at least one of the underlying EU information systems.[159]

75 Law enforcement access to data stored in the CIR may be granted where there are reasonable grounds to believe that consulting EU information systems will contribute to the prevention, detection or investigation of terrorist offences or where other serious criminal offences exist.[160] Access may be granted, in particular, where a competent authority suspects that the suspect, perpetrator or victim of a terrorist offence or other serious criminal offence is a person whose data are stored in the underlying systems.[161] Where the CIR indicates that a person's data are stored in one of the underlying systems, it will provide the querying user with a reference to the corresponding system (s).[162] The user may then submit a request to access the data stored in the system(s) for which the CIR found a match. Such access will be granted in line with the procedures and conditions that are laid down in the respective legal instruments establishing the underlying databases.[163]

---

[154] Art. 8 Regulation (EU) 2019/817 and Regulation (EU) 2019/818. Also see: Annex to the Commission Implementing Decision laying down technical details for European search portal user profiles, pursuant to Art. 8(2) of Regulation (EU) 2019/817 of the European Parliament and of the Council, 9.11.2021, 5052.

[155] It should be noted that the analysis of travel behaviour is also covered by passenger name record (PNR) data, which are neither the subject of this assessment nor included in the interoperability framework, at least for the time being. See Directive (EU) 2016/681 on the use of passenger name record (PNR) data for the prevention, detection, investigation and prosecution of terrorist offences and serious crime.

[156] Quintel, Luxembourg Law Working Paper 2018, 15.

[157] With regard to the EES, see, for instance, Art. 29 and 30 Regulation (EU) 2017/2226.

[158] COM(2016) 194 final, 6.

[159] Art. 7(1) Regulation (EU) 2019/817 and Regulation (EU) 2019/818.

[160] Art. 22(1) Regulation (EU) 2019/817 and Regulation (EU) 2019/818.

[161] Art. 22(1) Regulation (EU) 2019/817 and Regulation (EU) 2019/818.

[162] Art. 22(2) Regulation (EU) 2019/817 and Regulation (EU) 2019/818.

[163] Art. 22(3) Regulation (EU) 2019/817 and Regulation (EU) 2019/818.

Access to the underlying systems for national LEAs is to be provided via a central access point, which will receive access requests from operational units or designated authorities and verify whether the conditions for access are satisfied.[164] In cases of urgency, verification may take place ex post.[165] Member States are free to decide whether to establish such a verifying authority within the same organization as the designated authority that will submit an access request. **76**

Generally, law enforcement access to data stored in the underlying systems must be necessary in a specific case and proportionate in relation to an overriding public security concern. In addition, there must be reasonable grounds that access may substantially contribute to the prevention, detection and investigation of the respective criminal offence. Furthermore, a prior search in the national databases must be carried out, where possible.[166] Hence, the conditions for accessing the underlying databases are generally more stringent than the requirements that need to be satisfied to access the CIR, in the sense that they require a necessity and proportionality assessment, a relevant criminal offence and a prior search in the national databases. It could be argued that the information indicated in a CIR search is far less intrusive and does not reveal a large amount of personal data. In addition, the user should not take an adverse decision about the individual concerned solely based on the occurrence of a match in the CIR.[167] **77**

The threshold for national police authorities is lower when it comes to accessing the CIR to identify a person, for instance during a police check. For such purposes, a police authority may query the CIR with biometric data where a person is not able to identify himself or herself by means of an identity document or where the police authority doubts the person's identity or the authenticity of their identity document.[168] In such cases, the police authority would be permitted to query the CIR and, where data on that person are located, would be permitted to consult data such as the names, nationality, travel document and visa-related information, facial images and fingerprint data that are stored in the underlying systems.[169] Consequently, access to the CIR for identification purposes, both in terms of the way in which the query is carried out (with biometric data) and the datasets revealed to the querying user, is more intrusive than access for law enforcement purposes. **78**

How CIR identity searches will be carried out in practice remains to be seen once the interoperable system becomes fully operational. However, such identity checks increase the risk of discrimination and privacy intrusions based on appearance. **79**

Regarding Europol access to data stored in the underlying databases and in the interoperability components, similar conditions as the ones applicable to access by national LEAs apply, with the difference that the Agency is supposed to support Member State action and that Europol staff are not permitted to carry out prior searches in national databases.[170] Furthermore, the processing of information obtained by Europol after consulting the data will be subject to the authorization of the Member State of origin when it comes to the data retained in the underlying systems.[171] **80**

---

[164] See, for instance, Art. 51 Regulation (EU) 2018/1240, Art. 26 Regulation (EU) 2017/2226, Art. 3 Regulation (EC) No 767/2008 or Art. 20 Regulation (EU) No 603/2013.

[165] See, for instance, Art. 3(2) Regulation (EC) No 767/2008.

[166] See, for instance, Art. 26 Regulation (EU) 2017/2226.

[167] Recital 36 Regulation (EU) 2019/817 and Regulation (EU) 2019/818. See also Vavoula, European Journal of Migration and Law 2021, 626.

[168] Art. 20(1)(a), (b) and (c) Regulation (EU) 2019/817 and Regulation (EU) 2019/818.

[169] Art. 20(3) Regulation (EU) 2019/817 and Regulation (EU) 2019/818. The police authority would not be granted access to data stored in the SIS.

[170] Quintel, KritV 2018, 332.

[171] Art. 33(5) Regulation (EU) 2017/2226.

Evidently, Europol's mandate allows neither for identity checks in the CIR nor for the verification of different identities linked in the MID.

81 For Europol staff to obtain access, a distinct operational unit will have to submit a request for consultation to a designated access point. The latter will be established within the Agency and is supposed to act independently of the requesting unit.

5. The role of EU Agencies in the interoperable system

82 Systematic data sharing between Europol, Frontex and national competent authorities have been intensified over the course of several years and structural data exchanges are being implemented not only between Europol, Frontex and national LEAs, but also within wider structures that include additional actors.

83 One of the objectives of interoperability is to facilitate and streamline access by national and EU Agencies to information stored in EU large-scale information systems that were not exclusively established for law enforcement purposes. With the establishment of the AFSJ and the entry into force of the Lisbon Treaty, EU Agencies were attributed new competences in order to pool both technical and specialized expertise at EU level with a view to enhancing cooperation among Member States and between the EU and national level.[172]

84 EU Agencies have started to play a more pivotal role in migration and border management. Instead of only national authorities handling implementation of EU asylum policy, the institutionalization of practical cooperation through EU Agencies has brought players such as Frontex, the European Asylum Support Office (EASO, now the European Union Asylum Agency, EUAA) and Europol to the forefront of such matters.[173] These Agencies are increasingly involved in information exchanges and the training of national staff such as border guards and asylum officers, in the identification, security screening and risk analysis of TCNs, and in removal assistance.[174] While operationally assisting the national competent authorities in the Member States, these Agencies have developed their expertise and naturally expanded their own mandate, later codified either in the form of specialized centres in the respective agency or in legislation and by amending the Agency's constituting act.

85 These Agencies' increasing opportunities for processing TCNs' personal data have gone hand in hand with the revision of the operational and the establishment of new EU large-scale information systems. Two EU Agencies in particular, namely Frontex and Europol, have progressively engaged in the processing of TCNs' personal data, given that they are responsible to assist in the identification, registration and carrying out of secondary security checks on TCNs. Furthermore, both Agencies contribute to tackling cross-border crime such as migrant smuggling and trafficking in human beings, thereby exchanging personal data with Member State authorities and additional EU bodies.

86 Frontex is a particularly interesting case, because it was established as a border control agency with an arguably limited mandate. Within a relatively short timeframe, the Agency turned into a powerful information hub. Relatively quickly, Frontex developed into one of the fastest-growing EU Agencies in terms of both budget and staff.[175]

87 Its transformation into the European Border and Coast Guard Agency was finalized in October 2016. Since then, Frontex has been in charge of monitoring the EU's

---

[172] Weyembergh/Armada/Briere, New Journal of European Criminal Law 2015, 258 (259).

[173] Tsourdi, German Law Journal 2020, 506 (507).

[174] Davis, Washington University Global Studies Law Review 2020, 261 (281).

[175] See Niemann/Speyer, JCMS 2018, 23; Ferraro/De Capitani, ERA Forum 2016, 385; Rijpma, Study for the LIBE Committee.

external borders and, together with the Member State authorities and Europol, of identifying and registering TCNs, including assessing potential security threats. Frontex has progressively become more active in the field of security and will have additional competences for processing personal data when consulting EU information systems.[176] With the establishment of the ETIAS and the interoperability regime, Frontex will obtain even more powers in terms of data processing activities. For instance, the ETIAS Central Unit that is to be established within Frontex[177] will be responsible for verifying whether personal data that trigger a hit during an ETIAS application are present in other information systems, including Europol and Interpol databases.[178] In addition, the ETIAS Central Unit will verify hits in the system, initiate consultation processes with Member States and Europol and will have specific responsibility with regard to the definition of the algorithms applied to the ETIAS screening rules.[179] Under the Interoperability Regulations, the ETIAS Central Unit will play a pivotal role regarding the multiple identity detection and the manual verification of different identities.[180] Thus, the legislative instruments of the underlying systems and the Interoperability Regulations codify Frontex's strengthened mandate and access rights to TCNs' personal data.[181]

Hence, Frontex has been attributed an entirely new role in relation to the EU large- **88** scale information systems. Both the ETIAS and the Interoperability Regulations contribute to the enormous step up for the Agency in terms of accessing, searching, comparing and verifying personal data stored in both the underlying systems and the interoperability components. In addition, the Agency was granted new operational tasks that involve the processing of personal data.

A similar situation arises with regard to Europol. Like Frontex, Europol was given a **89** bigger role so as to be able to search, access and consult data from the EU information systems and interoperability components. Even before the Interoperability Regulations were proposed, Europol's access to the EU information systems had become somehow self-evident and both the Interoperability Regulations and the 2022 recast Europol Regulation contribute to the Agency's new role in the context of migration management and border control. The outcome is the same as in Frontex's case, only in reverse: Europol, as an EU LEA, has accumulated more and more tasks in migration management and border control.

The Final Report by the so-called Future Group on Travel Intelligence and Border **90** Management dated September 2021 highlighted the new cooperation opportunities that the new architecture of EU information systems for borders, migration and security provides. In the Report, Europol and the Frontex suggest ways to merge the capacity of different authorities at national and EU level in order to maximize operational benefits.[182] In particular, the Agencies propose making it easier for law enforcement and border authorities to proactively share strategic information, trends and patterns regarding TCNs.[183]

The growing involvement of these two EU Agencies in the processing of TCNs' **91** personal data may raise concerns regarding the data protection rules applicable to the

---

[176] Radjenovic, EPRS 2018, 3.

[177] Art. 7(1) Regulation (EU) 2018/1240.

[178] Art. 7(2)(a) Regulation (EU) 2018/1240.

[179] See Art. 22, Art. 28 and Art. 29 Regulation (EU) 2018/1240.

[180] See Art. 26(1)(c), Art. 57 and Art. 69 Regulation (EU) 2019/817 and Regulation (EU) 2019/818.

[181] Quintel, EPL 2020, 205 et seqq.

[182] Europol and Frontex, 'Annex to the Final Report of the Future Group on Travel Intelligence and Border Management', September 2021.

[183] ibid., 13.

respective Agency, as certain provisions leave room for interpretation. Europol's recast Regulation was adopted in May 2022.[184] It broadened the Agency's mandate to enable it to analyse large and complex datasets. Frontex, on the other hand, had already obtained a revised legal framework in 2019 that allows the Agency to, among other things, cooperate with Europol in the fight against cross-border crime and terrorism.[185]

92 A third EU agency, Eurojust, is more restricted than Europol and Frontex and does not have the same operational capacity to process personal data as the other two Agencies do. Its role in terms of access to EU large-scale IT systems is marginal. Under the Interoperability Regulations, the Agency may appoint a representative to attend meetings of the Interoperability Advisory Group and meetings of the Management Boards of the different systems.[186] However, neither the Eurodac and VIS nor the ETIAS or the EES Regulations mention Eurojust in relation to access.

93 Ultimately, the opportunities for Eurojust to access, search and process personal data in the EU large-scale systems are more restricted than those attributed to Europol and Frontex. On the one hand, Eurojust's rights to access those systems are much more limited than those of the other two Agencies. On the other hand, Eurojust is much more dependent on instructions it receives from the Member States. While Europol and Frontex may access and use personal data stored in the EU systems more autonomously, Eurojust relies on consent given by the respective Member State that issued an alert or input data into a system.

94 In addition, the Agency is (for the time being) far less involved in matters concerning migration and border control and hence does not use personal data from AFSJ in its daily operations. This seems logical given Eurojust's role, which only kicks in when a judicial investigation or prosecution is envisaged, that is much later in the process.[187] Nevertheless, Eurojust is progressively coordinating cross-border cases of organized crime that are related to illegal immigrant smuggling.[188]

95 Likewise, the EPPO's role is negligible when it comes to interoperability and most of the underlying information systems. However, authorized EPPO staff have direct access to data in the ECRIS-TCN and are entitled to query ECRIS-TCN to identify which Member States hold criminal record information on a TCN.[189] Yet, EPPO staff may neither rectify nor delete data in the ECRIS-TCN nor may they enter any new information into the system.[190]

96 Another EU Agency that is involved in migration- and asylum-related matters is the European Union Asylum Agency (EUAA),[191] formerly EASO.[192] The EUAA is not

---

[184] Regulation (EU) 2022/991 amending Regulation (EU) 2016/794, as regards Europol's cooperation with private parties, the processing of personal data by Europol in support of criminal investigations, and Europol's role in research and innovation.

[185] Art. 10(1)(q) Regulation (EU) 2019/1896 on the European Border and Coast Guard.

[186] See, for instance, Art. 62 Regulation (EU) 2019/817.

[187] Quintel, p. 187.

[188] Eurojust, 'Report on Eurojust's Casework in the Field of Migrant Smuggling' (2018) available from <http://www.eurojust.europa.eu> (last accessed: 13.10.2023). It should be noted that the report refers to an increase in the number of migrant smuggling cases referred to Eurojust from 1.7% to 2.7% in the period between 2012 and 2014, which is still marginal. According to Eurojust's 2020 Annual Report, in 2020, the Agency coordinated 217 migrant smuggling investigations, 118 of which were carried over from previous years. The increase in caseload is thus marginal. Interestingly, the annual report highlights the fact that the investigations were often carried out in close cooperation with Europol, see: Eurojust, 'Annual Report 2020' (2020) https://www.eurojust.europa.eu/ar2020/7-casework-crime-type/77-migrant-smuggling (last accessed: 13.10.2023).

[189] Art. 14(1) Regulation (EU) 2019/816.

[190] This also applies to Europol and Eurojust, see Art. 7(3) Regulation (EU) 2019/816.

[191] Regulation (EU) 2021/2303 on the European Union Agency for Asylum.

[192] Regulation (EU) No 439/2010 establishing a European Asylum Support Office.

permitted to access any of the EU systems. However, in the future, the EUAA might have limited access to Eurodac to collect and insert biometric data into the system.[193] Furthermore, the Agency's role in information exchanges with both national and EU authorities, data analysis and risk assessment is growing, as illustrated below.

C. Interoperable risk detection, automated data matching and AI-based functionalities

Interoperable systems are intended to enable competent authorities to take better and more informed decisions based on all the available data processed in the different AFSJ databases. With the aim of enhancing the efficiency and effectiveness of information sharing within the EU, interoperability pursues a complete information awareness approach by granting access to numerous authorities at different levels. The propagation of databases into multi-purpose apparatuses and their connection to form a single interoperable system creates new opportunities in terms of data exploitation and data analysis, which were previously processed separately and according to specific purposes. Additional purposes, further datasets containing new categories of TCNs and more actors adding and retrieving data – all this will enable the systems to generate novel processing operations and to employ extended functions. **97**

Data quality is relevant for the result of algorithmic data analyses and decision-making, as erroneous data will reproduce any flaws and will affect the result of an analysis exponentially. Although the interoperable system is to improve decision-making processes and increase the accuracy of data, this assumption could contradict reports that show that the currently operational EU large-scale information systems contain erroneous data that would be inserted into the interoperability components.[194] **98**

In addition, algorithms and other AI techniques may be biased and thus allow for discrimination.[195] Often, algorithms are trained using low-quality data, insufficiently homogenous data or data that represent only certain parts of the population. Furthermore, if algorithms are trained on datasets that include pre-existing biases, they run the risk of replicating both the implicit and inherent biases of such earlier results.[196] **99**

With interoperability, those existing errors and biases could be multiplied and could, instead of enhancing information sharing between different authorities, lead to an overload of wrong matches, which the competent authorities would then have to rectify.[197] **100**

In the law enforcement context, this may have additional consequences for individuals, as the results of algorithmic profiling may be less visible.[198] Such disempowerment would be added to the privacy and data protection issues, which are often the last **101**

---

[193] COM(2020) 614 final, Art. 13(7).

[194] European Data Protection Supervisor, 'EDPS Opinion 4/2018 on the Proposals for Two Regulations Establishing a Framework for Interoperability between EU Large-Scale Information Systems' (2018), point 36. Even if the Interoperability Regulations require a minimum threshold for the quality of the data to be inserted into the system, the operational databases that will be connected will first have to be cleaned of erroneous datasets.

[195] ibid., point 480.

[196] Vavoula, European Journal of Migration and Law 2021, 471.

[197] Quintel, p. 88.

[198] Van Brakel in van der Sloot/Broeders/Schrijvers, Exploring the Boundaries of Big Data, p. 117.

line of defence for vulnerable people such as asylum seekers or victims of human trafficking approaching EU external borders.[199]

I. Problems related to data quality

102 Within an interoperable system, problems that already exist in the currently operational EU systems could be magnified, in particular where different authorities at both national and EU level are responsible for inputting data into and accessing data in the databases.[200]

103 As mentioned in the above, sharing personal data in an interoperable system and between various authorities raises concerns regarding the quality of the data being introduced into the underlying systems and subsequently merged in the networked structure.

104 Data quality has raised concerns for several years and has been assessed in various studies and academic contributions.[201] In 2019, the European Court of Auditors found that EU information systems still lacked accurate data.[202] However, in order to generate reliable results, the data used for analyses purposes must be of a high quality, as otherwise matching these data could lead to false positives and thus wrongful conclusions about the individuals concerned. Consequently, where the underlying systems contain erroneous data, those errors will be propagated in the interoperable network and lead to a multitude of wrong matches that the competent authorities will have to handle.

105 eu-LISA, the Agency responsible for operating the large-scale IT systems, is a key stakeholder when it comes to ensuring data quality. Under its founding act[203] and the Interoperability Regulations, eu-LISA is to establish automated data quality control mechanisms, common data quality indicators and minimum quality standards for the storage of data in the underlying databases and the relevant interoperability components.[204]

106 In addition, the interoperability components may only start operating after the successful completion of a comprehensive test of data quality control mechanisms, common data quality indicators and minimum quality standards.[205] Assuming that such assessment includes the testing of the underlying systems, this is a welcome safeguard.

107 The implementation of data quality by the Member States will be assessed on a yearly basis and the Commission will make recommendations in relation to which the Member States will have to provide an action plan and follow up by means of progress reports.[206] This is a rather weak accountability mechanism and no real enforcement is envisaged. Yet, the evaluation report is also to be submitted to the European Data Protection Board (EDPB) and the European Data Protection Supervisor (EDPS).[207]

---

199 European Data Protection Supervisor, 'EDPS Opinion 9/2020 Opinion on the New Pact on Migration and Asylum', 30.11.2020, 6 point 7.

200 Quintel, EPL 2020, 205 et seqq.

201 See, for instance, FRA, 'Under watchful eyes – biometrics, EU IT-systems and fundamental rights', 2018, 16, Vavoula, European Journal of Migration and Law 2021, 457–484 or Fuster, Study for the LIBE Committee of the European Parliament, 42.

202 European Court of Auditors, 'EU information systems supporting border control – a strong tool, but more focus needed on timely and complete data', 2019, 29–30.

203 Art. 12 Regulation (EU) 2018/1726.

204 Art. 37(1) and (2) Regulation (EU) 2019/817 and Regulation (EU) 2019/818.

205 Art. 68(2)(d), (3)(d) and (4)(e) Regulation (EU) 2019/817 and Regulation (EU) 2019/818.

206 Art. 37(5) Regulation (EU) 2019/817 and Regulation (EU) 2019/818.

207 Art. 37(5) Regulation (EU) 2019/817 and Regulation (EU) 2019/818.

Therefore, the national data protection authorities (DPAs) and the EDPS, which is responsible for supervising EU institutions, bodies, offices and agencies, will be made aware of potential issues in the systems. Together with their mandate under the individual founding acts of the underlying databases, the supervisory authorities at both levels could use their powers in order to be able to effectively supervise the different data flows within the interoperability framework.[208]

In principle, this would mean that the national DPAs and the EDPS would have to act on low-quality data issues notified by eu-LISA in the yearly reports. This would require eu-LISA to notify, for each dataset of low quality, the respective data controller, hence the authority that entered the data into the underlying database and the interoperability component, respectively, in order for the DPAs or the EDPS to identify the source of any erroneous data. In addition, all the data generated by the system itself based on the initial input data would have to be traceable in order to be able to correct subsequent results. Whether that would be feasible and indicated in the report, for instance by means of logs, remains to be seen. In addition, depending on the reactiveness of the individual DPA, in practice some authorities might be less diligent than others. **108**

Nevertheless, even if applied effectively, data must only adhere to a *minimum* quality standard, whereas achieving reliable results from automated decision-making operations requires high-quality data.[209] In addition, the age for mandatory facial images and fingerprints stored in the underlying systems was lowered, which may have additional consequences for data quality.[210] Such lowering may have repercussions with regard to the quality of data owing to the physical changes that may occur much faster in children.[211] **109**

II. Algorithmic testing and inherent biases

It is very likely that, in future, both the underlying systems and the interoperability components will increasingly use automated biometric matching and facial recognition technologies to identify *bona fide* travellers and detect fraudulent documents. **110**

Automation in border control can decrease discrimination and increase efficiency in border control. From a practical point of view, the biometric matching algorithms' performance has improved remarkably in recent years, including in a visa and border control context. Well-performing facial recognition algorithms already outperform human experts when it comes to facial recognition, are significantly faster and still deliver results when humans get tired. In addition, automated border controls and facial recognition technologies are indeed believed to be less discriminatory.[212] However, contrary to such confidence in automated systems, these tools are far from neutral and do not necessarily lead to less discrimination.[213] **111**

---

[208] The challenges with regard to supervising the interoperable system also apply with regard to ensuring data quality in the systems.

[209] See also Vavoula, European Journal of Migration and Law 2021, 457–484.

[210] See, for instance, Ecorys/BV Fraunhofer IGD/Vrije Universiteit Amsterdam, 'Feasibility and implications of lowering the fingerprinting age for children and on storing a scanned copy of the visa applicant's travel document in the Visa Information System (VIS)', 2018. The study concluded that the practical problems relating to the accurate collection of fingerprints of children below the age of six lead to the conclusion that this option currently lacks both necessity and proportionality.

[211] Vavoula, p. 423. See also Srinivas et al., 'Face Recognition Algorithm Bias: Performance Differences on Images of Children and Adults' (2019).

[212] FRA in eu-LISA, Smart border pilot project – technical report annexes, p. 307–335.

[213] FRA, 'Bias in Algorithms – Artificial Intelligence and Discrimination', 2022.

112 Algorithmic decision-making can have crucial shortcomings in terms of acquisition and testing, over-reliance on technology, inherent biases and fundamental rights implications more generally. In addition, facial recognition technologies build on the processing of biometric data, which are defined as special categories of personal data under data protection law and require higher safeguards. Some of the related concerns are discussed in this and the subsequent section.

113 One of the problems related to the use of algorithmic decision-making tools used by public authorities is that instead of developing the algorithms themselves, they commonly rely on external providers' biometric matching algorithms. This means that, on the one hand, the end users may not understand why a system performs in a certain way and how it came to a certain conclusion. On the other hand, it is not always clear what datasets were used to train a specific system.

114 Hence, the system will produce an output or result that is based on the input of a particular dataset, but it may not always be clear how the system generated this output. This particularly holds true where systems rely on black-box algorithms that deliver results without any explanation as to how the result was configured.

115 Reliance on vendor algorithms without having sufficient insight into their training requires testing of the system to determine its reliability in a real-life scenario. While the quality of synthetic data[214] has improved in recent years, their accuracy is not sufficient to perform reliable testing of a large-scale system such as the one that will form part of the interoperability framework.

116 Therefore, actual people's real data are necessary to test the systems, which means that large datasets of operational personal data representing the entire world population would be required to reliably test an algorithm used in the interoperable system. If the testing data were to be based solely on white Caucasian males and merely to be audited in a testing environment, the results of algorithmic matching would be less accurate when being applied to women of colour in a real-life scenario. In addition, the data used for testing purposes cannot be the same data as the training data, since using the same data would lead to the same result and, thus, potentially to unrepresentative outcomes. As mentioned above, besides the need for good-quality data, operational data are needed to train the algorithms to achieve the most accurate results. Where the results of biased analyses are inserted into the systems, this – just like low-quality data – will multiply wrong matches.

117 Since increasing the quantity of the datasets will exponentially increase the reliability of the testing results, it will likewise become increasingly challenging to compile a testing dataset that will be based on the consent of the data subjects whose personal data will be used for testing. Likewise, the acquisition of such large testing datasets will be extremely expensive. Consequently, the most reliable solution would be to test the algorithmic systems with operational data that are already processed by the systems. The *ECJ* held in a *Digi*[215] that the use of an internal database for the purposes of testing

---

[214] Synthetic data are artificial data that are generated from original data and a model that is trained to reproduce the characteristics and structure of the original data. This means that synthetic data and original data should deliver very similar results when undergoing the same statistical analysis. The degree to which synthetic data are an accurate proxy for the original data is a measure of the utility of the method and the model. Hence, synthetic data are not personal data. However, a privacy assurance assessment should be performed to ensure that the resulting synthetic data are not actual personal data. See EDPS, 'Synthetic Data' <https://edps.europa.eu/press-publications/publications/techsonar/synthetic-data_en/> (last accessed: 13.10.2023).

[215] ECJ 20.10.2022 – case C-77/21, ECLI:EU:C:2022:805 – *Digi Távközlési és Szolgáltató Kft. v Nemzeti Adatvédelmi és Információszabadság Hatóság*. The case concerned Digi, one of Hungary's main media and online providers. Digi created a database of one third of its users for the purposes of testing and

and correcting errors may be based on the legitimate interest of the tester. However, in the specific context of EU large-scale systems and interoperability, legitimate interest might not be an adequate legal basis, as it generally does not apply to processing carried out by public authorities in the performance of their tasks.[216] In addition, the risk of discrimination is more prevalent on account of the nature and vulnerability of the individuals whose data are stored in the system. With regard to police cooperation databases included in the connected system, individuals will most likely not be aware of the fact that their personal data are retained and, thus, any subsequent processing would require careful consideration of all the fundamental rights and interests at stake.[217]

In this context, the algorithms used for the analyses must be free of prejudices that could **118** have an impact on the outcome. Since algorithms are created by humans, there is a danger that human bias may be replicated and further exacerbated where the results of algorithmic analyses in one system are further disseminated via the interoperable network. Where algorithms are not trained and tested using reliable data or where algorithms are not reviewable, any discrimination may remain inherently anchored in the system.

Despite a general lack of court decisions on algorithmic profiling, the *ECJ* has held **119** that algorithms must be sufficiently reliable, not discriminatory and must be limited to what is necessary.[218] In addition, any check must be carried out against up-to-date and reliable databases and must be reviewable.

The need for such safeguards is all the greater where personal data are subject to **120** automated processing. Those considerations in particular apply where the processing of personal data includes sensitive data so-called special categories of personal data.[219] Special categories of personal data are personal data revealing racial or ethnic origin, political opinions, religious or philosophical beliefs, or trade union membership, and the processing of genetic data, biometric data for the purpose of uniquely identifying a natural person, data concerning health or data concerning a natural person's sex life or sexual orientation, the processing of which is prohibited under Art. 9(1) GDPR.

In the *La Quadrature du Net and Others* case, the ECJ found that, with regard to special **121** categories of personal data, algorithmic profiling must not be based on sensitive data in isolation.[220] In addition, the *ECJ* set a high benchmark with regard to inferred data[221] that

---

correcting errors in its main database. The test database was hacked. Digi notified the breach. The DPA fined it for violating purpose limitation. The *ECJ* held that further processing is allowed if (a) there is a concrete, logical and sufficiently close link between the purposes of the initial collection and the further processing and (b) the further processing does not deviate from the legitimate expectations of subscribers.

[216] Art. 6(1)(f) GDPR.

[217] Additional data protection-related questions may arise with regard to the applicable data protection regime, for instance concerning the restriction of data protection rights. Furthermore, in the law enforcement context, the processing of personal data may evidently not be based on the legitimate interest of the data controller (Art. 6(1)(f) GDPR), as was the case in the judgment, since this legal basis does not exist under the LED.

[218] In Opinion 1/15, the *ECJ* held that PNR data may, when combined, reveal sensitive information about passengers, see ECJ 26.7.2017 – Opinion 1/15, ECLI:EU:C:2017:592 para. 128.

[219] ibid., para. 141.

[220] ECJ 6.10.2020 – joined cases C-511/18, C-512/18 and C-520/18, ECLI:EU:C:2020:791 para. 181 – *La Quadrature du Net and Others*. See also ECJ 26.7.2017 – Opinion 1/15, ECLI:EU:C:2017:592 para. 165. See also Vavoula, European Journal of Migration and Law 2021, 457. It should be noted that the AG in his Opinion on the PNR Directive found that the stricter approach that the Court has followed in relation to electronic communications cannot be transposed as such to the systems for processing PNR data. Hence, any transposition strictu sensu of the *ECJ's* approach in that case law may not be appropriate in relation to the migration and border control context. Nevertheless, certain findings may apply and should even require higher standards where vulnerable individuals are concerned. See AG Pitruzzella 27.1.2022 – case C-817/19, ECLI:EU:C:2022:65 para. 199 – *Ligue des droits humains v Conseil des ministres*.

[221] ECJ 1.8.2022 – case C-184/20, ECLI:EU:C:2022:601 – *OT v Vyriausioji tarnybinės etikos komisija*.

may ultimately lead to special categories of personal data.[222]In the EU information systems, certain data may be used as proxies and, by inference, amount to special categories of personal data. For instance, the nationality or place of birth of a TCN could be used to deduce information such as his or her race, religious belief or ethnic origin.

122 Those sets of data are used for the ETIAS screening rules, the abovementioned algorithm enabling the profiling of TCNs in order to indicate security, illegal immigration or high epidemic risks. Data such as nationality, home address, education or current occupation are to allow profiling and risk assessment that will in the future be done to single out passengers who may pose such risks. In addition, the screening rules will take into account statistics from the EES on rates of overstayers and refusals of entry, which in turn are based on the nationality of the TCNs.[223]

123 While the ETIAS watchlist will be based on data matching rather than algorithmic profiling, it may nevertheless affect individuals' ability to scrutinize why a certain decision was taken about them. In addition, the data used for matching might have undergone analyses prior to being inserted into the watchlist. The ETIAS watchlist will consist of data related to persons who are suspected of having committed or taken part in a terrorist offence or other serious criminal offence.[224] Such information will be entered into the watchlist by Europol and will include personal data such as name, address, nationality, sex and information related to the travel document.[225]

124 The above also means that it will become increasingly challenging to distinguish between ordinary and special categories of personal data. On the one hand, this may require higher protection standards for those datasets that could include particularly sensitive data. On the other hand, it could mean that such data are not processed in isolation and could therefore be used for algorithmic profiling. Ultimately, using inferred special categories of personal data for algorithmic profiling in the EU information systems to single out high-risk passengers by way of automation may lead to indirect discrimination and less protection, since these sensitive data are not processed in isolation. Such indirect discrimination is addressed neither in the founding acts of the underlying systems nor in the Interoperability Regulations.

125 In that vein, one future challenge will be to clarify to what extent authorities rely on technological output to take decisions and whether human intervention[226] and human oversight are effective in diminishing discriminatory biases in automated systems.

126 Against that background, it would also be crucial to ascertain whether TCNs are always aware that their biometric data are matched and, in future, if they are aware of the consequences algorithmic results in the interoperable system may have for them in terms of fundamental rights repercussions.

127 Eventually, it will be extremely challenging for individuals to exercise their right to an explanation and to an effective judicial remedy, as explainability of the decision-making processes in the systems will decrease with additional automated functionalities. Even if those processes were to be made more transparent, the information provided to individuals might be very technical and not specifically useful. In the migration and

---

[222] In accordance with Art. 9(1) of the GDPR, special categories of personal data are personal data revealing racial or ethnic origin, political opinions, religious or philosophical beliefs or trade union membership, and the processing of genetic data, biometric data for the purpose of uniquely identifying a natural person, data concerning health or data concerning a natural person's sex life or sexual orientation.

[223] Art. 63(1)(e) and (f) Regulation (EU) 2017/2226.

[224] Art. 34(1) Regulation (EU) 2018/1240.

[225] Art. 34(3) and (4) Regulation (EU) 2018/1240.

[226] ECJ 6.10.2020 – joined cases C-511/18, C-512/18 and C-520/18, ECLI:EU:C:2020:791 para. 182 – *La Quadrature du Net also 7.12.2023 – case C-634/21 ECLI:EU:C:2023:957 – OQ v Land Hessen.*

asylum context, language barriers or a general distrust/fear of authorities may also become an insurmountable obstacle to the effective exercise of individuals' rights.

III. The use of AI Act-based technologies

Artificial intelligence (AI) could be described as a set of techniques used to train machines to approximate some aspects of human or animal cognition.[227] A broader definition of the term 'AI' may include the use of technology to generate profiles, to employ algorithms or machine-learning techniques to detect suspicious patterns and behaviours.[228] Large quantities of data are needed for such analyses so as to be able to find new correlations and predict behaviour, trends or patterns.[229] **128**

AI technologies are typically based on algorithms that make predictions to support or even fully automate decision-making. The main goals of using AI in this way include to increase efficiency and operate systems at a large scale.[230] **129**

It could be argued that some EU information systems, such as the ETIAS, the EES or the VIS, anticipate incorporating AI-based tools. ETIAS and the VIS will employ algorithmic profiling using screening rules when examining applications for residence permits, visas and travel authorizations. The EES envisages the processing of facial images and the use of facial recognition technologies.[231] This type of technology enables biometric identification. In accordance with the EDPB, facial recognition technologies use AI or machine-learning components.[232] **130**

The predictive risk assessments to be carried out in ETIAS might also be understood as using certain AI-based features. The pre-vetting of TCNs by way of matching against the ETIAS screening rules and the watchlist will be built into an algorithm that will make it possible to identify travellers who fit pre-defined risk profiles.[233] In addition, a 2020 study for the Commission envisaged an AI tool in ETIAS for 'individual risk assessment in case of a "hit" in the first automatic risk assessment, facilitating further review by a member state'.[234] **131**

Several EU Agencies are likewise investing in AI or machine-learning technologies. The European Commission and the EU Agencies in the AFSJ are exploring other applications in this field, including in the context of further developing the EUROSUR system and the EU Innovation Hub. The EU Innovation Hub for Internal Security is a collaborative network aimed at projects that provide the latest innovation updates to support the work of internal security actors in the EU and its Member States.[235] Such projects notably include predictive data analytics and related tools **132**

---

[227] Vavoula, European Journal of Migration and Law 2021, 457.

[228] ibid.

[229] De Hert/Sajfert EDPL 2019, 338–351.

[230] FRA, 'Bias in Algorithms – Artificial Intelligence and Discrimination', 2022, 7 <https://fra.europa.eu/sites/default/files/fra_uploads/fra-2022-bias-in-algorithms_en.pdf> (last accessed: 13.10.2023).

[231] Art. 15 Regulation (EU) 2017/2226. See eu-LISA, 'Artificial Intelligence in the Operational Management of Large-scale IT Systems', 2020.

[232] European Data Protection Board, 'EDPB Guidelines 05/2022 on the use of facial recognition technology in the area of law enforcement Version 1.0', 12.5.2022, 3.

[233] Dumbrava, EPRS 2021, 19.

[234] Deloitte, 'Opportunities and challenges for the use of artificial intelligence in border control, migration and security', 2020, 19 and 91–92.

[235] Europol, 'EU Innovation Hub for Internal Security', 17.10.2022, <https://www.europol.europa.eu/operations-services-innovation/innovation-lab/eu-innovation-hub-for-internal-security> (last accessed: 13.10.2023).

using state-of-the-art machine-learning and AI methods to prevent, detect, analyse and combat criminal activities.[236]

133 In addition, Europol is involved in pilot projects that analyse TCNs' personal data[237] and, in the framework of the research and innovation provisions under its recast Regulation, the Agency aims at further extending its mandate and the role of Europol in innovative undertakings for law enforcement purposes.

134 Generally speaking, the recast Europol Regulation introduced new opportunities for the Agency to process large and complex datasets, put forward a strengthened mandate for Europol to cooperate effectively with private parties, third countries and other EU Agencies, and reinforced Europol's role in research and innovation. The provisions on research and innovation signify additional possibilities for Europol to engage in rather undefined processing.[238] Yet, as the EDPS emphasized in his Opinion on the European Strategy of Data, the provisions are broadly defined and relevant data protection principles may not be fully taken into account.[239]

135 Established within the organizational structure of Frontex, the European surveillance system EUROSUR provides a common framework for the exchange of information and cooperation between Member States' border surveillance authorities and Frontex. For that purpose, so-called National Coordination Centres (NCCs) and Frontex exchange information, data and intelligence in situational awareness pictures in order to detect and monitor unauthorized crossings of the external Schengen borders.[240]

136 In addition, EUROSUR is to increasingly operate fusion services, which will use analyses derived from large-scale information systems for the purpose of detecting changing routes and methods used for illegal immigration and cross-border crime.[241] EUROSUR follows an intelligence- and risk analysis-driven approach and is instrumental in establishing national and European situational pictures at borders, carrying out risk analysis and supporting reaction capabilities. A situational picture is defined as 'an aggregation of georeferenced near-real-time data and information received from different authorities, sensors, platforms and other sources'.[242]

137 In recent years, the EUAA has heavily invested in state-of-the-art systems to allow the forecasting of asylum-related migration trends.[243] For that purpose, large amounts of big data are harvested and analysed by means of machine-learning techniques.[244]

---

[236] See, for instance, the AIDA project, which is funded to the tune of 7.6m EUR by the EU <https://cordis.europa.eu/project/id/883596> (last accessed: 13.10.2023).

[237] European Data Protection Supervisor, 'EDPS Opinion on a Prior Consultation Requested by Europol on a pilot project for a European Police Records Index System (EPRIS) (Case 2022-0265)', 25.4.2022.

[238] Quintel, EDPL 2022, 90–102.

[239] European Data Protection Supervisor, 'Opinion 4/2021 EDPS Opinion on the Proposal for Amendment of the Europol Regulation', 8.3.2021, 3 and para. 33. See also Vavoula/Mitsilegas, 'Strengthening Europol's Mandate', 2021, PE 694.200, 41.

[240] Commission Staff Working Document, 'Evaluation of the Regulation (EU) No 1052/2013 of the European Parliament and of the Council of 22 October 2013 establishing the European Border Surveillance System (EUROSUR)', 12.9.2018, SWD(2018) 410 final, 7.

[241] Art. 29(2)(h) Regulation (EU) 2019/1896.

[242] Dumbrava, EPRS 2021, 9.

[243] Migration-related applications of 'big data' and 'digital traces' are currently gaining traction, using 'big data', for example, from a mobile phone or social media 'digital footprints' in addition to more traditional data sources, such as administrative records. See Napierała/Hilton/Forster/Carammia, International Migration Review 2022, 33–62.

[244] Melachrinos/Carammia/Wilkin in Fargues/Rango, Migration in West and North Africa and across the Mediterranean, p. 98. Yet, no matter how sophisticated the technology or how insightful the participants, neither of these approaches was able to predict the pandemic or its effects on displacement and international protection, nor can they be invoked to simulate the post-COVID-19 world.

With a view to anticipating asylum-related pressure at EU level, the EUAA engages in 138
big data analytics, such as media-covered events in origin countries[245] that are selected on the basis of the effect such events may have on asylum-related migration in the EU. These data are aggregated in the so-called EUAA Push Factor Index (PFI).[246] The PFI extracts disruptive events from big data on push factors and seeks to find correlations with irregular arrivals and asylum applications in EU countries.[247]

In addition, eu-LISA and the EUAA are to 'explore together, based on their expertise, 139
and with the Member States, innovative solutions including the use of Artificial Intelligence and machine-learning for technical practical tools used in the asylum procedure.'[248]

The Artificial Intelligence (AI) Act, which was adopted in March 2024, aims at 140
ensuring that AI systems placed on the EU market adhere to certain standards and prohibits specific high-risk AI technologies.

Although criticism was raised regarding the lack of a fundamental rights-based 141
approach of the AI Act proposal, it could be argued that the Act offers more protection for individuals in terms of safeguards and prohibitions of certain processing operations than is currently the case.[249] In order to close any protection gaps, it is welcome that EU large-scale systems that could include AI-based functionalities in the future, must comply with the requirements of the AI Act.[250]

In any event, the necessity for and proportionality of the use of AI should be included 142
in any future endeavour to embed AI-based functionalities in the EU large-scale systems. This discussion should be held in relation to the purpose, legal basis and context of each system so as to be able to evaluate the impact on fundamental rights of each system and its AI functionality. However, this may be increasingly challenging in an interoperability framework that will continuously evolve and be further expanded by means of additional systems that include new purposes, types of data and categories of data subjects and that will grant access to additional authorities.

Finally, individuals whose personal data will be processed by way of AI analyses 143
should be aware of their rights. As regards implementation of the right to complain in the border context, the use of AI may have risks for and negative impacts on individuals' possibility for challenging the use of a certain technology or exercising the right to an explanation.

Furthermore, one crucial aspect when it comes to effective remedies is that indivi- 144
duals need to know that AI or AI-based technologies were used and where and how to complain. Ultimately, if the result of a certain automated decision would go to court, there will be a need to guarantee equality of arms, meaning that all the information available needs to be taken into account when challenging a decision.

---

245 The EUAA uses the Global Database on Events, Language and Tone (GDELT) Project <www.gdeltproject.org/> (last accessed: 13.10.2023).

246 European Union Asylum Agency, Data Analysis and Research, available at: https://euaa.europa.eu/asylum-knowledge/data-analysis-and-research.

247 Melachrinos/Carammia/Wilkin in Fargues/Rango (eds), Migration in West and North Africa and across the Mediterranean, p. 112.

248 Eu-LISA/EASO, 'Cooperation Plan 2020-2022 of eu-LISA and EASO', 3 <https://euaa.europa.eu/sites/default/files/CP_EASO_eu-LISA.pdf> (last accessed: 13.10.2023).

249 See, for instance: Edri et al, 'An EU Artificial Intelligence Act for Fundamental Rights – A Civil Society Statement' (Edri et al., 20.11.2021) <https://edri.org/wp-content/uploads/2021/12/Political-statement-on-AI-Act.pdf> (last accessed: 13.10.2023).

250 In accordance with Article 111 of the final draft of the AI Act, AI systems which are components of the EU large-scale IT systems must comply with the Act by 31 December 2030.

D. Data protection concerns in connection with interoperable information exchanges at different levels

145 Data exchanges among different authorities and between the national and EU level, as well as with third countries or private parties have been increasingly stepped up over the past few years.[251] Particularly within the AFSJ, processing of personal data is often opaque, which makes it difficult to ascertain where the data originated from and which entity complemented the datasets with additional analyses. Interoperability and the intensification of data exchanges between different authorities at different levels make it even more challenging to comprehend the data flows in the complex, interconnected environment.

146 Improving the exchange of information between LEAs in the EU is of paramount importance for tackling cross-border crime. However, the question is how this can be done in the right way and in a necessary and proportionate manner. Interoperability will revolutionize the way in which EU large-scale systems are governed and raises concerns regarding data protection standards, in particular the purpose limitation principle, which stipulates that personal data should be collected for specified, explicit and legitimate purposes and not be further processed in a manner that is incompatible with those purposes.[252] This is to enable individuals whose personal data are processed to anticipate a certain expected outcome and thereby builds upon the transparency principle.[253]

147 While some of the revisions of the operational systems and the recently adopted regulations respond to the needs that have emerged with changing migratory flows[254] – and may, in fact, be necessary and proportionate – adding new objectives to each system and establishing interoperability will have consequences for this key data protection principle.[255]

148 On the one hand, data flows between the different authorities at different levels are becoming more and more intense, which makes it difficult to retrace the initial source of information and identify the responsible controller. On the other hand, EU Agencies have been attributed new competences in relation to the processing of TCNs' personal data. In addition, their mandates have been broadened to accommodate new tasks and functions, reaching into additional fields. Particularly in the context of migration, such increased competences and mandates could lead to a blurring of the boundaries between migration and criminal law.

149 The purpose limitation principle also has particular relevance in the context of law enforcement access to each individual system, as the primary purposes of initially setting up the AFSJ databases were, except for the SIS, of a non-law enforcement nature. With the revision of operational systems and the establishment of new systems,

---

[251] Quintel, p. 216.

[252] Art. 5(1)(b) GDPR. See also Quintel, p. 223.

[253] Art. 5(1)(a) GDPR.

[254] While the number of irregular arrivals has decreased over time, the share of migrants arriving from countries with recognition rates lower than 25 % rose from 14 % in 2015 to 57 % in 2018. In addition, there has been an increasing number of complex cases, as the arrival of TCNs with clear international protection needs in 2015/16 has been partly replaced by the arrival of people with more divergent recognition rates. Furthermore, notwithstanding the EU-wide decrease in irregular arrivals since 2015, the number of applications for international protection has continued to climb. See European Commission, COM(2020) 614 final, 1.

[255] '[Personal] data must be processed fairly for specified purposes[…]'. See: Quintel, Luxembourg Law Working Paper 2018, 17.

more purposes were added to the initial ones and streamlined law enforcement access was added as an ancillary objective. Interoperability will fundamentally change the current architecture of AFSJ large-scale IT systems and introduce a shift from separated silos to an interconnected framework in which personal data will be stored on a centralized basis.[256]

This creates new processing operations and may provide information to authorities that they would normally not have direct access to in the underlying system.[257] The right to the protection of personal data is not an absolute right and must be balanced against other fundamental rights and interests. However, new processing operations must be sufficiently justified and need to have undergone a necessity and proportionality assessment.[258] **150**

The assimilation of migration management, border control and asylum with security concerns first materialized through the revision of AFSJ databases. Rendering those databases interoperable is, for the time being, the last exemplification in a series of steps towards manifesting such an assimilation. However, the system as it currently stands is by no means intended to be static or final. Rather, interoperability should be seen as an expandable toolbox that can be extended by added functionalities, access possibilities and databases. The Screening Regulation, the Prüm II or the API Regulations could be seen as such extensions.[259] **151**

Linking more and more data from different sources makes it challenging to define clear purposes for which the data are to be processed. One the one hand, this makes it difficult for individuals to exercise their rights under EU data protection law. On the other hand, it will become increasingly challenging for DPAs to supervise the interoperable framework of EU large-scale information systems. **152**

I. EU data protection rules in different contexts

In 2016, seven years after the entry into force of the Lisbon Treaty and the CFR becoming legally binding, the EU data protection reform had become both necessary and possible. Since then, the *CJEU* has progressively bolstered the rights of data subjects through its case law, relying on Art. 7 and 8 CFR. In addition to Art. 7 and 8 CFR, Art. 16 of the TFEU became a strong legal basis for the Union to legislate on data protection matters. Both the provisions that form part of the EU data protection reform and the rights under Art. 7 and 8 CFR apply to everyone in the EU, irrespective of nationality. **153**

While most of the TCNs who have been the subject of the debate here may not consider the right to data protection as important or may not even be aware that that right exists and applies equally to them as to EU citizens, data protection is often their last line of defence.[260] **154**

Detecting the applicable data protection instrument is of particular importance in the context of migration management, border control and asylum. Under EU data protection law, the purpose of the processing and the authority processing the data determine the applicability of different sets of rules. Hence, while EU data protection law grants **155**

[256] Quintel, Luxembourg Law Working Paper 2018, 9.

[257] EDPS, 'Reflection Paper on the Interoperability of Information Systems in the Area of Freedom, Security and Justice', 17.11.2017.

[258] Interference may be justified if it is proportionate, provided for by law, genuinely meets the objectives of a general interest or the need to protect the rights and freedoms of others, Art. 52(1) CFR.

[259] See also Quintel, p. 43.

[260] EDPS, 'Opinion 9/2020 EDPS Opinion on the New Pact on Migration and Asylum', 30.11.2020, 6 point 7.

strong rights to individuals in the field of border control, migration and asylum (GDPR), in a security-related context competent authorities need to be able to apply data protection rules in a more flexible manner and are granted more leeway to restrict the rights of individuals (LED). The delineation of these different types of data protection rules may, however, prove difficult, as events of recent years and the aftermath of the migration crisis have not only led to the above-mentioned revision of many legal instruments in that AFSJ but have also blurred the line between migration and security, migration law and criminal law.

156 TCNs such as visa applicants, (irregular) migrants and asylum seekers will become subject to certain types of profiling measures when they apply for a visa in the EU or are registered in a receiving country. In order to determine whether an individual may be granted a visa, an applicant's personal data are examined by the respective authorities and will be matched against other data sets in the interoperable system, risk indicators and the ETIAS watchlist. Likewise, where ETIAS applicants are pre-vetted to ascertain whether they pose a public security, illegal immigration or public health risk, their personal data are automatically processed and compared with the ETIAS screening rules in addition to being matched against data in the underlying EU systems and the interoperability components. In the case of asylum applications, information regarding the route via which the person applying for international protection arrived in the recipient state is scrutinized by analysing data from multiple sources. Such administrative processing to determine visa or ETIAS eligibility and refugee status falls within the scope of the GDPR. However, when processing is carried out for the prevention, investigation, detection or prosecution of criminal offences, the LED applies. Hence, where national competent authorities such as the police, prosecutors or criminal judges process personal data for preventative and investigatory purposes, such processing falls within the scope of the Directive.

157 Like the GDPR, the LED was adopted in May 2016 as the first legally binding horizontal instrument setting out rules for both the domestic and cross-border processing of personal data in the field of law enforcement, with the aim of establishing a comprehensive EU data protection regime.[261]

158 As the Directive is not a full harmonization instrument, its scope and application are dependent on its transposition in the individual Member States. In order for the LED to apply, both its personal and material scope need to be satisfied, meaning that a competent LEA needs to process personal data for law enforcement purposes, i.e. for the prevention, detection, investigation and prosecution of criminal offences.[262] However, various Member States have included authorities within the LED's scope that might not be viewed as traditional criminal law enforcement authorities.[263] In addition, in certain Member States, any authority processing personal data for law enforcement purposes can become a competent authority within the meaning of the LED while carrying out law enforcement processing operations. Where Member States have criminalized irregular entry into their territory, irregular migrants' personal data could then be processed within the scope of the Directive.

---

[261] Sajfert/Quintel, 'Data Protection Directive (EU) 2016/680 for Police and Criminal Justice Authorities' (SSRN, 10.12.2018) <https://papers.ssrn.com/sol3/papers.cfm?abstract_id=3285873> (last accessed: 13.10.2023) and Marquenie, Computer Law & Security Review 2017 (33), 324.

[262] See Art. 1(1) and Art. 3(7) Directive 2016/680 for a definition of 'competent authority'.

[263] Traditional LEAs are authorities such as the police, prosecutors and criminal courts. However, in Germany, for instance, processing by administrative authorities to prosecute administrative fines (*Ordnungswidrigkeiten*) falls within the scope of the LED. In Sweden, the border and coast guard applies the Directive to certain types of processing. In Denmark and Belgium, the Financial Intelligence Unit processes personal data within the scope of the LED.

This may lead to a broadening of the Directive's scope to the detriment of the GDPR and the Directive's application in situations where this may not be justified. This may be the case where competent border authorities and/or LEAs insert, access and subsequently process personal data from the underlying EU information systems, or, in future, the interoperability components. Where competent authorities apply the LED instead of the GDPR in the migration and border control context, many of the rights of data subjects may be restricted and obligations for controllers applied in a more flexible manner than under the Regulation. **159**

Therefore, one of the grey areas between the GDPR and the LED is that of border control, migration and asylum. Particularly in the migration context, the blurring of the scope of the GDPR and the LED may lead to the processing of migrants' and other TCNs' personal data within the scope of the Directive. LEAs could also process TCNs' personal data within the scope of the LED when carrying out identity checks. Depending on the grounds for return, and whether the authority carrying out such return is a competent authority within the scope of the LED in a Member State, personal data could be transferred to third countries within the scope of the Directive. **160**

The EU's data protection reform could be said to include a revision of the data protection rules applicable to EU Agencies so as to harmonize and make more coherent the rules that apply to EU institutions, bodies and agencies with those at national level. This was necessary because the rules applicable to EU institutions, bodies and agencies originated from a 2001 Regulation[264] and were outdated. Regulation (EU) 2018/1725 on the protection of personal data by Union institutions, bodies, offices and agencies (EUDPR)[265] was adopted in 2018. The EUDPR replicates the rules of the GDPR in its general chapters on administrative processing (Chapters I–IX, Chapters X–XII). In addition, it includes a chapter on so-called operational personal data (Chapter IX) that applies where personal data are processed by EU Agencies[266] for law enforcement purposes and provides a set of horizontal rules that are based on the LED.[267] **161**

Since December 2018, Frontex, eu-LISA and the EUAA have applied the EUDPR to their processing activities. The processing of personal data by Europol and Eurojust is governed by a *lex specialis–lex generalis* regime, which means that both Eurojust and Europol maintained a number of specific data protection rules in their founding acts while applying the general rules of the EUDPR to the so-called administrative processing of personal data. The rules of Chapter IX of the EUDPR apply to the processing of operational personal data as *lex generalis* and in addition to the specific rules.[268, 269] Chapter IX of the EUDPR remained unfinished with regard to the rules on international transfers and supervision by the EDPS. In terms of the processing of operational personal data by Europol and Eurojust, this does not pose major concerns, as the founding acts of both Agencies include provisions on super- **162**

264 Regulation (EC) No 45/2001 on the protection of individuals with regard to the processing of personal data by the Community institutions and bodies and on the free movement of such data.

265 Regulation (EU) 2018/1725 on the protection of natural persons with regard to the processing of personal data by the Union institutions, bodies, offices and agencies and on the free movement of such data, and repealing Regulation (EC) No 45/2001 and Decision No 1247/2002/EC.

266 The chapter applies to EU bodies, offices and agencies for the processing of personal data when carrying out activities that fall within the scope of chapter 4 or 5 of Title V of Part Three of the TFEU.

267 European Commission, 'Communication from the Commission to the European Parliament and the Council: First report on the application of the Data Protection Regulation for European Union institutions, bodies, offices and agencies (Regulation 2018/1725)', 14.10.2022, 15, COM(2022) 530 final.

268 See Art. 26(1) Regulation 2018/1727.

269 Art. 26(3) Regulation 2018/1727 and Art. 27a(1) Regulation 2022/991.

vision.[270] However, the Frontex Regulation, as regards those parts of the Agency's activities that are subject to the law enforcement chapter[271] in the EUDPR, does not include any specific provisions on EDPS powers, which leads to uncertainties regarding the supervision of those processing activities.[272] The same could hold true for the processing activities of the EUAA, should the latter process operational personal data in future, for instance when transmitting personal data to Frontex, Europol or Eurojust in the performance of their tasks.[273]

163 Consequently, the data protection framework applicable to different EU Agencies are characterized by a patchwork of data protection rules that take into account the specific needs of some of the Agencies. Stand-alone provisions applicable to specific Agencies may lead to a fragmentation of data protection standards and, with increased exchanges of personal data between the national and EU level, such fragmentation may lead to variations in terms of safeguards, obligations and supervision. The recast Europol Regulation, in particular, gives the Agency a lot of leeway to apply its own rules, which prevail over the rules under the EUDPR.

164 In addition, while the GDPR and the LED are to be seen as *leges generals*, some of the underlying EU information systems contain specific provisions on data protection that ought to prevail. Evidently, this adds to the fragmentation of rules and increases incoherence within the interoperable system. Both the interoperable data flows between national authorities and EU Agencies or among the Agencies themselves and the variations in terms of applicable data protection rules make the supervision of information exchanges challenging.

II. Supervision of multi-level data flows

165 In a world where more and more data are being used to analyse the movement of individuals, connecting information from different sources on a systematic basis may be a logical step so as to carry out such analyses more effectively. In addition, interoperable databases allow immediate data exchanges that are intended to facilitate and streamline decision-making by digital means.[274]

166 At the same time, it becomes more challenging to supervise data exchanges and sources of information in the interconnected system. Particularly where authorities exchange and further process personal data in order to use them for different purposes at both national and EU level, supervision becomes more intricate.

167 Owing to the complex landscape of information exchange channels and the multitude of actors, data processing activities within the AFSJ are opaque, which makes it difficult for data subjects to ascertain who is processing their personal data. Therefore, compliance with data protection principles to ensure clearly defined processing activities that are subject to strict supervision are of the utmost importance when it comes to guaranteeing fundamental rights standards. The independent oversight of personal data processing must be ensured pursuant to Art. 8(3) CFR, and it therefore applies horizontally to all areas regulated by EU law. In addition, the GDPR, the LED and the EUDPR regulate independent supervisions in specific areas.

---

[270] See Art. 40 and 42 Regulation 2018/1727 and Art. 43 and 44 Regulation 2022/991.
[271] See Art. 10(1)(q) and Art. 90 Regulation 2019/1896.
[272] COM(2022) 530 final, 17.
[273] Art. 32(2)(b) Regulation 2021/2303.
[274] See EDPS, 'Reflection Paper on the Interoperability of Information Systems in the Area of Freedom, Security and Justice', 17.11.2017.

Yet, Chapter VI of the EUDPR (on supervision) does not apply to the processing of operational personal data, and Chapter IX remained incomplete as far as supervision is concerned.

Furthermore, there will be situations in which certain processing activities will remain unknown to the data subject. For instance, the national supervisory authority under the LED in one Member State has no competence to scrutinize the processing activities of the competent (law enforcement) authorities in another Member State. Yet, where systematic data exchanges between those authorities take place, cooperation between the national supervisory authorities is crucial. However, such cooperation is time-consuming and will be even slower in a complex system such as the one that is envisaged by means of the interoperability of EU large-scale information systems. 168

With the blurring of the lines between migration and security, leading to the obscuring of different purposes and the dilution of responsibilities of different actors, it is challenging for supervisory authorities to get a concrete picture of processing activities and, hence, the risks involved for data subjects. In an environment in which data constantly move between different actors, it is difficult, if not impossible, to know which actor is carrying out each respective processing activity. In order to ascertain which authority is responsible for supervision, close cooperation between the DPAs will become increasingly relevant.[275] 169

To ensure effective supervision, DPAs should be able to follow data flows across the different networks instead of looking at each specific controller separately. To achieve such effective supervision of the complex network of different processors, closer cooperation between national DPAs and the EDPS to better understand the steps behind certain decision-making processes and better handle complaints is a move in the right direction.[276] 170

Just like the merging of previously disconnected EU systems under the Interoperability Regulations, and the increasing number of cases in which different authorities exchange personal data, supervisory authorities should gain a better overview of the connected systems so as to be able to provide more effective supervision.[277] Yet, national supervisory authorities often lack the resources for enforcement, and they obtained weaker powers as regards processing in a law enforcement context. In addition, cooperation between national DPAs and the EPDS is still far from satisfactory, particularly in the area of law enforcement.[278] Therefore, the rules on coordinated supervision[279] between national DPAs and the EDPS of EU large-scale information systems and relevant EU Agencies represent a first step to preparing a harmonized approach and ensuring the exchange of relevant information on supervision.[280] 171

E. Conclusion and outlook

Interoperability will drastically change the way in which competent authorities can access, retrieve and process personal data stored in the AFSJ databases. The interoper- 172

---

[275] Demková/Quintel, Cahiers Jean Monnet 2020, 616.
[276] Quintel, p. 87.
[277] Demková/Quintel, Cahiers Jean Monnet 2020, 616.
[278] Quintel, p. 87.
[279] Art. 62 Regulation 2018/1725.
[280] Demková/Quintel, Cahiers Jean Monnet 2020, 613.

able system abandons the traditional silo-based approach, pursuant to which these databases were set up according to specific purposes, with precise time limits and access conditions. Hence, the interoperable system will introduce a game-changing playing field on both sides, one for competent authorities and one for TCNs. Whether this game changer will be to the benefit to one, either or both remains to be seen once interoperability becomes operational.

173 The quality of law criteria, which were elaborated by the European Court of Human Rights (ECtHR), require a law to be adequately accessible, foreseeable, clear and precise. Hence, individuals must be able to have an adequate indication as to the application of the law in a given case and must be able to have access to it.[281]

174 The interoperability framework, together with the numerous implementing and delegated acts, may affect foreseeability on account of it being difficult to read all the provisions that need to be considered in combination. The interoperability framework combines multi-functional purposes from different areas of law with broad provisions, for instance with regard to law enforcement access. The complexity of each of the individual EU large-scale systems and the interoperability framework may lead to challenges regarding the foreseeability, accessibility and clarity of their founding acts.

175 The EU legislator's ambition was to connect all the underlying systems in order to facilitate the work of the competent authorities. However, it will be extremely challenging for individuals whose information will be stored in the interoperable system to understand how their data will be analysed and utilized, since the systems were adopted at different times, leading to an abundance of amendments to those systems that were adopted prior to others.

176 The proliferation of new systems and the interoperability framework signify a paradigm shift by streamlining law enforcement access to non-law enforcement databases and abolishing the cascading system of mandatory checks in national databases prior to accessing the EU systems. The consequences of such abolition and re-purposing are manifold and will lead to new access and processing possibilities for different authorities.

177 The ETIAS allows for the pre-vetting of TCNs by matching their personal data against screening rules and a watchlist that will be fed with data from Europol's analyses and consist of data relating to people who are suspected of having committed or taken part in a terrorist offence or other serious criminal offence. The ETIAS watchlist will be re-used by the VIS to carry out a risk assessment of visa applicants by automatically comparing their data with those in the watchlist and visa applications will be analysed using specific risk indicators.

178 Both national authorities and EU Agencies are investing heavily in AI technologies. Some of the underlying databases that interoperability will be built on could be said to anticipate the inclusion of AI-based functionalities. This will have an impact on the explainability of the systems' operation and the exercise of individual rights. In addition, AI-based technologies, just like any data-driven analysis, by their very nature raise concerns regarding their compliance with core EU data protection principles. Where personal data are entered into the systems and subsequently analysed in order to find risky patterns or to predict criminal behaviour, this represents a challenge for both the data minimization and the purpose limitation principles.

179 In the interoperable system, purposes/objectives will become increasingly mixed, in particular where migration databases become interconnected with law enforcement databases and new sets of data are generated by the system itself. In the context of

---

[281] Van der Sloot, JIPITEC 2020, 160 para. 1.

migration management and border control, detecting the applicable data protection instrument is of particular importance. Under EU data protection law, the purpose of the processing and the authority processing the data determine the applicability of different sets of rules. While EU data protection law grants strong rights to individuals in the field of border control, migration and asylum, in a security-related context competent authorities need to be able to apply data protection rules more flexibly and are granted more leeway to restrict individuals' data subject rights. Delineating those different types of data protection rules may, however, prove difficult.

An additional layer of complexity that needs to be taken into consideration arises **180** when authorities at national and EU level exchange personal data. On the one hand, data are exchanged indirectly through the EU large-scale information systems and the different interoperability components. On the other hand, Europol and Frontex in particular have evolved into notable information hubs at EU level, meaning that they receive enormous amounts of personal data from national authorities in order to feed these data into their analyses.

Where purposes are increasingly broadened, the blurring of the boundaries between **181** migration law enforcement and criminal law enforcement is inevitable.

To prevent an implicit lowering of data protection standards, it would be important **182** to clearly define the purposes of each processing operation in accordance with the purpose limitation principle.

PART VI
PERSPECTIVES

§ 21
On the future of security cooperation in the European Union

Steffen Zanger

Bibliography: Aden, 'EU Policy on Internal Security and the Subsidiarity Principle', E-IR 2021, 1; Al-Rodhan/Stoudmann, Definitions of Globalization: A Comprehensive Overview and a Proposed Definition, Geneva, 2006; Bendiek/Maat, 'The EU's Regulatory Approach to Cyber-security', SWP Working Paper 2019 (2), 1; Bermeo, 'On Democratic Backsliding', JoD 2016 (27:1), 5; Bigo, 'Globalization and Security' in Amenta/Nash/Scott (eds), The Wiley-Blackwell Companion to Political Sociology, Cambridge 2012, p. 204; Bigo, 'When Two Become One: Internal and External Securitisations in Europe' in Kelstrup/Williams (eds), International Relations Theory and the Politics of European Integration, London 2000, p. 171; Bossong, 'Policy networks for European internal security governance: toward a more systematic empirical and normative assessment', JTS 2020 (18), 190; Bossong/Carrapico, 'The Multidimensional Nature and Dynamic Transformation of European Borders and Internal Security' in Bossong/Carrapico (eds), EU Borders and Shifting Internal Security. Technology, Externalization and Accountability, Cham 2016, p. 1; Brandão, 'The internal – external nexus in the security narrative of the European Union', JANUS.NET, e-journal of International Relations 2015 (6:1), 1; Brayne, 'Big Data Surveillance: The Case of Policing', ASR 2017 (82:5), 977; Brownsword/Harel, 'Law, liberty and technology: criminal justice in the context of smart machines', International Journal of Law in Context 2019 (15:2), 107; Bulmer, 'Shop till you drop – The German executive as venue-shopper in Justice and home affairs' in Bendel/Ette/Parks (eds), The Europeanization of Control, Münster 2011, p. 41; Buzan/Waever/de Wilde, Security – A New Framework for Analysis, London 1998; Calcara/Csernatoni/Lavallée, 'Introduction' in Calcara/Csernatoni/Lavallée (eds), Emerging Security Technologies and EU Governance: Actors, Practices and Processes, Milton Park 2021, p. 1; Cameron, 'Metadata retention and national security: Privacy International and La Quadrature du Net', Common Market Law Review 2021 (58:5), 1433; Carrera/Colombi/Cortinovis, An Assessment of the State of the EU Schengen Area and its External Borders. A Merited Trust Model to Uphold Schengen Legitimacy, Study Requested by the LIBE committee, Strasbourg 2023; Christensen/Raynor/Gregersen, Disruptive Innovation: The Christensen Collection, Boston 2012; Closa/Kochenov, 'Introduction. How to Save the EU's Rule of Law and Should One Bother' in Closa/Kochenov (eds), Reinforcing Rule of Law Oversight in the European Union, Cambridge 2016, p. 1; Ette/Parks/Bendel, 'The Diversity of European Justice and Home Affairs Cooperation: A Model-Testing Exercise on its Development and Outcomes' in Bendel/Ette/Parks (eds), The Europeanization of Control – Venues and Outcomes of EU Justice and Home Affairs Cooperation, Münster 2011, p. 9; Fiott, 'Digitalization and hybrid threats', Hybrid CoE Paper 2022 (13), 1; Fletcher, 'EU Criminal Justice: Beyond Lisbon' in Eckes/Konstandinides (eds), Crime within the Area of Freedom, Security and Justice, Cambridge 2011, p. 10; Institute for Economics and Peace (ed.), Global Terrorism Index 2022: Measuring the Impact of Terrorism, Sydney 2022; Institute for Economics and Peace (ed.), Global Terrorism Index 2023: Measuring the Impact of Terrorism, Sydney 2023; Geddes, The Politics of Migration and Immigration in Europe, Thousand Oaks 2003; Geddes/Scholten, The Politics of Migration and Immigration in Europe, 2nd edn, Thousand Oaks 2016; Giannopoulos/Smith/Theocharidou, The Landscape of Hybrid Threats: A Conceptual Model, Luxemburg 2021; Gora/de Wilde, 'The essence of democratic backsliding in the European Union: deliberation and rule of law', Journal of European Public Policy 2022 (29:3), 342; Grabbe/Valášek, Refocus the European Union – Planet, Lifetime, Technology, Washington D.C. 2019; Guiraudon, 'European Integration and Migration Policy: Vertical Policy-making as Venue Shopping', JCMS 2000 (38:2), 251; Harvey, The Condition of Postmodernity, Cambridge 1989; Hoffmann-Riem, 'Artificial

Intelligence as a Challenge for Law and Regulation' in Wischmeyer/Rademacher (eds), Regulating Artificial Intelligence, Cham 2020, p. 1; Holesch/Kyriaz, 'Democratic backsliding in the European Union: the role of the Hungarian-Polish coalition', East European Politics 2021 (38:1), 1; Hosein, 'Policy Laundering, and Other Policy Dynamics' in Halpin/Trevorrow/Webb/Wright (eds), Cyberwar, Netwar and the Revolution in Military Affairs, London 2006, p. 228; Kay, 'Globalization, Power, and Security', Security Dialogue 2004 (35:1), 5; Klenk/Nullmeier/Wewer, 'Auf dem Weg zum Digitalen Staat? Stand und Perspektiven der Digitalisierung in Staat und Verwaltung' in Klenk/Nullmeier/Wewer (eds), Handbuch Digitalisierung in Staat und Verwaltung, Wiesbaden 2020, p. 1; Labasque, 'The Merits of Informality in Bilateral and Multilateral Cooperation', (2020) 33(3) IJICI, 492; Léonard, 'EU Border Security and Migration into the European Union. FRONTEX and Securitisation Through Practices', European Security 2010 (19:2), 231; Marchant, 'The Growing Gap Between Emerging Technologies and the Law' in Marchant/Allenby/Herkert (eds), The Growing Gap Between Emerging Technologies and Legal-Ethical Oversight. The International Library of Ethics, Law and Technology, Dordrecht 2011, p. 19; Mechkova/Lührmann/Lindberg, 'How Much Democratic Backsliding?', JoD 2017 (28:4), 162; Monsees/Lambach, 'Digital sovereignty, geopolitical imaginaries, and the reproduction of European identity', European Security 2022 (31:3), 377; Moser/Rittberger, 'The CJEU and EU (de-)constitutionalization: Unpacking jurisprudential responses', International Journal of Constitutional Law 2022 (20:3), 1038; Ní áin, Position of the United Nations Special Rapporteur on the promotion and protection of human rights and fundamental freedoms while countering terrorism on the human rights of adolescents/juveniles being detained in North-East Syria, Geneva 2022; von Ondarza/Ålander, 'After the Conference on the Future of Europe: Time to Make Reforms Happen', SWP Comment 2022 C 49; Orrù, 'Freedom, security and justice in the European Union: a short genealogy of the "Security Union"', Eunomia. Rivista di studi su pace e diritti umani 2022 (11:1), 143; Rüß/Lutz, 'Die novellierte Europol-Verordnung: Eine europäische Antwort auf das FBI?', GSZ 2022 (5), 221; Sandhu/Fussey, 'The 'uberization of policing'? How police negotiate and operationalise predictive policing technology', Policing and Society 2021 (31:1), 66; Slaughter, A New World Order, Princeton 2004; Solana et al., From Hybrid Peace to Human Security: Rethinking EU Strategy towards Conflict. The Berlin Report of the Human Security Study Group, London 2016; Sule, 'National Security and EU law restraints on Intelligence Activities' in Dietrich/Sule (eds), Intelligence Law and Policies in Europe, Munich/Oxford/Baden-Baden 2019, p. 335.

A. Introduction

1 After previous chapters provided insights into the structures, methods and state of the European Security Union, this final chapter of the Handbook gives an outlook on the way forward for security cooperation within the European Union's internal area. To do so, the interrelationship between disruptive trends on the one hand and the political and legal dynamics within the EU on the other must be examined.

2 As laid out by *Arne Pilniok*, the multi-level governance system for providing internal security in the EU has evolved and, particularly since the adoption of the Treaty of Lisbon, the role and significance of EU institutions have increased (→ § 4 mn. 4). By communitising the third pillar of the Union and thus introducing the ordinary legislative procedure for security matters, the normative influence of the Union has been extensively expanded. Member States' governments may even be enticed to have security matters regulated by the EU to achieve more restrictive results or avoid domestic controversies.[1] At the same time, CJEU case law[2] indicates that Member

[1] Guiraudon, JCMS 2000, 251; Hosein in Halpin et al., Cyberwar, Netwar and the Revolution in Military Affairs, p. 229.

[2] ECJ 6.10.2020 – case C-623/17, ECLI:EU:C:2020:790 – *Privacy International*; ECJ 6.10.2020 – joined cases, C-511/18, C-512/18 and C-520/18, ECLI:EU:C:2020:791 – *La Quadrature du Net*.

States' security measures are barely isolated from EU law (→ § 8 mn. 19; → § 10 mn. 9, mn. 11; → § 6 mn. 17).

Simultaneously, the EU – accelerated by technological progress – has become a central facilitator for Member State action in the field of security. The shared databases operated by the EU provide Member State authorities with information that is considered a requirement for the freedom of movement within the Union (→ § 20 mn. 3). Specialized agencies such as Europol also support the analysis of what would otherwise be overwhelming quantities of data, creating links to make raw information actionable.[3] 3

The EU has thus far not become a significant actor on executive, operational matters, though. The Member States are still responsible for providing executive security. They police[4] their respective populations and operate aligned yet distinct criminal justice systems.[5] And the Member States are even more restrictive when it comes to sharing or communitizing intelligence capabilities.[6] 4

The expansion of EU capabilities has thus focused on areas in which Member States have perceived added value, in that they have transferred tasks to the EU while retaining the core of their power. The incentives for transferring security competences to Brussels are improved coordination and access to information that would not be available on the national level in the face of new challenges in a globalized world. Furthermore, communitizing tasks can lead to the sharing of financial burdens.[7] 5

Yet, continuing the trajectory of slowly progressing European integration in the field of security is in no way a given. Not only are Eurosceptic and populist nationalist parties achieving successes in national and European elections,[8] the so-called Art. 7 TEU procedures against Poland and Hungary are also an indication of the erosion of a common understanding of the rule of law as the lowest common denominator for sharing sensitive information.[9] Furthermore, even traditional champions of European integration are hesitating to grant the CJEU oversight over their security agencies, contesting the Court's views on the scope of the national security exemptions set out in Art. 4(2) TEU (→ § 10 mn. 6, mn. 25). However, the Member States' efforts to shield security measures from the oversight of the CJEU and the application of EU law have born little success.[10] Still, the Member States have not transferred any executive competences. 6

That said, it is not clear how security cooperation will evolve in future. A structured approach is needed to prepare a medium-term scenario as to how the European Security Union is to develop. In a first step, this chapter discusses the impact of three disruptive trends on security provision and cooperation. Then, turning to the EU's plan to react to these developments, it establishes how the roles and responsibilities in the European Security Union are likely to evolve, taking legislative and non-legislative instruments into account. 7

---

[3] Art. 88(2)(a) TFEU; Art. 4 Regulation (EU) No 2016/794 on the European Union Agency for Law Enforcement Cooperation (Europol).

[4] Rüß/Lutz, GSZ 2022, 221 (226).

[5] Fletcher in Eckes/Konstandinides, Crime within the Area of Freedom, Security and Justice, p. 14.

[6] Labasque, IJICI 2020, 492 (492).

[7] See Aden, E-IR 2021, 1 (2 et seqq.).

[8] ibid., 1.

[9] ECJ 16.2.2022 – case C-156/21, ECLI:EU:C:2022:97 – *Hungary v Parliament and Council* and ECJ 16.2.2022 – case C-157/21, ECLI:EU:C:2022:98 – *Poland v Parliament and Council.*

[10] Sule in Dietrich/Sule, Intelligence Law and Policies in Europe, p. 358 (mn. 70); Cameron, Common Market Law Review 2021, 1433 (1458).

B. Disruptive trends

8 There is an infinite number of factors that influence the ways in which security in the EU and its Member States will be guaranteed in future and how the relevant actors cooperate. In order to be able to forecast their trajectory in the medium term, it is therefore necessary to limit the analysis to three disruptions that fundamentally change either the tasks or methods of the security providers. Focusing on fundamental trends ensures that the prognosis does not stray too far from a most likely scenario. By analogy with *Clay Christensen's* theory of disruptive innovation, these trends have the potential to make good governments fail in the long term if they ignore or fight developments that are not currently pressing issues but will eventually upset the status quo.[11]

9 While *Heather Grabbe* and *Tomáš Valášek* have identified climate change, the ageing EU population and technological change as the EU's main long-term policy challenges,[12] these factors are not directly transferable for the purposes of this chapter. Although climate change is already increasing the probability of natural disasters and will have a significant long-term impact on the EU's internal security, it is not a deciding factor that will disrupt security provision on a five-year timeline. Although a shrinking domestic labour force affects security providers seeking the necessary talent, it is mainly an issue that affects the common market and social security.

10 Taking a narrower focus on border security, *Raphael Bossong* and *Helena Carrapico* identified the growing role of technology, the externalization of public security and accountability gaps as key trends.[13] Within the framework of this chapter, account also needs to be taken of the internalization of external security in order to cover additional aspects of security cooperation in the area of freedom, security and justice (AFSJ). To get a holistic picture, accountability gaps will be addressed by looking at executive aggrandisement as a central challenge.

I. Technological progress

11 First, rapid technological innovation fundamentally changes the ways in which humans interact and perform tasks. It affects all sectors and spheres of live[14] on a global scale, including how governments do business. Overlapping innovations in the fields of artificial intelligence (AI) and machine learning, big data analysis, quantum computing, robotics, 3D-printing and biotech are progressing at 'unprecedented speed and scale'.[15] They allow a vast amount of easily available information to be utilized that has multiplied in recent decades and will continue to do so.[16] For security providers, this means that the behaviour of the communities they are tasked to protect is changing, as are the activities and tools of offenders. At the same time, law enforcement and intelligence agencies themselves are

[11] See Christensen/Raynor/Gregersen, Disruptive Innovation, p. 9 et seqq.

[12] Grabbe/Valášek, p. 2.

[13] Bossong/Carrapico in Bossong/Carrapico, EU Borders and Shifting Internal Security, p. 2 et seqq.

[14] Hoffmann-Riem in Wischmeyer/Rademacher, Regulating Artificial Intelligence, p. 4 (mn. 8); Klenk/Nullmeier/Wewer in Klenk/Nullmeier/Wewer, Handbuch Digitalisierung in Staat und Verwaltung, p. 3.

[15] Calcara/Csernatoni/Lavallée in Calcara/Csernatoni/Lavallée, Emerging Security Technologies and EU Governance, p. 4; Fiott, Hybrid CoE Paper 2022, 1 (7).

[16] Klenk/Nullmeier/Wewer in Klenk/Nullmeier/Wewer, Handbuch Digitalisierung in Staat und Verwaltung, p. 3.

adapting rapidly, not only to keep up with these changes but also to conduct their operations more effectively and with more accountability.[17]

1. Adjusting to a changing reality

The more our lives are becoming digital, the more threats are also evolving. Their 'nature [...] has not changed, but cyberspace provides a new delivery mechanism'.[18] In many instances, crime has become delocalized: Victims, crime scenes and offenders do not have to be in the same place or even in the same jurisdiction. Acts ranging from petty theft to warfare can be perpetrated remotely. Innovative technologies 'increase the speed, diffusion, and power of an attack'.[19] **12**

In addition, it is getting harder to detect crimes and identify their perpetrators. This also applies to crimes committed beyond the bounds of cyberspace – the use of encrypted communications and digital payments are only two examples of how incriminating evidence can more easily be concealed. In addition to new tools and methods used by threat actors, societal and industrial changes are creating and increasing vulnerabilities. As all industrial sectors, including critical infrastructure, private homes and personal information are becoming more and more connected, the number of potential threat vectors is increasing significantly. Thus, resilient systems are required.[20] **13**

2. Opportunities to innovate

That said, technology also provides security providers with opportunities to improve their operations. In their most basic form, manual processes are supported by or transferred 1:1 into a digital system, saving resources and making services more accessible.[21] While Member States' administrations still struggle when it comes to implementing this process, the potential inherent in the digital transformation is much bigger. Advanced digitization could transform structures and processes at large to provide more efficient and accountable solutions. These could range from collecting, accessing, linking and analysing evidence and threat-related information (for an example in the field of border management, → § 20 mn. 53) to using data to improve the security agencies' conduct and to deploy resources more efficiently and accountably – not only through the contested concept of predictive policing[22] but also using statistics to better understand operations. However, such innovation has its challenges. **14**

3. Challenges

To keep up with technological evolution, security providers have to change – comprehensively and constantly. There are several regulatory obstacles and obstacles to implementation, though.[23] First, regulatory gaps regarding new or emerging technologies need to be addressed.[24] However, governing processes that have not yet been established and technologies that are not fully developed is a particularly difficult **15**

---

[17] Brayne, ASR 2017, 977 (981).
[18] Giannopoulos/Smith/Theocharidou, p. 28.
[19] ibid.
[20] Grabbe/Valášek, p. 28.
[21] Klenk/Nullmeier/Wewer in Klenk/Nullmeier/Wewer, Handbuch Digitalisierung in Staat und Verwaltung, p. 5.
[22] Sandhu/Fussey, 'The 'uberization of policing'?', Policing and Society 2021, 66.
[23] Hoffmann-Riem in Wischmeyer/Rademacher, Regulating Artificial Intelligence, p. 5 (mn. 13 et seq.).
[24] Brownsword/Harel, 'Law, liberty and technology' International Journal of Law in Context 2019, 107.

endeavour.[25] Furthermore, there is consensus between the CJEU,[26] national courts[27] and academia (→ § 20 mn. 145) that these innovations, particularly in the field of big data analysis and AI, have serious implications for data protection and that their use has to be kept in compliance with applicable legislation. Particularly sensitive areas like the merging or linking of separate information systems and the use of biometric data may require a fundamental recalibration of the concept of data protection. In addition, minimising biases in algorithms and making their conclusions transparent for meaningful individual legal review remain a challenge.[28]

16 The use of new hardware and software can also create dependencies. Government agencies cannot fulfil their mandates without relying on solutions by private actors that are often outside their jurisdiction, and this raises questions around the need for digital sovereignty.[29] When it comes to implementation, technological evolution requires investment in digital solutions and infrastructure on the one hand and qualified personnel to develop, maintain and use such systems on the other. Although innovative technologies will eventually save administrations significant amounts of money, acquiring and setting them up requires costly up-front investments. Furthermore, qualified talent is scarce. The tasks involved lie outside of the traditional skills profiles of security professionals. Thus, recruiting experts, upskilling the workforce and external contracting pose additional challenges when it comes to implementation. This explains why Member States are open to more cooperation in this field so as to be able to pool scarce resources and share the financial burden.

II. The link between internal and external security

17 Second, external factors have increasingly affected public security within the EU's internal area. While the European Security Union is separate, in terms of scope and aims, from the Common Foreign and Security Policy (CFSP), with its specific intergovernmental-shaped structures and processes,[30] there is a long-established[31] overlap between the two policy areas.

18 These blurring lines[32] between the two concepts are acknowledged in the Security Union Strategy.[33] At the same time, maintaining internal security is the first of the EU's priorities to be listed in the Global Strategy.[34] This chapter will, though, only focus on the EU's internal area. In the internal sphere, external factors are operationalised as cross-cutting issues that are included in the European Commission's areas of action.

---

[25] Marchant in Marchant/Allenby/Herkert, The Growing Gap Between Emerging Technologies and Legal-Ethical Oversight, p. 24 et seqq.

[26] For example, ECJ 21.6.2019 – case C-817/19, ECLI:EU:C:2022:491 – *Ligue des droits humains*; ECJ 6.10.2020 – case C-623/17, ECLI:EU:C:2020:790 – *Privacy International*; ECJ 6.10.2020 – joined cases, C-511/18, C-512/18 and C-520/18, ECLI:EU:C:2020:791 – *La Quadrature du Net*.

[27] For example, BVerfG 16.2.2023 – 1 BvR 1547/19, NJW 2023, 1196.

[28] Art. 22(1) Regulation (EU) No 2016/679 on the protection of natural persons with regard to the processing of personal data and on the free movement of such data (General Data Protection Regulation (GDPR).

[29] Monsees/Lambach European Security 2022, 377.

[30] Art. 21 to 46 TEU.

[31] Bigo in Kelstrup/Williams, International Relations Theory and the Politics of European Integration, p. 171 (173 et seqq.).

[32] Brandão, JANUS.NET, e-journal of International Relations 2015, 1 (5 et seq.).

[33] European Commission, 'Communication on the EU Security Union Strategy, 24.7.2020, COM(2020) 605 final, 2, 14, 17, 26.

[34] EEAS, 'Shared Vision, Common Action: A Stronger Europe – A Global Strategy for the European Union's Foreign And Security Policy', June 2016, 9, 18.

When focusing on internal security provision, four developments on a meta level shape the way in which external factors influence the threat landscape.

1. Accelerating globalization/international dependencies

First, accelerating globalization has enormous economic, cultural and social potential, yet it also increases domestic vulnerabilities.[35] There is no universal definition of the term 'globalization',[36] but it has been described as 'the compression of time and space'.[37] Globalization is closely linked to the technological transformation described in the above and to economic dependencies, though it extends beyond that, as the COVID-19 pandemic showed. In addition to international (dis)information and communication flows, more and more people are travelling across continents and economic interdependencies are increasing. Supply chains have been globally integrated. **19**

Of course, the consequences of globalization have an impact on security provision within the AFSJ, but security itself is not globalised. *Didier Bigo* rejects the 'narrative of global (in)security',[38] for example in relation to the 'global war on terror', and denies the existence of global threats, describing them as a means to blur the distinction between the military, police and intelligence and consequently to circumvent rule-of-law safeguards in the post-9/11 era. As a result, the displacement of threats in itself poses challenges for free societies.[39] Yet, developments on a different continent can cause disruptions in Europe, and remote actors can exert both a direct and an indirect influence – legislators, policymakers and security providers are challenged by such close interrelations, given that they are bound by their jurisdictions but at times challenged outside of them. **20**

2. Geopolitical competition

Second, renewed geopolitical competition acts as a catalyst for many domestic security threats. The EU's internal discourse on hybrid threats was triggered by Russia's occupation of Crimea in 2014 (→ § 17 mn. 7). Consequently, Member States faced issues ranging from energy security, espionage and disinformation to cyber threats and organised crime and direct action.[40] The Union's Framework on Countering Hybrid Threats therefore stresses that the evolving security environment in Europe has changed 'dramatically'.[41] The all-out Russian war of aggression against Ukraine since February 2022 has only exacerbated these underlying conditions. **21**

In addition, China's increasing claims to power, paired with the United States' increasingly confrontational approach to its near-peer competitor, have to be taken into account in connection with internal security provision in Europe, for instance as regards the protection of critical infrastructure and supply chain security. **22**

While geopolitical competition first and foremost remains a foreign and security policy issue, it also affects several other policy fields, and internal security providers have to deal with the fallout from deteriorating relations elsewhere. **23**

---

[35] See Kay, Security Dialogue 2004, 5 (9).

[36] Al-Rodhan/Stoudmann, p. 9.

[37] Harvey, p. 240.

[38] Bigo in Amenta/Nash/Scott, The Wiley-Blackwell Companion to Political Sociology, p. 213.

[39] ibid.

[40] European Commission, 'Communication, on the Fifth Progress Report on the implementation of the EU Security Union Strategy', 13.12.2022, COM(2022) 745 final, 1.

[41] European Commission, 'Joint Communication to the European Parliament and the Council. Joint Framework on countering hybrid threats a European Union response', 6.4.2016, JOIN(2016) 18 final, 2.

3. Securitization of migration and asylum

24 Third, accelerating globalization and the abolition of internal borders in the Schengen Area have inverted the discourse on Justice and Home Affairs, particularly on migration and border management since the 1980s.[42] Rather than Member States 'losing control'[43] as sovereignty erodes in the face of bureaucratic European expansion, integration is now seen as a necessary response to functional pressure[44] created by the impact of global developments.[45] Global numbers of migrants and refugees are reaching record highs.[46]

25 The economic potential of migration is acknowledged by the EU and its Member States, and the right to asylum is enshrined in Art. 18 of the Charter of Fundamental Rights (CFR). Nevertheless, both developments are often viewed[47] through a securitised[48] lens in the AFSJ. While increased migration and flight do pose challenges to Member State administrations, securitised approaches pose risks to the human security[49] and fundamental rights[50] of those on the move. Neglecting such major issues affects the values of the EU.[51] Furthermore, political controversies over migration and asylum contribute to domestic social polarization and can aggravate other threats to public order. Politicised reactions are thus at risk of aggravating tensions.

4. Decline in transnational terrorism

26 Fourth, the decline in transnational terrorism shifts policy priorities. An increasing geopolitical disinterest in this issue is paired with a significant decline in terrorist violence since it peaked in 2018. By 2021, the number of terrorist attacks in the West, including the EU, had decreased by 68 % within a three-year period.[52] While western countries suffered 457 deaths from terrorist attacks between 2015 and 2017,[53] only one victim of terrorism died in the EU in 2021.[54] However, preventing the re-emergence of terrorism in the EU remains a foreign policy challenge. The 22 countries most affected by terrorism in 2021 are in the Global South.[55] Ten years of security assistance in the Sahel have failed, resulting in the highest numbers of casualties of terrorism worldwide.[56] Meanwhile, by the end of 2022, 65,000 people with links to the Islamic State, including 42,000 foreign nationals, were still in detention in dire conditions in northern Syria.[57] Besides a lack of due process and human rights violations, including the arbitrary detention of adolescents by the overwhelmed de facto authorities,[58] the

---

[42] Bigo in Amenta/Nash/Scott, The Wiley-Blackwell Companion to Political Sociology, p. 211.

[43] Geddes, p. 127.

[44] Ette/Parks/Bendel in Bendel/Ette/Parks, The Europeanization of Control, p. 16.

[45] Geddes/Scholten, p. 127.

[46] UNHCR, 'Refugee Data Finder', 2023 <https://www.unhcr.org/refugee-statistics/> (last accessed: 13.10.2023).

[47] Grabbe/Valášek, p. 3.

[48] Léonard, European Security 2010, 231; Buzan/Waever/de Wilde., p. 23 et seqq.

[49] Solana et al., p. 21 mn. 6.2.

[50] Especially Art. 3, 18 CFR.

[51] Art. 2 TEU.

[52] Institute for Economics and Peace, 2022, p. 2.

[53] ibid., p. 33.

[54] ibid., p. 39 et seq.

[55] ibid., p. 8.

[56] ibid., p. 60 et seqq.

[57] HRW, 'Syria: Repatriations Lag for Foreigners with Alleged ISIS Ties', 15.12.2022 available from (HRW, 15.12.2022) <https://www.hrw.org> (last accessed: 13.10.2023).

[58] Ní Aoláin, p. 3 et seq.

circumstances are at risk of contributing to the radicalization of minors growing up in such facilities. Furthermore, this 'army in waiting' is at risk of breaking out of detention sites.[59]

III. Executive aggrandisement

The last trend to be addressed in this chapter concerns the separation of powers and the rule of law. These separate phenomena – for different reasons – lead to a shift towards executives to the detriment of the two other branches of government. On the one hand, democratic backsliding weakens oversight over the executives within Member States. On the other hand, the EU is gaining executive capabilities more quickly than it is oversight capabilities. 27

1. Member States' backsliding

Freedom and democracy and respect for human dignity and human rights are fundamental values of the EU and are enshrined in Art. 2 TEU. Nevertheless, while they are still listed among the world's most liberal democracies, it has been established that many EU Member States have experienced some form of democratic backsliding.[60] This has been most prominently the case in Hungary and Poland.[61] 28

The concept of democratic backsliding is complex and has been interpreted in various ways. The minimum everyone can agree on is that it can be described as a 'state-led debilitation or elimination of any of the political institutions that sustain an existing democracy'.[62] Democratic backsliding is not a dichotomous process in which a democratic state becomes authoritarian; the concept describes an incremental deterioration along the spectrum of liberal democracy.[63] Without negating the significance of the long-term, system-altering effects of the erosion of democracy, this chapter focuses on the challenges this poses to the rule of law on account of its immediate impact on law enforcement and the judiciary. 29

In her landmark paper on the issue, *Nancy Berneo* coined the term 'executive aggrandisement' as one of the strategies of democratic backsliding that 30

> occurs when elected executives weaken checks on executive power one by one, undertaking a series of institutional changes that hamper the power of opposition forces to challenge executive preferences.[64]

Governments do so through legal means such as legislative reforms and often with broad popular support.[65] Executive aggrandisement mostly focuses on reducing oversight on the national level, although governments may also seek to reduce scrutiny by the EU.[66] 31

First, unchecked executive action, particularly by security providers, can lead to human rights violations and affect their overall effectiveness. Hollowing out the 32

---

[59] Storch et al., 'Operation Inherent Resolve. Lead Inspector General Report to the United States Congress October 1st, 2022 – December 31st 2022', 2023, 10.

[60] Gora/de Wilde, Journal of European Public Policy 2020, 342 (352).

[61] ibid., 345; Holesch/Kyriaz, East European Politics 2021, 1 (7).

[62] Bermeo, JoD 2016, 5.

[63] Mechkova/Lührmann/Lindberg, JoD 2017, 162.

[64] Bermeo, JoD 2016, 5 (10 et seq.).

[65] ibid.

[66] See Closa/Kochenov in Closa/Kochenov, Reinforcing Rule of Law Oversight in the European Union, p. 1 (1 et seqq.).

independent judiciary prevents victims of human rights violations from seeking legal redress. Political policing can increase, and the lack of accountability undermines the trust of the people in the authorities that should be serving them.

33 In addition, executive aggrandisement has direct implications for security cooperation within the EU. A Member State may be more hesitant when it comes to sharing information – for example putting it into an EU database – if it does not trust other Member States to use it responsibly. Diverging human rights and oversight standards therefore undermine the required trust when it comes to collaborating effectively in the borderless internal area. Conflicting levels of protection could thus impede the achievement of the goals of the European Security Union.

2. European executive detours

34 Meanwhile, the EU institutions are undergoing a contradictory development. They have been given more responsibility – and capabilities – as a facilitator, and in exceptional cases have become the operator of security measures. Hence, the need for oversight and accountability of these organs increases proportionally, but the structures and processes to ensure oversight and accountability have yet to develop at a similar pace, as is exemplified in the report published by the European Parliament's Frontex Scrutiny Working Group.[67]

35 *Virginie Guidauron* conceptionalised how Member States' executive branches used 'venue shopping' during the pre-Lisbon era to regulate migration and asylum processes.[68] They chose an international instead of a national venue to loosen judicial oversight and avoid national political constraints, set the agenda and exclude political opponents. The adoption of the Lisbon Treaty mitigated these effects, particularly by granting the CJEU oversight over the AFSJ and including the Charter of Fundamental Rights in primary EU law and creating secondary-law protection regimes.[69] Still, governments continue to shop around for venues, especially in the area of border security, migration and asylum,[70] thereby introducing restrictive legislation on third-country nationals.[71]

36 And, vice versa, the EU has been accused of the 'ad hoc legalization of EU Member States' malpractices and exceptionalism.'[72] Such 'policy laundering'[73] is applied in moments of actual or constructed crises to codify or introduce domestically unpopular practices in the European venue, avoiding domestic repercussions.

---

[67] European Parliament, 'Report on the fact-finding investigation on Frontex concerning alleged fundamental rights violations', 14.7.2021.

[68] Guiraudon, JCMS 200, 251.

[69] Bossong, JTS 2020, 190 (196); Ette/Parks/Bendel in Bendel/Ette/Parks, The Europeanization of Control, p. 25 et seq.

[70] Bossong, JTS 2020, 190 (196); Bulmer in Bendel/Ette/Parks, The Europeanization of Control, p. 41.

[71] The planned systematic collection of biometric data of all third-country short-term visitors (EES) as well as the linking of these with asylum and criminal databases is one recent example of such legislation, as is the introduction of travel authorizations for visa-exempt travellers, including algorithmic risk management; Regulation (EU) 2017/2226 establishing an Entry/Exit System (EES) to register entry and exit data and refusal of entry data of third-country nationals crossing the external borders of the Member States and determining the conditions for access to the EES for law enforcement purposes; Regulation (EU) 2018/1240 establishing a European Travel Information and Authorisation System (ETIAS); Regulation (EU) 2019/817 on establishing a framework for interoperability between EU information systems in the field of borders and visa.

[72] Carrera/Colombi/Cortinovis, p. 102.

[73] Hosein in Halpin et al., Cyberwar, Netwar and the Revolution in Military Affairs, p. 229.

C. The future of European security cooperation

After the first part of this chapter looked at disruptive trends, this section analyzes the EU's internal legislative and policy agenda. This framework and the trends are closely interconnected and, taken together, make it possible to create a scenario for the way ahead in the European Security Union. The following analysis focuses on the role of the EU institutions and will not look at developments within individual Member States. First, the division of roles and responsibilities within the Security Union is addressed before deducing its medium-term trajectory based on recently adopted or planned legislation and policies. 37

I. Roles and responsibilities

Anne-Marie Slaughter identified three tasks of trans-governmental networks[74] that can be used to delineate the roles and responsibilities of the EU (compared to the Member States) in the AFSJ. The following functions were identified: regulation, information exchange and implementing executive tasks. However, the EU goes further than just enabling information-sharing. It takes comprehensive action to facilitate Member States in the information space through coordination, digital enablers, funding and research. Hence, this function needs to be expanded. 38

In terms of its first, regulatory, function, the EU sets norms and reviews their implementation. It does so by adopting legislation and policies, not only prescribing and streamlining measures, but also determining responsibilities and creating rules on how activities are to be carried out. Despite the application of the principle of subsidiarity to Member State legislation,[75] and the Member States' prerogative as providers of security,[76] the EU holds far-reaching legislative competences on cross-border and transnational issues, such as border security,[77] asylum[78] and migration,[79] cybersecurity and money laundering[80]. However, Member States, as co-legislators within the Council, maintain a significant influence on the legislative files. In other policy areas where legislative powers remain at the national level, Member States do not act outside the scope of EU law and have to comply with its principles even when carrying out domestic security functions (→ § 8 mn. 50; → § 6 mn. 20). As well as the Council and European Parliament as co-legislators and the Commission as the executive branch of the Union, the CJEU also plays a crucial role, overseeing compliance with the normative framework and shaping it through its case law and claiming far-reaching jurisdiction over security matters, at times in the face of protests from many Member States.[81] 39

---

[74] Slaughter, p. 69 et seqq.

[75] Art. 69 TFEU.

[76] Art. 4(2) TEU; Art. 72 TFEU.

[77] Art. 77(2) TFEU.

[78] Art. 78(2) TFEU.

[79] Art. 79(2) TFEU.

[80] The EU's legislative competences for cybersecurity and money laundering are not explicitly granted in the Treaties, but have been derived from its general competence for the internal market as set out in Art. 114 TFEU, see Bendiek/Pander Maat, SWP Working Paper 2019, 3.

[81] For instance ECJ 21.6.2019 – case C-817/19, ECLI:EU:C:2022:491 – *Ligue des droits humains*; ECJ 6.10.2020 – case C-623/17, ECLI:EU:C:2020:790 – *Privacy International*; ECJ 6.10.2020 – joined cases, C-511/18, C-512/18 and C-520/18, ECLI:EU:C:2020:791 – *La Quadrature du Net.*

40 Second, the Commission and the EU agencies facilitate operational Member State action using a variety of tools. They provide the digital infrastructure and services to support the executive security measures that are essential to law enforcement in the internal area. The Schengen Information System alone was queried 12.7 billion times in 2022, for example.[82] To run and develop these services, the European Union Agency for the Operational Management of Large-Scale IT Systems in the Area of Freedom, Security and Justice (eu-LISA) had a budget of nearly 327 million EUR in 2023.[83]

41 But eu-LISA is only one of 12 EU agencies and bodies dealing with matters relating to the AFSJ. The total annual budget of these entities amounts to nearly 2 billion EUR.[84] Other agencies provide operational support and capabilities as well as knowledge, analysis, advice and training to Member States in their area of expertise. The importance of migration and border security in the EU's approach to security is exemplified by the fact that 1.35 billion EUR of the 2 billion EUR is provided to the three agencies[85] working on these issues. Frontex's budget alone increased from 97 million EUR in 2014[86] to 845 million EUR in 2023.[87] Further budgetary priorities include cybersecurity[88] and police cooperation.[89] The remaining agencies' budgets ranged between 9 EUR and 65 million EUR in 2023. In addition, the EU provides funding and support to research, most significantly through the Horizon Europe programme.

42 However, the support provided by EU institutions is generally below the threshold of executive action. In line with the Treaties, the Member States remain the primary executive security providers. As at 2023, the EU does not play a significant operational role. However, it has built certain capabilities to act in exceptional cases, and only at the request of a Member State, to take on operational roles in areas in which the requesting Member State lacks capability or capacity – in particular police investigations, border security and cybersecurity. This reserve function has clear limits, but it provides for structures and processes that pave the way to more communitized security provision within the scope of what Member States can accept. For example, Europol is mandated to provide operational support to national criminal investigations,[90] yet the agency has no executive powers when it does so.[91]

---

[82] eu-LISA, 'SIS II 2022 Annual Statistics', March 2023, 3.

[83] eu-LISA, 'Statement of Revenue and Expenditure for Financial Year 2023', 31.1.2023, 1.

[84] The AFSJ agencies are the following: European Union Agency for Law Enforcement Training (CEPOL), Europol, European body for the enhancement of judicial co-operation (Eurojust), eu-LISA, Frontex, European Monitoring Centre for Drugs and Drug Addiction (EMCDDA), European Union Agency for Cybersecurity (ENISA), European Union Agency for Asylum (EUAA), European Institute for Gender Equality (EIGE) and the Fundamental Rights Agency. Additionally, the European Cybersecurity Competence Centre (ECCC), as an executive agency, and the EPPO, as an independent secondary law body, deal with matters of the AFSJ.

[85] Frontex, eu-LISA and EUAA.

[86] Frontex, 'Annual Activity Report 2014', 12.5.2015, 50.

[87] Frontex, 'Management Board Decision 70/2022', 31.12.2022, 83.

[88] The European Cybersecurity Competence Centre (ECCC) has a budget of 195 million EUR for 2023 to strengthen cybersecurity through industrial policy; European Union Agency for Cybersecurity (ENISA) has an annual budget of 25 million EUR for 2023.

[89] The Europol 2023 budget amounts to 208 million EUR.

[90] Art. 4(1)(c) Regulation (EU) No 2016/794.

[91] Art. 4(5) Regulation (EU) No 2016/794.

II. Legislative and policy agenda

Having determined the roles the EU currently has, I will turn to an analysis of the legislative and policy agenda associated with the European Security Union. In order to create a scenario for the future of security provision in the AFSJ for the coming five years in relation to the disruptive trends discussed in the above, overarching themes, priorities as well as omissions in this roadmap will be identified. **43**

1. Primary law

Security cooperation within the EU is based on Art. 3(2) TEU, which sets out the objective of creating an AFSJ 'in which the free movement of persons is ensured in conjunction with appropriate measures with respect to external border controls, asylum, immigration and the prevention and combating of crime.' This is further specified in Art. 67 to 89 TFEU in conjunction with the Charter of Fundamental Rights. Hence, a change in this polity could cause wide-ranging shifts in security cooperation and provision. **44**

That said, a reform of primary law does not seem likely in the medium term. Although the European Parliament called for Treaty amendments[92] after the Conference on the Future of Europe,[93] no agreement with the Council and the Commission, which prefer to maintain the current polity without changes, is in sight.[94] Even if the recommendations of the Parliament were to be implemented, they would have limited impact on the AFSJ. The only amendment that is directly linked to this policy area calls for the strengthening of the Art. 7 TEU procedure,[95] which would probably not be adopted owing to resistance from Poland and Hungary at the very least. **45**

2. Secondary law

Thus, we need to take a closer look at developments relating to secondary law and European Commission policies to determine the probable pathway when it comes to the sharing of responsibilities between the Member States and EU. Not only does the Security Union Strategy outline the Commission's ambitions in this policy field for the period from 2020 to 2025, its implementation roadmap,[96] which was annexed to the progress reports,[97] lists concrete endeavours that are to be used to execute the strategy. Structured in line with the strategy's four pillars, these actions allow for the identification of the legislative agenda and policy priorities as well as the evolving roles of the EU in interrelation with the Member States. **46**

---

[92] European Parliament, 'European Parliament resolution of 9 June 2022 on the call for a Convention for the revision of the Treaties', 2022/2705(RSP).

[93] Conference on the Future of Europe, 'Report on the final outcome', May 2022, 6; unlike the European Parliament, the citizen-led conference called for reforms regarding 'Values and rights, rule of law, security', see Conference on the Future of Europe, 'Report on the final outcome', May 2022, 68 et seqq.

[94] Von Ondarza/Ålander, SWP Comment 2022 C 49, 1.

[95] Mn. 5 subpara. 4 of European Parliament resolution on the call for a Convention for the revision of the Treaties, 9.6.2022, 2022/2705(RSP).

[96] European Commission, 'Communication, on the Fourth Progress Report on the implementation of the EU Security Union Strategy', 25.5.2022, COM(2022) 252 final, Annex.

[97] European Commission, 'Communication, on the Fifth Progress Report on the implementation of the EU Security Union Strategy', 13.12.2022, COM(2022) 745 final.

a) Implementation roadmap

47 The implementation roadmap[98] comprises 46 deliverables, 20 legislative files and 26 policy initiatives. Regardless of the current status of implementation, it provides a comprehensive overview over the Union's legislative and non-legislative priorities and, further, shows how the roles of its institutions will be shaped by 2025.

48 The disruptive trends have an impact on policy planning across all four pillars of the strategy. Seventy per cent of the deliverables directly address the disruptive trend of rapid technological innovation. The same number of deliverables touch upon the internal–external security nexus. By contrast, no deliverable has the advancement of basic rights or the rule of law as its main goal, but the matter is integrated as a cross-cutting issue across other deliverables. Still, this prioritization reaffirms the preoccupation[99] with security in the AFSJ. Instead of strategically planning policies that aim to promote rule-of-law guarantees, it is still up to the CJEU and administrative oversight bodies to provide ex-post oversight over legislators and security providers.

49 Fifty-nine per cent of the deliverables in the roadmap serve the preparation and adoption of legislative files and policy documents relating to the European Security Union, thus fulfilling its norm-setting function. The remaining 41 % strengthen the role of the EU as a facilitator of Member State action mainly through support functions, capacity-building and the coordination of efforts to provide security. None of the deliverables would create an executive role for EU institutions.

50 The balance between the different roles, however, shifts between the four sections of the roadmap. Twenty-six per cent of the deliverables are listed under the first pillar of the strategy (A future-proof security environment), which focus on three themes: cybersecurity (→ § 16 mn. 1) (five deliverables), critical infrastructure protection (five deliverables) and drones (two deliverables). As regards the role of the EU in this area, 75 % of the deliverables are normative in nature. The remaining three aim at facilitating Member State action through capacity-building, coordination and the creation of a Joint Cyber Unit.[100]

51 Only 13 % of the deliverables are addressed under the second pillar of the strategy (Tackling evolving threats). No cohesive theme can be identified in relation to these deliverables, which encompass the digitization of law enforcement and justice authorities (two deliverables), the fight against child sexual abuse (two deliverables) and countering hybrid threats (two deliverables). Except for one deliverable aiming at building capacities for digital investigations, all the actions are normative in nature.

52 Thirty per cent of deliverables are addressed under the third pillar of the strategy (Protecting Europeans from terrorism and organised crime). The actions in this part of the strategy focus on preventing and responding to specific offences in these areas – mostly through normative action – on the one hand and on facilitating cooperation with third countries on the other.

53 The remaining 30 % of the deliverables are addressed under the fourth pillar (A strong European security ecosystem). It is the only section of the implementation roadmap with a facilitative rather than a normative focus. Through 12 of the 14 deliverables, the Union facilitates Member State action by strengthening Europol's mandate, expanding information-sharing, collaborating digitally and funding research.

---

[98] As annexed to the 4th progress report, COM(2022) 252 final.

[99] Orrù Eunomia, Rivista di studi su pace e diritti umani 2022, 143 (151).

[100] As the Joint Cyber Unit is comprised of Member State experts whose assistance the Member States can request, this deliverable is considered a facilitative and not an operational act in this context.

b) Empowerment of EU Agencies

Further legislative changes that were adopted prior to the Security Union Strategy also have to be taken into consideration due to their long-term impact on security provision within in EU. The establishment and subsequent extension of Frontex's mandate was the most prominent and the most controversial (→ § 19 mn. 7). While Frontex can perform operational functions in the field of integrated border management[101] and is building the first uniformed armed service of EU staff,[102] it cannot act operationally without the consent of the Member State when staff are deployed.[103] Frontex missions need to be integrated into the national chain of command of one of the Member States, which then retains primary responsibility.[104] Hence, Frontex is not itself an executive actor but facilitates Member State action. Yet, building and maintaining both capabilities and institutional memory might have a subliminal impact on the balance of power between the Member States and EU institutions. This is particularly true since transferring costs from the national level to the EU by deploying Frontex is an additional incentive to use these capacities. 54

The delayed[105] yet consequential reform of the EU's IT landscape, which facilitates migration and border control, is another example of legislation that was adopted prior to the Security Union Strategy (→ § 20 mn. 5). In addition to extending existing databases operated by eu-LISA,[106] three new information systems[107] are to be created and all information systems are to be linked as a result.[108] The Member States' border and migration agencies will gain far-reaching new capabilities on account of the data that are included in the information systems, which is also why the legislation comes with immense data protection challenges, particularly the wide-ranging collection, storage and use of the biometrical data of third-country nationals, algorithmic risk management and the linking of databases created for different purposes. 55

The European Public Prosecutor's Office (EPPO) is a further arm of the EU security architecture. The option of establishing this body was laid down in Art. 86 TFEU. In 2013, the Commission proposed a regulation for this purpose, which the Member States had still not agreed on by 2017. That is why the EPPO was established by way of enhanced cooperation[109] and why, as of 2023, 22 Member States are participating in the office. The EPPO is an executive law enforcement body by nature, yet several caveats regarding the separation of responsibilities between the Union und the Member States have to be taken into account. The EPPO's mandate is limited to prosecuting crimes against the financial interests of the Union[110] in contrast to the broader scope of criminal law, and the EPPO does not prosecute cases in an EU court, but in the affected Member States, which apply their criminal codes. Also, the EPPO is decentralised, with prosecutors located in the individual Member States. Investigations and prosecutions are generally conducted by a prosecutor appointed by and from the 56

[101] Art. 10(1) Regulation (EU) No 2019/1896 on the European Border and Coast Guard (Frontex-Regulation).

[102] Art. 54(1)(a) Frontex-Regulation.

[103] Art. 7(2) Frontex-Regulation.

[104] Art. 7(1) Frontex-Regulation.

[105] European Parliament, 'Priority question for written answer P-000834/2023', 10.3.2023, 1.

[106] Schengen Information System, Visa Information System, European Dactyloscopy.

[107] Entry-Exit System, European Travel Information and Authorization System, European Criminal Record Information System for Third Country Nationals.

[108] Interoperability of EU information systems for security, border and migration management.

[109] Art. 326–324 TFEU; Art. 1 Regulation (EU) No 2017/193 of 12 December 2017 on cooperation between national authorities responsible for the enforcement of consumer protection laws.

[110] Art. 4 Regulation (EU) No 2017/193.

Member State that holds jurisdiction over the case. Despite being an independent EU body with an executive mandate, Member States still carefully consider which powers to grant the EPPO and have put in place several safeguards to guarantee their sovereignty.

c) CJEU case law

57 Lastly, CJEU case law is integral to shaping the future of European security. According to Art. 19 TEU, the Court ensures that the law is obeyed in the interpretation and application of the Treaties. In doing that, it does not set policy or pass legislation. However, through its case law, the CJEU has been considered an 'engine of constitutionalization of the European Union'.[111] It has been instrumental in the juridification of the EU's Justice and Home Affairs.[112]

58 Despite the Member States claiming national security exceptions under Art. 4(2) TEU, the Court feels competent to ensure that national legislation is compliant on security matters with EU law and therefore acts as a gatekeeper. Further, the CJEU reviews EU legislation that is relevant to this field, aiming to balance security provisions with fundamental freedoms. These adjustments are essential when it comes to shaping not only the implementation of existing laws at the EU and the national level, but also future legislative procedures.

D. Conclusion

59 Despite geopolitical ruptures, the Security Union Strategy has proven to provide an adaptive framework that allows for adjustments to a changing threat landscape while addressing the underlying developments when it comes to preventing and mitigating incident impact and, ultimately, investigating and prosecuting crimes. Examining the European Commission's strategic planning in this regard while considering the impact of disruptive trends on the Security Union's trajectory, its development in the medium term becomes clearer.

60 The Security Union Strategy reflects wider disruptive shifts. Seventy per cent of legislative files and policy initiatives on internal security address technological innovation. The same percentage of deliverables relates to the internal–external security nexus. On the one hand, technological progress and its inherent risks – particularly in cyberspace – and a securitised approach to migration and asylum on the other are the two issues that receive by far the most attention from legislators and policymakers. Meanwhile, promoting fundamental rights and freedom is not an end in itself in dedicated legislative files, but these matters are included as cross-cutting issues in other legislation. The prioritization of *security* in the AFSJ is likely to increase even further. It is up to the CJEU and administrative oversight bodies to retroactively impose fundamental rights boundaries on security legislation. These trends will shape the medium-term development of security provision in the EU's internal area.

61 As regards the Member States, the European Union has been and will remain first and foremost a normative actor in the field of security. EU law and CJEU jurisprudence will continue to have a far-reaching impact on domestic security legislation and its implementation. At the same time, the EU is extending its role as a facilitator of

[111] Moser/Rittberger, International Journal of Constitutional Law 2022, 1038.
[112] ibid., 1059.

Member State action in areas in which the Member States lack capacity or capabilities and see the opportunity to save on scarce resources. Technological innovation and the availability of big data will drive this process forward, and the value added perceived by the Member States will increase the probability that the EU's role in this respect will continue to expand.

However, despite increased EU capacity-building as regards operational security **62** provision, it is unlikely that the Member States will permanently transfer any executive competences in these areas. The EU can only act in exceptional circumstances at the request of Member States within its respective legal framework, and this situation will most likely not change. Nevertheless, even if creating and maintaining such capabilities at the Union level mostly serves political purposes, it also has a long-term subliminal impact on the balance of power between the Member State authorities and the EU agencies as Brussels builds institutional knowledge and can in certain situations present itself as a viable operational alternative to Member State agencies.

There are clear indications of a consensus between EU institutions and Member **63** States governments on the division of their roles and responsibilities when it comes to implementing security legislation. In sum, the EU remains a security enabler, not an enforcer. At the same time, though, the Member States often seek to limit EU judicial oversight over their national security legislation and agencies, while the CJEU indicates that it sees itself as competent to review their legal bases. This rift has yet to be repaired.

Although security competences and accountability are inextricably linked – and **64** despite efforts to improve accountability – it is likely that security competences will continue to be expanded faster than oversight capacities. Even if EU oversight were not to be expanded, security agencies would not be acting in a legal vacuum, but would be bound by national legislation. Domestic courts would still engage in oversight. However, if, on the basis of EU legislation, Member States pass national security laws that are more restrictive than would have been politically possible in a purely domestic setting, how can such laws be shielded from the CJEU? Instead of the EU meeting the Member States' fundamental rights standards,[113] Member States will have to uniformly meet the rule-of-law standards of the Treaties to maintain the required trust when it comes to security cooperation.

[113] BVerfG 22.10.1986 – 2 BvR 197/83, NJW 1987, 577.

